Expert VB 2005 Business Objects

Second Edition

Rockford Lhotka

Apress®

Expert VB 2005 Business Objects, Second Edition

Copyright © 2006 by Rockford Lhotka

ISBN-13 (pbk): 978-1-59059-631-9

ISBN-10 (pbk): 1-59059-631-5

Printed and bound in the United States of America 9 8 7 6 5 4 3 2 1

Lead Editor: Jonathan Hassell

Technical Reviewer: Petar Kozul

Editorial Board: Steve Anglin, Ewan Buckingham, Gary Cornell, Jason Gilmore, Jonathan Gennick,
     Jonathan Hassell, James Huddleston, Chris Mills, Matthew Moodie, Dominic Shakeshaft,
     Jim Sumser, Keir Thomas, Matt Wade

Project Manager: Kylie Johnston

Copy Edit Manager: Nicole LeClerc

Copy Editor: Damon Larson

Assistant Production Director: Kari Brooks-Copony

Production Editor: Laura Cheu

Compositor: Linda Weidemann, Wolf Creek Press

Proofreader: April Eddy

Indexer: John Collin

Artist: Kinetic Publishing Services, LLC

Cover Designer: Kurt Krames

Manufacturing Director: Tom Debolski

Distributed to the book trade worldwide by Springer-Verlag New York, Inc., 233 Spring Street, 6th Floor, New York, NY 10013. Phone 1-800-SPRINGER, fax 201-348-4505, e-mail orders-ny@springer-sbm.com, or visit http://www.springeronline.com.

For information on translations, please contact Apress directly at 2560 Ninth Street, Suite 219, Berkeley, CA 94710. Phone 510-549-5930, fax 510-549-5939, e-mail info@apress.com, or visit http://www.apress.com.

The source code for this book is available to readers at http://www.apress.com in the Source Code section.

In memory of my Grandmother, Evylyn,
a true angel on earth, who now rests in heaven.

Contents at a Glance

Contents

About the Author

ROCKFORD LHOTKA is the author of numerous books, including *Expert C# 2005 Business Objects*. He is a Microsoft regional director, a Microsoft MVP, and an INETA speaker. Rockford speaks at many conferences and user groups around the world, and is a columnist for MSDN Online. Rockford is the principal technology evangelist for Magenic Technologies (www.magenic.com), one of the nation's premiere Microsoft gold certified partners dedicated to solving today's most challenging business problems using 100-percent Microsoft tools and technology.

About the Technical Reviewer

PETAR KOZUL is a senior consultant for ComputerPro, a Melbourne-based company focused on providing IT management, consulting, and enterprise solutions. He is the author of ActiveObjects, a suite of extensions for the CSLA .NET framework (http://csla.kozul.info). As an active member of the CSLA community, he has been using the framework since its inception. He graduated from the Royal Melbourne Institute of Techology (RMIT) with a degree in computer science. Petar has over 11 years experience in software design and development, with his primary focus on object-oriented solutions using Microsoft technologies. He has worked in several countries, including Croatia, Bosnia and Hercegovina, and Australia. His work has spanned a variety of industries in both the public and private sectors, including gaming, retail, medicine, and government.

Acknowledgments

This book started as a revision, and ended up being almost a complete rewrite to cover all the changes in .NET 2.0 and Visual Studio 2005. Thus, it turned into a really a big project, and I want to thank a number of people who helped make it come to fruition.

First, I'd like to thank my wife and sons for their love, patience, and support over the past many years. Without you, this would have been impossible! Moreover, I owe my wife special thanks for helping with the editing process, as she saved me many hours of work during my least favorite part of the writing process.

I'd also like to thank Greg Frankenfield and Paul Fridman for making Magenic such an awesome place to work. The support that you and the rest of Magenic have provided has been great, and I appreciate it very much! It is an honor to work with everyone there.

Special thanks to Brant Estes, a fellow Magenic employee who ported the original code into C# and kept it in sync with the VB code over the past few months. You saved me untold amounts of time—thank you, Brant!

The Magenic Managed Services Organization (MSO) team did a lot of testing and is largely responsible for the unit tests included with the framework. This fine group of people helped identify and eliminate numerous bugs and played a key role in keeping the VB and C# code bases in sync.

Thank you to Steve Lasker at Microsoft for helping figure out solutions to some Windows Forms data binding issues, and to Bill McCarthy for helping wrap the answer to one of those issues into the `BindingSourceRefresh` control.

The Apress editorial team put in a lot of time and effort and really helped shape this book into what you see here. I owe them all a debt of gratitude for their fine work.

Finally, I'd like to thank the scores of people who've sent me emails of support or encouragement, or just plain asked when the book would be done. The great community that has grown around these books and the CSLA .NET framework is wonderful, and I thank you all! I hope you find this book to be as rewarding to read as it has been for me to write.

Code well and have fun!

Introduction

This book is about application architecture, design, and development in .NET using object-oriented concepts. The focus is on business-focused objects called *business objects*, and how to implement them to work in various distributed environments, including web and client/server configurations. The book makes use of a great many .NET technologies, object-oriented design and programming concepts, and distributed architectures.

The first half of the book walks through the process of creating a framework to support object-oriented application development in .NET. This will include a lot of architectural concepts and ideas. It will also involve some in-depth use of advanced .NET techniques to create the framework.

The second half of the book makes use of the framework to build a sample application with several different interfaces. If you wish, it's perfectly possible to skip the first half of the book and simply make use of the framework to build object-oriented applications.

One of my primary goals in creating the CSLA .NET framework was to simplify .NET development. Developers using the framework in this book don't need to worry about the details of underlying technologies such as remoting, serialization, or reflection. All of these are embedded in the framework so that a developer using it can focus almost entirely on business logic and application design, rather than getting caught up in "plumbing" issues.

From .NET 1.0 to 2.0

This book is a major update to the previous edition: *Expert One-on-One Visual Basic .NET Business Objects*. This updated book takes advantage of new features of .NET 2.0 and applies lessons learned from using .NET 1.0 and 1.1 over the past few years.

This book is nearly identical to the *Expert C# 2005 Business Objects* book—the only difference between the two books is the syntax of the programming languages.

Both the VB and C# books are the most recent expressions of concepts I've been working on for nearly a decade. My goal all along has been to enable the productive use of object-oriented design in distributed n-tier applications. Over the years, both the technologies and my understanding and expression of the concepts have evolved greatly.

The VB 5 and 6 books that started this whole process discussed how to use VB, COM, DCOM, MTS, and COM+ to create applications using object-oriented techniques. (Or at least they were as object-oriented as was possible in VB 5/6 and COM.) They also covered the concept of *distributed objects*, whereby a given object is "spread" over multiple machines in a physical n-tier environment. In COM, this isn't a trivial thing to implement, and so these books included a fair amount of discussion relating to object state and state serialization techniques.

The end result was an architecture that I called *CSLA* (which stands for component-based, scalable, logical architecture). Over the years, I've received hundreds of emails from people who have used CSLA as a basis for their own architectures as they've built applications ranging from small, single-user programs to full-blown enterprise applications that power major parts of their businesses.

In .NET, the idea of *distributed objects* has given way to the more appropriate idea of *mobile objects*, where objects actually move between computers in an n-tier environment. At a high level, the architecture is comparable, but mobile objects provide a far more powerful way to implement object-oriented designs in distributed environments.

I've also received a handful of emails from people for whom CSLA .NET *wasn't* successful, but this isn't surprising. To use CSLA .NET effectively, you must become versed in object-oriented and component-based design, understand the concept of distributed objects, and develop a host of other skills. The mobile object architecture has many benefits, but it's not the simplest or the easiest to understand.

Designing CSLA .NET

One of the characteristics of .NET is that it often provides several ways to solve the same problem. Some of the approaches available will be better than others, but the best one for a given problem may not be immediately obvious. Before writing the .NET 1.0 books, I spent a lot of time trying various approaches to distributing objects. Although a variety have proven to work, in the end I've arrived at the one that best matches my original goals.

Before I discuss those goals, I think it's important to talk about one other issue that I wrestled with when writing this book. Given the large number of people using the concepts and code from the previous edition of the book, I wanted to preserve backward compatibility whenever possible. At the same time, this new edition of the book is an opportunity to not only use .NET 2.0 features, but also to apply lessons learned by using .NET over the past several years.

Applying those lessons means that using the new concepts and code requires changes to existing business objects and user interface code. I don't take backward compatibility lightly, yet it is important to advance the concepts to keep up with changes in technology and my views on both object-oriented and distributed computing.

When possible, I have minimized the impact on existing code, so the transition shouldn't be overly complex for most applications.

I have a specific set of goals for the architecture and the book. These goals are important, because they're key to understanding why I made many of the choices I did in terms of which .NET technologies to use, and how to use them. The goals are as follows:

- To support a fully object-oriented programming model
- To allow the developer to use the architecture without jumping through hoops
- To enable high scalability
- To enable high performance
- To provide all the capabilities and features of the original CSLA, namely
  - N-level undo on a per-object basis (edit, cancel, apply)
  - Management of validation rules
  - Management of authorization rules
  - Support for many types of UI based on the same objects
  - Support for data binding in Windows and Web Forms
  - Integration with distributed transaction technologies such as Enterprise Services and `System.Transactions`
- To simplify .NET by handling complex issues like serialization, remoting, and reflection
- To use the tools provided by Microsoft, notably IntelliSense and the Autocomplete feature in Visual Studio .NET

Of these, saving the developer from jumping through hoops—that is, allowing him or her to do "normal" programming—has probably had the largest impact. To meet all these goals without a framework, the developer would have to write a lot of extra code to track business rules, implement n-level undo, and support serialization of object data. All this code is important, but adds nothing to the business value of the application.

Fortunately, .NET offers some powerful technologies that help to reduce or eliminate much of this "plumbing" code. If those technologies are then wrapped in a framework, a business developer shouldn't have to deal with them at all. In several cases, this goal of simplicity drove my architectural decisions. The end result is that the developer can, for the most part, simply write a normal C# class and have it automatically enjoy all the benefits of n-level undo, business rule tracking, and so forth.

It has taken a great deal of time and effort, but I've certainly enjoyed putting this architecture and this book together, and I hope that you will find it valuable during the development of your own applications.

What's Covered in This Book?

This book covers the thought process behind the CSLA .NET 2.0 architecture, describes the construction of the framework that supports the architecture, and demonstrates how to create Windows Forms, Web Forms, and Web Services applications based on business objects written using the framework.

Chapter 1 is an introduction to some of the concepts surrounding distributed architectures, including logical and physical architectures, business objects, and distributed objects. Perhaps more importantly, this chapter sets the stage, showing the thought process that results in the remainder of the book.

Chapter 2 takes the architecture described at the end of Chapter 1 and uses it as the starting point for a code framework that enables the goals described earlier. By the end, you'll have seen the design process for the objects that will be implemented in Chapters 4 and 5; but before that, there's some other business to attend to.

Chapters 3 through 5 are all about the construction of the CSLA .NET framework itself. If you're interested in the code behind n-level undo, mobile object support, validation rules, authorization rules, and object persistence, then these are the chapters for you. In addition, they make use of some of the more advanced and interesting parts of the .NET Framework, including remoting, serialization, reflection, .NET security, Enterprise Services, System.Transactions, strongly named assemblies, dynamically loaded assemblies, application configuration files, and more.

The rest of the book then focuses on creating an application that makes use of the architecture and framework. Even if you're not particularly interested in learning all the lower-level .NET concepts from Chapters 3 through 5, you can take the framework and build applications based on it by reading Chapters 6 through 12.

In Chapter 6, I discuss the requirements of a sample application and create its database. The sample application uses SQL Server and creates not only tables but also stored procedures in order to enable retrieval and updating of data.

Chapter 7 discusses how to use each of the primary base classes in the CSLA .NET framework to create your own business objects. The basic code structure for editable and read-only objects, as well as collections and name/value lists, is discussed.

Chapter 8 creates the business objects for the application. This chapter really illustrates how you can use the framework to create a powerful set of business objects rapidly and easily for an application. The end result is a set of objects that not only model business entities, but also support n-level undo, data binding, and various physical configurations that can optimize performance, scalability, security, and fault tolerance, as discussed in Chapter 1.

Chapter 9 demonstrates how to create a Windows Forms interface to the business objects. Chapter 10 covers the creation of a Web Forms or an ASP.NET interface with comparable functionality.

In Chapter 11, Web Services is used to provide a programmatic interface to the business objects that any web service client can call.

Finally, Chapter 12 shows how to set up application servers using .NET Remoting, Enterprise Services, and Web Services. These application servers support the CSLA .NET framework and can be used interchangeably from the Windows Forms, Web Forms, and Web Services applications created in Chapters 8 through 11.

By the end, you'll have a framework that supports object-oriented application design in a practical, pragmatic manner. The framework implements a logical model that you can deploy in various physical configurations to optimally support Windows, web, and Web Services clients.

Framework License

LICENSE AND WARRANTY

The CSLA .NET framework is Copyright 2006 by Rockford Lhotka.

You can use this Software for any noncommercial purpose, including distributing derivative works. You can use this Software for any commercial purpose, except that you may not use it, in whole or in part, to create a commercial framework product.

In short, you can use CSLA .NET and modify it to create other commercial or business software, you just can't take the framework itself, modify it, and sell it as a product.

In return, the owner simply requires that you agree:

This Software License Agreement ("Agreement") is effective upon your use of CSLA .NET ("Software").

1. Ownership. The CSLA .NET framework is Copyright 2006 by Rockford Lhotka, Eden Prairie, MN, USA.

2. Copyright Notice. You must not remove any copyright notices from the Software source code.

3. License. The owner hereby grants a perpetual, non-exclusive, limited license to use the Software as set forth in this Agreement.

4. Source Code Distribution. If you distribute the Software in source code form, you must do so only under this License (i.e., you must include a complete copy of this License with your distribution).

5. Binary or Object Distribution. You may distribute the Software in binary or object form with no requirement to display copyright notices to the end user. The binary or object form must retain the copyright notices included in the Software source code.

6. Restrictions. You may not sell the Software. If you create a software development framework based on the Software as a derivative work, you may not sell that derivative work. This does not restrict the use of the Software for creation of other types of non-commercial or commercial applications or derivative works.

7. Disclaimer of Warranty. The Software comes "as is," with no warranties. None whatsoever. This means no express, implied, statutory, or other warranty, including without limitation, warranties of merchantability or fitness for a particular purpose, noninfringement, or the presence or absence of errors, whether or not discoverable. Also, you must pass this disclaimer on whenever you distribute the Software.

8. Liability. Neither Rockford Lhotka nor any contributor to the Software will be liable for any of those types of damages known as indirect, special, consequential, incidental, punitive, or exemplary related to the Software or this License, to the maximum extent the law permits, no matter what legal theory it's based on. Also, you must pass this limitation of liability on whenever you distribute the Software.

9. Patents. If you sue anyone over patents that you think may apply to the Software for a person's use of the Software, your license to the Software ends automatically.

   The patent rights, if any, licensed hereunder, only apply to the Software, not to any derivative works you make.

10. Termination. Your rights under this License end automatically if you breach it in any way.

    Rockford Lhotka reserves the right to release the Software under different license terms or to stop distributing the Software at any time. Such an election will not serve to withdraw this Agreement, and this Agreement will continue in full force and effect unless terminated as stated above.

11. Governing Law. This Agreement shall be construed and enforced in accordance with the laws of the state of Minnesota, USA.

12. No Assignment. Neither this Agreement nor any interest in this Agreement may be assigned by licensee without the prior express written approval of developer.

13. Final Agreement. This Agreement terminates and supersedes all prior understandings or agreements on the subject matter hereof. This Agreement may be modified only by a further writing that is duly executed by both parties.

14. Severability. If any term of this Agreement is held by a court of competent jurisdiction to be invalid or unenforceable, then this Agreement, including all of the remaining terms, will remain in full force and effect as if such invalid or unenforceable term had never been included.

15. Headings. Headings used in this Agreement are provided for convenience only, and shall not be used to construe meaning or intent.

What You Need to Use This Book

The code in this book has been verified to work against Microsoft Visual Studio 2005 Professional, and therefore against version 2.0 of the .NET Framework. The database is a SQL Server Express database, and SQL Server Express is included with Visual Studio 2005 Professional. The Enterprise version of VS 2005 and the full version of SQL Server are useful, but not necessary.

In order to run the tools and products listed previously, you'll need at least one PC with Windows 2000, Windows Server 2003, or Windows XP Professional Edition installed. To test CSLA .NET's support for multiple physical tiers, of course, you'll need an additional PC (or you can use Virtual PC or a similar tool) for each tier that you wish to add.

Conventions

I've used a number of different styles of text and layout in this book to differentiate between different kinds of information. Here are some examples of the styles used, and an explanation of what they mean.

Code has several fonts. If I'm talking about code in the body of the text, I use a fixed-width font like this: foreach. If it's a block of code that you can type as a program and run, on the other hand, then it will appear as follows:

```
if (Thread.CurrentPrincipal.Identity.IsAuthenticated)
{
  pnlUser.Text = Thread.CurrentPrincipal.Identity.Name;
  EnableMenus();
}
```

Sometimes, you'll see code in a mixture of styles, like this:

```
dgProjects.DataSource = ProjectList.GetProjectList();
DataBind();

// Set security
System.Security.Principal.IPrincipal user;
user = Threading.Thread.CurrentPrincipal;
```

When this happens, the code with a normal font is code you're already familiar with, or code that doesn't require immediate action. Lines in bold font indicate either new additions to the code since you last looked at it, or something that I particularly want to draw your attention to.

■**Tip** Advice, hints, and background information appear in this style.

■**Note** Important pieces of information are included as notes, like this.

Bullets appear indented, with each new bullet marked as follows:

• *Important words* are in italics.

How to Download Sample Code for This Book

Visit the Apress website at www.apress.com, and locate the title through the Search facility. Open the book's detail page and click the Source Code link. Alternatively, on the left-hand side of the Apress homepage, click the Source Code link, and select the book from the text box that appears.

Download files are archived in a zipped format, and need to be extracted with a decompression program such as WinZip or PKUnzip. The code is typically arranged with a suitable folder structure, so make sure that your decompression software is set to use folder names before extracting the files.

Author and Community Support

The books and CSLA .NET framework are also supported by both the author and a large user community.

The author maintains a website with answers to frequently asked questions, updates to the framework, an online discussion forum, and additional resources. Members of the community have created additional support websites and tools to assist in the understanding and use of CSLA .NET and related concepts.

For information and links to all these resources, visit www.lhotka.net/cslanet.

CHAPTER 1

Distributed Architecture

Object-oriented design and programming are big topics—there are entire books devoted solely to the process of object-oriented design, and other books devoted to using object-oriented programming in various languages and on various programming platforms. My focus in this book isn't to teach the basics of object-oriented design or programming, but rather to show how they may be applied to the creation of distributed .NET applications.

It can be difficult to apply object-oriented design and programming effectively in a physically distributed environment. This chapter is intended to provide a good understanding of the key issues surrounding distributed computing as it relates to object-oriented development. I'll cover a number of topics, including the following:

- How logical n-tier architectures help address reuse and maintainability

- How physical n-tier architectures impact performance, scalability, security, and fault tolerance

- The difference between data-centric and object-oriented application models

- How object-oriented models help increase code reuse and application maintainability

- The effective use of objects in a distributed environment, including the concepts of anchored and mobile objects

- The relationship between an architecture and a framework

This chapter provides an introduction to the concepts and issues surrounding distributed, object-oriented architecture. Throughout this book, you'll be exploring an n-tier architecture that may be physically distributed across multiple machines. The book will show how to use object-oriented design and programming techniques to implement a framework supporting this architecture. After that, a sample application will be created to demonstrate how the architecture and the framework support development efforts.

Logical and Physical Architecture

In today's world, an object-oriented application must be designed to work in a variety of physical configurations. Even the term "application" has become increasingly blurry due to all the hype around service-oriented architecture (SOA). If you aren't careful, you can end up building applications by combining several applications, which is obviously very confusing.

When I use the term "application" in this book, I'm referring to a set of code, objects, or components that's considered to be part of a single, logical unit. Even if parts of the application are in different .NET assemblies or installed on different machines, all the code is viewed as being part of a singular application.

Although such an application *might* run on a single machine, it's more likely that the application will run on a web server, or be split between a smart client and an application server. Given these varied physical environments, we're faced with the following questions:

- Where do the objects reside?
- Are the objects designed to maintain state, or should they be stateless?
- How is object-to-relational mapping handled when retrieving or storing data in the database?
- How are database transactions managed?

Before getting into discussing some answers to these questions, it's important to fully understand the difference between a *physical architecture* and a *logical architecture*. After that, I'll define objects and mobile objects, and show how they fit into the architectural discussion.

When most people talk about n-tier applications, they're talking about physical models in which the application is spread across multiple machines with different functions: a client, a web server, an application server, a database server, and so on. And this isn't a misconception—these are indeed n-tier systems. The problem is that many people tend to assume there's a one-to-one relationship between the tiers in a logical model and the tiers in a physical model, when in fact that's not always true.

A *physical* n-tier architecture is quite different from a *logical* n-tier (or n-layer) architecture. The latter has nothing to do with the number of machines or network hops involved in running the application. Rather, a logical architecture is all about separating different types of functionality. The most common logical separation is into a UI layer, a business layer, and a data layer that may exist on a single machine, or on three separate machines—the logical architecture doesn't define those details.

■**Note** There is a relationship between an application's logical and physical architectures: the logical architecture always has at least as many layers as the physical architecture has tiers. There may be more logical layers than physical ones (because one physical tier can contain several logical layers), but never fewer.

The sad reality is that many applications have no clearly defined logical architecture. Often the logical architecture merely defaults to the number of physical tiers. This lack of a formal, logical design causes problems because it reduces flexibility. If a system is designed to operate in two or three physical tiers, then changing the number of physical tiers at a later date is typically very difficult. However, if you start by creating a logical architecture of three layers, you can switch more easily between one, two, or three physical tiers later on.

Additionally, having clean separation between these layers makes your application more maintainable because changing one layer often has minimal impact on the other layers. Nowhere is this truer than with the Presentation layer, where the ability to switch between Windows Forms, Web Forms, Web Services, and future technologies like Windows Presentation Foundation (Avalon) is critical.

The flexibility to choose your physical architecture is important because the benefits gained by employing a physical n-tier architecture are different from those gained by employing a logical n-layer architecture. A properly designed logical n-layer architecture provides the following benefits:

- Logically organized code
- Easier maintenance
- Better reuse of code
- Better team-development experience
- Higher clarity in coding

On the other hand, a properly chosen physical n-tier architecture can provide the following benefits:

- Performance
- Scalability
- Fault tolerance
- Security

It goes almost without saying that if the physical or logical architecture of an application is designed poorly, there will be a risk of damaging the things that would have been improved had the job been done well.

Complexity

Experienced designers and developers often view a good n-tier architecture as a way of simplifying an application and reducing complexity, but this isn't necessarily the case. It's important to recognize that n-tier designs (logical and/or physical) are typically *more* complex than single-tier designs. Even novice developers can visualize the design of a form or a page that retrieves data from a file and displays it to the user, but novice developers often struggle with 2-tier designs, and are hopelessly lost in n-tier environments.

With sufficient experience, architects and developers typically find that the organization and structure of an n-tier model reduces complexity for large applications. However, even a veteran n-tier developer will often find it easier to avoid n-tier models when creating a simple form to display some simple data.

The point here is that n-tier architectures only simplify the process for large applications or complex environments. They can easily complicate matters if all you're trying to do is create a small application with a few forms that will be running on someone's desktop computer. (Of course, if that desktop computer is one of hundreds or thousands in a global organization, then the *environment* may be so complex that an n-tier solution provides simplicity.)

In short, n-tier architectures help to decrease or manage complexity when *any* of these are true:

- The application is large or complex.
- The application is one of many similar or related applications that *when combined* may be large or complex.
- The environment (including deployment, support, and other factors) is large or complex.

On the other hand, n-tier architectures can increase complexity when *all* of these are true:

- The application is small or relatively simple.
- The application isn't part of a larger group of enterprise applications that are similar or related.
- The environment isn't complex.

Something to remember is that even a small application is likely to grow, and even a simple environment will often become more complex over time. The more successful your application, the more likely that one or both of these will happen. If you find yourself on the edge of choosing an n-tier solution, it's typically best to go with it. You should expect and plan for growth.

This discussion illustrates why n-tier applications are viewed as relatively complex. There are a lot of factors, technical and non-technical, that must be taken into account. Unfortunately, it isn't possible to say definitively when n-tier does and doesn't fit. In the end, it's a judgment call that you, as an application architect, must make, based on the factors that affect your particular organization, environment, and development team.

Relationship Between Logical and Physical Models

Architectures such as Windows Distributed interNet Architecture (Windows DNA), represent a merger of logical and physical models. Such mergers seem attractive because they appear so simple and straightforward, but typically they aren't good in practice—they can lead people to design applications using a logical or physical architecture that isn't best suited to their needs.

■**Note** To be fair, Windows DNA didn't *mandate* that the logical and physical models be the same. Unfortunately, almost all of the printed material (even the mousepads) surrounding Windows DNA included diagrams and pictures that illustrated the "proper" Windows DNA implementation as an intertwined blur of physical and logical architecture. Although some experienced architects were able to separate the concepts, many more didn't, and created some horrendous results.

The Logical Model

When you're creating an application, it's important to start with a logical architecture that clarifies the roles of all components, separates functionality so that a team can work together effectively, and simplifies overall maintenance of the system. The logical architecture must also include enough layers so that you have flexibility in choosing a physical architecture later on.

Traditionally, you would devise at least a 3-layer logical model that separates the interface, the business logic, and the data-management portions of the application. Today that's rarely sufficient, because the "interface" layer is often physically split into two parts (browser and web server), and the "logic" layer is often physically split between a client or web server and an application server. Additionally, there are various application models that have been used to break the traditional Business Logic layer into multiple parts—model-view-controller and facade-data-logic being two of the most popular at the moment.

This means that the logical layers are governed by the following rules:

- The logical architecture includes layers in order to organize components into discrete roles.
- The logical architecture must have at least as many layers as the anticipated physical deployment will have tiers.

Following these rules, most modern applications have four to six logical layers. As you'll see, the architecture used in this book includes five logical layers.

The Physical Model

By ensuring that the logical model has enough layers to provide flexibility, you can configure your application into an appropriate physical architecture that will depend on your performance, scalability, fault tolerance, and security requirements. The more physical tiers included, the worse the performance will be; but there is the potential to increase scalability, security, and/or fault tolerance.

Performance and Scalability

The more physical tiers there are, the *worse* the performance? That doesn't sound right, but if you think it through, it makes perfect sense: *performance* is the speed at which an application responds to a user. This is different from *scalability*, which is a measure of how performance changes as load (such as increased users) is added to an application. To get optimal performance—that is, the fastest possible response time for a given user—the ideal solution is to put the client, the logic, and the data on the user's machine. This means no network hops, no network latency, and no contention with other users.

If you decide that you need to support multiple users, you might consider putting application data on a central file server. (This is typical with Access and dBASE systems, for example.) However, this immediately affects performance because of contention on the data file. Furthermore, data access now takes place across the network, which means you've introduced network latency and network contention, too. To overcome this problem, you could put the data into a managed environment such as SQL Server or Oracle. This will help to reduce data contention, but you're still stuck with the network latency and contention problems. Although improved, performance for a given user is still nowhere near what it was when everything ran directly on that user's computer.

Even with a central database server, scalability is limited. Clients are still in contention for the resources of the server, with each client opening and closing connections, doing queries and updates, and constantly demanding the CPU, memory, and disk resources that are being used by other clients. You can reduce this load by shifting some of the work to another server. An *application server*, possibly running Enterprise Services or Internet Information Services (IIS), can provide database connection pooling to minimize the number of database connections that are opened and closed. It can also perform some data processing, filtering, and even caching to offload some work from the database server.

These additional steps provide a dramatic boost to scalability, but again at the cost of performance. The user's request now has *two* network hops, potentially resulting in double the network latency and contention. For a single user, the system gets slower; but it is able to handle many times more users with acceptable performance levels.

In the end, the application is constrained by the most limiting resource. This is typically the speed of transferring data across the network—but if the database or application server is underpowered, it can become so slow that data transfer across the network isn't an issue. Likewise, if the application does extremely intense calculations and the client machines are slow, then the cost of transferring the data across the network to a relatively idle high-speed server can make sense.

Security

Security is a broad and complex topic, but by narrowing the discussion solely to consider how it's affected by physical n-tier decisions, it becomes more approachable. The discussion is no longer about authentication or authorization as much as it is about controlling physical access to the machines on which portions of the application will run. The number of physical tiers in an application has no impact on whether users can be authenticated or authorized, but physical tiers *can* be used to increase or decrease physical access to the machines on which the application executes.

For instance, in a 2-tier Windows Forms or Web Forms application, the machine running the UI code must have credentials to access the database server. Switching to a 3-tier model in which the data access code runs on an application server means that the machine running the UI code no longer needs those credentials, potentially making the system more secure.

Security requirements vary radically based on the environment and the requirements of your application. A Windows Forms application deployed only to internal users may need relatively little security, but a Web Forms application exposed to anyone on the Internet may need extensive security.

To a large degree, security is all about surface area: how many points of attack are exposed from the application? The surface area can be defined in terms of domains of trust.

Security and Internal Applications

Internal applications are totally encapsulated within a domain of trust: the client and all servers are running in a trusted environment. This means that virtually every part of the application is exposed to a potential hacker (assuming that the hacker can gain physical access to a machine on the network in the first place). In a typical organization, hackers can attack the client workstation, the web server, the application server, and the database server if they so choose. Rarely are there firewalls or other major security roadblocks *within* the context of an organization's LAN.

■**Note** Obviously, there *is* security. It is common to use Windows domain or Active Directory (AD) security on the clients and servers, but there's nothing stopping someone from attempting to communicate directly with any of these machines. Within a typical LAN, users can usually connect through the network to all machines due to a lack of firewall or physical barriers.

Because the internal environment is so exposed to start with, security should have little impact on the decisions regarding the number of physical tiers for the application. Increasing or decreasing the number of tiers will rarely have much impact on a hacker's ability to compromise the application from a client workstation on the LAN.

An exception to this rule comes when someone can use an application's own web services to access its servers in invalid ways. This problem was particularly acute with DCOM, because there were browsers that end users could use to locate and invoke server-side services. Thanks to COM, users could use Microsoft Excel to locate and interact with server-side COM components, thereby bypassing the portions of the application that were *supposed* to run on the client. This meant that the applications were vulnerable to power users who could use server-side components in ways their designers never imagined!

This problem is rapidly transferring to web services as Microsoft Office and other end-user applications start to allow power users to call web services from within macros. I expect to find power users calling web services in unexpected ways in the very near future.

The services in this book will be designed to prevent casual usage of the objects, even if a power user were to gain access to the service from their application.

In summary, although security shouldn't cause an increase or decrease in the number of physical tiers for internal applications, it *should* inform your design choices when exposing services from server machines.

Security and External Applications

For external applications, things are entirely different. This is really where SOA comes into play. Service orientation (SO) is all about assembling an "application" that spans trust boundaries. When part of your application is deployed outside your own network, that certainly crosses at least a security (trust) boundary.

In a client/server model, this would be viewed as a minimum of two tiers, since the client workstation is physically separate from any machines running behind the firewall.

But really, SO offers a better way to look at the problem: there are two totally separate applications. The client runs one application, and another application runs on your server. These two applications communicate with each other through clearly defined messages, and neither application is privy to the internal implementation of the other.

This provides a good way to deal with not only the security trust boundary, but also with the *semantic* trust boundary. What I mean by this is that the server application assumes that any data coming from the client application is flawed: either maliciously or due to a bug in the client. Even if the client has *security* access to interact with your server, the server application cannot assume that the semantic meaning of the data coming from the client is valid.

In short, because the client workstations are outside the domain of trust, you should assume that they're compromised and potentially malicious. You should assume that any code running on those clients will run incorrectly or not at all; in other words, the client input must be completely validated as it enters the domain of trust, even if the client includes code to do the validation.

Note I've had people tell me that this is an overly paranoid attitude, but I've been burned this way too many times. Any time an interface is exposed (Windows, web, XML, and so on) so that clients outside your control can use it, you should assume that the interface will be misused. Often, this misuse is unintentional—for example, someone may write a buggy macro to automate data entry. That's no different than if they made a typo while entering the data by hand, but user-entered data is always validated before being accepted by an application. The same must be true for automated data entry as well, or your application will fail.

This scenario occurs in three main architectures: smart/rich clients, web pages with DHTML/JavaScript, and AJAX-style web pages.

If you deploy a Windows Forms client application to external workstations, it should be designed as a stand-alone application that calls your server application through web services. Chapter 11 shows how you can do this with the object-oriented concepts in this book.

If you use JavaScript in your web pages to validate data or otherwise provide a richer experience for the user, your web UI code on the web server should assume that the browser didn't do anything it was supposed to. It is far too easy for a user to subvert your client-side JavaScript—as such, nothing running in the browser can be trusted.

And of course, more recently, web developers have started creating AJAX web pages that contain a *lot* of JavaScript code and do callbacks to the server through web services or specialized web pages. AJAX is an attempt to make browser-based applications approach the richness available to Windows applications. The same rules apply here: the code running in the browser should be viewed as a *separate* application that is not trusted by the server application.

In these latter two cases, it is important to realize that JavaScript is not object-oriented and is not at the same level of technology as .NET on the web server. You can apply the object-oriented concepts from this book on your web server, but the JavaScript and AJAX concepts in the browser are far more limited.

As you'll see, the object-oriented concepts and techniques shown in this book can be used to create smart client applications that call web services on your servers. They can be used to create those web services. They can also be used to create Web Forms applications, in which those web pages may use simple HTML, more complex client-side JavaScript, or even AJAX-based technologies.

Fault Tolerance

Fault tolerance is achieved by identifying points of failure and providing redundancy. Typically, applications have numerous points of failure. Some of the most obvious are as follows:

- The network feed to your user's buildings
- The power feed to your user's buildings
- The network feed and power feed to your data center
- The primary DNS host servicing your domain
- Your firewall, routers, switches, etc.
- Your web server
- Your application server
- Your database server
- Your internal LAN

In order to achieve high levels of fault tolerance, you need to ensure that if any one of these fails, some system will instantly kick in and fill the void. If the data center power goes out, a generator kicks in. If a bulldozer cuts your network feed, you'll need to have a second network feed coming in from the other side of the building, and so forth.

Considering some of the larger and more well-known outages of major websites in the past couple of years, it's worth noting that most of them occurred due to construction work cutting network or power feeds, or because their ISP or external DNS provider went down or was attacked. That said, there are plenty of examples of websites going down due to local equipment failure. The reason why the high-profile failures are seldom due to this type of problem is because large sites make sure to provide redundancy in these areas.

Clearly, adding redundant power, network, ISP, DNS, or LAN hardware will have little impact on application architecture. Adding redundant servers, on the other hand, *will* affect the n-tier application architecture—or at least the application design. Each time a physical tier is added, you need to ensure that you add redundancy to the servers in that tier. Thus, adding a fault-tolerant physical tier always means adding at least *two* servers to the infrastructure.

The more physical tiers, the more redundant servers there are to configure and maintain. This is why fault tolerance is typically expensive to achieve.

Not only that, but to achieve fault tolerance through redundancy, all servers in a tier must also be logically identical at all times. For example, at no time can a user be tied to a specific server, so no single server can ever maintain any user-specific information. As soon as a user is tied to a specific server, that server becomes a point of failure for that user. The result is that the user loses fault tolerance.

Achieving a high degree of fault tolerance isn't easy. It requires a great deal of thought and effort to locate all points of failure and make them redundant. Having fewer physical tiers in an architecture can assist in this process by reducing the number of tiers that must be made redundant.

To summarize, the number of physical tiers in an architecture is a trade-off between performance, scalability, security, and fault tolerance. Furthermore, the optimal configuration for a web application isn't the same as the one for an intranet application with smart client machines. If an application framework is to have any hope of broad appeal, it needs flexibility in the physical architecture so that it can support web and smart clients effectively, as well as provide both with optimal performance and scalability. Beyond that, it needs to work well in a service-oriented environment to create both client and server applications that interact through message-based communication.

A 5-Layer Logical Architecture

This book will explore a 5-layer logical architecture and show how you can implement it using object-oriented concepts. Once the logical architecture has been created, it will be configured into various physical architectures in order to achieve optimal results for Windows Forms, Web Forms, and Web Services interfaces.

■Note If you get any group of architects into a room and ask them to describe their ideal architecture, each one will come up with a different answer. I make no pretense that this architecture is the only one out there, nor do I intend to discuss all the possible options. My aim here is to present a coherent, distributed, object-oriented architecture that supports Windows, web, and Web Services interfaces.

In the framework used in this book, the logical architecture comprises the five layers shown in Figure 1-1.

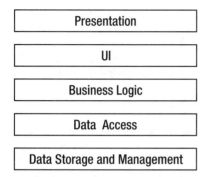

Figure 1-1. *The 5-layer logical architecture*

Remember that the benefit of a logical n-layer architecture is the separation of functionality into clearly defined roles or groups, in order to increase clarity and maintainability. Let's define each of the layers more carefully.

Presentation

At first, it may not be clear why I've separated presentation from the user interface (UI). Certainly, from a Windows perspective, presentation and UI are one and the same: They are graphical user interface (GUI) forms with which the user can interact.

From a web perspective (or from that of terminal-based programming), the distinction is probably quite clear. Typically, the browser merely presents information to the user and collects user input. In that case, all of the actual interaction logic—the code written to *generate* the output, or to *interpret* user input—runs on the web server (or mainframe), and not on the client machine.

Of course, in today's world, the browser might run JavaScript or even richer client-side code. But as discussed earlier in the chapter, none of this code can be trusted. It must be viewed as being a *separate* application that interacts with your application as it runs on the server. So even with code running in the browser, *your* application's UI code is running on your web server.

Knowing that the logical model must support both smart and web-based clients (along with even more limited clients, such as cell phones or other mobile devices), it's important to recognize that in many cases, the presentation will be physically separate from the UI logic. In order to accommodate this separation, it is necessary to design the applications around this concept.

■Note The types of presentation technologies continue to multiply, and each comes with a new and relatively incompatible technology with which we must work. It's virtually impossible to create a programming framework that entirely abstracts presentation concepts. Because of this, the architecture and framework will merely *support the creation* of varied presentations, not automate their creation. Instead, the focus will be on simplifying the other tiers in the architecture, for which technology is more stable.

User Interface

Now that I've addressed the distinction between presentation and UI, the latter's purpose is probably fairly clear. This layer includes the logic to decide what the user sees, the navigation paths, and how to interpret user input. In a Windows Forms application, this is the code behind the form. Actually, it's the code behind the form in a Web Forms application, too, but here it can also include code that resides in server-side controls; *logically*, that's part of the same layer.

In many applications, the UI code is very complex. For a start, it must respond to the user's requests in a nonlinear fashion. (It is difficult to control how users might click controls, or enter or leave the forms or pages.) The UI code must also interact with logic in the business layer to validate user input, to perform any processing that's required, or to do any other business-related action.

Basically, the goal is to write UI code that accepts user input and then provides it to the business layer, where it can be validated, processed, or otherwise manipulated. The UI code must then respond to the user by displaying the results of its interaction with the business layer. Was the user's data valid? If not, what was wrong with it? And so forth.

In .NET, the UI code is almost always event-driven. Windows Forms code is all about responding to events as the user types and clicks the form, and Web Forms code is all about responding to events as the browser round-trips the user's actions back to the web server. Although both Windows Forms and Web Forms technologies make heavy use of objects, the code that is typically written into the UI isn't object-oriented as much as procedural and event-based.

That said, there's great value in creating frameworks and reusable components that will support a particular type of UI. When creating a Windows Forms UI, developers can make use of visual inheritance and other object-oriented techniques to simplify the creation of the forms. When creating a Web Forms UI, developers can use ASP.NET user controls and custom server controls to provide reusable components that simplify page development.

Because there's such a wide variety of UI styles and approaches, I won't spend much time dealing with UI development or frameworks in this book. Instead, I'll focus on simplifying the creation of the Business Logic and Data Access layers, which are required for any type of UI.

Business Logic

Business logic includes all business rules, data validation, manipulation, processing, and security for the application. One definition from Microsoft is as follows: "The combination of validation edits, login verifications, database lookups, policies, and algorithmic transformations that constitute an enterprise's way of doing business."[1]

■**Note**   Again, while you may implement validation logic to run in a browser or other external client, that code can't be trusted. You must view the logic that runs under your control in the business layer as being the only *real* validation logic.

The business logic *must* reside in a separate layer from the UI code. While you may choose to duplicate some of this logic in your UI code to provide a richer user experience, the business layer must implement all the business logic, because it is the only point of central control and maintainability.

I believe that this particular separation between the responsibilities of the business layer and UI layer is absolutely critical if you want to gain the benefits of increased maintainability and reusability. This is because any business logic that creeps into the UI layer will reside within a *specific* UI, and will not be available to any other UIs that might be created later.

Any business logic written into (say) a Windows UI is useless to a web or Web Services interface, and must therefore be written into those as well. This instantly leads to duplicated code, which is a maintenance nightmare. Separation of these two layers can be done through techniques such as clearly defined procedural models, or object-oriented design and programming.

---

1. MSDN, "Business rule" definition, "Enterprise Glossary." See http://msdn.microsoft.com/library/default. asp?url=/library/en-us/vsentpro/html/veovrb.asp.

In this book, I'll show how to use object-oriented concepts to help separate the business logic from the UI.

It is important to recognize that a typical application will use business logic in a couple different ways. Most applications have some user interaction, such as forms in which the user views or enters data into the system. Most applications also have some very non-interactive processes, such as posting invoices, relieving inventory, or calculating insurance rates.

Ideally, the Business Logic layer will be used in a very rich and interactive way when the user is directly entering data into the application. For instance, when a user is entering a sales order, he or she expects that the validation of data, the calculation of tax, and the subtotaling of the order will happen literally as they type. This implies that the business layer can be physically deployed on the client workstation or on the web server to provide the high levels of interactivity users desire.

To support non-interactive processes, on the other hand, the Business Logic layer often needs to be deployed onto an application server, or as close to the database server as possible. For instance, the calculation of an insurance rate can involve extensive database lookups along with quite a bit of complex business processing. This is the kind of thing that should occur behind the scenes on a server, not on a user's desktop.

Fortunately, it is possible to deploy a logical layer on multiple physical tiers. Doing this does require some up-front planning and technical design, as you'll see in Chapter 2. The end result, however, is a single business layer that is potentially deployed on both the client workstation (or web server) and on the application server. This allows the application to provide high levels of interactivity when the user is working directly with the application, and efficient back-end processing for non-interactive processes.

Data Access

Data access code interacts with the Data Management layer to retrieve, insert, update, and remove information. The Data Access layer doesn't actually manage or store the data; it merely provides an interface between the business logic and the database.

Data access gets its own logical layer for much the same reason that the presentation is split from the UI. In some cases, data access will occur on a machine that's physically separate from the one on which the UI and/or business logic is running. In other cases, data access code will run on the same machine as the business logic (or even the UI) in order to improve performance or fault tolerance.

■**Note** It may sound odd to say that putting the Data Access layer on the same machine as the business logic can *increase* fault tolerance, but consider the case of web farms, in which each web server is identical to all the others. Putting the data access code on the web servers provides automatic redundancy of the Data Access layer along with the Business Logic and UI layers.

Adding an extra physical tier just to do the data access makes fault tolerance harder to implement, because it increases the number of tiers in which redundancy needs to be implemented. As a side effect, adding more physical tiers also reduces performance for a single user, so it's not something that should be done lightly.

Logically defining data access as a separate layer enforces a separation between the business logic and any interaction with a database (or any other data source). This separation provides the flexibility to choose later whether to run the data access code on the same machine as the business logic, or on a separate machine. It also makes it much easier to change data sources without affecting the application. This is important because it enables switching from one database vendor to another at some point.

This separation is useful for another reason: Microsoft has a habit of changing data access technologies every three years or so, meaning that it is necessary to rewrite the data access code to keep up (remember DAO, RDO, ADO 1.0, ADO 2.0, and now ADO.NET?). By isolating the data access code into a specific layer, the impact of these changes is limited to a smaller part of the application.

Data access mechanisms are typically implemented as a set of services, with each service being a procedure that's called by the business logic to retrieve, insert, update, or delete data. Although these services are often constructed using objects, it's important to recognize that the designs for an effective Data Access layer are really quite procedural in nature. Attempts to force more object-oriented designs for relational database access often result in increased complexity or decreased performance. I think the best approach is to implement the data access as a set of methods, but encapsulate those methods within objects to keep them logically organized.

■**Note** If you're using an object database instead of a relational database, then of course the data access code may be very object-oriented. Few of us get such an opportunity, however, because almost all data is stored in relational databases.

Sometimes the Data Access layer can be as simple as a series of methods that use ADO.NET directly to retrieve or store data. In other circumstances, the Data Access layer is more complex, providing a more abstract or even metadata-driven way to get at data. In these cases, the Data Access layer can contain a lot of complex code to provide this more abstract data access scheme. The framework created in this book doesn't restrict how you implement your Data Access layer. The examples in the book will work directly against ADO.NET, but you could also use a metadata-driven Data Access layer if you prefer.

Another common role for the Data Access layer is to provide mapping between the object-oriented business logic and the relational data in a data store. A good object-oriented model is almost never the same as a good relational database model. Objects often contain data from multiple tables, or even from multiple databases; or conversely, multiple objects in the model can represent a single table. The process of taking the data from the tables in a relational model and getting it into the object-oriented model is called *object-relational mapping* (ORM), and I'll have more to say on the subject in Chapter 2.

Data Storage and Management

Finally, there's the Data Storage and Management layer. Database servers such as SQL Server and Oracle often handle these tasks, but increasingly, other applications may provide this functionality, too, via technologies such as Web Services.

What's key about this layer is that it handles the physical creation, retrieval, update, and deletion of data. This is different from the Data Access layer, which *requests* the creation, retrieval, update, and deletion of data. The Data Management layer actually *implements* these operations within the context of a database or a set of files.

The business logic (via the Data Access layer) invokes the Data Management layer, but the layer often includes additional logic to validate the data and its relationship to other data. Sometimes, this is true relational data modeling from a database; other times, it's the application of business logic from an external application. What this means is that a typical Data Management layer will include business logic that is also implemented in the Business Logic layer. This time, the replication is unavoidable because relational databases are designed to enforce relational integrity; and that's just another form of business logic.

In summary, whether you're using stored procedures in SQL Server, or web service calls to another application, data storage and management is typically handled by creating a set of services or procedures that can be called as needed. Like the Data Access layer, it's important to recognize that the designs for data storage and management are typically very procedural.

Table 1-1 summarizes the five layers and their roles.

Table 1-1. *The Five Logical Layers and the Roles They Provide*

Layer	Roles
Presentation	Renders display and collects user input.
UI	Acts as an intermediary between the user and the business logic, taking user input and providing it to the business logic, then returning results to the user.
Business Logic	Provides all business rules, validation, manipulation, processing, and security for the application.
Data Access	Acts as an intermediary between the business logic and data management. Also encapsulates and contains all knowledge of data access technologies (such as ADO.NET), databases, and data structures.
Data Storage and Management	Physically creates, retrieves, updates, and deletes data in a persistent data store.

Everything I've talked about to this point is part of a *logical* architecture. Now it's time to move on and see how it can be applied in various *physical* configurations.

Applying the Logical Architecture

Given this 5-layer logical architecture, it should be possible to configure it into one, two, three, four, or five physical tiers in order to gain performance, scalability, security, or fault tolerance to various degrees, and in various combinations.

Note In this discussion, it is assumed that there is total flexibility to configure which logical layer runs where. In some cases, there are technical issues that prevent the physical separation of some layers. Fortunately, there are fewer such issues with the .NET Framework than there were with COM-based technologies.

There are a few physical configurations that I want to discuss in order to illustrate how the logical model works. These are common and important setups that are encountered on a day-to-day basis.

Optimal Performance Smart Client

When so much focus is placed on distributed systems, it's easy to forget the value of a single-tier solution. Point of sale, sales force automation, and many other types of application often run in stand-alone environments. However, the benefits of the logical n-layer architecture are still desirable in terms of maintainability and code reuse.

It probably goes without saying that everything can be installed on a single client workstation. An optimal performance smart client is usually implemented using Windows Forms for the presentation and UI, with the business logic and data access code running in the same process and talking to an Access (JET) or Microsoft SQL Server Express database. The fact that the system is deployed on a single physical tier doesn't compromise the logical architecture and separation, as shown in Figure 1-2.

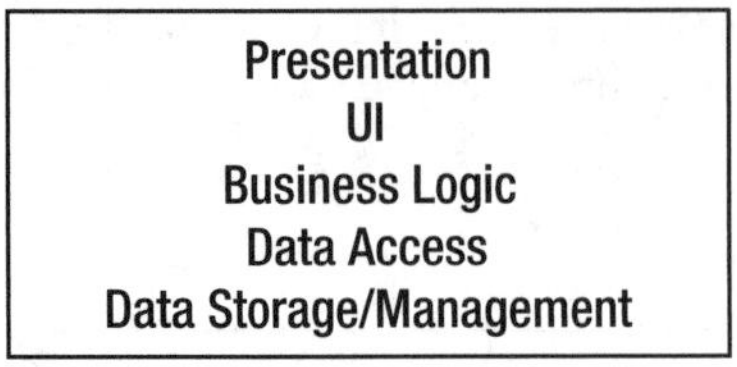

```
┌─────────────────────────────────┐
│          Presentation           │
│               UI                │
│         Business Logic          │
│          Data Access            │
│      Data Storage/Management    │
└─────────────────────────────────┘
```

Figure 1-2. *The five logical layers running on a single machine*

I think it's very important to remember that n-layer systems can run on a single machine in order to support the wide range of applications that require stand-alone machines. It's also worth pointing out that this is basically the same as 2-tier, "fat-client" physical architecture; the only difference in that case is that the Data Storage and Management tier would be running on a central database server, such as SQL Server or Oracle, as shown in Figure 1-3.

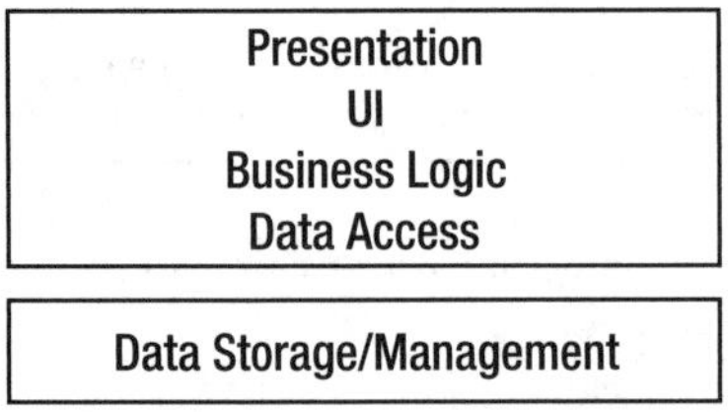

```
┌─────────────────────────────────┐
│          Presentation           │
│               UI                │
│         Business Logic          │
│          Data Access            │
└─────────────────────────────────┘
┌─────────────────────────────────┐
│      Data Storage/Management    │
└─────────────────────────────────┘
```

Figure 1-3. *The five logical layers with a separate database server*

Other than the location of the data storage, this is identical to the single-tier configuration, and typically the switch from single-tier to 2-tier revolves around little more than changing the database configuration string for ADO.NET.

High-Scalability Smart Client

Single-tier configurations are good for stand-alone environments, but they don't scale well. To support multiple users, it is common to use 2-tier configurations. I've seen 2-tier configurations support more than 350 concurrent users against SQL Server with very acceptable performance.

Going further, it is possible to trade performance to gain scalability by moving the Data Access layer to a separate machine. Single or 2-tier configurations give the best performance, but they don't scale as well as a 3-tier configuration would. A good rule of thumb is that if you have more than 50 to 100 concurrent users, you can benefit by making use of a separate server to handle the Data Access layer.

Another reason for moving the Data Access layer to an application server is security. Since the Data Access layer contains the code that directly interacts with the database, the machine on which it runs must have credentials to access the database server. Rather than having those credentials on the client workstation, they can be moved to an application server. This way, the user's computer won't have the credentials to interact directly with the database server, thus increasing security.

It is also possible to put the Business Logic layer on the application server. This is very useful for non-interactive processes such as batch updates or data-intensive business algorithms. Yet, at the same time, most applications allow for user interaction, and so there is a very definite need to have the Business Logic layer running on the client workstation to provide high levels of interactivity for the user.

As discussed earlier in the chapter, it is possible to deploy the same logical layer onto multiple physical tiers. Using this idea, the Data Access layer can be put on an application server, and the Business Logic layer on *both* the client workstation and the application server, as shown in Figure 1-4.

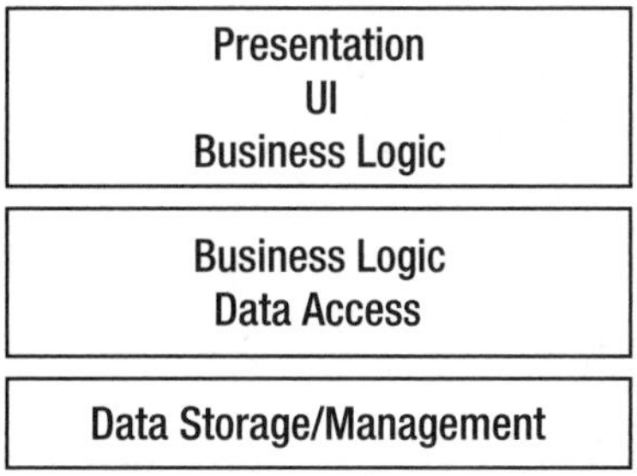

```
┌─────────────────────────────┐
│        Presentation         │
│             UI              │
│       Business Logic        │
└─────────────────────────────┘
┌─────────────────────────────┐
│       Business Logic        │
│        Data Access          │
└─────────────────────────────┘
┌─────────────────────────────┐
│   Data Storage/Management   │
└─────────────────────────────┘
```

Figure 1-4. *The five logical layers with separate application and database servers*

Putting the Data Access layer on the application server centralizes all access to the database on a single machine. In .NET, if the connections to the database for all users are made using the same user ID and password, you'll get the benefits of *connection pooling* for all your users. What this means immediately is that there will be far fewer connections to the database than there would be if each client machine connected directly. The actual reduction depends on the specific application, but often it means supporting 150 to 200 concurrent users with just two or three database connections!

Of course, all user requests now go across an extra network hop, thereby causing increased latency (and therefore decreased performance). This performance cost translates into a huge scalability gain, however, because this architecture can handle many more concurrent users than a 2-tier physical configuration.

With the Business Logic layer deployed on both the client and server, the application is able to fully exploit the strengths of both machines. Validation and a lot of other business processing can run on the client workstation to provide a rich and highly interactive experience for the user, while non-interactive processes can efficiently run on the application server.

If well designed, such an architecture can support *thousands* of concurrent users with adequate performance.

Optimal Performance Web Client

As with a Windows Forms application, the best performance is received from a web-based application by minimizing the number of physical tiers. However, the trade-off in a web scenario is different: in this case, it is possible to improve performance and scalability at the same time, but at the cost of security, as I will demonstrate.

To get optimal performance in a web application, it is desirable to run most of the code in a single process on a single machine, as shown in Figure 1-5.

The Presentation layer must be physically separate because it's running in a browser, but the UI, Business Logic, and Data Access layers can all run on the same machine, in the same process. In some cases, you might even put the Data Management layer on the same physical machine, though this is only suitable for smaller applications.

This minimizes network and communication overhead and optimizes performance. Figure 1-6 shows how it is possible to get very good scalability, because the web server can be part of a web farm in which all the web servers are running the same code.

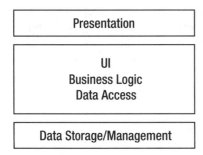

Figure 1-5. *The five logical layers as used for web applications*

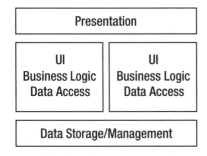

Figure 1-6. *The five logical layers deployed on a load-balanced web farm*

This setup provides very good database-connection pooling because each web server will be (potentially) servicing hundreds of concurrent users, and all database connections on a web server are pooled.

■**Note** In COM-based technologies such as ASP and Visual Basic 6, this configuration was problematic, because running COM components in the same process as ASP pages had drawbacks in terms of the manageability and stability of the system. Running the COM components in a COM+ server application addressed the stability issues, but at the cost of performance. These issues have been addressed in .NET, however, so this configuration is highly practical when using ASP.NET and other .NET components.

Unless the database server is getting overwhelmed with connections from the web servers in the web farm, a separate application server will rarely provide gains in scalability. If a separate application server is needed, there will be a reduction in performance because of the additional physical tier. (Hopefully, there will be a gain in scalability, because the application server can consolidate database connections across all the web servers.) It is important to consider fault tolerance in this case, because redundant application servers may be needed in order to avoid a point of failure.

Another reason for implementing an application server is to increase security, and that's the topic of the next section.

High-Security Web Client

As discussed in the earlier section on security, there will be many projects in which it's dictated that a web server can never talk directly to a database. The web server must run in a "demilitarized zone" (DMZ), sandwiched between the external firewall and a second internal firewall. The web server must communicate with another server through the internal firewall in order to interact with the database or any other internal systems.

As with the 3-tier Windows client scenario, there is tremendous benefit to also having the Business Logic layer deployed on both the web server and the application server. Such a deployment allows the Web Forms UI code to interact closely with the business logic when appropriate, while non-interactive processes can simply run on the application server.

This is illustrated in Figure 1-7, in which the dashed lines represent the firewalls.

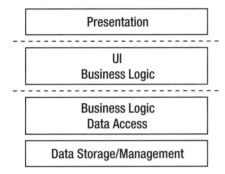

Figure 1-7. *The five logical layers deployed in a secure web configuration*

Splitting out the Data Access layer and running it on a separate application server increases the security of the application. However, this comes at the cost of performance—as discussed earlier, this configuration will typically cause a performance degradation of around 50 percent. Scalability, on the other hand, is fine: like the first web configuration, it can be achieved by implementing a web farm in which each web server runs the same UI and business logic code, as shown in Figure 1-8.

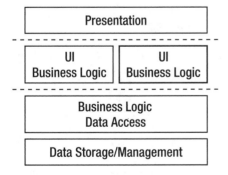

Figure 1-8. *The five logical layers in a secured environment with a web farm*

The Way Ahead

After implementing the framework to support this 5-layer architecture, I'll create a sample application with three different interfaces: Windows Forms, Web Forms, and Web Services. This will give you the opportunity to see firsthand how the framework supports the following models:

- High-scalability smart client
- Optimal performance web client
- Optimal performance web service

Due to the way the framework is implemented, switching to any of the other models just discussed will require only configuration file changes. The result is that you can easily adapt your application to any of the physical configurations without having to change your code.

Managing Business Logic

At this point, you should have a good understanding of logical and physical architectures, and how a 5-layer logical architecture can be configured into various n-tier physical architectures. In one way or another, all of these layers will use or interact with the application's data. That's obviously the case for the Data Management and Data Access layers, but the Business Logic layer must validate, calculate, and manipulate data; the UI transfers data between the Business Logic and Presentation layers (often performing formatting or using the data to make navigational choices); and the Presentation layer displays data to the user and collects new data as it's entered.

In an ideal world, all of the business logic would exist in the Business Logic layer, but in reality, this is virtually impossible to achieve. In a web-based UI, validation logic is often included in the Presentation layer, so that the user gets a more interactive experience in the browser. Unfortunately, any validation that's done in the web browser is unreliable, because it's too easy for a malicious user to bypass that validation. Thus, any validation done in the browser must be rechecked in the Business Logic layer as well.

Similarly, most databases enforce referential integrity, and often some other rules, too. Furthermore, the Data Access layer will very often include business logic to decide when and how data should be stored or retrieved from databases and other data sources. In almost any application, to a greater or a lesser extent, business logic gets scattered across all the layers.

There's one key truth here that's important: for each piece of application data, there's a fixed set of business logic associated with that data. If the application is to function properly, the business logic must be applied to that data at least once. Why "at least"? Well, in most applications, some of the business logic is applied more than once. For example, a validation rule applied in the Presentation layer can be reapplied in the UI layer or Business Logic layer before data is sent to the database for storage. In some cases, the database will include code to recheck the value as well.

Now, I'd like to look at some of the more common options. I'll start with three popular (but flawed) approaches. Then I'll discuss a compromise solution that's enabled through the use of mobile objects; such as the ones supported by the framework I'll create later in the book.

Potential Business Logic Locations

Figure 1-9 illustrates common locations for validation and manipulation business logic in a typical application. Most applications have the same logic in at least a couple of these locations.

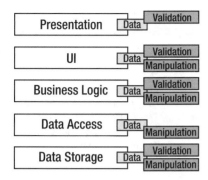

Figure 1-9. *Common locations for business logic in applications*

Business logic is put in a Web Presentation layer to give the user a more interactive experience—and put into a Windows UI for the same reason. The business logic is rechecked in the web UI (on the web server) because the browser isn't trustworthy. And database administrators put the logic into the database (via stored procedures and other database constructs) because they don't trust any application developers!

The result of all this validation is a lot of duplicated code, all of which has to be debugged, maintained, and somehow kept in sync as the business needs (and thus logic) change over time. In the real world, the logic is almost never *really* kept in sync, and so developers must constantly debug and maintain the code in a near-futile effort to make all of these redundant bits of logic agree with each other.

One solution is to force all of the logic into a single layer, thereby making the other layers as "dumb" as possible. There are various approaches to this, although (as you'll see) none of them provide an optimal solution.

Business Logic in the Data Management Tier

The classic approach is to put all logic into the database as the single, central repository. The presentation and UI then allow the user to enter absolutely anything (because any validation would be redundant), and the Business Logic layer now resides inside the database. The Data Access layer does nothing but move the data into and out of the database, as shown in Figure 1-10.

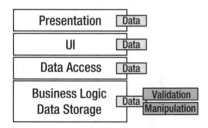

Figure 1-10. *Validation and business logic in the Data Management tier*

The advantage of this approach is that the logic is centralized, but the drawbacks are plentiful. For starters, the user experience is totally non-interactive. Users can't get any results, or even confirmation that their data is valid, without round-tripping the data to the database for processing. The database server becomes a performance bottleneck, because it's the only thing doing any actual work. Unfortunately, the hardest physical tier to scale up for more users is the database server, since it is difficult to use load-balancing techniques on it. The only real alternative is to buy bigger and bigger server machines.

Business Logic in the UI Tier

Another common approach is to put all of the business logic into the UI. The data is validated and manipulated in the UI, and the Data Storage layer just stores the data. This approach, as shown in Figure 1-11, is very common in both Windows and web environments, and has the advantage that the business logic is centralized into a single tier (and of course, one can write the business logic in a language such as C# or VB .NET).

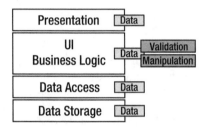

Figure 1-11. *Business logic deployed with only the UI*

Unfortunately, in practice, the business logic ends up being scattered throughout the UI and intermixed with the UI code itself, thereby decreasing readability and making maintenance more difficult. Even more importantly, business logic in one form or page isn't reusable when subsequent pages or forms are created that use the same data. Furthermore, in a web environment, this architecture also leads to a totally non-interactive user experience, because no validation can occur in the browser. The user must transmit his or her data to the web server for any validation or manipulation to take place.

■**Note** ASP.NET Web Forms' validation controls at least allow for basic data validation in the UI, with that validation automatically extended to the browser by the Web Forms technology itself. Though not a total solution, this is a powerful feature that does help.

Business Logic in the Middle (Business and Data Access) Tier

Still another option is the classic UNIX client/server approach, whereby the Business Logic and Data Access layers are merged, keeping the Presentation, UI, and Data Storage tiers as "dumb" as possible (see Figure 1-12).

Unfortunately, once again, this approach falls afoul of the non-interactive user experience problem: the data must round-trip to the Business Logic/Data Access tier for any validation or manipulation. This is especially problematic if the Business Logic/Data Access tier is running on a separate application server, because then you're faced with network latency and contention issues, too. Also, the central application server can become a performance bottleneck, because it's the only machine doing any work for all the users of the application.

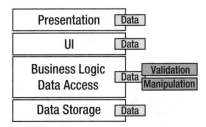

Figure 1-12. *Business logic deployed on only the application server*

Sharing Business Logic Across Tiers

I wish this book included the secret that allows you to write all your logic in one central location, thereby avoiding all of these awkward issues. Unfortunately, that's not possible with today's technology: putting the business logic only on the client, application server, or database server is problematic, for all the reasons given earlier. But something needs to be done about it, so what's left?

What's left is the possibility of centralizing the business logic in a Business Logic layer that's deployed on the client (or web server), so that it's accessible to the UI layer; and in a Business Logic layer that's deployed on the application server, so that it's able to interact efficiently with the Data Access layer. The end result is the best of both worlds: a rich and interactive user experience and efficient high-performance back-end processing when interacting with the database (or other data source).

In the simple cases in which there is no application server, the Business Logic layer is deployed only once: on the client workstation or web server, as shown in Figure 1-13.

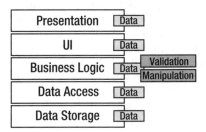

Figure 1-13. *Business logic centralized in the Business Logic layer*

Ideally, this business logic will run on the same machine as the UI code when interacting with the user, but on the same machine as the data access code when interacting with the database. (As discussed earlier, all of this could be on one machine or a number of different machines, depending on your physical architecture.) It must provide a friendly interface that the UI developer can use to invoke any validation and manipulation logic, and it must also work efficiently with the Data Access tier to get data in and out of storage.

The tools for addressing this seemingly intractable set of requirements are *mobile business objects* that encapsulate the application's data along with its related business logic. It turns out that a properly constructed business object can move around the network from machine to machine with almost no effort on your part. The .NET Framework itself handles the details, and you can focus on the business logic and data.

By properly designing and implementing mobile business objects, you allow the .NET Framework to pass your objects across the network *by value*, thereby automatically copying them from one machine to another. This means that with little extra code, you can have your business logic and business data move to the machine where the UI tier is running, and then shift to the machine where the Data Access tier is running when data access is required.

At the same time, if you're running the UI tier and Data Access tier on the same machine, then the .NET Framework doesn't move or copy your business objects. They're used directly by both tiers with no performance cost or extra overhead. You don't have to do anything to make this happen, either—.NET automatically detects that the object doesn't need to be copied or moved, and thus takes no extra action.

The Business Logic layer becomes portable, flexible, and mobile, and adapts to the physical environment in which you deploy the application. Due to this, you're able to support a variety of physical n-tier architectures with one code base, whereby your business objects contain no extra code to support the various possible deployment scenarios. What little code you need to implement to support the movement of your objects from machine to machine will be encapsulated in a framework, leaving the business developer to focus purely on the development of business logic.

Business Objects

Having decided to use business objects and take advantage of .NET's ability to move objects around the network automatically, it's now time to discuss business objects in more detail. I will discuss exactly what they are and how they can help you to centralize the business logic pertaining to your data.

The primary goal when designing any kind of software object is to create an abstract representation of some entity or concept. In ADO.NET, for example, a DataTable object represents a tabular set of data. DataTables provide an abstract and consistent mechanism by which you can work with *any* tabular data. Likewise, a Windows Forms TextBox control is an object that represents the concept of displaying and entering data. From the application's perspective, there is no need to have any understanding of how the control is rendered on the screen, or how the user interacts with it. It's just an object that includes a Text property and a handful of interesting events.

Key to successful object design is the concept of *encapsulation*. This means that an object is a black box: it contains logic and data, but the user of the object doesn't know *what* data or *how* the logic actually works. All they can do is interact with the object.

■**Note** Properly designed objects encapsulate both behavior or logic and the data required by that logic.

If objects are abstract representations of entities or concepts that encapsulate both data and its related logic, what then are *business objects*?

■**Note** Business objects are different from regular objects only in terms of what they represent.

Object-oriented applications are created to address problems of one sort or another. In the course of doing so, a variety of different objects are often used. Some of these objects will have no direct connection with the problem at hand (DataTable and TextBox objects, for example, are just abstract representations of computer concepts). However, there will be others that are closely related to the area or *domain* in which you're working. If the objects are related to the business for which you're developing an application, then they're business objects.

For instance, if you're creating an order entry system, your business domain will include things such as customers, orders, and products. Each of these will likely become business objects within your order entry application—the Order object, for example, will provide an abstract representation of the order being placed by a customer.

■**Note** Business objects provide an abstract representation of entities or concepts that are part of the business or problem domain.

Business Objects As Smart Data

I've already discussed the drawbacks of putting business logic into the UI tier, but I haven't thoroughly discussed the drawback of keeping the data in a generic representation such as a DataSet object. The data in a DataSet (or an array or XML document) is unintelligent, unprotected, and generally unsafe. There's nothing to prevent anyone from putting invalid data into any of these containers, and there's nothing to ensure that the business logic behind one form in the application will interact with the data in the same way as the business logic behind another form.

A DataSet or an XML document with an XSD (XML Schema Definition) might ensure that text cannot be entered where a number is required, or that a number cannot be entered where a date is required. At best, it might enforce some basic relational-integrity rules. However, there's no way to ensure that the values match other criteria, or that calculations or other processing is done properly against the data, without involving other objects. The data in a DataSet, an array, or an XML document isn't self-aware; it's not able to apply business rules or handle business manipulation or processing of the data.

The data in a business object, however, is what I like to call "smart data." The object not only contains the data, but also includes all the business logic that goes along with that data. Any attempt to work with the data must go through this business logic. In this arrangement, there is much greater assurance that business rules, manipulation, calculations, and other processing will be executed consistently everywhere in the application. In a sense, the data has become self-aware, and can protect itself against incorrect usage.

In the end, an object doesn't care whether it's used by a Windows Forms UI, a batch-processing routine, or a web service. The code using the object can do as it pleases; the object itself will ensure that all business rules are obeyed at all times.

Contrast this with a DataSet or an XML document, in which the business logic doesn't reside in the data container, but somewhere else—typically, a Windows form or a web form. If multiple forms or pages use this DataSet, there is no assurance that the business logic is applied consistently. Even if you adopt a standard that says that UI developers must invoke methods from a centralized class to interact with the data, there's nothing preventing them from using the DataSet directly. This may happen accidentally, or because it was simply easier or faster to use the DataSet than to go through some centralized routine.

■**Note** With consistent use of business objects, there's no way to bypass the business logic. The only way to the data is through the object, and the object always enforces the rules.

So, a business object that represents an invoice will include not only the data pertaining to the invoice, but also the logic to calculate taxes and amounts due. The object should understand how to post itself to a ledger, and how to perform any other accounting tasks that are required. Rather than passing raw invoice data around, and having the business logic scattered throughout the application, it is possible to pass an Invoice object around. The entire application can share not only the data, but also its associated logic. Smart data through objects can dramatically increase the ability to reuse code, and can decrease software-maintenance costs.

Anatomy of a Business Object

Putting all of these pieces together, you get an object that has an interface (a set of properties and methods), some implementation code (the business logic behind those properties and methods), and state (the data). This is illustrated in Figure 1-14.

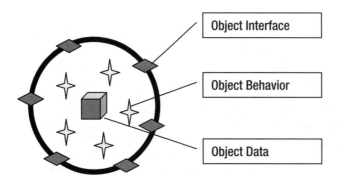

Object Interface

Object Behavior

Object Data

Figure 1-14. *A business object composed of state, implementation, and interface*

The hiding of the data and the implementation code behind the interface are keys to the successful creation of a business object. If the users of an object are allowed to "see inside" it, they will be tempted to cheat, and to interact with the logic or data in unpredictable ways. This danger is the reason that it will be important to take care when using the public keyword as you build your classes.

Any property, method, event, or field marked as public will be available to the users of objects created from the class. For example, you might create a simple class such as the following:

```
Public Class Project

  Private mId As Guid = Guid.NewGuid
  Private mName As String = ""

  Public ReadOnly Property Id() As Guid
    Get
      Return mId
    End Get
  End Property

  Public Property Name() As String
    Get
      Return mName
    End Get
    Set(ByVal value As String)
      If Len(value) > 50 Then
        Throw New Exception("Name too long")
      End If
```

```
        mName = value
    End Set
End Property
```

End Class

This defines a business object that represents a project of some sort. All that is known at the moment is that these projects have an ID value and a name. Notice, though, that the fields containing this data are `Private`—you don't want the users of your object to be able to alter or access them directly. If they were `Public`, the values could be changed without the object's knowledge or permission. (The `mName` field could be given a value that's longer than the maximum of 50 characters, for example.)

The properties, on the other hand, are `Public`. They provide a controlled access point to the object. The `Id` property is read-only, so the users of the object can't change it. The `Name` property allows its value to be changed, but enforces a business rule by ensuring that the length of the new value doesn't exceed 50 characters.

■**Note** None of these concepts are unique to business objects—they're common to all objects, and are central to object-oriented design and programming.

Mobile Objects

Unfortunately, directly applying the kind of object-oriented design and programming I've been talking about so far is often quite difficult in today's complex computing environments. Object-oriented programs are almost always designed with the assumption that all the objects in an application can interact with each other with no performance penalty. This is true when all the objects are running in the same process on the same computer, but it's not at all true when the objects might be running in different processes, or even on different computers.

Earlier in this chapter, I discussed various physical architectures in which different parts of an application might run on different machines. With a high-scalability smart client architecture, for example, there will be a client, an application server, and a data server. With a high-security web client architecture, there will be a client, a web server, an application server, and a data server. Parts of the application will run on each of these machines, interacting with each other as needed.

In these distributed architectures, you can't use a straightforward object-oriented design, because any communication between classic fine-grained objects on one machine and similar objects on another machine will incur network latency and overhead. This translates into a performance problem that simply can't be ignored. To overcome this problem, most distributed applications haven't used object-oriented designs. Instead, they consist of a set of procedural code running on each machine, with the data kept in a `DataSet`, an array, or an XML document that's passed around from machine to machine.

This isn't to say that object-oriented design and programming is irrelevant in distributed environments—just that it becomes complicated. To minimize the complexity, most distributed applications are object-oriented *within a tier*, but between tiers they follow a procedural or service-based model. The end result is that the application as a whole is neither object-oriented nor procedural, but a blend of both.

Perhaps the most common architecture for such applications is to have the Data Access layer retrieve the data from the database into a `DataSet`. The `DataSet` is then returned to the client (or the web server). The code in the forms or pages then interacts with the `DataSet` directly, as shown in Figure 1-15.

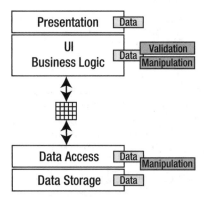

Figure 1-15. *Passing a DataSet between the Business Logic and Data Access layers*

This approach has the maintenance and code-reuse flaws that I've talked about, but the fact is that it gives pretty good performance in most cases. Also, it doesn't hurt that most programmers are pretty familiar with the idea of writing code to manipulate a DataSet, so the techniques involved are well understood, thus speeding up development.

A decision to stick with an object-oriented approach should be undertaken carefully. It's all too easy to compromise the object-oriented design by taking the data out of the objects running on one machine, sending the raw data across the network, and allowing other objects to use that data outside the context of the objects and business logic. Such an approach would break the encapsulation provided by the logical business layer.

Mobile objects are all about sending smart data (objects) from one machine to another, rather than sending raw data.

Through its remoting, serialization, and deployment technologies, the .NET Framework contains direct support for the concept of mobile objects. Given this ability, you can have your Data Access layer (running on an application server) create a business object and load it with data from the database. You can then send that business object to the client machine (or web server), where the UI code can use the object (as shown in Figure 1-16).

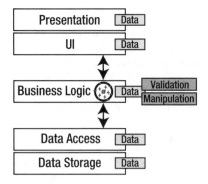

Figure 1-16. *Using a business object to centralize business logic*

In this architecture, smart data, in the form of a business object, is sent to the client, rather than raw data. Then the UI code can use the same business logic as the data access code. This reduces maintenance, because you're not writing some business logic in the Data Access layer, and some other business logic in the UI layer. Instead, all of the business logic is consolidated into a real, separate layer composed of business objects. These business objects will move across the network just like the DataSet did earlier, but they'll include the data *and* its related business logic—something the DataSet can't easily offer.

Note In addition, business objects will typically move across the network more efficiently than the DataSet. The approach in this book will use a binary transfer scheme that transfers data in about 30 percent of the size of data transferred using the DataSet. Also, the business objects will contain far less metadata than the DataSet, further reducing the number of bytes transferred across the network.

Effectively, you're sharing the Business Logic layer between the machine running the Data Access layer and the machine running the UI layer. As long as there is support for mobile objects, this is an ideal solution: it provides code reuse, low maintenance costs, and high performance.

A New Logical Architecture

Being able to directly access the Business Logic layer from both the Data Access layer and the UI layer opens up a new way to view the logical architecture. Though the Business Logic layer remains a separate concept, it's directly used by and tied into both the UI and Data Access layers, as shown in Figure 1-17.

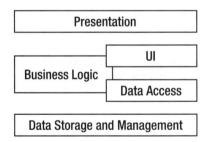

Figure 1-17. *The Business Logic layer tied to the UI and Data Access layers*

The UI layer can interact directly with the objects in the Business Logic layer, thereby relying on them to perform all validation, manipulation, and other processing of the data. Likewise, the Data Access layer can interact with the objects as the data is retrieved or stored.

If all the layers are running on a single machine (such as a smart client), then these parts will run in a single process and interact with each other with no network or cross-processing overhead. In more distributed physical configurations, the Business Logic layer will run on both the client *and* the application server, as shown in Figure 1-18.

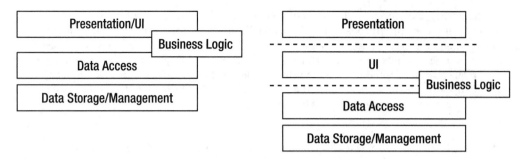

Figure 1-18. *Business logic shared between the UI and Data Access layers*

Local, Anchored, and Mobile Objects

Normally, one might think of objects as being part of a single application, running on a single machine in a single process. A distributed application requires a broader perspective. Some of the objects might only run in a single process on a single machine. Others may run on one machine, but may be called by code running on another machine. Still others may be mobile objects: moving from machine to machine.

Local Objects

By default, .NET objects are *local*. This means that ordinary .NET objects aren't accessible from outside the process in which they were created. Without taking extra steps in your code, it isn't possible to pass objects to another process or another machine (a procedure known as *marshaling*), either by value or by reference.

Anchored Objects

In many technologies, including COM, objects are always passed *by reference*. This means that when you "pass" an object from one machine or process to another, what actually happens is that the object remains in the original process, and the other process or machine merely gets a pointer, or reference, back to the object, as shown in Figure 1-19.

Other Machine Gets a Reference to Object

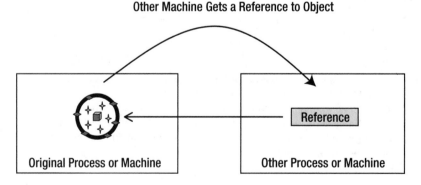

Figure 1-19. *Calling an object by reference*

By using this reference, the other machine can interact with the object. Because the object is still on the original machine, however, any property or method calls are sent across the network, and the results are returned back across the network. This scheme is only useful if the object is designed so that it can be used with very few method calls; just one is ideal! The recommended designs for MTS or COM+ objects call for a single method on the object that does all the work for precisely this reason, thereby sacrificing "proper" object-oriented design in order to reduce latency.

This type of object is stuck, or *anchored*, on the original machine or process where it was created. An anchored object never moves; it's accessed via references. In .NET, an anchored object is created by having it inherit from `MarshalByRefObject`:

```
Public Class MyAnchoredClass
  Inherits MarshalByRefObject

End Class
```

From this point on, the .NET Framework takes care of the details. Remoting can be used to pass an object of this type to another process or machine as a parameter to a method call, for example, or to return it as the result of a function.

Mobile Objects

The concept of mobile objects relies on the idea that an object can be passed from one process to another, or from one machine to another, *by value*. This means that the object is physically copied from the original process or machine to the other process or machine, as shown in Figure 1-20.

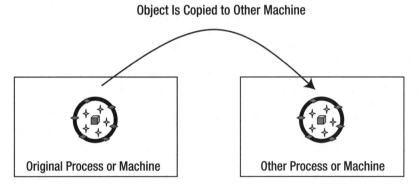

Figure 1-20. *Passing a physical copy of an object across the network*

Because the other machine gets a copy of the object, it can interact with the object locally. This means that there's effectively no performance overhead involved in calling properties or methods on the object—the only cost was in copying the object across the network in the first place.

Note One caveat here is that transferring a large object across the network can cause a performance problem. Returning a `DataSet` that contains a great deal of data can take a long time. This is true of all mobile objects, including business objects. You need to be careful in your application design in order to avoid retrieving very large sets of data.

Objects that can move from process to process or from machine to machine are *mobile objects*. Examples of mobile objects include the DataSet and the business objects created in this book. Mobile objects aren't stuck in a single place, but can move to where they're most needed. To create one in .NET, add the <Serializable()> attribute to your class definition. You may also optionally implement the ISerializable interface. I'll discuss this further in Chapter 2, but the following illustrates the start of a class that defines a mobile object:

```
<Serializable()> _
Public Class MyMobileClass

End Class
```

Again, the .NET Framework takes care of the details, so an object of this type can be simply passed as a parameter to a method call or as the return value from a function. The object will be copied from the original machine to the machine where the method is running.

It is important to understand that the *code* for the object isn't automatically moved across the network. Before an object can move from machine to machine, both machines must have the .NET assembly containing the object's code installed. Only the object's serialized data is moved across the network by .NET. Installing the required assemblies is often handled by ClickOnce or other .NET deployment technologies.

When to Use Which Mechanism

The .NET Framework supports all three of the mechanisms just discussed, so you can choose to create your objects as local, anchored, or mobile, depending on the requirements of your design. As you might guess, there are good reasons for each approach.

Windows Forms and Web Forms objects are all local—they're inaccessible from outside the processes in which they were created. The assumption is that other applications shouldn't be allowed to just reach into your program and manipulate your UI objects.

Anchored objects are important because they will always run on a specific machine. If you write an object that interacts with a database, you'll want to ensure that the object always runs on a machine that has access to the database. Because of this, anchored objects are typically used on application servers.

Many business objects, on the other hand, will be more useful if they *can* move from the application server to a client or web server, as needed. By creating business objects as mobile objects, you can pass smart data from machine to machine, thereby reusing your business logic anywhere the business data is sent.

Typically, anchored and mobile objects are used in concert. Later in the book, I'll show how to use an anchored object on the application server to ensure that specific methods are run *on that server*. Then mobile objects will be passed as parameters to those methods, which will cause those mobile objects to move from the client to the server. Some of the anchored server-side methods will return mobile objects as results, in which case the mobile object will move from the server back to the client.

Passing Mobile Objects by Reference

There's a piece of terminology here that can get confusing. So far, I've loosely associated anchored objects with the concept of "passing by reference," and mobile objects as being "passed by value." Intuitively, this makes sense, because anchored objects provide a reference, though mobile objects provide the actual object (and its values). However, the terms "by reference" and "by value" have come to mean other things over the years.

The original idea of passing a value "by reference" was that there would be just one set of data—one object—and any code could get a reference to that single entity. Any changes made to that entity by any code would therefore be immediately visible to any other code.

The original idea of passing a value "by value" was that a copy of the original value would be made. Any code could get a copy of the original value, but any changes made to that copy weren't reflected in the original value. That makes sense, because the changes were made to a copy, not to the original value.

In distributed applications, things get a little more complicated, but the previous definitions remain true: an object can be passed by reference so that all machines have a reference to the same object on a server. And an object can be passed by value so that a copy of the object is made. So far, so good. However, what happens if you mark an object as `<Serializable()>` (i.e., mark it as a mobile object), and then *intentionally* pass it by reference? It turns out that the object is passed by value, but the .NET Framework attempts to provide the illusion that the object was passed by reference.

To be more specific, in this scenario, the object is copied across the network just as if it were being passed by value. The difference is that the object is then returned back to the calling code when the method is complete, and the reference to the original object is replaced with a reference to this new version, as shown in Figure 1-21.

Object Is Copied to Other Machine

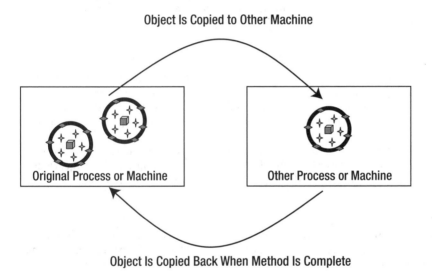

Object Is Copied Back When Method Is Complete

Figure 1-21. *Passing a copy of the object to the server and getting a copy back*

This is potentially very dangerous, since *other* references to the original object continue to point to that original object—only this one particular reference is updated. You can potentially end up with two different versions of the same object on the machine, with some references pointing to the new one and some to the old one.

■**Note** If you pass a mobile object by reference, you must always make sure to update *all* references to use the new version of the object when the method call is complete.

You can choose to pass a mobile object by value, in which case it's passed one way: from the caller to the method. Or you can choose to pass an mobile object by reference, in which case it's passed two ways: from the caller to the method and from the method back to the caller. If you want to get back any changes the method makes to the object, use "by reference." If you don't care about or don't want any changes made to the object by the method, use "by value."

Note that passing a mobile object by reference has performance implications—it requires that the object be passed back across the network to the calling machine, so it's slower than passing by value.

Complete Encapsulation

Hopefully, at this point, your imagination is engaged by the potential of mobile objects. The flexibility of being able to choose between local, anchored, and mobile objects is very powerful, and opens up new architectural approaches that were difficult to implement using older technologies such as COM.

I've already discussed the idea of sharing the Business Logic layer across machines, and it's probably obvious that the concept of mobile objects is exactly what's needed to implement such a shared layer. But what does this all mean for the *design* of the layers? In particular, given a set of mobile objects in the business layer, what's the impact on the UI and Data Access layers with which the objects interact?

Impact on the UI Layer

What it means for the UI layer is simply that the business objects will contain all the business logic. The UI developer can code each form or page using the business objects, thereby relying on them to perform any validation or manipulation of the data. This means that the UI code can focus entirely on displaying the data, interacting with the user, and providing a rich, interactive experience.

More importantly, because the business objects are mobile , they'll end up running in the same process as the UI code. Any property or method calls from the UI code to the business object will occur locally without network latency, marshaling, or any other performance overhead.

Impact on the Data Access Layer

A traditional Data Access layer consists of a set of methods or services that interact with the database, and with the objects that encapsulate data. The data access code itself is typically outside the objects, rather than being encapsulated within the objects. This, however, breaks encapsulation, since it means that the objects' data must be externalized to be handled by the data access code.

The framework created in this book allows for the data access code to be encapsulated within the business objects, or externalized into a separate set of objects. As you'll see in Chapter 7, there are both performance and maintainability benefits to including the data access code directly inside each business object. However, there are security and manageability benefits to having the code external.

Either way, the concept of a Data Access layer is of key importance. Maintaining a strong logical separation between the data access code and business logic is highly beneficial, as discussed earlier in this chapter. Obviously, having a totally separate set of data access objects is one way to clearly implement a Data Access layer. However, logical separation doesn't require putting the logic in separate classes. It is enough to put the data access code in clearly defined data access methods. As long as no data access code exists outside those methods, separation is maintained.

Architectures and Frameworks

The discussion so far has focused mainly on architectures: logical architectures that define the separation of responsibilities in an application, and physical architectures that define the locations where the logical layers will run in various configurations. I've also discussed the use of object-oriented design and the concepts behind mobile objects.

Although all of these are important and must be thought through in detail, you really don't want to have to go through this process every time you need to build an application. It would be preferable to have the architecture and design solidified into reusable code that could be used to build all your applications. What you want is an *application framework*. A framework codifies an architecture and design in order to promote reuse and increase productivity.

The typical development process starts with analysis, followed by a period of architectural discussion and decision making. Next comes the application design: first, the low-level concepts to support the architecture, and then the business-level concepts that actually matter to the end users. With the design completed, developers typically spend a fair amount of time implementing the low-level functions that support the business coding that comes later.

All of the architectural discussions, decision making, designing, and coding can be a lot of fun. Unfortunately, it doesn't directly contribute anything to the end goal of writing business logic and providing business functionality. This low-level supporting technology is merely "plumbing" that must exist in order to create actual business applications. It's an overhead that in the long term you should be able to do once, and then reuse across many business application–development efforts.

In the software world, the easiest way to reduce overhead is to increase reuse, and the best way to get reuse out of an architecture (both design and coding) is to codify it into a framework.

This doesn't mean that *application* analysis and design are unimportant—quite the opposite! People typically spend far too little time analyzing business requirements and developing good application designs to meet those business needs. Part of the reason is that they often end up spending substantial amounts of time analyzing and designing the "plumbing" that supports the business application, and then run out of time to analyze the business issues themselves.

What I'm proposing here is to reduce the time spent analyzing and designing the low-level plumbing by creating a framework that can be used across many business applications. Is the framework created in this book ideal for every application and every organization? Certainly not! You'll have to take the architecture and the framework and adapt them to meet your organization's needs. You may have different priorities in terms of performance, scalability, security, fault tolerance, reuse, or other key architectural criteria. At the very least, though, the remainder of this book should give you a good start on the design and construction of a distributed, object-oriented architecture and framework.

Conclusion

In this chapter, I've focused on the theory behind distributed systems—specifically, those based on mobile objects. The key to success in designing a distributed system is to keep clear the distinction between a logical and a physical architecture.

Logical architectures exist to define the separation between the different types of code in an application. The goal of a good logical architecture is to make code more maintainable, understandable, and reusable. A logical architecture must also define enough layers to enable any physical architectures that may be required.

A physical architecture defines the machines on which the application will run. An application with several logical layers can still run on a single machine. You also might configure that same logical architecture to run on various client and server machines. The goal of a good physical architecture is to achieve the best trade-off between performance, scalability, security, and fault tolerance within your specific environment.

The trade-offs in a physical architecture for a smart client application are very different from those for a web application. A Windows application will typically trade performance against scalability, and a web application will typically trade performance against security.

In this book, I'll be using a 5-layer logical architecture consisting of presentation, UI, business logic, data access, and data storage. Later in the book, this architecture will be used to create Windows, web, and Web Services applications, each with a different physical architecture. The next chapter will start the process of designing the framework that will make this possible.

CHAPTER 2

■■■

Framework Design

In Chapter 1, I discussed some general concepts about physical and logical n-tier architecture, including a 5-layer model for describing systems logically. In this chapter, I'll take that 5-layer logical model and expand it into a framework design. Specifically, this chapter will map the logical layers against the technologies illustrated in Figure 2-1.

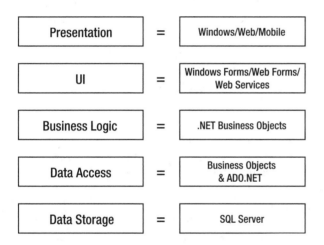

Figure 2-1. *Mapping the logical layers to technologies*

The framework itself will focus on the Business Logic and Data Access layers. This is primarily due to the fact that there are already powerful technologies for building Windows, web (browser-based and Web Services), and mobile UIs and presentations. Also, there are already powerful data-storage options available, including SQL Server, Oracle, DB2, XML documents, and so forth.

Recognizing that these preexisting technologies are ideal for building the Presentation and UI layers, as well as for handling data storage, allows business developers to focus on the parts of the application that have the least technological support, where the highest return on investment occurs through reuse. Analyzing, designing, implementing, testing, and maintaining business logic is incredibly expensive. The more reuse achieved, the lower long-term application costs become. The easier it is to maintain and modify this logic, the lower costs will be over time.

■**Note** This is not to say that additional frameworks for UI creation or simplification of data access are bad ideas. On the contrary, such frameworks can be very complementary to the ideas presented in this book; and the combination of several frameworks can help lower costs even further.

When I set out to create the architecture and framework discussed in this book, I started with the following set of high-level guidelines:

- Simplify the task of creating object-oriented applications in a distributed .NET environment.

- The Windows, web, and Web Services interface developer should never see or be aware of SQL, ADO.NET, or other raw data concepts, but should instead rely on a purely object-oriented model of the problem domain.

- Business object developers should be able to use "natural" coding techniques to create their classes—that is, they should employ everyday coding using fields, properties, and methods. Little or no extra knowledge should be required.

- The business classes should provide total encapsulation of business logic, including validation, manipulation, calculation, security, and data access. Everything pertaining to an entity in the problem domain should be found within a single class.

- It should be relatively easy to create code generators, or templates for existing code-generation tools, to assist in the creation of business classes.

- Provide an n-layer logical architecture that can be easily reconfigured to run on one to four physical tiers.

- Use complex features in .NET—but those should be largely hidden and automated (remoting, serialization, security, deployment, and so forth).

- The concepts present in version 1.x of the framework from the .NET 1.x Framework should carry forward, including object-undo capabilities, broken rule tracking, and object-state tracking (IsNew, IsDirty, IsDeleted).

In this chapter, I'll focus on the design of a framework that allows business developers to make use of object-oriented design and programming with these guidelines in mind. Having walked through the design of the framework, Chapters 3 through 5 will dive in and implement the framework itself, focusing first on the parts that support UI development, and then on providing scalable data access and object-relational mapping for the objects. Before I get into the design of the framework, however, let's discuss some of the specific goals I was attempting to achieve.

Basic Design Goals

When creating object-oriented applications, the ideal situation is that any nonbusiness objects will already exist. This includes UI controls, data access objects, and so forth. In that case, all developers need to do is focus on creating, debugging, and testing the business objects themselves, thereby ensuring that each one encapsulates the data and business logic needed to make the application work.

As rich as the .NET Framework is, however, it doesn't provide all the nonbusiness objects needed in order to create most applications. All the basic tools are there, but there's a fair amount of work to be done before you can just sit down and write business logic. There's a set of higher-level functions and capabilities that are often needed, but aren't provided by .NET right out of the box.

These include the following:

- N-level undo capability
- Tracking broken business rules to determine whether an object is valid
- Tracking whether an object's data has changed (is it "dirty"?)
- Strongly typed collections of child objects (parent-child relationships)
- A simple and abstract model for the UI developer
- Full support for data binding in both Windows Forms and Web Forms
- Saving objects to a database and getting them back again
- Custom authentication
- Integrated authorization rules
- Other miscellaneous features

In all of these cases, the .NET Framework provides all the pieces of the puzzle, but they must be put together to match your specialized requirements. What you *don't* want to do, however, is to have to put them together for every business object or application. The goal is to put them together *once*, so that all these extra features are automatically available to all the business objects and applications.

Moreover, because the goal is to enable the implementation of *object-oriented* business systems, the core object-oriented concepts must also be preserved:

- Abstraction
- Encapsulation
- Polymorphism
- Inheritance

The result will be a framework consisting of a number of classes. The design of these classes will be discussed in this chapter, and their implementation will be discussed in Chapters 3 through 5.

■**Tip** The Diagrams folder in the Csla project in the code download includes FullCsla.cd, which shows all the framework classes in a single diagram. You can also get a PDF document showing that diagram from www. lhotka.net/cslanet/csla20.aspx.

Before getting into the details of the framework's design, let's discuss the desired set of features in more detail.

N-Level Undo Capability

Many Windows applications provide their users with an interface that includes OK and Cancel buttons (or some variation on that theme). When the user clicks an OK button, the expectation is that any work the user has done will be saved. Likewise, when the user clicks a Cancel button, he expects that any changes he's made will be reversed or undone.

Simple applications can often deliver this functionality by saving the data to a database when the user clicks OK, and discarding the data when they click Cancel. For slightly more complex applications, the application must be able to undo any editing on a single object when the user presses the Esc key. (This is the case for a row of data being edited in a DataGridView: if the user presses Esc, the row of data should restore its original values.)

When applications become much more complex, however, these approaches won't work. Instead of simply undoing the changes to a single row of data in real time, you may need to be able to undo the changes to a row of data at some later stage.

Note   It is important to realize that the n-level undo capability implemented in the framework is *optional* and is designed to incur no overhead if it is not used.

Consider the case of an Invoice object that contains a collection of LineItem objects. The Invoice itself contains data that the user can edit, plus data that's derived from the collection. The TotalAmount property of an Invoice, for instance, is calculated by summing up the individual Amount properties of its LineItem objects. Figure 2-2 illustrates this arrangement.

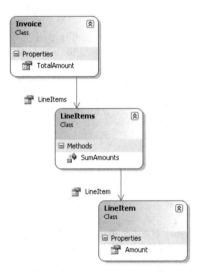

Figure 2-2. *Relationship between the Invoice, LineItems, and LineItem classes*

The UI may allow the user to edit the LineItem objects, and then press Enter to accept the changes to the item, or Esc to undo them. However, even if the user chooses to accept changes to some LineItem objects, they can still choose to cancel the changes on the Invoice itself. Of course, the only way to reset the Invoice object to its original state is to restore the states of the LineItem objects as well; including any changes to specific LineItem objects that might have been "accepted" earlier.

As if this weren't enough, many applications have more complex hierarchies of objects and subobjects (which I'll call *child objects*). Perhaps the individual LineItem objects each have a collection of Component objects beneath them. Each one represents one of the components sold to the customer that make up the specific line item, as shown in Figure 2-3.

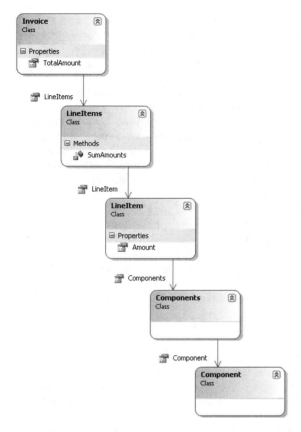

Figure 2-3. *Class diagram showing a more complex set of class relationships*

Now things get even more complicated. If the user edits a Component object, those changes ultimately impact the state of the Invoice object itself. Of course, changing a Component also changes the state of the LineItem object that owns the Component.

The user might accept changes to a Component, but cancel the changes to its parent LineItem object, thereby forcing an undo operation to reverse *accepted* changes to the Component. Or in an even more complex scenario, the user may accept the changes to a Component and its parent LineItem, only to cancel the Invoice. This would force an undo operation that reverses all those changes to the child objects.

Implementing an undo mechanism to support such n-level scenarios isn't trivial. The application must implement code to take a snapshot of the state of each object before it's edited, so that changes can be reversed later on. The application might even need to take more than one snapshot of an object's state at different points in the editing process, so that the object can revert to the appropriate point based on when the user chooses to accept or cancel any edits.

■Note This multilevel undo capability flows from the user's expectations. Consider a typical word processor, in which the user can undo multiple times to restore the content to ever-earlier states.

And the collection objects are every bit as complex as the business objects themselves. The application must handle the simple case in which a user edits an existing LineItem, but it must also handle the case in which a user adds a new LineItem and then cancels changes to the parent or grandparent, resulting in the new LineItem being discarded. Equally, it must handle the case in which the user *deletes* a LineItem and then cancels changes to the parent or grandparent, thereby causing that deleted object to be restored to the collection as though nothing had ever happened.

N-level undo is a perfect example of complex code that shouldn't be written into every business object. Instead, this functionality should be written *once*, so that all business objects support the concept and behave the way we want them to. This functionality will be incorporated directly into the business object framework—but at the same time, the framework must be sensitive to the different environments in which the objects will be used. Although n-level undo is of high importance when building sophisticated Windows user experiences, it's virtually useless in a typical web environment.

In web-based applications, the user typically doesn't have a Cancel button. They either accept the changes, or navigate away to another task, allowing the application to simply discard the changed object. In this regard, the web environment is much simpler, so if n-level undo isn't useful to the web UI developer, it shouldn't incur any overhead if it isn't used. The framework design will take into account that some UI types will use the concept, though others will simply ignore it.

N-level undo is optional and won't incur any overhead if it isn't used by the UI developer.

Tracking Broken Business Rules

A lot of business logic involves the enforcement of *business rules*. The fact that a given piece of data is required is a business rule. The fact that one date must be later than another date is a business rule. Some business rules are the result of calculations, though others are merely toggles. In any case, a business or validation rule is either broken or not. And when one or more rules are broken, the object is invalid.

Because all rules ultimately return a Boolean value, it is possible to abstract the concept of validation rules to a large degree. Every rule is implemented as a bit of code. Some of the code might be trivial, such as comparing the length of a string and returning false if the value is zero. Other code might be more complex, involving validation of the data against a lookup table or through a numeric algorithm. Either way, a rule can be expressed as a method that returns a Boolean result.

The .NET Framework provides the Delegate concept, making it possible to formally define a method signature for a type of method. A Delegate defines a reference type (an object) that represents a method. Essentially, delegates turn methods into objects, allowing you to write code that treats the method like an object; and of course they also allow you to invoke the method.

I'll use this capability in the framework to formally define a method signature for all validation rules. This will allow the framework to maintain a list of validation rules for each object, enabling relatively simple application of those rules as appropriate. With that done, every object can easily maintain a list of the rules that are broken at any point in time.

■**Note** There are commercial business rule engines and other business rule products that strive to take the business rules out of the software and keep it in some external location. Some of these are powerful and valuable. For most business applications, however, the business rules are typically coded directly into the software. When using object-oriented design, this means coding them into the objects.

A fair number of business rules are of the toggle variety: required fields, fields that must be a certain length (no longer than, no shorter than), fields that must be greater than or less than other fields, and so forth. The common theme is that business rules, when broken, immediately make the object invalid. In short, an object is valid if *no* rules are broken, but invalid if *any* rules are broken.

Rather than trying to implement a custom scheme in each business object in order to keep track of which rules are broken and whether the object is or isn't valid at any given point, this behavior can be abstracted. Obviously, the rules *themselves* are often coded into an application, but the tracking of which rules are broken and whether the object is valid can be handled by the framework.

■**Tip** Defining a validation rule as a method means you can create libraries of reusable rules for your application. The framework in this book actually includes a small library with some of the most common validation rules so you can use them in applications without having to write them at all.

The result is a standardized mechanism by which the developer can check all business objects for validity. The UI developer should also be able to retrieve a list of currently broken rules to display to the user (or for any other purpose).

Additionally, this provides the underlying data required to implement the System. ComponentModel.IDataErrorInfo interface defined by the .NET Framework. This interface is used by the ErrorProvider and DataGridView controls in Windows Forms to automate the display of validation errors to the user.

The list of broken rules is obviously linked to the framework's n-level undo capability. If the user changes an object's data so that the object becomes invalid, but then cancels the changes, the original state of the object must be restored. The reverse is true as well: an object may start out invalid (perhaps because a required field is blank), so the user must edit data until it becomes valid. If the user later cancels the object (or its parent, grandparent, etc.), then the object must become *invalid* once again, because it will be restored to its original invalid state.

Fortunately, this is easily handled by treating the broken rules and validity of each object as part of that object's state. When an undo operation occurs, not only is the object's core state restored, but so is the list of broken rules associated with that state. The object and its rules are restored together.

Tracking Whether the Object Has Changed

Another concept is that an object should keep track of whether its state data has been changed. This is important for the performance and efficiency of data updates. Typically, data should only be updated into the database if the data has actually changed. It's a waste of effort to update the database with values it already has! Although the UI developer *could* keep track of whether any values have changed, it's simpler to have the object take care of this detail, and it allows the object to better encapsulate its behaviors.

This can be implemented in a number of ways, ranging from keeping the previous values of all fields (allowing comparisons to see if they've changed), to saying that *any* change to a value (even "changing" it to its original value) will result in the object being marked as having changed.

Rather than having the framework dictate one cost over the other, it will simply provide a generic mechanism by which the business logic can tell the framework whether each object has been changed. This scheme supports both extremes of implementation, allowing you to make a decision based on the requirements of a specific application.

Strongly Typed Collections of Child Objects

The .NET Framework includes the System.Collections.Generic namespace, which contains a number of powerful collection objects, including List(Of T), Dictionary(Of TKey, TValue), and others.

There's also `System.ComponentModel.BindingList(Of T)`, which provides collection behaviors and full support for data binding.

A Short Primer on Generics

Generic types are a new feature in .NET 2.0. A generic type is a template that defines a set of behaviors, but the specific data type is specified when the type is *used* rather than when it is created. Perhaps an example will help.

Consider the `ArrayList` collection type. It provides powerful list behaviors, but it stores all its items as type `Object`. While you can wrap an `ArrayList` with a strongly typed class, or create your own collection type in many different ways, the items in the list are always stored in memory as type `object`.

The new `List(Of T)` collection type has the same behaviors as `ArrayList`, but it is strongly typed—all the way to its core. The type of the indexer, enumerator, `Remove()`, and other methods are all defined by the *generic type parameter*, `T`. Even better, the items in the list are stored in memory as type `T`, not type `Object`.

So what is `T`? It is the type provided when the `List(Of T)` is created. For instance:

```
Dim myList As New List(Of Integer)
```

In this case, `T` is `Integer`, meaning that `myList` is a strongly typed list of `Integer` values. The public properties and methods of `myList` are all of type `Integer`, and the values it contains are stored internally as `Integer` values.

Not only do generic types offer type safety due to their strongly typed nature, but they typically offer substantial performance benefits because they avoid storing values as type `Object`.

Strongly Typed Collections of Child Objects

Sadly, the basic functionality provided by even the generic collection classes isn't enough to integrate fully with the rest of the framework. As mentioned previously, the business objects need to support some relatively advanced features, such as undo capabilities. Following this line of reasoning, the n-level undo capabilities discussed earlier must extend into the collections of child objects, thereby ensuring that child object states are restored when an undo is triggered on the parent object. Even more complex is the support for adding and removing items from a collection, and then undoing the addition or the removal if an undo occurs later on.

Also, a collection of child objects needs to be able to indicate if any of the objects it contains are dirty. Although the business object developer could easily write code to loop through the child objects to discover whether any are marked as dirty, it makes a lot more sense to put this functionality into the framework's collection object. That way, the feature is simply available for use. The same is true with validity: if any child object is invalid, then the collection should be able to report that it's invalid. If all child objects are valid, then the collection should report itself as being valid.

As with the business objects themselves, the goal of the business framework will be to make the creation of a strongly typed collection as close to normal .NET programming as possible, while allowing the framework to provide extra capabilities common to all business objects. What I'm defining here are two sets of behaviors: one for business objects (parent and/or child) and one for collections of business objects. Though business objects will be the more complex of the two, collection objects will also include some very interesting functionality.

Simple and Abstract Model for the UI Developer

At this point, I've discussed some of the business object features that the framework will support. One of the key reasons for providing these features is to make the business object support Windows- and web-style user experiences with minimal work on the part of the UI developer. In fact, this should be an overarching goal when you're designing business objects for a system. The UI developer should be able to rely on the objects to provide business logic, data, and related services in a consistent manner.

Beyond all the features already covered are the issues of creating new objects, retrieving existing data, and updating objects in some data store. I'll discuss the *process* of object persistence later in the chapter, but first this topic should be considered from the UI developer's perspective. Should the UI developer be aware of any application servers? Should they be aware of any database servers? Or should they simply interact with a set of abstract objects? There are three broad models to choose from:

- UI-in-charge
- Object-in-charge
- Class-in-charge

To a greater or lesser degree, all three of these options hide information about how objects are created and saved and allow us to exploit the native capabilities of .NET. In the end, I'll settle on the option that hides the most information (keeping development as simple as possible) and best allows you to exploit the features of .NET.

Note Inevitably, the result will be a compromise. As with many architectural decisions, there are good arguments to be made for each option. In your environment, you may find that a different decision would work better. Keep in mind, though, that this particular decision is fairly central to the overall architecture of the framework, so choosing another option will likely result in dramatic changes throughout the framework.

To make this as clear as possible, the following discussion will assume the use of a physical n-tier configuration, whereby the client or web server is interacting with a separate application server, which in turn interacts with the database. Although not all applications will run in such configurations, it will be much easier to discuss object creation, retrieval, and updating in this context.

UI-in-Charge

One common approach to creating, retrieving, and updating objects is to put the UI in charge of the process. This means that it's the UI developer's responsibility to write code that will contact the application server in order to retrieve or update objects.

In this scheme, when a new object is required, the UI will contact the application server and ask it for a new object. The application server can then instantiate a new object, populate it with default values, and return it to the UI code. The code might be something like this:

```
Dim svr As AppServer = _
  CType(Activator.GetObject(GetType(AppServer), _
  "http://myserver/myroot/appserver.rem"), AppServer)
Dim cust  As Customer = svr.CreateCustomer
```

Here the object of type AppServer is anchored, so it always runs on the application server. The Customer object is mobile, so although it's created on the server, it's returned to the UI by value.

■**Note**   This code example uses the .NET Remoting technology to contact a web server and have it instantiate an object on the server. In Chapter 4, you'll see how to do this with Web Services and Enterprise Services as well. Sometime late in 2006, Microsoft plans to release the Windows Communication Foundation (WCF), code-name Indigo, to replace and update all these technologies. The design in Chapter 4 will leave the door open to easily add support for WCF when it becomes available.

This may seem like a lot of work just to create a new, empty object, but it's the retrieval of default values that makes it necessary. If the application has objects that don't need default values, or if you're willing to hard-code the defaults, you can avoid some of the work by having the UI simply create the object on the client workstation. However, many business applications have configurable default values for objects that must be loaded from the database; and that means the application server must load them.

Retrieving an *existing* object follows the same basic procedure. The UI passes criteria to the application server, which uses the criteria to create a new object and load it with the appropriate data from the database. The populated object is then returned to the UI for use. The UI code might be something like this:

```
Dim svr As AppServer = _
  CType(Activator.GetObject(GetType(AppServer), _
  "http://myserver/myroot/appserver.rem"), AppServer)
Dim cust As Customer = svr.GetCustomer(myCriteria)
```

Updating an object happens when the UI calls the application server and passes the object to the server. The server can then take the data from the object and store it in the database. Because the update process may result in changes to the object's state, the newly saved and updated object is then returned to the UI. The UI code might be something like this:

```
Dim svr As AppServer = _
  CType(Activator.GetObject(GetType(AppServer), _
  "http://myserver/myroot/appserver.rem"), AppServer)
cust = svr.UpdateCustomer(cust)
```

Overall, this model is straightforward—the application server must simply expose a set of services that can be called from the UI to create, retrieve, update, and delete objects. Each object can simply contain its business logic, without the object developer having to worry about application servers or other details.

The drawback to this scheme is that the UI code must know about and interact with the application server. If the application server is moved, or some objects come from a different server, then the UI code must be changed. Moreover, if a Windows UI is created to use the objects, and then later a web UI is created that uses those same objects, you'll end up with duplicated code. Both types of UI will need to include the code in order to find and interact with the application server.

The whole thing is complicated further if you consider that the physical configuration of the application should be flexible. It should be possible to switch from using an application server to running the data access code *on the client* just by changing a configuration file. If there's code scattered throughout the UI that contacts the server any time an object is used, then there will be a lot of places where developers might introduce a bug that prevents simple configuration file switching.

Object-in-Charge

Another option is to move the knowledge of the application server into the objects themselves. The UI can just interact with the objects, allowing them to load defaults, retrieve data, or update themselves. In this model, simply using the New keyword creates a new object:

```
Dim cust As New Customer
```

Within the object's constructor, you would then write the code to contact the application server and retrieve default values. It might be something like this:

```
Public Sub New()
  Dim svr As AppServer = _
    CType(Activator.GetObject(GetType(AppServer), _
    "http://myserver/myroot/appserver.rem"), AppServer)

  Dim values() As Object = svr.GetCustomerDefaults

  ' Copy the values into our local fields
End Sub
```

Notice that the above code does *not* take advantage of the built-in support for passing an object by value across the network. Ideally, the code would look more like this:

```
Public Sub New()
  Dim svr As AppServer = _
    CType(Activator.GetObject(GetType(AppServer), _
    "http://myserver/myroot/appserver.rem"), AppServer)

  Me = svr.CreateCustomer
End Sub
```

But it won't work because you can't change the value of Me. While the compiler won't complain, at runtime the value won't be set.

This means you're left to retrieve the data in some other manner (Array, Hashtable, DataSet, an XML document, or some other data structure) and then load it into the object's fields. The end result is that you have to write code on both the server and in the business class in order to manually copy the data values.

Given that both the UI-in-charge and class-in-charge techniques avoid all this extra coding, let's just abort the discussion of this option and move on.

Class-in-Charge (Factory Pattern)

The UI-in-charge approach uses .NET's ability to pass objects by value, but requires the UI developer to know about and interact with the application server. The object-in-charge approach enables a very simple set of UI code, but makes the object code prohibitively complex by making it virtually impossible to pass the objects by value.

The class-in-charge option provides a good compromise by providing reasonably simple UI code that's unaware of application servers, while also allowing the use of .NET's ability to pass objects by value, thus reducing the amount of "plumbing" code needed in each object. Hiding more information from the UI helps create a more abstract and loosely coupled implementation, thus providing better flexibility.

■**Note** The class-in-charge approach is a variation on the Factory design pattern, in which a "factory" method is responsible for creating and managing an object. In many cases, these factory methods are Shared methods that may be placed directly into a business class—hence the class-in-charge moniker.[1]

In this model, I'll make use of the concept of Shared factory methods on a class. A Shared method can be called directly, without requiring an instance of the class to be created first. For instance, suppose that a Customer class contains the following code:

```
<Serializable()> _
Public Class Customer

  Public Shared Function NewCustomer() As Customer
    Dim svr As AppServer = _
      CType(Activator.GetObject(GetType(AppServer), _
      "http://myserver/myroot/appserver.rem"), AppServer)

    Return svr.CreateCustomer
  End Function
End Class
```

Then the UI code could use this method without first creating a Customer object, as follows:

```
Dim cust As Customer = Customer.NewCustomer
```

A common example of this tactic within the .NET Framework itself is the Guid class, whereby a Shared method is used to create new Guid values, as follows:

```
Dim myGuid As Guid = Guid.NewGuid
```

This accomplishes the goal of making the UI code reasonably simple; but what about the Shared method and passing objects by value? Well, the NewCustomer() method contacts the application server and asks it to create a new Customer object with default values. The object is created on the server and then returned back to the NewCustomer() code, which is running *on the client*. Now that the object has been passed back to the client by value, the method simply returns it to the UI for use.

Likewise, you can create a Shared method in the class in order to load an object with data from the data store, as shown:

```
  Public Shared Function GetCustomer(ByVal criteria As String) As Customer

    Dim svr As AppServer = _
      CType(Activator.GetObject(GetType(AppServer), _
      "http://myserver/myroot/appserver.rem"), AppServer)

    Return svr.GetCustomer(criteria)
  End Function
```

Again, the code contacts the application server, providing it with the criteria necessary to load the object's data and create a fully populated object. That object is then returned by value to the GetCustomer() method running on the client, and then back to the UI code.

---

1. Erich Gamma, Richard Helm, Ralph Johnson, and John Vlissides, *Design Patterns: Elements of Reusable Object-Oriented Software* (Addison-Wesley, 1995).

As before, the UI code remains simple:

```
Dim cust As Customer = Customer.GetCustomer(myCriteria)
```

The class-in-charge model requires that you write Shared factory methods in each class, but keeps the UI code simple and straightforward. It also takes full advantage of .NET's ability to pass objects across the network by value, thereby minimizing the plumbing code in each object. Overall, it provides the best solution, which will be used (and explained further) in the chapters ahead.

Supporting Data Binding

For more than a decade, Microsoft has included some kind of data binding capability in its development tools. Data binding allows developers to create forms and populate them with data with almost no custom code. The controls on a form are "bound" to specific fields from a data source (such as a DataSet or a business object).

With .NET 2.0, Microsoft has dramatically improved data binding for both Windows Forms and Web Forms. The primary benefits or drivers for using data binding in .NET development include the following:

- Data binding offers good performance, control, and flexibility.
- Data binding can be used to link controls to properties of business objects.
- Data binding can dramatically reduce the amount of code in the UI.
- Data binding is sometimes *faster* than manual coding, especially when loading data into list boxes, grids, or other complex controls.

Of these, the biggest single benefit is the dramatic reduction in the amount of UI code that must be written and maintained. Combined with the performance, control, and flexibility of .NET data binding, the reduction in code makes it a very attractive technology for UI development.

In both Windows Forms and Web Forms, data binding is read-write, meaning that an element of a data source can be bound to an editable control so that changes to the value in the control will be updated back into the data source as well.

Data binding in .NET 2.0 is very powerful. It offers good performance with a high degree of control for the developer. Given the coding savings gained by using data binding, it's definitely a technology that needs to be supported in the business object framework.

Enabling the Objects for Data Binding

Although data binding can be used to bind against any object or any collection of homogeneous objects, there are some things that object developers can do to make data binding work better. Implementing these "extra" features enables data binding to do more work for us, and provide the user with a superior experience. The .NET DataSet object, for instance, implements these extra features in order to provide full data binding support to both Windows Forms and Web Forms developers.

The IEditableObject Interface

All editable business objects should implement the interface called System.ComponentModel. IEditableObject. This interface is designed to support a simple, one-level undo capability, and is used by simple forms-based data binding and complex grid-based data binding alike.

In the forms-based model, IEditableObject allows the data binding infrastructure to notify the business object before the user edits it, so that the object can take a snapshot of its values. Later, the application can tell the object whether to apply or cancel those changes, based on the user's actions. In the grid-based model, each of the objects is displayed in a row within the grid. In this case, the interface allows the data binding infrastructure to notify the object when its row is being edited, and then whether to accept or undo the changes based on the user's actions. Typically, grids perform an undo operation if the user presses the Esc key, and an accept operation if the user presses Enter or moves off that row in the grid by any other means.

The INotifyPropertyChanged Interface

Editable business objects need to raise events to notify data binding any time their data values change. Changes that are caused directly by the user editing a field in a bound control are supported automatically—however, if the object updates a property value through *code*, rather than by direct user editing, the object needs to notify the data binding infrastructure that a refresh of the display is required.

The .NET Framework defines `System.ComponentModel.INotifyPropertyChanged`, which should be implemented by any bindable object. This interface defines the `PropertyChanged` event that data binding can handle to detect changes to data in the object.

The IBindingList Interface

All business *collections* should implement the interface called `System.ComponentModel.IBindingList`. The simplest way to do this is to have the collection classes inherit from `System.ComponentModel.BindingList(Of T)`. This generic class implements all the collection interfaces required to support data binding:

- `IBindingList`
- `IList`
- `ICollection`
- `IEnumerable`
- `ICancelAddNew`
- `IRaiseItemChangedEvents`

As you can see, being able to inherit from `BindingList(Of T)` is very valuable. Otherwise, the business framework would need to manually implement all these interfaces.

This interface is used in grid-based binding, in which it allows the control that's displaying the contents of the collection to be notified by the collection any time an item is added, removed, or edited, so that the display can be updated. Without this interface, there's no way for the data binding infrastructure to notify the grid that the underlying data has changed, so the user won't see changes as they happen.

Along this line, when a child object within a collection changes, the collection should notify the UI of the change. This implies that every collection object will listen for events from its child objects (via `INotifyPropertyChanged`), and in response to such an event will raise its own event indicating that the collection has changed.

Events and Serialization

The events that are raised by business collections and business objects are all valuable. Events support the data binding infrastructure and enable utilization of its full potential. Unfortunately, there's a conflict between the idea of objects raising events and the use of .NET serialization via the `<Serializable()>` attribute.

When an object is marked as `<Serializable()>`, the .NET Framework is told that it can pass the object across the network by value. As part of this process, the object will be automatically converted into a byte stream by the .NET runtime. It also means that any other objects *referenced* by the object will be serialized into the same byte stream, unless the field representing it is marked with the `<NonSerialized()>` attribute. What may not be immediately obvious is that *events create an object reference behind the scenes*.

When an object declares and raises an event, that event is delivered to *any* object that has a handler for the event. Windows Forms often handle events from objects, as illustrated in Figure 2-4.

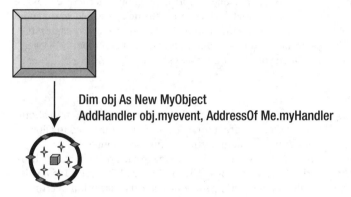

Dim obj As New MyObject
AddHandler obj.myevent, AddressOf Me.myHandler

Figure 2-4. *A Windows form referencing a business object*

How does the event get delivered to the handling object? Well, it turns out that behind every event is a *delegate*—a strongly typed reference that points back to the handling object. This means that any object that raises events can end up with bidirectional references between the object and the other object/entity that is handling those events, as shown in Figure 2-5.

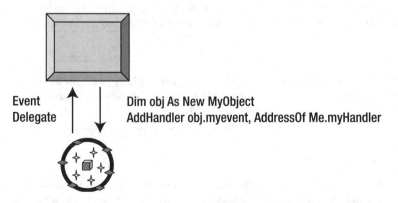

Event   **Dim obj As New MyObject**
Delegate   **AddHandler obj.myevent, AddressOf Me.myHandler**

Figure 2-5. *Handling an event on an object causes a back reference to the form.*

Even though this back reference isn't visible to developers, it's completely visible to the .NET serialization infrastructure. When serializing an object, the serialization mechanism will trace this reference and attempt to serialize any objects (including forms) that are handling the events!

Obviously, this is rarely desirable. In fact, if the handling object is a form, this will fail outright with a runtime error, because forms aren't serializable.

■**Note** If any non-serializable object handles events that are raised by a serializable object, you'll be unable to serialize the object because the .NET runtime serialization process will error out.

Solving this means marking the events as `<NonSerialized()>`. It turns out that this requires a bit of special syntax when dealing with events. Specifically, a more explicit block structure must be used to declare the event. This approach allows manual declaration of the delegate field so that it is possible to mark that field as `<NonSerialized()>`. The `BindingList(Of T)` class already declares its event in this manner, so this issue only pertains to the implementation of `INotifyPropertyChanged` (or any custom events you choose to declare in your business classes).

The IDataErrorInfo Interface

Earlier, I discussed the need for objects to implement business rules and expose information about broken rules to the UI. The `System.ComponentModel.IDataErrorInfo` interface is designed to allow data binding to request information about broken validation rules from a data source.

Given that the object framework will already help the objects manage a list of all currently broken validation rules, you'll already have the tools needed to easily implement `IDataErrorInfo`. This interface defines two methods. The first allows data binding to request a text description of errors at the object level, while the second provides a text description of errors at the property level.

By implementing this interface, the objects will automatically support the feedback mechanisms built into the Windows Forms `DataGridView` and `ErrorProvider` controls.

Object Persistence and Object-Relational Mapping

One of the biggest challenges facing a business developer building an object-oriented system is that a good object model is almost never the same as a good relational data model. Because most data is stored in relational databases using a relational model, we're faced with the significant problem of translating that data into an object model for processing, and then changing it back to a relational model later on to persist the data from the objects back into the data store.

■**Note** The framework in this book doesn't *require* a relational model, but since that is the most common data storage technology, I focus on it quite a bit. You should remember that the concepts and code shown in this chapter can be used against XML files, object databases, or almost any other data store you are likely to use.

Relational vs. Object Modeling

Before going any further, let's make sure we're in agreement that object models aren't the same as relational models. Relational models are primarily concerned with the efficient storage of data, so that replication is minimized. Relational modeling is governed by the rules of normalization, and almost all databases are designed to meet at least the third normal form. In this form, it's quite likely that the data for any given business concept or entity is split between multiple tables in the database in order to avoid any duplication of data.

Object models, on the other hand, are primarily concerned with modeling *behavior*, not data. It's not the data that defines the object, but the role the object plays within your business domain.

Every object should have one clear responsibility and a limited number of behaviors focused on fulfilling that responsibility.

■**Tip** I recommend the book *Object Thinking*, by David West (DV-Microsoft Professional, 2004), for some good insight into behavioral object modeling and design. Though my ideas differ somewhat from those in *Object Thinking*, I use many of the concepts and language from that book in my own object-oriented design work and in this book.

For instance, a `Customer` object may be responsible for *adding and editing customer data*. A `CustomerInfo` object in the same application may be responsible for *providing read-only access to customer data*. Both objects will use the same data from the same database and table, but they provide different behaviors.

Similarly, an `Invoice` object may be responsible for *adding and editing invoice data*. But invoices include some customer data. A naive solution is to have the `Invoice` object make use of the aforementioned `Customer` object, but that's not a good answer. That `Customer` object should only be used in the case where the application is adding or editing customer data—something that isn't occurring while working with invoices. Instead, the `Invoice` object should directly interact with the customer data that it needs to do its job.

Through these two examples, it should be clear that sometimes multiple objects will use the same relational data. In other cases, a single object will use relational data from different data entities. In the end, the same customer data is being used by three different objects. The point, though, is that each one of these objects has a clearly defined responsibility that defines the object's *behavior*. Data is merely a resource that the object needs to implement that behavior.

Behavioral Object-Oriented Design

It is a common trap to think that data in objects needs to be normalized like it is in a database. A better way to think about objects is to say that *behavior* should be normalized. The goal of object-oriented design is to avoid replication of *behavior*, not data.

■**Note** In object-oriented design, *behavior* should be normalized, not data.

At this point, most people are struggling. Most developers have spent years programming their brains to think relationally, and this view of object-oriented design flies directly in the face of that conditioning. Yet the key to the successful application of object-oriented design is to divorce object thinking from relational or data thinking.

Perhaps the most common objection at this point is this: if two objects (say, `Customer` and `Invoice`) both use the same data (say, the customer's name), how do you make sure that consistent business rules are applied to that data? And this is a good question.

The answer is that the behavior must be normalized. Business rules are merely a form of behavior. The business rule specifying that the customer name value is required, for instance, is just a behavior associated with that particular value.

Earlier in the chapter, I discussed the idea that a validation rule can be reduced to a method defined by a `Delegate`. A `Delegate` is just an object that points to a method, so it is quite possible to view the `Delegate` itself as the rule. Following this train of thought, every rule then becomes an object.

Behavioral object-oriented design relies heavily on the concept of *collaboration*. Collaboration is the idea that an object should collaborate with other objects to do its work. If an object starts to become complex, you can break the problem into smaller, more digestible parts by moving some of the sub-behaviors into other objects that collaborate with the original object to accomplish the overall goal.

In the case of a required customer name value, there's a `Rule` object that defines that behavior. Both the `Customer` and `Invoice` objects can collaborate with that `Rule` object to ensure that the rule is consistently applied. As you can see in Figure 2-6, the actual rule is only implemented once, but is used as appropriate—effectively normalizing that behavior.

It could be argued that the `CustomerName` concept should become an object of its own, and that this object would implement the behaviors common to the field. While this sounds good in an idealistic sense, it has serious performance and complexity drawbacks when implemented on development platforms such as .NET. Creating a custom object for every field in your application can rapidly become overwhelming, and such an approach makes the use of technologies like data binding very complex.

My approach of normalizing the rules themselves provides a workable compromise—providing a high level of code reuse while still offering good performance and allowing the application to take advantage of all the features of the .NET platform.

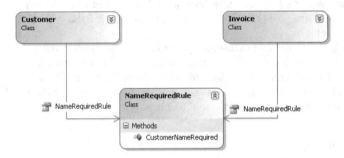

Figure 2-6. *Normalizing the customer name required behavior*

In fact, the idea that a string value is required is so pervasive that it can be normalized to a general `StringRequired` rule that can be used by any object with a required property anywhere in an application. In Chapter 5, I'll implement a `CommonRules` class containing several common validation rules of this nature.

Object-Relational Mapping

If object models aren't the same as relational models (or some other data models that we might be using), some mechanism is needed by which data can be translated from the Data Storage and Management layer up into the object-oriented Business Logic layer.

■**Note** This is a well-known issue within the object-oriented community. It is commonly referred to as the *impedance mismatch problem*, and one of the best discussions of it can be found in David Taylor's book, *Object Technology: A Manager's Guide, 2nd Edition* (Addison-Wesley, 1997).

Several object-relational mapping (ORM) products exist for the .NET platform from various vendors. In truth, however, most ORM tools have difficulty working against object models defined using behavioral object-oriented design. Unfortunately, most of the ORM tools tend to create "superpowered" `DataSet` equivalents, rather than true behavioral business objects. In other words, they create a data-centric representation of the business data and wrap it with business logic.

The difference between such a data-centric object model and what I am proposing in this book are subtle but important. Behavioral object modeling creates objects that are focused on the object's behavior, not on the data it contains. The fact that objects contain data is merely a side effect of implementing behavior; the data is not the identity of the object. Most ORM tools, by contrast, create objects based around the data, with the *behavior* being a side effect of the data in the object.

Beyond the philosophical differences, the wide variety of mappings you might need and the potential for business logic to drive variations in the mapping from object to object make it virtually impossible to create a generic ORM product that can meet everyone's needs.

Consider the `Customer` object example discussed earlier. While the customer data may come from one database, it is totally realistic to consider that some data may come from SQL Server while other data comes through screen-scraping a mainframe screen. It's also quite possible that the business logic will dictate that some of the data is updated in some cases, but not in others. Issues like these are virtually impossible to solve in a generic sense, and so solutions almost always revolve around custom code. The most a typical ORM tool can do is provide support for simple cases, in which objects are updated to and from standard, supported, relational data stores. At most, they'll provide hooks with which their behavior can be customized. Rather than trying to build a generic ORM product as part of this book, I'll aim for a much more attainable goal.

The framework in this book will define a standard set of four methods for creating, retrieving, updating, and deleting objects. Business developers will implement these four methods to work with the underlying data management tier by using ADO.NET, the XML support in .NET, Web Services, or any other technology required to accomplish the task. In fact, if you have an ORM (or some other generic data access) product, you'll often be able to invoke that tool from these four methods just as easily as using ADO.NET directly.

■**Note** The approach taken in this book and the associated framework is very conducive to code generation. Many people use code generators to automate the process of building common data access logic for their objects—thus achieving high levels of productivity while retaining the ability to create a behavioral object-oriented model.

The point is that the framework will simplify object persistence to the point at which all developers need to do is implement these four methods in order to retrieve or update data. This places no restrictions on the object's ability to work with data, and provides a standardized persistence and mapping mechanism for all objects.

Preserving Encapsulation

As I noted at the beginning of the chapter, one of my key goals is to design this framework to provide powerful features while following the key object-oriented concepts, including *encapsulation*.

Encapsulation is the idea that all of the logic and data pertaining to a given business entity is held within the object that represents that entity. Of course, there are various ways in which one can interpret the idea of encapsulation—nothing is ever simple!

One approach is to encapsulate business data and logic in the business object, and then encapsulate data access and ORM behavior in some other object: a persistence object. This provides a nice separation between the business logic and data access, and encapsulates both types of behavior, as shown in Figure 2-7.

Figure 2-7. *Separation of ORM logic into a persistence object*

Although there are certainly some advantages to this approach, there are drawbacks, too. The most notable of these is that it can be challenging to efficiently get the data from the persistence object into or out of the business object. For the persistence object to load data into the business object, it must be able to bypass business and validation processing in the business object, and somehow load raw data into it directly. If the persistence object tries to load data into the object using the object's public properties, you'll run into a series of issues:

- The data already in the database is presumed valid, so a lot of processing time is wasted unnecessarily revalidating data. This can lead to a serious performance problem when loading a large group of objects.

- There's no way to load read-only property values. Objects often have read-only properties for things such as the primary key of the data, and such data obviously must be loaded into the object, but it can't be loaded via the normal interface (if that interface is properly designed).

- Sometimes properties are interdependent due to business rules, which means that some properties must be loaded before others or errors will result. The persistence object would need to know about all these conditions so that it could load the right properties first. The result is that the persistence object would become *very* complex, and changes to the business object could easily break the persistence object.

On the other hand, having the persistence object load raw data into the business object breaks encapsulation in a big way, because one object ends up directly tampering with the internal fields of another. This could be implemented using reflection, or by designing the business object to expose its private fields for manipulation. But the former is slow, and the latter is just plain bad object design: it allows the UI developer (or any other code) to manipulate these fields, too. That's just asking for the abuse of the objects, which will invariably lead to code that's impossible to maintain.

A much better approach, therefore, is to view encapsulation to mean that *all* the logic for the business entity should be in the object—that is, the logic to support the UI developer (validation, calculation, and so on) *and* the data access logic. This way, the object encapsulates all responsibility for its data—it has sole control over the data from the moment it leaves the database until the time it returns to the database, as shown in Figure 2-8.

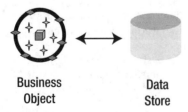

Figure 2-8. *Business object directly managing persistence to the data store*

This is a simpler way of doing things, because it keeps all of the logic for the entity within the boundaries of a single object, and all the code within the boundaries of a single class. Any time there's a need to alter, enhance, or maintain the logic for an entity, you know *exactly* where to find it. There's no ambiguity regarding whether the logic is in the business object, the persistence object, or possibly both—there's only one object.

The new approach also has the benefit of providing optimal performance. Because the data access code is *inside* the object, that code can interact directly with the object's `Private` instance fields. There's no need to break encapsulation, or to resort to trickery such as reflection (or deal with the resulting performance issues).

The drawback to this approach is that the data access code ends up inside the business class; potentially blurring the line between the Business Logic layer and the Data Access layer in the n-layer logical model. The framework will help to mitigate this by formally defining four methods into which the data access code will be written, providing a clear and logical location for all data access code within each object.

On balance, then, I prefer this second view, because it allows total encapsulation of all data and logic pertaining to a business entity with very high performance. Better still, this is accomplished using techniques and technologies that are completely supported within the .NET Framework, without the need to resort to any complex or hard-to-code workarounds (such as using reflection to load the data).

That said, the framework directly supports the idea of having a separate persistence object that implements the Data Access layer. If you choose to take such an approach, it is up to you to determine how to transfer the data from the persistence object into the business object. You may choose to use reflection to load field values directly, you may pass XML documents or data transfer objects (DTOs) between the two objects, or you may simply open an ADO.NET `DataReader` and hand it back to the business object.

Supporting Physical N-Tier Models

The question that remains, then, is how to support physical n-tier models if the UI-oriented and data-oriented behaviors reside in *one* object?

UI-oriented behaviors almost always involve a lot of properties and methods—a very fine-grained interface with which the UI can interact in order to set, retrieve, and manipulate the values of an object. Almost by definition, this type of object *must* run in the same process as the UI code itself, either on the Windows client machine with Windows Forms, or on the web server with Web Forms.

Conversely, data-oriented behaviors typically involve very few methods: create, fetch, update, and delete. They must run on a machine where they can establish a physical connection to the database server. Sometimes, this is the client workstation or web server, but often it means running on a physically separate application server.

This point of apparent conflict is where the concept of *mobile objects* enters the picture. It's possible to pass a business object from an application server to the client machine, work with the object, and then pass the object back to the application server so that it can store its data in the database. To do this, there needs to be some black-box component running as a service on the application server with which the client can interact. This black-box component does little more than accept the object from the client, and then call methods on the object to retrieve or update data as required. But the object itself does all the real work. Figure 2-9 illustrates this concept, showing how the *same physical business object* can be passed from application server to client, and vice versa, via a generic router object that's running on the application server.

In Chapter 1, I discussed anchored and mobile objects. In this model, the business object is mobile, meaning that it can be passed around the network by value. The router object is anchored, meaning that it will always run on the machine where it's created.

In the framework, I'll refer to this router object as a *data portal*. It will act as a portal for all data access for all the objects. The objects will interact with this portal in order to retrieve default values (create), fetch data (read), update or insert data (update), and remove data (delete). This means that the data portal will provide a standardized mechanism by which objects can perform all CRUD operations.

The end result will be that each business class will include a factory method that the UI can call in order to load an object based on data from the database, as follows:

```
Public Shared Function GetCustomer(ByVal customerId As String) As Customer
    Return DataPortal.Fetch(Of Customer)(New Criteria(customerId))
End Function
```

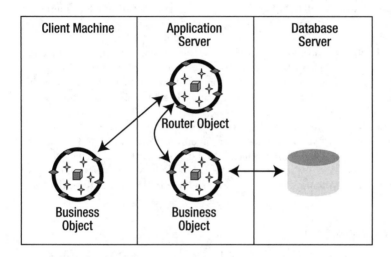

Figure 2-9. *Passing a business object to and from the application server*

The actual data access code will be contained within each of the business objects. The data portal will simply provide an anchored object on a machine with access to the database server, and will invoke the appropriate CRUD methods on the business objects themselves. This means that the business object will also implement a method that will be called by the data portal to actually load the data. That method will look something like this:

```
Private Sub DataPortal_Fetch(ByVal criteria As Criteria)
    ' Code to load the object's fields with data goes here
End Sub
```

The UI won't know (or need to know) how any of this works, so in order to create a Customer object, the UI will simply write code along these lines:

```
Dim cust As Customer = Customer.GetCustomer("ABC")
```

The framework, and specifically the data portal, will take care of all the rest of the work, including figuring out whether the data access code should run on the client workstation or on an application server.

Using the data portal means that all the logic remains encapsulated within the business objects, while physical n-tier configurations are easily supported. Better still, by implementing the data portal correctly, you can switch between having the data access code running on the client machine and placing it on a separate application server just by changing a configuration file setting. The ability to change between different physical configurations with no changes to code is a powerful, valuable feature.

Custom Authentication

Application security is often a challenging issue. Applications need to be able to authenticate the user, which means that they need to verify the user's identity. The result of authentication is not only that the application knows the identity of the user, but that the application has access to the user's role membership and possibly other information about the user—collectively, I'll refer to this as the user's profile data. This profile data can be used by the application for various purposes, most notably authorization.

The framework directly supports integrated security. This means that you can use objects within the framework to determine the user's Windows identity and any domain or Active Directory (AD) groups to which they belong. In some organizations, this is enough: all the users of the organization's applications are in the Windows NT domain or AD, and by having them log in to a workstation or a website using integrated security, the applications can determine the user's identity and roles (groups).

In other organizations, applications are used by at least some users who are *not* part of the organization's NT domain or AD. They may not even be members of the organization in question. This is very often the case with web and mobile applications, but it's surprisingly common with Windows applications as well. In these cases, you *can't* rely on Windows integrated security for authentication and authorization.

To complicate matters further, the ideal security model would provide user profile and role information not only to server-side code, but also to the code on the client. Rather than allowing the user to attempt to perform operations that will generate errors due to security at some later time, the UI should gray out the options, or not display them at all. This requires that the developer have consistent access to the user's identity and profile at all layers of the application, including the UI, Business Logic, and Data Access layers.

Remember that the layers of an application may be deployed across multiple physical tiers. Due to this fact, there must be a way of transferring the user's identity information across tier boundaries. This is often called *impersonation*.

Implementing impersonation isn't too hard when using Windows integrated security, but it's often problematic when relying solely on, say, COM+ role-based security, because there's no easy way to make the user's COM+ role information available to the UI developer.

■**Note** In May 2002, Juval Lowy wrote an article for MSDN magazine in which he described how to create custom .NET security objects that merge NT domain or AD groups and COM+ roles so that both are available to the application.[2]

The business framework will provide support for both Windows integrated security *and* custom authentication, in which you define how the user's credentials are validated and the user's profile data and roles are loaded. This custom security is a model that you can adapt to use any existing security tables or services that already exist in your organization. The framework will rely on Windows itself to handle impersonation when using Windows integrated or AD security, and will handle impersonation itself when using custom authentication.

---

2. Juval Lowy, "Unify the Role-Based Security Models for Enterprise and Application Domains with .NET" (MSDN, May 2002). See http://msdn.microsoft.com/msdnmag/issues/02/05/rolesec.

Integrated Authorization

Applications also need to be able to authorize the user to perform (or not perform) certain operations, or view (or not view) certain data. Such authorization is typically handled by associating users with roles, and then indicating which roles are allowed or disallowed for specific behaviors.

■Note Authorization is just another type of business logic. The decisions about what a user can and can't do or can and can't see within the application are business decisions. Although the framework will work with the .NET Framework classes that support authentication, it's up to the business objects to implement the rules themselves.

Earlier, I discussed authentication and how the framework will support both Windows integrated or AD authentication, and custom authentication. Either way, the result of authentication is that the application has access to the list of roles (or groups) to which the user belongs. This information can be used by the application to authorize the user as defined by the business.

While authorization can be implemented manually within the application's business code, the business framework can help formalize the process in some cases. Specifically, objects must use the user's role information to restrict what properties the user can view and edit. There are also common behaviors—such as loading, deleting, and saving an object—that are subject to authorization.

As with validation rules, authorization rules can be distilled to a set of fairly simple yes/no answers. A user either can or can't read a given property. The business framework will include code to help a business object developer easily restrict which object properties a user can or can't read or edit. In Chapters 7 and 8, you'll also see a common pattern that can be implemented by all business objects to control whether an object can be retrieved, deleted, or saved.

Not only does this business object need access to this authorization information, but the UI does as well. Ideally, a good UI will change its display based on how the current user is allowed to interact with an object. To support this concept, the business framework will help the business objects expose the authorization rules such that they are accessible to the UI layer without duplicating the authorization rules themselves.

Framework Design

So far, I've been focused on the major goals for the framework. Having covered the guiding principles, let's move on to discuss the design of the framework so it can meet these goals. In the rest of this chapter, I'll walk through the various classes that will combine to create the framework. After covering the design, Chapters 3 through 5 will dive into the implementation of the framework code.

A comprehensive framework can be a large and complex entity. There are usually many classes that go into the construction of a framework, even though the end users of the framework—the business developers—only use a few of those classes directly. The framework discussed here and implemented in Chapters 3 through 5 accomplishes the goals I've just discussed, along with enabling the basic creation of object-oriented n-tier business applications. For any given application or organization, this framework will likely be modified and enhanced to meet specific requirements. This means that the framework will grow as you use and adapt it to your environment.

The CSLA .NET framework contains a lot of classes and types, which can be overwhelming if taken as a whole. Fortunately, it can be broken down into smaller units of functionality to better understand how each part works. Specifically, the framework can be divided into the following functional groups:

- Business object creation
- N-level undo functionality
- Data binding support
- Validation rules
- A data portal enabling various physical configurations
- Transactional and nontransactional data access
- Authentication and authorization
- Helper types and classes

For each functional group, I'll focus on a subset of the overall class diagram, breaking it down into more digestible pieces.

Business Object Creation

First, it's important to recognize that the key classes in the framework are those that business developers will use as they create business objects, but that these are a small subset of what's available. In fact, many of the framework classes are never used *directly* by business developers. Figure 2-10 shows only those classes the business developer will typically use.

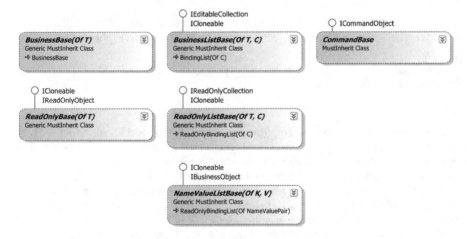

Figure 2-10. *Framework classes used directly by business developers*

Obviously, the business developer may periodically interact with other classes as well, but these are the ones that will be at the center of most activity. Classes or methods that the business developer shouldn't have access to will be scoped to prevent accidental use.

Table 2-1 summarizes each class and its intended purpose.

Table 2-1. *Business Framework Base Classes*

Class	Purpose
BusinessBase(Of T)	Inherit from this class to create a single editable business object such as Customer, Order, or OrderLineItem.
BusinessListBase(Of T, C)	Inherit from this class to create an editable collection of business objects such as PaymentTerms or OrderLineItems.
CommandBase	Inherit from this class to implement a command that should run on the application server, such as implementation of a Customer.Exists or an Order.ShipOrder command.
ReadOnlyBase(Of T)	Inherit from this class to create a single read-only business object such as OrderInfo or ProductStatus.
ReadOnlyListBase(Of T, C)	Inherit from this class to create a read-only collection of objects such as CustomerList or OrderList.
NameValueListBase(Of K, V)	Inherit from this class to create a read-only collection of key/value pairs (typically for populating drop-down list controls) such as PaymentTermsCodes or CustomerCategories.

Let's discuss each class in a bit more detail.

BusinessBase

The BusinessBase class is the base from which all editable (read-write) business objects will be created. In other words, to create a business object, inherit from BusinessBase, as shown here:

```
<Serializable()> _
Public Class Customer
  Inherits BusinessBase(Of Customer)

End Class
```

When creating a subclass, the business developer must provide the specific type of new business object as a type parameter to BusinessBase(Of T). This allows the generic BusinessBase type to expose strongly typed methods corresponding to the specific business object type.

Behind the scenes, BusinessBase(Of T) inherits from Csla.Core.BusinessBase, which implements the majority of the framework functionality to support editable objects. The primary reason for pulling the functionality out of the generic class into a normal class is to enable polymorphism.

Polymorphism is what allows you to treat all subclasses of a type as though they were an instance of the base class. For instance, all Windows Forms—Form1, Form2, and so forth—can all be treated as type Form. You can write code like this:

```
Dim form As Form = New Form2
form.Show()
```

This is polymorphic behavior, in which the variable form is of type Form, but references an object of type Form2. The same code would work with Form1, because both inherit from the base type Form.

It turns out that generic types are not polymorphic like normal types.

Another reason for inheriting from a non-generic base class is to make it simpler to customize the framework. If needed, you can create alternative editable base classes starting with the functionality in Core.BusinessBase.

Csla.Core.BusinessBase and the classes from which it inherits provide all the functionality discussed earlier in this chapter, including n-level undo, tracking of broken rules, "dirty" tracking, object persistence, and so forth. It supports the creation of root (top-level) objects and child objects. Root objects are objects that can be retrieved directly from and updated or deleted within the database. Child objects can only be retrieved or updated in the context of their parent object.

■**Note** Throughout this book, it is assumed that you are building business applications, in which case almost all objects are ultimately stored in the database at one time or another. Even if an object isn't persisted to a database, you can still use BusinessBase to gain access to the n-level undo, validation rule tracking, and "dirty" tracking features built into the framework.

For example, an Invoice is typically a root object, though the LineItem objects contained by an Invoice object are child objects. It makes perfect sense to retrieve or update an Invoice, but it makes no sense to create, retrieve, or update a LineItem without having an associated Invoice. To make this distinction, BusinessBase includes a method that can be called to indicate that the object is a child object: MarkAsChild(). By default, business objects are assumed to be root objects, unless this method is invoked. This means that a child object might look like this:

```
<Serializable()>
Public Class Child
  Inherits  BusinessBase(Of Child)

  Private Sub New()
    MarkAsChild()
  End Sub
End Class
```

The BusinessBase class provides default implementations of the data access methods that exist on all root business objects. These methods will be called by the data portal mechanism. These default implementations all raise an error if they're called. The intention is that the business objects can opt to override these methods if they need to support, create, fetch, insert, update, or delete operations. The names of these methods are as follows:

- DataPortal_Create()
- DataPortal_Fetch()
- DataPortal_Insert()
- DataPortal_Update()
- DataPortal_DeleteSelf()
- DataPortal_Delete()

Though Overridable implementations of these methods are in the base class, developers will typically implement strongly typed versions of DataPortal_Create(), DataPortal_Fetch(), and DataPortal_Delete(), as they all accept a criteria object as a parameter. The Overridable methods declare this parameter as type Object, of course; but a business object will typically want to use the actual data type of the criteria object itself. This is discussed in more detail in Chapters 7 and 8.

The data portal also supports three other (optional) methods for pre- and post-processing and exception handling. The names of these methods are as follows:

- DataPortal_OnDataPortalInvoke()
- DataPortal_OnDataPortalInvokeComplete()
- DataPortal_OnDataPortalException()

BusinessBase provides a great deal of functionality to the business objects, whether root or child. Chapter 3 will cover the implementation of BusinessBase itself, and Chapters 7 and 8 will show how to create business objects using BusinessBase.

BusinessListBase

The BusinessListBase class is the base from which all editable *collections* of business objects will be created. Given an Invoice object with a collection of LineItem objects, BusinessListBase will be the base for creating that collection:

```
<Serializable()> _
Public Class LineItems
  Inherits BusinessListBase(Of LineItems, LineItem)

End Class
```

When creating a subclass, the business developer must provide the specific types of their new business collection, and the child objects the collection contains, as type parameters to BusinessListBase(Of T, C). This allows the generic type to expose strongly typed methods corresponding to the specific business collection type and the type of the child objects.

The result is that the business collection automatically has a strongly typed indexer, along with strongly typed Add() and Remove() methods. The process is the same as if the object had inherited from System.ComponentModel.BindingList(Of T), except that *this* collection will include all the functionality required to support n-level undo, object persistence, and the other business object features.

■**Note** BusinessListBase inherits from System.ComponentModel.BindingList(Of T), so it starts with all the core functionality of a data-bindable .NET collection.

The BusinessListBase class also defines the data access methods and the MarkAsChild() method discussed in the previous BusinessBase section. This allows retrieval of a collection of objects directly (rather than a single object at a time), if that's what is required by the application design.

CommandBase

Most applications consist not only of interactive forms or pages (which require editable objects and collections), but also of non-interactive processes. In a 1- or 2-tier physical model, these processes run on the client workstation or web server, of course. But in a 3-tier model, they should run on the application server to have optimal access to the database server or other back-end resources.

Common examples of non-interactive processes include tasks as simple as checking to see if a specific customer or product exists, and as complex as performing all the back-end processing required to ship an order or post an invoice.

The CommandBase class provides a clear starting point for implementing these types of behaviors. A command object is created on the client and initialized with the data it needs to do its work on the server. It is then executed on the server through the data portal. Unlike other objects, however, command objects implement a special execute method:

```
DataPortal_Execute()
```

The optional pre-, post-, and exception data portal methods can also be implemented if desired. But the `DataPortal_Execute()` method is the important one, since that is where the business developer writes the code to implement the non-interactive back-end processing.

I'll make use of `CommandBase` in Chapter 8 when implementing the sample application objects.

ReadOnlyBase

Sometimes, applications don't want to expose an editable object. Many applications have objects that are read-only or display-only. Read-only objects need to support object persistence only for retrieving data, not for updating data. Also, they don't need to support any of the n-level undo or other editing-type behaviors, because they're created with read-only properties.

For editable objects, there's `BusinessBase`, which has a property that can be set to indicate whether it's a parent or child object. The same base supports both types of objects, allowing dynamic switching between parent and child at runtime.

Making an object read-only or read-write is a bigger decision, because it impacts the *interface* of the object. A read-only object should only include read-only properties as part of its interface, and that isn't something you can toggle on or off at runtime. By implementing a specific base class for read-only objects, they can be more specialized, and have less overhead.

The `ReadOnlyBase` class is used to create read-only objects, as follows:

```
<Serializable()> _
Public Class StaticContent
  Inherits ReadOnlyBase(Of StaticContent)

End Class
```

Classes shouldn't implement any read-write properties. Were they to do so, it would be entirely up to the code in the object to handle any undo, persistence, or other features for dealing with the changed data. If an object has editable properties, it should subclass from `BusinessBase`.

ReadOnlyListBase

Not only do applications sometimes need read-only business objects, but they also commonly require immutable *collections* of objects. The `ReadOnlyListBase` class lets you create strongly typed collections of objects whereby the object and collection are both read-only.

```
<Serializable()> _
Public Class StaticList
  Inherits ReadOnlyListBase(Of StaticList, ChildType)

End Class
```

As with `ReadOnlyBase`, this object supports only the retrieval of data. It has no provision for updating data or handling changes to its data. While the child objects in such a collection may inherit from `ReadOnlyBase`, they don't have to. More commonly, the child objects in a read-only collection are just simple .NET objects that merely expose read-only properties.

NameValueListBase

The `NameValueListBase` class is designed specifically to support the idea of lookup tables or lists of read-only key/value data such as categories, customer types, product types, and so forth. The goal of this class is to simplify the process of retrieving such data and displaying it in common controls like drop-down lists, combo boxes, and other list controls.

```
<Serializable()> _
Public Class CodeList
  Inherits NameValueListBase(Of Integer, String)

End Class
```

While the business developer does need to create a specific class for each type of name/value data, inheriting from this base class largely trivializes the process.

N-Level Undo Functionality

The implementation of n-level undo functionality is quite complex, and involves heavy use of reflection. Fortunately, we can use inheritance to place the implementation in a base class, so that no business object needs to worry about the undo code. In fact, to keep things cleaner, this code is in its *own* base class, separate from any other business object behaviors, as shown in Figure 2-11.

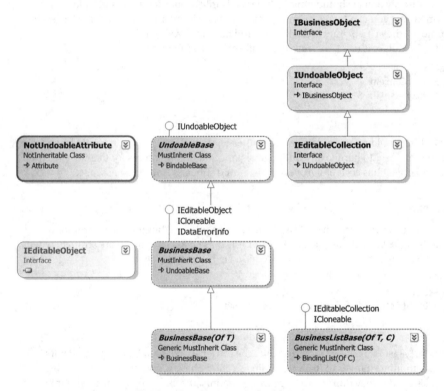

Figure 2-11. *Separating n-level undo into Core.UndoableBase*

At first glance, it might appear that you could use .NET serialization to implement undo functionality: what easier way to take a snapshot of an object's state than to serialize it into a byte stream? Unfortunately, this isn't as easy as it might sound, at least when it comes to restoring the object's state.

Taking a snapshot of a <Serializable()> object is easy, and can be done with code similar to this:

```
<Serializable()> _
Public Class Customer

    Public Function Snapshot() As Byte()
      Using m As New MemoryStream
        Dim f As New BinaryFormatter

        f.Serialize(m, Me)
        m.Position = 0
        return m.ToArray()
      End Using
    End Function
End Class
```

This converts the object into a byte stream, returning that byte stream as an array of type Byte. That part is easy—it's the restoration that's tricky. Suppose that the user now wants to undo the changes, requiring that the byte stream be restored back into the object. The code that deserializes a byte stream looks like this:

```
<Serializable()> _
Public Class Customer

    Public Function Deserialize(ByVal state As Byte()) As Customer
      Using m As New MemoryStream(state)
        Dim f As New BinaryFormatter

        Return CType(f.Deserialize(m), Customer)
      End Using
    End Function
End Class
```

Notice that this function returns a *new customer object*. It doesn't restore the existing object's state; it creates a new object. Somehow, you would have to tell any and all code that has a reference to the existing object to use this new object. In some cases, that might be easy to do, but it isn't always trivial. In complex applications, it's hard to guarantee that other code elsewhere in the application doesn't have a reference to the original object—and if you don't somehow get that code to update its reference to this new object, it will continue to use the old one.

What's needed is some way to restore the object's state *in place*, so that all references to the current object remain valid, but the object's state is restored. This is the purpose of the UndoableBase class.

UndoableBase

The BusinessBase class inherits from UndoableBase, and thereby gains n-level undo capabilities. Because all business objects inherit from BusinessBase, they too gain n-level undo. Ultimately, the n-level undo capabilities are exposed to the business object and to UI developers via three methods:

- BeginEdit() tells the object to take a snapshot of its current state, in preparation for being edited. Each time BeginEdit() is called, a new snapshot is taken, allowing the state of the object to be trapped at various points during its life. The snapshot will be kept in memory so the data can be easily restored to the object if CancelEdit() is called.

- CancelEdit() tells the object to restore the object to the most recent snapshot. This effectively performs an undo operation, reversing one level of changes. If CancelEdit() is called the same number of times as BeginEdit(), the object will be restored to its original state.

- `ApplyEdit()` tells the object to discard the most recent snapshot, leaving the object's current state untouched. It accepts the most recent changes to the object. If `ApplyEdit()` is called the same number of times as `BeginEdit()`, all the snapshots will be discarded, essentially making any changes to the object's state permanent.

Sequences of `BeginEdit()`, `CancelEdit()`, and `ApplyEdit()` calls can be combined to respond to the user's actions within a complex Windows Forms UI. Alternatively, you can totally ignore these methods, taking no snapshots of the object's state. In such a case, the object will incur no overhead from n-level undo, but it also won't have the ability to undo changes. This is common in web applications in which the user has no option to cancel changes. Instead, the user simply navigates away to perform some other action or view some other data.

Supporting Child Objects

As it traces through a business object to take a snapshot of the object's state, `UndoableBase` may encounter child objects. For n-level undo to work for complex objects as well as simple objects, any snapshot of object state must extend down through all child objects as well as the parent object.

I discussed this earlier with the `Invoice` and `LineItem` example. When `BeginEdit()` is called on an `Invoice`, it must *also* take snapshots of the states of all its `LineItem` objects, because they're technically part of the state of the `Invoice` object itself. To do this while preserving encapsulation, each individual object takes a snapshot of its own state so that no object data is ever made available outside the object—thus preserving encapsulation for each object.

In that case, `UndoableBase` simply calls a method on the child object to cascade the `BeginEdit()`, `CancelEdit()`, or `ApplyEdit()` call to that object. It is then up to the individual child object to take a snapshot of its own data. In other words, each object is responsible for managing its own state, including taking a snapshot and potentially restoring itself to that snapshot later.

`UndoableBase` implements `Core.IUndoableObject`, which simplifies the code in the class. This interface defines the methods required by `UndoableBase` during the undo process.

A child object could also be a collection derived from `BusinessListBase`. Notice that `BusinessListBase` implements the `Core.IEditableCollection` interface, which inherits from the `Core.IUndoableObject` interface.

NotUndoableAttribute

The final concept to discuss regarding n-level undo is the idea that some data might not be subject to being in a snapshot. Taking a snapshot of an object's data takes time and consumes memory—if the object includes read-only values, there's no reason to take a snapshot of them. Because the values can't be changed, there's no benefit in restoring them to the same value in the course of an undo operation.

To accommodate this scenario, the framework includes a custom attribute named `NotUndoableAttribute`, which you can apply to fields within your business classes, as follows:

```
<NotUndoable()> _
Private mReadonlyData As String
```

The code in `UndoableBase` simply ignores any fields marked with this attribute as the snapshot is created or restored, so the field will always retain its value regardless of any calls to `BeginEdit()`, `CancelEdit()`, or `ApplyEdit()` on the object.

Data Binding Support

As I discussed earlier in the chapter, the .NET data binding infrastructure directly supports the concept of data binding to objects and collections. However, an object can provide more complete behaviors by implementing a few interfaces in the framework base classes. Table 2-2 lists the interfaces and their purposes.

Table 2-2. *.NET Data Binding Interfaces*

Interface	Purpose
IBindingList	Defines data binding behaviors for collections, including change notification, sorting, and filtering (implemented by BindingList(Of T))
ICancelAddNew	Defines data binding behaviors for collections to allow data binding to cancel the addition of a new child object (implemented by BindingList(Of T))
IRaiseItemChangedEvents	Indicates that a collection object will raise a ListChanged event to indicate that one of its child objects has raised a PropertyChanged event (implemented by BindingList(Of T))
IEditableObject	Defines single-level undo behavior for a business object, allowing the object to behave properly with in-place editing in a DataGridView
INotifyPropertyChanged	Defines an event allowing an object to notify data binding when a property has been changed
IDataErrorInfo	Defines properties used by the DataGridView and ErrorProvider controls to automatically show descriptions of broken validation rules within the object

The IBindingList interface is a well-defined interface that (among other things) raises a single event to indicate that the contents of a collection have changed. Fortunately, there's the System. ComponentModel.BindingList(Of T) base class that already implements this interface, so virtually no effort is required to gain these benefits.

The System.ComponentModel.INotifyPropertyChanged interface members are a bit more complex. This interface defines a single PropertyChanged event that a business object should raise any time a property value is changed. As discussed earlier, in a serializable object, events must be declared using a more explicit syntax than normal so the delegate references can be marked as <NonSerialized()>.

The BindableBase class exists to encapsulate this event declaration and related functionality. This acts as the ultimate base class for BusinessBase(Of T), while BindingList(Of T) is the base class for BusinessListBase(Of T, C), as shown in Figure 2-12.

Combined with implementing System.ComponentModel.IEditableObject and System. ComponentModel.IDataErrorInfo in BusinessBase, the objects can now fully support data binding in both Windows Forms and Web Forms.

While BusinessListBase won't support sorting of a collection, Chapter 5 will implement a SortedBindingList class that provides a sorted view against any collection derived from IList(Of T) (which in turn means any BindingList(Of T)). Such a sorted view provides superior performance and stability as compared to directly sorting a collection in place.

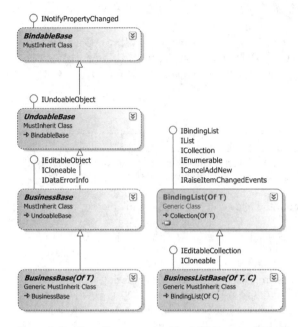

Figure 2-12. *Class diagram with BindableBase and BindingList(Of T)*

Validation Rules

Recall that one of the framework's goals is to simplify the tracking of broken business rules. An important side benefit of this is that the UI developer will have read-only access to the list of broken rules, which means that the descriptions of the broken rules can be displayed to the user in order to explain what's making the object invalid.

The support for tracking broken business rules will be available to *all* editable business objects, so it's implemented at the BusinessBase level in the framework.

To provide this functionality, each business object will have an associated collection of broken business rules.

Additionally, a "rule" is defined as a method that returns a Boolean value indicating whether the business requirement was met. In the case that the result is False (the rule is broken), a rule also returns a text description of the problem for display to the user.

To automate this process, each business object will have an associated list of rule methods for each property in the object.

Figure 2-13 illustrates all the framework classes required to implement both the management of rule methods and maintenance of the list of broken rule descriptions.

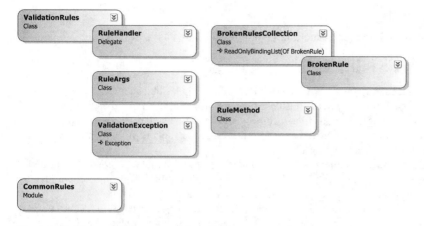

Figure 2-13. *Classes implementing the validation rules behavior*

A business object taps into this functionality through methods exposed on `BusinessBase`. The end result is that a business property is always coded in a consistent manner. In the following example, the highlighted line of code triggers the validation rules behavior:

```
Public Property Name() As String
  Get
    If CanReadProperty() Then
      Return mName
    Else
      Throw New System.Security.SecurityException("Property get not allowed")
  End Get
  Set(ByVal value As String)
    If CanWriteProperty() Then
      If mName <> value Then
        mName = value
        PropertyHasChanged()
      End If
    Else
      Throw New System.Security.SecurityException("Property set not allowed")
    End If
  End Set
End Property
```

You'll see more complete use of the validation rules functionality in Chapter 8, during the implementation of the sample application.

There are three types of functionality displayed in Figure 2-13. The `ValidationRules`, `RuleHandler`, `RuleArgs`, and `ValidationException` classes manage the rule methods associated with the properties of an object. The `BrokenRulesCollection` and `BrokenRule` classes maintain a list of currently broken validation rules for an object. Finally, the `CommonRules` class implements a set of commonly used validation rules, such as `StringRequired`.

Managing Rule Methods

Business rules are defined by a specific method signature as declared in the RuleHandler delegate:

```
Public Delegate Function RuleHandler( _
  ByVal target As Object, ByVal e RuleArgs) As Boolean
```

Each business object contains an instance of the ValidationRules object, which in turn maintains a list of rules for each property in the business object. Within ValidationRules, there is an optimized data structure that is used to efficiently store and access a list of rules for each property. This allows the business object to request that validation rules for a specific property be executed; or that all rules for all properties be executed.

Each rule method returns a Boolean value to indicate whether the rule was satisfied. If a rule is broken, it returns False. A RuleArgs object is passed to each rule method. This object includes a Description property that the rule can set to describe the nature of a broken rule.

As ValidationRules executes each rule method, it watches for a response. When it gets a negative response, it adds an item to the BrokenRulesCollection for the business object. On the other hand, a positive response causes removal of any corresponding item in BrokenRulesCollection.

Finally, there's the ValidationException class. A ValidationException is *not* thrown when a rule is broken, since the broken rule is already recorded in BrokenRulesCollection. Instead, ValidationException is thrown by BusinessBase itself in the case that there's an attempt to save the object to the database when it's in an invalid state.

Maintaining a List of Broken Rules

The ValidationRules object maintains a list of rule methods associated with an object. It also executes those methods to check the rules, either for a specific property or for all properties. The end result of that process is that descriptions for broken rules are recorded into the BrokenRulesCollection associated with the business object.

The BrokenRulesCollection is a list of BrokenRule objects. Each BrokenRule object represents a validation rule that is currently broken by the data in the business object. These BrokenRule objects are added and removed from the collection by ValidationRules as part of its normal processing.

The BusinessBase class uses its BrokenRulesCollection to implement an IsValid property. IsValid returns True only if BrokenRulesCollection contains no items. If it does contain items, then the object is in an invalid state.

The primary point of interest with the BusinessRulesCollection is that it is designed to not only maintain a list of current broken rules, but also to provide read-only access to the UI. This is the reason for implementing a specialized collection object that can change its own data, but that the UI sees as being read-only. On top of that, the base class implements support for data binding so that the UI can display a list of broken rule descriptions to the user by simply binding the collection to a list or grid control.

Additionally, the implementation of IDataErrorInfo makes use of the BrokenRulesCollection to return error text for the object or for individual properties. Supporting this interface allows the DataGridView and ErrorProvider controls to automatically display validation error text to the user.

Implementing Common Rules

If you consider the validation rules applied to most properties, there's a set of common behaviors that occur time and time again. For example, there's the idea that a string value is required, or that a string has a maximum length.

Rather than requiring every business application to implement these same behaviors over and over again, you can have them be supplied by the framework. As you'll see in Chapter 3, the implementation will make use of reflection—so there's a performance cost. If your particular application finds that performance cost to be too high, you can always do what you would have done anyway—that is, write the rule implementation directly into the application. In most cases, however, the benefit of code reuse will outweigh the small performance cost incurred by reflection.

Data Portal

Supporting object persistence—the ability to store and retrieve an object from a database—can be quite complex. I discussed this earlier in the chapter when talking about basic persistence and the concept of ORM.

As you'll see in Chapter 8, business objects will either encapsulate data access logic within the objects, or they will delegate the data access behavior to a persistence object. At the same time, however, you don't want to be in a position in which a change to your physical architecture requires every business object in the system to be altered. The ability to easily switch between having the data access code run on the client machine and having it run on an application server is the goal; with that change driven by a configuration file setting.

On top of this, when using an application server, not every business object in the application should be directly exposed by the server. This would be a maintenance and configuration nightmare, because it would require updating configuration information on all client machines any time a business object is added or changed.

■**Note** This is a lesson learned from years of experience with DCOM and MTS/COM+. Exposing large numbers of components, classes, and methods from a server almost always results in a tightly coupled and fragile relationship between clients and the server.

Instead, it would be ideal if there were one consistent entry point to the application server, so that every client could simply be configured to know about that single entry point and never have to worry about it again. This is exactly what the data portal concept provides, as shown in Figure 2-14.

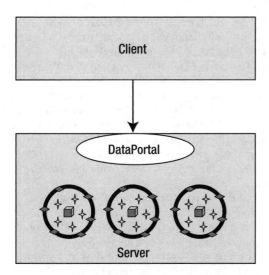

Figure 2-14. *The data portal provides a consistent entry point to the application server.*

The data portal provides a single point of entry and configuration for the server. It manages communication with the business objects while they're on the server running their data access code. Additionally, the data portal concept provides the following other key benefits:

- Centralized security when calling the application server
- A consistent object persistence mechanism (all objects persist the same way)
- Abstraction of the network transport between client and server (enabling support for remoting, Web Services, Enterprise Services, and future protocols)
- One point of control to toggle between running the data access code locally and via remoting

The data portal functionality is designed in several parts, as shown in Table 2-3.

Table 2-3. *Parts of the Data Portal Concept*

Area	Functionality
Client-side `DataPortal`	Functions as the primary entry point to the data portal infrastructure, for use by code in business objects
Client-side proxy classes	Implement the channel adapter pattern to abstract the underlying network protocol from the application
Message objects	Transfer data to and from the server, including security information, application context, the business object's data, the results of the call, and any server-side exception data
Server-side host classes	Expose single points of entry for different server hosts, such as remoting, Web Services, and Enterprise Services
Server-side data portal	Implements transactional and nontransactional data access behaviors, delegating all actual data access to appropriate business objects

Let's discuss each area of functionality in turn.

Client-Side DataPortal

The client-side `DataPortal` is implemented as a `Module`, which means that any `Public` methods it exposes become available to business object code without the need to create a `DataPortal` object. The methods it provides are `Create()`, `Fetch()`, `Update()`, `Delete()`, and `Execute()`. Business objects and collections use these methods to retrieve and update data, or in the case of a `CommandBase`-derived object, to execute server code on the server.

The client-side `DataPortal` has a great deal of responsibility, however, since it contains the code to read and act on the client's configuration settings. These settings control whether the "server-side" data portal components will actually run on the server or locally on the client. It also looks at the business object itself, since a `<RunLocal()>` attribute can be used to force persistence code to run on the client, even if the configuration says to run it on the server.

Either way, the client-side `DataPortal` always delegates the call to the server-side data portal, which handles the actual object persistence behaviors.

However, if the client configuration indicates that the server-side data portal will really run on a server, the configuration will also specify which network transport should be used. It is the client-side `DataPortal` that reads that configuration and loads the appropriate client-side proxy object. That proxy object is then responsible for handling the network communication.

As an object is implemented, its code will use the client-side `DataPortal` to retrieve and update the object's information. An automatic result is that the code in the business object won't need to know about network transports or whether the application is deployed into a 1-, 2-, or n-tier physical environment. The business object code always looks something like this:

```
Public Shared Function GetCustomer(ByVal id As String) As Customer
  Return DataPortal.Fetch(Of Customer)(New Criteria(id))
End Function
```

An even more important outcome is that any UI code using these business objects will look something like this:

```
Dim cust As Customer = Customer.GetCustomer(myId)
```

Neither of these code snippets changes, regardless of whether you've configured the server-side data portal to run locally, or on a remote server via remoting, Web Services, Enterprise Services, or (in the future) WCF. All that changes is the application's configuration file.

Client-Side Proxies

While it is the client-side DataPortal that reads the client configuration to determine the appropriate network transport, the client-side proxy classes actually take care of the details of each network technology. There is a different proxy class for each technology: remoting, Web Services, and Enterprise Services.

The design also allows for a business application to provide its own proxy class to use other protocols. This means you can write your own TCP sockets protocol if you are so inclined.

The remoting and Web Services proxies use the HTTP protocol for communication across the network. This makes both of them firewall- and Internet-friendly. The Enterprise Services proxy uses DCOM for communication across the network. This is substantially faster than HTTP, but harder to configure for firewalls or the Internet. Both HTTP and DCOM can be configured to encrypt data on the wire and so provide quite high levels of security if needed.

Every client-side proxy has a corresponding server-side host class. This is because each transport protocol requires that both ends of the network connection use the same technology.

The client-side DataPortal simply creates an instance of the appropriate client-side proxy and then delegates the request (Create, Fetch, Update, Delete, or Execute) to the proxy object. The proxy object is responsible for establishing a network connection to the server-side host object and delegating the call across the network.

The proxy must also pass other message data, such as security and application context, to the server. Similarly, the proxy must receive data back from the server, including the results of the operation, application context information, and any exception data from the server.

To this last point, if an exception occurs on the server, the full exception details are returned to the client. This includes the nature of the exception, any inner exceptions, and the stack trace related to the exception. Ideally, this exception information will be used on the client to rethrow the exception, giving the illusion that the exception flowed naturally from the code on the server back to the code on the client.

Message Objects

When the client-side DataPortal calls the server-side data portal, several types of information are passed from client to server. Obviously, the data method call (Create, Update, Insert, etc.) itself is transferred from client to server. But other information is also included, as follows:

- Client-side context data (such as the client machine's culture setting)
- Application-wide context data (as defined by the application)
- The user's principal and identity security objects (if using custom security)

Client-side context data is passed one way, from the client to the server. This information may include things like the client workstation's culture setting—thus allowing the server-side code to also use that context when servicing requests for that user. This can be important for localization of an application when a server may be used by workstations in different nations.

Application-wide context data is passed both from client to server and from server back to client. You may use this context data to pass arbitrary application-specific data between client and server on each data portal operation. This can be useful for debugging, as it allows you to build up a trace log of the call as it goes from client to server and back again.

If the application is using custom authentication, then the custom principal and identity objects representing the user are passed from client to server. This means the code on the server will run under the same security context as the client. If you are using Windows integrated or AD security, then Windows itself can be configured to handle the impersonation.

When the server-side data portal has completed its work, the results are returned to the client. Other information is also included, as follows:

- Application-wide context data (as defined by the application)

- Details about any server-side exception that may have occurred

Again, the application-wide context data is passed from client to server and from server to client.

If an exception occurs on the server, the details about that exception are returned to the client. This is important for debugging, as it means you get the full details about any issues on the server. It is also important at runtime, since it allows you to write exception handling code on the client to gracefully handle server-side exceptions—including data-oriented exceptions such as duplicate key or concurrency exceptions.

All the preceding bulleted items are passed to and from the server on each data portal operation. Keeping in mind that the data portal supports several verbs, it is important to understand what information is passed to and from the server to support each verb. This is listed in Table 2-4.

Table 2-4. *Data Passed to and from the Server for Data Portal Operations*

Verb	To Server	From Server
Create	Type of object to create and (optional) criteria about new object	New object loaded with default values
Fetch	Criteria for desired object	Object loaded with data
Update	Object to be updated	Object after update (possibly containing changed data)
Delete	Criteria for object to be deleted	Nothing
Execute	Object to be executed (must derive from CommandBase)	Object after execution (possibly containing changed data)

Notice that the Create, Fetch, and Delete operations all require criteria information about the object to be created, retrieved, or removed. At a minimum, the criteria object must specify the type of object you are trying to create, retrieve, or delete. It may also contain any other data you need to describe your particular business object. A criteria object can be created one of two ways:

- By creating a nested class within your business class

- By creating a class that inherits from CriteriaBase

When a criteria class is nested within a business class, the .NET type system can be used to easily determine the type of class in which the criteria is nested. The CriteriaBase class, on the other hand, directly includes a property you must set, indicating the type of the business object.

In either case, your criteria class should include properties containing any specific information you need in order to identify the specific object to be created, retrieved, or removed.

Server-Side Host Objects

I've already discussed the client-side proxy objects and how each one has a corresponding server-side host object. In Chapter 4, I'll create three host objects, one for each protocol: remoting, Web Services, and Enterprise Services. It is also possible to add new host objects without altering the core framework, providing broad extensibility. Any new host object would need a corresponding client-side proxy, of course.

Server-side host objects are responsible for two things: first, they must accept inbound requests over the appropriate network protocol from the client, and those requests must be passed along to the server-side data portal components; second, the host object is responsible for running inside the appropriate server-side host technology.

Microsoft provides a couple server-side host technologies for hosting application server code: Internet Information Services (IIS) and Enterprise Services.

It is also possible to write your own Windows service that could act as a host technology, but I strongly recommend against such an approach. By the time you write the host and add in security, configuration, and management support, you'll have recreated most or all of either IIS or Enterprise Services. Worse, you'll have opened yourself up for unforeseen security and stability issues.

The remoting and Web Services host objects are designed to run within the IIS host. This way, they can take advantage of the management, stability, and security features inherent in IIS. The Enterprise Services host object is designed to run within Enterprise Services, taking advantage of its management, stability, and security features.

Both IIS and Enterprise Services provide a robust process model and thread management, and so provide very high levels of scalability.

Server-Side Data Portal

At its core, the server-side data portal components provide an implementation of the message router design pattern. The server-side data portal accepts requests from the client and routes those requests to an appropriate handler—in this case, a business object.

■**Note** I say "server-side" here, but keep in mind that the server-side data portal components may run either on the client workstation or on a remote server. Refer to the client-side DataPortal discussion regarding how this selection is made. The data portal is implemented to minimize overhead as much as possible when configured to run locally or remotely, so it is appropriate for use in either scenario.

For Create, Fetch, and Delete operations, the server-side data portal requires type information about your business object. Typically, this is provided via the criteria object. For update and execute operations, the business object itself is passed to the server-side data portal.

But the server-side data portal is more than a simple message router. It also provides optional access to the transactional technologies available within .NET, namely Enterprise Services (MTS/COM+) and the new System.Transactions namespace.

The business framework defines a custom attribute named TransactionalAttribute that can be applied to methods within business objects. Specifically, you can apply it to any of the data access methods that your business object might implement to create, fetch, update, or delete data, or to execute server-side code. This allows you to use one of three models for transactions, as listed in Table 2-5.

Table 2-5. *Transaction Options Supported by the Data Portal*

Option	Description	Transactional Attribute
Manual	You are responsible for implementing your own transactions using ADO.NET, stored procedures, etc.	None or <Transactional (TransactionalTypes.Manual)>
Enterprise Services	Your data access code will run within a COM+ distributed transactional context, providing distributed transactional support	<Transactional (TransactionalTypes. EnterpriseServices)>
System.Transactions	Your data access code will run within a TransactionScope from System.Transactions, automatically providing basic or distributed transactional support as required	<Transactional (TransactionalTypes. TransactionScope)>

This means that in the business object, there may be an update method (overriding the one in BusinessBase) marked to be transactional:

```
<Transactional(TransactionalTypes.TransactionScope)> _
Protected Overrides Sub DataPortal_Update()
  ' Data update code goes here
End Sub
```

At the same time, the object might have a fetch method in the same class that's *not* transactional:

```
Private Sub DataPortal_Fetch(ByVal criteria As Criteria)
  ' Data retrieval code goes here
End Sub
```

This facility means that you can control transactional behavior at the method level, rather than at the class level. This is a powerful feature, because it means that you can do your data retrieval outside of a transaction to get optimal performance, and still do updates within the context of a transaction to ensure data integrity.

The server-side data portal examines the appropriate method on the business object before it routes the call to the business object itself. If the method is marked as <Transactional(TransactionalTypes.EnterpriseServices)>, then the call is routed to a ServicedDataPortal object that is configured to require a COM+ distributed transaction. The ServicedDataPortal then calls the SimpleDataPortal, which delegates the call to your business object, but only after it is running within a distributed transaction.

If the method is marked with <Transactional(TransactionalTypes.TransactionScope)>, the call is routed to a TransactionalDataPortal object that is configured to run within a System. Transactions.TransactionScope. A TransactionScope is powerful because it provides a lightweight transactional wrapper in the case that you are updating a single database; but it automatically upgrades to a distributed transaction if you are updating multiple databases. In short, you get the benefits of COM+ distributed transactions if you need them, but you don't pay the performance penalty if you don't need them. Either way, your code is transactionally protected.

If the method doesn't have the attribute, or is marked as `<Transactional(TransactionalTypes.Manual)>`, the call is routed directly to the `SimpleDataPortal`, as illustrated in Figure 2-15.

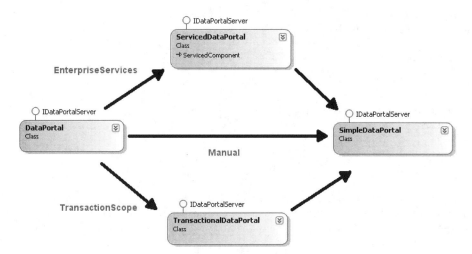

Figure 2-15. *Routing calls through transactional wrappers*

Data Portal Behaviors

Now that you have a grasp of the areas of functionality required to implement the data portal concept, let's discuss the specific data behaviors the data portal will support. The behaviors were listed earlier, in Table 2-4.

Create

The "create" operation is intended to allow the business objects to load themselves with values that must come from the database. Business objects don't need to support or use this capability, but if they need to initialize default values, then this is the mechanism to use.

There are many types of applications for which this is important. For instance, order entry applications typically have extensive defaulting of values based on the customer. Inventory management applications often have many default values for specific parts, based on the product family to which the part belongs. Medical records also often have defaults based on the patient and physician involved.

When the `Create()` method of the `DataPortal` is invoked, it's passed a `Criteria` object. As I've explained, the data portal will either use reflection against the `Criteria` object or will rely on the type information in `CriteriaBase` to determine the type of business object to be created. Using that information, the data portal will then use reflection to create an instance of the business object itself. However, this is a bit tricky, because all business objects will have `Private` or `Protected` constructors to prevent direct creation by code in the UI:

```
<Serializable()> _
Public Class Employee
  Inherits BusinessBase(Of Employee)
```

```
Private Sub New()
  ' prevent direct creation
End Sub

<Serializable()> _
Private Class Criteria
  Private mSsn As String
  Public ReadOnly Property Ssn() As String
    Get
      Return mSsn
    End Get
  End Property

  Public Sub New(ByVal ssn As String)
    mSsn = ssn
  End Sub
End Class

End Class
```

Business objects will expose Shared factory methods to allow the UI code to create or retrieve objects. Those factory methods will invoke the client-side DataPortal. (I discussed this "class-in-charge" concept earlier in the chapter.) As an example, an Employee class may have a Shared factory method, such as the following:

```
Public Shared Function NewEmployee() As Employee
  Return DataPortal.Create(Of Employee)()
End Function
```

Notice that no Employee object is created on the client here. Instead, the factory method asks the client-side DataPortal for the Employee object. The client-side DataPortal passes the call to the server-side data portal. If the data portal is configured to run remotely, the business object is created on the server; otherwise, the business object is created locally on the client.

Even though the business class has only a Private constructor, the server-side data portal uses reflection to create an instance of the class.

The alternative is to make the constructor Public—in which case the UI developer will need to learn and remember that they must use the Shared factory methods to create the object. Making the constructor Private provides a clear and direct reminder that the UI developer *must* use the Shared factory method, thus reducing the complexity of the interface for the UI developer. Keep in mind that *not* implementing the default constructor won't work either, because in that case, the compiler provides a Public default constructor on your behalf.

Once the server-side data portal has created the business object, it calls the business object's DataPortal_Create() method, passing the Criteria object as a parameter. At this point, code *inside* the business object is executing, so the business object can do any initialization that's appropriate for a new object. Typically, this will involve going to the database to retrieve any configurable default values.

When the business object is done loading its defaults, the server-side data portal returns the fully created business object back to the client-side DataPortal. If the two are running on the same machine, this is a simple object reference; but if they're configured to run on separate machines, then the business object is serialized across the network to the client (that is, it's passed by value), so the client machine ends up with a local copy of the business object. The UML sequence diagram in Figure 2-16 illustrates this process.

You can see how the UI interacts with the business object *class* (the Shared factory method), which then creates a Criteria object and passes it to the client-side DataPortal. The client-side DataPortal then delegates the call to the server-side data portal (which may be running locally or remotely, depending on the configuration). The server-side data portal then creates an instance of the business object itself, and calls the business object's DataPortal_Create() method so it can populate itself with default values. The resulting business object is then ultimately returned to the UI.

Alternatively, the DataPortal_Create() method could request the default data values from a persistence object in another assembly, thus providing a clearer separation between the Business Logic and Data Access layers.

In a physical n-tier configuration, remember that the Criteria object starts out on the client machine and is passed by value to the application server. The business object itself is created on the application server, where it's populated with default values. It's then passed back to the client machine by value. This architecture truly takes advantage of the mobile object concept.

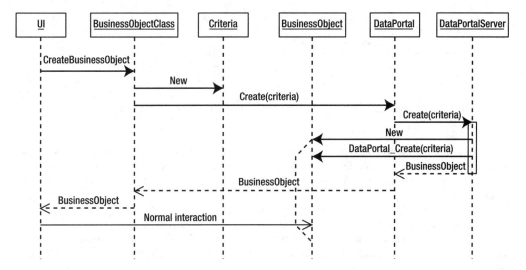

Figure 2-16. *UML sequence diagram for the creation of a new business object*

Fetch

Retrieving a preexisting object is very similar to the creation process just discussed. Again, a Criteria object is used to provide the data that the object will use to find its information in the database. The Criteria class is nested within the business object class and/or inherits from CriteriaBase, so the server-side data portal code can determine the type of business object desired and then use reflection to create an instance of the class.

The UML sequence diagram in Figure 2-17 illustrates all of this.

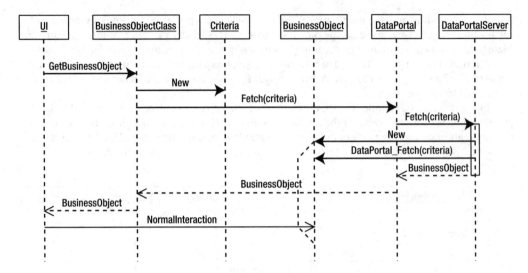

Figure 2-17. *UML sequence diagram for the retrieval of an existing business object*

The UI interacts with the factory method, which in turn creates a Criteria object and passes it to the client-side DataPortal code. The client-side DataPortal determines whether the server-side data portal should run locally or remotely, and then delegates the call to the server-side data portal components.

The server-side data portal uses reflection to determine the assembly and type name for the business class and creates the business object itself. After that, it calls the business object's DataPortal_Fetch() method, passing the Criteria object as a parameter. Once the business object has populated itself from the database, the server-side data portal returns the fully populated business object to the UI.

Alternatively, the DataPortal_Fetch() method could delegate the fetch request to a persistence object from another assembly, thus providing a clearer separation between the Business Logic and Data Access layers.

As with the "create" process, in an n-tier physical configuration, the Criteria object and business object move by value across the network as required. You don't have to do anything special beyond marking the classes as <Serializable()>—the .NET runtime handles all the details on your behalf.

Update

The update process is a bit different from the previous operations. In this case, the UI already has a business object with which the user has been interacting, and this object needs to save its data into the database. To achieve this, all editable business objects have a Save() method (as part of the BusinessBase class from which all business objects inherit). The Save() method calls the DataPortal to do the update, passing the business object itself, Me, as a parameter.

The thing to remember when doing updates is that the object's data will likely change as a result of the update process. Any changed data must be placed back into the object.

There are two common scenarios illustrating how data changes during an update. The first is when the database assigns the primary key value for a new object. That new key value needs to be put into the object and returned to the client. The second scenario is when a timestamp is used to implement optimistic first-write-wins concurrency. In this case, every time the object's data is inserted or updated, the timestamp value must be refreshed in the object with the new value from the database. Again, the updated object must be returned to the client.

This means that the update process is *bidirectional*. It isn't just a matter of sending the data to the server to be stored, but also a matter of returning the object *from* the server after the update has completed, so that the UI has a current, valid version of the object.

Due to the way .NET passes objects by value, it may introduce a bit of a wrinkle into the overall process. When passing the object to be saved over to the server, .NET makes a copy of the object from the client onto the server, which is exactly what is desired. However, after the update is complete, the object must be returned to the client. When an object is returned from the server to the client, a new copy of the object is made on the client, which isn't really the desired behavior.

Figure 2-18 illustrates the initial part of the update process.

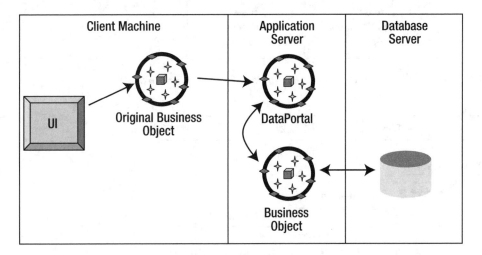

Figure 2-18. *Sending a business object to the data portal to be inserted or updated*

The UI has a reference to the business object and calls its Save() method. This causes the business object to ask the data portal to save the object. The result is that a copy of the business object is made on the server, where it can save itself to the database. So far, this is pretty straightforward.

Note Notice that the business object has a Save() method, but the data portal infrastructure has methods named Update(). Although this is a bit inconsistent, remember that the business object is being called by UI developers, and I've found that it's more intuitive for the typical UI developer to call Save() than Update(), especially since the Save() call can trigger an Insert, an Update, or even a Delete operation.

However, once this part is done, the updated business object is returned to the client, and the UI must update its references to use the *newly updated* object instead, as shown in Figure 2-19.

This is fine, too—but it's important to keep in mind that you can't continue to use the old business object; you must update all object references to use the newly updated object. Figure 2-20 is a UML sequence diagram that shows the overall update process.

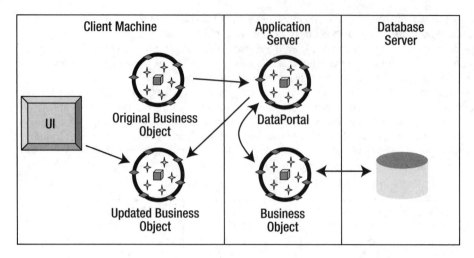

Figure 2-19. *Data portal returning the inserted or updated business object to the UI*

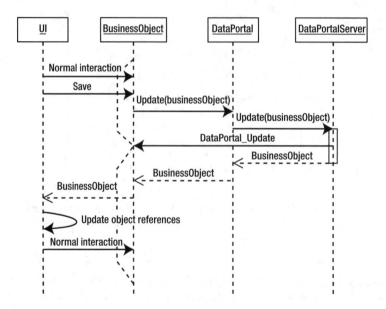

Figure 2-20. *UML sequence diagram for the updating of a business object*

You can see that the UI calls the `Save()` method on the business object, which results in a call to the client-side `DataPortal`'s `Update()` method, passing the business object as a parameter. As usual, the client-side `DataPortal` determines whether the server-side data portal is running locally or remotely, and then delegates the call to the server-side data portal.

The server-side data portal then simply calls the `DataPortal_Update()` method on the business object so that the object can save its data into the database. If the object were a new object, then `DataPortal_Insert()` would have been called, and if the object had been marked for deletion, then `DataPortal_DeleteSelf()` would have been called.

These methods may implement the code to insert, update, or delete the object directly within the business class, or they may delegate the call to a persistence object in another assembly.

At this point, two versions of the business object exist: the original version on the client and the newly updated version on the application server. However, the best way to view this is to think of the original object as being obsolete and invalid at this point. Only the newly updated version of the object is valid.

Once the update is done, the new version of the business object is returned to the UI; the UI can then continue to interact with the new business object as needed.

■**Note** The UI must update any references from the old business object to the newly updated business object as soon as the new object is returned from the data portal.

In a physical n-tier configuration, the business object is automatically passed by value to the server, and the updated version is returned by value to the client. If the server-side data portal is running locally, however, simple object references are passed. This avoids the overhead of serialization and so forth.

Delete

The final operation, and probably the simplest, is to delete an object from the database. The framework actually supports two approaches to deleting objects.

The first approach is called *deferred deletion*. In this model, the object is retrieved from the database and is marked for deletion by calling a Delete() method on the business object. Then the Save() method is called to cause the object to update itself to the database (thus actually doing the Delete operation). In this case, the data will be deleted by the DataPortal_DeleteSelf() method.

The second approach, called *immediate deletion*, consists of simply passing criteria data to the server, where the object is deleted immediately within the DataPortal_Delete() method.

This second approach provides superior performance because you don't need to load the object's data and return it to the client. Instead, you simply pass the criteria fields to the server, where the object deletes its data.

The framework supports both models, providing you with the flexibility to allow either or both in your object models, as you see fit.

Deferred deletion follows the same process as the update process I just discussed, so let's explore immediate deletion. In this case, a Criteria object is created to describe the object to be deleted, and the data portal is invoked to do the deletion. Figure 2-21 is a UML diagram that illustrates the process.

Because the data has been deleted at this point, you have nothing to return to the UI, so the overall process remains pretty straightforward. As usual, the client-side DataPortal delegates the call to the server-side data portal. The server-side data portal creates an instance of the business object and invokes its DataPortal_Delete() method, providing the Criteria object as a parameter.

The business logic to do the deletion itself is encapsulated within the business object, along with all the other business logic relating to the object. Alternatively, the business object could delegate the deletion request to a persistence object in another assembly.

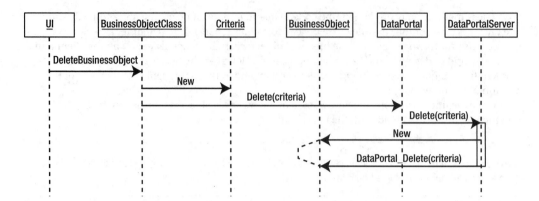

Figure 2-21. *UML sequence diagram for immediate deletion of a business object*

Custom Authentication

As discussed earlier in the chapter, many environments include users who aren't part of a Windows domain or AD. In such a case, relying on Windows integrated security for the application is problematic at best, and you're left to implement your own security scheme. Fortunately, the .NET Framework includes several security concepts, along with the ability to customize them to implement your own security as needed.

The following discussion applies to you only in the case that Windows integrated security doesn't work for your environment. In such a case, you'll typically maintain a list of users and their roles in a database, or perhaps in an LDAP server. The custom authentication concepts discussed here will help you integrate the application with that preexisting security database.

Custom Principal and Identity Objects

The .NET Framework includes a couple of built-in *principal* and *identity* objects that support Windows integrated security or generic security. You can also create your own principal and identity objects by creating classes that implement the IPrincipal and IIdentity interfaces from the System.Security.Principal namespace.

Implementations of principal and identity objects will be specific to your environment and security requirements. However, the framework will include a BusinessPrincipalBase class to streamline the process.

When you create a custom principal object, it must inherit from BusinessPrincipalBase. Code in the data portal ensures that only a WindowsPrincipal or BusinessPrincipalBase object is passed between client and server, depending on the application's configuration.

In many cases, your custom principal object will require very little code. The base class already implements the IPrincipal interface, and it is quite likely that you'll only need to implement the IsInRole() method to fit your needs.

However, you will need to implement a custom identity object that implements IIdentity. Typically, this object will populate itself with user profile information and a list of user roles from a database. Essentially, this is just a read-only business object, and so you'll typically inherit from ReadOnlyBase. Such an object might be declared like this:

```
<Serializable()> _
Public Class CustomIdentity
  Inherits ReadOnlyBase(Of CustomIdentity)

  Implements IIdentity

  ' implement here
End Class
```

You'll also need to implement a Login method that the UI code can call to initiate the process of authenticating the user's credentials (username and password) and loading data into the custom identity object. This is often best implemented as a Shared factory method on the custom principal class. In many cases, this factory method will look something like this:

```
Public Shared Sub Login(ByVal username As String, ByVal password As String)
  Dim identity As CustomIdentity = _
    CustomIdentity.GetIdentity(username, password)
  If identity.IsAuthenticated Then
    Dim principal As IPrincipal = New CustomPrincipal(identity)
    Csla.ApplicationContext.User = principal
  End If
End Sub
```

The GetIdentity method is a normal factory method in CustomIdentity that just calls the data portal to load the object with data from the database. A corresponding Logout method may look like this:

```
Public Shared Sub Logout()
  Dim identity As CustomIdentity = CustomIdentity.UnauthenticatedIdentity()
  Dim principal As IPrincipal = New CustomPrincipal(identity)
  Csla.ApplicationContext.User = principal
End Sub
```

The UnauthenticatedIdentity() method is actually a variation on the factory concept, but in this case, it probably doesn't use the data portal. Instead, it merely needs to create an instance of CustomIdentity, in which IsAuthenticated returns False.

Integrated Authorization

Virtually all applications rely on some form of authorization. At the very least, there is typically control over which users have access to the application at all. But more commonly, applications need to restrict which users can view or edit specific bits of data at either the object or property level. This is often accomplished by assigning users to roles and then specifying which roles are allowed to view or edit various data.

To help control whether the current user can view or edit individual properties, the business framework will allow the business developer to specify the roles that are allowed or denied the ability to view or edit each property. Typically, these role definitions will be set up as the object is created, and they may be hard-coded into the object or loaded from a database, as you choose.

With the list of allowed and denied roles established, the framework is able to implement CanReadProperty() and CanWriteProperty() methods that can be called within each property's get and set code. The result is that a typical property looks like this:

```
Public Property Name() As String
  Get
    CanReadProperty(True)
    return mName
  End Get
  Set(ByVal value As String)
    CanWriteProperty(True)
    If mName <> value Then
      mName = value
      PropertyHasChanged()
    End If
  End Set
End Property
```

The CanReadProperty() and CanWriteProperty() methods check the current user's roles against the list of roles allowed and denied read and write access to this particular property. If the authorization rules are violated, a security exception is thrown; otherwise, the user is allowed to read or write the property. There are other overloads of these methods as well, offering variation in coding simplicity, control, and performance. These will be fully explored in Chapter 3.

The CanReadProperty() and CanWriteProperty() methods are Public in scope. This is important because it allows code in the UI layer to ask the object about the user's permissions to read and write each property. The UI can use this information to alter its display to give the user visual cues as appropriate. In Chapter 9, you'll see how this capability can be exploited by an extender control in Windows Forms to eliminate most authorization code in a typical application. While the story isn't quite as compelling in Web Forms, Chapter 10 will demonstrate how to leverage this capability in a similar manner.

Helper Types and Classes

Most business applications require a set of common behaviors not covered by the concepts discussed thus far. These behaviors are a grab bag of capabilities that can be used to simplify common tasks that would otherwise be complex. These include the items listed in Table 2-6.

Table 2-6. *Helper Types and Classes*

Type or Class	Description
SafeDataReader	Wraps any IDataReader (such as SqlDataReader) and converts all null values from the database into non-null empty or default values
ObjectAdapter	Fills a DataSet or DataTable with information from an object or a collection of objects
DataMapper	Maps data from an IDictionary to an object's properties, or from one object's properties to another object's properties
SmartDate	Implements a DateTime data type that understands how to translate values transparently between DateTime and string representations, and also understands the concept of an empty date
SortedBindingList	Provides a sorted view of any IList(Of T); if the underlying collection is editable, then the view will also be editable

Let's discuss each of these in turn.

SafeDataReader

Most of the time, applications don't care about the difference between a null value and an empty value (such as an empty string or a zero)—but databases often do. When retrieving data from a database, an application needs to handle the occurrence of unexpected null values with code such as the following:

```
If dr.IsDBNull(idx) Then
  myValue = ""
Else
  myValue = dr.GetString(idx)
End If
```

Clearly, doing this over and over again throughout the application can get very tiresome. One solution is to fix the database so that it doesn't allow nulls when they provide no value, but this is often impractical for various reasons.

■Note Here's one of my pet peeves: allowing nulls in a column in which you care about the difference between a value that was never entered and the empty value (" ", or 0, or whatever) is fine. Allowing nulls in a column where you *don't* care about the difference merely complicates your code for no good purpose, thereby decreasing developer productivity and increasing maintenance costs.

As a more general solution, the framework includes a utility class that uses SqlDataReader (or any IDataReader implementation) in such a way that you never have to worry about null values again. Unfortunately, the SqlDataReader class isn't inheritable—it can't be subclassed directly. Instead, it is wrapped using containment and delegation. The result is that your data access code works the same as always, except that you never need to write checks for null values. If a null value shows up, SafeDataReader will automatically convert it to an appropriate empty value.

Obviously, if you *do* care about the difference between a null and an empty value, you can just use a regular SqlDataReader to retrieve the data. In this case, .NET 2.0 includes the new Nullable(Of T) generic type that helps manage null database values. This new type is very valuable when you do care about null values: when business rules dictate that an "empty" value like 0 is different from null.

ObjectAdapter

Many reporting technologies, such as Crystal Reports, don't offer the ability to generate a report directly against objects. Unfortunately, these technologies are designed to only generate reports directly against a database or DataSet; yet many applications need to generate reports against business objects, leaving the developer in a difficult position.

The ObjectAdapter implements a Fill() method that copies data from an object or a collection of objects into a DataTable or a DataSet. The resulting DataSet can then be used as a data source for reporting technologies that can't run directly against objects.

While not useful for large sets of data, this technology can be very useful for generating small printouts against small amounts of data. For a more complete discussion of ObjectAdapter and reporting with objects, see Chapter 5.

DataMapper

In Chapter 10, you will see how to implement an ASP.NET Web Forms UI on top of business objects. This chapter will make use of the new data binding capabilities in Web Forms 2.0. In this technology, the Insert and Update operations provide the data from the form in IDictionary objects (name/value pairs). The values in these name/value pairs must be loaded into corresponding properties in the business object. You end up writing code much like this:

```
cust.Name = e.Values("Name").ToString
cust.Address1 = e.Values("Address1").ToString
cust.City = e.Values("City").ToString
```

Similarly, in Chapter 11, you'll see how to implement a Web Services interface on top of business objects. When data is sent or received through a web service, it goes through a proxy object: an object with properties containing the data, but no other logic or code. Since the goal is to get the data into or out of a business object, this means copying the data from one object's properties to the other. You end up writing code much like this:

```
cust.Name = message.Name
cust.Address1 = message.Address1
cust.City = message.City
```

In both cases, this is repetitive, boring code to write. One alternative, though it does incur a performance hit, is to use reflection to automate the copy process. This is the purpose of the DataMapper class: to automate the copying of data to reduce all those lines of code to one simple line. It is up to you whether to use DataMapper in your applications.

SmartDate

Dates are a perennial development problem. Of course, there's the DateTime data type, which provides powerful support for manipulating dates, but it has no concept of an "empty" date. The trouble is that many applications allow the user to leave date fields empty, so you need to deal with the concept of an empty date within the application.

On top of this, date formatting is problematic—rather, formatting an ordinary date value is easy, but again you're faced with the special case whereby an "empty" date must be represented by an empty string value for display purposes. In fact, for the purposes of data binding, we often want any date properties on the objects to be of type String so that the user has full access to the various data formats as well as the ability to enter a blank date into the field.

Dates are also a challenge when it comes to the database: the date data types in the database don't understand the concept of an empty date any more than .NET does. To resolve this, date columns in a database typically *do* allow null values, so a null can indicate an empty date.

■**Note** Technically, this is a misuse of the null value, which is intended to differentiate between a value that was never entered and one that's empty. Unfortunately, we're typically left with no choice, because there's no way to put an empty date value into a date data type.

You may be able to use Nullable(Of DateTime) as a workable data type for your date values. But even that isn't always perfect, because Nullable(Of DateTime) doesn't offer specialized formatting and parsing capabilities for working with dates. Nor does it really understand the concept of an empty date: it isn't possible to compare actual dates with empty dates, yet that is often a business requirement.

The SmartDate type is an attempt to resolve this issue. Repeating the problem with SqlDataReader, the DateTime data type isn't inheritable, so SmartDate can't just subclass DateTime to create a more powerful data type. Instead, it uses containment and delegation to create a new type that provides the capabilities of the DateTime data type while also supporting the concept of an empty date.

This isn't as easy at it might at first appear, as you'll see when the SmartDate class is implemented in Chapter 5. Much of the complexity flows from the fact that applications often need to compare an empty date to a real date, but an empty date might be considered very small or very large. You'll see an example of both cases in the sample application in Chapter 8.

The SmartDate class is designed to support these concepts, and to integrate with the SafeDataReader so that it can properly interpret a null database value as an empty date.

SortedBindingList

The business framework will base its collections on BindingList(Of T), thus automatically supporting data binding as well as collection behaviors. The BindingList(Of T) class is an implementation of the IBindingList interface. This interface not only defines basic data binding behaviors, but also exposes methods for sorting the contents of the collection. Unfortunately, BindingList(Of T) doesn't implement this sorting behavior.

It would be possible to implement the sorting behaviors directly within the BusinessListBase and ReadOnlyBindingList classes. Unfortunately, it turns out that sorting a collection in place is somewhat complex. The complexity arises because IBindingList also supports the idea of removing the sort—thus presumably returning the collection's contents to their original order. That necessitates keeping a list of the original position of all items when a sort is applied. Add to this the question of where to position newly added items, and things can get quite complex.

ADO.NET provides one possible solution through its use of DataView objects that are used to provide sorted views of a DataTable. Taking a cue from ADO.NET, SortedBindingList provides a sorted view of any IList(Of T) collection, including all collection objects that inherit from BindingList(Of T). By implementing a sorted view, all the complexity of manipulating the original collection is avoided. The original collection remains intact and unchanged, and SortedBindingList just provides a sorted view of the collection.

That said, SortedBindingList will provide an *editable* view of a collection if the original source collection is editable. In other words, editing a child object in a SortedBindingList *directly* edits the child object in the source collection. Similarly, adding or removing an item from a SortedBindingList directly adds or removes the item from the original collection.

Namespace Organization

At this point, I've walked through all the classes that will make up the business framework. Given that there are quite a few classes and types required to implement the framework, there's a need to organize them for easier discovery and use. The solution for this is to organize the types into a set of *namespaces*.

Namespaces allow you to group classes together in meaningful ways so that you can program against them more easily. Additionally, namespaces allow different classes to have the same name as long as they're in different namespaces. From a business perspective, you might use a scheme like the following:

```
MyCompany.MyApplication.FunctionalArea.Class
```

A convention like this immediately indicates that the class belongs to a specific functional area within an application and organization. It also means that the application could have multiple classes with the same names:

```
MyCompany.MyApplication.Sales.Product
MyCompany.MyApplication.Manufacturing.Product
```

It's quite likely that the concept of a "product" in sales is different from that in manufacturing, and this approach allows reuse of class names to make each part of the application as clear and self-documenting as possible.

The same is true when you're building a framework. Classes should be grouped in meaningful ways so that they're comprehensible to the end developer. Additionally, use of the framework can be simplified for the end developer by putting little-used or obscure classes in separate namespaces. This way, the business developer doesn't typically see them via IntelliSense.

Consider the UndoableBase class, which isn't intended for use by a business developer: it exists for use within the framework only. Ideally, when business developers are working with the framework, they won't see UndoableBase via IntelliSense unless they go looking for it by specifically navigating to a specialized namespace. The framework has some namespaces that are to be used by end developers, and others that are intended for internal use.

All the namespaces in the framework are prefixed with *component-based, scalable, logical architecture* (CSLA).

■Note CSLA was the name of the COM-based business object framework about which I wrote in the mid-to-late 1990s. In many ways, this book brings the basic concepts and capabilities of that architecture into the .NET environment. In fact, .NET enables the CSLA concepts, though COM has often hindered them.

Table 2-7 lists the namespaces used in the CSLA .NET framework.

Table 2-7. *Namespaces Used in the CSLA .NET Framework*

Namespace	Description
Csla	Contains the types most commonly used by business developers
Csla.Core	Contains the types that provide core functionality for the framework; not intended for use by business developers
Csla.Data	Contains the optional types used to support data access operations; often used by business developers, web UI developers, and web service developers
Csla.DataPortalClient	Contains the types that support the client-side DataPortal behaviors; used when creating a custom data portal proxy
Csla.Properties	Contains code generated by Visual Studio for the Csla project; not intended for use by business developers
Csla.Security	Contains the types supporting authorization; used when creating a custom principal object
Csla.Server	Contains the types supporting the server-side data portal behaviors; not intended for use by business developers
Csla.Server.Hosts	Contains the types supporting server-side data portal hosts; used when creating a custom data portal host
Csla.Validation	Contains the types supporting validation and business rules; often used when creating rule methods
Csla.Web	Contains the CslaDataSource control; used by web UI developers
Csla.Web.Design	Contains the supporting types for the CslaDataSource control; not intended for use by business developers
Csla.WebServiceHost	Contains the Web Services data portal host; not intended for use by business developers
Csla.Windows	Contains controls to assist with Windows Forms data binding; used by Windows UI developers

For instance, the primary base classes intended for use by business developers go into the `Csla` namespace itself. They are named as follows:

- `Csla.BusinessBase(Of T)`
- `Csla.BusinessListBase(Of T, C)`
- `Csla.ReadOnlyBase(Of T)`
- `Csla.ReadOnlyListBase(Of T, C)`
- `Csla.NameValueListBase(Of K, V)`
- `Csla.CommandBase`

The rest of the classes and types in the framework are organized into the remaining namespaces based on their purposes. You'll see how they all fit and are implemented in Chapters 3 through 5.

The end result is that a typical business developer can simply use the `Csla` namespace as follows:

`using Csla;`

and all the developer will see are the classes intended for use during business development. All the other classes and concepts within the framework are located in other namespaces, and therefore won't appear in IntelliSense by default, unless the developer specifically imports those namespaces.

When using custom authentication, you'll likely import the `Csla.Security` namespace. But if you're not using that feature, you can ignore those classes and they won't clutter up the development experience. Similarly, `Csla.Data` and `Csla.Validation` may be used in some cases, as you'll see in Chapter 8. If the types they contain are useful, they can be brought into a class with an `Imports` statement; otherwise, they are safely out of the way.

Conclusion

This chapter has examined some of the key design goals for the CSLA .NET business framework. The key design goals include the following:

- N-level undo capability
- Tracking broken validation rules to tell if an object is valid
- Tracking whether an object's data has changed (whether or not it's "dirty")
- Support for strongly typed collections of child objects
- Providing a simple and abstract model for the UI developer
- Full support for data binding in both Windows Forms and Web Forms
- Saving objects to a database and getting them back again
- Custom authentication
- Integrated authorization
- Other miscellaneous features

I've also walked you through the design of the framework itself, providing a high-level glimpse into the purpose and rationale behind each of the classes that will make it up. With each class, I discussed how it relates back to the key goals to provide the features and capabilities of the framework.

The chapter closed by defining the namespaces that contain the framework classes. This way, they're organized so that they're easily understood and used.

Chapter 3 will implement the portions of the framework primarily geared toward supporting the UI and data binding. Then, Chapter 4 will implement the data portal and object persistence. Chapter 5 will wrap up loose ends by implementing the helper classes, such as `SmartDate`, `SafeDataReader`, and others.

With the framework complete, the rest of the book will walk through the design and implementation of a sample application using object-oriented concepts and the CSLA .NET framework. Those chapters will explore how the framework functions and how it meets the goals set forth in this chapter.

CHAPTER 3

■■■

Business Framework Implementation

In Chapter 1, I discussed the concepts behind the use of business objects and distributed objects. In Chapter 2, I explored the design of the business framework. In this chapter, we're going to start creating the CSLA .NET framework. The focus in this chapter is on the functionality required to support editable and read-only objects and collections. Specifically, the goal is to create the following classes, along with all supporting classes and functionality:

- Csla.BusinessBase(Of T)
- Csla.BusinessListBase(Of T, C)
- Csla.ReadOnlyBase(Of T)
- Csla.ReadOnlyListBase(Of T, C)

These four base classes are the primary classes from which most business objects will inherit. Chapter 5 will cover the other base classes: CommandBase and NameValueListBase.

BusinessBase and BusinessListBase rely on quite a number of other classes. For instance, Csla.BusinessBase inherits from Csla.Core.BusinessBase, which inherits from Csla.Core.UndoableBase. It also makes use of the ValidationRules and AuthorizationRules classes.

The end result is that this chapter will cover the creation of the four base classes, plus the types and classes in the Csla.Core namespace and most of the types from the Csla.Validation and Csla. Security namespaces. Table 3-1 lists all the classes discussed in this chapter.

Table 3-1. *Classes Required to Support Editable and Read-Only Business Objects*

Type	Description
Csla.Core.IBusinessObject	Interface implemented by all editable and read-only base classes
Csla.Core.IUndoableObject	Interface implemented by all editable base classes
Csla.Core.IEditableCollection	Interface implemented by all editable collection base classes
Csla.Core.IReadOnlyObject	Interface implemented by all read-only base classes
Csla.Core.IReadOnlyCollection	Interface implemented by all read-only collection base classes
Csla.Core.ICommandObject	Interface implemented by CommandBase
Csla.Core.ObjectCloner	Clones any serializable object

Continued

Table 3-1. *Continued*

Type	Description
Csla.Core.BindableBase	Implements INotifyPropertyChanged
Csla.NotUndoableAttribute	Used to mark a field such that n-level undo ignores the field's value
Csla.Core.UndoableBase	Implements n-level undo functionality
Csla.Core.BusinessBase	Implements editable object functionality and data binding support
Csla.Core.ReadOnlyBindingList	Inherits from BindingList(Of T) to implement read-only behaviors
Csla.Validation.RuleHandler	Defines the method signature for rule methods
Csla.Validation.RuleArgs	Defines the arguments passed to a rule handler method
Csla.Validation.RuleMethod	Contains information about a rule method
Csla.Validation.ValidationRules	Maintains a list of rules associated with each object property
Csla.Validation.BrokenRule	Represents a single broken rule in the BrokenRulesCollection
Csla.Validation.BrokenRulesCollection	Maintains a list of currently broken validation rules for a business object
Csla.Security.RolesForProperty	Maintains a list of roles allowed or denied access for a specific object property
Csla.Security.AuthorizationRules	Maintains a list of roles allowed or denied access for all object properties by using RolesForProperty objects
Csla.BusinessBase	Base class from which editable business classes will inherit
Csla.BusinessListBase	Base class from which editable business collection classes will inherit
Csla.ReadOnlyBase	Base class from which read-only business classes will inherit
Csla.ReadOnlyListBase	Base class from which read-only business collection classes will inherit

The reasoning behind the existence of these classes, and the explanation of how they're organized into namespaces, were covered in Chapter 2. In this chapter, I'll focus mostly on the actual implementation of each assembly and class.

This chapter will cover the creation of each class in turn. Obviously, this is a lot to cover, so the chapter will only include the critical code from each class. You'll want to download the code for the book from the Apress website (www.apress.com) so you can see each complete class or type as it is discussed.

Setting Up the CSLA .NET Project

Open Visual Studio 2005 and create a new Class Library project named Csla. I recommend immediately saving the project using File ➤ Save All. Make sure the option to create a directory for the solution is checked, as shown in Figure 3-1.

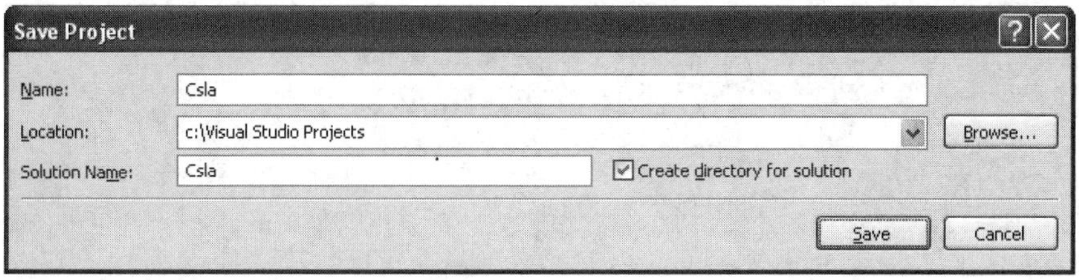

Figure 3-1. *Saving the blank Csla solution*

Of course, the `Class1.vb` file needs to be removed in preparation for adding the classes that belong to the framework.

Creating the Directory Structure

To keep all the source files in the project organized, the project needs a set of folders. Table 3-2 lists the folders to add to the project.

Table 3-2. *Folders in the Csla Project*

Folder	Purpose
Core	Contains the `Csla.Core` types
Data	Contains the `Csla.Data` types
DataPortal	Contains files in the `Csla` namespace that are part of the data portal functionality (see Chapter 4)
DataPortal\Client	Contains `Csla.DataPortal`, along with the `Csla.DataPortalClient` proxy classes (see Chapter 4)
DataPortal\Hosts	Contains the `Csla.Server.Hosts` host classes (see Chapter 4)
DataPortal\Server	Contains the `Csla.Server` types that implement the server-side data portal functionality (see Chapter 4)
Security	Contains the `Csla.Security` types
Validation	Contains the `Csla.Validation` types

By organizing the various files into folders, the project will be far easier to create and manage. Some of the folders listed here won't be used until Chapter 4, but it is worth getting them all set up now to be ready.

There's an additional `Diagrams` folder in the code download, containing many of the diagrams (or pieces of them at least) used to create the graphics in this book.

Supporting Localization

The CSLA .NET framework supports localization. For a framework, the key to supporting localization is to avoid using any string literal values that might be displayed to the end user. The .NET Framework and Visual Studio 2005 offer features to assist in this area through the use of resources.

In the Solution Explorer window, double-click on the Properties node under the `Csla` project to bring up the project's properties windows. Click on the Resources tab to navigate to the built-in resource editor. Figure 3-2 shows this editor with several of the string resources from `Resources.resx`.

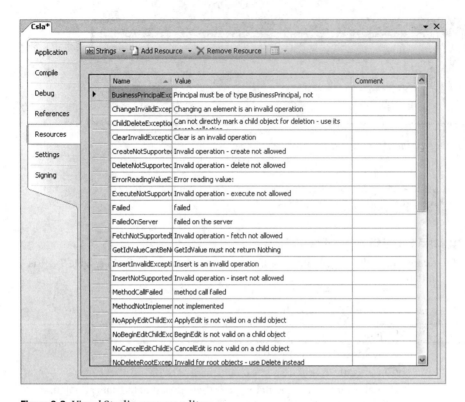

Figure 3-2. *Visual Studio resource editor*

The complete set of resources is available in the Resources.resx file in the download. Additionally, a number of people around the world have been kind enough to translate the resources to various languages. As this is an ongoing process, please refer to www.lhotka.net/cslanet/download.aspx for updates to the framework and resource files.

Now that the basic project has been set up, let's walk through each class or type in turn. To keep things organized, I'll follow the basic order from Table 3-1 (with a couple of exceptions). This way, the namespaces can be built one at a time.

Csla.Core Namespace

The Csla.Core namespace contains types that are not intended for business developers. Rather, these types are intended for use by the CSLA .NET framework itself. This is a primary motivation for putting them into their own namespace—to help keep them out of sight of business developers during normal development.

These types may also be useful to people who wish to extend the framework. For instance, Core.BusinessBase could easily act as a starting point for creating some different or more advanced BusinessBase-style class. Likewise, Core.ReadOnlyBindingList is useful as a base for creating any type of read-only collection that supports data binding.

IBusinessObject Interface

Generic types like BindingList(Of T) are very powerful because they allow a developer to easily create a strongly typed instance of the generic type. For instance

```
Dim myStringList As BindingList(Of String)
```

defines a strongly typed collection of type String. Similarly

```
Dim myIntList As BindingList(Of Integer)
```

defines a strongly typed collection of type Integer. Since both myStringList and myIntList are "of type" BindingList(Of T), you might think they are polymorphic—that you could write one method that could act on both fields. But you can't. Generic types are *not* inherited, and thus do not come from the same type. This is highly counterintuitive at first glance, but nonetheless is a fact of life when working with generic types.

Since CSLA .NET makes use of generic types (BusinessBase(Of T), BusinessListBase(Of T, C), etc.), this is a problem. There are cases in which a UI developer will want to treat all business objects the same—or at least be able to use the .NET type system to determine whether an object is a business object or not.

In order to treat instances of a generic type polymorphically, or to do type checks to see if those instances come from the same type, the generic type must inherit from a non-generic base class or implement a non-generic interface. In the case of BindingList(Of T), the generic type implements IBindingList. So both myStringList and myIntList can be treated as IBindingList types.

To provide this type of polymorphic behavior to CSLA .NET business objects, all business base classes will implement Csla.Core.IBusinessObject. This, then, is the ultimate base type for all business objects. Here's the code for IBusinessObject:

```
Namespace Core

  Public Interface IBusinessObject
  End Interface

End Namespace
```

Notice that this interface has no members (methods, properties, etc). This is because there are no common behaviors across both read-only and editable business objects. The interface remains incredibly useful, however, because it allows code to easily detect whether an object is a business object, through code like this:

```
If TypeOf theObject Is Csla.Core.IBusinessObject Then
  ' theObject is a business object
End If
```

The next couple of interfaces will have more members.

IUndoableObject Interface

In the same way that IBusinessObject provides a form of polymorphism and commonality across all business objects, IUndoableObject does the same thing for editable business objects—specifically those that inherit from BusinessBase(Of T) and BusinessListBase(Of T, C).

This polymorphic ability will be of critical importance in the implementation of UndoableBase later in the chapter. UndoableBase needs to be able to treat all editable objects the same in order to implement the n-level undo functionality.

Here's the code for IUndoableObject:

```
Namespace Core

  Public Interface IUndoableObject
    Inherits IBusinessObject

    Sub CopyState()
    Sub UndoChanges()
    Sub AcceptChanges()
  End Interface

End Namespace
```

First notice that this interface inherits from the IBusinessObject interface. This means that all editable objects implementing this interface will automatically be business objects in the broader sense.

All editable objects support n-level undo. The n-level undo support implemented by UndoableBase requires that every object implement the three methods listed in this interface.

Putting these methods in an interface is a double-edged sword. On one hand, it clearly defines the methods and will make it easier to implement UndoableBase. On the other hand, these methods are now potentially available to any code using a business object. In other words, a UI developer could write code to call these methods—almost certainly causing nasty bugs and side effects, because these methods aren't designed for public use.

This is a difficult design decision when building frameworks. In this case, the benefits of having a common interface for use by UndoableBase appears to outweigh the potential risk of a UI developer doing something foolish by calling the methods directly.

To help minimize this risk, the actual implementation methods in the base classes will keep these methods Private. That way, they can only be called by directly casting the object to the IUndoableObject type.

IEditableCollection Interface

While a BusinessListBase(Of T, C) is both a business object and an editable object, it is also a collection. It turns out that collections need one extra behavior beyond a simple editable object, so the IEditableCollection interface adds that extra method:

```
Namespace Core

  <System.Diagnostics.CodeAnalysis.SuppressMessage( _
    "Microsoft.Naming", "CA1711:IdentifiersShouldNotHaveIncorrectSuffix")> _
  Public Interface IEditableCollection
    Inherits IUndoableObject

    Sub RemoveChild(ByVal child As Core.BusinessBase)
  End Interface

End Namespace
```

The RemoveChild() method will be important later in the chapter, during the implementation of BusinessBase and BusinessListBase, and specifically for the implementation of the System.ComponentModel.IEditableObject interface. This interface has some tricky requirements for interaction between a child object in a collection and the collection itself.

Also notice the SuppressMessage attribute applied to the interface. Some versions of Visual Studio 2005 offer a code-analysis feature. This is a powerful feature that can be used to proactively find bugs and other problems with your code. It applies a set of naming standards to your code as part of its analysis, which is often good. Sometimes, however, you don't want to follow the recommendation. In that case, this attribute can be applied to tell code analysis to be silent on a specific issue. You'll see this type of attribute used here and there throughout the code in Chapters 3 through 5.

IReadOnlyObject Interface

In the same way that IBusinessObject provides a form of polymorphism and commonality across all business objects, IReadOnlyObject does the same thing for read-only business objects—specifically those that inherit from ReadOnlyBase(Of T).

It turns out that all read-only objects support a method for authorization: CanReadProperty(). This method is defined in the interface as follows:

```
Public Interface IReadOnlyObject
  Inherits IBusinessObject

  Function CanReadProperty(ByVal propertyName As String) As Boolean
End Interface
```

The CanReadProperty() method will be discussed later in the chapter.

IReadOnlyCollection Interface

The IReadOnlyCollection interface exists purely to support polymorphism for read-only collection objects that inherit from ReadOnlyListBase(Of T, C). As such, it is an empty interface.

```
Public Interface IReadOnlyCollection
  Inherits IBusinessObject

End Interface
```

You can use this interface to easily determine if a business object is a read-only collection as needed within your business or UI code.

ICommandObject Interface

The final common interface is ICommandObject. Like IReadOnlyCollection, this is an empty interface:

```
Public Interface ICommandObject
  Inherits IBusinessObject

End Interface
```

Again, you can use this interface to easily determine if a business object inherits from CommandBase within your business or UI code.

ObjectCloner Class

All read-only and editable objects will implement the System.ICloneable interface. This interface defines a Clone() method that returns an exact copy of the original object. Also remember that all business objects will be mobile objects: marked with the <Serializable()> attribute.

■Tip The primary reason I'm including this cloning implementation is to reinforce the concept that business objects and any objects they reference must be serializable. Having implemented a Clone() method as part of the framework, it becomes very easy to create a test harness that attempts to clone each of your business objects, clearly establishing that they are all totally serializable.

Creating a clone of a serializable object is easily accomplished through the use of the BinaryFormatter object in the System.Runtime.Serialization.Formatters.Binary namespace. Still, the implementation is a few lines of code. Rather than replicating this code in every base class, it can be centralized in a single object. All the base classes can then collaborate with this object to perform the clone operation.

The class contains the following code:

```
Namespace Core

  Friend Module ObjectCloner

    Public Function Clone(ByVal obj As Object) As Object

      Using buffer As New MemoryStream()
        Dim formatter As New BinaryFormatter()

        formatter.Serialize(buffer, obj)
        buffer.Position = 0
        Dim temp As Object = formatter.Deserialize(buffer)
        Return temp
      End Using

    End Function

  End Module

End Namespace
```

This code is implemented in a Module, as there is no reason to create an instance of the class. Also notice that it has a scope of Friend, making it only available to classes within the CSLA .NET framework.

The Clone() method itself uses the BinaryFormatter to serialize the object's state into an in-memory buffer. All objects referenced by the business object are also automatically serialized into the same buffer. The combination of an object and all the objects it references, directly or indirectly, is called an *object graph*.

The in-memory buffer is immediately deserialized to create a copy of the original object graph. The buffer is then disposed, as it could consume a fair amount of memory, depending on the size of the fields in your objects.

The resulting copy is returned to the calling code.

BindableBase Class

Editable objects that derive from Csla.BusinessBase will support data binding. One key interface for Windows Forms data binding is System.ComponentModel.INotifyPropertyChanged. This interface simply declares a single event: PropertyChanged.

In Chapter 2, I discussed the issue of serializing objects that declare events. If a non-serializable object handles the event, then serialization will fail, because it will attempt to serialize the non-serializable object. Having just discussed the ObjectCloner class, it is clear that all business objects must be serializable.

To avoid this issue, events must be declared in a more complex manner than normal. Specifically, they must be declared using a block structure such that it is possible to manually declare the delegate field. That way, the field can be marked with the <NonSerialized()> attribute to prevent serialization from attempting to serialize a non-serializable event handler.

To be slightly more clever, the implementation can maintain two delegate fields, one serializable and one not. As event handlers are added, the code can check to see if the handler is contained within a serializable object or not, and can add the event handler to the appropriate delegate.

All this functionality is encapsulated in Csla.Core.BindableBase. This is the base class from which Csla.BusinessBase will ultimately derive. Here's the code:

```
Namespace Core

  <Serializable()> _
  Public MustInherit Class BindableBase

    Implements System.ComponentModel.INotifyPropertyChanged

    Protected Sub New()

    End Sub

    <NonSerialized()> _
    Private mNonSerializableHandlers As PropertyChangedEventHandler
    Private mSerializableHandlers As PropertyChangedEventHandler

    <System.Diagnostics.CodeAnalysis.SuppressMessage( _
      "Microsoft.Design", "CA1062:ValidateArgumentsOfPublicMethods")> _
    Public Custom Event PropertyChanged As PropertyChangedEventHandler _
                          Implements INotifyPropertyChanged.PropertyChanged
      AddHandler(ByVal value As PropertyChangedEventHandler)
        If value.Method.IsPublic AndAlso _
          (value.Method.DeclaringType.IsSerializable OrElse _
          value.Method.IsStatic) Then
          mSerializableHandlers = _
            DirectCast(System.Delegate.Combine( _
              mSerializableHandlers, value), PropertyChangedEventHandler)
        Else
          mNonSerializableHandlers = _
            DirectCast(System.Delegate.Combine( _
              mNonSerializableHandlers, value), PropertyChangedEventHandler)
        End If
      End AddHandler

      RemoveHandler(ByVal value As PropertyChangedEventHandler)
        If value.Method.IsPublic AndAlso _
          (value.Method.DeclaringType.IsSerializable OrElse _
          value.Method.IsStatic) Then
          mSerializableHandlers = DirectCast( _
            System.Delegate.Remove( _
              mSerializableHandlers, value), PropertyChangedEventHandler)
```

```vb
      Else
        mNonSerializableHandlers = DirectCast( _
          System.Delegate.Remove( _
            mNonSerializableHandlers, value), PropertyChangedEventHandler)
      End If
    End RemoveHandler

    RaiseEvent(ByVal sender As Object, ByVal e As PropertyChangedEventArgs)
      Dim nonSerializableHandlers As PropertyChangedEventHandler = _
        mNonSerializableHandlers
      If nonSerializableHandlers IsNot Nothing Then
        nonSerializableHandlers.Invoke(sender, e)
      End If
      Dim serializableHandlers As PropertyChangedEventHandler = _
        mSerializableHandlers
      If serializableHandlers IsNot Nothing Then
        serializableHandlers.Invoke(sender, e)
      End If
    End RaiseEvent
  End Event

  <EditorBrowsable(EditorBrowsableState.Advanced)> _
  Protected Overridable Sub OnIsDirtyChanged()

    OnUnknownPropertyChanged()

  End Sub

  <EditorBrowsable(EditorBrowsableState.Advanced)> _
  Protected Overridable Sub OnUnknownPropertyChanged()

    Dim properties() As PropertyInfo = _
      Me.GetType.GetProperties(BindingFlags.Public Or BindingFlags.Instance)
    For Each item As PropertyInfo In properties
      RaiseEvent PropertyChanged( _
        Me, New PropertyChangedEventArgs(item.Name))
    Next

  End Sub

  <EditorBrowsable(EditorBrowsableState.Advanced)> _
  Protected Overridable Sub OnPropertyChanged(ByVal propertyName As String)
    RaiseEvent PropertyChanged( _
      Me, New PropertyChangedEventArgs(propertyName))
  End Sub

End Class

End Namespace
```

It's important that this class is marked as `<Serializable()>`. Ultimately, all business objects will be serializable, and that means that any classes they inherit from must also be marked as such. Also, the class is declared as `MustInherit`. This means that an instance of this class can't be created directly.

Before declaring the event itself, the code declares two delegate fields. These fields will hold delegate references to all event handlers registered to receive the `PropertyChanged` event:

```
<NonSerialized()> _
Private mNonSerializableHandlers As PropertyChangedEventHandler
Private mSerializableHandlers As PropertyChangedEventHandler
```

Notice that one is declared with the `<NonSerialized()>` attribute, while the other is not. The `BinaryFormatter` will ignore the first one and all objects referenced by that delegate field. Objects referenced by the second field will be serialized as normal.

The event declaration uses a block structure, including `AddHandler`, `RemoveHandler`, and `RaiseEvent` sections. Notice how the code in the `AddHandler` and `RemoveHandler` sections checks to see if the event handler is contained within a serializable object:

```
If value.Method.IsPublic AndAlso _
  (value.Method.DeclaringType.IsSerializable OrElse _
  value.Method.IsStatic) Then
```

If the event handler is contained in a serializable object, it is added or removed from the serializable delegate; otherwise it is added or removed from the non-serialized delegate.

The thing about events and inheritance is that an event can only be raised by code in the class in which it is declared. This is because the event member can only be accessed directly from the class in which it is defined. It *can't* be raised by code in classes that inherit from this class. This means that business objects can't raise the `PropertyChanged` event directly, even though that is the goal. To solve this problem, the code follows a standard .NET design pattern by creating a `Protected` method that in turn raises the event:

```
<EditorBrowsable(EditorBrowsableState.Advanced)> _
Protected Overridable Sub OnPropertyChanged(ByVal propertyName As String)
  RaiseEvent PropertyChanged( _
    Me, New PropertyChangedEventArgs(propertyName))
End Sub
```

Any classes that inherit from the base class can call this method when they want to raise the event.

This method is marked with the `<EditorBrowsable()>` attribute, indicating that this is an advanced method. In VB, this means that the method appears in the All tab in IntelliSense, and won't appear in the Common tab. In C#, this means that the method won't appear in IntelliSense unless the IDE is set to show advanced members.

The `OnUnknownPropertyChanged()` method covers a special case, different from the `OnPropertyChanged()` method. Where `OnPropertyChanged()` raises the `PropertyChanged` event for a single property, `OnUnknownPropertyChanged()` raises the event for *all* properties of the object:

```
<EditorBrowsable(EditorBrowsableState.Advanced)> _
Protected Overridable Sub OnUnknownPropertyChanged()

  Dim properties() As PropertyInfo = _
    Me.GetType.GetProperties(BindingFlags.Public Or BindingFlags.Instance)
  For Each item As PropertyInfo In properties
    RaiseEvent PropertyChanged( _
      Me, New PropertyChangedEventArgs(item.Name))
  Next

End Sub
```

There are a number of cases in which the object's state will change in such a way that it isn't possible to know which properties actually changed. In that case, this blanket notification approach ensures that data binding is aware that *something* changed, so the UI updates as needed.

To do this, the method uses reflection to get a list of all the Public properties on the business object, and then raises the PropertyChanged event for each item in the list. Since only Public properties can be bound through data binding, this ensures that data binding will refresh any properties that are bound to the UI. The result is a base class that allows business objects to raise the PropertyChanged event, thereby supporting data binding and serialization.

NotUndoableAttribute Class

As discussed in Chapter 2, editable business objects and collections will support n-level undo functionality. Sometimes, however, objects may have values that shouldn't be included in the snapshot that's taken before an object is edited. (These may be read-only values, or recalculated values, or values that are simply so big—large images, perhaps—that you choose not to support undo for them.)

The custom attribute NotUndoable is used to allow a business developer to indicate that a field shouldn't be included in the undo operation.

The UndoableBase class, which will implement the n-level undo operations, will detect whether this attribute has been placed on any fields. If so, it will simply ignore that field within the undo process, neither taking a snapshot of its value nor restoring it in the case of a cancel operation.

▉Note Since this attribute will be used by business developers as they write normal business code, it will be in the Csla namespace along with all the other types intended for use directly by business developers. It is also in the main project directory rather than in the Core subdirectory.

The NotUndoableAttribute class contains the following code:

```
<AttributeUsage(AttributeTargets.Field)> _
Public NotInheritable Class NotUndoableAttribute
  Inherits Attribute

End Class
```

The <AttributeUsage()> attribute specifies that this attribute can be applied only to fields. Beyond that, the <NotUndoable()> attribute is merely a marker to indicate that certain actions should (or shouldn't) be taken by the n-level undo implementation, so there's no real code here at all.

UndoableBase Class

The UndoableBase class is where all the work to handle n-level undo for an object will take place. This is pretty complex code that makes heavy use of reflection to find all the fields in each business object, take snapshots of their values, and then (potentially) restore their values later in the case of an undo operation.

Remember, nothing *requires* the use of n-level undo. In many web scenarios, as demonstrated in Chapter 10, there's no need to use these methods at all. A flat UI with no Cancel button has no requirement for undo functionality, so there's no reason to incur the overhead of taking a snapshot of the object's data. On the other hand, when creating a complex Windows Forms UI that involves modal dialog windows to allow editing of child objects (or even grandchild objects), it is often best to call these methods to provide support for the OK and Cancel buttons on each of the dialog windows.

■Tip Typically, a snapshot of a business object's fields is taken before the user or an application is allowed to interact with the object. That way, you can always undo back to that original state. The BusinessBase and BusinessListBase classes will include a BeginEdit() method that will trigger the snapshot process, a CancelEdit() method to restore the object's state to the last snapshot, and an ApplyEdit() method to commit any changes since the last snapshot.

The reason this snapshot process is so complex is that the values of *all* fields in each object must be copied, and each business object is essentially composed of several classes all merged together through inheritance and aggregation. This causes problems when classes have fields with the same names as fields in the classes they inherit from, and it causes particular problems if a class inherits from another class in a different assembly.

Since this will be a base class from which Csla.BusinessBase will ultimately derive, it must be marked as <Serializable()>. It should also be declared as MustInherit, so that no one can create an instance of this class directly. All business objects need to utilize the INotifyPropertyChanged interface implemented in BindableBase so they'll inherit from that, too. Finally, the n-level undo functionality relies on the Csla.Core.IUndoableObject interface, so that will be implemented in this class (and in BusinessListBase later in the chapter):

```
<Serializable()> _
Public MustInherit Class UndoableBase
  Inherits Csla.Core.BindableBase

  Implements IUndoableObject

End Class
```

With that base laid down, I can start to discuss how to implement the undo functionality. There are three operations involved: taking a snapshot of the object state, restoring the object state in case of an undo, and discarding the stored object state in case of an accept operation.

Additionally, if this object has child objects that implement Csla.Core.IUndoableObject, those child objects must also perform the store, restore, and accept operations. To achieve this, any time the algorithm encounters a field that's derived from either of these types, it will cascade the operation to that object so it can take appropriate action.

The three operations will be implemented by a set of three methods:

- CopyState()
- UndoChanges()
- AcceptChanges()

CopyState

The CopyState() method will take a snapshot of the object's current data and store it in a System.Collections.Generic.Stack(Of T) object.

Stacking the Data

Since this is an implementation of n-level undo capability, each object could end up storing a number of snapshots. As each undo or accept operation occurs, it will get rid of the most recent snapshot stored; this is the classic behavior of a "stack" data structure. Fortunately, the .NET Framework includes a prebuilt Stack(Of T) class that implements the required functionality. It is declared as follows:

```
<NotUndoable()> _
Private mStateStaStack(Of T)ck As New Stack(Of Byte())
```

This field is marked as `<NotUndoable()>` to prevent taking a snapshot of previous snapshots. `CopyState()` should just record the fields that contain actual business data. Once a snapshot has been taken of the object's data, the snapshot will be serialized into a single byte stream. That byte stream is then put on the stack. From there, it can be retrieved and deserialized to perform an undo operation if needed.

Taking a Snapshot of the Data

The process of taking a snapshot of each field value in an object is a bit tricky. Reflection is used to walk through all the fields in the object. During this process, each field is checked to determine if it has the `<NotUndoable()>` attribute. If so, the field is ignored.

The big issue is that field names may not be unique within an object. To see what I mean, consider the following two classes:

```
Public Class BaseClass

  Dim mId As Integer

End Class

Public Class SubClass
  Inherits BaseClass

  Dim mId As Integer

End Class
```

Here, each class has its own field named `mId`—and in most circumstances, that's not a problem. However, when using reflection to walk through all the fields in a `SubClass` object, it will return *two* `mId` fields: one for each of the classes in the inheritance hierarchy.

To get an accurate snapshot of an object's data, `CopyState()` needs to accommodate this scenario. In practice, this means prefixing each field name with the name of the class to which it belongs. Instead of two `mId` fields, the result is `BaseClass!mId` and `SubClass!mId`. The use of an exclamation point for a separator is arbitrary, but *some* character is necessary to separate the class name from the field name.

As if this weren't complex enough, reflection works differently with classes that are subclassed from other classes in the *same* assembly than with classes that are subclassed from classes in a *different* assembly. If in the example above, `BaseClass` and `SubClass` are in the same assembly, one technique can be used, but if they're in different assemblies, a different technique will be necessary. Of course, `CopyState()` should deal with both scenarios so the business developer doesn't have to worry about these details.

■**Note** Not all the code for `UndoableBase` is listed in the book. I'm only covering the key parts of the algorithm. For the rest of the code, please refer to the download.

The following method deals with all of the preceding issues. I'll walk through how it works after the listing.

```vb
<EditorBrowsable(EditorBrowsableState.Never)> _
Protected Friend Sub CopyState() Implements IUndoableObject.CopyState

  Dim currentType As Type = Me.GetType
  Dim state As New HybridDictionary()
  Dim fields() As FieldInfo
  Dim field As FieldInfo
  Dim fieldName As String

  Do
    ' get the list of fields in this type
    fields = currentType.GetFields( _
                        BindingFlags.NonPublic Or _
                        BindingFlags.Instance Or _
                        BindingFlags.Public)

    For Each field In fields
      ' make sure we process only our variables
      If field.DeclaringType Is currentType Then
        ' see if this field is marked as not undoable
        If Not NotUndoableField(field) Then
          ' the field is undoable, so it needs to be processed
          Dim value As Object = field.GetValue(Me)

          If GetType(Csla.Core.IUndoableObject). _
              IsAssignableFrom(field.FieldType) Then
            ' make sure the variable has a value
            If Not value Is Nothing Then
              ' this is a child object, cascade the call
              DirectCast(value, IUndoableObject).CopyState()
            End If

          Else
            ' this is a normal field, simply trap the value
            fieldName = field.DeclaringType.Name & "!" & field.Name
            state.Add(fieldName, value)

          End If

        End If

      End If
    Next

    currentType = currentType.BaseType

  Loop Until currentType Is GetType(UndoableBase)

  ' serialize the state and stack it
  Using buffer As New MemoryStream
    Dim formatter As New BinaryFormatter
    formatter.Serialize(buffer, state)
    mStateStack.Push(buffer.ToArray)
  End Using
  CopyStateComplete()
```

```
End Sub

Protected Overridable Sub CopyStateComplete()

End Sub
```

This method is scoped as `Protected Friend`, which is a bit unusual. The method needs `Protected` scope because `BusinessBase` will subclass `UndoableBase`, and the `BeginEdit()` method in `BusinessBase` will need to call `CopyState()`. That part is fairly straightforward.

The method also needs `Friend` scope, however, because child business objects will be contained within business collections. When a collection needs to take a snapshot of its data, what that really means is that the objects *within* the collection need to take snapshots of their data. `BusinessListBase` will include code that goes through all the business objects it contains, telling each business object to take a snapshot of its state. This will be done via the `CopyState()` method, which means that `BusinessListBase` needs the ability to call this method, too. Since it's in the same project, this is accomplished with `Friend` scope.

To take a snapshot of data, there needs to be somewhere to store the various field values before they are pushed onto the stack. A `HybridDictionary` is ideal for this purpose, as it stores name/value pairs. It also provides high-speed access to values based on their names, which will be important for the undo implementation. Finally, the `HybridDictionary` object supports .NET serialization, which means that it can be serialized and passed by value across the network as part of a business object.

The `CopyState()` routine is essentially a big loop that starts with the outermost class in the object's inheritance hierarchy and walks back up through the chain of classes until it gets to `UndoableBase`. At that point, it can stop—it knows that it has a snapshot of all the business data.

At the end of the method there's a call to `CopyStateComplete()`. Notice that `CopyStateComplete()` is an `Overridable` method with no implementation. The idea is that a subclass can override this method if additional actions should be taken once the object's state is copied. While this method won't be overridden in the framework, it provides an extensibility point for advanced business developers.

Getting a List of Fields

It's inside the loop where the real work occurs. The first step is to get a list of all the fields corresponding to the current class:

```
' get the list of fields in this type
fields = currentType.GetFields( _
                      BindingFlags.NonPublic Or _
                      BindingFlags.Instance Or _
                      BindingFlags.Public)
```

It doesn't matter whether the fields are `Public`—they all need to be recorded regardless of scope. What's more important is to only record instance fields, not those declared as `Shared`. The result of this call is an array of `FieldInfo` objects, each of which corresponds to a field in the business object.

Avoiding Double-Processing of Fields

As discussed earlier, the `FieldInfo` array could include fields from the base classes of the current class. Due to the way the Just-in-Time (JIT) compiler optimizes code within the same assembly, if some base classes are in the same assembly as the actual business class, the same field name may be listed in multiple classes! As the code walks up the inheritance hierarchy, it could end up processing those fields twice. To avoid this, the code only looks at the fields that *directly* belong to the class currently being processed:

```
For Each field As FieldInfo In fields
  ' make sure we process only our variables
  If field.DeclaringType Is currentType Then
```

Skipping <NotUndoable()> Fields

At this point in the proceedings, it has been established that the current `FieldInfo` object refers to a field within the object that's part of the current class in the inheritance hierarchy. However, a snapshot of the field should only be taken if it doesn't have the `<NotUndoable()>` attribute:

```
  ' see if this field is marked as not undoable
  If Not NotUndoableField(field) Then
```

Having reached this point, it is clear that the field value needs to be part of the snapshot, so there are two possibilities: this may be a regular field or it may be a reference to a child object that implements `Csla.Core.IUndoableObject`.

Cascading the Call to Child Objects or Collections

If the field is a reference to a `Csla.Core.IUndoableObject`, the `CopyState()` call must be cascaded to that object so that it can take its own snapshot:

```
    If GetType(Csla.Core.IUndoableObject). _
      IsAssignableFrom(field.FieldType) Then
      ' make sure the variable has a value
      If Not value Is Nothing Then
        ' this is a child object, cascade the call
        DirectCast(value, IUndoableObject).CopyState()
      End If
```

If an object were to "reach into" another object and manipulate its state, it would break encapsulation. Instead, it is up to that other object to manage its own state. By cascading the `CopyState()` call to the child object, it is up to that child object to take a snapshot of its own state. Keep in mind that if the child object is derived from `BusinessListBase`, the call will automatically be cascaded down to each individual child object in the collection.

■**Tip** Of course, the `GetValue()` method returns everything as type `object`, so the result is casted to `Csla.Core.IUndoableObject` in order to call the method.

Later on, the methods to undo or accept any changes will work the same way—that is, they'll cascade the calls to any child objects. This way, all objects handle undo without breaking encapsulation.

Taking a Snapshot of a Regular Field

With a regular field, the code simply stores the field value into the `Hashtable` object, associating that value with the combined class name and field name:

```
        ' this is a normal field, simply trap the value
        fieldName = field.DeclaringType.Name & "!" & field.Name
        state.Add(fieldName, value)
```

Note that these "regular" fields might actually be complex types in and of themselves. All that is known is that the field doesn't reference an editable business object, since the value didn't implement Csla.Core.IUndoableObject. It could be a simple value such as an Integer or String, or it could be a complex object (as long as that object is marked as <Serializable()>).

Having gone through every field for every class in the object's inheritance hierarchy, the Hashtable will contain a complete snapshot of all the data in the business object.

■**Note** This snapshot will include some fields put into the BusinessBase class to keep track of the object's status (such as whether it's new, dirty, deleted, etc.). The snapshot will also include the collection of broken rules that will be implemented later. An undo operation will restore the object to its previous state in *every* way.

Serializing and Stacking the Hashtable

At this point, the object's field values have been recorded, but the snapshot is in a complex data type: a Hashtable. To further complicate matters, some of the elements contained in the Hashtable might be references to more complex objects. In that case, the Hashtable just has a reference to the existing object, not a copy or a snapshot at all.

Fortunately, there's an easy answer to both issues. The BinaryFormatter can be used to convert the Hashtable to a byte stream, reducing it from a complex data type to a very simple one for storage. Better yet, the very process of serializing the Hashtable will *automatically* serialize any objects to which it has references.

This does require that all objects referenced by any business objects must be marked as <Serializable()>, so that they can be included in the byte stream. If referenced objects aren't serializable, the serialization attempt will result in a runtime error. Alternatively, any non-serializable object references can be marked as <NotUndoable()> so that the undo process simply ignores them.

The code to do the serialization is fairly straightforward:

```
' serialize the state and stack it
Using buffer As New MemoryStream
  Dim formatter As New BinaryFormatter
  formatter.Serialize(buffer, state)
  mStateStack.Push(buffer.ToArray)
End Using
```

This code is quite comparable to the cloning code implemented earlier in the ObjectCloner class.

The BinaryFormatter object serializes the Hashtable (and any objects to which it refers) into a stream of bytes in an in-memory buffer. The byte stream is simply extracted from the in-memory buffer and pushed onto the stack:

```
mStateStack.Push(buffer.ToArray)
```

Converting a MemoryStream to a byte array is not an issue since the MemoryStream is implemented to store its data in a byte array. The ToArray() method simply returns a reference to that existing array, so no data is copied.

The act of conversion to a byte array is important, however, because a byte array is serializable, while a MemoryStream object is not. If the business object is passed across the network by value *while it is being edited*, the stack of states needs to be serializable.

■**Tip** Passing objects across the network while they're being edited is not *anticipated*, but since business objects are serializable, you can't prevent the business developer from doing just that. If the stack were to reference a MemoryStream, the business application would get a runtime error as the serialization failed, and that's not acceptable. Converting the data to a byte array avoids accidentally crashing the application on the off chance that the business developer decides to pass an object across the network as it's being edited.

At this point, we're a third of the way through implementing n-level undo support. It is now possible to create a stack of snapshots of an object's data. It is time to move on and discuss the undo and accept operations.

UndoChanges

The UndoChanges() method is the reverse of CopyState(). It takes a snapshot of data off the stack, deserializes it back into a Hashtable, and then takes each value from the Hashtable and restores it into the appropriate object field. Like CopyState(), once this method is complete, an Overridable UndoChangesComplete() method is called to allow subclasses to take additional actions. This method will be overridden later in Csla.Core.BusinessBase.

The hard issues of walking through the types in the object's inheritance hierarchy and finding all the fields in the object were solved in the implementation of CopyState(). The structure of UndoChanges() will therefore be virtually identical, except that it will restore field values rather than take a snapshot.

Since the overall structure of UndoChanges() is essentially the reverse of CopyState(), I won't show the entire code here. Rather, I'll focus on the key functionality.

EditLevel

It is possible for a business developer to accidentally trigger a call to UndoChanges() when there is no state to restore. If this condition isn't caught, it will cause a runtime error. To avoid such a scenario, the first thing the UndoChanges() method does is to get the "edit level" of the object by retrieving the Count property from the stack object. If the edit level is 0, then there's no state to restore, and UndoChanges() just exits without doing any work.

This edit level concept will become even more important later during the implementation of BusinessListBase, and so you'll notice that the value is implemented as a property.

Re-Creating the Hashtable Object

Where CopyState() serializes the Hashtable into a byte array at the end of the process, the first thing UndoChanges() needs to do is pop the most recently added snapshot off the stack and deserialize it to re-create the Hashtable object containing the detailed values:

```
Dim state As HybridDictionary
Using buffer As New MemoryStream(mStateStack.Pop())
  buffer.Position = 0
  Dim formatter As New BinaryFormatter()
  state = _
    CType(formatter.Deserialize(buffer), HybridDictionary)
End Using
```

This is the reverse of the process used to put the Hashtable onto the stack in the first place. The result of this process is a Hashtable containing all the data that was taken in the original snapshot.

Restoring the Object's State Data

With the `Hashtable` containing the original object values restored, it is possible to loop through the fields in the object in the same manner as `CopyState()`.

When the code encounters a child business object that implements `Csla.Core.IUndoableObject`, it cascades the `UndoChanges()` call to that child object so that it can do its own restore operation. Again, this is done to preserve encapsulation—only the code within a given object should manipulate that object's data.

With a "normal" field, its value is simply restored from the `Hashtable`:

```
' this is a regular field, restore its value
fieldName = field.DeclaringType.Name & "!" & field.Name
field.SetValue(Me, state.Item(fieldName))
```

At the end of this process, the object will be reset to the state it had when the most recent snapshot was taken. All that remains is to implement a method to *accept* changes, rather than to undo them.

AcceptChanges

`AcceptChanges()` is actually the simplest of the three methods. If changes are being accepted, it means that the current values in the object are the ones that should be kept, and the most recent snapshot is now meaningless and can be discarded. Like `CopyState()`, once this method is complete, an `Overridable` `AcceptChangesComplete()` method is called to allow subclasses to take additional actions.

In concept, this means that all `AcceptChanges()` needs to do is discard the most recent snapshot:

```
mStateStack.Pop()
```

However, it is important to remember that the object may have child objects, and they need to know to accept changes as well. This requires looping through the object's fields to find any child objects that implement `Csla.Core.IUndoableObject`. The `AcceptChanges()` method call must be cascaded to them, too.

The process of looping through the fields of the object is the same as in `CopyState()` and `UndoChanges()`. The only difference is where the method call is cascaded:

```
' the field is undoable so see if it is editable
If GetType(Csla.Core.IUndoableObject). _
  IsAssignableFrom(field.FieldType) Then
  Dim value As Object = field.GetValue(Me)
  ' make sure the variable has a value
  If Not value Is Nothing Then
    ' it is a child object so cascade the call
    DirectCast(value, IUndoableObject).AcceptChanges()
  End If
End If
```

Simple field values don't need any processing. Remember that the idea is that the current values have been accepted—so there's no need to change those current values at all.

BusinessBase Class

The next class listed in Table 3-1 is `Csla.Core.BusinessBase`. This class will implement most of the functionality for a single editable object, and combine the n-level undo, validation rules, and authorization rules, along with some data binding support. Given that the validation and authorization classes are later in the chapter, you may need to look forward in the chapter to see the full implementation of each feature.

Like all base classes, this class must be serializable and `MustInherit`. It inherits from `UndoableBase` (and therefore also from `BindableBase`):

```
Namespace Core

  <Serializable()> _
  Public MustInherit Class BusinessBase
    Inherits UndoableBase

    Implements System.ComponentModel.IEditableObject
    Implements ICloneable
    Implements IDataErrorInfo
```

Not only does this class inherit from `UndoableBase`, but it also implements `System.ComponentModel.IEditableObject` and `System.ComponentModel.IDataErrorInfo` to provide data binding support. It also implements `System.ICloneable`, and so the object will have a `Clone()` method.

This class pulls together a lot of functionality. The goal is to abstract all this functionality into a set of easily understood behaviors that simplify the creation of business objects. Table 3-3 lists the functional areas.

Table 3-3. *Functional Areas Implemented in Csla.Core.BusinessBase*

Functional Area	Description
Tracking object status	Keeps track of whether the object is new, old, dirty, clean, or marked for deletion
N-level undo	Provides access to the underlying n-level undo functionality implemented in `UndoableBase`, and implements the `IEditableObject` interface
Root, parent, and child behaviors	Implement behaviors so that the object can function as either a stand-alone object, a parent object, or a child of another object or collection
Validation rules	Provide abstract access to the validation rules behavior (discussed later in the chapter) and implement the `IDataErrorInfo` interface
Authorization rules	Provide abstract access to the authorization rules behavior (discussed later in the chapter)
Cloning	Implements the `ICloneable` interface

■**Tip** Of course, there will also be code in `BusinessBase` to support data access—a topic discussed in Chapter 4. In this chapter, the focus is on the behaviors that support the creation of the user interface and the implementation of non–data access business logic.

Tracking Object Status

All editable business objects should keep track of whether the object has just been created, whether its data has been changed, or whether it has been marked for deletion. Using the validation rules functionality, the object can also keep track of whether it's valid. Table 3-4 lists the object status properties in `BusinessBase`.

Table 3-4. *Object Status Properties*

Property	Description
IsNew	Indicates whether the object's primary identifying value in memory corresponds to a corresponding primary key in a database—if not, the object is new
IsDirty	Indicates whether the object's data in memory is known to be different from data in the database—if different, the object is dirty
IsValid	Indicates whether the object currently has any broken validation rules—if so, the object is not valid
IsSavable	Combines IsValid and IsDirty—only a valid and dirty object is savable
IsDeleted	Indicates whether the object is marked for deletion

I will now discuss the concepts behind an object being new, dirty, valid, and marked for deletion.

IsNew

When an object is "new," it means that the object exists in memory, but not in the database or other persistent store. If the object's data resides in the database, then the object is considered to be "old." I typically think of it this way: if the primary key value in the object corresponds to an existing primary key value in the database, then the object is old; otherwise it is new.

The value behind the IsNew property is stored in an mIsNew field. When an object is first created, this value defaults to the object being new:

```
Private mIsNew As Boolean = True
```

If the object is then loaded with data from the database, the mIsNew field is set to False, through a protected MarkOld() method:

```
Protected Overridable Sub MarkOld()
  mIsNew = False
  MarkClean()
End Sub
```

Notice that this process also sets the object to a "clean" status—a concept discussed later for the IsDirty property. When an object's data has just been loaded from the database, it is safe to assume that the object's data matches the data in the database and so has not been changed—and thus is "clean."

There's also a corresponding MarkNew() method:

```
Protected Overridable Sub MarkNew()
  mIsNew = True
  mIsDeleted = False
  MarkDirty()
End Sub
```

Typically, this method is called upon deletion of an existing object, but it can be used any time the business developer knows that the object does not correspond to data in the database. In such a case, not only is the object "new," but it must also be "dirty," because the data in the object does not match data in the database. The concept of being marked for deletion will be discussed later with the IsDeleted property, but a new object shouldn't be marked for deletion, and so this flag is set to False.

Knowing whether an object is new or old will allow for implementation of the data access code in Chapter 4. The IsNew property will control the choice of whether to insert or update data into the database.

Sometimes, the IsNew property can be useful to the UI developer as well. Some UI behaviors may be different for a new object than an existing object. The ability to edit the object's primary key data is a good example—this is often editable only up to the point that the data has been stored in the database. When the object becomes "old," the primary key is fixed.

IsDirty

An object is considered to be "dirty," or changed, when the values in the object's fields do not match the values in the database. If the values in the object's fields do match the values in the database, then the object is not dirty. It is virtually impossible to always know whether the object's values match those in the database, so the implementation shown here acts on a "best guess." The implementation relies on the business developer to indicate when an object has been changed and thus has become dirty.

The current status of the value is maintained in a field:

```
Private mIsDirty As Boolean = True
```

The value is then exposed as a property:

```
<Browsable(False)> _
Public Overridable ReadOnly Property IsDirty() As Boolean
  Get
    Return mIsDirty
  End Get
End Property
```

Notice that this property is marked as Overridable. This is important because sometimes a business object isn't simply dirty because its data has changed. For instance, consider a business object that contains a collection of child objects—even if the business object's data hasn't changed, it will be dirty if any of its child objects have changed. In this case, the business developer will need to override the IsDirty property to provide a more sophisticated implementation. This will be clearly illustrated in Chapter 7, in the implementation of the example business objects.

Also notice that the property is adorned with the <Browsable()> attribute from the System. ComponentModel namespace. This attribute tells data binding not to automatically bind this property. Without this attribute, data binding would automatically display this property in grids and on forms—and typically, this property shouldn't be displayed. This attribute is used on other properties in BusinessBase as well.

The IsDirty property defaults to True, since a new object's field values won't correspond to values in the database. If the object's values are subsequently loaded from the database, this value will be changed to False when MarkOld() is called. Remember that MarkOld() calls a MarkClean() method:

```
<EditorBrowsable(EditorBrowsableState.Advanced)> _
Protected Sub MarkClean()
  mIsDirty = False
  OnUnknownPropertyChanged()
End Sub
```

This method not only sets the value to False, but calls the OnUnknownPropertyChanged() method implemented in Csla.Core.BindableBase to raise the PropertyChanged event for all object properties. This notifies data binding that the object has changed, so Windows Forms can refresh the display for the user.

There's a corresponding MarkDirty() method as well. This method will be called from various points in an object's lifetime, including any time a property value is changed, or when the MarkNew() method is called.

When a property value has been changed, a specific `PropertyChanged` event will be raised for that property.

If `MarkDirty()` is called at other times, when a specific property value *wasn't* changed, then the `PropertyChanged` event for all object properties should be raised. That way, data binding is notified of the change if *any* object property is bound to a UI control.

To be clear, the goal is to ensure that at least one `PropertyChanged` event is raised any time the object's state changes. If a specific property were changed, then the `PropertyChanged` event should be raised *for that property*. But if there's no way to tell which properties were changed (like when the object is persisted to the database) there's no real option but to raise `PropertyChanged` for every property.

Implementing this requires a couple of overloads of the `MarkDirty()` method:

```
Protected Sub MarkDirty()
  MarkDirty(False)
End Sub
```

```
<EditorBrowsable(EditorBrowsableState.Advanced)> _
Protected Sub MarkDirty(ByVal supressEvent As Boolean)
  mIsDirty = True
  If Not supressEvent Then
    OnUnknownPropertyChanged()
  End If
End Sub
```

The first overload can be called by a business developer if they want to manually mark the object as changed. This is intended for use when unknown properties may have changed.

The second overload is called by the `PropertyHasChanged()` method:

```
Protected Sub PropertyHasChanged(ByVal propertyName As String)
  ValidationRules.CheckRules(propertyName)
  MarkDirty(True)
  OnPropertyChanged(propertyName)
End Sub
```

The `PropertyHasChanged()` method is called by the business developer to indicate that a specific property has changed. Notice that in this case, any validation rules for the property are checked (the details on this are discussed later in the chapter). Then the object is marked as being dirty by raising the `PropertyChanged` event for the specific property that was changed.

■**Tip** This method is `Overridable`, allowing you to add extra steps to the process if needed. Additionally, this means you can override the behavior to implement field-level dirty tracking if desired.

Calling `PropertyHasChanged()` by passing the property name as a string value would mean hard-coding the property name in code. String literals are notoriously difficult to maintain, so there's an overload to automatically glean the property name at runtime:

```
<System.Runtime.CompilerServices.MethodImpl( _
  System.Runtime.CompilerServices.MethodImplOptions.NoInlining)> _
Protected Sub PropertyHasChanged()
  Dim propertyName As String = _
    New System.Diagnostics.StackTrace(). _
    GetFrame(1).GetMethod.Name.Substring(4)
  PropertyHasChanged(propertyName)
End Sub
```

This implementation uses System.Diagnostics to retrieve the name of the method or property that called PropertyHasChanged(). The <MethodImpl()> attribute prevents the compiler from merging this code directly into the property itself, since that would confuse the System.Diagnostics call.

There is a performance penalty (akin to using reflection) to calling System.Diagnostics like this, but I am usually happy to pay that price to avoid using string literals for property names through a business class. Using this method, a business object's property will look like this:

```
Public Property Name() As String
  Get
    CanReadProperty(True)
    Return mName
  End Get
  Set(ByVal value As String)
    CanWriteProperty(True)
    If mName <> value Then
      mName = value
      PropertyHasChanged()
    End If
  End Set
End Property
```

The PropertyHasChanged() call doesn't require the property name because it is automatically retrieved using System.Diagnostics. If you feel the performance penalty for that approach is too high, you can always hard-code the property name as a parameter to every PropertyHasChanged() method call.

Either way, the property's validation rules are checked, the IsDirty property is set to True, and the appropriate PropertyChanged event is raised.

IsValid

An object is considered to be valid if it has no currently broken validation rules. The Csla.Validation namespace is covered later in the chapter and provides management of the business rules. The IsValid property merely exposes a flag indicating whether the object currently has broken rules or not:

```
<Browsable(False)> _
Public Overridable ReadOnly Property IsValid() As Boolean
  Get
    Return ValidationRules.IsValid
  End Get
End Property
```

As with IsDirty, this property is marked with the <Browsable()> attribute so data binding defaults to ignoring the property.

IsSavable

An object should only be saved to the database if it is valid and its data has changed. The IsValid property indicates whether the object is valid, and the IsDirty property indicates whether the object's data has changed. The IsSavable property is a simple helper to combine those two properties into one:

```
<Browsable(False)> _
Public Overridable ReadOnly Property IsSavable() As Boolean
  Get
    Return IsDirty AndAlso IsValid
  End Get
End Property
```

The primary purpose for this property is to allow a Windows Forms UI developer to bind the `Enabled` property of a Save button such that the button is only enabled if the object can be saved.

IsDeleted

The CSLA .NET framework provides for deferred or immediate deletion of an object. The *immediate* approach directly deletes an object's data from the database without first loading the object into memory. It requires prior knowledge of the object's primary key value(s), and is discussed in Chapter 4, as it is directly linked to data access.

The *deferred* approach requires that the object be loaded into memory. The user can then view and manipulate the object's data, and may decide to delete the object, in which case the object is marked for deletion. The object is not immediately deleted, but rather it is deleted if and when the object is saved to the database. At that time, instead of inserting or updating the object's data, it is deleted from the database.

This approach is particularly useful for child objects in a collection. In such a case, the user may be adding and updating some child objects at the same time as deleting others. All the insert, update, and delete operations occur in a batch when the collection is saved to the database.

Whether an object is marked for deletion or not is tracked by the `mIsDeleted` field and exposed through an `IsDeleted` property. As with `IsDirty`, there's a `Protected` method to allow the object to be marked for deletion when necessary:

```
Protected Sub MarkDeleted()
  mIsDeleted = True
  MarkDirty()
End Sub
```

Of course, marking the object as deleted is another way of changing its data, so the `MarkDirty()` method is called to indicate that the object's state has been changed.

The `MarkDeleted()` method is called from the `Delete()` and `DeleteChild()` methods. The `Delete()` method is used to mark a non-child object for deferred deletion, while `DeleteChild()` is called by a parent object (like a collection) to mark the child object for deferred deletion:

```
Public Sub Delete()
  If Me.IsChild Then
    Throw New NotSupportedException(My.Resources.ChildDeleteException)
  End If

  MarkDeleted()
End Sub

Friend Sub DeleteChild()
  If Not Me.IsChild Then
    Throw New NotSupportedException(My.Resources.NoDeleteRootException)
  End If

  MarkDeleted()
End Sub
```

Both methods do the same thing: call `MarkDelete()`. But `Delete()` is scoped as `Public` and can only be called if the object is *not* a child object (a topic covered later in the discussion about parent and child object behaviors). Conversely, `DeleteChild()` can only be called if the object *is* a child. Since it is intended for use by `BusinessListBase`, it is scoped as `Friend`.

N-Level Undo

UndoableBase implements the basic functionality to take snapshots of an object's data and then perform undo or accept operations using these snapshots. These methods were implemented as Protected methods, so they're not available for use by code in the UI. The BusinessBase class will implement three standard methods for use by the UI code, as described in Table 3-5.

Table 3-5. *Object-Editing Methods in BusinessBase*

Method	Description
BeginEdit()	Initiates editing of the object. Triggers a call to CopyState().
CancelEdit()	Indicates that the user wants to undo her recent changes. Triggers a call to UndoChanges().
ApplyEdit()	Indicates that the user wants to keep her recent changes. Triggers a call to AcceptChanges().

The System.ComponentModel.IEditableObject interface also ties into n-level undo as well as supporting data binding. This interface is used by Windows Forms data binding to control the editing of objects—specifically, to provide a single level of undo behavior.

When using n-level undo, the UI should start by calling BeginEdit(). If the user then clicks a Cancel button, the CancelEdit() method can be called. If the user clicks a Save or an Accept button, then ApplyEdit() can be called. See Chapter 8 for an example of using n-level undo within a rich Windows Forms UI.

Calling BeginEdit() multiple times will cause stacking of states. This allows complex hierarchical interfaces to be created, in which each form has its own Cancel button that triggers a call to CancelEdit().

It is important to recognize that every BeginEdit() call *must* have a corresponding CancelEdit() or ApplyEdit() call. Refer to the UndoableBase implementation regarding the use of a Stack object to maintain the list of states.

BeginEdit, CancelEdit, and ApplyEdit Methods

The basic edit methods are intended for use by UI developers so they can control when an object's state is trapped and restored. They delegate the work to the methods in UndoableBase, but include other code to interact appropriately with the IEditableObject implementation:

```
Public Sub BeginEdit()
  mBindingEdit = True
  CopyState()
End Sub

Public Sub CancelEdit()
  UndoChanges()
End Sub

Protected Overrides Sub UndoChangesComplete()
  mBindingEdit = False
  ValidationRules.SetTarget(Me)
  AddBusinessRules()
  OnUnknownPropertyChanged()
  MyBase.UndoChangesComplete()
End Sub
```

```
Public Sub ApplyEdit()
  mBindingEdit = False
  mNeverCommitted = False
  AcceptChanges()
End Sub
```

The primary action in each method is to delegate to the corresponding method in UndoableBase. The mBindingEdit and mNeverCommitted fields are used by the implementation of IEditableObject.

Notice the overridden UndoChangesComplete() method. This is required because there are actions that must be taken any time the object's state has been restored. While it may seem that these actions could be taken in the CancelEdit() method, remember that a business object's state can also be restored by its parent object through UndoableBase—without ever calling CancelEdit() on the child object. Overriding UndoChangesComplete() means that these lines of code will run after CancelEdit() is either called directly on this object or on its parent object.

The code in UndoChangesComplete() sets the mBindingEdit flag, reestablishes the object's validation rules, and raises the PropertyChanged event for all properties on the object—thus ensuring that data binding is aware that the object's state has changed. The ValidationRules class will be implemented later in the chapter, but it manages a list of business rules for each property. It also maintains a list of currently broken business rules. The list of broken business rules is part of the object's state and is subject to n-level undo.

The list of rules associated with each property is really a list of delegate references, which can be broken by serialization. To prevent any such issues, that list isn't subject to serialization or n-level undo. Instead, after resetting the object's state with UndoChanges(), the business rules are simply reassociated with the properties by calling the AddBusinessRules() method. The SetTarget() method is also called to ensure that ValidationRules has a current reference to the business object.

This will be much clearer later in the chapter as you look at the ValidationRules and BrokenRulesCollection classes.

System.ComponentModel.IEditableObject

The System.ComponentModel.IEditableObject interface is used by the Windows Forms data binding infrastructure to control undo operations in two cases:

- If an object is a child of a collection and is being edited in a grid control, the IEditableObject interface will be used so that the user can start editing a row of the grid (that is, the object) and then press Esc to undo any edits he has made on the row.

- When binding controls from a Windows Form to an object's properties, the IEditableObject interface will be used to tell the object that editing has *started*. It will *not* be used to tell the object when editing is complete, or whether the user requests an undo. It's up to the UI code to handle these cases.

When using data binding to bind an object to a form, you can allow the data binding infrastructure to tell the object that editing has started. I typically don't rely on that feature, preferring to call BeginEdit() myself. Since I have to call CancelEdit() and ApplyEdit() manually anyway, I prefer simply to control the entire process.

■Note The BeginEdit() and CancelEdit() methods on this interface are different from the Public methods a developer may call directly. The rules for using the interface apply to data binding, and you should not confuse them with the rules for calling BeginEdit(), CancelEdit(), or ApplyEdit() manually.

IEditableObject is most important when an object is being edited within a grid control. In that case, this interface is the *only* way to get the editing behavior that's expected by users.

Clearly, implementing the interface requires understanding of how it is used. The interface defines three methods, as described in Table 3-6.

Table 3-6. *IEditableObject Interface Methods*

Method	Description
BeginEdit()	This is called by data binding to indicate the start of an edit process. However, it may be called by the Windows Forms data binding infrastructure *many times* during the same edit process, and only the first call should be honored.
CancelEdit()	This is called by data binding to indicate that any changes since the first BeginEdit() call should be undone. However, it may be called by the Windows Forms data binding infrastructure *many times* during the same edit process, and only the first call should be honored.
EndEdit()	This is called by data binding to indicate that the edit process is complete, and that any changes should be kept intact. However, it may be called by the Windows Forms data binding infrastructure *many times* during the same edit process, and only the first call should be honored.

Note The official Microsoft documentation on these methods is somewhat inconsistent with their actual behavior. In the documentation, only BeginEdit() is noted for being called multiple times, but experience has shown that any of these methods may be called multiple times.

While these methods are certainly *similar* to the edit methods implemented earlier, there are some key differences in the way these new methods work. Consider BeginEdit(), for example. *Every* call to the existing BeginEdit() method will result in a new snapshot of the object's state, while only the *first* call to IEditableObject.BeginEdit() should be honored. Any subsequent calls (and they do happen during data binding) should be ignored. The same is true for the other two methods.

Remember, data binding only uses a single level of undo. By definition, this means that only the first call to BeginEdit() through the IEditableObject interface has any meaning.

To implement the behavior of the IEditableObject methods properly, the object needs to keep track of whether the edit process has been started and when it ends. At the same time, though, it is important to preserve the existing BeginEdit() functionality. This means implementing separate methods for IEditableObject, which will call the preexisting n-level undo methods when appropriate.

There is one other complication to deal with as well. When a collection of objects is bound to a Windows Forms grid control, the user can dynamically add and remove child objects in the collection by using the grid control. When an object is removed in this manner, the grid control does not notify the collection object. Instead, it notifies the child object, and it's up to the child object to remove itself from the collection.

It is then up to the child to interact with its parent collection to be removed from the collection itself. For this to happen, the child object needs a reference to its parent collection. This is expressed through a Protected property named Parent, which is discussed later in the chapter, in the "Root, Parent, and Child Behaviors" section.

A flag is used to ignore multiple calls to the IEditableObject methods:

```
<NotUndoable()> _
Private mBindingEdit As Boolean
Private mNeverCommitted As Boolean = True
```

Notice that mBindingEdit is declared with the <NotUndoable()> attribute. This field controls interaction with the UI, not internal object state; and because of this, there's no reason to make it part of the object's snapshot data, as that would just waste memory.

A second flag is also declared, and is used to track whether ApplyEdit() has been called on the object. This value was set to False in the ApplyEdit() implemented earlier, and will be used to control whether a child object should remove itself from its parent collection.

The three interface methods are implemented as follows:

```
Private Sub IEditableObject_BeginEdit() _
  Implements System.ComponentModel.IEditableObject.BeginEdit
  If Not mBindingEdit Then
    BeginEdit()
  End If
End Sub

Private Sub IEditableObject_CancelEdit() _
  Implements System.ComponentModel.IEditableObject.CancelEdit
  If mBindingEdit Then
    CancelEdit()
    If IsNew AndAlso mNeverCommitted AndAlso _
      EditLevel <= EditLevelAdded Then
      If Not Parent Is Nothing Then
        Parent.RemoveChild(Me)
      End If
    End If
  End If
End Sub

Private Sub IEditableObject_EndEdit() _
  Implements System.ComponentModel.IEditableObject.EndEdit
  If mBindingEdit Then
    ApplyEdit()
  End If
End Sub
```

Notice that the methods are declared using syntax to explicitly implement the IEditableObject interface. This is required because BeginEdit() and CancelEdit() are already public methods in the class, and this avoids any naming conflict. All three methods call the corresponding edit methods implemented earlier.

The mBindingEdit field is used to determine whether the BeginEdit() method has been called already so any subsequent method calls can be ignored. The mBindingEdit field is set to True when an edit process is started, and to False when either CancelEdit() or ApplyEdit() is called.

The mNeverCommitted field tracks whether the ApplyEdit() method has ever been called. If it hasn't ever been called, and data binding attempts to cancel the edit operation, this flag is used to control whether the object should remove itself from its parent collection. The mNeverCommitted field starts out True and is set to False if ApplyEdit() is called.

With this mechanism in place, the implementation of IEditableObject.BeginEdit() calls only the real BeginEdit() method if no edit session is currently underway. With the implementation of the n-level undo methods and System.ComponentModel.IEditableObject, business objects now provide full control over editing and undo capabilities, both to the UI developer and to Windows Forms data binding.

Root, Parent, and Child Behaviors

Chapter 2 introduced the idea that a business object can be a root, parent, and/or child object. A definition of each can be found in Table 3-7.

Table 3-7. *Root, Parent, and Child Object Definitions*

Object Type	Definition
Root	An object that can be directly retrieved or updated via the data portal
Parent	An object that contains other business objects as part of its state
Child	An object that is contained by another business object

A root object may be a stand-alone object. It may also be a parent if it contains child objects. A child object could also be a parent if it, in turn, contains other child objects. An example of a root and parent object is an Invoice, while an example of a child object would be a LineItem object within that Invoice. Child objects are related to root objects via a containment relationship, as illustrated by the class diagram in Figure 3-3.

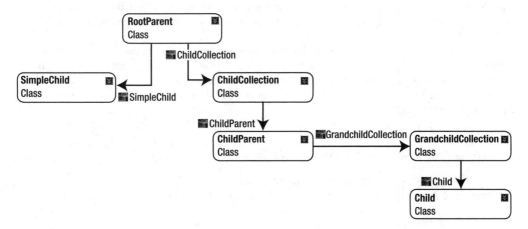

Figure 3-3. *Class diagram showing how root, child, and grandchild objects are related*

MarkAsChild

The business programmer makes the choice about whether an object is a child or not through code. By default, an object is a root object, and is only considered to be a child object if the MarkAsChild() method is called in the object's constructor. The MarkAsChild() method looks like this:

```
Protected Sub MarkAsChild()
  mIsChild = True
End Sub
```

The mIsChild field is used to maintain whether the object is a child, and that value is exposed via an IsChild property:

```
<NotUndoable()> _
Private mIsChild As Boolean

Protected Friend ReadOnly Property IsChild() As Boolean
  Get
    Return mIsChild
  End Get
End Property
```

Notice that the field is declared using the `<NotUndoable()>` attribute. Since this value will never change during the lifetime of the object, there's no reason to include it in an n-level undo snapshot. The `IsChild` property will be used within other `BusinessBase` code, and may be useful to the business developer, so it's declared as `Protected`.

There are certain behaviors that are valid only for root objects, and others that apply only to child objects. These rules will be enforced by throwing exceptions when an invalid operation is attempted. The `Delete()` and `DeleteChild()` methods implemented earlier are examples of this approach.

Parent Property

If a business object is a child of a collection, then it will maintain a reference to its parent business object. As you saw earlier, this is required for implementation of `System.ComponentModel.IEditableObject`.

To avoid circular reference issues with n-level undo and serialization, the field holding this reference must be declared with the `<NotUndoable()>` and `<NonSerialized()>` attributes. Without these attributes, `UndoableBase` will go into an infinite loop during `CopyState()`, and .NET serialization will create a much larger byte stream during serialization than is required. The value will also be exposed through a property:

```
<NotUndoable()> _
<NonSerialized()> _
Private mParent As Core.IEditableCollection

<EditorBrowsable(EditorBrowsableState.Advanced)> _
Protected ReadOnly Property Parent() As Core.IEditableCollection
  Get
    Return mParent
  End Get
End Property
```

Due to the fact that the `mParent` field is not serializable, its value must be restored by the parent collection any time that deserialization occurs. To make this possible, the collection will call a `Friend` method on the business object:

```
Friend Sub SetParent(ByVal parent As Core.IEditableCollection)
  If Not IsChild Then
    Throw New InvalidOperationException(My.Resources.ParentSetException)
  End If
  mParent = parent
End Sub
```

This method is only valid if the object is a child object, and all it does is store the parent object reference in the `mParent` field.

Edit Level Tracking for Child Objects

N-level undo of collections of child objects is pretty complex, a fact that will become clear in the implementation of BusinessListBase. The biggest of several problems arises when a new child object is added to the collection, and then the collection's parent object is "canceled." In that case, the child object must be removed from the collection as though it were never there—the collection must be reset to its original state. To support this, child objects must keep track of the *edit level* at which they were added.

UndoableBase made use of an EditLevel property that returned a number corresponding to the number of times the object's state had been copied for later undo. From a UI programmer's perspective, the edit level is the number of times BeginEdit() has been called, minus the number of times CancelEdit() or ApplyEdit() has been called.

An example might help. Suppose that there is an Invoice object with a collection of LineItem objects. If BeginEdit() is called on the Invoice, then its edit level is 1. Since it cascades that call down to its child collection, the collection and all child objects are also at edit level 1.

If a new child object is added to the collection, it would be added at edit level 1. If the Invoice object is then *canceled*, the user expects the Invoice object's state to be restored to what it was originally—effectively, back to the level 0 state. Of course, this includes the child collection, which means that the collection somehow needs to realize that the newly added child object should be discarded. To do this, the BusinessListBase code will loop through its child objects looking for any that were added at an edit level higher than the current edit level.

In this example, when the Invoice is canceled, its edit level immediately goes to 0. It cascades that call to the child collection, which then also has an edit level of 0. The collection scans its child objects looking for any that were added at an edit level greater than 0, and finds the new child object that was added at edit level 1. It then knows that this child object can be removed.

This implies that business objects—if they're child objects—must keep track of the edit level at which they were added. This can be done with a simple field and a Friend property to set and retrieve its value:

```
Private mEditLevelAdded As Integer

Friend Property EditLevelAdded() As Integer
  Get
    Return mEditLevelAdded
  End Get
  Set(ByVal Value As Integer)
    mEditLevelAdded = Value
  End Set
End Property
```

The purpose and use of this functionality will become much clearer in the implementation of the BusinessListBase class later in this chapter.

Validation Rules

As discussed in Chapter 2, most business objects will be validating data based on various business rules. The actual implementation to manage an object's validation rules and maintain a list of broken business rules will be discussed later, in the "Csla.Validation Namespace" section. However, the BusinessBase class encapsulates that behavior and exposes it in an easy-to-use manner.

ValidationRules Object

The validation rules and broken rules will be managed by a `ValidationRules` object, and `BusinessBase` will collaborate with this object to manage all validation rule behaviors. A reference to this object is kept by `BusinessBase`, and is exposed through a property:

```
Private mValidationRules As Validation.ValidationRules

Protected ReadOnly Property ValidationRules() _
  As Validation.ValidationRules
  Get
    If mValidationRules Is Nothing Then
      mValidationRules = New Validation.ValidationRules(Me)
    End If
    Return mValidationRules
  End Get
End Property
```

The property implements a lazy loading approach, so the `ValidationRules` object is created only on first use. This is ideal, since an object that doesn't use any of the validation rules functionality won't even incur the overhead of creating the object.

The `ValidationRules` object maintains a list of validation rules for each property on the object. These rules are configured by the business developer in an `AddBusinessRules()` method, defined in `BusinessBase`, and overridden in the business class:

```
Protected Overridable Sub AddBusinessRules()
End Sub
```

This method is called when the object is created through the constructor in the `BusinessBase` class:

```
Protected Sub New()
  AddBusinessRules()
  AddAuthorizationRules()
End Sub
```

An `AddAuthorizationRules()` method is also called, and will be discussed shortly in the "Authorization Rules" section.

`AddBusinessRules()` must also be called when the business object is deserialized. This will happen after a clone operation or when the object moves across the network via the data portal. It is not efficient to try to maintain the list of rule delegates for each property during serialization and deserialization. Instead, when the object is deserialized, it can simply call `AddBusinessRules()` to reestablish the rule references:

```
<OnDeserialized()> _
Private Sub OnDeserializedHandler(ByVal context As StreamingContext)
  ValidationRules.SetTarget(Me)
  AddBusinessRules()
  OnDeserialized(context)
End Sub

<EditorBrowsable(EditorBrowsableState.Advanced)> _
Protected Overridable Sub OnDeserialized( _
  ByVal context As StreamingContext)
  ' do nothing - this is here so a subclass
  ' could override if needed
End Sub
```

The `<OnDeserialized()>` attribute is used to tell the .NET serialization infrastructure to call this method once deserialization is complete. This attribute comes from the `System.Runtime.Serialization` namespace, and is one of a set of attributes you can use to decorate methods that are to be called by the .NET Framework during the serialization and deserialization of an object.

Inside this method, the `AddBusinessRules()` method is called. Before that, however, the `ValidationRules` object needs to be given a reference to the business object so it can properly apply the validation rules to the properties. Finally, an `Overridable OnDeserialized` method is invoked so that the business developer can respond to the deserialization operation if desired.

The `ValidationRules` object maintains a list of currently broken rules. This was used earlier in the implementation of the `IsValid` property, but there's value in exposing the collection itself:

```
<Browsable(False)> _
<EditorBrowsable(EditorBrowsableState.Advanced)> _
Public Overridable ReadOnly Property BrokenRulesCollection() _
  As Validation.BrokenRulesCollection
  Get
    Return ValidationRules.GetBrokenRules
  End Get
End Property
```

Within `ValidationRules`, this collection is implemented to be read-only. Even though the collection is exposed as a `Public` property, it can't be changed by the UI. However, the UI can display the list of broken rules to the user if so desired.

System.ComponentModel.IDataErrorInfo

Windows Forms data binding uses the `IDataErrorInfo` interface to interrogate a data source for validation errors. This interface allows a data source, such as a business object, to provide human-readable descriptions of errors at the object and property levels. This information is used by grid controls and the `ErrorProvider` control to display error icons and tooltip descriptions.

The `ValidationRules` object will provide a list of broken rules for each property on the object, making it relatively easy to implement `IDataErrorInfo`:

```
Private ReadOnly Property [Error]() As String _
  Implements System.ComponentModel.IDataErrorInfo.Error
  Get
    If Not IsValid Then
      Return ValidationRules.GetBrokenRules.ToString

    Else
      Return ""
    End If
  End Get
End Property

Private ReadOnly Property Item(ByVal columnName As String) As String _
  Implements System.ComponentModel.IDataErrorInfo.Item
  Get
    Dim result As String = ""
    If Not IsValid Then
      Dim rule As Validation.BrokenRule = _
        ValidationRules.GetBrokenRules.GetFirstBrokenRule(columnName)
```

```
        If rule IsNot Nothing Then
          result = rule.Description()
        End If
      End If
      Return result
    End Get
  End Property
```

The Error property returns a text value describing the validation errors for the object as a whole. The indexer returns a text value describing any validation error for a specific property. In this implementation, only the first validation error in the list is returned. In either case, if there are no errors, an empty string value is returned—telling data binding that there are no broken rules to report.

Authorization Rules

In a manner similar to validation rules, authorization rules are managed by an AuthorizationRules object. The BusinessBase class collaborates with AuthorizationRules to implement authorization rules for each property. To simplify usage of this feature, BusinessBase encapsulates and abstracts the underlying behavior.

Step one is to declare a field and property for the rules:

```
<NotUndoable()> _
Private mAuthorizationRules As Security.AuthorizationRules

Protected ReadOnly Property AuthorizationRules() _
  As Security.AuthorizationRules
  Get
    If mAuthorizationRules Is Nothing Then
      mAuthorizationRules = New Security.AuthorizationRules
    End If
    Return mAuthorizationRules
  End Get
End Property
```

BusinessBase also declares an Overridable AddAuthorizationRules() method that the business developer can override in a business class. The business developer should write code in this method to specify which roles are allowed and denied access to read and write specific properties:

```
Protected Overridable Sub AddAuthorizationRules()
End Sub
```

The BusinessBase constructor automatically calls AddAuthorizationRules() so that any role-property relationships are established when the object is first created.

The BusinessBase class also defines methods so that both the business object developer and UI developer can find out whether the current user is allowed to read or write to a specific property. The CanReadProperty() methods indicate whether the user can read a specific property, while the CanWriteProperty() methods do the same for altering a property. Both have several overloads. Only the CanReadProperty() methods will be shown here, and you can look at the CanWriteProperty() methods in the downloaded code.

The primary CanReadProperty() implementation enforces the authorization rules for a property, making use of the AuthorizationRules object:

```vbnet
<EditorBrowsable(EditorBrowsableState.Advanced)> _
Public Overridable Function CanReadProperty( _
  ByVal propertyName As String) As Boolean

  Dim result As Boolean = True
  If AuthorizationRules.HasReadAllowedRoles(propertyName) Then
    ' some users are explicitly granted read access
    ' in which case all other users are denied
    If Not AuthorizationRules.IsReadAllowed(propertyName) Then
      result = False
    End If

  ElseIf AuthorizationRules.HasReadDeniedRoles(propertyName) Then
    ' some users are explicitly denied read access
    If AuthorizationRules.IsReadDenied(propertyName) Then
      result = False
    End If
  End If
  Return result
End Function
```

The AuthorizationRules object can maintain a list of roles explicitly granted access to a property, and a separate list of roles explicitly denied access. This algorithm first checks to see if there are any roles granted access, and if so, it assumes all other roles are denied. On the other hand, if no roles are explicitly granted access, it assumes *all* roles have access—except those in the denied list.

Notice that the method is Overridable, so a business developer can override this behavior to implement a different authorization algorithm if needed. The CanWriteProperty() method operates in the same manner and is also Overridable.

As with the PropertyHasChanged() method earlier in the chapter, the CanReadProperty() implementation requires a string parameter indicating the property name. That forces the use of string literals in the business object, which should be avoided for maintainability. To assist in this effort, there's an overloaded version that uses System.Diagnostics to retrieve the property name, just like PropertyHasChanged().

There's a third overload as well. Notice that the CanReadProperty() implementation returns a Boolean result, allowing the calling code to decide what to do if access is denied. That's fine, but within a business object's property, denied access will almost always trigger a security exception to be thrown. The final overload simplifies business object property code by throwing this exception automatically:

```vbnet
<System.Runtime.CompilerServices.MethodImpl( _
  System.Runtime.CompilerServices.MethodImplOptions.NoInlining)> _
Public Function CanReadProperty(ByVal throwOnFalse As Boolean) As Boolean

  Dim propertyName As String = _
    New System.Diagnostics.StackTrace(). _
    GetFrame(1).GetMethod.Name.Substring(4)
  Dim result As Boolean = CanReadProperty(propertyName)
  If throwOnFalse AndAlso result = False Then
    Throw New System.Security.SecurityException( _
      String.Format("{0} ({1})", _
      My.Resources.PropertyGetNotAllowed, propertyName))
  End If
  Return result
End Function
```

This version of the method uses `System.Diagnostics` to retrieve the property name. But if access is denied, it optionally throws an exception. This allows code in a property to enforce property read and write authorization with just two lines of code and no string literals.

The Boolean parameter to this method is only required to create a different method signature. Otherwise, the only difference would be the return type (or lack thereof), which isn't sufficient for method overloading.

System.ICloneable

The `BusinessBase` class implements the `System.ICloneable` interface. This interface defines a `Clone()` method that can be called to create a clone, or copy, of an object. The `Csla.Core.ObjectCloner` class implements a general cloning solution that works against any serializable object, making it very easy to implement a `Clone()` method.

However, there are cases in which a business developer might not want to return an *exact* clone of an object. To accommodate this case, the cloning will be handled by an `Overridable` method so that the business developer can override the method and replace the cloning mechanism with their own, if needed:

```
Private Function Clone() As Object Implements ICloneable.Clone
  Return GetClone()
End Function

<EditorBrowsable(EditorBrowsableState.Advanced)> _
Protected Overridable Function GetClone() As Object
  Return ObjectCloner.Clone(Me)
End Function
```

Notice that neither of these methods is `Public`. The only way to invoke this `Clone()` method is through the `ICloneable` interface. Later in the chapter, `BusinessBase(Of T)` will implement a strongly typed `Public Clone()` method by virtue of being a generic type.

The `GetClone()` method is `Protected` in scope to allow customization of the cloning process by a business developer. While a straight copy of the object is typically the required behavior, sometimes a business object needs to do extra work when creating a clone of itself.

ReadOnlyBindingList Class

The final type in the `Csla.Core` namespace is the `ReadOnlyBindingList(Of C)` class. This implements a read-only collection based on `System.ComponentModel.BindingList(Of T)`. The standard `BindingList(Of T)` class implements a read-write collection that supports data binding, but there are numerous cases in which a read-only collection is useful. For example, `ReadOnlyBindingList` is the base class for `Csla.ReadOnlyListBase`, `Csla.NameValueListBase`, and `Csla.Validation.BrokenRulesCollection`.

This class inherits from `BindingList`. It is also serializable and `MustInherit`, like all the framework base classes:

```
<Serializable()> _
Public MustInherit Class ReadOnlyBindingList(Of C)
  Inherits System.ComponentModel.BindingList(Of C)

  Implements Core.IBusinessObject

End Class
```

All the basic collection and data binding behaviors are already implemented by `BindingList`. Making the collection read-only is a matter of overriding a few methods to prevent alteration of the collection. Of course, the collection has to be read-write at *some* point, in order to get data into the collection at all. To control whether the collection is read-only or not, there's a field and a property:

```
Private mIsReadOnly As Boolean = True

Public Property IsReadOnly() As Boolean
  Get
    Return mIsReadOnly
  End Get
  Protected Set(ByVal value As Boolean)
    mIsReadOnly = value
  End Set
End Property
```

Notice that while the IsReadOnly property is Public for reading, it is Protected for changing. This way, any code can determine if the collection is read-only or read-write, but only a subclass can lock or unlock the collection.

The class contains a constructor that turns off the options to edit, remove, or create items in the collection by setting some properties in the BindingList base class:

```
Protected Sub New()
  AllowEdit = False
  AllowRemove = False
  AllowNew = False
End Sub
```

The rest of the class overrides the methods in BindingList that control alteration of the collection. Each override checks the IsReadOnly property and throws an exception when an attempt is made to change the collection when it is in read-only mode.

The only complicated overrides are ClearItems() and RemoveItem(). This is because AllowRemove is typically set to False and must be temporarily changed to True to allow the operation (when the collection is not in read-only mode). For instance, here's the ClearItems() method:

```
Protected Overrides Sub ClearItems()
  If Not IsReadOnly Then
    Dim oldValue As Boolean = AllowRemove
    AllowRemove = True
    MyBase.ClearItems()
    AllowRemove = oldValue
  Else
    Throw New NotSupportedException(My.Resources.ClearInvalidException)
  End If
End Sub
```

The original AllowRemove value is restored after the operation is complete. This completes all the types in the Csla.Core namespace. The rest of the implementation is available in the code download for the book. Let's move on and discuss the types in the Csla.Validation namespace.

Csla.Validation Namespace

The Csla.Validation namespace contains types that assist the business developer in implementing and enforcing business rules. The Csla.Core.BusinessBase class, discussed earlier in the "Business-Base Class" section, illustrated how some of the functionality in the Csla.Validation namespace will be used. This includes managing a list of business rules for each of the object's properties and maintaining a list of currently broken business rules.

Obviously, the framework can't implement the actual business rules and validation code—that will vary from application to application. However, business rules follow a very specific pattern in that they are either broken or not. The result of a rule being checked is a Boolean value and a human-readable description of why the rule is broken. This makes it possible to check the rules and then maintain a list of broken rules—including human-readable descriptions of each rule.

RuleHandler Delegate

Given that rules follow a specific pattern, it is possible to define a method signature that covers virtually all business rules. In .NET, a method signature can be formally defined using a delegate; here's the definition for a rule method:

```
Public Delegate Function RuleHandler( _
  ByVal target As Object, ByVal e As RuleArgs) As Boolean
```

Every rule is implemented as a method that returns a Boolean result: True if the rule is satisfied, False if the rule is broken. The object containing the data to be validated is passed as the first argument, and the second argument is a RuleArgs object that can be used to pass extra rule-specific information. This means that a business rule in a business class looks like this:

```
Private Function CustNameRequired( _
  ByVal target As Object, ByVal e As RuleArgs) As Boolean

  If Len(CType(target, Customer).Name) = 0 Then
    e.Description = "Customer name required"
    Return False
  Else
    Return True
  End If
End Function
```

If the length of the target object's Name property is zero, then the rule is not satisfied, so it returns False. It also sets the Description property of the RuleArgs object to a human-readable description of why the rule is broken.

This illustrates a rule that would be implemented within a single business class. By using reflection, it is possible to write entirely reusable rule methods that can be used by any business class. You'll see some examples of this in the "Common Business Rules" section of Chapter 5 when I discuss the CommonRules class.

RuleArgs Class

The RuleHandler delegate specifies the use of the RuleArgs object as a parameter to every rule method. This follows the general pattern used throughout .NET of passing an EventArgs parameter to all event handlers. Business rules aren't event handlers, so RuleArgs doesn't inherit from EventArgs, but it follows the same basic principal:

```
Public Class RuleArgs

  Private mPropertyName As String
  Private mDescription As String
  Public ReadOnly Property PropertyName() As String
    Get
      Return mPropertyName
    End Get
  End Property
```

```
Public Property Description() As String
  Get
    Return mDescription
  End Get
  Set(ByVal Value As String)
    mDescription = Value
  End Set
End Property

Public Sub New(ByVal propertyName As String)
  mPropertyName = propertyName
End Sub

Public Overrides Function ToString() As String
    Return mPropertyName
End Function
```

```
End Class
```

The goal is to be able to pass data into and out of the rule method in a clearly defined manner. At a minimum, `RuleArgs` passes the name of the property to be validated into the rule method, and passes back any broken rule description out of the rule method. To do this, it simply contains a read-only `PropertyName` property and a read-write `Description` property.

More important is the fact that the author of a rule method can create a subclass of `RuleArgs` to provide *extra* information. For instance, implementing a maximum value rule implies that the maximum allowed value can be provided to the rule. To do this, the rule author would create a subclass of `RuleArgs`. You'll see an example of this in the "Common Business Rules" section of Chapter 5, in which I discuss the `CommonRules` class.

RuleMethod Class

The `ValidationRules` class will maintain a list of rules for each property. This implies that `ValidationRules` has information about each rule method. This is the purpose of the `RuleMethod` class. It stores information about each rule, including the target object containing the data the rule should validate, a delegate reference to the rule method itself, a unique name for the rule, and any custom `RuleArgs` object that should be passed to the rule method. This information is stored in a set of fields with associated properties. The fields are declared like this:

```
Private mTarget As Object
Private mHandler As RuleHandler
Private mRuleName As String = ""
Private mArgs As RuleArgs
```

The `RuleMethod` class is scoped as `Friend`, as it is used by other classes in the `Csla.Validation` namespace, but shouldn't be used by code outside the framework.

The unique rule name associated with each rule is derived automatically by combining the name of the rule method with the string representation of the `RuleArgs` object. By default, this is the name of the property with which it is associated:

```
mRuleName = mHandler.Method.Name & "!" & mArgs.ToString
```

Because the rule name must be unique, any custom subclasses of `RuleArgs` should be sure to override `ToString()` to return a value that includes any custom data that is part of the arguments object.

When the business developer associates a rule method with a property, `ValidationRules` creates a `RuleMethod` object to maintain all this information. This `RuleMethod` object is what's actually associated with the property, thus providing all the information needed to invoke the rule when appropriate.

In fact, the `RuleMethod` object handles the invocation of the rule method itself by exposing an `Invoke()` method:

```
Public Function Invoke() As Boolean
  Return mHandler.Invoke(mTarget, mArgs)
End Function
```

When `ValidationRules` is asked to check the business rules, it merely loops through its list of `RuleMethod` objects, asking each one to invoke the rule it represents. As you can see, the `Invoke()` method simply invokes the method via the delegate reference, passing in a reference to the object to be validated (the business object) and the `RuleArgs` object associated with the rule.

ValidationRules Class

The `ValidationRules` class is the primary class in the `Csla.Validation` namespace. Every business object that uses the validation rules functionality will contain its own `ValidationRules` object. `ValidationRules` relies on the other classes in `Csla.Validation` to do its work. Together, these classes maintain the list of rules for each property and the list of currently broken rules.

Managing Rules for Properties

You've already seen how a business rule is defined based on the `RuleHandler` delegate. A key part of what `ValidationRules` does is keep a list of such rule methods for each of the business object's properties.

Referencing the Business Object

Remember that each rule method accepts a `target` parameter, which is the object containing the data to be validated. This target is always the business object, so `ValidationRules` keeps a reference to the business object. This reference is provided via the constructor and can be reset through the `SetTarget()` method—both of which you've seen in the implementation of `Csla.Core.BusinessBase`:

```
<NonSerialized()> _
Private mTarget As Object

Friend Sub New(ByVal businessObject As Object)
  SetTarget(businessObject)
End Sub

Friend Sub SetTarget(ByVal businessObject As Object)
  mTarget = businessObject
End Sub
```

Notice that the `mTarget` field is marked as `<NonSerialized()>`. This is important because otherwise the `BinaryFormatter` would trace the circular reference between the business object and the `ValidationRules` object, causing a bloated serialization byte stream. No failure would result, but the size of the byte stream would be larger than needed, which may cause a performance issue in some cases.

Associating Rules with Properties

To provide good performance in managing the list of rules for each property, `ValidationRules` uses an optimal data structure. Specifically, it has a dictionary with an entry for each property. Each entry in the dictionary contains a list of the rules for that property. This provides for very fast lookup to get the list of rules for a specific property, since the dictionary can jump right to the property's entry.

The dictionary is strongly typed, keyed by the property name, and used for storing strongly typed lists of `RuleMethod` objects:

```
<NonSerialized()> _
Private mRulesList As _
  Generic.Dictionary(Of String, List(Of RuleMethod))
```

The business developer calls an `AddRule()` method to associate a rule method with a property on the business object. There are two versions of this method, the simplest accepting just a rule method delegate and the name of the property:

```
Public Sub AddRule( _
  ByVal handler As RuleHandler, ByVal propertyName As String)

  ' get the list of rules for the property
  Dim list As List(Of RuleMethod) = GetRulesForProperty(propertyName)

  ' we have the list, add our new rule
  list.Add(New RuleMethod(mTarget, handler, propertyName))
End Sub
```

The `GetRulesForProperty()` method returns the list of `RuleMethod` objects associated with the property. If such a list doesn't already exist, it creates an empty list and adds it to the dictionary. This is another example of lazy object creation. If there are no rules for a property, no list object is ever added to the dictionary, thus reducing the overhead of the whole process.

In fact, the dictionary object itself is created on demand as well, so if no business rules are ever associated with properties for an object, even that little bit of overhead is avoided.

The other `AddRule()` implementation provides an increased level of control. Its method signature is as follows:

```
Public Sub AddRule(ByVal handler As RuleHandler, ByVal args As RuleArgs)
```

This overload allows the business developer to provide a specific `RuleArgs` object that will be passed to the rule method when it is invoked. This is required for any rule methods that require custom `RuleArgs` subclasses, so it will be used any time extra information needs to be passed to the rule method.

The combination of the `RuleMethod` class, the dictionary and list object combination, and the `AddRule()` methods covers the management of the rules associated with each property.

Checking Validation Rules

Once a set of rule methods have been associated with the properties of a business object, there needs to be a way to invoke those rules. Typically, when a single property is changed on a business object, only the rules for that property need to be checked. At other times, the rules for *all* the object's properties need to be checked. This is true when an object is first created, for instance, since multiple properties of the object could start out with invalid values.

To cover these two cases, `ValidationRules` implements two `CheckRules()` methods. The first checks the rules for a specific property:

```
Public Sub CheckRules(ByVal propertyName As String)
  Dim list As List(Of RuleMethod)
  ' get the list of rules to check
  If RulesList.ContainsKey(propertyName) Then
    list = RulesList.Item(propertyName)
    If list Is Nothing Then Exit Sub

    ' now check the rules
    Dim rule As RuleMethod
    For Each rule In list
      If rule.Invoke() Then
        BrokenRulesList.Remove(rule)
      Else
        BrokenRulesList.Add(rule)
      End If
    Next
  End If
End Sub
```

This method checks to see if the RulesList (the dictionary) contains an entry for the specified property. If so, it retrieves the list of RuleMethod objects and loops through them, asking each one to invoke its underlying rule method.

If a rule returns True, then BrokenRulesList.Remove() is called to ensure that the rule isn't listed as a broken rule. If the rule returns False, then BrokenRulesList.Add() is called to ensure that the rule *is* listed as a broken rule. The BrokenRulesList class is part of the Csla.Validation namespace, and will be discussed shortly.

The other CheckRules() implementation checks all the rules that have been added to the ValidationRules object:

```
Public Sub CheckRules()
  ' get the rules for each rule name
  Dim de As Generic.KeyValuePair(Of String, List(Of RuleMethod))
  For Each de In RulesList

    Dim list As List(Of RuleMethod) = _
      de.Value

    ' now check the rules
    Dim rule As RuleMethod
    For Each rule In list
      If rule.Invoke() Then
        BrokenRulesList.Remove(rule)
      Else
        BrokenRulesList.Add(rule)
      End If
    Next
  Next
End Sub
```

This method simply loops through all items in the RulesList dictionary. Every entry in the dictionary is a list of RuleMethod objects, so it then loops through each list, invoking all the rules. The rule is then added or removed from BrokenRulesList based on the result.

At this point, it should be clear how ValidationRules associates rule methods with properties and is then able to check those rules for a specific property or for the business object as a whole.

Maintaining a List of Broken Rules

The ValidationRules object also maintains a list of currently broken validation rules. This list was used in the CheckRules() methods, and is declared as follows:

```
Private mBrokenRules As BrokenRulesCollection

Private ReadOnly Property BrokenRulesList() As BrokenRulesCollection
  Get
    If mBrokenRules Is Nothing Then
      mBrokenRules = New BrokenRulesCollection
    End If
    Return mBrokenRules
  End Get
End Property
```

Notice that the mBrokenRules field is not adorned with either the <NotUndoable()> or <NonSerialized()> attributes. The list of currently broken rules is directly part of a business object's state, and so it is subject to n-level undo operations and to being transferred across the network along with the business object.

This way, if a business developer transfers an invalid object across the network or makes a clone, the object remains invalid, with its list of broken rules intact.

The BrokenRulesList value is also exposed via a Public method. To any external consumer, such as code in the UI, this is a read-only collection:

```
Public Function GetBrokenRules() As BrokenRulesCollection
  Return BrokenRulesList
End Function
```

The reason the collection is exposed publicly is to allow UI developers to use the list of broken rules as they see fit. Remember that a broken rule includes a human-readable description of the rule, and so it is perfectly reasonable to display this list to the end user in some circumstances.

BrokenRule Class

When a rule method returns False in a CheckRules() method, the broken rule is recorded into a BrokenRulesCollection. That collection contains a list of BrokenRule objects, each one representing a single broken business rule. The BrokenRule object exposes read-only properties for the rule name, a human-readable description of the broken rule, and the name of the property that is broken. The class is available in the code download for the book.

BrokenRulesCollection Class

The BrokenRulesCollection class is used by ValidationRules to maintain the list of currently broken rules. Each broken rule is represented by a BrokenRule object. The collection inherits from Csla. Core.ReadOnlyBindingList and so is a read-only collection:

```
<Serializable()> _
Public Class BrokenRulesCollection
  Inherits Core.ReadOnlyBindingList(Of BrokenRule)

  Friend Sub New()
    ' limit creation to this assembly
  End Sub

End Class
```

The collection also includes a `Friend` constructor, thus ensuring that an instance of the object can only be created from within the CSLA .NET framework. Also, though the collection is read-only, it does provide some `Friend` methods to allow `ValidationRules` to add and remove items. These methods are used in the `CheckRules()` methods to ensure that broken rules are only in the list when appropriate:

```
Friend Overloads Sub Add(ByVal rule As RuleMethod)
  Remove(rule)
  IsReadOnly = False
  Add(New BrokenRule(rule))
  IsReadOnly = True
End Sub

Friend Overloads Sub Remove(ByVal rule As RuleMethod)
  ' we loop through using a numeric counter because
  ' removing items in a For..Each isn't reliable
  IsReadOnly = False
  For index As Integer = 0 To Count - 1
    If Me(index).RuleName = rule.RuleName Then
      RemoveAt(index)
      Exit For
    End If
  Next
  IsReadOnly = True
End Sub
```

The `Add()` method is pretty straightforward. To avoid possible duplicate object issues, it first ensures that the broken rule isn't already in the list by calling the `Remove()` method. Then it changes the collection to be read-write, adds the rule to the collection, and sets the collection back to be read-only.

While it could just see if the collection contains the broken rule, removing and re-adding the rule is better, because it ensures that the human-readable description for the rule is current. The rule method could have changed the description over time.

The `Remove()` method is a bit more complex. It has to scan through the collection to find a rule with the same rule name. Notice that no exception is thrown if the item isn't in the collection. If it isn't there, that's fine—then there's just no need to remove it.

There are two other methods in `BrokenRulesCollection` worth mentioning. Both provide information about the contents of the collection.

The `GetFirstBrokenRule()` method scans the list and returns the first broken rule (if any) for a specified property. You may recall that this method was used in `Csla.Core.BusinessBase` to implement the `IDataErrorInfo` interface.

The second is an overridden `ToString()` method that concatenates the human-readable descriptions of all broken rules into a single string value. This too is used in the `IDataErrorInfo` implementation to return all the errors for the entire object.

ValidationException

The `ValidationException` class allows CSLA .NET to throw a custom exception to indicate that a validation problem has been found. This exception is thrown by the `Save()` method in `BusinessBase`.

This exception class doesn't add any new information to the base `Exception` class from the .NET Framework. Thus its code is very simple, since it merely declares a set of constructors, each of which delegates to the `Exception` base class. (You can look at the code from the code download for the book.)

The reason ValidationException exists is to allow UI code to easily catch a ValidationException as being separate from other exceptions that might be thrown by the Save() method. For instance, UI code might look like this:

```
Try
  customer = customer.Save()

Catch ex As ValidationException
  ' handle validation exceptions

Catch ex As Exception
  ' handle other exceptions
End Try
```

Custom exceptions, even if they offer no extra information, are often very valuable in this way.

At this point, the Csla.Validation namespace is complete, except for CommonRules, which will be discussed in Chapter 5. The framework now supports validation rules and broken rule tracking.

Csla.Security Namespace

The Csla.Security namespace includes both authentication and authorization functionality. In this chapter, only the authorization classes will be explored, leaving authentication for Chapter 4.

Authorization supports the idea that each business object property can have a list of roles that are allowed and denied access. You've already seen some of the authorization implemented in Csla.Core.BusinessBase with the CanReadProperty() and CanWriteProperty() methods. Those methods made use of a Csla.Validation.AuthorizationRules object.

Every business object that uses authorization rules will have an associated AuthorizationRules object that manages the list of roles associated with each property. The AuthorizationRules object will use a RolesForProperty collection to manage those roles.

RolesForProperty Class

The RolesForProperty class is responsible for maintaining the list of roles explicitly allowed and denied access to a specific property. The AuthorizationRules class will provide public methods for interaction with the authorization functionality. All the code in RolesForProperty exists to support AuthorizationRules. The RolesForProperty class itself is scoped as Friend, because it is only used within the framework.

Primarily, RolesForProperty just maintains four lists, declared as follows:

```
Private mReadAllowed As New List(Of String)
Private mReadDenied As New List(Of String)
Private mWriteAllowed As New List(Of String)
Private mWriteDenied As New List(Of String)
```

Each list is just a collection of string values—each entry representing a role or group that is allowed or denied access to read or write the property. Each of the four lists is exposed via a read-only property so that AuthorizationRules can interact with the list as needed.

More interesting, however, are the methods that compare a user's roles with the list of allowed or denied roles. For instance, the IsReadAllowed() method returns a Boolean indicating whether a user has a role that allows reading of the property:

```
Public Function IsReadAllowed(ByVal principal As IPrincipal) As Boolean
  Dim result As Boolean
  For Each role As String In ReadAllowed
    If principal.IsInRole(role) Then
      result = True
      Exit For
    End If
  Next
  Return result
End Function
```

The method accepts a System.Security.Principal.IPrincipal object—the standard security object in the .NET Framework. All IPrincipal objects expose an IsInRole() method that can be used to determine if the user is in a specific role. Using this property, the IsReadAllowed() method loops through the list of roles allowed to read the current property to determine if the user is in any of the roles. If the user is in one of the allowed roles, then the method returns True; otherwise, it returns False to indicate that the user isn't allowed to read the property.

The IsReadDenied(), IsWriteAllowed(), and IsWriteDenied() methods work the same way. Together, these methods help simplify the implementation of AuthorizationRules.

AccessType Enum

The AuthorizationRules class will provide access to the list of roles allowed or denied read or write access to each property. When implementing the GetRolesForProperty() method that returns this information, the calling code needs to specify the operation (read, write and allow, deny) for which the roles should be returned. The AccessType enumerated value defines the following options:

```
Public Enum AccessType
  ReadAllowed
  ReadDenied
  WriteAllowed
  WriteDenied
End Enum
```

This enumerated value will be used in the AuthorizationRules class. It may also be used by business developers if they need access to the list of roles—perhaps to implement some type of custom authorization for a specific object.

AuthorizationRules Class

The AuthorizationRules class is the core of the authorization rules implementation. Every business object has its own AuthorizationRules object, and the business object collaborates with AuthorizationRules to implement the authorization rules for the object.

As with validation rules, authorization rules are implemented to use lazy object creation to minimize overhead. That way, if a business object doesn't use the feature, there's little to no cost to having it in the framework.

It also uses a similar design by using a dictionary object to associate a RolesForProperty object with each business object property. This dictionary is created on demand:

```
Private mRules As Dictionary(Of String, RolesForProperty)

Private ReadOnly Property Rules() _
  As Dictionary(Of String, RolesForProperty)
  Get
    If mRules Is Nothing Then
      mRules = New Dictionary(Of String, RolesForProperty)
    End If
    Return mRules
  End Get
End Property
```

Each entry in the dictionary is indexed by the property name and contains a RolesForProperty object to manage the list of allowed and denied roles for the property.

Retrieving Roles

Following the idea of lazy object creation, the GetRolesForProperty() method returns the list of roles for a property, creating it if it doesn't exist:

```
Private Function GetRolesForProperty( _
  ByVal propertyName As String) As RolesForProperty
  Dim currentRoles As RolesForProperty = Nothing
  If Not Rules.ContainsKey(propertyName) Then
    currentRoles = New RolesForProperty
    Rules.Add(propertyName, currentRoles)

  Else
    currentRoles = Rules.Item(propertyName)
  End If
  Return currentRoles
End Function
```

This method is scoped as Private because it is only used by other methods in the class. There is a public overload of GetRolesForProperty() that returns the list of roles for the property—for a specific type of access (read, write and allow, deny):

```
<EditorBrowsable(EditorBrowsableState.Advanced)> _
Public Function GetRolesForProperty(ByVal propertyName As String, _
  ByVal access As AccessType) As String()

  Dim currentRoles As RolesForProperty = GetRolesForProperty(propertyName)
  Select Case access
    Case AccessType.ReadAllowed
      Return currentRoles.ReadAllowed.ToArray
    Case AccessType.ReadDenied
      Return currentRoles.ReadDenied.ToArray
    Case AccessType.WriteAllowed
      Return currentRoles.WriteAllowed.ToArray
    Case AccessType.WriteDenied
      Return currentRoles.WriteDenied.ToArray
  End Select
  Return Nothing
End Function
```

This method may be used by business developers if they need access to the list of roles—perhaps to implement some type of custom authorization for a specific object. It is implemented here for flexibility—not because the framework needs the functionality directly—and so the `<EditorBrowsable()>` attribute is used to designate this as an advanced method.

Associating Roles with Properties

Of course, the business object needs to be able to associate lists of roles with its properties. The `AuthorizationRules` object exposes a set of methods for this purpose—one for each access type. For instance, the `AllowRead()` method adds roles to the list of roles allowed to read a specific property:

```
Public Sub AllowRead( _
  ByVal propertyName As String, ByVal ParamArray roles() As String)
  Dim currentRoles As RolesForProperty = GetRolesForProperty(propertyName)
  For Each item As String In roles
    currentRoles.ReadAllowed.Add(item)
  Next
End Sub
```

This method accepts the name of the property and an array of role names. It uses the `GetRolesForProperty()` method to retrieve the appropriate `RolesForProperty` object from the dictionary, and then appends the roles to the `ReadAllowed` list.

The `DenyRead()`, `AllowWrite()`, and `DenyWrite()` methods work in a similar fashion.

Checking Roles

The final behavior implemented by `AuthorizationRules` is to allow a business object to authorize the current user to read or write to a property. The `Csla.Core.BusinessBase` class implemented the actual algorithm for this purpose, but `AuthorizationRules` provides methods to make that possible.

■Tip Remember that the methods in `BusinessBase` were `Overridable`, so a business developer could implement their own authorization algorithm by using `AuthorizationRules` if the algorithm in `BusinessBase` is inadequate.

For each access type, there are two methods. One indicates where there are any roles associated with the property for the specific access type, and the other checks the current user's roles against the roles for the property. For the read-allowed access type, the following methods are implemented:

```
Public Function HasReadAllowedRoles( _
  ByVal propertyName As String) As Boolean
  Return (GetRolesForProperty(propertyName).ReadAllowed.Count > 0)
End Function

Public Function IsReadAllowed(ByVal propertyName As String) As Boolean
  Return GetRolesForProperty(propertyName). _
    IsReadAllowed(ApplicationContext.User)
End Function
```

The `HasReadAllowedRoles()` method returns `True` if there are any roles explicitly allowing read access to the specified property. Recall that the `CanReadProperty()` method in `BusinessBase` uses this method to decide how to apply authorization rules.

■**Note** The principal object is retrieved from `Csla.ApplicationContext`. This class is discussed in Chapter 4. Its `User` property returns the proper principal object in both ASP.NET and other environments, and should be used rather than `System.Threading.Thread.CurrentPrincipal` or `HttpContext.Current.User`.

The `IsReadAllowed()` method retrieves the `IPrincipal` object for the current user and collaborates with the underlying `RolesForProperty` object to determine if the user has a role that matches any of the roles in the list of roles that can read the specified property.

The deny-read, allow-write, and deny-write access types each have a pair of methods implemented in a similar manner. Combined, these methods provide the tools needed by `BusinessBase` to implement the `CanReadProperty()` and `CanWriteProperty()` methods.

This concludes not only the `Csla.Security` discussion, but all the supporting classes required for the main base classes in the `Csla` namespace itself. The rest of the chapter will cover the base classes typically used by business developers when creating their own editable and read-only business objects.

Csla Namespace

The rest of the chapter will cover the implementation of the four primary base classes a business developer will use to create editable and read-only business objects and collections:

- `Csla.BusinessBase(Of T)`
- `Csla.BusinessListBase(Of T, C)`
- `Csla.ReadOnlyBase(Of T)`
- `Csla.ReadOnlyListBase(Of T, C)`

Let's walk through each of these in turn.

BusinessBase Class

The `Csla.BusinessBase` class is the primary base class for creating both editable root and editable child objects. This includes objects such as `Invoice`, `Customer`, `OrderLineItem`, and so forth.

Given the code in `Csla.Core.BusinessBase`, implementing this new base class will be relatively straightforward. In fact, the only methods this class will contain are those that rely on .NET generics to be strongly typed.

Like all the framework base classes, `Csla.BusinessBase` is serializable and `abstract`. This class is also a generic template:

```
<Serializable()> _
Public MustInherit Class BusinessBase(Of T As BusinessBase(Of T))
  Inherits Core.BusinessBase

End Class
```

The use of generics here is a bit tricky. The type parameter, T, is constrained to only allow types that inherit from `BusinessBase(Of T)`. This is a self-referencing generic and ensures that `BusinessBase(Of T)` can only be used as a base class when the subclass itself is provided as T. For instance, a business class looks like this:

```
<Serializable()> _
Public Class Customer
  Inherits Csla.BusinessBase(Of Customer)

End Class
```

The purpose behind doing this is so that BusinessBase(Of T) can implement methods that return the business object itself in a strongly typed manner. For instance, in Chapter 4, BusinessBase(Of T) will implement a Save() method that (in the preceding example) would return an object of type Customer.

■**Note** This use of generics not only provides strong typing for methods, but hides the generic types from the UI developer, making their code more readable. In this example, the UI developer will see only a Customer class with strongly typed methods.

The BusinessBase class implements functionality in three areas: overriding System.Object methods, a strongly typed Clone() method, and data access methods. The data access methods will be added in Chapter 4; this chapter will only deal with the first two areas.

System.Object Overrides

A well-implemented business object should always override three methods from the base System.Object type. Remember that all .NET objects ultimately inherit from System.Object, and so all objects have default implementations of these methods. Unfortunately, the default implementation is not ideal, and better implementations can (and should) be provided by every business object.

These three methods are Equals(), GetHashCode(), and ToString(). To implement each of these methods, the business object must have some unique identifying field—a primary key, in a sense. Such a unique identifier can be used to determine equality between objects, to return a unique hash code, and to return a meaningful string representation for the object.

Obviously, the BusinessBase class can't automatically determine a unique identifying value for every business object a developer might create. To get such a value, the class instead implements a MustOverride method that *must* be implemented by the business developer to return the object's unique key value:

```
Protected MustOverride Function GetIdValue() As Object
```

This forces any subclass of BusinessBase to implement a GetIdValue() method that returns a unique value identifying the business object. This value can then be used to implement the three System.Object method overrides:

```
Public Overloads Overrides Function Equals(ByVal obj As Object) As Boolean
  If TypeOf obj Is T Then
    Dim id As Object = GetIdValue()
    If id Is Nothing Then
      Throw New ArgumentException(My.Resources.GetIdValueCantBeNull)
    End If
    Return DirectCast(obj, T).GetIdValue.Equals(id)

  Else
    Return False
  End If
End Function
```

```
Public Overrides Function GetHashCode() As Integer
  Dim id As Object = GetIdValue()
  If id Is Nothing Then
    Throw New ArgumentException(My.Resources.GetIdValueCantBeNull)
  End If
  Return id.GetHashCode
End Function

Public Overrides Function ToString() As String
  Dim id As Object = GetIdValue()
  If id Is Nothing Then
    Throw New ArgumentException(My.Resources.GetIdValueCantBeNull)
  End If
  Return id.ToString
End Function
```

In each case, the result of GetIdValue() is checked to see if it is Nothing. If so, an exception is thrown, since these implementations require a non-null value.

The GetHashCode() and ToString() implementations are very simple, as they just use the object's ID value to generate a hash code or a string value, respectively.

The Equals() method is a bit more interesting. It compares the business object to see if it is equal to the object passed as a parameter. The first thing it does is check the type of the parameter to see if that object is the same type as the business object:

```
If TypeOf obj Is T Then
```

Notice the use of the generic type, T, to represent the type of the business object. If the types are different, then obviously the objects can't be equal to each other. If the types are the same, then the obj parameter is casted to type T (the type of the business object), and its ID value is retrieved by calling its GetIdValue() method.

This clearly demonstrates why T is constrained to types that inherit from BusinessBase(Of T). Without that constraint on the generic type, there would be no guarantee that the obj parameter would implement GetIdValue().

If the two ID values match, then the objects are considered to be equal.

You should remember that these are merely default implementations of the three methods. If a business object needs a different implementation, it is perfectly acceptable to override one or all of these methods in a business class and ignore these implementations.

Clone Method

Earlier in the chapter, I discussed the ICloneable interface and the concept of cloning. The Csla. Core.ObjectCloner class contains code to clone any serializable object, and Csla.Core. BusinessBase implemented the ICloneable interface, delegating to an Overridable GetClone() method to do the work. Recall that the Clone() method implemented at that time was not Public in scope.

The reason for this is so that a strongly typed Clone() method could be implemented in the generic base class. ICloneable.Clone() returns a value of type object, but the following Clone() method is strongly typed:

```
Public Overridable Function Clone() As T
  Return DirectCast(GetClone(), T)
End Function
```

This implementation returns an object of type T, which is the type of the business object. So in the Customer class example, this would return an object of type Customer. Notice that it delegates the call to the same Overridable GetClone() method, so the business developer can override the default cloning behavior if he needs to implement a variation.

Other than the data access support that will be added in Chapter 4, the BusinessBase class is now complete.

BusinessListBase Class

While BusinessBase is the primary base class for building business objects, the framework must also support *collections* of business objects. Both the UndoableBase and Csla.Core.BusinessBase classes made accommodations for the BusinessListBase class discussed here. Remember the use of Csla.Core.IUndoableObject and Csla.Core.IEditableCollection in the implementation of those classes. BusinessListBase will implement IEditableCollection to interact with those other classes.

BusinessListBase needs to support many of the same features implemented in Csla.Core.BusinessBase. Table 3-8 lists all the functional areas included in the class. Of course, the implementation of each of these is quite different for a collection of objects than for a single object.

Table 3-8. *Functional Areas Implemented in BusinessListBase*

Functional Area	Description
Tracking object status	Keeps track of whether the collection is dirty and valid
Root and child behaviors	Implement behaviors so the collection can function as a root object or as a child of another object or collection
N-level undo	Integrates with the n-level undo functionality implemented in UndoableBase, and implements the IEditableCollection interface
Cloning	Implements the ICloneable interface

As with all base classes, this one is serializable and MustInherit. To support both data binding and collection behaviors, it inherits from System.ComponentModel.BindingList(Of T):

```
<Serializable()> _
Public MustInherit Class BusinessListBase( _
  Of T As BusinessListBase(Of T, C), C As Core.BusinessBase)
  Inherits System.ComponentModel.BindingList(Of C)

  Implements Core.IEditableCollection
  Implements ICloneable

End Class
```

Notice that in addition to inheriting from BindingList(Of T), this class implements Csla.Core.IEditableCollection and System.ICloneable.

Also take a look at the generic type parameters, T and C. The T type is constrained, just as with Csla.BusinessBase, ensuring that T will be the type of the business collection subclassing BusinessListBase. The C type represents the type of child object contained within the collection. It is constrained to be of type Csla.Core.BusinessBase, ensuring that the collection will only contain business objects. The end result is that a business collection is declared like this:

```
<Serializable()> _
Public Class LineItems
  Inherits Csla.BusinessListBase(Of LineItems, LineItem)

End Class
```

This indicates that the collection contains business objects defined by a `LineItem` class that inherits from `Csla.BusinessBase(Of LineItem)`.

With this basis established, let's move on and discuss each functional area in the class.

Tracking Object Status

The `IsDirty` and `IsValid` concepts are relatively easy to implement. A collection is "dirty" if it contains child objects that are dirty, added, or removed. A collection's "validity" can be determined by finding out if all its child objects are valid. An invalid child object means that the entire collection is in an invalid state. Here are the properties:

```
Public ReadOnly Property IsDirty() As Boolean
  Get
    ' any deletions make us dirty
    If DeletedList.Count > 0 Then Return True

    ' run through all the child objects
    ' and if any are dirty then the
    ' collection is dirty
    For Each Child As C In Me
      If Child.IsDirty Then Return True
    Next
    Return False
  End Get
End Property

Public Overridable ReadOnly Property IsValid() As Boolean
  Get
    ' run through all the child objects
    ' and if any are invalid then the
    ' collection is invalid
    For Each child As C In Me
      If Not child.IsValid Then Return False
    Next
    Return True
  End Get
End Property
```

Remember that the generic type `C` is the type of the child objects contained in the collection. As you can see, all the real work is done by the child objects, so the collection's state is really driven by the state of its children.

Root and Child Behaviors

The idea that a collection can be a root object or a child object is particularly important. It's fairly obvious that a collection can be a child object—an `Invoice` root object will have a `LineItems` collection that contains `LineItem` objects, so the `LineItems` collection is itself a child object. However, collection objects can also be root objects.

An application may have a root object called `Categories`, which contains a list of `Category` objects. It's quite possible that there's no root object to act as a parent for `Categories`—it may simply be an editable list of objects. To support this concept, `BusinessListBase`, like `BusinessBase` itself, must support these two modes of operation. In root mode, some operations are legal while others are not; in child mode, the reverse is true.

As in BusinessBase, the collection object needs to know whether it's a root or a child object:

```
<NotUndoable()> _
Private mIsChild As Boolean = False

Protected ReadOnly Property IsChild() As Boolean
  Get
    Return mIsChild
  End Get
End Property

Protected Sub MarkAsChild()
  mIsChild = True
End Sub
```

This functionality is the same in BusinessBase, and it allows the business developer to mark the object as a child object when it's first created. The IsChild property will be used in the rest of BusinessListBase to adjust the behavior of the object (such as exercising control over deletion) accordingly.

N-Level Undo

As with a regular business object, a collection needs to support n-level undo. The functionality in BusinessListBase must integrate with UndoableBase. This means that BusinessListBase must implement the Csla.Core.IEditableCollection interface, which inherits from Csla.Core. IUndoableObject.

Implementing the interface requires that the class implement CopyState(), UndoChanges(), and AcceptChanges() methods that store and restore the collection's state as appropriate. Because a collection can also be a root object, it needs Public methods named BeginEdit(), CancelEdit(), and ApplyEdit(), like BusinessBase. In either scenario, the process of taking a snapshot of the collection's state is really a matter of having all the child objects take a snapshot of their individual states.

The undo operation for a collection is where things start to get more complicated. Undoing all the child objects isn't too hard, since the collection can cascade the request to each child object. At the collection level, however, an undo means restoring any objects that were deleted and removing any objects that were added, so the collection's list of objects ends up the same as it was in the first place.

There's a fair amount of code in BusinessListBase just to deal with deletion of child objects in order to support n-level undo. As with the rest of the framework, if n-level undo isn't used, then no overhead is incurred by these features.

Edit Level Tracking

The hardest part of implementing n-level undo functionality is that not only can child objects be added or deleted, but they can also be "undeleted" or "unadded" in the case of an undo operation.

Csla.Core.BusinessBase and UndoableBase use the concept of an *edit level*. The edit level allows the object to keep track of how many BeginEdit() calls have been made to take a snapshot of its state without corresponding CancelEdit() or ApplyEdit() calls. More specifically, it tells the object how many states have been stacked up for undo operations.

BusinessListBase needs the same edit level tracking as in BusinessBase. However, a collection won't actually stack its states. Rather, it cascades the call to each of its child objects so that they can stack their *own* states. Because of this, the edit level can be tracked using a simple numeric counter. It merely counts how many unpaired BeginEdit() calls have been made:

```
' keep track of how many edit levels we have
Private mEditLevel As Integer
```

The implementations of CopyState(), UndoChanges(), and AcceptChanges() will alter this value accordingly.

Reacting to Insert, Remove, or Clear Operations

Collection base classes don't implement Add() or Remove() methods directly, since those are implemented by Collection(Of T), which is the base class for BindingList(Of T). However, they *do* need to perform certain operations any time that an insert or remove operation occurs. To accommodate this, BindingList(Of T) invokes certain Overridable methods when these events occur. These methods can be overridden to respond to the events.

Child objects also must have the ability to remove themselves from the collection. Remember the implementation of System.ComponentModel.IEditableObject in Clsa.Core.BusinessBase— that code included a parent reference to the collection object, and code to call a RemoveChild() method. This RemoveChild() method is part of the IEditableCollection interface implemented by BusinessListBase.

The following code handles the insert and remove operations, as well as the implementation of the RemoveChild() method:

```
Private Sub RemoveChild(ByVal child As Core.BusinessBase) _
  Implements Core.IEditableCollection.RemoveChild
  Remove(DirectCast(child, C))
End Sub

Protected Overrides Sub InsertItem(ByVal index As Integer, ByVal item As C)
  ' when an object is inserted we assume it is
  ' a new object and so the edit level when it was
  ' added must be set
  item.EditLevelAdded = mEditLevel
  item.SetParent(Me)
  MyBase.InsertItem(index, item)
End Sub

Protected Overrides Sub RemoveItem(ByVal index As Integer)
  ' when an object is 'removed' it is really
  ' being deleted, so do the deletion work
  DeleteChild(Me(index))
  MyBase.RemoveItem(index)
End Sub
```

The RemoveChild() method is called by a child object contained within the collection. This is called when a Windows Forms grid control requests that the child remove itself from the collection via the System.ComponentModel.IEditableObject interface.

Note In reality, this shouldn't be a common occurrence. Windows Forms 2.0 uses a new interface, ICancelAddNew, that is implemented by BindingList(Of T). This interface notifies the *collection* that the child should be removed, rather than notifying the child object itself. The code in the RemoveItem() method takes care of the ICancelAddNew case automatically, so this code is really here to support backward compatibility for anyone explicitly calling the IEditableObject interface on child objects.

The InsertItem() method is called when an item is being added to the collection. The EditLevelAdded property is changed when a new child object is added to the collection, thus telling the child object the edit level at which it's being added. Recall that this property was implemented in BusinessBase to merely record the value so that it can be checked during undo operations. This value will be used in the collection's UndoChanges() and AcceptChanges() methods later on.

Also notice that the child object's SetParent() method is called to make sure its parent reference is correct. This way, if needed, it can call the collection's RemoveChild() method to remove itself from the collection.

The RemoveItem() method is called when an item is being removed from the collection. To support the concept of undo, the object isn't *actually* removed, because it might need to be restored later. Rather, a DeleteChild() method is called, passing the object being removed as a parameter. You'll see the implementation of this method shortly. For now, it's enough to know that it keeps track of the object in case it must be restored later.

Deleted Object Collection

To ensure that the collection can properly "undelete" objects in case of an undo operation, it needs to keep a list of the objects that have been "removed." The first step in accomplishing this goal is to maintain an internal list of deleted objects.

Along with implementing this list, there needs to be a ContainsDeleted() method so that the business or UI logic can find out whether the collection contains a specific deleted object.

BindingList(Of T) already includes a Contains() method so that the UI code can ask the collection if it contains a specific item. Since a BusinessListBase collection is unusual in that it contains two lists of objects, it's appropriate to allow client code to ask whether an object is contained in the deleted list, as well as in the nondeleted list:

```
Private mDeletedList As List(Of C)

<EditorBrowsable(EditorBrowsableState.Advanced)> _
Protected ReadOnly Property DeletedList() As List(Of C)
  Get
    If mDeletedList Is Nothing Then
      mDeletedList = New List(Of C)
    End If
    Return mDeletedList
  End Get
End Property

<EditorBrowsable(EditorBrowsableState.Advanced)> _
Public Function ContainsDeleted(ByVal item As C) As Boolean
  Return DeletedList.Contains(item)
End Function
```

Notice that the list of deleted objects is kept as a List(Of C)—a strongly typed collection of child objects. That list is then exposed through a Protected property so that it is available to subclasses. Subclasses have access to the nondeleted items in the collection, so this just follows the same scoping model. The list object is created on demand to minimize overhead in the case that no items are ever removed from the collection.

Deleting and Undeleting Child Objects

Given the list for storing deleted child objects, it is now possible to implement the methods to delete and undelete objects as needed.

Deleting a child object is really a matter of marking the object as deleted and moving it from the active list of child objects to DeletedList. Undeleting occurs when a child object has restored its state so that it's no longer marked as deleted. In that case, the child object must be moved from DeletedList back to the list of active objects in the collection.

The permutations here are vast. The ways in which combinations of calls to BeginEdit(), Add(), Remove(), CancelEdit(), and ApplyEdit() can be called are probably infinite. Let's look at some relatively common scenarios, though, to get a good understanding of what happens as child objects are deleted and undeleted.

First, consider a case in which the collection has been loaded with data from a database, and the database included one child object: A. Then, the UI called BeginEdit() on the collection and added a new object to the collection: B. Figure 3-4 shows what happens if those two objects are removed and then CancelEdit() is called on the collection object.

■**Tip** In Figure 3-4, EL is the mEditLevel value in the collection, ELA is the mEditLevelAdded value in each child object, and DEL is the IsDeleted value in each child object.

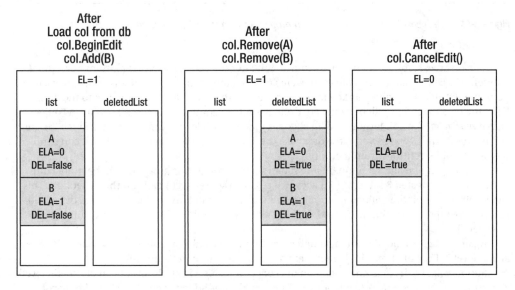

Figure 3-4. *Edit process in which objects are removed and CancelEdit() is called*

After both objects have been removed from the collection, they're marked for deletion and moved to the DeletedList collection. This way, they *appear* to be gone from the collection, but the collection still has access to them if needed.

After the CancelEdit() call, the collection's edit level goes back to 0. Since child A came from the database, it was "added" at edit level 0, so it sticks around. Child B, on the other hand, was added at edit level 1, so it goes away. Also, child A has its state reset as part of the CancelEdit() call (remember that CancelEdit() causes a cascade effect, so each child object restores its snapshot values). The result is that because of the undo operation, child A is no longer marked for deletion.

Another common scenario follows the same process, but with a call to ApplyEdit() at the end, as shown in Figure 3-5.

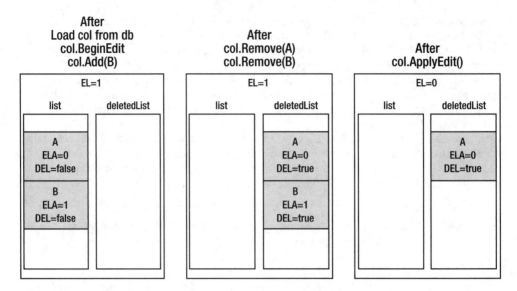

Figure 3-5. *Edit process in which objects are removed and ApplyEdit() is called*

The first two steps are identical, of course, but after the call to ApplyEdit(), things are quite different. Since changes to the collection were accepted rather than rejected, the changes became permanent. Child A remains marked for deletion, and if the collection is saved back to the database, the data for child A will be removed. Child B is totally gone at this point. It was a new object added *and deleted* at edit level 1, and all changes made at edit level 1 were accepted. Since the collection knows that B was never in the database (because it was *added* at edit level 1), it can simply discard the object entirely from memory.

Let's look at one last scenario. Just to illustrate how rough this gets, this will be more complex. It involves nested BeginEdit(), CancelEdit(), and ApplyEdit() calls on the collection. This can easily happen if the collection contains child or grandchild objects, and they are displayed in a Windows Forms UI that uses modal dialog windows to edit each level (parent, child, grandchild, etc.).

Again, child A is loaded from the database and child B is added at edit level 1. Finally, C is added at edit level 2. Then all three child objects are removed, as shown in Figure 3-6.

Suppose ApplyEdit() is now called on the collection. This will apply all edits made at edit level 2, putting the collection back to edit level 1. Since child C was added at edit level 2, it simply goes away, but child B sticks around because it was added at edit level 1, which is illustrated in Figure 3-7.

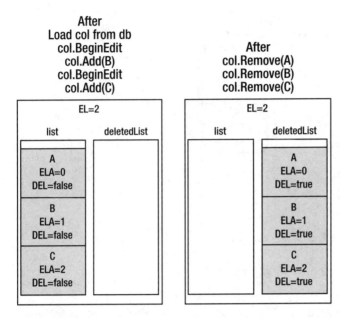

Figure 3-6. *A more complex example with nested edit method calls*

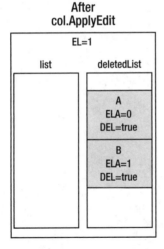

Figure 3-7. *The result after calling ApplyEdit()*

Both objects remain marked for deletion because the changes made at edit level 2 were *applied*. Were CancelEdit() called now, the collection would return to the same state as when the first BeginEdit() was called, meaning that only child A (not marked for deletion) would be left.

Alternatively, a call to ApplyEdit() would commit all changes made at edit level 1: child A would continue to be marked for deletion, and child B would be totally discarded since it was added and deleted at edit level 1. Both of these possible outcomes are illustrated in Figure 3-8.

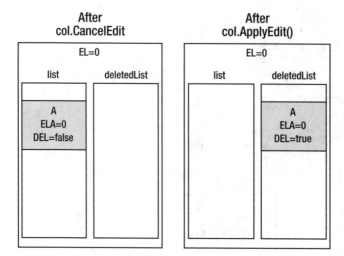

Figure 3-8. *Result after calling either CancelEdit() or ApplyEdit()*

Having gone through all that, let's take a look at the code that will implement these behaviors. The DeleteChild() and UnDeleteChild() methods deal with marking the child objects as deleted and moving them between the active items in the collection and the DeletedList object:

```
Private Sub DeleteChild(ByVal child As C)
  ' mark the object as deleted
  child.DeleteChild()
  ' and add it to the deleted collection for storage
  DeletedList.Add(child)
End Sub

Private Sub UnDeleteChild(ByVal child As C)
  ' we are inserting an _existing_ object so
  ' we need to preserve the object's editleveladded value
  ' because it will be changed by the normal add process
  Dim SaveLevel As Integer = child.EditLevelAdded
  Add(child)
  child.EditLevelAdded = SaveLevel

  ' since the object is no longer deleted, remove it from
  ' the deleted collection
  DeletedList.Remove(child)
End Sub
```

On the surface, this doesn't seem too complicated—but look at the code that deals with the child's EditLevelAdded property in the UnDeleteChild() method. Recall the InsertItem() method implemented earlier. That method assumes that any child being added to the collection is a new object, and therefore sets its edit level value to the collection's current value. However, the InsertItem() method will be run when this *preexisting* object is reinserted into the collection, altering *its* edit level. This would leave the child object with an incorrect edit level value.

The problem is that in this case, the child object isn't a new object; it is a preexisting object that is just being restored to the collection. To solve this, the object's edit level value is stored in a temporary field, the child object is re-added to the collection, and then the child object's edit level value is reset to the original value, effectively leaving it unchanged.

CopyState

Everything has so far laid the groundwork for the n-level undo functionality. All the pieces now exist to make it possible to implement the CopyState(), UndoChanges(), and AcceptChanges() methods, and then the BeginEdit(), CancelEdit(), and ApplyEdit() methods.

The CopyState() method needs to take a snapshot of the collection's current state. It is invoked when the BeginEdit() method is called on the root object (either the collection itself, or the collection's parent object). At that time, the root object takes a snapshot of its own state and calls CopyState() on any child objects or collections so they can take snapshots of their states as well.

```
Private Sub CopyState() Implements Core.IEditableCollection.CopyState
  Dim Child As C

  ' we are going a level deeper in editing
  mEditLevel += 1

  ' cascade the call to all child objects
  For Each Child In Me
    Child.CopyState()
  Next

  ' cascade the call to all deleted child objects
  For Each Child In DeletedList
    Child.CopyState()
  Next
End Sub
```

As CopyState() takes a snapshot of the collection's state, it increases the edit level by one. Remember that UndoableBase relied on the Stack object to track the edit level, but this code just uses a simple numeric counter. Remember, a collection has no state of its own, so there's nothing to add to a stack of states. Instead, a collection is only responsible for ensuring that all the objects it *contains* take snapshots of their states. All it needs to do is keep track of how many times CopyState() has been called, so the collection can properly implement the adding and removing of child objects, as described earlier.

Notice that the CopyState() call is also cascaded to the objects in DeletedList. This is important because those objects might, at some point, get restored as active objects in the collection. Even though they're not active at the moment (because they're marked for deletion), they need to be treated the same as regular nondeleted objects.

Overall, this process is *fairly* straightforward: the CopyState() call is just cascaded down to the child objects. The same can't be said for UndoChanges() or AcceptChanges().

UndoChanges

The UndoChanges() method is more complex than the CopyState() method. It too cascades the call down to the child objects, deleted or not, but it also needs to find any objects that were added since the latest snapshot. Those objects must be removed from the collection and discarded, since an undo operation means that it must be as though they were never added. Furthermore, it needs to find any objects that were deleted since the latest snapshot. Those objects must be re-added to the collection.

Here's the complete method:

```
Private Sub UndoChanges() Implements Core.IEditableCollection.UndoChanges
  Dim child As C
  Dim index As Integer

  ' we are coming up one edit level
  mEditLevel -= 1
  If mEditLevel < 0 Then mEditLevel = 0

  ' Cancel edit on all current items
  For index = Count - 1 To 0 Step -1
    child = Me(index)
    child.UndoChanges()
    ' if item is below its point of addition, remove
    If child.EditLevelAdded > mEditLevel Then
      RemoveAt(index)
    End If
  Next

  ' cancel edit on all deleted items
  For index = DeletedList.Count - 1 To 0 Step -1
    child = DeletedList.Item(index)
    child.UndoChanges()
    If child.EditLevelAdded > mEditLevel Then
      ' if item is below its point of addition, remove
      DeletedList.RemoveAt(index)
    Else
      ' if item is no longer deleted move back to main list
      If Not child.IsDeleted Then UnDeleteChild(child)
    End If
  Next
End Sub
```

First of all, mEditLevel is decremented to indicate that one call to CopyState() has been countered.

Notice that the loops going through the collection itself and the DeletedList collections go from bottom to top, using a numeric index value. This is important because it allows safe removal of items from each collection. Neither a For...Each loop or a forward-moving numeric index would allow removal of items from the collections without causing a runtime error.

UndoChanges() is called on all child objects in the collection so that they can restore their individual states. After a child object's state has been restored, the child object's edit level is checked to see when it was added to the collection. If the collection's new edit level is less than the edit level when the child object was added, then it is a new child object that now must be discarded.

```
  ' if item is below its point of addition, remove
  If child.EditLevelAdded > mEditLevel Then
    RemoveAt(index)
  End If
```

The same process occurs for the objects in DeletedList—again, UndoChanges() is called on each child object. Then there's a check to see if the child object was a newly added object that can now be discarded:

```
  If child.EditLevelAdded > mEditLevel Then
    ' if item is below its point of addition, remove
    DeletedList.RemoveAt(index)
```

A bit more work is required when dealing with the deleted child objects. It is possible that the undo operation needs to undelete an object. Remember that the IsDeleted flag is automatically maintained by UndoChanges(), so it is possible that the child object is no longer marked for deletion. In such a case, the object must be moved back into the active list:

```
Else
    ' if item is no longer deleted move back to main list
    If Not child.IsDeleted Then UnDeleteChild(child)
End If
```

At the end of the process, the collection object and all its child objects will be in the state they were when CopyState() was last called. Any changes, additions, or deletions will have been undone.

AcceptChanges

The AcceptChanges() method isn't nearly as complicated as UndoChanges(). It also decrements the mEditLevel field to counter one call to CopyState(). The method then cascades the AcceptChanges() call to each child object so that the child object can accept its own changes. The only complex bit of code is that the "edit level added" value of each child must also be altered:

```
Private Sub AcceptChanges() _
    Implements Core.IEditableCollection.AcceptChanges
    Dim child As C
    Dim index As Integer

    ' we are coming up one edit level
    mEditLevel -= 1
    If mEditLevel < 0 Then mEditLevel = 0

    ' cascade the call to all child objects
    For Each child In Me
        child.AcceptChanges()
        ' if item is below its point of addition, lower point of addition
        If child.EditLevelAdded > mEditLevel Then child.EditLevelAdded = mEditLevel
    Next

    ' cascade the call to all deleted child objects
    'For Each Child In deletedList
    For index = DeletedList.Count - 1 To 0 Step -1
        child = DeletedList.Item(index)
        child.AcceptChanges()
        ' if item is below its point of addition, remove
        If child.EditLevelAdded > mEditLevel Then
            DeletedList.RemoveAt(index)
        End If
    Next
End Sub
```

While looping through the collection and DeleteList, the code makes sure that no child object maintains an EditLevelAdded value that's higher than the collection's new edit level.

Think back to the LineItem example, and suppose the collection were at edit level 1 and the changes were *accepted*. In that case, the newly added LineItem object is to be kept—it's valid. Because of this, its EditLevelAdded property needs to be the same as the collection object's, so it needs to be set to 0 as well.

This is important, because there's nothing to stop the user from starting a *new* edit session and raising the collection's edit level to 1 again. If the user *then* cancels the operation, the collection shouldn't remove the previous LineItem object accidentally. It was already accepted once, and it should *stay* accepted.

This method won't be removing any items from the collection as changes are accepted, so the simpler `For...Each` looping structure can be used rather than the bottom-to-top numeric looping structure needed in the `UndoChanges()` method.

When looping through the `DeletedList` collection, however, the bottom-to-top approach is still required. This is because `DeletedList` may contain child items that were newly added to the collection and then were marked for deletion. Since they are *new* objects, they have no corresponding data in the database, and so they can simply be dropped from the collection in memory. In such a case, those child objects will be removed from the list based on their edit level value.

This completes all the functionality needed to support n-level undo, allowing `BusinessListBase` to integrate with the code in the `UndoableBase` class.

BeginEdit, CancelEdit, and ApplyEdit

With the n-level undo methods complete, it is possible to implement the methods that the UI will need in order to control the edit process on a collection. Remember, though, that this control is only valid if the collection is a root object. If it's a child object, then its edit process should be controlled by its parent object. This requires a check to ensure that the object isn't a child before allowing these methods to operate:

```
Public Sub BeginEdit()
  If Me.IsChild Then
    Throw New _
      NotSupportedException(My.Resources.NoBeginEditChildException)
  End If

  CopyState()
End Sub

Public Sub CancelEdit()
  If Me.IsChild Then
    Throw New _
      NotSupportedException(My.Resources.NoCancelEditChildException)
  End If

  UndoChanges()

End Sub

Public Sub ApplyEdit()
  If Me.IsChild Then
    Throw New _
      NotSupportedException(My.Resources.NoApplyEditChildException)
  End If

  AcceptChanges()
End Sub
```

All three methods are very straightforward and allow developers to create a UI that starts editing a collection with `BeginEdit()`, lets the user interact with the collection, and then either cancels or accepts the changes with `CancelEdit()` or `ApplyEdit()`, respectively.

System.ICloneable

The `BusinessListBase` class implements the `System.ICloneable` interface. This interface defines a `Clone()` method that can be called to create a clone, or copy, of an object. The `Csla.Core.ObjectCloner` class implements a general cloning solution that works against any serializable object, making it very easy to implement a Clone() method. Additionally, BusinessListBase is a generic class, so it can implement a strongly typed Clone() method like Csla.BusinessBase.

As in Csla.Core.BusinessBase, the clone operation is implemented through an Overridable method named GetClone(), allowing the business developer to override the default cloning behavior if desired:

```
Private Function ICloneable_Clone() As Object Implements ICloneable.Clone
  Return GetClone()
End Function

<EditorBrowsable(EditorBrowsableState.Advanced)> _
Protected Overridable Function GetClone() As Object
  Return ObjectCloner.Clone(Me)
End Function

Public Overloads Function Clone() As T
  Return DirectCast(GetClone(), T)
End Function
```

The ICloneable.Clone() and strongly typed Clone() methods delegate to GetClone() to do their work. Other than the data access functionality that will be added in Chapter 4, this concludes the functionality for the BusinessListBase class.

ReadOnlyBase Class

With BusinessBase and BusinessListBase finished (at least for the time being), a business developer has the tools needed to build editable objects and collections. However, most applications also include a number of read-only objects and collections. An application might have a read-only object that contains system configuration data, or a read-only collection of ProductType objects that are used just for lookup purposes.

■**Tip** Chapter 5 will include a NameValueListBase class designed specifically to handle name/value lookup data.

The ReadOnlyBase class will provide a base on which business developers can build a read-only object. The chapter will conclude with the ReadOnlyListBase, which supports read-only *collections* of data.

By definition, a read-only object is quite simple: it's just a container for data, possibly with authorization or formatting logic to control how that data is accessed. It doesn't support editing of the data, so there's no need for n-level undo, change events, or much of the other complexity built into UndoableBase and BusinessBase. In fact, other than data access logic, the base class can only implement the CanReadProperty() authorization methods and the ICloneable interface.

Like all base classes, this one is serializable and MustInherit. It will also implement Csla.Core.IBusinessObject to provide some level of polymorphic behavior even though this is a generic class:

```
<Serializable()> _
Public MustInherit Class ReadOnlyBase(Of T As ReadOnlyBase(Of T))

  Implements ICloneable
  Implements Core.IReadOnlyObject

End Class
```

Like `Csla.BusinessBase`, the generic type `T` is constrained to be the type of business object being created, so a business class is declared like this:

```
<Serializable()> _
Public Class DefaultCustomerData
  Inherits Csla.ReadOnlyBase(Of DefaultCustomerData)

End Class
```

Like all good objects, it should override the core `System.Object` methods just like `BusinessBase(Of T)`. To do this, the class defines a `GetIdValue()` method and uses its result to implement `Equals()`, `GetHashCode()`, and `ToString()` in exactly the same manner as `BusinessBase(Of T)` did earlier.

Presumably, any business object based on this class would consist entirely of read-only properties or methods that just return values. Chapter 4 will add data access functionality to this class, supporting only the reading of data from the database, with no update possible.

Let's walk through the implementation of authorization rules and the `ICloneable` interface.

Authorization Rules

The authorization rules behavior in `ReadOnlyBase` is virtually identical to that in `BusinessBase`, with the exception that only read operations need to be checked. Since the intent is to create a read-only object, there's no reason to support checking authorization rules for writing to a property.

An `AuthorizationRules` object will be used to manage the roles for each property:

```
<NotUndoable()> _
Private mAuthorizationRules As New Security.AuthorizationRules

Protected ReadOnly Property AuthorizationRules() _
  As Security.AuthorizationRules
  Get
    Return mAuthorizationRules
  End Get
End Property
```

Then the same `CanReadProperty()` methods are implemented as in `BusinessBase`. I won't repeat them here, as they are literally the exact same code: three different overloads of the method to support different scenarios. And the primary implementation is an `Overridable` method, allowing a business developer to alter the authorization behavior if needed.

System.ICloneable

The `ICloneable` interface is implemented as well. The `Clone()` method for the interface itself is accessible only via the interface. There's also a `Public` strongly typed method that returns an object of type `T`. Both of these methods delegate to an `Overridable` method named `GetClone()`, which in turn delegates to `Csla.Core.ObjectCloner` to do the actual work.

Again, this is the same code as in `BusinessBase` and `BusinessListBase`, so I won't repeat it here. This completes the `ReadOnlyBase` class. The chapter will wrap up by covering `ReadOnlyListBase`.

ReadOnlyListBase Class

Like the `ReadOnlyBase` class, `ReadOnlyListBase` is quite simple to create. It is designed to make it easy for a business developer to create a business collection that doesn't allow items to be added or removed. Presumably, it will be used to contain read-only child objects, but any type of child object is allowed.

The `Csla.Core.ReadOnlyBindingList` class implemented earlier in the chapter already handles all the details, except for implementing `ICloneable` and data access. The data access code will be added in Chapter 4, so only the `ICloneable` functionality will be added here.

The `ReadOnlyListBase` class is defined like this:

```
<Serializable()> _
Public MustInherit Class ReadOnlyListBase( _
  Of T As ReadOnlyListBase(Of T, C), C)
  Inherits Core.ReadOnlyBindingList(Of C)

  Implements Csla.Core.IReadOnlyCollection
  Implements ICloneable

End Class
```

Like `BusinessListBase`, it accepts two generic type parameters. Type `T` is constrained to be a subclass of this base class and refers to the type of the collection being created. Type `C` is the type of the child object to be contained within the collection, and it can be any type. Again, it would make the most sense for the child type to be some form of read-only object, but that's not required by the collection class. A business collection would be declared like this:

```
<Serializable()> _
Public Class CustomerList
  Inherits  Csla.ReadOnlyListBase(Of CustomerList, CustomerInfo)

End Class
```

This indicates that the collection will be containing child objects of type `CustomerInfo`.

System.ICloneable

The class implements `System.ICloneable` like all base classes in CSLA .NET. The implementation is identical to that in `BusinessListBase`, so I won't duplicate it here. The clone operation is available via `ICloneable` and through a `Public` strongly typed `Clone()` method.

Other than the data access code that will be implemented in Chapter 4, this completes the read-only collection base class and this chapter.

Conclusion

This chapter has applied the concepts from Chapter 1 to implement about a third of the framework discussed in Chapter 2. At this point, the framework provides enough functionality for a business developer to build object-oriented systems that support useful concepts such as the following:

- N-level undo
- Validation rules
- Authorization rules
- Data binding
- Change tracking
- Strongly typed collections
- Editable and read-only objects
- Root and child objects

Chapters 4 and 5 will finish the business framework. Chapter 4 will focus on implementing the data portal concept and supporting object persistence. Then Chapter 5 will wrap up by implementing a variety of functionality to support a business developer in building an application using mobile objects.

From Chapter 6 on, the focus will be on designing and building a simple business application that illustrates how the classes in the framework can be used to build applications based on mobile business objects.

CHAPTER 4

■■■

Data Access and Security

Chapter 3 combined the concepts from Chapter 1 with the framework design from Chapter 2 to implement much of the CSLA .NET framework. The focus in Chapter 3 was on creating editable and read-only business objects and collections to support the UI developer. This chapter will continue the process by adding data access to the framework. This will entail making some minor changes to some of the base classes created in Chapter 4. Chapter 1 introduced the concept of mobile objects, including the idea that in an ideal world, business logic would be available both on the client work-station (or web server) and on the application server. The implementation of data access in this chapter is specifically designed to leverage the concept of mobile objects by enabling objects to move between client and server. When on the client, all the data binding and UI support from Chapter 3 is available to a UI developer; and when on the server, the objects will be able to persist themselves to the database (or other data store).

Chapter 2 discussed the idea of a *data portal*. The data portal combines the channel adapter and message router design patterns to provide a simple, clearly defined point of entry to the server for all data access operations. In fact, the data portal entirely hides whether a server is involved, allowing an application to switch between 2-tier and 3-tier physical deployments without changing any code.

The UI developer is entirely unaware of the use of a data portal. Instead, the UI developer will interact *only* with the business objects created by the business developer.

The business developer will make use of a `Csla.DataPortal` class to create, retrieve, update, and delete all business object data. This `DataPortal` class is the single entry point to the entire data portal infrastructure, which enables mobile objects and provides access to server-side resources such as distributed transaction support. The key features enabled by the data portal infrastructure include:

- Enabling mobile objects
- Hiding the network transport (channel adapter)
- Exposing a single point of entry to the server (message router)
- Exposing server-side resources (database engine, distributed transactions, etc.)
- Unifying context (passing context data to/from client and server)
- Using Windows integrated (AD) security
- Using CSLA .NET custom authentication (including impersonation)

Meeting all those needs means that the data portal is a very complex entity. While to a business developer, it appears to consist only of the simple `Csla.DataPortal` class, there's actually a lot going on behind that class.

You should also know that the *foundation* for custom authentication in the data portal will be created in this chapter, but the details of creating a custom .NET principal object for the data portal will be discussed in Chapter 5 and then in the sample application in Chapter 8.

Figure 4-1 shows the primary classes created in this chapter.

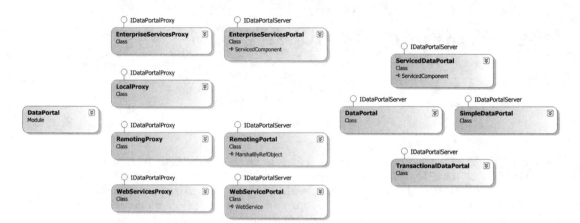

Figure 4-1. *Types required to implement data access, mobile objects, and security*

This chapter also includes many cases that support those shown in Figure 4-1. While the concept behind these classes was covered in Chapter 2, this chapter will reprise those discussions, providing insight into the implementation.

Data Portal Design

One of the primary goals of object-oriented programming is to encapsulate all the functionality (data and implementation) for a domain entity into a single class. This means, for instance, that all the data and implementation logic for the concept of a customer should be in a Customer class.

In many cases, the business logic in an object directly supports a rich, interactive user experience. This is especially true for Windows Forms applications, in which the business object implements validation and calculation logic that should be run as the user enters values into each field on a form. To achieve this, the objects should be running on the client workstation or web server to be as close to the user as possible.

At the same time, most applications have back-end processing that is not interactive. In an n-tier deployment, this non-interactive business logic should run on an application server. Yet good object-oriented design dictates that all business logic should be encapsulated within objects rather than spread across the application. This can be challenging when an object needs to both interact with the user *and* perform back-end processing. Effectively, the object needs to be on the client sometimes and on the application server other times.

The idea of mobile objects solves this problem by allowing an object to physically move from one machine to another. This means it really is possible to have an object run on the client to interact with the user, then move to the application server to do back-end work like interacting with the database.

A key goal of the data portal is to enable the concept of mobile objects. In the end, not only will objects be able to go to the application server to persist their data to a database, but they will also be able to handle any other non-interactive back-end business behaviors that should run on the application server.

Channel Adapter and Message Router Patterns

The data portal combines two common design patterns: channel adapter and message router.

The channel adapter pattern provides a great deal of flexibility for n-tier applications by allowing the application to switch between 2-tier and 3-tier models, as well as switching between various network protocols.

The message router pattern helps to decouple the client and server by providing a clearly defined, single point of entry for all server interaction. Each call to the server is routed to an appropriate server-side object.

Channel Adapter

Chapter 1 discussed the costs and benefits of physical n-tier deployments. Ideally, an application will use as few physical tiers as possible. At the same time, it is good to have the flexibility to switch from a 2-tier to a 3-tier model, if needed, to meet future scalability or security requirements.

Switching to a 3-tier model means that there's now a network connection between the client (or web server) and the application server. Today, .NET directly supports three technologies for such communication, and Windows Communication Foundation (WCF) will add another in the near future. To avoid being locked into a single network communication technology, the data portal will apply the channel adapter design pattern.

The channel adapter pattern allows the specific network technology to be changed through configuration rather than through code. A side effect of the implementation shown in this chapter is that *no network* is also an option. Thus, the data portal provides support for 2-tier or 3-tier deployment. In the 3-tier case, it supports various network technologies, all of which are configurable without changing any code.

Figure 4-2 illustrates the flow of a client call to the `Csla.DataPortal` class as it goes through all the optional channels to the server-side `Csla.Server.DataPortal` object.

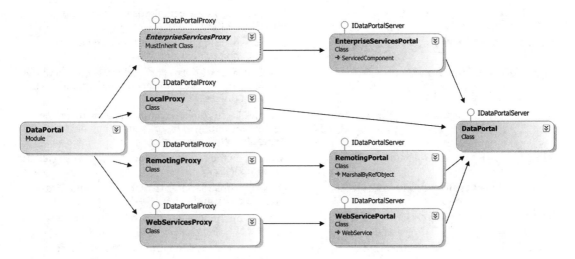

Figure 4-2. *Flow of a client call through the data portal*

Switching from one channel to another is done by changing a configuration file, not by changing code. Notice that the `LocalProxy` channel communicates directly with the `Csla.Server.DataPortal` object on the right. This is because it entirely bypasses the network, interacting with the object in memory on the client. All the other channel proxies use network communication to interact with the server-side object.

Tip The data portal will also allow you to create your own proxy/host combination so you can support network channels other than the three implemented in this chapter.

Table 4-1 lists the types required to implement the channel adapter portion of the data portal.

Table 4-1. *Types Required for the Channel Adapter*

Type	Description
Csla.MethodCaller	Utility class that encapsulates the use of reflection to find method information and invoke methods
Csla.Server.CallMethodException	Exception thrown by the data portal when an exception occurs while calling a data access method
Csla.RunLocalAttribute	Attribute applied to a business object's data access methods to force the data portal to *always* run that method on the client, bypassing the configuration settings
Csla.DataPortalEventArgs	EventArgs subclass passed as a parameter for events raised by Csla.DataPortal
Csla.DataPortal	Primary entry point to the data portal infrastructure; used by business developers
Csla.Server.DataPortal	Portal to the message router functionality on the server; acts as a single point of entry for all server communication
Csla.Server.IDataPortalServer	Interface defining the methods required for data portal host objects
Csla.DataPortalClient.IDataPortalProxy	Interface defining the methods required for client-side data portal proxy objects
Csla.DataPortalClient.LocalProxy	Loads Csla.Server.DataPortal directly into memory on the client and runs all "server-side" operations in the client process
Csla.DataPortalClient.RemotingProxy	Uses .NET Remoting to communicate with a remoting server running in IIS or within a custom host (typically a Windows service)
Csla.Server.Hosts.RemotingPortal	Exposed on the server by IIS or a custom host; called by RemotingProxy
Csla.DataPortalClient.EnterpriseServicesProxy	Uses Enterprise Services (DCOM) to communicate with a server running in COM+
Csla.Server.Hosts.EnterpriseServicesPortal	Exposed on the server by Enterprise Services; called by EnterpriseServicesProxy
Csla.DataPortalClient.WebServicesProxy	Uses Web Services to communicate with a service hosted in IIS
Csla.Server.Hosts.WebServicePortal	Exposed on the server as a web service by IIS; called by WebServicesProxy

The point of the channel adapter is to allow a client to call Csla.DataPortal without your having to worry about how that call will be relayed to the Csla.Server.DataPortal object. Once the call makes it to the server-side DataPortal object, the message router pattern becomes important.

Message Router

One important lesson to be learned from the days of COM and MTS/COM+ is that it isn't wise to expose large numbers of classes and methods from a server. When a server exposes dozens or even hundreds of objects, the client must be aware of all of them in order to function.

Having the client aware of every server-side object results in tight coupling and fragility. A change to the server typically changes the server's public API, breaking all clients—often even those that aren't even using the object that was changed.

One way to avoid this fragility is to add a layer of abstraction. Specifically, you can implement the server to have a single point of entry that exposes a limited number of methods. This keeps the server's API very clear and concise, minimizing the need for a server API change. The data portal will expose just the five methods listed in Table 4-2.

Table 4-2. *Methods Exposed by the Data Portal Server*

Method	Purpose
Create	Creates a new object, loading it with default values from the database
Fetch	Retrieves an existing object, first loading it with data from the database
Update	Inserts, updates, or deletes data in the database corresponding to an existing object
Delete	Deletes data in the database corresponding to an existing object
Execute	Executes a command object (subclass of CommandBase as described in Chapter 5) on the server

Of course, the next question is how, with a single point of entry, do your clients get at the dozens or hundreds of objects on the server? It isn't like they aren't needed! This is the purpose of the message router.

The single point of entry to the server routes all client calls to the appropriate server-side object. If you think of each client call as a message, then this component routes messages to your server-side objects. In CSLA .NET, the message router is Csla.Server.DataPortal. Notice that it is also the endpoint for the channel adapter pattern discussed earlier; the data portal knits the two patterns together into a useful whole.

For Csla.Server.DataPortal to do its work, all server-side objects must conform to a standard design so the message router knows how to invoke them. Remember, the message router merely routes messages to objects—it is the object that actually does useful work in response to the message.

Figure 4-3 illustrates the flow of a call through the message router implementation.

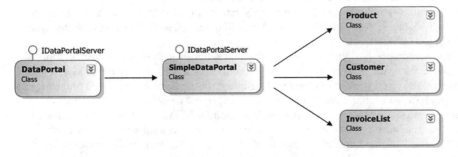

Figure 4-3. *Flow of a client call through the message router*

The DataPortal class (on the left of Figure 4-3) represents the Csla.Server.DataPortal—which was the rightmost entity in Figure 4-2. It relies on a SimpleDataPortal object to do the actual message routing, a fact that will become important shortly for support of distributed transactions.

The SimpleDataPortal object routes each client call (message) to the actual business object that can handle the message. These are the same business classes and objects that make up the application's business logic layer.

In other words, the *same exact objects* used by the UI on the client are also called by the data portal on the server. This allows the objects to run on the client to interact with the user, and on the server to do back-end processing as needed.

Table 4-3 lists the classes needed, in addition to Csla.Server.DataPortal, to implement the message router behavior.

Table 4-3. *Types Required for the Message Router*

Type	Description
Csla.Server.SimpleDataPortal	Entry point to the server, implementing the message router behavior and routing client calls to the appropriate business object on the server
Csla.CriteriaBase	Optional base class for use when building criteria objects; criteria objects contain the criteria or key data needed to create, retrieve, or delete an object's data
Csla.MethodCaller	Utility class that encapsulates the use of reflection to find method information and to invoke methods

Notice that neither the channel adapter nor message router explicitly deal with moving objects between the client and server. This is because the .NET runtime typically handles object movement automatically as long as the objects are marked as <Serializable()>. The exception to this is when using Web Services. In that case, as you'll see later in the chapter, manual serialization and deserialization of the objects is required.

The Csla.CriteriaBase class listed in Table 4-3 is optionally used to define the message sent from a client to the server for Create, Fetch, and Delete data portal operations. It exists primarily to support business objects created using code-generation tools. During the implementation of SimpleDataPortal later in the chapter, you'll see how this base class is used.

Distributed Transaction Support

There are several different technologies that support database transactions, including transactions in the database itself, ADO.NET, Enterprise Services, and System.Transactions. When updating a single database (even multiple tables), any of them will work fine, and your decision will often be based on which is fastest or easiest to implement.

If your application needs to update multiple databases, however, the options are a bit more restrictive. Transactions that protect updates across multiple databases are referred to as *distributed transactions*. In SQL Server, you can implement distributed transactions within stored procedures. Outside the database, you can use Enterprise Services or System.Transactions.

Distributed transaction technologies use the Microsoft Distributed Transaction Coordinator (DTC) to manage the transaction across multiple databases. There is a substantial performance cost to enlisting the DTC in a transaction. Your application, the DTC, and the database engine(s) all need to interact throughout the transactional process to ensure that a consistent commit or rollback occurs, and this interaction takes time.

Historically, you had to pick one transactional approach for your application. This often meant using distributed transactions even when they weren't required—and paying that performance cost.

The new System.Transactions namespace offers a compromise through the TransactionScope object. It starts out using nondistributed transactions (like those used in ADO.NET), and thus offers high performance for most applications. However, as soon as your code uses a *second* database within a transaction, TransactionScope automatically enlists the DTC to protect the transaction. This means you get the benefits of distributed transactions when you need them, but you don't pay the price for them when they aren't needed.

The data portal allows the developer to specify which transactional technology to use for each of a business object's data access methods. To do this, the message router portion of the data portal uses some extra classes, as shown in Figure 4-4. Notice that this is basically the same diagram as Figure 4-3, but with extra types to support the transactional technologies.

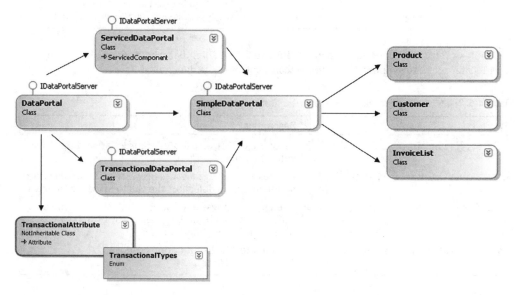

Figure 4-4. *Types supporting transactional technologies in the data portal*

The Csla.Server.DataPortal object uses the TransactionalAttribute to determine what type of transactional approach should be used for each call by the client. Ultimately, all calls end up being handled by SimpleDataPortal, which routes the call to an appropriate business object. The real question is whether SimpleDataPortal (and thus the business object) run within a preexisting transactional context or not.

The TransactionalAttribute is applied to the data access methods on the business object itself. Csla.Server.DataPortal looks at the business object's data access method that will ultimately be invoked by SimpleDataPortal, and finds the value of the TransactionalAttribute (if any). Table 4-4 lists the options for this attribute.

Table 4-4. *Transactional Options Supported by the Data Portal*

Attribute	Result
None	The business object does not run within a preexisting transactional context and so must implement its own transactions using stored procedures or ADO.NET.
`<Transactional(TransactionalTypes.Manual)>`	Same as "none" in the previous entry.
`<Transactional(TransactionalTypes.EnterpriseServices)>`	The business object runs within a COM+ distributed transactional context.
`<Transactional(TransactionalTypes.TransactionScope)>`	The business object runs within a `System.Transactions.TransactionalScope` transaction.

Table 4-5 lists the types required, in addition to `Csla.Server.DataPortal` and `Csla.Server.SimpleDataPortal`, to support transactional technologies in the data portal.

Table 4-5. *Types Required to Implement Transactional Support*

Type	Description
`Csla.Server.ServicedDataPortal`	Creates a COM+ distributed transaction and then delegates the call to `SimpleDataPortal`
`Csla.Server.TransactionalDataPortal`	Creates a `System.Transactions.TransactionScope` transaction and then delegates the call to `SimpleDataPortal`
`Csla.TransactionalAttribute`	Used by a business developer to indicate the type of transactional technology expected by each business object data access method
`Csla.TransactionalTypes`	Enumerates the list of options used by `TransactionalAttribute`

By extending the message router concept to add transactional support, the data portal makes it very easy for a business developer to leverage either Enterprise Services or `System.Transactions` as needed. At the same time, the complexity of both technologies is reduced by abstracting them within the data portal.

Context and Location Transparency

A key goal for the data portal is to provide a consistent environment for the business objects. At a minimum, this means that both client and server should run under the same user identity (impersonation) and the same culture (localization). The business developer should be able to pass other arbitrary information between client and server as well.

In addition to context information, exception data from the server should flow back to the client with full fidelity. This is important for debugging and at runtime. The UI often needs to know the specifics about any server-side exceptions in order to properly notify the user about what happened and then to take appropriate steps.

Figure 4-5 shows the objects used to flow data from the client to the server and back again to the client.

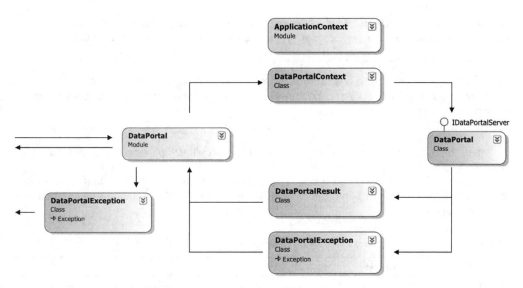

Figure 4-5. *Context and exception data flow to and from the server*

The arrows pointing off the left side of the diagram indicate communication with the calling code—typically the business object's factory methods. A business object calls Csla.DataPortal to invoke one of the data portal operations. Csla.DataPortal calls Csla.Server.DataPortal (using the channel adapter classes not shown here), passing a DataPortalContext object along with the actual client request.

The DataPortalContext object contains several types of context data, as listed in Table 4-6.

Table 4-6. *Context Data Contained Within DataPortalContext*

Context Data	Description
GlobalContext	Collection of context data that flows from client to server and then from server back to client; changes on either end are carried across the network
ClientContext	Collection of context data that flows from client to server; changes on the server are *not* carried back to the client
Principal	Client's IPrincipal object, which flows to the server if custom authentication is being used
IsRemotePortal	A flag indicating whether Csla.Server.DataPortal is actually running on a server or not
ClientCulture	Client thread's culture, which flows from the client to the server
ClientUICulture	Client thread's UI culture, which flows from the client to the server

The GlobalContext and ClientContext collections are exposed to both client and server code through Shared methods on the Csla.ApplicationContext class. All business object and UI code will use properties on the Csla.ApplicationContext class to access any context data.

When a call is made from the client to the server, the client's context data must flow to the server; the data portal does this by using the DataPortalContext object.

The Csla.Server.DataPortal object accepts the DataPortalContext object and uses its data to ensure that the server's context is set up properly before invoking the actual business object code.

This means that by the time the business developer's code is running on the server, the server's IPrincipal, culture, and Csla.ApplicationContext are set to match those on the client.

■**Caution** The exception to this is when using Windows integrated (AD) security. In that case, you must config-ure the server technology (such as IIS) to use Windows impersonation or the server will not impersonate the user identity from the client.

There are two possible outcomes of the server-side processing. Either it succeeds or it throws an exception.

If the call to the business object succeeds, Csla.Server.DataPortal returns a DataPortalResult object back to Csla.DataPortal on the client. The DataPortalResult object contains the information listed in Table 4-7.

Table 4-7. *Context Data Contained Within DataPortalResult*

Context Data	Description
GlobalContext	Collection of context data that flows from client to server and then from server back to client; changes on either end are carried across the network
ReturnObject	The business object being returned from the server to the client as a result of the data portal operation

Csla.DataPortal puts the GlobalContext data from DataPortalResult into the client's Csla.ApplicationContext, thus ensuring that any changes to that collection on the server are reflected on the client. It then returns the ReturnObject value as the result of the call itself.

You may use the bidirectional transfer of GlobalContext data to generate a consolidated list of debugging or logging information from the client, to the server, and back again to the client.

On the other hand, if an exception occurs on the server, either within the data portal itself, or more likely within the business object's code, that exception must be returned to the client. Either the business object or the UI on the client can use the exception information to deal with the exception in an appropriate manner.

In some cases, it can be useful to know the exact state of the business object graph on the server when the exception occurred. To this end, the object graph is also returned in the case of an exception. Keep in mind that it is returned *as it was at the time of the exception*, so the objects are often in an indeterminate state.

If an exception occurs on the server, Csla.Server.DataPortal catches the exception and wraps it as an InnerException within a Csla.Server.DataPortalException object. This DataPortalException object contains the information listed in Table 4-8.

Table 4-8. *Context Data Contained Within Csla.Server.DataPortalException*

Context Data	Description
InnerException	The actual server-side exception (which may also have InnerException objects of its own)
StackTrace	The stack trace information for the server-side exception
DataPortalResult	A DataPortalResult object (as discussed previously) containing both GlobalContext and the business object from the server

Again, Csla.DataPortal uses the information in the exception object to restore the Csla.ApplicationContext object's GlobalContext. Then it throws a Csla.DataPortalException, which is initialized with the data from the server.

The Csla.DataPortalException object is designed for use by business object or UI code. It provides access to the business object as it was on the server at the time of the exception. It also overrides the StackTrace property to append the server-side stack trace to the client-side stack trace, so the result shows the entire stack trace from where the exception occurred on the server all the way back to the client code.

Note Csla.DataPortal *always* throws a Csla.DataPortalException in case of failure. You must use either its InnerException or BusinessException properties, or the GetBaseException() method to retrieve the original exception that occurred.

In addition to Csla.DataPortal and Csla.Server.DataPortal, the types in Table 4-9 are required to implement the context behaviors discussed previously.

Table 4-9. *Types Required to Implement Context Passing and Location Transparency*

Type	Description
Csla.ApplicationContext	Provides access to the ClientContext and GlobalContext collection objects, as well as other context information
Csla.DataPortalException	Exception thrown by the data portal in case of any server-side exceptions; the server-side exception is an InnerException within the DataPortalException
Csla.Server.DataPortalContext	Transfers context data from the client to the server on every data portal operation
Csla.Server.DataPortalResult	Transfers context and result data from the server to the client on every successful data portal operation
Csla.Server.DataPortalException	Transfers context and exception data from the server to the client on every unsuccessful data portal operation

This infrastructure ensures that business code running on the server will share the same key context data as the client. It also ensures that the client's IPrincipal object is transferred to the server when the application is using custom authentication. The framework's support for custom authentication will be discussed in Chapter 5.

At this point, you should have a good understanding of the various areas of functionality provided by the data portal, and the various classes and types used to implement that functionality. The rest of the chapter will walk through those classes. As with Chapter 3, not all code is shown in this chapter, so you'll want to get the code download for the book (available at www.apress.com) to follow along.

Enhancing the Base Classes

In order to support persistence, the ability to save and restore from the database, objects need to implement methods that can be called by the UI. They also need to implement methods that can be called by the data portal on the server.

Figure 4-6 shows the basic process flow when the UI code wants to get a new business object or load a business object from the database.

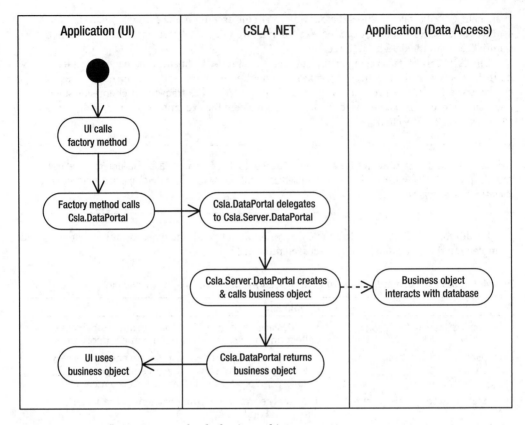

Figure 4-6. *Process flow to create or load a business object*

Following the class-in-charge model from Chapter 2, you can see that the UI code calls a factory method on the business class. The factory method then calls the appropriate method on the Csla.DataPortal class to create or retrieve the business object. The Csla.Server.DataPortal object then creates the object and invokes the appropriate data access method (DataPortal_Create() or DataPortal_Fetch()). The populated business object is returned to the UI, which can then use it as needed by the application.

Immediate deletion follows the same basic process, with the exception that no business object is returned to the UI as a result.

The BusinessBase and BusinessListBase classes need to implement a Save() method to make the update process work, as illustrated by Figure 4-7.

The process is almost identical to creating or loading an object, except that the UI starts off by calling the Save() method *on the object to be saved*, rather than invoking a factory method on the business class.

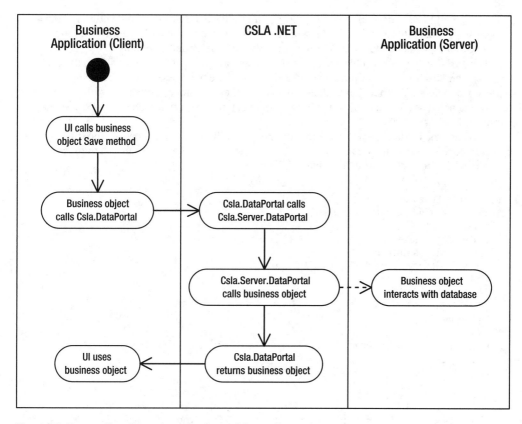

Figure 4-7. *Process flow for saving a business object*

Factory Methods and Criteria

Chapter 2 discussed the class-in-charge model and factory methods. When the UI needs to create or retrieve a business object, it will call a factory method that abstracts that behavior. These factory methods are just Shared methods, and you can put them in any class you choose. While some people put them in their own *factory class*, I prefer to put them in the business class for the object they create or retrieve, as I think it makes them easier to find.

This means a Customer class will include Shared factory methods such as GetCustomer() and NewCustomer(), both of which return a Customer object as a result. It may also implement a DeleteCustomer() method, which would return nothing. The implementation of these methods would typically look like this:

```
Public Shared Function NewCustomer() As Customer
   Return DataPortal.Create(Of Customer)()
End Function

Public Shared Function GetCustomer(ByVal id As Integer) As Customer
   Return DataPortal.Fetch(Of Customer)(New Criteria(id))
End Function

Public Shared Sub DeleteCustomer(ByVal id As Integer)
   DataPortal.Delete(New Criteria(id))
End Sub
```

The Criteria class used in the GetCustomer() method will either be nested within the business class, or must inherit from Csla.CriteriaBase. The former is the typical approach for classes written by hand, while the latter is intended for use with code-generation tools.

The purpose of a criteria object is to convey at least one piece of information from the client to the server. The only *required* piece of data is the type of the business object to be created, retrieved, or deleted. The data portal determines this either by looking at the class within which the criteria object is nested, or by retrieving a Type object from the criteria object in the case that it inherits from Csla.CriteriaBase.

In reality, most criteria objects include other information to uniquely identify the specific object to be retrieved. In this Customer example, the customer's unique ID value is a number.

A nested criteria class would look like this:

```
<Serializable()> _
Public Class Customer
  Inherits  BusinessBase(Of Customer)
  <Serializable()> _
  Private Class Criteria
    Private mId As Integer
    Public ReadOnly Property Id() As Integer
      Get
        Return mId
      End Get
    End Property

    Public Sub New(ByVal id As Integer)
      mId = id
    End Sub
  End Class
End Class
```

The same criteria class inheriting from Csla.CriteriaBase would look like this:

```
<Serializable()> _
Friend Class Criteria
  Inherits CriteriaBase
  Private mId As Integer
  Public ReadOnly Property Id() As Integer
    Get
      Return mId
    End Get
  End Property

  Public Sub New(ByVal id As Integer)
    MyBase.New(GetType(Customer))
    mId = id
  End Sub
End Class
```

Either way, the data portal can discover that the criteria object is looking for a Customer object, and so a Customer object will be created by the data portal. This will become clearer later, in the implementation of Csla.Server.SimpleDataPortal.

Save Methods

The factory methods, combined with the support for deleting child objects implemented in Chapter 3, cover creating, retrieving, and deleting objects. This leaves inserting and updating.

In both of these cases, the object already exists in memory, and so the Save() method is an instance method on any editable object.

One Save() method can be used to support inserting and updating an object's data because all editable objects have an IsNew property. Recall from Chapter 3 that the definition of a "new" object is that the object's primary key value doesn't exist in the database. This means that if IsNew is True, then Save() causes an insert operation; otherwise, Save() causes an update operation.

Csla.BusinessBase and Csla.BusinessListBase are the base classes for all editable business objects, and both these base classes implement Save() methods:

```vbnet
Public Overridable Function Save() As T
  If Me.IsChild Then
    Throw New NotSupportedException( _
      My.Resources.NoSaveChildException)
  End If

  If EditLevel > 0 Then
    Throw New Validation.ValidationException( _
      My.Resources.NoSaveEditingException)
  End If

  If Not IsValid Then
    Throw New Validation.ValidationException( _
      My.Resources.NoSaveInvalidException)
  End If

  If IsDirty Then
    Return DirectCast(DataPortal.Update(Me), T)
  Else
    Return DirectCast(Me, T)
  End If
End Function

Public Function Save(ByVal forceUpdate As Boolean) As T

  If forceUpdate AndAlso IsNew Then
    MarkOld()
    MarkDirty(True)
  End If
  Return Me.Save()
End Function
```

The first Save() method is the primary one that does the real work. It implements a set of common rules that make sense for most objects. Specifically, it does the following:

- Ensures that the object is not a child (since child objects must be saved as part of their parent)

- Makes sure that the object isn't currently being edited (a check primarily intended to assist with debugging)

- Checks to see if the object is valid; invalid objects can't be saved

- Ensures the object is dirty; there's no sense saving unchanged data into the database

Notice that the method is Overridable, so if a business developer needs a different set of rules for an object, it is possible to override this method and implement something else.

The second Save() method exists to support Web Services (discussed in Chapter 10). It allows a web service author to create a new instance of the object, load it with data, and then *force* the object to do an update (rather than an insert) operation. The reason for this is that when creating a web service to update data, the application calling the web service often passes *all* the data needed to update the database; there's no need to retrieve the existing data just to overwrite it. This optional overload of Save() gives you that option.

This is done by first calling MarkOld() to set IsNew to False, and then calling MarkDirty() to set IsDirty to True. This feature can also be useful for some stateless Web Forms implementations as well.

In either case, it is the DataPortal.Update() call that ultimately triggers the data portal infrastructure to move the object to the application server so it can interact with the database.

It is important to notice that the Save() method returns an instance of the business object. Recall that .NET doesn't actually move objects across the network; rather, it makes *copies* of the objects. The DataPortal.Update() call causes .NET to copy this object to the server so the copy can update itself into the database. That process could change the state of the object (especially if you are using primary keys assigned by the database or timestamps for concurrency). The resulting object is then copied back to the client and returned as a result of the Save() method.

■**Note** It is critical that the UI update all its references to use the new object returned by Save(). Failure to do this means that the UI will be displaying and editing old data from the old version of the object.

Data Portal Methods

As noted earlier, the data portal places certain constraints on business objects. Specifically, it needs to know what methods it can invoke on the server. The data portal will invoke the methods listed in Table 4-10, though not all framework base classes need to implement all the methods. Collectively, I'll refer to these methods as the DataPortal_XYZ methods.

Table 4-10. *Business Object Methods Invoked by the Data Portal*

Method	Purpose
DataPortal_Create()	An editable business object implements this method to load itself with default values required for a new object.
DataPortal_Fetch()	An editable or read-only business object implements this method to load itself with existing data from the database.
DataPortal_Insert()	An editable business object implements this method to insert its data into the database.
DataPortal_Update()	An editable business object implements this method to update its data in the database.
DataPortal_DeleteSelf()	An editable business object implements this method to delete its data from the database.
DataPortal_Delete()	An editable business object implements this method to delete its data from the database based on its primary key values only.
DataPortal_Execute()	A command object (see Chapter 5) implements this method to execute arbitrary code on the application server.
DataPortal_OnDataPortalInvoke()	This method is invoked on all objects before one of the preceding methods is invoked.

Method	Purpose
DataPortal_OnDataPortalInvokeComplete()	This method is invoked on all objects after any of the preceding methods have been invoked.
DataPortal_OnDataPortalException()	This method is invoked on an object if an exception occurs on the server; in this case, DataPortal_OnDataPortalInvokeComplete would not typically be invoked.

There are several ways the framework might ensure that the appropriate methods are implemented on each business object. A formal interface or abstract base class could be used to force business developers to implement each method. Alternatively, a base class could implement Overridable methods with default behaviors that could optionally be overridden by a business developer. Finally, it is possible to use reflection to dynamically invoke the methods.

Since not all objects will implement all the methods listed in Table 4-10, the idea of an interface or base class with MustOverride methods isn't ideal. Another negative side effect of those approaches is that the methods end up being publicly available, so a UI developer could call them. Of course, that would be problematic, since these methods will be designed to be called only by the data portal infrastructure. Finally, defining the methods at such an abstract level prevents the use of strong typing. Since the data types of the parameters being passed to the server by the client are defined by the business application, there's no way the framework can anticipate all the types—meaning that the parameters must be passed as type Object or another very generic base type.

Implementing default Overridable methods is an attractive option because it doesn't force the business developer to implement methods that will never be called. This is the approach I used in CSLA .NET 1.0, and will use in this chapter as well. However, this approach suffers from the same lack of strong typing as the interface or abstract base class approach.

Which brings us to the use of reflection. Reflection is much maligned as being slow, and it is in fact slower than making a native method call. However, it offers substantial benefits as well, most notably the ability to implement strongly typed data access methods on the business objects. The purpose behind reflection is to allow dynamic loading of types and then to allow dynamic invocation of methods on those types. And that's exactly what the data portal does.

Note The performance cost of reflection is typically negligible within the data portal. This is because the overhead of network communication and data access is so high that any overhead due to reflection usually becomes inconsequential.

Remember that the message router pattern implies that CSLA .NET has no reference to any business assembly. Business assemblies are loaded dynamically based on the request coming from the client. Reflection is used to dynamically load the assemblies and to create instances of business objects based on the classes built by the business developer.

Using reflection to also invoke the DataPortal_XYZ methods on the objects means that the business developer can write strongly typed versions of those methods. After all, the business developer knows the exact type of the parameters she is sending from the client to the server, and can write data access methods to accept those types. For instance, a DataPortal_Fetch() method may look like this:

```
Private Sub DataPortal_Fetch(ByVal criteria As MyCriteria)
  ' load data into object from database
End Sub
```

If this method were defined by CSLA .NET, it couldn't use the `MyCriteria` type because that type is specific to the business application. Instead, the framework would have to define the method using `Object` as the parameter type, as I did in CSLA .NET 1.0. In that case, a business developer must write code like this:

```
Protected Overrides Sub DataPortal_Fetch(ByVal criteria As Object)
  MyCriteria crit = CType(criteria, MyCriteria)
  ' load data into object from database
End Sub
```

For the purposes of backward compatibility, the implementation in this chapter will support both the old and new strongly typed models.

To support the old model, the base classes in the framework need to include `Protected Overridable` methods with default behaviors for the key `DataPortal_XYZ` methods that a business developer might override. For those methods that aren't appropriate for a given base class, `Private` methods are implemented in the base class that throw an exception.

For example, `Csla.Core.BusinessBase` includes the following code:

```
Protected Overridable Sub DataPortal_Create(ByVal criteria As Object)
  Throw New NotSupportedException( _
    My.Resources.CreateNotSupportedException)
End Sub
```

This provides a base method definition that a business class can override. The Visual Studio 2005 IDE makes it very easy to override methods by simply typing the keyword `Overrides` into the editor and getting an IntelliSense list of the `Overridable` methods in the base class.

Notice that the default implementation throws an exception. If the business developer *doesn't* override this method (or provide a strongly typed equivalent), but does implement a factory method that calls `DataPortal.Create()`, this exception will be the result.

■**Tip** Notice the use of a string resource rather than a literal string for the exception's message. This is done to enable localization. Since the text value comes from the resource (resx) file for the project, it will automatically attempt to use the resources for the current culture on the executing thread.

The same thing is done for `DataPortal_Fetch()`, `DataPortal_Insert()`, `DataPortal_Update()`, `DataPortal_DeleteSelf()`, and `DataPortal_Delete()`. Since a subclass of `BusinessBase` is an editable object, all the data portal operations are valid. Likewise, the same default methods are implemented in `BusinessListBase`. Again, it is the base for editable collections, and so all operations are valid.

`Csla.ReadOnlyBase` and `Csla.ReadOnlyListBase` are used to create read-only objects. As such, only the `DataPortal.Fetch()` operation is valid. This means that only `DataPortal_Fetch()` is implemented as a `Protected Overridable` default. All the other `DataPortal_XYZ` methods are implemented with `Private` scope, and they all throw exceptions if they are called. This ensures that read-only objects can only be retrieved—never inserted, updated, or deleted.

This completes the enhancements to the business object base classes that are required for the data portal to function. Chapter 5 will implement a couple more base classes, and they too will have comparable features.

Now let's move on and implement the data portal itself, feature by feature. The data portal is designed to provide a set of core features, including

- Implementing a channel adapter
- Supporting distributed transactional technologies
- Implementing a message router
- Transferring context and providing location transparency

The remainder of the chapter will walk through each functional area in turn, discussing the implementation of the classes supporting the concept. Though the data portal support for custom authentication and impersonation will be covered in this chapter, the Csla.Security. BusinessPrincipalBase class will be covered in Chapter 5.

The data portal is exposed to the business developer through the Csla.DataPortal class. This class implements a set of Shared methods to make it as easy as possible for the business developer to create, retrieve, update, or delete objects. All the channel adapter behaviors are hidden behind the Csla.DataPortal class.

The Csla.DataPortal class makes use of methods from the Csla.MethodCaller class.

Csla.MethodCaller Class

In fact, MethodCaller is used by many other classes in the data portal infrastructure, as it wraps the use of reflection in several ways. Csla.DataPortal, Csla.Server.DataPortal, and Csla.Server. SimpleDataPortal in particular all need to retrieve information about methods on the business class, and SimpleDataPortal needs to invoke those methods. The MethodCaller class contains methods to provide all these behaviors.

GetMethod

Chief among the behaviors is the GetMethod() method. This method is used to locate a specific method on the business class or object. Once the method has been located, other code can retrieve the attributes for that method, or the method can be invoked.

This method is somewhat complex. Recall that the data portal will call strongly typed methods based on the type of criteria object provided by the business object's factory method. This means that GetMethod() must locate the matching method on the business class—not only by method name, but by checking the parameter types as well.

The process flow is illustrated in Figure 4-8.

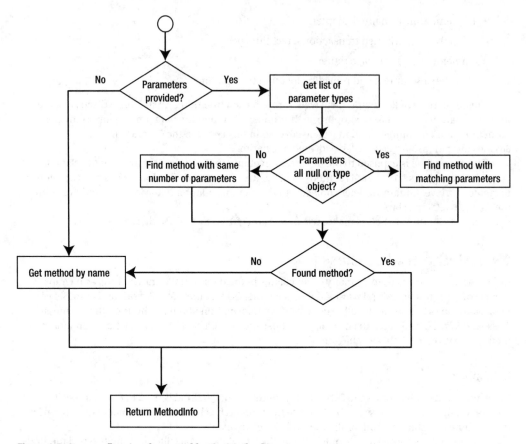

Figure 4-8. *Process flow implemented by GetMethod()*

Here's the method in its entirety:

```
Public Function GetMethod(ByVal objectType As Type, _
  ByVal method As String, ByVal ParamArray parameters() As Object) _
  As MethodInfo

  Dim flags As BindingFlags = _
    BindingFlags.FlattenHierarchy Or _
    BindingFlags.Instance Or _
    BindingFlags.Public Or _
    BindingFlags.NonPublic

  Dim result As MethodInfo = Nothing

  ' try to find a strongly typed match
  If parameters.Length > 0 Then
    ' put all param types into an array of Type
    Dim paramsAllNothing As Boolean = True
    Dim types As New List(Of Type)
    For Each item As Object In parameters
      If item Is Nothing Then
        types.Add(GetType(Object))
```

```vb
      Else
        types.Add(item.GetType)
        paramsAllNothing = False
      End If
    Next

    If paramsAllNothing Then
      ' all params are Nothing so we have
      ' no type info to go on
      Dim oneLevelFlags As BindingFlags = _
        BindingFlags.DeclaredOnly Or _
        BindingFlags.Instance Or _
        BindingFlags.Public Or _
        BindingFlags.NonPublic
      Dim typesArray() As Type = types.ToArray

      ' walk up the inheritance hierarchy looking
      ' for a method with the right number of
      ' parameters
      Dim currentType As Type = objectType
      Do
        Dim info As MethodInfo = _
          currentType.GetMethod(method, oneLevelFlags)
        If info IsNot Nothing Then
          If info.GetParameters.Length = parameters.Length Then
            ' got a match so use it
            result = info
            Exit Do
          End If
        End If
        currentType = currentType.BaseType
      Loop Until currentType Is Nothing

    Else
      ' at least one param has a real value
      ' so search for a strongly typed match
      result = objectType.GetMethod(method, flags, Nothing, _
        CallingConventions.Any, types.ToArray, Nothing)
    End If
End If

' no strongly typed match found, get default
If result Is Nothing Then
  Try
    result = objectType.GetMethod(method, flags)

  Catch ex As AmbiguousMatchException
    Dim methods() As MethodInfo = objectType.GetMethods
    For Each m As MethodInfo In methods
      If m.Name = method AndAlso _
      m.GetParameters.Length = parameters.Length Then
        result = m
        Exit For
      End If
```

```
        Next
        If result Is Nothing Then
          Throw
        End If
      End Try
    End If

    Return result
  End Function
```

Let's walk through the key parts of the process. First, assuming parameters were passed in for the method, the parameter *types* are put into a list:

```
' put all param types into an array of Type
Dim paramsAllNothing As Boolean = True
Dim types As New List(Of Type)
For Each item As Object In parameters
  If item Is Nothing Then
    types.Add(GetType(Object))

  Else
    types.Add(item.GetType)
    paramsAllNothing = False
  End If
Next
```

The reason for doing this is twofold. First, if there is at least one parameter that is not Nothing, then this list is needed for a call to reflection to get the matching method. Second, the loop determines whether there actually are any non-Nothing parameters. If not, the search for a matching method can only by done by parameter count, not data type.

Note In the general case, this could be problematic, because a Nothing value along with some non-Nothing values could result in an ambiguous match. For the purposes of the data portal, however, this is not an issue because the parameters involved are very clearly defined.

If all the parameter values are Nothing, then the search is done based on parameter count rather than parameter type. This is complicated, however, by the fact that preference is given to methods lower on the inheritance hierarchy. In other words, if both a base class and subclass have methods of the same name and number of parameters, preference is given to the subclass.

To accomplish this, the code loops through the specific class types, starting with the outermost class and working up through the inheritance chain—ultimately to System.Object:

```
Dim currentType As Type = objectType
Do
  Dim info As MethodInfo = _
    currentType.GetMethod(method, oneLevelFlags)
  If info IsNot Nothing Then
    If info.GetParameters.Length = parameters.Length Then
      ' got a match so use it
      result = info
      Exit Do
    End If
  End If
  currentType = currentType.BaseType
Loop Until currentType Is Nothing
```

As soon as a match is found, the loop is terminated and the result is used.

The other case occurs when at least one parameter is not Nothing. In such a case, reflection can be used in a simpler manner to locate a method with matching parameter types:

```
' at least one param has a real value
' so search for a strongly typed match
result = objectType.GetMethod(method, flags, Nothing, _
  CallingConventions.Any, types.ToArray, Nothing)
```

One way or the other, the result is typically a MethodInfo object for the correct method. However, it is possible that no match was found. In that case, as in the case in which no parameters were passed at all, a search is done based purely on the method's name:

```
result = objectType.GetMethod(method, flags)
```

Finally, it is possible for this check to find multiple matches—an ambiguous result. When that happens, an exception is thrown. In such a case, as a last-ditch effort, all methods on the business class are scanned to see if there's a match based on method name and parameter count:

```
Dim methods() As MethodInfo = objectType.GetMethods
For Each m As MethodInfo In methods
  If m.Name = method AndAlso _
  m.GetParameters.Length = parameters.Length Then
    result = m
    Exit For
  End If
Next
```

If even that fails, then the AmbiguousMatchException is thrown so that the business developer knows that something is seriously wrong with the data access methods in their business class.

The end result of GetMethod() is a MethodInfo object describing the method on the business class. This MethodInfo object is used by other methods in MethodCaller and in other data portal code.

CallMethod

The Csla.Server.SimpleDataPortal object (discussed later in the chapter) will ultimately invoke methods on business objects based on the MethodInfo object returned from GetMethod(). To support this, MethodCaller implements two different CallMethod() overloads:

```
Public Function CallMethod(ByVal obj As Object, _
  ByVal method As String, ByVal ParamArray parameters() As Object) As Object

  Dim info As MethodInfo = _
    GetMethod(obj.GetType, method, parameters)
  If info Is Nothing Then
    Throw New NotImplementedException( _
      method & " " & My.Resources.MethodNotImplemented)
  End If

  Return CallMethod(obj, info, parameters)
End Function

Public Function CallMethod(ByVal obj As Object, _
  ByVal info As MethodInfo, ByVal ParamArray parameters() As Object) _
  As Object
```

```
' call a Public method on the object
Dim result As Object
Try
  result = info.Invoke(obj, parameters)

Catch e As Exception
  Throw New CallMethodException( _
    info.Name & " " & My.Resources.MethodCallFailed, _
    e.InnerException)
End Try
Return result
End Function
```

The first version accepts the method name as a String value, while the second accepts a MethodInfo object. In the first case, GetMethod() is called to retrieve a matching MethodInfo object. If one isn't found, an exception is thrown; otherwise, the second version of CallMethod() is invoked.

The second version of CallMethod() actually invokes the method by using the MethodInfo object. The interesting bit here is the way exceptions are handled. Since reflection is being used to invoke the business method, any exceptions that occur in the business code end up being wrapped within a *reflection* exception.

To business developers, the exception from reflection isn't very useful. They want the actual exception that occurred within their business method. To resolve this, when an exception is thrown as the business method is invoked, it is caught, and the InnerException of the reflection exception is wrapped within a new Csla.Server.CallMethodException.

Effectively, the reflection exception is stripped off and discarded, leaving only the original exception thrown within the business code. That exception is then wrapped within a CSLA .NET exception so the name of the failed business method can be returned as well.

CallMethodIfImplemented

The CallMethodIfImplemented() method is similar to the CallMethod() methods mentioned previously, but it doesn't throw an exception if the method doesn't exist on the business class.

```
Public Function CallMethodIfImplemented(ByVal obj As Object, _
  ByVal method As String, ByVal ParamArray parameters() As Object) As Object

  Dim info As MethodInfo = _
    GetMethod(obj.GetType, method, parameters)
  If info IsNot Nothing Then
    Return CallMethod(obj, info, parameters)

  Else
    Return Nothing
  End If
End Function
```

This is the same basic code as the first CallMethod() implementation, except that it doesn't throw an exception if the method isn't found. Instead, it simply returns a value of Nothing.

CallMethodIfImplemented() is used by Csla.Server.SimpleDataPortal to invoke optional methods on the business class—methods that should be invoked if implemented by the business developer, but which shouldn't cause failure if they aren't implemented at all. An example is DataPortal_OnDataPortalInvoke(), which is purely optional, but should be called if it has been implemented by the business developer.

GetObjectType

The final method in `MethodCaller` is used by both `Csla.DataPortal` and `Csla.Server.DataPortal` to determine the type of business object involved in the data portal request. It uses the criteria object supplied by the factory method in the business class to find the type of the business object itself.

This method supports the two options discussed earlier: where the criteria class is nested within the business class and where the criteria object inherits from `Csla.CriteriaBase`:

```
Public Function GetObjectType(ByVal criteria As Object) As Type

    If criteria.GetType.IsSubclassOf(GetType(CriteriaBase)) Then
        ' get the type of the actual business object
        ' from CriteriaBase
        Return CType(criteria, CriteriaBase).ObjectType

    Else
        ' get the type of the actual business object
        ' based on the nested class scheme in the book
        Return criteria.GetType.DeclaringType
    End If
End Function
```

If the criteria object is a subclass of `Csla.CriteriaBase`, then the code simply casts the object to type `CriteriaBase` and retrieves the business object type by calling the `ObjectType` property.

With a nested criteria class, the code gets the type of the criteria object and then returns the `DeclaringType` value from the `Type` object. The `DeclaringType` property returns the type of the class within which the criteria class is nested.

Csla.Server.CallMethodException

The `MethodCaller` class throws a custom `Csla.Server.CallMethodException` in the case that an exception occurs while calling a method on the business object. The purpose behind throwing this exception is to supply the name of the business method that generated the exception, and to provide the original exception details as an `InnerException`.

More importantly, it preserves the stack trace from the original exception. The original stack trace shows the details about where the exception occurred, and is very useful for debugging. Without a bit of extra work, this information is lost as the method call comes back through reflection.

Remember that `MethodCaller.CallMethod()` uses reflection to invoke the business method. When an exception occurs in the business method, a reflection exception is thrown—with the original business exception nested inside. `CallMethod()` strips off the reflection exception and provides the original business exception as a parameter during the creation of the `CallMethodException` object. In the constructor of `CallMethodException`, the stack trace details from that original exception are stored for later use:

```
Public Sub New(ByVal message As String, ByVal ex As Exception)
    MyBase.New(message, ex)
    mInnerStackTrace = ex.StackTrace
End Sub
```

Then in the `StackTrace` property of `CallMethodException`, the stack trace for the `CallMethodException` itself is combined with the stack trace from the original exception:

```
Public Overrides ReadOnly Property StackTrace() As String
  Get
    Return String.Format("{0}{1}{2}", _
      mInnerStackTrace, vbCrLf, MyBase.StackTrace)
  End Get
End Property
```

The result is that the complete stack trace is available—showing the flow from the original exception all the way back to the UI in most cases.

Csla.RunLocalAttribute Class

The data portal routes client calls to the server based on the client application's configuration settings in its config file. If the configuration is set to use an actual application server, the client call is sent across the network using the channel adapter pattern. However, there are cases in which the business developer knows that there's no need to send the call across the network—even if the application is configured that way.

The most common example of this is in the creation of new business objects. The `DataPortal.Create()` method is called to create a new object, and it in turn triggers a call to the business object's `DataPortal_Create()` method, where the object can load itself with default values from the database. But what if an object doesn't need to load defaults from the database? In that case, there's no reason to go across the network at all, and it would be nice to short-circuit the call so that particular object's `DataPortal_Create()` would run on the client.

This is the purpose behind the `RunLocalAttribute`. A business developer can mark a data access method with this attribute to tell `Csla.DataPortal` to force the call to run on the client, regardless of how the application is configured in general. Such a business method would look like this:

```
<RunLocal()> _
Private Sub DataPortal_Create(ByVal criteria As Criteria)
  ' set default values here
End Sub
```

The attribute class itself is quite straightforward:

```
<AttributeUsage(AttributeTargets.Method)> _
Public NotInheritable Class RunLocalAttribute
  Inherits Attribute
End Class
```

As with all custom attributes, it inherits from `System.Attribute`. The `<AttributeUsage()>` attribute is used to restrict this attribute so it can only be applied to methods—not classes, properties, etc.

Csla.DataPortalEventArgs Class

The `Csla.DataPortal` class will raise a couple events that can be handled by the business logic or UI code on the client. These events are raised immediately before and after the data portal calls the server. A `DataPortalEventArgs` object is provided as a parameter to these events. This object includes information of value when handling the event:

```vbnet
Public Class DataPortalEventArgs
  Inherits EventArgs

  Private mDataPortalContext As Server.DataPortalContext

  Public ReadOnly Property DataPortalContext() As Server.DataPortalContext
    Get
      Return mDataPortalContext
    End Get
  End Property

  Public Sub New(ByVal dataPortalContext As Server.DataPortalContext)
    mDataPortalContext = dataPortalContext
  End Sub
End Class
```

The DataPortalContext property returns the Csla.Server.DataPortalContext object that is passed to the server as part of the client message. The DataPortalContext class will be implemented later in the chapter, but it includes the user's Principal object (if using custom authentication), the client's culture information, and the ClientContext and GlobalContext collections.

This information can be used by code handling the event to better understand all the information being passed to the server as part of the client message.

Csla.DataPortal Class

The primary entry point for the entire data portal infrastructure is the Csla.DataPortal class. Business developers use the methods on this class to trigger all the data portal behaviors. This class is involved in both the channel adapter implementation and in handling context information. This section will focus on the channel adapter code in the class, while the context-handling code will be discussed later in the chapter.

The Csla.DataPortal class exposes five primary methods, described in Table 4-11, that can be called by business logic.

Table 4-11. *Methods Exposed by the Client-Side DataPortal*

Method	Description
Create()	Calls Csla.Server.DataPortal, which then invokes the DataPortal_Create() method
Fetch()	Calls Csla.Server.DataPortal, which then invokes the DataPortal_Fetch() method
Update()	Calls Csla.Server.DataPortal, which then invokes the DataPortal_Insert(), DataPortal_Update(), or DataPortal_DeleteSelf() methods, as appropriate
Delete()	Calls Csla.Server.DataPortal, which then invokes the DataPortal_Delete() method
Execute()	Calls Csla.Server.DataPortal, which then invokes the DataPortal_Execute() method

The class also raises two events that the business developer or UI developer can handle. The DataPortalInvoke event is raised before the server is called, and the DataPortalInvokeComplete event is raised after the call the to the server has returned.

Behind the scenes, each DataPortal method determines the network protocol to be used when contacting the server in order to delegate the call to Csla.Server.DataPortal. Of course, Csla.Server.DataPortal ultimately delegates the call to Csla.Server.SimpleDataPortal and then to the business object on the server.

The `Csla.DataPortal` class is designed to expose `Shared` methods. As such, it is a `Module`:

```
Public Module DataPortal

End Module
```

This ensures that an instance of `Csla.DataPortal` won't be created.

Data Portal Events

The class defines two events, `DataPortalInvoke` and `DataPortalInvokeComplete`:

```
Public Event DataPortalInvoke As Action(Of DataPortalEventArgs)
Public Event DataPortalInvokeComplete As Action(Of DataPortalEventArgs)

Private Sub OnDataPortalInvoke(ByVal e As DataPortalEventArgs)
  RaiseEvent DataPortalInvoke(e)
End Sub

Private Sub OnDataPortalInvokeComplete(ByVal e As DataPortalEventArgs)
  RaiseEvent DataPortalInvokeComplete(e)
End Sub
```

These follow the standard approach by providing helper methods to raise the events.

Also notice the use of the `Action(Of T)` generic template. This is provided by the .NET framework as a helper when declaring events that have a custom `EventArgs` subclass as a single parameter. There's also a corresponding `EventHandler(Of T)` template to help when declaring the standard `sender` and `EventArgs` pattern for event methods.

RunLocal

In each of the five public methods, `DataPortal` must determine whether the business developer has applied the `<RunLocal()>` attribute to the business method on their business class. The `RunLocal()` method checks for the attribute, returning a Boolean indicating whether it exists or not:

```
Private Function RunLocal(ByVal method As MethodInfo) As Boolean
  Return Attribute.IsDefined(method, GetType(RunLocalAttribute))
End Function
```

While not strictly necessarily, this helper method streamlines the more complex code elsewhere in the class.

Creating the Proxy Object

The primary function of `Csla.DataPortal` is to determine the appropriate network protocol (if any) to be used when interacting with `Csla.Server.DataPortal`. Each protocol is managed by a proxy object that implements the `Csla.DataPortalClient.IDataPortalProxy` interface. This interface will be discussed shortly, but for now it is enough to know that it ensures that all proxy classes implement the methods required by `Csla.DataPortal`.

The proxy object to be used is defined in the application's configuration file. That's the `web.config` file for ASP.NET applications, and *myprogram*.`exe.config` for Windows applications (where *myprogram* is the name of your program). Within Visual Studio, a Windows configuration file is named `app.config`, so I'll refer to them as `app.config` files from here forward.

Config files can include an <appSettings> section to store application settings, and it is in this section that the CSLA .NET configuration settings are located. The following shows how this section would look for an application set to use the .NET Remoting technology:

```
<appSettings>
  <add key="CslaDataPortalProxy"
       value="Csla.DataPortalClient.RemotingProxy, Csla"/>
  <add key="CslaDataPortalUrl"
       value="http://servername/sitename/RemotingPortal.rem"/>
</appSettings>
```

Of course, servername and sitename would correspond to a real web server and virtual root.

The CslaDataPortalProxy key defines the proxy class that should be used by Csla.DataPortal. The CslaDataPortalUrl key is defined and used by the proxy object itself. Different proxy objects may require or support different keys for their own configuration data.

The GetDataPortalProxy() method uses this information to create an instance of the correct proxy object:

```
Private mLocalPortal As DataPortalClient.IDataPortalProxy
Private mPortal As DataPortalClient.IDataPortalProxy

Private Function GetDataPortalProxy( _
  ByVal forceLocal As Boolean) As DataPortalClient.IDataPortalProxy

  If forceLocal Then
    If mLocalPortal Is Nothing Then
      mLocalPortal = New DataPortalClient.LocalProxy
    End If
    Return mLocalPortal

  Else
    If mPortal Is Nothing Then

      Dim proxyTypeName As String = ApplicationContext.DataPortalProxy
      If proxyTypeName = "Local" Then
        mPortal = New DataPortalClient.LocalProxy

      Else
        Dim typeName As String = _
          proxyTypeName.Substring(0, proxyTypeName.IndexOf(",")).Trim
        Dim assemblyName As String = _
          proxyTypeName.Substring(proxyTypeName.IndexOf(",") + 1).Trim
        mPortal = DirectCast(Activator.CreateInstance(assemblyName, _
          typeName).Unwrap, DataPortalClient.IDataPortalProxy)
      End If
    End If
    Return mPortal
  End If
End Function
```

For both local and remote proxy objects, once the proxy has been created, it is cached in a Shared field. (Remember that all fields, methods, and properties in a Module are effectively Shared.) This avoids recreating the proxy object for every data portal call.

If the forceLocal parameter is True, then only a local proxy is returned. The Csla.DataPortalClient.LocalProxy object is a special proxy that doesn't use any network protocols at all, but rather runs the "server-side" data portal components directly within the client process. This class will be covered later in the chapter.

When forceLocal is False, the real work begins. First, the proxy string is retrieved from the CslaDataPortalProxy key in the config file by calling the ApplicationContext.DataPortalProxy property. The ApplicationContext class is covered later in the chapter, but this property reads the config file and returns the value associated with the CslaDataPortalProxy key.

If that key value is "Local", then again an instance of the LocalProxy class is created and returned. The ApplicationContext.DataPortalProxy method also returns a LocalProxy object if the key is not found in the config file. This makes LocalProxy the default proxy.

If some other config value is returned, then it is parsed and used to create an instance of the appropriate proxy class:

```
Dim typeName As String = _
  proxyTypeName.Substring(0, proxyTypeName.IndexOf(",")).Trim
Dim assemblyName As String = _
  proxyTypeName.Substring(proxyTypeName.IndexOf(",") + 1).Trim
mPortal = DirectCast(Activator.CreateInstance(assemblyName, _
  typeName).Unwrap, DataPortalClient.IDataPortalProxy)
```

In the preceding <appSettings> example, notice that the value is a comma-separated value with the full class name on the left and the assembly name on the right. This follows the .NET standard for describing classes that are to be dynamically loaded.

The config value is parsed to pull out the full type name and assembly name. Then Activator.CreateInstance() is called to create an instance of the object. The .NET runtime automatically loads the assembly if needed.

The object returned from Activator.CreateInstance() isn't the actual proxy object. Instead, it is an internal .NET object representing the underlying object. The Unwrap() method returns the real proxy object that was dynamically loaded.

The final result is that the appropriate proxy object is loaded into memory and returned for use by the code in Csla.DataPortal.

Data Access Methods

The next step is to implement the five primary methods in the client-side DataPortal. Most of the hard work is handled by the code implemented thus far in the "Channel Adapter" section and in the MethodCaller class, so implementing these will be pretty straightforward. All five will follow the same basic flow:

- Get the MethodInfo for the business method to be ultimately invoked.
- Get the data portal proxy object.
- Create a DataPortalContext object.
- Raise the DataPortalInvoke event.
- Delegate the call to the proxy object (and thus to the server).
- Handle and throw any exceptions.
- Restore the GlobalContext returned from the server.
- Raise the DataPortalInvokeComplete event.
- Return the resulting business object (if appropriate).

Let's look at the Fetch() method in detail, followed by the minor differences required to implement the other four methods.

Fetch

There are two Fetch() methods: a generic one to provide a strongly typed result, and the actual implementation:

```
Public Function Fetch(Of T)(ByVal criteria As Object) As T
  Return DirectCast(Fetch(criteria), T)
End Function

Public Function Fetch(ByVal criteria As Object) As Object

  Dim result As Server.DataPortalResult

  Dim method As MethodInfo = _
    MethodCaller.GetMethod( _
      MethodCaller.GetObjectType(criteria), "DataPortal_Fetch", criteria)

  Dim proxy As DataPortalClient.IDataPortalProxy
  proxy = GetDataPortalProxy(RunLocal(method))

  Dim dpContext As New Server.DataPortalContext( _
    GetPrincipal, proxy.IsServerRemote)

  OnDataPortalInvoke(New DataPortalEventArgs(dpContext))

  Try
    result = proxy.Fetch(criteria, dpContext)

  Catch ex As Server.DataPortalException
    result = ex.Result
    If proxy.IsServerRemote Then
      ApplicationContext.SetGlobalContext(result.GlobalContext)
    End If
    Throw New DataPortalException("DataPortal.Fetch " & _
      My.Resources.Failed, ex.InnerException, result.ReturnObject)
  End Try

  If proxy.IsServerRemote Then
    ApplicationContext.SetGlobalContext(result.GlobalContext)
  End If

  OnDataPortalInvokeComplete(New DataPortalEventArgs(dpContext))

  Return result.ReturnObject
End Function
```

The generic method simply casts the result so that the calling code doesn't have to. Remember that the data portal can return virtually any type of object, and so the actual Fetch() method implementation must deal with results of type Object.

Looking at the code, you should see all the steps listed in the preceding bulleted list. The first is to retrieve the MethodInfo for the business method that will be ultimately invoked on the server:

```
Dim method As MethodInfo = _
  MethodCaller.GetMethod( _
    MethodCaller.GetObjectType(criteria), "DataPortal_Fetch", criteria)
```

This MethodInfo object is immediately used to determine whether the <RunLocal()> attribute has been applied to the method on the business class. This value is used as a parameter to the GetDataPortalProxy() method, which returns the appropriate proxy object for server communication:

```
proxy = GetDataPortalProxy(RunLocal(method))
```

Next, a DataPortalContext object is created and initialized. The details of this object and the means of dealing with context information are discussed later in the chapter.

```
Dim dpContext As New Server.DataPortalContext( _
  GetPrincipal, proxy.IsServerRemote)
```

Then the DataPortalInvoke event is raised, notifying client-side business or UI logic that a data portal call is about to take place:

```
OnDataPortalInvoke(New DataPortalEventArgs(dpContext))
```

Finally, the Fetch() call itself is delegated to the proxy object:

```
result = proxy.Fetch(criteria, dpContext)
```

All a proxy object does is relay the method call across the network to Csla.Server.DataPortal, so you can almost think of this as delegating the call directly to Csla.Server.DataPortal, which in turn delegates to Csla.Server.SimpleDataPortal. The ultimate result is that the business object's DataPortal_XYZ methods are invoked on the server.

Note Remember that the default is that the "server-side" code actually runs in the client process on the client workstation (or web server). Even so, the full sequence of events described here occur—just much faster than if network communication were involved.

An exception could occur while calling the server. The most likely cause of such an exception is that an exception occurred in the business logic running on the server, though exceptions can also occur because of network issues or similar problems. When an exception does occur in business code on the server, it will be reflected here as a Csla.Server.DataPortalException, which is caught and handled:

```
result = ex.Result
If proxy.IsServerRemote Then
  ApplicationContext.SetGlobalContext(result.GlobalContext)
End If
Throw New DataPortalException("DataPortal.Fetch " & _
  My.Resources.Failed, ex.InnerException, result.ReturnObject)
```

The Csla.Server.DataPortalException returns the business object from the server exactly as it was when the exception occurred. It also returns the GlobalContext information from the server so that it can be used to update the client's context data. Ultimately, the data from the server is used to create a Csla.DataPortalException that is thrown back to the business object. It can be handled by the business object or the UI code as appropriate.

Notice that the Csla.DataPortalException object contains not only all the exception details from the server, but also the business object from the server. This object can be useful when debugging server-side exceptions.

More commonly, an exception won't occur. In that case, the result returned from the server includes the GlobalContext data from the server, which is used to update the context on the client:

```
If proxy.IsServerRemote Then
  ApplicationContext.SetGlobalContext(result.GlobalContext)
End If
```

The details around context are discussed later in the chapter. With the server call complete, the `DataPortalInvokeComplete` event is raised:

```
OnDataPortalInvokeComplete(New DataPortalEventArgs(dpContext))
```

Finally, the business object created and loaded with data on the server is returned to the factory method that called `DataPortal.Fetch()` in the first place.

Remember that in a physical n-tier scenario, this is a copy of the object that was created on the server. .NET serialized the object on the server, transferred its data to the client, and deserialized it on the client. This object being returned as a result of the `Fetch()` method exists on the client workstation and so can be used by other client-side objects and UI components in a very efficient manner.

Create

The `Create()` method works in virtually the same manner as `Fetch()`. The only difference is in how the type of business object is managed. When retrieving an existing object, some criteria information is virtually always required. But when creating a new object that is to be loaded with default values, a criteria object may or may not be useful. In many cases, there's no need for criteria at all when creating a new object.

However, the criteria object is central to the `MethodCaller.GetObjectType()` method and the determination of the type of business object to be created. To make the criteria object optional, `Create()` takes a slightly different approach. The `Public` methods look like this:

```
Public Function Create(Of T)(ByVal criteria As Object) As T
  Return DirectCast(Create(GetType(T), criteria), T)
End Function

Public Function Create(Of T)() As T
  Return DirectCast(Create(GetType(T), Nothing), T)
End Function

Public Function Create(ByVal criteria As Object) As Object
  Return Create(MethodCaller.GetObjectType(criteria), criteria)
End Function
```

Again, there's the generic version that returns a casted value. But there's also a version that doesn't require a criteria object as a parameter. Finally, there's a loosely typed version that returns a value of type `Object`.

All three implementations delegate to a `Private` version of the method that accepts not only the criteria object, but also a `Type` object specifying the type of business object to be created. The generic versions of the method get this by calling `GetType(T)`, while the loosely typed version uses the same `GetObjectType()` method used in the `Fetch()` method earlier.

The private implementation of `Create()` follows the same structure as `Fetch()`, with the exception of how it calls `GetMethod()` in the first step. That code is bolded here:

```
Private Function Create( _
  ByVal objectType As Type, ByVal criteria As Object) As Object

  Dim result As Server.DataPortalResult

  Dim method As MethodInfo = _
    MethodCaller.GetMethod(objectType, "DataPortal_Create", criteria)
```

Because the business object type was passed in as a parameter, it can be used directly, rather than calling `MethodCaller.GetObjectType()`, like in the `Fetch()` method.

Following this approach, when the `Create()` call is delegated to the proxy object (and thus to `Csla.Server.DataPortal` and the other server-side code), the object type is passed as a parameter:

```
result = proxy.Create(objectType, criteria, dpContext)
```

This way, the type of business object to be created flows from the `Csla.DataPortal` through to the server-side code.

Update

The `Update()` method is similar again, but it doesn't get a criteria object as a parameter. Instead, it gets passed the business object itself:

```
Public Function Update(ByVal obj As Object) As Object
```

This way, it can pass the business object to `Csla.Server.DataPortal`, which ultimately calls the object's `DataPortal_Insert()`, `DataPortal_Update()`, or `DataPortal_DeleteSelf()` method, causing the object to update the database. It also checks to see if the business object inherits from `Csla.CommandBase` (discussed in Chapter 5), and if so, it invokes the object's `DataPortal_Execute()` method instead.

The only major difference from `Fetch()` is in how the `MethodInfo` object is retrieved for the business method to be called:

```
Dim method As MethodInfo
Dim methodName As String
If TypeOf obj Is CommandBase Then
  methodName = "DataPortal_Execute"

ElseIf TypeOf obj Is Core.BusinessBase Then
  Dim tmp As Core.BusinessBase = DirectCast(obj, Core.BusinessBase)
  If tmp.IsDeleted Then
    methodName = "DataPortal_DeleteSelf"
  Else
    If tmp.IsNew Then
      methodName = "DataPortal_Insert"

    Else
      methodName = "DataPortal_Update"
    End If
  End If
Else
  methodName = "DataPortal_Update"
End If
```

```
method = MethodCaller.GetMethod(obj.GetType, methodName)
```

The decision tree regarding which method to call is more complex in this case, because the decision is based on the type of the business object involved. Therefore, the logic here is a bit more interesting than in the `Fetch()` method.

If the object inherits from `CommandBase`, the `DataPortal_Execute()` method will be invoked. If it is a subclass of `Csla.Core.BusinessBase`, then the method to be called is determined by the state of the object. Any other objects (most likely a subclass of `Csla.BusinessListBase`) will have their `DataPortal_Update()` method invoked.

The rest of the process is fundamentally the same as `Create()` and `Fetch()`.

CHAPTER 4 ■ DATA ACCESS AND SECURITY   197

Execute

The Update() method includes code to call DataPortal_Execute() on a business object that inherits from Csla.CommandBase. That's fine, but may not be intuitive to a business developer. The Execute() method is intended to make the data portal API more intuitive.

Since the Update() method already handles Csla.CommandBase subclasses, the Execute() method simply delegates to Update() to do its work:

```
Public Function Execute(Of T As CommandBase)(ByVal obj As T) As T
  Return DirectCast(Update(CObj(obj)), T)
End Function
```

```
Public Function Execute(ByVal obj As CommandBase) As CommandBase
  Return DirectCast(Update(obj), CommandBase)
End Function
```

Notice that the parameters and types of both methods are constrained to only accept objects that subclass Csla.CommandBase. All the real work occurs in the Update() method.

Delete

The final Csla.DataPortal method is Delete(), which is virtually identical to Fetch(). It also receives a criteria object as a parameter, which it uses to get a Type object for the business class, and so forth.

The Delete() method exists to support the *immediate* deletion of an object, without having to retrieve the object first. Instead, it accepts a criteria object that identifies which object's data should be deleted. Ultimately, the server-side DataPortal calls the business object's DataPortal_Delete() method to perform the delete operation.

■**Tip** Remember that a delete operation doesn't need to actually delete data from the database. It could just as easily set a deleted flag on a row of data. The specific implementation of a delete operation is up to the business developer as he codes the DataPortal_Delete() method in his object.

Nothing is returned from this method, as it doesn't generate a business object. If the delete operation itself fails, it should throw an exception, which will be returned to the client as an indicator of failure.

At this point, the role of Csla.DataPortal as gateway to the data portal overall should be clear. The other end of the channel adapter is the Csla.Server.DataPortal class, which is also the entry point to the message router pattern. The details of Csla.Server.DataPortal will be discussed later in the chapter, as part of the message router section. First though, let's walk through the various proxy and host classes that implement the four channels implemented by CSLA .NET.

Csla.Server.IDataPortalServer

Each channel comes in two parts: a proxy on the client and a host on the server. Csla.DataPortal calls the proxy, which in turn transfers the call to the host by using its channel. The host then delegates the call to a Csla.Server.DataPortal object. To ensure that all the parts of this chain can reliably interact, there are two interfaces: Csla.Server.IDataPortalServer and Csla.DataPortalClient.IDataPortalProxy.

The IDataPortalServer interface defines the methods common across the entire process:

```
Public Interface IDataPortalServer
  Function Create( _
    ByVal objectType As Type, _
    ByVal criteria As Object, _
    ByVal context As DataPortalContext) As DataPortalResult
  Function Fetch( _
    ByVal criteria As Object, _
    ByVal context As DataPortalContext) As DataPortalResult
  Function Update( _
    ByVal obj As Object, _
    ByVal context As DataPortalContext) As DataPortalResult
  Function Delete( _
    ByVal criteria As Object, _
    ByVal context As DataPortalContext) As DataPortalResult
End Interface
```

Notice that these are the same method signatures as implemented by the methods in Csla.DataPortal, making it very easy for that class to delegate its calls through a proxy and host all the way to Csla.Server.DataPortal.

Csla.DataPortalClient.IDataPortalProxy

All the proxy classes implement a common Csla.DataPortalClient.IDataPortalProxy interface so they can be used by Csla.DataPortal. This interface inherits from Csla.Server.IDataPortalServer, ensuring that all proxy classes will have the same methods as all server-side host classes:

```
Public Interface IDataPortalProxy
  Inherits Server.IDataPortalServer
  ReadOnly Property IsServerRemote() As Boolean
End Interface
```

In addition to the four data methods, proxy classes need to report whether they interact with an actual server-side host or not. As you'll see, at least one proxy interacts with a *client-side* host. Recall that in Csla.DataPortal, the IsServerRemote property was used to control whether the context data was set and restored. If the "server-side" code is running inside the client process, then much of that work can be bypassed, improving performance.

Csla.DataPortalClient.LocalProxy

The default option for a "network" channel is not to use the network at all, but rather to run the "server-side" code inside the client process. This option offers the best performance, though possibly at the cost of security or scalability. The various trade-offs of n-tier deployments were discussed in Chapter 1.

Even when running the "server-side" code in-process on the client, the data portal uses a proxy for the local "channel": Csla.DataPortalClient.LocalProxy. As with all proxy classes, this one implements the Csla.DataPortalClient.IDataPortalProxy interface, exposing a standard set of methods and properties for use by Csla.DataPortal.

Because this proxy doesn't actually use a network protocol, it is the simplest of all the proxies:

```vb
Public Class LocalProxy

  Implements DataPortalClient.IDataPortalProxy

  Private mPortal As Server.IDataPortalServer = _
    New Server.DataPortal

  Public Function Create( _
    ByVal objectType As System.Type, ByVal criteria As Object, _
    ByVal context As Server.DataPortalContext) As Server.DataPortalResult _
    Implements Server.IDataPortalServer.Create

    Return mPortal.Create(objectType, criteria, context)

  End Function

  Public Function Fetch( _
    ByVal criteria As Object, _
    ByVal context As Server.DataPortalContext) As Server.DataPortalResult _
    Implements Server.IDataPortalServer.Fetch

    Return mPortal.Fetch(criteria, context)

  End Function

  Public Function Update( _
    ByVal obj As Object, _
    ByVal context As Server.DataPortalContext) As Server.DataPortalResult _
    Implements Server.IDataPortalServer.Update

    Return mPortal.Update(obj, context)

  End Function

  Public Function Delete( _
    ByVal criteria As Object, _
    ByVal context As Server.DataPortalContext) As Server.DataPortalResult _
    Implements Server.IDataPortalServer.Delete

    Return mPortal.Delete(criteria, context)

  End Function

  Public ReadOnly Property IsServerRemote() As Boolean _
    Implements IDataPortalProxy.IsServerRemote
    Get
      Return False
    End Get
  End Property
End Class
```

All this proxy does is directly create an instance of Csla.Server.DataPortal:

```vb
Private mPortal As Server.IDataPortalServer = _
  New Server.DataPortal
```

Each of the data methods (Create(), Fetch(), etc.) simply delegates to this object. The result is that the client call is handled by a Csla.Server.DataPortal object running within the client AppDomain and on the client's thread. Due to this, the IsServerRemote property returns False.

Csla.DataPortalClient.RemotingProxy

More interesting is the .NET Remoting channel. This is implemented on the client by the RemotingProxy class, and on the server by the RemotingPortal class. When Csla.DataPortal delegates a call into RemotingProxy, it uses .NET Remoting to pass that call to a RemotingPortal object on the server. That object then delegates the call to a Csla.Server.DataPortal object.

Because .NET Remoting automatically serializes objects across the network, the RemotingProxy class is not much more complex than LocalProxy:

```vb
Public Class RemotingProxy

  Implements DataPortalClient.IDataPortalProxy

#Region " Configure Remoting "

  Shared Sub New()

    ' create and register a custom HTTP channel
    ' that uses the binary formatter
    Dim properties As New Hashtable
    properties("name") = "HttpBinary"

    If ApplicationContext.AuthenticationType = "Windows" Then
      ' make sure we pass the user's Windows credentials
      ' to the server
      properties("useDefaultCredentials") = True
    End If

    Dim formatter As New BinaryClientFormatterSinkProvider

    Dim channel As New HttpChannel(properties, formatter, Nothing)

    ChannelServices.RegisterChannel(channel, EncryptChannel)

  End Sub

  Private Shared ReadOnly Property EncryptChannel() As Boolean
    Get
      Dim encrypt As Boolean = _
        (ConfigurationManager.AppSettings("CslaEncryptRemoting") = "true")
      Return encrypt
    End Get
  End Property

#End Region

    Private mPortal As Server.IDataPortalServer

  Private ReadOnly Property Portal() As Server.IDataPortalServer
    Get
      If mPortal Is Nothing Then
        mPortal = CType( _
          Activator.GetObject(GetType(Server.Hosts.RemotingPortal), _
          ApplicationContext.DataPortalUrl.ToString), _
          Server.IDataPortalServer)
      End If
      Return mPortal
    End Get
  End Property
```

```vbnet
  Public Function Create( _
    ByVal objectType As System.Type, ByVal criteria As Object, _
    ByVal context As Server.DataPortalContext) As Server.DataPortalResult _
    Implements Server.IDataPortalServer.Create

    Return Portal.Create(objectType, criteria, context)

  End Function

  Public Function Fetch( _
    ByVal criteria As Object, _
    ByVal context As Server.DataPortalContext) As Server.DataPortalResult _
    Implements Server.IDataPortalServer.Fetch

    Return Portal.Fetch(criteria, context)

  End Function

  Public Function Update( _
    ByVal obj As Object, _
    ByVal context As Server.DataPortalContext) As Server.DataPortalResult _
    Implements Server.IDataPortalServer.Update

    Return Portal.Update(obj, context)

  End Function

  Public Function Delete( _
    ByVal criteria As Object, _
    ByVal context As Server.DataPortalContext) As Server.DataPortalResult _
    Implements Server.IDataPortalServer.Delete

    Return Portal.Delete(criteria, context)

  End Function

  Public ReadOnly Property IsServerRemote() As Boolean _
    Implements IDataPortalProxy.IsServerRemote
    Get
      Return True
    End Get
  End Property
End Class
```

In fact, the data methods themselves are identical. This is because the `Portal` property abstracts the creation of the portal object itself, and because .NET Remoting offers a feature called *location transparency*, which means code can call methods on a client-side proxy as though the methods were being called directly on the server-side object. The fact that the method call is actually relayed across the network is transparent to the client code.

The `Portal` property itself uses `Activator.GetObject()` to create an instance of a .NET Remoting proxy for the server-side object:

```
Private mPortal As Server.IDataPortalServer

Private ReadOnly Property Portal() As Server.IDataPortalServer
  Get
    If mPortal Is Nothing Then
      mPortal = CType( _
        Activator.GetObject(GetType(Server.Hosts.RemotingPortal), _
        ApplicationContext.DataPortalUrl.ToString), _
        Server.IDataPortalServer)
    End If
    Return mPortal
  End Get
End Property
```

The `Activator.GetObject()` call doesn't actually create an instance of a server-side object. It merely creates an instance of a client-side proxy for the server object. The server configuration controls how server-side objects are created, and in this case, one will be created for each method call from a client.

The only other interesting bit of code is the `Shared` constructor, in which .NET Remoting is configured. A `Shared` constructor is guaranteed to run before any method on a class is invoked, including a regular constructor. In other words, this code will run before anything else runs within the `RemotingProxy` class. This ensures that .NET Remoting is configured before any other code runs in the proxy.

The configuration of remoting is a bit complex, as it employs some optimizations. It sets up a custom configuration for the `HttpChannel`, making sure that the `BinaryFormatter` is used, rather than the default `SoapFormatter`. The code also ensures that the user's Windows credentials are passed across the network if Windows authentication is being used:

```
' create and register a custom HTTP channel
' that uses the binary formatter
Dim properties As New Hashtable
properties("name") = "HttpBinary"

If ApplicationContext.AuthenticationType = "Windows" Then
  ' make sure we pass the user's Windows credentials
  ' to the server
  properties("useDefaultCredentials") = True
End If

Dim formatter As New BinaryClientFormatterSinkProvider
Dim channel As New HttpChannel(properties, formatter, Nothing)
```

Finally, when the remoting channel itself is registered, it may be encrypted. Control over whether it is encrypted is provided through an `<appSettings>` key named `CslaEncryptRemoting`, the value of which is returned from the `EncryptChannel` property. This is used, along with the `Hashtable` defined earlier, to configure the channel:

```
ChannelServices.RegisterChannel(channel, EncryptChannel)
```

The end result is that the client is ready to use HTTP to communicate with the server, where a virtual root in IIS is configured to serve up `Csla.Server.Hosts.RemotingPortal` objects.

Csla.Server.Hosts.RemotingPortal

You've seen the client proxy for the .NET Remoting channel. It requires that a `RemotingPortal` object be hosted on an IIS server. To expose a server-side object through remoting, that object must inherit from System.MarshalByRefObject. Such objects are often referred to as MBROs (marshal-by-refer-ence objects). This base class ensures that the object will run on the server and that it can return information to the client so the client can create a proxy for the server-side object. Remember the Activator.GetObject() call in RemotingProxy. That call relies on the MBRO ability to return proxy information to the client.

The RemotingPortal object's job is simple. It accepts a call from the client and delegates it to an instance of Csla.Server.DataPortal:

```vbnet
Public Class RemotingPortal
  Inherits MarshalByRefObject

  Implements Server.IDataPortalServer

  Public Function Create( _
    ByVal objectType As System.Type, _
    ByVal criteria As Object, _
    ByVal context As Server.DataPortalContext) As Server.DataPortalResult _
    Implements Server.IDataPortalServer.Create

    Dim portal As New Server.DataPortal
    Return portal.Create(objectType, criteria, context)

  End Function

  Public Function Fetch( _
    ByVal criteria As Object, _
    ByVal context As Server.DataPortalContext) As Server.DataPortalResult _
    Implements Server.IDataPortalServer.Fetch

    Dim portal As New Server.DataPortal
    Return portal.Fetch(criteria, context)

  End Function

  Public Function Update( _
    ByVal obj As Object, _
    ByVal context As Server.DataPortalContext) As Server.DataPortalResult _
    Implements Server.IDataPortalServer.Update

    Dim portal As New Server.DataPortal
    Return portal.Update(obj, context)

  End Function

  Public Function Delete( _
    ByVal criteria As Object, _
    ByVal context As Server.DataPortalContext) As Server.DataPortalResult _
    Implements Server.IDataPortalServer.Delete

    Dim portal As New Server.DataPortal
    Return portal.Delete(criteria, context)

  End Function
End Class
```

Notice that it not only inherits from `MarshalByRefObject`, but it also implements `IDataPortalServer`. Recall that this is the common interface required to implement the components of the channel adapter within the data portal.

Each of the methods simply accepts the client's call, creates an instance of `Csla.Server.DataPortal`, and delegates the call.

■**Note** I'm not doing any caching of object references on the server because the remoting object will be exposed as a `SingleCall` object, meaning that a new instance is created and destroyed on every client call. This provides optimal safety on the server by ensuring that one client doesn't try to reuse another client's object.

The reason this code is so simple is because remoting is doing all the hard work. Remoting automatically deserializes the objects passed in as parameters, and serializes the objects being returned as results. If an exception occurs on the server, remoting automatically serializes the exception and returns it to the client instead of the normal result. As you'll see, not all network technologies make things quite so simple.

Chapter 8 will show how to host the `RemotingPortal` in IIS and use it from a client. The following steps summarize the process:

1. Set up a virtual root in IIS.

2. Put `Csla.dll` into the `Bin` directory.

3. Add a `<system.runtime.remoting>` section to `web.config`.

The required `<system.runtime.remoting>` section looks like this:

```
<system.runtime.remoting>
  <application>
    <service>
      <wellknown mode="SingleCall" objectUri="RemotingPortal.rem"
            type="Csla.Server.Hosts.RemotingPortal, Csla"/>
    </service>
    <channels>
      <channel ref="http">
        <serverProviders>
          <provider ref="wsdl"/>
          <formatter ref="soap" typeFilterLevel="Full"/>
          <formatter ref="binary" typeFilterLevel="Full"/>
        </serverProviders>
      </channel>
    </channels>
  </application>
</system.runtime.remoting>
```

This configures ASP.NET to expose the `Csla.Server.Hosts.RemotingPortal` class such that clients can create instances of the class through remoting over HTTP.

Csla.DataPortalClient.EnterpriseServicesProxy

.NET Remoting is a powerful client/server technology, since it easily works with HTTP over port 80 to a web server. However, it isn't as fast as the older Distributed COM (DCOM) protocol used by Enterprise Services. DCOM isn't as easy to use with firewalls, but it offers performance benefits and additional security options that may be attractive.

Another advantage of using Enterprise Services is that the server-side code can be hosted in COM+ rather than in IIS. While IIS has proven to be a highly scalable and reliable host technology, COM+ is often preferred as a host on application servers. It isn't always appropriate or desirable to expose an application server via HTTP, or to install the extra components required by IIS on the server. COM+ provides a viable alternative.

The EnterpriseServicesProxy class uses the .NET support for Enterprise Services to call a server-side object hosted within COM+. This is a bit different from .NET Remoting, however, because the COM references are used. To make this work nicely, EnterpriseServicesProxy is actually a base class that a client application can use to easily create an Enterprise Services client proxy. Similarly, the corresponding server-side EnterpriseServicesPortal class is a base class that the application can use to easily create a server-side object to host in COM+.

This way, the client application can reference its specific server-side object in COM+, ensuring that each application is isolated from other applications using that same server.

EnterpriseServicesProxy implements IDataPortalProxy, and thus the four standard data methods. It also defines a MustOverride method that must be implemented by the subclass to create an instance of the appropriate COM+ server object:

```
Protected MustOverride Function GetServerObject() As _
  Server.Hosts.EnterpriseServicesPortal
```

Each of the data methods simply delegates the call to this server-side object:

```
Public Function Fetch( _
  ByVal criteria As Object, _
  ByVal context As Server.DataPortalContext) As Server.DataPortalResult _
  Implements Server.IDataPortalServer.Fetch

  Dim svc As Server.Hosts.EnterpriseServicesPortal = GetServerObject()
  Try
    Return svc.Fetch(criteria, context)

  Finally
    If svc IsNot Nothing Then
      svc.Dispose()
    End If
  End Try
End Function
```

Notice the Try...Catch block, which ensures that the proxy for the server object is disposed. Normally, you would expect to see a Using statement in such a case; unfortunately, COM+-hosted objects don't work that way.

A client application creates its own subclass with the following steps:

1. Create a Class Library project to contain both the proxy and host classes.

2. Add a subclass of Csla.Server.Hosts.EnterpriseServicesPortal to the assembly.

3. Add a subclass of Csla.DataPortalClient.EnterpriseServicesProxy to the assembly.

4. Override GetServerObject() to return an instance of the class defined in step 2.

5. Set the CslaDataPortalProxy key in the application's config file.

You'll see a complete example of this process in Chapter 12. A subclass of EnterpriseServicesProxy looks like this:

```
Public Class MyEnterpriseServicesProxy
  Inherits Csla.DataPortalClient.EnterpriseServicesProxy

  Protected Overrides Function GetServerObject() As _
      Csla.Server.Hosts.EnterpriseServicesPortal
    Return New MyEnterpriseServicesPortal
  End Function

  ' proxy implementation provided by base class
End Class
```

All that's required for a subclass is to implement the GetServerObject() method. This method is simple to implement because the assembly references the COM+ component on the server. In this example, the assembly contains a class named MyEnterpriseServicesPortal, which is a subclass of Csla.Server.Hosts.EnterpriseServicesPortal.

The CslaDataPortalProxy key in the application config file needs to look like this:

```
<add key="CslaDataPortalProxy"
     value="MyAssembly.MyEnterpriseProxy,MyAssembly " />
```

where MyAssembly is the name of the assembly and namespace needed to find the application's custom proxy class.

Csla.Server.Hosts.EnterpriseServicesPortal

Before a client application can create a subclass of EnterpriseServicesProxy, it needs to create an assembly containing a subclass of EnterpriseServicesPortal. The purpose of this subclass is to provide a unique assembly name for this application within COM+. Where IIS allows you to define numerous virtual roots that expose the same assemblies, COM+ requires different assembly names to achieve isolation between applications.

In order to run within the Enterprise Services environment, the class inherits from System.EnterpriseServices.ServicedComponent and has a couple Enterprise Services attributes applied:

```
<EventTrackingEnabled(True)> _
<ComVisible(True)> _
Public MustInherit Class EnterpriseServicesPortal
  Inherits ServicedComponent

  Implements Server.IDataPortalServer
```

The <EventTrackingEnabled()> attribute ensures that the object reports its status to COM+ so that the "spinning balls" work properly in the management console. The <ComVisible()> attribute is required so that the class is exposed as a COM class, allowing COM+ to interact with it as needed.

Because EnterpriseServicesPortal is a ServicedComponent, the Csla.dll assembly needs some extra configuration:

- The Csla project references System.EnterpriseServices.dll.
- The project/assembly is signed with a key file.
- The project includes an EnterpriseServicesSettings.cs file with some key attributes.

Figure 4-9 shows the Project Properties page where the key file is specified to sign the assembly. Enterprise Services requires that assemblies be signed before they can run within COM+.

Enterprise Services also requires that an assembly include some attributes to describe how it should be used within COM+. I prefer to put these attributes into a file named EnterpriseServicesSettings.vb, though they can technically go into any file in the project. The settings are as follows:

```
Imports System.EnterpriseServices

' EnterpriseServices settings
<Assembly: ApplicationActivation(ActivationOption.Library)>
<Assembly: ApplicationName("CSLA .NET DataPortal")>
<Assembly: Description("CSLA .NET Serviced DataPortal")>
<Assembly: ApplicationAccessControl(False)>
```

The ApplicationActivation() setting indicates that the assembly should run within the process that calls it, not within a separate process hosted by COM+. This is important since Csla.dll must be allowed to run within many different processes, including Windows Forms, ASP.NET, and COM+.

The ApplicationName() and Description() settings are optional, but are used to describe the COM+ component. Finally, the ApplicationAccessControl() setting indicates that COM+ shouldn't apply its own method-level security when clients try to call Csla.dll objects.

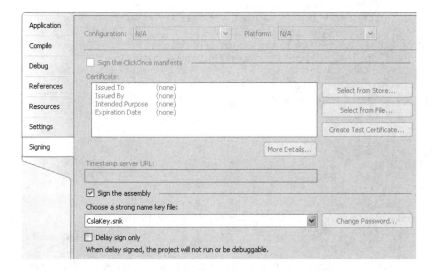

Figure 4-9. *Signing an assembly using the Project Properties designer*

The EnterpriseServicesPortal class implements IDataPortalServer, and thus the four data methods. As with RemotingPortal, these methods simply delegate the call to a Csla.Server. DataPortal object:

```
Public Function Fetch( _
  ByVal criteria As Object, _
  ByVal context As Server.DataPortalContext) As Server.DataPortalResult _
  Implements Server.IDataPortalServer.Fetch

  Dim portal As New Server.DataPortal
  Return portal.Fetch(criteria, context)
End Function
```

Like remoting, Enterprise Services automatically serializes and deserializes objects as they move between client and server. However, there's one extra issue that must be covered when hosting within COM+. Due to the way .NET assemblies are dynamically loaded, the .NET serialization process is unable to automatically discover business assemblies—even if they are already loaded into memory. To overcome this problem, the class has a Shared constructor that sets up an event handler to work around the serialization issue:

```
Shared Sub New()
  SerializationWorkaround()
End Sub

Private Shared Sub SerializationWorkaround()
  ' hook up the AssemblyResolve
  ' event so deep serialization works properly
  ' this is a workaround for a bug in the .NET runtime
  Dim currentDomain As AppDomain = AppDomain.CurrentDomain

  AddHandler currentDomain.AssemblyResolve, _
    AddressOf ResolveEventHandler
End Sub

Private Shared Function ResolveEventHandler( _
  ByVal sender As Object, ByVal args As ResolveEventArgs) As [Assembly]

  ' get a list of all the assemblies loaded in our appdomain
  Dim list() As [Assembly] = AppDomain.CurrentDomain.GetAssemblies()

  ' search the list to find the assemby that was not found automatically
  ' and return the assembly from the list
  Dim asm As [Assembly]

  For Each asm In list
    If asm.FullName = args.Name Then
      Return asm
    End If
  Next

  ' if the assembly wasn't already in the appdomain, then try to load it
  Return [Assembly].Load(args.Name)
End Function
```

The AssemblyResolve event is raised by .NET itself when it can't find a requested assembly. The handler code shown here merely loops through the assemblies *already loaded* in the AppDomain to find the assembly and return it. This effectively works around the serialization issue by "helping" .NET find the assembly.

■Note The underlying issue here is that .NET maintains several lists of loaded assemblies, and the deserialization process only checks *some* of the lists to find assemblies. Dynamically loaded assemblies aren't found by default, but this code solves the problem by handling the AssemblyResolve event.

The EnterpriseServicesPortal base class handles virtually all the details, allowing a subclass to look like this:

```
<EventTrackingEnabled(True)> _
<ComVisible(True)> _
Public Class MyEnterpriseServicesPortal
  Inherits Csla.Server.Hosts.EnterpriseServicesPortal

  ' implementation provided by base class
End Class
```

I refer to the assembly containing this subclass as the proxy/host assembly because it will also contain the subclass of EnterpriseServicesProxy. However, because the assembly contains a sub-class of EnterpriseServicesPortal, it needs to meet the requirements for any assembly hosted in Enterprise Services, namely:

- The assembly must be signed with a key file, similar to Csla.dll (see Figure 4-9).
- The assembly must reference System.EnterpriseServices.dll.
- Like Csla.dll, the assembly must include some key <Assembly: > attributes.

I typically put the attributes required by Enterprise Services into an EnterpriseServicesSettings.vb file in the project. The attributes look like this:

```
Imports System.EnterpriseServices

' EnterpriseServices settings
<Assembly: ApplicationActivation(ActivationOption.Server)>
<Assembly: ApplicationName("My Application")>
<Assembly: Description("My Application Description")>
<Assembly: ApplicationAccessControl(False)>
```

Replace My Application and My Application Description with an appropriate name and description for your business application. The ApplicationActivation() setting specifies that this component should run within a process hosted by COM+. It is this setting that allows the component to act as a host on the server to accept calls from remote clients.

■**Note** The ApplicationActivation() setting here is different from the one used for Csla.dll. This is because Csla.dll needs to run *inside your application's process*, while this separate proxy/host assembly needs to run in a COM+ process.

After building the assembly, follow these steps to install and configure the assembly for use:

1. Use the .NET command line utility regsvcs.exe to install the assembly into COM+.
2. Create a directory to store the server configuration.
3. Add application.config and application.manifest files to the directory created in step 2.
4. Use the Component Services management console to set the application root directory to the directory created in step 2, as shown in Figure 4-10.
5. Use the Component Services management console to set any other application settings as appropriate for your environment.

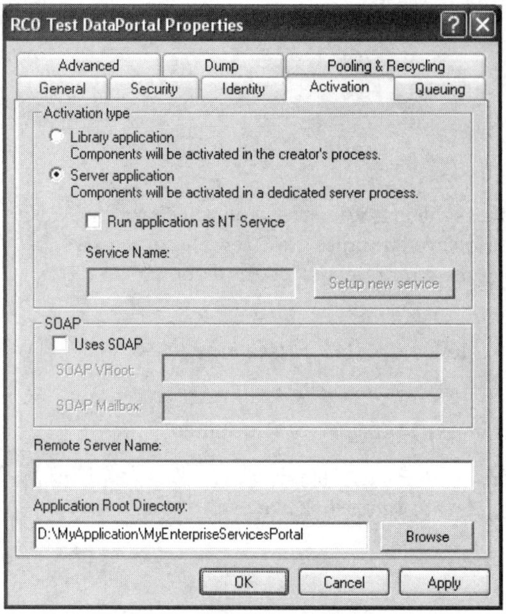

Figure 4-10. *Setting the application root directory*

The `application.config` file is actually named `application.config`. It is a standard .NET config file that contains the normal .NET configuration you would put into any `app.config` file, including the CSLA .NET configuration settings. For instance, it might look like this:

```
<?xml version="1.0" encoding="utf-8" ?>
<configuration>
  <appSettings>
    <add key="CslaAuthentication" value="Csla"/>
  </appSettings>
</configuration>
```

The `application.manifest` file is required by Enterprise Services and looks like this:

```
<?xml version="1.0" encoding="UTF-8" standalone="yes"?>
<assembly xmlns="urn:schemas-microsoft-com:asm.v1" manifestVersion="1.0">
</assembly>
```

At this point, you can create your client-side proxy assembly, including a subclass of `EnterpriseServicesProxy`. Make sure to reference this new server-side assembly so that you can implement the `GetServerObject()` method as discussed earlier. Again, a fully working example of this process is covered in Chapter 12.

When you deploy the client application, you'll also need to install the COM+ proxy on every client workstation. Deployment of COM+ proxies is outside the scope of this book, but in short, you need to use the Component Services management console on the server to create a setup `msi` file for the COM+ application, and then run that `msi` on every client workstation.

Csla.DataPortalClient.WebServicesProxy

The final channel implemented in CSLA .NET uses Web Services as a network transport. Unfortunately, Web Services is not designed as a client/server technology, but rather as an interop technology. Due to this, Web Services is not normally able to support the concept of mobile objects.

The WebServicesProxy and corresponding WebServicePortal classes will overcome this limitation by manually using the .NET BinaryFormatter to serialize and deserialize the objects. The result of such serialization is a byte array, and so the web services used in this implementation will accept byte arrays as parameters and return byte arrays as results.

Additionally, Web Services doesn't normally return .NET exceptions with full fidelity. In a client/server application, it is desirable to return all the details about any server-side exceptions to the client for debugging purposes. The WebServicesProxy and WebServicePortal classes will overcome this limitation as well.

■**Note** The web service channel implemented here is primarily intended to be an example of how you can implement mobile objects using technologies less capable than remoting or Enterprise Services. You could apply similar concepts to build a channel over raw TCP sockets, SMTP email, or other network transports.

As with all the other proxy/host combinations, WebServicesProxy has one job: to connect to the server (web service, in this case) and deliver the client call to the server. To this end, it has a web reference to the web service.

■**Note** Setting up the web reference was a little tricky. Before creating the WebServicesProxy class, I had to implement the WebServicePortal class (discussed later) and temporarily host Csla.dll in a virtual root. That allowed me to add a web reference from the Csla project. Once that web reference was established, I was able to create WebServicesProxy because the required types from the web service were available.

The web reference defines a WebServiceHost namespace, and within that namespace a WebServicePortal class. These types are used to create an instance of the server object:

```
Private Function GetPortal() As WebServiceHost.WebServicePortal
  Dim wsvc As New WebServiceHost.WebServicePortal
  wsvc.Url = ApplicationContext.DataPortalUrl.ToString
  Return wsvc
End Function
```

Notice that it explicitly sets the proxy object's Url property based on the DataPortalUrl property read from the client application's <appSettings> config file section. This allows your application to specify the URL for the server through a config file, rather than having to alter either your business code or the code in the Csla project any time that URL changes.

Each data method then calls this web service to relay the client call to the server. But Web Services doesn't properly serialize object graphs for client/server purposes. Web Services uses the .NET XmlSerializer object to serialize objects; and XmlSerializer only serializes Public read-write fields and properties, ignoring private fields and read-only properties. It is absolutely not sufficient to implement mobile objects as required by CSLA .NET.

To overcome this limitation, each of the data methods in WebServicesProxy explicitly uses the .NET BinaryFormatter to serialize and deserialize objects:

```
Public Function Fetch( _
  ByVal criteria As Object, _
  ByVal context As Server.DataPortalContext) As Server.DataPortalResult _
  Implements Server.IDataPortalServer.Fetch
```

```
Dim result As Object
Dim request As New Server.Hosts.WebServicePortal.FetchRequest
request.Criteria = criteria
request.Context = context

Using wsvc As WebServiceHost.WebServicePortal = GetPortal()
  result = Deserialize(wsvc.Fetch(Serialize(request)))
End Using

If TypeOf result Is Exception Then
  Throw DirectCast(result, Exception)
End If
Return DirectCast(result, Server.DataPortalResult)
End Function
```

Before making the web service call, the criteria object and CSLA .NET context object are both put into a FetchRequest object, which is then serialized. The FetchRequest class is just a data transfer object (DTO) and is defined by Csla.Server.Hosts.WebServicePortal. Both these classes will be discussed shortly.

The Serialize() and Deserialize() methods are helper methods that invoke the BinaryFormatter to serialize and deserialize objects. Since BinaryFormatter is used by both remoting and Enterprise Services, this code is literally duplicating what those other technologies do natively:

```
Private Shared Function Serialize(ByVal obj As Object) As Byte()
  If Not obj Is Nothing Then
    Using buffer As New MemoryStream
      Dim formatter As New BinaryFormatter
      formatter.Serialize(buffer, obj)
      Return buffer.ToArray
    End Using

  Else
    Return Nothing
  End If
End Function

Private Shared Function Deserialize(ByVal obj As Byte()) As Object

  If Not obj Is Nothing Then
    Using buffer As New MemoryStream(obj)
      Dim formatter As New BinaryFormatter
      Return formatter.Deserialize(buffer)
    End Using

  Else
    Return Nothing
  End If
End Function
```

The Serialize() method is quite comparable to the Clone() method implemented by the ObjectCloner class in Chapter 3, and Deserialize() simply reverses the process: converting a byte array back into the original object graph.

Back in the Fetch() method, once the FetchRequest object is loaded with data, it is serialized with the Serialize() helper and passed to the server:

```
result = Deserialize(wsvc.Fetch(Serialize(request)));
```

The result of the web service call is deserialized using the Deserialize() helper and is put into a field of type Object. This is important because the result could either be a Csla.Server. DataPortalResult object or a subclass of System.Exception. If an exception was thrown on the server, it is returned to the client in serialized form; otherwise, a normal result is returned. Either way, the Fetch() method has to handle the result:

```
if (result is Exception)
  throw (Exception)result;
return (Server.DataPortalResult)result;
```

In the case of a server-side exception, the exception is rethrown on the client. Remember that the data portal only returns Csla.Server.DataPortalException type exceptions, which contain the full server-side stack trace and other details. This implementation achieves full parity with .NET Remoting or Enterprise Services, returning the complete server-side exception details through Web Services.

On the other hand, if a normal result was returned, then that result is simply passed back to Csla.DataPortal so it can process it normally.

Because the Csla.dll assembly has a preexisting web reference to the Csla.Server.Hosts. WebServicePortal class, no special client configuration is required. The client's config file merely needs to specify the use of the web service proxy and the server's URL.

Csla.Server.Hosts.WebServicePortal

The WebServicesProxy calls a web service, implemented in the Csla.Server.Hosts. WebServicePortal class. Unlike the other server-side host classes, this one doesn't implement IDataPortalServer. The interface exposed by the web service is quite different from IDataPortalServer, because the web service accepts and returns byte arrays rather than native .NET types.

You've already seen how the WebServicesProxy manually serializes and deserializes the data sent to and from the web service. Now let's look at the other end of the process. The same Serialize() and Deserialize() helper methods are used on the server too, as you can see in the Fetch() implementation:

```
<WebMethod()> _
Public Function Fetch(ByVal requestData As Byte()) As Byte()
  Dim request As FetchRequest = _
    DirectCast(Deserialize(requestData), FetchRequest)

  Dim portal As New Server.DataPortal
  Dim result As Object
  Try
    result = portal.Fetch(request.Criteria, request.Context)

  Catch ex As Exception
    result = ex
  End Try
  Return Serialize(result)
End Function
```

The method accepts a byte array as a parameter, which is immediately deserialized to create a server-side copy of the FetchRequest object created on the client:

```
Dim request As FetchRequest = _
  DirectCast(Deserialize(requestData), FetchRequest)
```

The FetchRequest class is a DTO that simply defines the data to be passed from client to server when Fetch() is called. It looks like this:

```
<Serializable()> _
Public Class FetchRequest

  Private mCriteria As Object
  Public Property Criteria() As Object
    Get
      Return mCriteria
    End Get
    Set(ByVal value As Object)
      mCriteria = value
    End Set
  End Property

  Private mContext As Server.DataPortalContext
  Public Property Context() As Server.DataPortalContext
    Get
      Return mContext
    End Get
    Set(ByVal value As Server.DataPortalContext)
      mContext = value
    End Set
  End Property
End Class
```

■**Tip** The concept of a DTO comes from Martin Fowler's excellent book, *Patterns of Enterprise Application Architecture* (Addison-Wesley Professional, 2002).

A Fetch() request requires both the criteria object and context data from the client. The whole purpose behind the FetchRequest class is to combine all the data into a single unit that can be easily serialized and deserialized.

Once the FetchRequest object has been deserialized, the Fetch() method on a Csla.Server.DataPortal object is called:

```
result = portal.Fetch(request.Criteria, request.Context)
```

This is no different from any of the other host classes discussed earlier in the chapter, except that the call is wrapped in a Try...Catch block. Remember that Web Services doesn't pass server-side exceptions back to the client with full fidelity. To ensure that the full details are returned, any exceptions are caught and are specifically returned as a result to the client.

Notice how the result field is declared as type Object and ends up either containing the DataPortalResult object from the Fetch() call, or the Exception object caught by the Try...Catch. Either way, it is serialized and returned to the client:

```
Return Serialize(result)
```

As with WebServicesProxy, the goal here is basically to replicate the functionality that remoting and Enterprise Services provide automatically.

Since WebServicePortal inherits from System.Web.Services.WebService, it is all ready to be exposed as a web service. All that is needed is a virtual root and an asmx file. When a client application wants to expose a web service data portal, it needs to do the following:

1. Set up a virtual root

2. Put `Csla.dll` into the `Bin` directory

3. Create an `asmx` file referencing `WebServicePortal` in the virtual directory

The `asmx` file needs to contain the following single line:

```
<%@ WebService Language="VB" Class="Csla.Server.Hosts.WebServicePortal" %>
```

This tells ASP.NET to find the web service implementation in the `Csla.Server.Hosts.`
`WebServicePortal` class. Recall that `Csla.dll` already includes a web reference to a web service
matching this description, so the client needs only to set up the appropriate `Url` entry in their
config file's `<appSettings>` section.

At this point, you've seen the code that implements the channel adapter, including the `Csla.`
`DataPortal` class used by business developers and all the channel proxy and host implementations.
Let's move on now to discuss the server-side portions of the data portal, starting with distributed
transaction support, and then moving on to the message router pattern.

Distributed Transaction Support

Though it may use different network channels to do its work, the primary job of `Csla.DataPortal` is
to delegate the client's call to an object on the server. This object is of type `Csla.Server.DataPortal`,
and its primary responsibility is to route the client's call to `Csla.Server.SimpleDataPortal`, which
actually implements the message router behavior.

The reason `Csla.Server.DataPortal` is involved in this process is so it can establish a distributed transactional context if requested by the business object. The CSLA .NET framework allows
a business developer to choose between manually handling transactions, using Enterprise Services
(COM+) transactions, or using `System.Transactions`.

The business developer indicates his preference through the use of the custom `Csla.`
`TransactionalAttribute`. Earlier in the chapter, Table 4-4 listed all the possible options when
using this attribute on a `DataPortal_XYZ` method.

Csla.TransactionalTypes

The `TransactionalTypes` enumerated list contains all the options that can be specified with the
`<Transactional()>` attribute when it is applied to a `DataPortal_XYZ` method on a business object:

```
Public Enum TransactionalTypes
  EnterpriseServices
  TransactionScope
  Manual
End Enum
```

This type is used to define the parameter value for the constructor in `Csla.`
`TransactionalAttribute`.

Csla.TransactionalAttribute

The `<Transactional()>` attribute can be optionally applied to a `DataPortal_XYZ` method in a business class to tell the data portal what type of transactional technology should be used when the
method is invoked by the data portal on the server. The default, if the attribute isn't used, is
`TransactionalTypes.Manual`—meaning that the developer is responsible for handling any transactions in his own code.

This class is a straightforward implementation of a custom attribute, inheriting from `System.`
`Attribute`:

```
<AttributeUsage(AttributeTargets.Method)> _
Public NotInheritable Class TransactionalAttribute
  Inherits Attribute

  Private mType As TransactionalTypes

  Public Sub New()
    mType = TransactionalTypes.EnterpriseServices
  End Sub

  Public Sub New(ByVal transactionType As TransactionalTypes)
    mType = transactionType
  End Sub

  Public ReadOnly Property TransactionType() As TransactionalTypes
    Get
      Return mType
    End Get
  End Property
End Class
```

The `<AttributeUsage()>` attribute restricts this new attribute so it can only be applied to methods. The parameterless constructor defaults to using `TransactionalTypes.EnterpriseServices`. This is done for backward compatibility with earlier versions of CSLA .NET, in which the only option was to use Enterprise Services. In most cases, it will be preferable to use the newer `TransactionScope` option to trigger the use of `System.Transactions`.

Csla.Server.DataPortal

Ultimately, all client calls go through the channel adapter and are handled on the server by an instance of `Csla.Server.DataPortal`. This object uses the value of the `<Transactional()>` attribute (if any) on the `DataPortal_XYZ` method of the business class to determine how to route the call to `Csla.Server.SimpleDataPortal`. The call will go via one of the following three routes:

- The `Manual` option routes directly to `SimpleDataPortal`.
- The `EnterpriseServices` option routes through `Csla.Server.ServicedDataPortal`.
- The `TransactionScope` option routes through `Csla.Server.TransactionalDataPortal`.

The `Csla.Server.DataPortal` object also takes care of establishing the correct context on the server based on the context provided by the client. The details of this process are discussed later in the chapter.

`Csla.Server.DataPortal` implements `IDataPortalServer`, and thus the four data methods. Each of these methods follows the same basic flow:

- Set up the server's context.
- Get the `MethodInfo` for the business method to be ultimately invoked.
- Check the `<Transactional()>` attribute on that `MethodInfo` object.
- Route the call based on the `<Transactional()>` attribute.
- Clear the server's context.
- Return the result provided by `SimpleDataPortal`.

Let's look first at the `Create()` method to see how this is implemented, followed by the differences in other methods.

Create

The Create() method implements the steps listed previously:

```
Public Function Create( _
  ByVal objectType As System.Type, _
  ByVal criteria As Object, _
  ByVal context As Server.DataPortalContext) As Server.DataPortalResult _
  Implements Server.IDataPortalServer.Create

  Try
    SetContext(context)

    Dim result As DataPortalResult

    Dim method As MethodInfo = _
      MethodCaller.GetMethod(objectType, "DataPortal_Create", criteria)

    Select Case TransactionalType(method)
      Case TransactionalTypes.EnterpriseServices
        Dim portal As New ServicedDataPortal
        Try
          result = portal.Create(objectType, criteria, context)

        Finally
          portal.Dispose()
        End Try

      Case TransactionalTypes.TransactionScope
        Dim portal As New TransactionalDataPortal
        result = portal.Create(objectType, criteria, context)

      Case Else
        Dim portal As New SimpleDataPortal
        result = portal.Create(objectType, criteria, context)
    End Select

    ClearContext(context)
    Return result

  Catch
    ClearContext(context)
    Throw
  End Try
End Function
```

After setting the server's context (a topic discussed later in the chapter), the MethodInfo object for the DataPortal_Create() method on the business class is retrieved:

```
Dim method As MethodInfo = _
    MethodCaller.GetMethod(objectType, "DataPortal_Create", criteria)
```

This uses the same MethodCaller.GetMethod() implementation discussed and used earlier in the chapter. Next, a TransactionType() helper method is called to retrieve the value of the <Transactional()> attribute associated with this method. The helper looks like this:

```
Private Shared Function TransactionalType( _
  ByVal method As MethodInfo) As TransactionalTypes

  Dim result As TransactionalTypes
  If IsTransactionalMethod(method) Then
    Dim attrib As TransactionalAttribute = _
      DirectCast(Attribute.GetCustomAttribute( _
        method, GetType(TransactionalAttribute)), _
      TransactionalAttribute)
    result = attrib.TransactionType

  Else
    result = TransactionalTypes.Manual
  End If
  Return result
End Function
```

If there is no <Transactional()> attribute on the method, then the Manual type is returned as a default. Otherwise, the TransactionalAttribute object associated with the attribute is retrieved and its TransactionType property value is returned.

Back in the Create() method, the resulting value is used in a Select statement to properly route the call. If EnterpriseServices was specified, then an instance of Csla.Server. ServicedDataPortal is created and the call is delegated to that object:

```
Case TransactionalTypes.EnterpriseServices
  Dim portal As New ServicedDataPortal
  Try
    result = portal.Create(objectType, criteria, context)

  Finally
    portal.Dispose()
  End Try
```

As with all Enterprise Services objects, a Try...Finally block is used to ensure that the object is properly disposed when the call is complete. The details of the ServicedDataPortal class will be covered shortly.

If TransactionScope was specified, then an instance of Csla.Server.TransactionalDataPortal is created and the call is delegated to that object:

```
Case TransactionalTypes.TransactionScope
  Dim portal As New TransactionalDataPortal
  result = portal.Create(objectType, criteria, context)
```

The details of the TransactionalDataPortal class will be covered shortly.

Finally, the default is to allow the business developer to handle any transactions manually. In that case, an instance of Csla.Server.SimpleDataPortal is created directly, and the call is delegated to that object:

```
Case Else
  Dim portal As New SimpleDataPortal
  result = portal.Create(objectType, criteria, context)
```

Both ServicedDataPortal and TransactionalDataPortal delegate their calls to SimpleDataPortal too—so in the end, all client calls are handled by SimpleDataPortal. By calling it directly, without involving any transactional technologies, this default approach allows the business developer to handle any transactions as she sees fit.

Once the Create() call is complete, the server's context is cleared (details discussed later), and the result is returned to the client:

```
Return result
```

If an exception occurs during the processing, it is caught, the server's context is cleared, and the exception is rethrown so it can be handled by Csla.DataPortal, as discussed earlier in the chapter.

Fetch and Delete

The Fetch() and Delete() methods work basically the same as Create(). The only difference is in how the MethodInfo object is retrieved. Remember that Create() gets the type of the business object passed as a parameter, while Fetch() and Delete() need to infer the type based on the criteria object. The Fetch() code looks like this:

```
Dim method As MethodInfo = _
  MethodCaller.GetMethod( _
    MethodCaller.GetObjectType(criteria), _
    "DataPortal_Fetch", criteria)
```

This overload of GetMethod() tries to find a strongly typed DataPortal_Fetch() method with a parameter that matches the type of the criteria object. Otherwise, it finds one with a parameter of type Object.

The remainder of the Fetch() and Delete() methods is fundamentally identical to Create().

Update

The Update() method is more complex. This is because Update() handles BusinessBase and CommandBase subclasses differently from other objects. The specific DataPortal_XYZ method to be invoked varies based on the base class of the business object. This complicates the process of retrieving the MethodInfo object:

```
Dim method As MethodInfo
Dim methodName As String
If TypeOf obj Is CommandBase Then
  methodName = "DataPortal_Execute"

ElseIf TypeOf obj Is Core.BusinessBase Then
  Dim tmp As Core.BusinessBase = DirectCast(obj, Core.BusinessBase)
  If tmp.IsDeleted Then
    methodName = "DataPortal_DeleteSelf"
  Else
    If tmp.IsNew Then
      methodName = "DataPortal_Insert"

    Else
      methodName = "DataPortal_Update"
    End If
  End If
Else
  methodName = "DataPortal_Update"
End If

method = MethodCaller.GetMethod(obj.GetType, methodName)
```

The same `GetMethod()` call is used as in `Fetch()` and `Delete()`, but the *name* of the method is determined based on the type and state of the business object itself. If the business object is a subclass of `CommandBase`, then the method name is `DataPortal_Execute`. For any other objects that don't inherit from `BusinessBase`, the method name is `DataPortal_Update`.

If the business object is a subclass of `BusinessBase`, however, the object's state becomes important. If the object is marked for deletion, then the method name is `DataPortal_DeleteSelf`. If the object is new, the name is `DataPortal_Insert`; otherwise, it is `DataPortal_Update`.

Once the `MethodInfo` object has been retrieved, the rest of the code is essentially the same as in the other three methods.

Now let's discuss the two remaining classes that set up an appropriate transaction context.

Csla.Server.ServicedDataPortal

The `ServicedDataPortal` has one job: to create a distributed COM+ transactional context within which `SimpleDataPortal` (and thus the business object) will run. When a call is routed through `ServicedDataPortal`, a distributed transactional context is created, ensuring that the business object's `DataPortal_XYZ` methods run within that context.

Normally, to run within a COM+ distributed transaction, an object must inherit from `System.EnterpriseServices.ServicedComponent`. This is a problem for typical business objects, since you don't *usually* want them to run within COM+, and no one likes all the deployment complexity that comes with a `ServicedComponent`.

`ServicedDataPortal` allows business objects to avoid this complexity. It does inherit from `ServicedComponent`, and includes the appropriate Enterprise Services attributes to trigger the use of a distributed transaction. But it turns out that when a `ServicedComponent` running in a transactional context calls a normal .NET object, *that object also runs in the transaction*. This is true even when the normal .NET object doesn't inherit from `ServicedComponent`.

The use of this concept is illustrated in Figure 4-11.

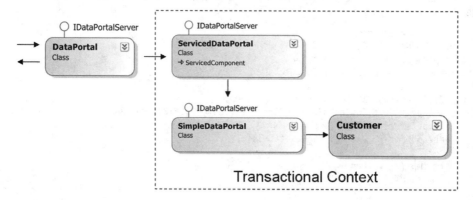

Figure 4-11. *Using ServicedDataPortal to wrap a business object in a transaction*

Once the transactional context is established by `ServicedDataPortal`, all normal .NET objects invoked from that point forward run within the same context.

`ServicedDataPortal` itself inherits from `System.EnterpriseServices.ServicedComponent`, and includes some key attributes:

```
<Transaction(TransactionOption.Required)> _
<EventTrackingEnabled(True)> _
<ComVisible(True)> _
Public Class ServicedDataPortal
  Inherits ServicedComponent

  Implements IDataPortalServer
```

The `<Transaction()>` attribute specifies that this object *must* run within a COM+ transactional context. If it is called by another object that already established such a context, this object will run within that context; otherwise, it will create a new context.

The `<EventTrackingEnabled()>` attribute indicates that this object will interact with COM+ to enable the "spinning balls" in the Component Services management console. This is only important (or even visible) if the data portal is running within COM+ on the server—meaning that the `EnterpriseServicesProxy` is used by the client to interact with the server.

The `<ComVisible()>` attribute makes this class visible to COM, which is a requirement for any class that is to be hosted in COM+.

Because `ServicedDataPortal` inherits from `ServicedComponent`, the `Csla.dll` assembly itself must be configured so it can be hosted in COM+. Because the assembly already includes the `Csla.Server.Hosts.EnterpriseServicesPortal` class, all the necessary configuration already exists. This was discussed earlier in the chapter.

The class also implements the `IDataPortalServer` interface, ensuring that it implements the four data methods. Each of these methods has another Enterprise Services attribute—`<AutoComplete()>`:

```
<AutoComplete(True)> _
Public Function Create( _
  ByVal objectType As System.Type, _
  ByVal criteria As Object, _
  ByVal context As Server.DataPortalContext) As Server.DataPortalResult _
  Implements Server.IDataPortalServer.Create

  Dim portal As New SimpleDataPortal
  Return portal.Create(objectType, criteria, context)
End Function
```

The `<AutoComplete()>` attribute is used to tell COM+ that this method will vote to commit the transaction unless it throws an exception. In other words, if an exception is thrown, the method votes to roll back the transaction; otherwise, it votes to commit the transaction.

This fits with the overall model of the data portal, which relies on the business object to throw exceptions in case of failure. The data portal uses the exception to return important information about the failure back to the client. `ServicedDataPortal` also relies on the exception to tell COM+ to roll back the transaction.

Notice how the `Create()` method simply creates an instance of `SimpleDataPortal` and delegates the call to that object. This is the same as `Csla.Server.DataPortal` did for manual transactions; except in this case, `SimpleDataPortal` and the business object are wrapped in a distributed transactional context.

The other three data methods are implemented in the same manner.

Csla.Server.TransactionalDataPortal

`TransactionalDataPortal` is designed in a manner very similar to `ServicedDataPortal`. Rather than using Enterprise Services, however, this object uses the transactional capabilities provided by the new `System.Transactions` namespace, and in particular the new `TransactionScope` object.

This class simply implements IDataPortalServer:

```
Public Class TransactionalDataPortal

  Implements IDataPortalServer
```

This ensures that it implements the four data methods. Each of these methods follows the same structure: create a TransactionScope object and delegate the call to an instance of SimpleDataPortal. For instance, here's the Create() method:

```
Public Function Create( _
  ByVal objectType As System.Type, _
  ByVal criteria As Object, _
  ByVal context As Server.DataPortalContext) As Server.DataPortalResult _
  Implements Server.IDataPortalServer.Create

  Dim result As DataPortalResult
  Using tr As New TransactionScope
    Dim portal As New SimpleDataPortal
    result = portal.Create(objectType, criteria, context)
    tr.Complete()
  End Using
  Return result
End Function
```

The first thing this method does is create a TransactionScope object from the System.Transactions namespace. Just the act of instantiating such an object creates a transactional context. It is not a *distributed* transactional context, but a lighter-weight context. If the business object interacts with more than one database, however, it will automatically become a distributed transaction.

The Using block here ensures both that the TransactionScope object will be properly disposed, and perhaps more importantly, that the transaction will be committed or rolled back as appropriate. If the object is disposed before the Complete() method is called, then the transaction is rolled back. Again, this model relies on the underlying assumption that the business code will throw an exception to indicate failure. This is the same model that is used by ServicedDataPortal, and really by the data portal infrastructure overall.

Within the Using block, the code creates an instance of SimpleDataPortal and delegates the call to that object, which in turn calls the business object. Assuming no exception is thrown by the business object, the Complete() method is called to indicate that the transaction should be committed.

The other three methods are implemented in the same manner. Regardless of which transactional model is used, all calls end up being handled by a SimpleDataPortal object, which implements the message router concept.

Message Router

The message router functionality picks up where the channel adapter leaves off. The channel adapter gets the client call from the client to the server, ultimately calling Csla.Server.DataPortal. Recall that every host class (LocalPortal, RemotingPortal, etc.) ends up delegating every method call to an instance of Csla.Server.DataPortal. That object routes the call to a Csla.Server.SimpleDataPortal object, possibly first setting up a transactional context.

The focus in this section of the chapter will primarily be on Csla.Server.SimplePortal, as it is this class that implements the message router behavior to call the appropriate methods on the right business object. First though, let's take a brief look at `Csla.CriteriaBase` and the role it plays in the message router implementation.

Csla.CriteriaBase

The `CriteriaBase` class has been discussed previously in the chapter, in the context of using it as a base class for defining a criteria class. Here's the code for the class:

```
<Serializable()> _
Public MustInherit Class CriteriaBase

  Private mObjectType As Type

  Public ReadOnly Property ObjectType() As Type
    Get
      Return mObjectType
    End Get
  End Property

  Protected Sub New(ByVal type As Type)
    mObjectType = type
  End Sub
End Class
```

The purpose of this base class is to ensure that the data portal infrastructure has access to the type of business object required for a create, retrieve, or delete operation. As has been discussed, the data portal supports both nesting a criteria class within the business class itself and having the criteria class inherit from `CriteriaBase`.

Csla.Server.SimpleDataPortal

The core of the message router behavior is the `SimpleDataPortal` class. In the final analysis, after going through the channel adapter and transactional behaviors, all client calls end up being handled on the server by an instance of `SimpleDataPortal`. This class is the counterpart to the client-side `Csla.DataPortal`, since it is this class that interacts directly with the business objects designed by the business developer.

`SimpleDataPortal` implements the four data methods defined by `IDataPortalServer`: `Create()`, `Fetch()`, `Update()`, and `Delete()`. Each of these methods follows the same basic processing flow:

1. Create or get an instance of the business object.

2. Call the object's `DataPortal_OnDataPortalInvoke()` method (if implemented).

3. Call the appropriate `DataPortal_XYZ` method on the object.

4. Set the object's status (new, dirty, etc.) as appropriate.

5. Call the object's `DataPortal_OnDataPortalInvokeComplete()` method (if implemented).

6. In case of exception, call the object's `DataPortal_OnDataPortalException()` method (if implemented) and throw a `Csla.Server.DataPortalException`.

7. Return the resulting business object (if appropriate).

Let's look at the `Create()` method in detail, followed by the minor differences required to implement the other four methods.

Create

The Create() method illustrates every step in the preceding list:

```
Public Function Create( _
  ByVal objectType As System.Type, _
  ByVal criteria As Object, _
  ByVal context As Server.DataPortalContext) As Server.DataPortalResult _
  Implements Server.IDataPortalServer.Create

  Dim obj As Object = Nothing

  Try
    ' create an instance of the business object
    obj = Activator.CreateInstance(objectType, True)

    ' tell the business object we're about to make a DataPortal_xyz call
    MethodCaller.CallMethodIfImplemented( _
      obj, "DataPortal_OnDataPortalInvoke", _
      New DataPortalEventArgs(context))

    ' tell the business object to fetch its data
    MethodCaller.CallMethod(obj, "DataPortal_Create", criteria)

    ' mark the object as new
    MethodCaller.CallMethodIfImplemented(obj, "MarkNew")

    ' tell the business object the DataPortal_xyz call is complete
    MethodCaller.CallMethodIfImplemented( _
      obj, "DataPortal_OnDataPortalInvokeComplete", _
      New DataPortalEventArgs(context))

    ' return the populated business object as a result
    Return New DataPortalResult(obj)

  Catch ex As Exception
    Try
      ' tell the business object there was an exception
      MethodCaller.CallMethodIfImplemented( _
        obj, "DataPortal_OnDataPortalException", _
        New DataPortalEventArgs(context), ex)
    Catch
      ' ignore exceptions from the exception handler
    End Try
    Throw New DataPortalException("DataPortal.Create " & _
      My.Resources.FailedOnServer, ex, New DataPortalResult(obj))
  End Try
End Function
```

The first step is to create an instance of the business object. This is done using the CreateInstance() method of the System.Activator class:

```
obj = Activator.CreateInstance(objectType, True)
```

The objectType parameter is passed from the client. Recall that in Csla.DataPortal, the type of the object to be created was determined and passed as a parameter to the Create() method.

It is also important to recognize that the constructors on business classes are not Public. They are either Private or Protected, thus forcing the UI developer to use the factory methods to create or retrieve business objects. This use of `Activator.CreateInstance()` tells .NET to create an instance of the class using the constructor even though it isn't `Public`.

If it isn't already loaded into memory, the .NET runtime will automatically load the assembly containing the business object class. This is handled automatically by `Activator.CreateInstance()`, following the normal assembly-loading process always used by .NET.

■**Tip** To ensure .NET can find your business assembly, it must be in the same directory as the client application's `.exe` file, in the `Bin` directory. Alternatively, you may install the assembly into the .NET global assembly cache (GAC).

The next step in the process is to tell the business object that it is about to be invoked by the data portal. This is done by calling the object's `DataPortal_OnDataPortalInvoke()` method:

```
MethodCaller.CallMethodIfImplemented( _
    obj, "DataPortal_OnDataPortalInvoke", _
    New DataPortalEventArgs(context))
```

Notice the use of the `CallMethodIfImplemented()` method on the `MethodCaller` class. This method was discussed earlier in the chapter, and it invokes the named method if it exists on the object, but does not throw an exception if the method isn't there. This is a way of invoking methods that are considered optional on the business object.

A business developer can implement this method to do any preprocessing prior to an actual `DataPortal_XYZ` method being called. And that's the very next step:

```
MethodCaller.CallMethod(obj, "DataPortal_Create", criteria)
```

This isn't optional, so `MethodCaller.CallMethod()` is used. If it doesn't find a matching method, it will throw an exception. Recall that it tries to invoke a method that has a strongly typed parameter matching the type of the criteria object; otherwise, it will invoke one with a parameter of type `Object`.

Since the `Create()` method is creating a new object, the business object's `MarkNew()` method is invoked to ensure that the object's status is set to being new and dirty:

```
MethodCaller.CallMethodIfImplemented(obj, "MarkNew")
```

Though the `MarkNew()` method is implemented by `Csla.Core.BusinessBase`, it isn't implemented by `Csla.BusinessListBase`; thus, it is considered optional.

■**Note** Technically, the data portal can be used to interact with objects that *don't* inherit from a CSLA .NET base class. While I won't cover this in the book, any object that follows the criteria scheme and implements the appropriate `DataPortal_XYZ` methods can be used with the data portal. This is another reason that calling methods like `MarkNew()` is optional.

Now that the `DataPortal_Create()` method has been invoked, the object is notified that the data portal processing is complete:

```
MethodCaller.CallMethodIfImplemented( _
    obj, "DataPortal_OnDataPortalInvokeComplete", _
    New DataPortalEventArgs(context))
```

Finally, the newly created object is wrapped in a `Csla.Server.DataPortalResult` object and returned:

```
Return New DataPortalResult(obj)
```

That concludes the normal sequence of events in the method. Of course, it is possible that an exception occurred during the processing. In that case, the exception is caught and the object is notified that an exception occurred:

```
Try
  ' tell the business object there was an exception
  MethodCaller.CallMethodIfImplemented( _
      obj, "DataPortal_OnDataPortalException", _
      New DataPortalEventArgs(context), ex)
Catch
  ' ignore exceptions from the exception handler
End Try
```

This optional call to `DataPortal_OnDataPortalException()` is wrapped in its own `Try...Catch` statement. Even if an exception occurs while calling *this* method, the code needs to continue. There's very little that could be done if the exception-handling code has an exception, so such an exception is simply ignored.

In any case, the exception is wrapped in a `Csla.Server.DataPortalException`, which is thrown back to `Csla.DataPortal`:

```
Throw New DataPortalException("DataPortal.Create " & _
    My.Resources.FailedOnServer, ex, New DataPortalResult(obj))
```

Remember that `DataPortalException` contains the original exception as an `InnerException`, and also traps the stack trace from the server exception so that it is available on the client. Also keep in mind that all the proxy/host channel implementations ensure that the exception is returned to the client with full fidelity, so `Csla.DataPortal` gets the full exception detail regardless of the network channel used.

At this point, you should understand how the flow of the data methods is implemented. The remaining methods follow the same flow with minor variations.

Fetch

The `Fetch()` method follows the same basic flow as `Create()`. The primary difference is in how the business object is created. Where `Create()` is passed the type of the business object as a parameter, `Fetch()` calls a `CreateBusinessObject()` helper method:

```
obj = CreateBusinessObject(criteria)
```

This helper method examines the criteria object to determine the type of business object to be created:

```
Private Shared Function CreateBusinessObject( _
  ByVal criteria As Object) As Object

  Dim businessType As Type

  If criteria.GetType.IsSubclassOf(GetType(CriteriaBase)) Then
    ' get the type of the actual business object
    ' from CriteriaBase
    businessType = CType(criteria, CriteriaBase).ObjectType
```

```
Else
  ' get the type of the actual business object
  ' based on the nested class scheme in the book
  businessType = criteria.GetType.DeclaringType
End If

' create an instance of the business object
Return Activator.CreateInstance(businessType, True)
End Function
```

If the criteria object inherits from Csla.CriteriaBase, then the ObjectType property is used to get the business object type. Otherwise, it is assumed that the criteria object's class is nested within the business class, and so the DeclaringType property is used to determine the business class.

In either case, Activator.CreateInstance() is used to create an instance of the business object, just as it was in the Create() method.

Once the object's data is loaded using the DataPortal_Fetch() method, the MarkOld() method is invoked to ensure that IsNew and IsDirty are both False.

Update

The Update() method is more complex. Remember that the Update() process adapts itself to the type of business object being updated, so it checks to see if the object is a subclass of BusinessBase or CommandBase and behaves appropriately. Also recall that the actual business object is passed as a parameter to Update(), so this method doesn't need to create an instance of the business object at all.

Processing a BusinessBase Object

It starts right out by checking to see if the business object is a subclass of BusinessBase. If the object is a subclass, then it is casted to type Csla.Core.BusinessBase so that the object's state can easily be checked:

```
If TypeOf obj Is Core.BusinessBase Then
  Dim busObj As Core.BusinessBase = DirectCast(obj, Core.BusinessBase)
  If busObj.IsDeleted Then
    If Not busObj.IsNew Then
      ' tell the object to delete itself
      MethodCaller.CallMethod(busObj, "DataPortal_DeleteSelf")
    End If
    ' mark the object as new
    MethodCaller.CallMethodIfImplemented(busObj, "MarkNew")

  Else
    If busObj.IsNew Then
      ' tell the object to insert itself
      MethodCaller.CallMethod(busObj, "DataPortal_Insert")

    Else
      ' tell the object to update itself
      MethodCaller.CallMethod(busObj, "DataPortal_Update")
    End If
    ' mark the object as old
    MethodCaller.CallMethodIfImplemented(busObj, "MarkOld")
  End If
```

If the object's IsDeleted property returns True, then the object should be deleted. It is possible that the object is also *new*, in which case there's actually nothing to delete; otherwise, the DataPortal_DeleteSelf() method is invoked:

```
If busObj.IsDeleted Then
  If Not busObj.IsNew Then
    ' tell the object to delete itself
    MethodCaller.CallMethod(busObj, "DataPortal_DeleteSelf")
  End If
  ' mark the object as new
  MethodCaller.CallMethodIfImplemented(busObj, "MarkNew")
```

In either case, the MarkNew() method is invoked to reset the object's state to new and dirty. The definition of a "new" object is that its primary key value isn't in the database—and since that data was just deleted, the object certainly meets that criteria. The definition of a "dirty" object is that its data values don't match values in the database—and again, the object now certainly meets that criteria as well.

If the object wasn't marked for deletion, then it needs to be either inserted or updated. If IsNew is True, then DataPortal_Insert() is invoked:

```
If busObj.IsNew Then
  ' tell the object to insert itself
  MethodCaller.CallMethod(busObj, "DataPortal_Insert")
```

Similarly, if the object isn't new, then DataPortal_Update() is invoked. In either case, the object's primary key and data values now reflect values in the database, so the object is clearly not new or dirty. The MarkOld() method is called to set the object's state accordingly:

```
MethodCaller.CallMethodIfImplemented(busObj, "MarkOld")
```

Processing a CommandBase Object

If the business object inherits from Csla.CommandBase, things are simpler. In this case, only the object's DataPortal_Execute() method is invoked:

```
ElseIf TypeOf obj Is CommandBase Then
  ' tell the object to update itself
  MethodCaller.CallMethod(obj, "DataPortal_Execute")
```

A command object should implement all server-side code in its DataPortal_Execute() method.

Processing All Other Objects

For any other objects (most commonly subclasses of BusinessListBase), the DataPortal_Update() method is invoked, followed by an optional call to MarkOld():

```
MethodCaller.CallMethod(obj, "DataPortal_Update")
MethodCaller.CallMethodIfImplemented(obj, "MarkOld")
```

As in Create() and Fetch(), the DataPortal_OnDataPortalInvoke() method is called before any of this other processing, and DataPortal_OnDataPortalInvokeComplete() is called once it is all done. The business object is returned as a result, wrapped in a DataPortalResult object.

Any exceptions are handled in the same way as in Create() or Fetch().

Delete

In contrast to Update(), the Delete() method is the simplest of the four. Like Fetch(), it creates an instance of the business object based on the criteria object:

```
obj = CreateBusinessObject(criteria)
```

Then it calls `DataPortal_OnDataPortalInvoke()`, followed by `DataPortal_Delete()`, and then `DataPortal_OnDataPortalInvokeComplete()`. Since the result is that the object's data was deleted, there's no business object to return. Thus an empty `DataPortalResult` is returned:

```
Return New DataPortalResult
```

This is required to return the global context data from the server back to the client—just in case the business object changed the global context during the delete operation.

The exception handling for `Delete()` is the same as in the other three methods.

That completes the `SimpleDataPortal` class and the message router behavior. Notice how all client calls are automatically routed to a dynamically created business object based on the type of business object required. `SimpleDataPortal` is entirely unaware of the particulars of any business application; it blindly routes client calls to the appropriate destinations.

Context and Location Transparency

The final major area of functionality provided by the data portal is that it manages context information to provide a level of location transparency between the client and server. Specifically, it allows the business application to pass data from the client to the server and from the server to the client on each data portal call, in addition to the actual call itself.

The data portal uses this capability itself in order to pass security and culture information from the client to the server.

You've already seen most of the code that implements the context-passing behaviors. `Csla.DataPortal` is responsible for passing the client context to the server and for updating the client's context with any changes from the server. `Csla.Server.DataPortal` is responsible for setting the server's context based on the data passed from the client, and for returning the global context from the server back to the client.

To maintain the context and pass it between client and server, several objects are used. Let's discuss them now.

Csla.Server.DataPortalContext

Earlier in the chapter, you saw how the `Csla.DataPortal` class implements `Shared` methods used by business developers to interact with the data portal. Each of those methods dealt with context data—creating a `DataPortalContext` object to pass to the server. On the server, `Csla.Server.DataPortal` uses the data in `DataPortalContext` to set up the server's context to match the client.

Of course, the phrase "on the server" is relative, since the data portal could be configured to use the `LocalProxy`. In that case, the "server-side" components actually run in the same process as your client code. Obviously, the context data is *already* present in that case, so there's no need to transfer it; and the data portal includes code to short-circuit the process when the server-side data portal components are running locally.

Creating the DataPortalContext Object

The `DataPortalContext` object is created and initialized in `Csla.DataPortal` within each data method:

```
Dim dpContext As New Server.DataPortalContext( _
    GetPrincipal, proxy.IsServerRemote)
```

The `DataPortalContext` object is a container for the set of context data to be passed from the client to the server. The data it contains is defined by the fields declared in `DataPortalContext`:

```
Private mPrincipal As IPrincipal
Private mRemotePortal As Boolean
Private mClientCulture As String
Private mClientUICulture As String
Private mClientContext As HybridDictionary
Private mGlobalContext As HybridDictionary
```

These data elements were described in Table 4-6, earlier in the chapter. The key here is that DataPortalContext is marked as <Serializable()>, and therefore when it is serialized, all the values in these fields are also serialized.

The values are loaded when the DataPortalContext object is created:

```
Public Sub New( _
  ByVal principal As IPrincipal, ByVal isRemotePortal As Boolean)

  If isRemotePortal Then
    mPrincipal = principal
    mRemotePortal = isRemotePortal
    mClientCulture = _
      System.Threading.Thread.CurrentThread.CurrentCulture.Name
    mClientUICulture = _
      System.Threading.Thread.CurrentThread.CurrentUICulture.Name
    mClientContext = Csla.ApplicationContext.GetClientContext
    mGlobalContext = Csla.ApplicationContext.GetGlobalContext
  End If
End Sub
```

The two culture values are pulled directly off the client's current Thread object. The mClientContext and mGlobalContext values are set based on the values in Csla.ApplicationContext, which will be discussed later.

Each of the values is exposed through a corresponding property so they can be used to set up the context data on the server.

Setting the Server Context

The server's context is set by Csla.Server.DataPortal as the first step in each of the four data methods. The work is handled by the SetContext() method in Csla.Server.DataPortal. This method follows this basic flow:

1. Do nothing if the "server" code is running on the client.

2. Otherwise, call ApplicationContext to set the client and global context collections.

3. Then set the server Thread to use the client's culture settings.

4. If using custom authentication, set the server Thread to use the IPrincipal supplied from the client.

Let's walk through the code in SetContext() that implements these steps. First is the check to see if the "server" code is actually running locally in the client process (using the LocalProxy in the channel adapter):

```
If Not context.IsRemotePortal Then Exit Sub
```

If the server code is running locally, then there's no sense setting any context data, because it is already set up. If the server code really is running remotely, though, the context data does need to be set up on the server, starting by restoring the client and global context data:

```
ApplicationContext.SetContext( _
  context.ClientContext, context.GlobalContext)
```

The `ApplicationContext` class will be discussed shortly. Remember that the client context comes from the client to the server only, while the global context will ultimately be returned to the client, reflecting any changes made on the server. The `ApplicationContext` also has an `ExecutionLocation` property that can be used by business code to determine whether the code is currently executing on the client or the server. This value must be set to indicate that execution is on the server:

```
ApplicationContext.SetExecutionLocation( _
  ApplicationContext.ExecutionLocations.Server)
```

Like the client context, the two culture values flow from the client to the server. They are used to set the current `Thread` object on the server to match the client settings:

```
System.Threading.Thread.CurrentThread.CurrentCulture = _
  New System.Globalization.CultureInfo(context.ClientCulture)
System.Threading.Thread.CurrentThread.CurrentUICulture = _
  New System.Globalization.CultureInfo(context.ClientUICulture)
```

Of the two, perhaps the most important is the `CurrentUICulture`, as this is the setting that dictates the language used when retrieving resource values such as those used throughout the CSLA .NET framework.

Finally, if custom authentication is being used, the `IPrincipal` object representing the user's identity is passed from the client to the server. It must be set on the current `Thread` or `HttpContext` as the `CurrentPrincipal` or `User` to effectively impersonate the user on the server. This is handled by `Csla.ApplicationContext`:

```
If ApplicationContext.AuthenticationType = "Windows" Then
  ' When using integrated security, Principal must be Nothing
  If context.Principal Is Nothing Then
    ' Set .NET to use integrated security
    AppDomain.CurrentDomain.SetPrincipalPolicy( _
      PrincipalPolicy.WindowsPrincipal)
    Exit Sub

  Else
    Throw New System.Security.SecurityException( _
      My.Resources.NoPrincipalAllowedException)
  End If
End If

' We expect the Principal to be of the type BusinessPrincipal
If context.Principal IsNot Nothing Then
  If TypeOf context.Principal Is Security.BusinessPrincipalBase Then
    ApplicationContext.User = context.Principal

  Else
    Throw New System.Security.SecurityException( _
      My.Resources.BusinessPrincipalException & " " & _
      CType(context.Principal, Object).ToString())
  End If

Else
  Throw New System.Security.SecurityException( _
    My.Resources.BusinessPrincipalException & " Nothing")
End If
```

There's a lot going on here, so let's break it down a bit. First, there's the check to ensure that custom authentication is being used. If Windows integrated (AD) security is being used, then Windows itself handles any impersonation, based on the configuration of the host (IIS, COM+, etc.). In that case, the IPrincipal value passed from the client must be Nothing, or else it is invalid, so the code throws an exception.

■Tip The check of the principal object's type is done to ensure that both the client and server are using the same authentication scheme. If the client is using custom authentication and the server is using Windows integrated security, this exception will be thrown. Custom authentication is discussed more fully in Chapter 5.

If the server is configured to use custom authentication, however, the rest of the code is executed. In that case, the first step is to make sure that the client did pass a valid IPrincipal object to the server. "Valid" in this case means that it isn't Nothing and that the object inherits from Csla. Security.BusinessPrincipalBase. Given a valid IPrincipal object, the server's principal value is set to match that of the client.

An invalid IPrincipal value results in an exception being thrown.

Clearing the Server Context

Once all the server-side processing is complete, the server clears the context values on its Thread object. This is done to prevent other code from accidentally gaining access to the client's context or security information. Csla.Server.DataPortal handles this in its ClearContext() method:

```
Private Shared Sub ClearContext(ByVal context As DataPortalContext)
  ' if the dataportal is not remote then
  ' do nothing
  If Not context.IsRemotePortal Then Exit Sub

  ApplicationContext.Clear()
  If ApplicationContext.AuthenticationType <> "Windows" Then
    ApplicationContext.User = Nothing
  End If
End Sub
```

This method is called at the end of each data method in Csla.Server.DataPortal. Notice that it calls Csla.ApplicationContext to clear the client and global context values. Then if custom authentication is being used, Csla.ApplicationContext is called to set the principal value to Nothing, removing the IPrincipal value from the client.

Csla.Server.DataPortalResult

Using the DataPortalContext object, Csla.DataPortal and Csla.Server.DataPortal convey client context data to the server. That's great for the client context, client culture, and client IPrincipal, but the global context data needs to be returned to the client when the server is done. This is handled by Csla.Server.DataPortalResult on a successful call, and Csla.Server.DataPortalException in the case of a server-side exception.

The Csla.Server.DataPortalResult object is primarily responsible for returning the business object that was created, retrieved, or updated on the server back to the client. However, it also contains the global context collection from the server:

```
Private mGlobalContext As HybridDictionary

Public ReadOnly Property GlobalContext() As HybridDictionary
  Get
    Return mGlobalContext
  End Get
End Property
```

When the DataPortalResult object is created by Csla.Server.SimpleDataPortal, it automatically pulls the global context data from Csla.ApplicationContext:

```
Public Sub New(ByVal returnObject As Object)
  mReturnObject = returnObject
  mGlobalContext = ApplicationContext.GetGlobalContext
End Sub
```

This way, the global context data is carried back to the client along with the business object.

Csla.Server.DataPortalException

Where Csla.Server.DataPortalResult returns the business object and context to the client for a successful server-side operation, Csla.Server.DataPortalException returns that data in the case of a server-side exception. Obviously, the primary responsibility of DataPortalException is to return the details about the exception, including the server-side stack trace, back to the client. This information is captured when the exception is created:

```
Public Sub New( _
  ByVal message As String, ByVal ex As Exception, _
  ByVal result As DataPortalResult)

  MyBase.New(message, ex)
  mInnerStackTrace = ex.StackTrace
  mResult = result
End Sub
```

Notice that a DataPortalResult object is required as a parameter to the constructor. This DataPortalResult object is returned to the client as part of the exception, thus ensuring that both the business object (exactly as it was when the exception occurred) and the global context from the server are returned to the client as well.

Csla.ApplicationContext

Both the client and global context information used by all the classes just discussed are ultimately managed by Csla.ApplicationContext. This class is responsible for providing access to context information to the CSLA .NET framework, the business objects, and the UI code. In many ways, ApplicationContext is similar to the idea of HttpContext within an ASP.NET application.

Client and Global Context Collections

On the surface, it seems like maintaining a set of globally available information is easy—just use a Shared field and be done with it. Unfortunately, things are quite a bit more complex when building a framework that must operate in a multithreaded server environment. Remember that the server-side components of the data portal may run in ASP.NET on an IIS server when either .NET Remoting or Web Services are used as a network channel. And in the future, WCF (Indigo) will run in a similar server configuration.

In these cases, the server may be supporting many clients at the same time. All the client requests are handled by the *same Windows process* and by the *same .NET AppDomain*. It turns out that Shared fields exist at the AppDomain level: meaning that a given Shared field is shared across all threads in an AppDomain. This is problematic because multiple client requests are handled within the *same* AppDomain, but on different threads. So Shared fields aren't the answer.

The solution is different in ASP.NET and in any other .NET code. Either way, the .NET Framework illustrates the right answer. Look at CurrentPrincipal: it is associated with the current Thread object, which provides an answer for any code running outside of ASP.NET. Within ASP.NET, there's the HttpContext object, which is automatically maintained by ASP.NET itself.

So when outside ASP.NET, the answer is to associate the context data directly with the current Thread object, and when inside ASP.NET, the context data can be stored using the HttpContext.

Let's discuss the Thread option first. While the .NET Thread object already has a property for CurrentPrincipal, it doesn't have a property for CslaContext. But it does have a concept called *named slots*. Every Thread object has a collection associated with it. Each entry in this collection is referred to as a *slot*. Slots can be referred to by a key, or *name*: hence the term *named slot*. The GetNameDataSlot() method on the Thread object returns access to a specific slot as an object of type LocalDataStoreSlot. You can then use the Thread object's GetData() and SetData() methods to get and set data in that slot.

While this is a bit more complex than dealing with a conventional collection, you can think of named slots as being like a collection of arbitrary values associated with a Thread object.

When running in ASP.NET, things are a bit simpler, because HttpContext has an Items collection. This is a dictionary of name/value pairs that is automatically maintained by ASP.NET and is available to your code. Within ASP.NET, this is the only safe place to put shared data like context data, because ASP.NET may switch your code to run on different threads in certain advanced scenarios.

Providing Public Access

The ApplicationContext class stores the client and global context data in named slots on the current thread or in the Items collection of HttpContext. It abstracts all the complexity, simply exposing the context data as a pair of collection objects via Public properties that can be used by other framework code, business code, or UI code. For instance, here's the ClientContext property:

```
Public ReadOnly Property ClientContext() As HybridDictionary
  Get
    Dim ctx As HybridDictionary = GetClientContext()
    If ctx Is Nothing Then
      ctx = New HybridDictionary
      SetClientContext(ctx)
    End If
    Return ctx
  End Get
End Property
```

The client context data is a standard .NET HybridDictionary object: a collection of name/value pairs much like Session in ASP.NET.

■**Note** HybridDictionary is used because it self-optimizes, keeping its data in an array format if there are few elements, and switching to a hashtable if there are many elements in the collection. This provides an automatic trade-off between memory consumption and fast lookup of items based on the name value.

The HybridDictionary is stored in a named slot or HttpContext entry called Csla. ClientContext. When a business object or some UI code calls the ClientContext property to get the client context collection, the value is retrieved from the slot or HttpContext by calling a GetClientContext() helper method:

```
Friend Function GetClientContext() As HybridDictionary
  If HttpContext.Current Is Nothing Then
    Dim slot As System.LocalDataStoreSlot = _
      Thread.GetNamedDataSlot("Csla.ClientContext")
    Return CType(Thread.GetData(slot), HybridDictionary)

  Else
    Return CType(HttpContext.Current.Items("Csla.ClientContext"), _
      HybridDictionary)
  End If
End Function
```

This method is Friend because portions of the framework need lower-level access than is provided by the standard ClientContext and GlobalContext properties.

The DataPortalContext object needs to pass the context to the server, but if the context values have never been used, it should pass Nothing. The two public properties automatically create instances of an empty HybridDictionary, but there's no sense passing an empty object across when Nothing would do better.

If this is the first time the value has been requested, it won't exist, of course. In that case, the value retrieved from the (previously nonexistent) slot or HttpContext item will be Nothing, and so a new HybridDictionary is created:

```
If ctx Is Nothing Then
  ctx = New HybridDictionary
  SetClientContext(ctx)
End If
```

Not only is a new object created, but it is put into the named slot or HttpContext item by calling a SetClientContext() helper method.

```
Private Sub SetClientContext(ByVal clientContext As HybridDictionary)
  If HttpContext.Current Is Nothing Then
    Dim slot As System.LocalDataStoreSlot = _
      Thread.GetNamedDataSlot("Csla.ClientContext")
    Threading.Thread.SetData(slot, clientContext)

  Else
    HttpContext.Current.Items("Csla.ClientContext") = clientContext
  End If
End Sub
```

This makes it available to any other code running on the same thread. The ApplicationContext.GlobalContext property works exactly the same way, storing its data in an entry named Csla.GlobalContext.

Providing Framework-Only Access

The standard ClientContext and GlobalContext properties, along with the GetClientContext() and GetGlobalContext() methods, provide access to the context data both publicly and to the client-side DataPortal.

On the other end of the process, Csla.Server.DataPortal needs to take the values provided by the client and use them to set the slots on the server's Thread object or into the server's HttpContext. This is done by calling a SetContext() method:

```
Friend Sub SetContext( _
  ByVal clientContext As HybridDictionary, _
  ByVal globalContext As HybridDictionary)

  SetClientContext(clientContext)
  SetGlobalContext(globalContext)
End Sub
```

This method simply sets both the values. This works even if the values passed from the client are Nothing, ensuring that the server context is identical to that on the client.

Similarly, Csla.Server.DataPortal needs to be able to clear the context on the server. It does this by calling a Clear() method:

```
Public Sub Clear()
  SetContext(Nothing, Nothing)
End Sub
```

Clearing the context merely means that the context values from the client should be removed from the thread or HttpContext. The easiest way to do this is simply to set the values to Nothing.

User Property

When code is running outside ASP.NET, it relies on System.Threading.Thread.CurrentPrincipal to maintain the user's principal object. On the other hand, when code is running inside ASP.NET, the only reliable way to find the user's principal object is through HttpContext.Current.User.

Normally, this would mean that you would have to write code to detect whether HttpContext.Current is Nothing, and only use System.Threading if HttpContext isn't available. The User property automates this process on your behalf:

```
Public Property User() As IPrincipal
  Get
    If HttpContext.Current Is Nothing Then
      Return Thread.CurrentPrincipal

    Else
      Return HttpContext.Current.User
    End If
  End Get
  Set(ByVal value As IPrincipal)
    If HttpContext.Current IsNot Nothing Then
      HttpContext.Current.User = value
    End If
    Thread.CurrentPrincipal = value
  End Set
End Property
```

In general, Csla.ApplicationContext.User should be used in favor of using either System.Threading or HttpContext directly, since it automatically adjusts to the environment in which your code is running. With CSLA .NET–based applications, this is particularly important, because your client code could be a Windows Forms application, but your server code could be running within ASP.NET. Remember that your business objects run in *both locations* and so must behave properly both inside and outside ASP.NET.

Config File Settings

Csla.ApplicationContext not only manages the client and global context collections, it also provides a central location for retrieval of any other context or settings values global to the application. These values come from two locations: the application's config file and settings that are directly maintained in memory.

The .NET Framework already provides the System.Configuration namespace to provide access to the application's config file. But it is often best to encapsulate lower-level plumbing code for commonly accessed values. The way config files are read changed from .NET 1.1 to 2.0, directly highlighting the value of hiding the use of .NET Framework functions of this sort. By encapsulating the use of System.Configuration, the framework needs to be changed in only one place if Microsoft changes the approach again in the future.

Additionally, by encapsulating the reading of config values, the framework can provide meaningful default values in the case that the setting isn't found in the config file. For instance, the DataPortalProxy property looks like this:

```
Public ReadOnly Property DataPortalProxy() As String
  Get
    Dim result As String = _
      ConfigurationManager.AppSettings("CslaDataPortalProxy")
    If Len(result) = 0 Then
      result = "Local"
    End If
    Return result
  End Get
End Property
```

If a proxy type and assembly are specified for the channel adapter, then they are returned; otherwise, the default value of Local is returned.

Other settings that are encapsulated as properties on ApplicationContext are DataPortalUrl and AuthenticationType.

ExecutionLocation Property

The final value maintained by ApplicationContext is a property called ExecutionLocation. This property can be used by business code to determine whether it is currently executing on the client or on the server.

This is particularly useful when writing data access code, since that code could run on either the client or the server, depending on whether the channel adapter uses LocalProxy or one of the remote proxies. Remember that LocalProxy is designed such that the "server-side" code runs on the client!

The property value is of type ExecutionLocations, defined by the following enumerated type:

```
Public Enum ExecutionLocations
  Client
  Server
End Enum
```

The ExecutionLocation value is global to both the client and server, so it is stored in a field within the Module. This is shared by all threads on the server, but that's OK because it will always return the Server value when on the server, and Client when on the client.

```
Private mExecutionLocation As ExecutionLocations = ExecutionLocations.Client

Public ReadOnly Property ExecutionLocation() As ExecutionLocations
  Get
    Return mExecutionLocation
  End Get
End Property
```

The value defaults to Client. This is fine, as it should only be set to Server in the case that the Csla.Server.DataPortal class explicitly sets it to Server. Recall that in that DataPortal class there's a SetContext() method that only runs in the case that the server-side components really are running on the server. In that case, it calls the SetExecutionLocation() method on ApplicationContext:

```
Friend Sub SetExecutionLocation(ByVal location As ExecutionLocations)
  mExecutionLocation = location
End Sub
```

This way, the value is set to Server only when the code is known to physically be executing in a separate AppDomain, process, and probably computer, from the client.

At this point, you have walked through all the various types and classes used to implement the core mobile object and data access functionality in the framework.

Conclusion

This chapter has walked through the various types and classes in the framework that enable both mobile objects and data access. The details of mobile objects are managed by a concept called the data portal. You should understand that the data portal incorporates several areas of functionality:

- Channel adapter
- Distributed transactional support
- Message router
- Context and location transparency

The channel adapter provides for flexibility in terms of how (or if) the client communicates with an application server to run server-side code. The distributed transactional support abstracts the use of Enterprise Services or System.Transactions. The message router handles the routing of client calls to your business components on the server, minimizing the coupling between client and server by enabling a single point of entry to the server. Behind the scenes, the data portal provides transparent context flow from the client to the server and back to the client. This includes implementing impersonation when using custom authentication.

The base classes from Chapter 3 were updated to integrate with the data portal concept and to support data access. Mostly, this revolves around the five DataPortal_XYZ methods:

- DataPortal_Create()
- DataPortal_Fetch()
- DataPortal_Update()
- DataPortal_Execute()
- DataPortal_Delete()

Chapter 3 walked through the support for editable and read-only business objects. Chapter 4 has now added on mobile object and data access concepts. Chapter 5 will complete the framework by discussing custom authentication and by covering a set of broadly useful base classes and objects that simplify the creation of business applications.

CHAPTER 5

■ ■ ■

Completing the Framework

This is the third chapter covering the implementation of the CSLA .NET framework. The framework is based on the concepts from Chapter 1 and the design in Chapter 2. Chapters 3 and 4 walked through implementing support for editable and read-only business objects and collections, including the concept of mobile objects and support for object persistence.

This chapter will conclude the implementation of the framework by completing support for custom authentication and adding several classes that are useful when building business applications. The following topic areas will be addressed:

- Additional business base classes
- Custom authentication
- Sorting collections
- Date handling
- Common business rules
- Data access
- Reporting
- Windows data binding
- Web data binding

The additional base classes will support the execution of arbitrary code on the application server and the retrieval of lists of name/value data. Both are common tasks in business applications, and the CommandBase and NameValueListBase classes are designed to make it easier for a business developer to accomplish those tasks.

Custom authentication has been discussed already, and much support for the idea was put into the data portal in Chapter 4. The code in Chapter 4 relies on a base class named BusinessPrincipalBase, which is what will be covered in this chapter.

The BusinessListBase and ReadOnlyListBase classes in Chapter 3 provide powerful functionality to support data binding. But they don't directly support sorting of the data in the collections. It turns out to be much better to avoid sorting collections in place, and rather to provide a sorted *view* of a collection instead. The SortedBindingList class provides a sorted, updatable view of any collection implementing IList(Of T). That includes collections based on the base classes from Chapter 3.

There are many views on what makes good UI design. One common view holds that the user should be free to enter arbitrary text, and it is up to the application to try and make sense of the entry. Nowhere is this truer than with date values, and the SmartDate type is designed to simplify how a business developer uses dates and exposes them to the UI.

In Chapter 3, the BusinessBase class implemented support for validation rules. Each rule is a method with a signature that conforms to the RuleHandler delegate. Using reflection, it is possible to implement a set of broadly reusable rules for common scenarios—such as the rule that a string value is required or has a maximum length, or that a numeric value has a minimum or maximum value. The `Csla.Validation.CommonRules` class implements a set of such common validation rules that a business developer may use when appropriate.

When it comes to data access, the .NET Framework provides powerful support through ADO.NET—yet dealing with data remains somewhat complex. For instance, database columns often store null values, but the application wants simpler, empty values (an empty string instead of a null, for instance). The `SafeDataReader` eliminates null values from the data, transforming them into appropriate empty values instead.

Another common issue when dealing with data, especially in Web Forms and Web Services, is that data must be copied from business objects into and out of other types of object. This is especially true when building web services, since data coming into a web service is contained in a proxy object, and that data must be moved into or out of your business objects. The `DataMapper` class helps streamline this process, reducing the amount of code you must write and maintain.

Reporting is typically handled by a report-generation tool such as SQL Reporting Services or Crystal Reports. These tools generate their reports directly from the database. However, sometimes an application needs to generate a printout based on data in your business objects. Unfortunately, most reporting tools can't work directly with objects—they require a `DataSet` instead. The `ObjectAdapter` is designed to use data from business objects to fill `DataTable` objects within a `DataSet`, thus enabling the use of such reporting tools.

Much of Chapter 3 focused on ensuring that business objects support Windows Forms data binding. Chapter 3 also added authorization code to business objects, making them aware of whether each property can be read or changed. The `ReadWriteAuthorization` control helps automate the process of building a UI that enables or disables controls based on whether properties can be read or changed.

It turns out that there's a quirk (either a bug or an odd implementation choice) in the way Windows Forms data binding works. The `BindingSourceRefresh` control helps work around this quirk (the details will be discussed later in the chapter).

Finally, there's the new Web Forms data binding in ASP.NET 2.0. Web Forms data binding is now bidirectional, simplifying both the display and update of data. Unfortunately, the data source controls provided with ASP.NET are not designed to work with objects that contain business logic, meaning that they aren't useful when working with CSLA .NET business objects. The `CslaDataSource` control is an ASP.NET data source control that is designed to work with objects containing business logic. This control allows the full use of Web Forms data binding with business objects.

Additional Base Classes

Chapter 3 covered the base classes to support the creation of editable and read-only objects and collections. While that covers most cases, business applications often need to execute arbitrary code on the server, and almost all applications need to retrieve lists of name/value data to populate combo box controls or other list controls.

CommandBase

Most applications execute some arbitrary code on the server. For instance, an application might need to know whether a customer's data exists in the database. The application doesn't need to retrieve the customer data; it just needs to confirm whether it exists.

Another example is the shipping of an order. Shipping an order can be a very intensive process: updating the order status, relieving inventory quantities, printing a pick list document, initiating an invoice, and more. None of this is interactive, and it all needs to be done on the application server to efficiently interact with the database.

When building an object-oriented business logic layer, everything should be represented by an object in the object model. Thus, operations like the preceding examples should be naturally reflected within the object model in the Business Logic layer.

To determine whether a customer's data is in the database, the UI developer should write code like the following:

```
If Customer.Exists(id) Then
```

The implementation of the Exists() method obviously needs to execute some server-side code to check whether that customer ID value exists in the database.

Similarly, the UI code to ship an order should look like this:

```
Order.Ship(id)
```

The implementation of the Ship() method needs to execute extensive server-side code to perform the shipping process.

So the question, then, is how to implement the Exists() and Ship() methods by using objects in the business object model. Keeping in mind that objects are defined by their behavior, it seems likely that there will be CustomerExists and OrderShipper objects in the object model. Each of these objects will be instantiated on the client, and then will move to the application server to run their code.

The Csla.CommandBase base class is designed to enable this scenario, making it easy for a business developer to create this type of object. You'll see examples of implementing Exists() commands in Chapter 7. The implementation of an Order.Ship() method using an OrderShipper class might look like this:

```
<Serializable()> _
Public Class Order
  Inherits  BusinessBase(Of Order)

  Public Shared Sub Ship(ByVal id As Integer)
    OrderShipper.ShipOrder(id)
  End Sub

  <Serializable()> _
  Private Class OrderShipper
    Inherits  CommandBase

    Public Shared Sub ShipOrder(ByVal id As Integer)
      DataPortal.Execute(New OrderShipper(id))
    End Sub

    Private mId As Integer

    Private Sub New(ByVal id As Integer)
      mId = id
    End Sub

    Protected Overrides Sub DataPortal_Execute()
      ' this method runs on the server and
      ' uses the mId value to ship the order
    End Sub
  End Class
End Class
```

Command objects like OrderShipper are often Private nested classes within a Public business class such as Order. They are invoked by methods in the Public business class as needed, thus providing a clean, abstract interface for the UI developer. The flow is illustrated in Figure 5-1.

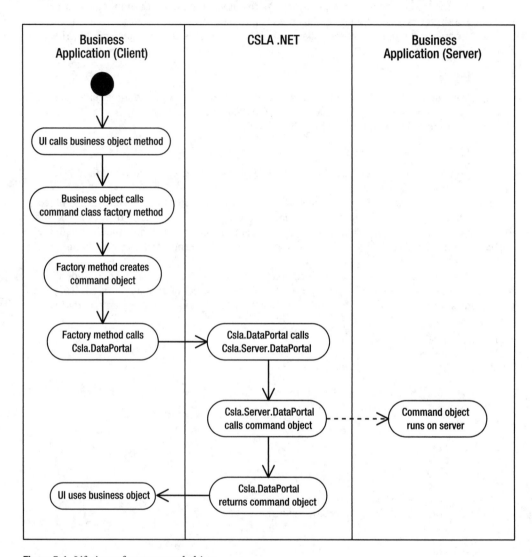

Figure 5-1. *Lifetime of a command object*

The command object itself, OrderShipper, is instantiated on the client in the ShipOrder() method. Notice that the order ID value is stored in the OrderShipper object at this point, so the object knows which order is to be shipped.

The DataPortal.Execute() method is then called to send the command object to the application server, where its DataPortal_Execute() method is invoked. The code to support this process within the data portal was implemented in Chapter 4. The DataPortal_Execute() method then contains all the code that is to run on the server—in this case, all the code required to ship an order.

Once `DataPortal_Execute()` is complete, the command object is returned to the client, thus allowing the object to report on its status. While `OrderShipper` doesn't do this, in Chapter 8 you'll see this concept used to implement `Exists()` commands.

The `Csla.CommandBase` class itself is relatively straightforward. Like all CSLA .NET base classes, it is serializable and has a non-public constructor. It also implements the `Csla.Core.ICommandObject` interface to allow polymorphic comparisons in your code:

```
<Serializable()> _
Public MustInherit Class CommandBase

  Implements Core.ICommandObject

  Protected Sub New()

  End Sub
End Class
```

Recall that in Chapter 4, all the framework base classes were enhanced to include default implementations of the `DataPortal_XYZ` methods: throwing exceptions if any of them were invoked. The same is true of `CommandBase`. All the `DataPortal_XYZ` methods are implemented as `Private` methods, except for `DataPortal_Execute()`, which is a `Protected Overridable` method:

```
Protected Overridable Sub DataPortal_Execute()
  Throw New NotSupportedException(My.Resources.ExecuteNotSupportedException)
End Sub
```

Of course, the default implementation throws an exception in this method, too. The command object only has value if the business developer overrides this method in his business class.

The `DataPortal_OnDataPortalInvoke()`, `DataPortal_OnDataPortalInvokeComplete()`, and `DataPortal_OnDataPortalException()` methods are also declared as `Protected` and `Overridable`.

NameValueListBase

Most business applications need to retrieve and display lists of name/value data. Commonly, this data is displayed in combo box or list controls, and is used to validate user entry to ensure the values are within the list.

A common example is customer payment terms. Customers are required to pay invoices within a certain amount of time: net 30 for 30 days, net 60 for 60 days, COD for cash on delivery, and so forth. An application dealing with customer payments will almost certainly have a table in the database containing the list of valid payment terms. This list will be displayed to the user on various forms and pages, and is used to ensure that every `Customer` object's `PaymentTerms` property is one of the items in the list.

It is quite practical to use the `ReadOnlyListBase` class from Chapter 3 to create your own name/value list. But this is such a common application requirement that it is better to create a more targeted base class to further minimize the code required to implement name/value lists. The `Csla.NameValueListBase` provides this targeted abstraction. A business developer can construct a name/value list like this:

```
<Serializable()> _
Public Class PaymentTerms
  Inherits  Csla.NameValueListBase(Of Integer, String)

  Private Sub New()
    ' require use of factory methods
  End Sub
```

```vbnet
   Public Shared Function GetList() As PaymentTerms
      Return DataPortal.Fetch(Of PaymentTerms)( _
        New Criteria(GetType(PaymentTerms)))
   End Function

   Private Sub DataPortal_Fetch(ByVal criteria As Criteria)
      IsReadOnly = False
      ' load data from database
      IsReadOnly = True
   End Sub
End Class
```

The goal of the `NameValueListBase` class is to allow the business developer to write as little code as possible when implementing a strongly typed name/value list. As you can see, the developer needs only to create a `Private` constructor, a factory method, and the `DataPortal_Fetch()` method, which contains the data access code to load the list with data.

NameValueListBase Declaration

Name/value lists are read-only collections that expose a list of child objects. Each child object contains a name and a value. Of course, the framework doesn't know the data types of the name and value ahead of time, but generics can help overcome that issue. A nested `NameValuePair` class will be declared within `NameValueListBase`, using generic type parameters to define the types for the name and value.

The `NameValueListBase` class takes two generic type parameters, one for the name (key) and the other for the value:

```vbnet
<Serializable()> _
Public MustInherit Class NameValueListBase(Of K, V)
  Inherits Core.ReadOnlyBindingList(Of NameValuePair)

  Implements ICloneable
  Implements Core.IBusinessObject
```

It also inherits from `Csla.Core.ReadOnlyBindingList`, specifying that the type of item contained in the collection is `NameValueListBase(Of K, V).NameValuePair`.

NameValuePair Class

The `NameValuePair` class defines the child objects to be contained in the collection: each of which contains a name (key) and value. It is defined as a nested class *inside* the `NameValueListBase` class:

```vbnet
  <Serializable()> _
  Public Class NameValuePair

    Private mKey As K
    Private mValue As V

    Public ReadOnly Property Key() As K
      Get
        Return mKey
      End Get
    End Property
```

```
  Public Property Value() As V
    Get
      Return mValue
    End Get
    Set(ByVal value As V)
      mValue = value
    End Set
  End Property

  Public Sub New(ByVal key As K, ByVal value As V)
    mKey = key
    mValue = value
  End Sub
End Class
```

Because it is nested inside NameValueListBase, it has access to the K and V generic type parameters. These type parameters are used to define the types of the key and value items stored in each child object.

Thanks to the code in the Csla.Core.ReadOnlyBindingList and in the .NET BindingList base classes, all the hard work is already done. The NameValueListBase is now a fully functioning read-only collection of name/value data. It even supports data binding to Windows Forms and Web Forms.

Key and Value Properties and Methods

However, it is relatively hard to use for validating data. There's no easy way to find a value given a key, or a key given a value. To simplify these common tasks, the class includes Key and Value properties:

```
Public Function Value(ByVal key As K) As V
  For Each item As NameValuePair In Me
    If item.Key.Equals(key) Then
      Return item.Value
    End If
  Next
  Return Nothing
End Function

Public Function Key(ByVal value As V) As K
  For Each item As NameValuePair In Me
    If item.Value.Equals(value) Then
      Return item.Key
    End If
  Next
  Return Nothing
End Function
```

The Value property accepts a key (name) and returns the value corresponding to that key. The Key property does the reverse, accepting a value and returning the first matching key value. In either case, if the value is not found, then the default value of the generic type is returned. If the generic type is a reference type, this will be Nothing; otherwise, it is typically 0 or False.

Similarly, there are ContainsKey() and ContainsValue() methods:

```
Public Function ContainsKey(ByVal key As K) As Boolean
  For Each item As NameValuePair In Me
    If item.Key.Equals(key) Then
      Return True
    End If
  Next
```

```
      Return False
    End Function

    Public Function ContainsValue(ByVal value As V) As Boolean
      For Each item As NameValuePair In Me
        If item.Value.Equals(value) Then
          Return True
        End If
      Next
      Return False
    End Function
```

Collectively, these properties and methods make it easy for a UI or business developer to use the name/value list to validate values and to translate between keys and values.

ICloneable Implementation

As with the framework base classes from Chapter 3, the ICloneable interface is implemented. This is done using the Csla.ObjectCloner class:

```
    Private Function ICloneable_Clone() As Object Implements ICloneable.Clone
      Return GetClone()
    End Function

    <EditorBrowsable(EditorBrowsableState.Advanced)> _
    Protected Overridable Function GetClone() As Object
      Return ObjectCloner.Clone(Me)
    End Function

    Public Overloads Function Clone() As NameValueListBase(Of K, V)
      Return DirectCast(GetClone(), NameValueListBase(Of K, V))
    End Function
```

The strongly typed Clone() method is Public, while the loosely typed implementation can only be accessed through the ICloneable interface.

Data Access

The final functionality required is support for data access. As with all business objects, the data portal will be used to invoke an appropriate DataPortal_XYZ method. Since this base class only supports read-only lists, only the DataPortal_Fetch() method is marked as Protected:

```
    Protected Overridable Sub DataPortal_Fetch(ByVal criteria As Object)
      Throw New NotSupportedException(My.Resources.FetchNotSupportedException)
    End Sub
```

This is comparable to the functionality added to BusinessBase or ReadOnlyBase in Chapter 4. The business developer must override or overload this method to implement the data access code that loads the name/value data from the database.

As with the other CSLA .NET base classes, the DataPortal_OnDataPortalInvoke(), DataPortal_OnDataPortalInvokeComplete(), and DataPortal_OnDataPortalException() methods are also declared as Protected and Overridable.

The primary difference from the base class code added in Chapter 4 is that NameValueListBase also includes a Protected criteria class:

```
<Serializable()> _
Protected Class Criteria
  Inherits CriteriaBase

  Public Sub New(ByVal collectionType As Type)
    MyBase.New(collectionType)
  End Sub
End Class
```

The `Csla.DataPortal.Fetch()` method requires a criteria object as a parameter. At a minimum, that criteria object must provide the data portal with the type of the business object to be created. Normally, the type can be determined by looking at the class within which the criteria class is nested, because that is the business class itself. But in this case, the criteria class is nested inside the *base* class rather than the business class itself, so that technique won't work. The data portal would end up trying to instantiate an instance of `NameValueListBase` rather than the actual business class.

This problem can be avoided because the `Criteria` class is a subclass of `Csla.CriteriaBase`. Remember that in Chapter 4 the data portal was designed to use `CriteriaBase` to find the specific type of business object to be created. The `Criteria` class has a constructor that requires the business developer to provide the type of the name/value list object to be created. In the following `PaymentTerms` example, the factory method uses this constructor when creating the `Criteria` object:

```
Public Shared Function GetList() As PaymentTerms
  Return DataPortal.Fetch(Of PaymentTerms)( _
    New Criteria(GetType(PaymentTerms)))
End Function
```

This ensures that the data portal knows that it is a `PaymentTerms` object that is to be created. This `Criteria` class works for the common case in which the entire set of name/value data is to be retrieved.

■**Note** If the business developer needs to retrieve a filtered list, he'll need to declare his own criteria class within his business class; just as for any other root business object.

This concludes the `NameValueListBase` class. The framework now has all its base classes: `BusinessBase`, `BusinessListBase`, `ReadOnlyBase`, `ReadOnlyListBase`, `CommandBase`, and `NameValueListBase`. Together these provide the base functionality to create most common types of business objects.

Custom Authentication

In Chapter 4, the data portal was implemented to support either Windows integrated (AD) or custom authentication. Either way, the result is that the current thread always has a valid principal object and associated identity object, allowing the authorization code from Chapter 3 to verify the user's roles as appropriate.

When using custom authentication, the data portal requires that the custom principal object inherit from the `Csla.Security.BusinessPrincipalBase` class. A business application will implement its own principal and identity classes so it can authenticate the user and load the user's roles as appropriate for the application.

The following shows a basic `CustomPrincipal` class (which makes use of a `CustomIdentity` class in the subsequent code):

```vb
<Serializable()> _
Public Class CustomPrincipal
  Inherits  Csla.Security.BusinessPrincipalBase

  Private Sub New(ByVal identity As IIdentity)
    MyBase.New(identity)
  End Sub

  Public Shared Function Login( _
    ByVal username As String, ByVal password As String) As Boolean

    Dim identity As CustomIdentity = _
      CustomIdentity.GetIdentity(username, password)
    If identity.IsAuthenticated Then
      CustomPrincipal principal = new CustomPrincipal(identity)
      Csla.ApplicationContext.User = principal
    End If
    Return identity.IsAuthenticated
  End Function

  Public Shared Sub Logout()
    Dim identity As CustomIdentity = _
      CustomIdentity.UnauthenticatedIdentity()
    Dim principal As New CustomPrincipal(identity)
    Csla.ApplicationContext.User = principal
  End Sub

  Public Overrides Function IsInRole(ByVal role As String) As Boolean
    Dim identity As CustomIdentity = CType(Me.Identity, CustomIdentity)
    Return identity.IsInRole(role)
  End Function
End Class
```

The BusinessPrincipalBase class implements System.Security.Principal.IPrincipal, which is the requirement for any .NET principal object. Notice that a CustomPrincipal object doesn't really do much work—all the hard work is handled by the identity object:

```vb
<Serializable()> _
Public Class CustomIdentity
  Inherits  ReadOnlyBase(Of CustomIdentity)

  Implements IIdentity

  Private mRoles As New List(Of String)
  Private mIsAuthenticated As Boolean
  Private mName As String = ""

  Public ReadOnly Property AuthenticationType() As String _
    Implements System.Security.Principal.IIdentity.AuthenticationType
    Get
      Return "Csla"
    End Get
  End Property
```

```vb
Public ReadOnly Property IsAuthenticated() As Boolean _
  Implements System.Security.Principal.IIdentity.IsAuthenticated
  Get
    Return mIsAuthenticated
  End Get
End Property

Public ReadOnly Property Name() As String _
  Implements System.Security.Principal.IIdentity.Name
  Get
    Return mName
  End Get
End Property

Protected Overrides Function GetIdValue() As Object
  Return mName
End Function

Friend Function IsInRole(ByVal role As String) As Boolean
  Return mRoles.Contains(role)
End Function

Private Sub New()
  ' require use of factory methods
End Sub

<Serializable()> _
Private Class Criteria

  Private mUsername As String
  Public ReadOnly Property Username() As String
    Get
      Return mUsername
    End Get
  End Property

  Private mPassword As String
  Public ReadOnly Property Password() As String
    Get
      Return mPassword
    End Get
  End Property

  Public Sub New(ByVal username As String, ByVal password As String)
    mUsername = username
    mPassword = password
  End Sub
End Class

Friend Shared Function UnauthenticatedIdentity() As PTIdentity

  Return New PTIdentity

End Function
```

```
    Friend Shared Function GetIdentity( _
      ByVal username As String, ByVal password As String) As PTIdentity

      Return DataPortal.Fetch(Of PTIdentity)(New Criteria(username, password))

    End Function

    Private Overloads Sub DataPortal_Fetch(ByVal criteria As Criteria)
      ' validate user identity against the database
      ' and load the user's roles
    End Sub
  End Class
```

This CustomIdentity class inherits from Csla.ReadOnlyBase, and so is a fully functional business object in its own right. This means it has a Private constructor and a factory method that the CustomPrincipal object can call to authenticate the user. It also has another factory method that returns an unauthenticated version of the object to support anonymous or guest users.

The DataPortal_Fetch() method needs to include the data access code to authenticate the username and password values against the database. The mIsAuthenticated field should be set accordingly. And if the credentials are valid, DataPortal_Fetch() must also load the user's roles into the mRoles list.

Chapter 8 will implement a working custom principal and identity class as part of a sample application.

BusinessPrincipalBase

To integrate a custom principal object with the data portal, the framework provides the Csla.BusinessPrincipalBase class. This class implements the System.Security.Principal.IPrincipal interface, but with the intent that business developers will override the implementation to meet their application requirements:

```
  <Serializable()> _
  Public Class BusinessPrincipalBase
    Implements IPrincipal

    Private mIdentity As IIdentity

    Public Overridable ReadOnly Property Identity() As IIdentity _
      Implements IPrincipal.Identity
      Get
        Return mIdentity
      End Get
    End Property

    Public Overridable Function IsInRole(ByVal role As String) As Boolean _
      Implements IPrincipal.IsInRole

      Return False
    End Function

    Protected Sub New(ByVal identity As IIdentity)
      mIdentity = identity
    End Sub
  End Class
```

The Identity property is easy enough, and is a standard implementation. When the principal object is created, an identity object must be supplied, and the Identity property merely returns a reference to that object.

The IsInRole() method is used to determine whether the current user is in a given role. When business developers implement custom principal and identity classes, they will write code to retrieve and store the user's list of roles. This means they need to override the IsInRole() method to check that list on request.

Because all the real work occurs in the classes implemented by the business developer, this is all the code required in BusinessPrincipalBase.

Sorting Collections

The BusinessListBase and ReadOnlyListBase classes implemented in Chapter 3 provide support for data binding and integration with the rest of the CSLA .NET framework. But they don't support sorting of the data in the collections. This is intentional, as it is better to provide a sorted *view* of a collection than to try and sort the collection in place.

The concept of sorting a collection in place is supported by the IBindingList interface, which is implemented by the BindingList(Of T) base class. However, BindingList(Of T) doesn't implement sorting, so the sort-related methods on IBindingList provide no useful behavior.

It seems like you would want to be able to just grab any collection and sort it, but that turns out to be quite problematic. The sort methods also allow "unsorting" by removing the sort. The expectation is that the list will return to its original order. But this implies that the sort algorithm is reversible, which isn't always true. Alternatively, it requires that the collection maintain an internal list of the items *in their original order* so that order can be restored. Either solution is somewhat complex.

There's also the issue of editing the collection while it is sorted. When new items are added, do they go on the end of the list? In sorted or unsorted order? What happens when you remove the sort, and where do those new items go? What if the user edits an item such that the sort order would change? Does that item's location change if the sort is removed?

Finally, what if you want to have different sorted views of the data at one time? Sorting in place means only one sort can be applied at a time.

To avoid all these issues, the Csla.SortedBindingList class implements a sorted view of any IList(Of T) collection. The IList(Of T) interface is a low-level interface defined by the .NET Framework. This interface is used by most collection types, including arrays. This means that SortedBindingList can be used to get a sorted view of arrays and many other types of collections—including views of business collections based on BusinessListBase and ReadOnlyListBase.

The word *view* doesn't completely convey what SortedBindingList will do. It could imply a snapshot, or read-only view of the original collection—but that's inaccurate. Instead, the word *view* is used here in the same way a DataView provides a view of a DataTable: the "view" is live and updatable. Changes to the view immediately affect the original collection, and changes in the original collection are immediately reflected in the view.

This means a UI developer can write code like this:

```
Dim customers As CustomerList = CustomerList.GetList()
Dim sortedList As _
  New SortedBindingList(Of CustomerList.CustomerInfo)(customers)
sortedList.ApplySort("Name", ListSortDirection.Ascending)
```

A normal customer collection is retrieved, and is then passed to the constructor of a new SortedBindingList object. Then the ApplySort() method is used to apply a sort to the data based on the Name property. The original collection is untouched, but sortedList now provides a sorted view of the collection.

SortedBindingList

The SortedBindingList class implements key collection and data binding interfaces: IList(Of T), IBindingList, and IEnumerable(Of T):

```
Public Class SortedBindingList(Of T)

  Implements IList(Of T)
  Implements IBindingList
  Implements IEnumerable(Of T)
```

Table 5-1 describes each interface.

Table 5-1. *Interfaces Implemented by SortedBindingList*

Interface	Description
IList(Of T)	Defines an interface for collections that contain objects that can be individually accessed by index
IBindingList	Defines an interface for collections that support data binding in Windows Forms
IEnumerable(Of T)	Defines an interface for collections to expose an enumerator object, which performs simple iteration over the items in the collection

Implementing these three interfaces means that SortedBindingList implicitly implements IList, IEnumerable, and ICollection as well. In the end, SortedBindingList looks and works like any BindingList(Of T) collection, but behind the scenes it is merely an updatable, sorted view of some other list or collection.

This means that SortedBindingList does not maintain its own collection of data. All the data is maintained within the original collection. That's why the constructor requires a reference to that original collection and the reference is maintained in an instance field named mList:

```
Private mList As IList(Of T)
Private mSupportsBinding As Boolean
Private mBindingList As IBindingList
Private mSorted As Boolean
Private mInitiatedLocally As Boolean
Private mSortBy As PropertyDescriptor
Private mSortOrder As ListSortDirection = ListSortDirection.Ascending
Private mSortIndex As New List(Of ListItem)

Public Sub New(ByVal list As IList(Of T))
  mList = list

  If TypeOf mList Is IBindingList Then
    mSupportsBinding = True
    mBindingList = DirectCast(mList, IBindingList)
    AddHandler mBindingList.ListChanged, AddressOf SourceChanged
  End If
End Sub
```

Not only is the source object reference stored, but if it implements IBindingList, then it is cast to that type, and a second reference is maintained. In that case, its ListChanged event is handled as well. I'll discuss handling of the ListChanged event later. First, it is important to understand some of the key plumbing code used in SortedBindingList.

Implementing a read-only sorted view of a collection is relatively straightforward, but implementing a view that is bidirectionally updatable is quite complex. And that's exactly what SortedBindingList does.

Acting As a View

Let's look at the simple things first. The original collection, as an ICollection, has a set of properties, such as Count and SyncRoot, that are simply exposed by SortedBindingList. For instance, here's the Count property:

```
Public ReadOnly Property Count() As Integer _
  Implements System.Collections.ICollection.Count, _
  System.Collections.Generic.ICollection(Of T).Count
  Get
    Return mList.Count
  End Get
End Property
```

This technique is repeated for all the ICollection, IList, and IEnumerable properties. The notable exception to this is the default property, which is quite a bit more complex and is discussed later.

If the original collection implements IBindingList, it has a broader set of properties. It might be editable and it might not. It might allow adding of new items or not. All these capabilities are exposed through its IBindingList interface, and SortedBindingList merely assumes the same settings. For instance, here's the AllowEdit property:

```
Public ReadOnly Property AllowEdit() As Boolean _
  Implements System.ComponentModel.IBindingList.AllowEdit
  Get
    If mSupportsBinding Then
      Return mBindingList.AllowEdit

    Else
      Return False
    End If
  End Get
End Property
```

Recall from the constructor that if the original collection doesn't implement IBindingList, then mSupportsBinding will be False. In that case, AllowEdit returns False because in-place editing isn't valid unless the original collection implements IBindingList. This technique is repeated for all the IBindingList properties.

Applying a Sort

The IBindingList interface allows a sort to be applied to a collection, either ascending or descending, based on a single property. This is done through the ApplySort() method.

ApplySort Method

SortedBindingList implements two overloads of ApplySort(), making it possible to apply a sort based on the string name of the property, as well as by a PropertyDescriptor as required by IBindingList:

```
Public Sub ApplySort( _
  ByVal propertyName As String, _
  ByVal direction As System.ComponentModel.ListSortDirection)
```

```
    mSortBy = Nothing

    If Len(propertyName) > 0 Then
      Dim itemType As Type = GetType(T)
      For Each prop As PropertyDescriptor In _
            TypeDescriptor.GetProperties(itemType)
        If prop.Name = propertyName Then
          mSortBy = prop
          Exit For
        End If
      Next
    End If

    ApplySort(mSortBy, direction)
  End Sub

  Public Sub ApplySort( _
    ByVal [property] As System.ComponentModel.PropertyDescriptor, _
    ByVal direction As System.ComponentModel.ListSortDirection) _
    Implements System.ComponentModel.IBindingList.ApplySort

    mSortBy = [property]
    mSortOrder = direction
    DoSort()
  End Sub
```

The first overload creates a PropertyDescriptor for the named property and calls the second overload. The second overload will also be called directly by data binding. It sets the mSortBy and mSortOrder fields to indicate the sort parameters, and calls DoSort(). The reason these two instance fields are used to store the parameters is that these values are also exposed by Public properties such as SortDirection:

```
  Public ReadOnly Property SortDirection() As _
    System.ComponentModel.ListSortDirection _
    Implements System.ComponentModel.IBindingList.SortDirection
    Get
      Return mSortOrder
    End Get
  End Property
```

The DoSort() method actually does the sorting by assembling the key values into a private collection and then sorting those values. Associated with each key value is a reference to the corresponding item in the original collection.

ListItem Class

Associating the value of the property by which to sort with a reference to the corresponding child object in the original collection requires a key/value list, which in turn requires a key/value class. The ListItem class maintains a relationship between a key and a reference to the corresponding child object.

The key value is the value of the property from the child object on which the collection is to be sorted. For example, when sorting a collection of Customer objects by their Name property, the key value will be the contents of the Name property from the corresponding child object.

Rather than maintaining an actual object reference, ListItem maintains the *index* value of the child item in the original collection. This is referred to as the *base index*.

```vb
Private Class ListItem
  Implements IComparable(Of ListItem)

  Private mKey As Object
  Private mBaseIndex As Integer

  Public ReadOnly Property Key() As Object
    Get
      Return mKey
    End Get
  End Property

  Public Property BaseIndex() As Integer
    Get
      Return mBaseIndex
    End Get
    Set(ByVal value As Integer)
      mBaseIndex = value
    End Set
  End Property

  Public Sub New(ByVal key As Object, ByVal baseIndex As Integer)
    mKey = key
    mBaseIndex = baseIndex
  End Sub

  Public Function CompareTo(ByVal other As ListItem) As Integer _
    Implements System.IComparable(Of ListItem).CompareTo

    Dim target As Object = other.Key

    If TypeOf Key Is IComparable Then
      Return DirectCast(Key, IComparable).CompareTo(target)

    Else
      If Key.Equals(target) Then
        Return 0

      Else
        Return Key.ToString.CompareTo(target.ToString)
      End If
    End If
  End Function

  Public Overrides Function ToString() As String
    Return Key.ToString
  End Function
End Class
```

In addition to associating the property value to the base index of the child object in the original collection, ListItem implements IComparable(Of T). This interface enables the .NET Framework to sort a collection of ListItem objects. This interface requires implementation of the CompareTo() method, which is responsible for comparing one ListItem object to another.

Of course, it is the key value that is to be compared, so CompareTo() simply compares the value of its Key property to the Key property from the other ListItem object. If the type of the key value implements IComparable, then the call simply delegates to that interface:

```
If TypeOf Key Is IComparable Then
    Return DirectCast(Key, IComparable).CompareTo(target)
```

Otherwise things are a bit more complex. Obviously, any objects can be compared for equality, so that part is straightforward:

```
If Key.Equals(target) Then
    Return 0
```

However, if the type of the key value doesn't implement IComparable, then there's no easy way to see if one is greater than the other. To overcome this problem, both values are converted to their string representations, which are then compared to each other:

```
Return Key.ToString.CompareTo(target.ToString)
```

While this is not perfect, it is the best we can do. And really this is an extreme edge case since most types are comparable, including strings, numeric types, and dates. Given that most properties are of those types, this solution works well in almost every case.

DoSort Method

Given the ListItem class and the sorting capabilities of the .NET Framework, the DoSort() method is not hard to implement:

```
Private Sub DoSort()
    Dim index As Integer

    mSortIndex.Clear()

    If mSortBy Is Nothing Then
        For Each obj As T In mList
            mSortIndex.Add(New ListItem(obj, index))
            index += 1
        Next

    Else
        For Each obj As T In mList
            mSortIndex.Add(New ListItem(mSortBy.GetValue(obj), index))
            index += 1
        Next
    End If

    mSortIndex.Sort()
    mSorted = True

    OnListChanged(New ListChangedEventArgs(ListChangedType.Reset, 0))
End Sub
```

If mSortBy is Nothing (which is quite possible, as it is optional), then each child object is sorted as is. In other words, it is the value of the child object itself that determines the sort order, rather than any specific property on the child object. In this case, DoSort() loops through every item in the original collection, creating a ListItem object for which the key value is the child object itself and the index is the location of the child object within the original collection:

```
For Each obj As T In mList
    mSortIndex.Add(New ListItem(obj, index))
    index += 1
Next
```

This scenario is quite common when creating a sorted view against an array of type `String` or `Integer`, since there's no meaning in setting an `mSortBy` value for those types.

For more complex child objects, however, an `mSortBy` value is typically supplied. In that case, a bit of reflection is used to retrieve the specified property value from the child object. That property value is then used as the key value for the `ListItem` object:

```
For Each obj As T In mList
  mSortIndex.Add(New ListItem(mSortBy.GetValue(obj), index))
  index += 1
Next
```

Remember that `mSortBy` is a `System.ComponentModel.PropertyDescriptor` object corresponding to the key property. `PropertyDescriptor` provides a `GetValue()` method that retrieves the property value from the specified child object.

Whether or not `mSortBy` is `Nothing`, the end result is a list of `ListItem` objects in a generic `List(Of ListItem)` collection named `mSortIndex`. The `List(Of T)` class provides a `Sort()` method that sorts the items in the list. Since `ListItem` implements `IComparable(Of T)`, that interface is used to order the sort, meaning that the items end up sorted based on the key property value in each `ListItem` object.

Since sorting changes the order of items in the list, the view object's `ListChanged` event is raised to tell data binding that the view collection has effectively been reset. Keep in mind that the original collection is entirely unaffected by this process, and doesn't raise any events due to the sort being applied.

Viewing the Sorted Values

You may be wondering how descending sorts are handled, since the `Sort()` method of `List(Of T)` performed an ascending sort in the `DoSort()` method. Ascending and descending sorts are handled by the view object's default property.

The `IList` interface requires that a default property be implemented. To retrieve an item, `SortedBindingList` must be able to cross-reference from the sorted position of the item to the original position of the item in the original collection. The `OriginalIndex()` helper method performs this cross-reference operation:

```
Private Function OriginalIndex(ByVal sortedIndex As Integer) As Integer
  If mSortOrder = ListSortDirection.Ascending Then
    Return mSortIndex.Item(sortedIndex).BaseIndex
  Else
    Return mSortIndex.Item(mSortIndex.Count - 1 - sortedIndex).BaseIndex
  End If
End Function
```

The method checks to see whether the sort is ascending or descending. The supplied index value is then cross-referenced into the `mSortIndex` list to find the *actual* index of the child item in the original collection. In the case of an ascending sort, a straight cross-reference from the position in `mSortIndex` to the original collection is used. And in the case of a descending sort, the cross-reference process merely starts at the bottom of `mSortIndex` and works toward the top.

The default property simply uses this helper method to retrieve or set the object from the original collection that corresponds to the location in the sorted index:

```
Default Public Overloads Property Item(ByVal index As Integer) As T _
  Implements System.Collections.Generic.IList(Of T).Item
  Get
    If mSorted Then
      Return mList(OriginalIndex(index))
```

```
      Else
        Return mList(index)
      End If
    End Get
    Set(ByVal value As T)
      If mSorted Then
        mList(OriginalIndex(index)) = value
      Else
        mList(index) = value
      End If
    End Set
  End Property
```

Notice that the child object is ultimately returned from the original collection. The data in SortedBindingList is merely used to provide a sorted cross-reference to those objects.

In the case that a sort hasn't been applied at all, no cross-reference is performed and the child object is returned from the original collection based directly on the index value:

```
      Return mList(index)
```

The same technique is used in the Set block as well. Additionally, the IList interface requires implementation of a loosely typed Item property:

```
Private Property Item1(ByVal index As Integer) As Object _
    Implements System.Collections.IList.Item
    Get
      Return Me(index)
    End Get
    Set(ByVal value As Object)
      Me(index) = CType(value, T)
    End Set
End Property
```

This property delegates its work to the strongly typed default property implemented previously.

Collection Enumerator

There are two ways to get items from a collection: the default property and an enumerator. The enumerator is used by the For...Each statement to loop through all items in the collection. Obviously, it too needs to perform a cross-reference process, so a For...Each loop goes through the sorted index and returns the corresponding item from the original collection.

There are two steps to this process. First, the custom enumerator class must understand how to perform the cross-reference process. Second, SortedBindingList needs to expose a GetEnumerator() method that returns an instance of this custom enumerator (or the original collection's enumerator if no sort has been applied).

Custom Enumerator Class

An enumerator is an object that implements either IEnumerator or IEnumerator(Of T). These interfaces define a Current property and MoveNext() and Reset() methods. You can think of an enumerator object as being a cursor or pointer into the collection. Table 5-2 describes these elements.

Table 5-2. *Properties and Methods of an Enumerator Object*

Member	Behavior
Current	Returns a reference to the current child object in the collection
MoveNext()	Moves to the next child object in the collection, making that the current object
Reset()	Moves to just above the top of the collection, so a subsequent MoveNext() call moves to the very first item in the collection

When you use a For...Each statement in your code, the compiler generates code behind the scenes to get an enumerator object from the collection, and to call the Reset(), MoveNext(), and Current elements to iterate through the items in the collection.

Because an enumerator object is a cursor or pointer into the collection, it must maintain a current index position. The SortedEnumerator class used by SortedBindingList also needs to know the sort order and must have access to the original collection itself:

```
Private Class SortedEnumerator

  Implements IEnumerator(Of T)

  Private mList As IList(Of T)
  Private mSortIndex As List(Of ListItem)
  Private mSortOrder As ListSortDirection
  Private mIndex As Integer

  Public Sub New( _
    ByVal list As IList(Of T), _
    ByVal sortIndex As List(Of ListItem), _
    ByVal direction As ListSortDirection)

    mList = list
    mSortIndex = sortIndex
    mSortOrder = direction
    Reset()
  End Sub
```

The constructor accepts a reference to the original collection, a reference to the mSortIndex list containing the sorted list of ListItem objects, and the sort direction. The mIndex field is used to maintain a pointer to the current position of the enumerator within the collection.

The Reset() method simply sets index to immediately before the first item in the collection. Of course, when using a descending sort, this is actually immediately *after* the last item in the collection, because the enumerator will walk through the list from bottom to top in that case:

```
Public Sub Reset() Implements System.Collections.IEnumerator.Reset
  If mSortOrder = ListSortDirection.Ascending Then
    mIndex = -1
  Else
    mIndex = mSortIndex.Count
  End If
End Sub
```

The MoveNext() method increments mIndex, moving to the next item in the collection. Again, when using a descending sort, it actually decrements mIndex, thus moving from the bottom of the collection toward the top.

```
Public Function MoveNext() As Boolean _
Implements System.Collections.IEnumerator.MoveNext

  If mSortOrder = ListSortDirection.Ascending Then
    If mIndex < mSortIndex.Count - 1 Then
      mIndex += 1
      Return True

    Else
      Return False
    End If

  Else
    If mIndex > 0 Then
      mIndex -= 1
      Return True

    Else
      Return False
    End If
  End If
End Function
```

The MoveNext() method returns a Boolean value, returning False when there are no more items in the collection. In other words, when it reaches the bottom of the list (or the top when doing a descending sort), it returns False to indicate that there are no more items.

The Current property simply returns a reference to the child object corresponding to the current value of mIndex. Of course, mIndex is pointing to an item in the *sorted list*, and so that value must be cross-referenced back to an item in the original collection. This is the same as in the default property earlier:

```
Public ReadOnly Property Current() As T _
  Implements System.Collections.Generic.IEnumerator(Of T).Current
  Get
    Return mList(mSortIndex(mIndex).BaseIndex)
  End Get
End Property

Private ReadOnly Property CurrentItem() As Object _
  Implements System.Collections.IEnumerator.Current
  Get
    Return mList(mSortIndex(mIndex).BaseIndex)
  End Get
End Property
```

Because SortedEnumerator implements IEnumerator(Of T), it actually has two Current properties—one strongly typed for IEnumerator(Of T) itself, and the other loosely typed for IEnumerator (from which IEnumerator(Of T) inherits).

Both do the same thing, using the mIndex value to find the appropriate ListItem object in the sorted list, and then using the BaseIndex property of ListItem to retrieve the corresponding item in the original collection. That child object is then returned as a result.

GetEnumerator Method

Collection objects must implement a GetEnumerator() method. This is required by the IEnumerable interface, which is the most basic interface for collection or list objects in the .NET Framework. In the case of SortedBindingList, both strongly typed and loosely typed GetEnumerator() methods must be implemented:

```
Public Function GetEnumerator() As _
  System.Collections.Generic.IEnumerator(Of T) _
  Implements System.Collections.Generic.IEnumerable(Of T).GetEnumerator

  If mSorted Then
    Return New SortedEnumerator(mList, mSortIndex, mSortOrder)
  Else
    Return mList.GetEnumerator
  End If
End Function

Private Function GetItemEnumerator() As System.Collections.IEnumerator _
  Implements System.Collections.IEnumerable.GetEnumerator

  Return GetEnumerator()
End Function
```

These methods merely return an instance of an enumerator object for use by For...Each statements that wish to iterate through the items in the collection.

If the view is not currently sorted, then it can simply ask the original collection for *its* enumerator. The original collection's enumerator will already iterate through all the child objects in the collection in their original order:

```
Return mList.GetEnumerator
```

On the other hand, if a sort has been applied, then an instance of the custom SortedEnumerator (implemented in the preceding code) is returned:

```
Return New SortedEnumerator(mList, mSortIndex, mSortOrder)
```

Either way, the compiler-generated code for the For...Each statement has an enumerator object that iterates through the items in the collection.

Removing the Sort

The IBindingList interface allows for removal of the sort. The result should be that the items in the collection return to their original order. This is handled by an UndoSort() method:

```
Private Sub UndoSort()
  mSortIndex.Clear()
  mSortBy = Nothing
  mSortOrder = ListSortDirection.Ascending
  mSorted = False

  OnListChanged(New ListChangedEventArgs(ListChangedType.Reset, 0))
End Sub
```

Removing a sort is just a matter of setting mSorted to False and clearing the various sort-related fields. Most important is calling Clear() on mSortIndex, as that releases any possible object references to items in the original collection.

Because removing the sort alters the order of items in the view, the ListChanged event is raised to tell the UI that it needs to refresh its display of the collection.

Adding and Removing Items

Now we get to the complex issues. Remember that SortedBindingList is an *updatable* view of the original collection. This means that when the user adds or removes an item from the original collection, that change is immediately reflected in the view; the view is even re-sorted, if appropriate. Conversely, if the user adds or removes an item from the view, that change is immediately reflected in the original collection. There's some work involved in keeping the view and collection in sync.

Also remember that collections may raise ListChanged events as they are changed. Table 5-3 lists the add and remove operations and how they raise events.

Table 5-3. *Events Raised During Add and Remove Operations*

Operation	Event Behavior
AddNew()	Called by data binding to add an item to the end of the collection; an ItemAdded type ListChanged event is raised by the collection
Insert()	Inserts an item into the collection; an ItemAdded type ListChanged event is raised by the collection
RemoveAt()	Removes an item from the collection; an ItemDeleted type ListChanged event is raised by the collection

A ListChanged event is raised when the user adds or removes an item from the original collection. This event must be handled and sometimes reraised by the view. This is illustrated in Figure 5-2.

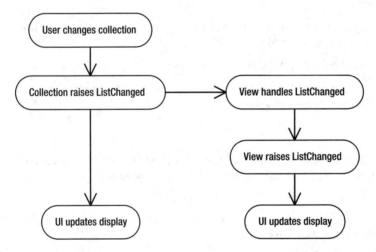

Figure 5-2. *Flow of events when the user changes the original collection*

Figure 5-2 shows the simple case, in which both the original collection and the view are bound to separate controls on the UI, and an update to the original collection is made.

However, when the user adds or removes an item through the view, the view raises a ListChanged event as well as updating the original collection. Of course, updating the original collection triggers *its* ListChanged event. If you're not careful, this could result in duplicate events being raised, as shown in Figure 5-3.

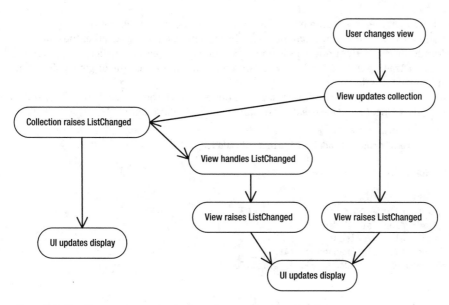

Figure 5-3. *Duplicate events raised when the user changes the view*

In this case, the UI control bound to the sorted view gets the ListChanged event twice, which is wasteful. But when the change is applied to the original collection, its event could flow back to the view and then to the UI.

Figure 5-4 shows what *should* happen when the user changes the view.

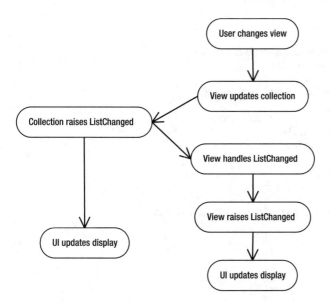

Figure 5-4. *Flow of events with no duplicate events being raised*

Making this happen means keeping track of whether the user added or removed an object directly in the original collection or through the view. The view needs to know whether the change was initiated locally, on the view, or not. This is tracked by the mInitiatedLocally field, which is set to True before SortedBindingList performs any add or remove operations on the original collection, and is set to False when it is done.

Adding and removing items to and from the view is done through the AddNew(), Insert(), and RemoveAt() methods. AddNew() and RemoveAt() are handled in a similar manner:

```
Public Function AddNew() As Object _
  Implements System.ComponentModel.IBindingList.AddNew

  Dim result As Object

  If mSupportsBinding Then
    mInitiatedLocally = True
    result = mBindingList.AddNew
    mInitiatedLocally = False
    OnListChanged(New ListChangedEventArgs( _
      ListChangedType.ItemAdded, mBindingList.Count - 1))

  Else
    result = Nothing
  End If

  Return result
End Function

Public Sub RemoveAt(ByVal index As Integer) _
  Implements System.Collections.IList.RemoveAt, _
  System.Collections.Generic.IList(Of T).RemoveAt

  If mSorted Then
    mInitiatedLocally = True
    Dim baseIndex As Integer = OriginalIndex(index)
    ' remove the item from the source list
    mList.RemoveAt(baseIndex)
    ' delete the corresponding value in the sort index
    mSortIndex.RemoveAt(index)
    ' now fix up all index pointers in the sort index
    For Each item As ListItem In mSortIndex
      If item.BaseIndex > baseIndex Then
        item.BaseIndex -= 1
      End If
    Next
    OnListChanged( _
      New ListChangedEventArgs(ListChangedType.ItemDeleted, index))
    mInitiatedLocally = False

  Else
    mList.RemoveAt(index)
  End If
End Sub
```

Remember that mBindingList is a reference to the original collection object's implementation of the IBindingList interface. So this code merely sets mInitiatedLocally to True and then delegates the AddNew() call to the original collection. Similarly, the RemoveAt() call is delegated to the original collection through its IList(Of T) interface.

I've also optimized the RemoveAt() implementation, so when an item is removed from the middle of the list, the entire sorted index isn't rebuilt. This offers substantial performance improvements when dealing with larger-sized lists.

■Note The important thing here is that SortedBindingList doesn't maintain a local copy of the collection's data. Instead, it delegates all calls directly to the original collection itself.

The original collection performs the requested operation and adds or removes the child object. Of course, that triggers a ListChanged event from the original collection. Recall that in the constructor of SortedBindingList, the original collection's ListChanged event was handled by the SourceChanged() method. I'll cover the SourceChanged() method in a moment, and you'll see how the ListChanged event is suppressed when the add or remove operation is initiated by the view itself.

The Insert() method is simpler:

```
Public Sub Insert(ByVal index As Integer, ByVal item As T) _
  Implements System.Collections.Generic.IList(Of T).Insert

  mList.Insert(index, item)
End Sub

Private Sub Insert(ByVal index As Integer, ByVal value As Object) _
  Implements System.Collections.IList.Insert

  Insert(index, CType(value, T))
End Sub
```

When a new item is inserted into the view, it is really inserted into the original collection. This results in the original collection raising its ListChanged event, and in turn the view then raises its ListChanged event (in the SourceChanged() method in the following code). The end result is that the view raises the ListChanged event exactly once, which is the desired goal.

Responding to Changed Data

The source collection's ListChanged event is handled by the SourceChanged() method. This allows SortedBindingList to re-sort the data if it is changed in the original collection, thus keeping the view current. It also means that the event can be reraised by the view so that any UI components bound to the sorted view are also aware that the underlying data has changed.

If no sort has been applied, then the only thing the SourceChanged() method needs to do is reraise the event:

```
Private Sub SourceChanged( _
  ByVal sender As Object, ByVal e As ListChangedEventArgs)

  If mSorted Then
    Select Case e.ListChangedType
        ' update sorted view based on type of change
    End Select

  Else
    OnListChanged(e)
  End If
End Sub
```

The OnListChanged() method raises the ListChanged event from the SortedBindingList object. Notice that the exact same event is raised, so in this case the UI is blissfully unaware that SortedBindingList is a view over the original collection.

However, if the view is sorted, then things are far more complex. In this case, the view must be updated appropriately based on the underlying change in the original collection. The ListChanged event can indicate different types of changes, each of which must be handled in a different manner. The code that goes in the preceding Select block takes care of these details. Let's go through each Case of that block.

Adding a New Item

If a new item was added to the original collection, then the sorted view must also add a new ListItem object to the sorted index. It is possible for an item to be added in the middle or at the end of the original collection.

If the item was added at the end of the original collection, the new ListItem object needs to contain the new child object's key property value and the index location of the item in the original collection.

But if the item was inserted in the middle of the original collection, then all the cross-reference indexes in the sort index become potentially invalid. The simplest way to ensure that they are all correct is to call DoSort() and rebuild the sort index completely:

```
Case ListChangedType.ItemAdded
 Dim newItem As T = mList(e.NewIndex)
  If e.NewIndex = mList.Count - 1 Then
    Dim newKey As Object
    If mSortBy IsNot Nothing Then
      newKey = mSortBy.GetValue(newItem)
    Else
      newKey = newItem
    End If

    If mSortOrder = ListSortDirection.Ascending Then
      mSortIndex.Add(New ListItem(newKey, e.NewIndex))

    Else
      mSortIndex.Insert(0, New ListItem(newKey, e.NewIndex))
    End If
    If Not mInitiatedLocally Then
      OnListChanged( _
        New ListChangedEventArgs( _
          ListChangedType.ItemAdded, SortedIndex(e.NewIndex)))
    End If

  Else
    DoSort()
  End If
```

The hard work occurs if the new item was added to the end of the original collection. In that case, the item's key property value is retrieved based on the value of mSortBy; just like in the DoSort() method.

Then a new ListItem object is created and inserted into the list—at the end for an ascending sort, and at the beginning for a descending sort. This ensures that the new item appears at the very bottom of a grid or list control when the sorted view is a data source for such a UI control.

Finally, if the addition of the new item was not initiated locally, then a ListChanged event is raised to tell the UI about the new item. This is important, because if the new item *was* added locally to the view, then no ListChanged event should be raised at this point; instead, the event is raised by the local AddNew() method itself.

Removing an Item

When an item is removed from the original collection, a ListChanged event is raised. SortedBindingList handles this event. If the removal was initiated by the original collection, then the view is simply re-sorted:

```
Case ListChangedType.ItemDeleted
  If Not mInitiatedLocally Then
    DoSort()
  End If
```

This is the easiest approach, since it causes automatic removal of the ListItem object corresponding to the removed item, and recalculation of all the cross-reference index values between the sorted list and the original collection.

Notice that if the removal was initiated by the view itself, then the view isn't re-sorted. This is because the RemoveAt() method in SortedBindingList removes both the original item and the corresponding ListItem object, and recalculates all the cross-reference index values.

By using a combination of delegation to the original collection and implementation of a cross-reference scheme between the sorted list and the original list, SortedBindingList provides a bidirectionally updatable, sorted view of any IList(Of T) array or collection.

Date Handling

One common view of good UI design holds that the user should be free to enter arbitrary text, and it is up to the application to make sense of the entry. Nowhere is this truer than with date values, and the SmartDate type is designed to simplify how a business developer uses dates and exposes them to the UI.

Examples of free-form date entry are easy to find. Just look at widely used applications like Microsoft Money or Intuit's Quicken. In these applications, users are free to enter dates in whatever format is easiest for them. Additionally, various shortcuts are supported; for example, the + character means tomorrow, while – means yesterday.

Most users find this approach more appealing than being forced to enter a date in a strict format through a masked edit control, or having to always use the mouse to use a graphical calendar control. Of course, being able to *additionally* support a calendar control is also a great UI design choice.

Date handling is also quite challenging because the standard DateTime data type doesn't have any comprehension of an "empty" or "blank" date.

Many applications have date values that may be empty for a time and are filled in later. Consider a sales order, in which the shipment date is unknown when the order is entered. That date should remain blank or empty until an actual date *is* known. Without having the concept of an empty date, an application will require the user to enter an invalid "placeholder" date until the real date is known; and that's just poor application design.

■**Tip** In the early 1990s, I worked at a company where all "far-future" dates were entered as 12/31/99. Guess how much trouble the company had around Y2K, when all of its never-to-be-delivered orders started coming due!

It is true that the Nullable(Of T) type can be applied to a DateTime value like this: Nullable(Of DateTime). This allows a date to be "empty" in a limited sense. Unfortunately, that isn't enough for many applications, since an actual date value can't be meaningfully compared to Nothing. Is Nothing greater than or less than a given date? With Nullable(Of T), the answer is an exception; which is not a very useful answer.

Additionally, data binding doesn't deal well with Nothing values, and so exposing a Nothing value from a business object's property often complicates the UI code.

SmartDate

The Csla.SmartDate type is designed to augment the standard .NET DateTime type to make it easier to work with date values. In particular, it provides the following key features:

- Automatic translation between String and DateTime types

- Translation of shortcut values to valid dates

- Understanding of the concept of an "empty" date

- Meaningful comparison between a date and an empty date

- Backward compatibility with SmartDate from the previous edition of this book

The DateTime data type is marked NotInheritable, meaning that a new type can't inherit from it to create a different data type. However, it is possible to use containment and delegation to "wrap" a DateTime value with extra functionality. That's exactly how the SmartDate type is implemented. Like DateTime itself, SmartDate is a value type:

```
<Serializable()> _
Public Structure SmartDate

  Implements IComparable

  Private mDate As Date
  Private mEmptyIsMax As Boolean
  Private mFormat As String
  Private mInitialized As Boolean
```

Notice that it has an mDate instance field, which is the underlying DateTime value of the SmartDate.

Supporting empty date values is more complex than it might appear. An empty date still has meaning, and in fact it is possible to compare a regular date to an empty date and get a valid result.

Consider the previous sales order example. If the shipment date is unknown, it will be empty. But effectively, that empty date is infinitely far in the future. Were you to compare that empty shipment date to any other date, the shipment date would be the larger of the two.

Conversely, there are cases in which an empty date should be considered to be smaller than the smallest possible date.

This concept is important, as it allows for meaningful comparisons between dates and empty dates. Such comparisons make implementation of validation rules and other business logic far simpler. You can, for instance, loop through a set of Order objects to find all the objects with a shipment date less than today; without the need to worry about empty dates:

```
For Each order As Order In OrderList
  If order.ShipmentDate <= Today Then
```

Assuming ShipmentDate is a SmartDate, this will work great, and any empty dates will be considered to be larger than any actual date value.

The mEmptyIsMax field keeps track of whether the SmartDate instance should consider an empty date to be the smallest or largest possible date value. If it is True, then an empty date is considered to be the largest possible value.

The mFormat field stores a .NET format string that provides the default format for converting a DateTime value into a string representation.

The mInitialized field keeps track of whether the SmartDate has been initialized. Remember that SmartDate is a Structure, not an object. This severely restricts how the type's fields can be initialized.

Initializing the Structure

As with any Structure, SmartDate can be created with or without calling a constructor. This means a business object could declare SmartDate fields using any of the following:

```
Private mDate1 As SmartDate
Private mDate2 As New SmartDate(False)
Private mDate3 As New SmartDate(Today)
Private mDate4 As New SmartDate(Today, True)
Private mDate5 As New SmartDate("1/1/2005", True)
Private mDate6 As New SmartDate("", True)
```

In the first two cases, the SmartDate will start out being empty, with empty meaning that it has a value *smaller* than any other date.

The mDate3 value will start out containing the current date. It if is set to an empty value later, that empty value will correspond to a value *smaller* than any other date.

The next two values are initialized either to the current date or a fixed date based on a String value. In both cases, if the SmartDate is set to an empty value later, that empty value will correspond to a value *larger* than any other date.

Finally, mDate6 is initialized to an empty date value, where that value is *larger* than any other date.

Handling this initialization is a bit tricky, since a Structure can't have a default constructor. Yet even in the case of mDate1, some initialization is required. This is the purpose of the mInitialized instance field. It, of course, defaults to a value of False, and so can be used in the properties of the Structure to determine whether the Structure has been initialized. As you'll see, this allows SmartDate to initialize itself the first time a property is called; assuming it hasn't been initialized previously.

All the constructors follow the same basic flow. Here's one of them:

```
Public Sub New(ByVal value As String, ByVal emptyIsMin As Boolean)
  mEmptyIsMax = Not emptyIsMin
  Me.Text = value
  mInitialized = True
End Sub
```

In this constructor, the Text property is used to set the date value based on the value parameter passed into the constructor. This includes translation of an empty String value into the appropriate empty date value.

Also look at the emptyIsMin parameter. Remember that SmartDate actually maintains an mEmptyIsMax field—the exact *opposite* of the parameter's meaning. This is why the parameter value is negated as mEmptyIsMax is assigned. This is a bit awkward, but necessary for preserving backward compatibility with the SmartDate type from the previous edition of this book, and thus previous versions of CSLA .NET.

■Note This highlights a key design consideration for frameworks in general. Backward compatibility is a key feature of frameworks, since breaking compatibility means going through every bit of code based on the framework to adjust to the change. While sometimes awkward, it is often worth adding extra code to a framework in order to preserve backward compatibility.

The reason the field is the reverse of the property is that the *default* value for a SmartDate is that EmptyIsMin is True. Given that you can't initialize fields in a Structure, it is simpler to accept the default value for a Boolean, which is False. Hence the use of mEmptyIsMax as a field, since if it is False (the default), then EmptyIsMin is True by default.

Supporting Empty Dates

SmartDate already has a field to control whether an empty date represents the largest or smallest possible date. This field is exposed as a property so that other code can determine how dates are handled:

```
Public ReadOnly Property EmptyIsMin() As Boolean
  Get
    Return Not mEmptyIsMax
  End Get
End Property
```

SmartDate also implements an IsEmpty property so that code can ask if the SmartDate object represents an empty date:

```
Public ReadOnly Property IsEmpty() As Boolean
  Get
    If Not mEmptyIsMax Then
      Return Me.Date.Equals(Date.MinValue)
    Else
      Return Me.Date.Equals(Date.MaxValue)
    End If
  End Get
End Property
```

Notice the use of the mEmptyIsMax flag to determine whether an empty date is to be considered the largest or smallest possible date for comparison purposes. If it is the smallest date, then it is empty if the date value equals DateTime.MinValue; if it is the largest date, it is empty if the value equals DateTime.MaxValue.

Conversion Functions

Given this understanding of empty dates, it is possible to create a couple of functions to convert dates to text (or text to dates) intelligently. For consistency with other .NET types, SmartDate will also include a Parse() method to convert a String into a SmartDate. These will be Shared methods so that they can be used even without creating an instance of SmartDate. Using these methods, a developer can write business logic such as this:

```
Dim userDate As DateTime = SmartDate.StringToDate(userDateString)
```

Table 5-4 shows the results of this function, based on various user text inputs.

Table 5-4. *Results of the StringToDate Method Based on Various Inputs*

User Text Input	EmptyIsMin	Result of StringToDate()
String.Empty	True (default)	DateTime.MinValue
String.Empty	False	DateTime.MaxValue
Any text that can be parsed as a date	True or False (ignored)	A date value

StringToDate() converts a string value containing a date into a DateTime value. It understands that an empty String should be converted to either the smallest or the largest date, based on an optional parameter.

It also handles translation of shortcut values to valid date values. The characters ., +, and – correspond to today, tomorrow, and yesterday, respectively. Additionally, the values t, today, tom, tomorrow, y, and yesterday work in a similar manner. These text values are defined in the project's Resource.resx file, and so are subject to localization for other languages.

Here's the code:

```
Public Shared Function StringToDate(ByVal value As String) As Date
    Return StringToDate(value, True)
End Function

Public Shared Function StringToDate( _
  ByVal value As String, ByVal emptyIsMin As Boolean) As Date

    If Len(value) = 0 Then
        If emptyIsMin Then
            Return Date.MinValue

        Else
            Return Date.MaxValue
        End If

    ElseIf IsDate(value) Then
        Return CDate(value)

    Else
        Select Case LCase(Trim(value))
            Case My.Resources.SmartDateT, My.Resources.SmartDateToday, "."
                Return Now

            Case My.Resources.SmartDateY, My.Resources.SmartDateYesterday, "-"
                Return DateAdd(DateInterval.Day, -1, Now)

            Case My.Resources.SmartDateTom, My.Resources.SmartDateTomorrow, "+"
                Return DateAdd(DateInterval.Day, 1, Now)

            Case Else
                Throw New ArgumentException(My.Resources.StringToDateException)
        End Select
    End If
End Function
```

Given a String of nonzero length, this function attempts to parse it directly to a DateTime field. If that fails, then the various shortcut values are checked. If that fails as well, then an exception is thrown to indicate that the String value couldn't be parsed into a date.

SmartDate can translate dates the other way as well, such as converting a DateTime field into a String and retaining the concept of an empty date. Again, an optional parameter controls whether an empty date represents the smallest or the largest possible date. Another parameter controls the format of the date as it's converted to a String. Table 5-5 illustrates the results for various inputs.

Table 5-5. *Results of the DateToString Method Based on Various Inputs*

User Date Input	EmptyIsMin	Result of DateToString()
DateTime.MinValue	True (default)	String.Empty
DateTime.MinValue	False	DateTime.MinValue
DateTime.MaxValue	True (default)	DateTime.MaxValue
DateTime.MaxValue	False	String.Empty
Any other valid date	True or False (ignored)	String representing the date value

Add the following code to the same region:

```
Public Shared Function DateToString( _
  ByVal value As Date, ByVal formatString As String) As String

  Return DateToString(value, formatString, True)
End Function

Public Shared Function DateToString( _
  ByVal value As Date, ByVal formatString As String, _
  ByVal emptyIsMin As Boolean) As String

  If emptyIsMin AndAlso value = Date.MinValue Then
    Return ""
  ElseIf Not emptyIsMin AndAlso value = Date.MaxValue Then
    Return ""
  Else
    Return String.Format("{0:" + formatString + "}", value)
  End If
End Function
```

This functions as a mirror to the StringToDate() method. This means it is possible to start with an empty String, convert it to a DateTime, and then convert that DateTime back into an empty String.

Notice that this method requires a format string, which defines how the DateTime value is to be formatted as a String. This is used to create a complete .NET format string such as {0:d}.

Finally, there's the Parse() method, which accepts a String value and returns a SmartDate. There are two variations on this method:

```
Public Shared Function Parse(ByVal value As String) As SmartDate
  Return New SmartDate(value)
End Function

Public Shared Function Parse( _
  ByVal value As String, ByVal emptyIsMin As Boolean) As SmartDate

  Return New SmartDate(value, emptyIsMin)
End Function
```

The first uses the default True value for EmptyIsMin, while the second allows the caller to specify the value. Neither is hard to implement given the constructors already present in the code.

Text Functions

Next, let's implement functions in SmartDate that support both text and DateTime access to the underlying DateTime value. When business code wants to expose a date value to the UI, it will often want to expose it as a String. (Exposing it as a DateTime precludes the possibility of the user entering a blank value for an empty date, and while that's great if the date is required, it isn't good for optional date values.)

Exposing a date as text requires the ability to format the date properly. To make this manageable, the mFormat field is used to control the format used for outputting a date. SmartDate includes a property so that the business developer can alter this format value to override the default:

```
Public Property FormatString() As String
  Get
    If mFormat Is Nothing Then
      mFormat = "d"
    End If
    Return mFormat
  End Get
  Set(ByVal value As String)
    mFormat = value
  End Set
End Property
```

The default value is d for the short date format. This is handled in the Get block, which is important given that the mFormat field will default to a value of Nothing unless explicitly set to something else.

Given the FormatString property, the Text property can use the StringToDate() and DateToString() methods to translate between text and date values. This property can be used to retrieve or set values using String representations of dates, where an empty String is appropriately handled:

```
Public Property Text() As String
  Get
    Return DateToString(Me.Date, FormatString, Not mEmptyIsMax)
  End Get
  Set(ByVal value As String)
    Me.Date = StringToDate(value, Not mEmptyIsMax)
  End Set
End Property
```

This property is used in the constructors as well, meaning that the same rules for dealing with an empty date apply during object initialization, as when setting its value via the Text property.

There's one other text-oriented method to implement: ToString(). All objects in .NET have a ToString() method, which ideally returns a useful text representation of the object's contents. In this case, it should return the formatted date value:

```
Public Overrides Function ToString() As String
  Return Me.Text
End Function
```

Since the Text property already converts the SmartDate value to a String, this is easy to implement.

Date Functions

It should be possible to treat a SmartDate like a regular DateTime—as much as possible, anyway. Since it's not possible for it to inherit from DateTime, there's no way for it to be treated *just* like a regular DateTime. The best approximation is to implement a Date property that returns the internal value:

```
Public Property [Date]() As Date
  Get
    If Not mInitialized Then
      mDate = Date.MinValue
      mInitialized = True
    End If
    Return mDate
  End Get
  Set(ByVal value As Date)
    mDate = value
    mInitialized = True
  End Set
End Property
```

Notice the use of the mInitialized field to determine whether the SmartDate has been initialized. If the SmartDate instance was declared without explicitly calling one of the constructors, then it will not have been initialized, so the mDate field needs to be set before it can be returned. It is set to DateTime.MinValue because that is the empty date when mEmptyIsMax is False (which it is by default).

IComparable

SmartDate implements the IComparable interface, which defines a CompareTo() method. The CompareTo() method is used by the .NET Framework in various ways, most notably to support sorting within sorted collections and lists. This CompareTo() method is overloaded to also include a strongly typed CompareTo() that directly accepts a SmartDate:

```
Public Function CompareTo(ByVal obj As Object) As Integer _
    Implements IComparable.CompareTo

  If TypeOf obj Is SmartDate Then
    Return CompareTo(DirectCast(obj, SmartDate))

  Else
    Throw New ArgumentException(My.Resources.ValueNotSmartDateException)
  End If
End Function

Public Function CompareTo(ByVal value As SmartDate) As Integer
  If Me.IsEmpty AndAlso value.IsEmpty Then
    Return 0
  Else
    Return Me.Date.CompareTo(value.Date)
  End If
End Function
```

Because empty dates are maintained as DateTime.MinValue or DateTime.MaxValue, they will automatically sort to the top or bottom of the list based on the setting of mEmptyIsMax. For ease of use, SmartDate also includes similar CompareTo() overloads that accept String and DateTime.

Date Manipulation

SmartDate should provide arithmetic manipulation of the date value. Since the goal is to emulate a regular DateTime data type, it should provide at least Add() and Subtract() methods:

```
Public Function Add(ByVal value As TimeSpan) As Date
  If IsEmpty Then
    Return Me.Date
  Else
    Return Me.Date.Add(value)
  End If
End Function

Public Function Subtract(ByVal value As TimeSpan) As Date
  If IsEmpty Then
    Return Me.Date
  Else
    Return Me.Date.Subtract(value)
  End If
End Function

Public Function Subtract(ByVal value As Date) As TimeSpan
  If IsEmpty Then
    Return TimeSpan.Zero
  Else
    Return Me.Date.Subtract(value)
  End If
End Function
```

Notice the special handling of empty SmartDate values. Adding or subtracting any value to an empty value results in an empty or zero value as appropriate. In any other case, the addition or subtraction is delegated to the actual underlying DateTime value in mDate.

Overloading Operators

To make SmartDate as similar to DateTime as possible, it needs to overload the operators that are overloaded by DateTime, including equality, comparison, addition, and subtraction.

Equality

Equality and inequality operators delegate to the override of the Equals() method:

```
Public Overloads Overrides Function Equals(ByVal obj As Object) As Boolean
  If TypeOf obj Is SmartDate Then
    Dim tmp As SmartDate = DirectCast(obj, SmartDate)
    If Me.IsEmpty AndAlso tmp.IsEmpty Then
      Return True
    Else
      Return Me.Date.Equals(tmp.Date)
    End If

  ElseIf TypeOf obj Is Date Then
    Return Me.Date.Equals(DirectCast(obj, Date))

  ElseIf TypeOf obj Is String Then
    Return Me.CompareTo(CStr(obj)) = 0

  Else
    Return False
  End If
End Function
```

```
Public Shared Operator =( _
  ByVal obj1 As SmartDate, ByVal obj2 As SmartDate) As Boolean

  Return obj1.Equals(obj2)
End Operator

Public Shared Operator <>( _
  ByVal obj1 As SmartDate, ByVal obj2 As SmartDate) As Boolean

  Return Not obj1.Equals(obj2)
End Operator
```

The Equals() method is relatively complex. This is because it supports the idea of comparing a SmartDate to another SmartDate, to a String value, or to a regular DateTime value. In each case, it honors the idea of an empty date value.

Then the equality and inequality operators simply delegate to the Equals() method. There are overloads of the equality and inequality operators to allow a SmartDate to be directly compared to a DateTime or String value.

Comparison

In addition to equality, it is possible to compare SmartDate values to see if they are greater than or less than another SmartDate, String, or DateTime value. This is easily accomplished given the implementation of the CompareTo() methods earlier. For instance, here are a couple of the comparison operators:

```
Public Shared Operator >( _
  ByVal obj1 As SmartDate, ByVal obj2 As SmartDate) As Boolean

  Return obj1.CompareTo(obj2) > 0
End Operator

Public Shared Operator <( _
  ByVal obj1 As SmartDate, ByVal obj2 As SmartDate) As Boolean

  Return obj1.CompareTo(obj2) < 0
End Operator
```

Along with greater than and less than, there are greater than or equals, and less than or equals operators that work in a similar manner. And as with equality and inequality, there are overloads of all these operators for String and DateTime comparison as well.

Addition and Subtraction

The Add() and Subtract() methods implemented earlier are also made available through operators:

```
Public Shared Operator +( _
  ByVal start As SmartDate, ByVal span As TimeSpan) As SmartDate

  Return New SmartDate(start.Add(span), start.EmptyIsMin)
End Operator

Public Shared Operator -( _
  ByVal start As SmartDate, ByVal span As TimeSpan) As SmartDate

  Return New SmartDate(start.Subtract(span), start.EmptyIsMin)
End Operator
```

```
Public Shared Operator -( _
  ByVal start As SmartDate, ByVal finish As SmartDate) As TimeSpan

  Return start.Subtract(finish.Date)
End Operator
```

Combined, all these methods and operators mean that a SmartDate can be treated almost exactly like a DateTime.

Database Format

The final bit of code in SmartDate exists to help simplify data access. This is done by implementing a method that allows a SmartDate value to be converted to a format suitable for writing to the database. Though SmartDate already has methods to convert a date to text and text to a date, it doesn't have any good way of getting a date formatted properly to write to a database. Specifically, it needs a way to either write a valid date or write a null value if the date is empty.

In ADO.NET, a null value is usually expressed as DBNull.Value, so it is possible to implement a method that returns either a valid DateTime object or DBNull.Value:

```
Public ReadOnly Property DBValue() As Object
  Get
    If Me.IsEmpty Then
      Return DBNull.Value

    Else
      Return Me.Date
    End If
  End Get
End Property
```

Since SmartDate already implements an IsEmpty() property, the code here is pretty straightforward. If the value is empty, DBNull.Value is returned, which can be used to put a null value into a database via ADO.NET. Otherwise, a valid date value is returned.

At this point, you've seen the implementation of the core SmartDate functionality. While using SmartDate is certainly optional, it does offer business developers an easy way to handle dates that must be represented as text, and to support the concept of an empty date. Later in the chapter, the SafeDataReader will also include some data access functionality to make it easy to save and restore a SmartDate from a database.

This same approach can be used to make other data types "smart" if you so desire. Even with the Nullable(Of T) support from the .NET Framework, dealing with empty values often requires extra coding, which is often most efficiently placed in a framework class like SmartDate.

Common Business Rules

The BusinessBase class implemented in Chapter 3 includes support for validation rules. Each rule is a method with a signature that conforms to the RuleHandler delegate. A business object can implement business rules conforming to this delegate, and then associate those rule methods with the properties of the business object.

Most applications use a relatively small, common set of validation rules—such as that a string value is required or has a maximum length, or that a numeric value has a minimum or maximum value. Using reflection, it is possible to create highly reusable rule methods—which is the purpose behind the Csla.Validation.CommonRules class.

Obviously, using reflection incurs some performance cost, so these reusable rule methods may or may not be appropriate for every application. However, the code reuse offered by these methods is very powerful, and most applications won't be adversely affected by this use of reflection. In the end, whether you decide to use these rule methods or not is up to you.

Tip If reflection-based rules are problematic for your application, you can implement hard-coded rule methods on a per-object basis.

If you find the idea of these reusable rules appealing and useful, you may opt to create your own library of reusable rules as part of your application. In that case, you'll want to add a class to your project similar to CommonRules, and you can use the rule methods from CommonRules as a guide for building your own reusable rule methods.

CommonRules

The RuleHandler delegate specifies that every rule method accepts two parameters: a reference to the object containing the data, and a RuleArgs object that is used to pass extra information into and out of the rule method.

The base RuleArgs object has a PropertyName property that provides the rule method with the name of the property to be validated. It also includes a Description property that the rule method should set for a broken rule to describe why the rule was broken.

StringRequired

The simplest type of rule method is one that doesn't require any information beyond that provided by the basic RuleArgs parameter. For instance, the StringRequired() rule method only needs a reference to the object containing the value and the name of the property to be validated:

```
Public Function StringRequired( _
  ByVal target As Object, ByVal e As RuleArgs) As Boolean

  Dim value As String = _
    CStr(CallByName(target, e.PropertyName, CallType.Get))
  If Len(value) = 0 Then
    e.Description = _
      String.Format(My.Resources.StringRequiredRule, e.PropertyName)
    Return False

  Else
    Return True
  End If
End Function
```

A CallByName() helper method is used to abstract the use of reflection to retrieve the property value based on the property name. It simply uses reflection to get a PropertyInfo object for the specified property, and then uses it to retrieve the property value.

If the property value is an empty string, then the rule is violated, so the Description property of the RuleArgs object is set to describe the nature of the rule. Then False is returned from the rule method to indicate that the rule is broken. Otherwise, the rule method simply returns True to indicate that that rule is not broken.

This rule is used within a business object by associating it with a property. A business object does this by overriding the AddBusinessRules() method defined by BusinessBase. Such code would look like this (assuming a Using statement for Csla.Validation):

```
<Serializable()> _
Public Class Customer
  Inherits  BusinessBase(Of Customer)

  Protected Overrides Sub AddBusinessRules()
    ValidationRules.AddRule( _
      AddressOf CommonRules.StringRequired,  "Name")
  End Sub
  ' rest of class…
End Class
```

This associates the rule method with the Name property so that the PropertyHasChanged() call within the property's Set block will automatically invoke the rule. You'll see this and other rule methods used in Chapter 8 within the sample application's business objects.

StringMaxLength

A slightly more complex variation is one in which the rule method needs extra information beyond that provided by the basic RuleArgs parameter. In these cases, the RuleArgs class must be subclassed to create a new object that adds the extra information. A rule method to enforce a maximum length on a string, for instance, requires the maximum length value.

Custom RuleArgs Class

Here's a subclass of RuleArgs that provides the maximum length value:

```
Public Class MaxLengthRuleArgs
  Inherits RuleArgs

  Private mMaxLength As Integer

  Public ReadOnly Property MaxLength() As Integer
    Get
      Return mMaxLength
    End Get
  End Property

  Public Sub New(ByVal propertyName As String, ByVal maxLength As Integer)
    MyBase.New(propertyName)
    mMaxLength = maxLength
  End Sub

  Public Overrides Function ToString() As String
    Return MyBase.ToString & "!" & mMaxLength.ToString
  End Function
End Class
```

All subclasses of RuleArgs will follow this basic structure. First, the extra data to be provided is stored in a field and exposed through a property:

```
Private mMaxLength As Integer

Public ReadOnly Property MaxLength() As Integer
  Get
    Return mMaxLength
  End Get
End Property
```

The data provided here will obviously vary based on the needs of the rule method. The constructor must accept the name of the property to be validated, and of course, the extra data. The property name is provided to the RuleArgs base class, and the extra data is stored in the field declared in the preceding code:

```
Public Sub New(ByVal propertyName As String, ByVal maxLength As Integer)
    MyBase.New(propertyName)
    mMaxLength = maxLength
End Sub
```

Finally, the ToString() method is overridden. This is required. Recall that in Chapter 3, this value is used to uniquely identify the corresponding rule within the list of broken rules for an object. The ToString() value of the RuleArgs object is combined with the name of the rule method to generate the unique rule name.

This means that the ToString() implementation must return a string representation of the rule that is unique within a given business object. Typically, this can be done by combining the name of the rule (from the RuleArgs base class) with whatever extra data you are storing in your custom object:

```
Public Overrides Function ToString() As String
    Return MyBase.ToString & "!" & mMaxLength.ToString
End Function
```

The RuleArgs base class implements a ToString() method that returns a relatively unique value (the name of the property). By combining this with the extra data stored in this custom class, the resulting name should be unique within the business object.

Rule Method

With the custom RuleArgs class defined, it can be used to implement a rule method. The StringMaxLength() rule method looks like this:

```
Public Function StringMaxLength(ByVal target As Object, _
    ByVal e As RuleArgs) As Boolean

    Dim max As Integer = DirectCast(e, MaxLengthRuleArgs).MaxLength
    If Len(CallByName( _
        target, e.PropertyName, CallType.Get).ToString) > max Then
        e.Description = _
        String.Format(My.Resources.StringMaxLengthRule, e.PropertyName, max)
        Return False
    Else
        Return True
    End If
End Function
```

This is similar to the StringRequired() rule method, except that the RuleArgs parameter is cast to the MaxLengthRuleArgs type so that the MaxLength value can be retrieved. That value is then compared to the length of the specified property from the target object to see if the rule is broken or not.

Note It might seem like the RuleArgs parameter should just be of type MaxLengthRuleArgs. But it is important to remember that this method must conform to the RuleHandler delegate defined in Chapter 3; and that defines the parameter as type RuleArgs.

A business object's AddBusinessRules() method would associate a property to this rule like this:

```
Protected Overrides Sub AddBusinessRules()
    ValidationRules.AddRule( _
      AddressOf CommonRules.StringMaxLength, _
      New CommonRules.MaxLengthRuleArgs("Name", 50))
End Sub
```

Remember that in Chapter 3 the ValidationRules.AddRule() method included an overload that accepted a rule method delegate along with a RuleArgs object. In this case, the RuleArgs object is an instance of MaxLengthRuleArgs, initialized with the property name and the maximum length allowed for the property.

The CommonRules class includes other similar rule method implementations that you may choose to use as is, or as the basis for creating your own library of reusable rules for an application.

Data Access

Almost all applications employ some data access. Obviously, the CSLA .NET framework puts heavy emphasis on enabling data access through the data portal, as described in Chapter 4. Beyond the basic requirement to create, read, update, and delete data, however, there are other needs.

During the process of reading data from a database, many application developers find themselves writing repetitive code to eliminate null database values. SafeDataReader is a wrapper around any ADO.NET data reader object that automatically eliminates any null values that might come from the database.

When creating many web applications using either Web Forms or Web Services, data must be copied into and out of business objects. In the case of Web Forms data binding, data comes from the page in a dictionary of name/value pairs, which must be copied into the business object's properties. With Web Services, the data sent or received over the network often travels through simple data transfer objects (DTOs). The properties of those DTOs must be copied into or out of a business object within the web service. The DataMapper class contains methods to simplify these tasks.

SafeDataReader

Null values should be allowed in database columns for only two reasons. The first is when the business rules dictate that the application cares about the difference between a value that was never entered and a value that is zero (or an empty string). In other words, the end user actually cares about the difference between "" and null, or between 0 and null. There are applications where this matters—where the business rules revolve around whether a field ever had a value (even an empty one) or never had a value at all.

The second reason for using a null value is when a data type doesn't intrinsically support the concept of an empty field. The most common example is the SQL DateTime data type, which has no way to represent an empty date value; it *always* contains a valid date. In such a case, null values in the database column are used specifically to indicate an empty date.

Of course, these two reasons are mutually exclusive. When using null values to differentiate between an empty field and one that never had a value, you need to come up with some other scheme to indicate an empty DateTime field. The solution to this problem is outside the scope of this book—but thankfully, the problem itself is quite rare.

The reality is that very few applications ever care about the difference between an empty value and one that was never entered, so the first scenario seldom applies. If it *does* apply to your application, then dealing with null values at the database level isn't an issue, because you'll use nullable types from the database all the way through to the UI. In this case, you can ignore SafeDataReader entirely, as it has no value for your application.

But for *most* applications, the only reason for using null values is the second scenario, and this one is quite common. Any application that uses date values, and for which an empty date is a valid entry, will likely use null to represent an empty date.

Unfortunately, a whole lot of poorly designed databases allow null values in columns where *neither* scenario applies, and we developers have to deal with them. These are databases that contain null values even if the application makes no distinction between a 0 and a null.

Writing defensive code to guard against tables in which null values are erroneously allowed can quickly bloat data access code and make it hard to read. To avoid this, the SafeDataReader class takes care of these details automatically, by eliminating null values and converting them into a set of default values.

As a rule, data reader objects are NotInheritable, meaning that you can't simply subclass an existing data reader class (such as SqlDataReader) and extend it. However, like the SmartDate class with DateTime, it is quite possible to encapsulate, or "wrap," a data reader object.

Creating the SafeDataReader Class

To ensure that SafeDataReader can wrap *any* data reader object, it relies on the root System.Data. IDataReader interface that's implemented by all data reader objects. Also, since SafeDataReader is to *be* a data reader object, it must implement that interface as well:

```
Public Class SafeDataReader

  Implements IDataReader

  Private mDataReader As IDataReader

  Protected ReadOnly Property DataReader() As IDataReader
    Get
      Return mDataReader
    End Get
  End Property

  Public Sub New(ByVal dataReader As IDataReader)
    mDataReader = dataReader
  End Sub
```

The class defines a field to store a reference to the *real* data reader that it is encapsulating. That field is exposed as a Protected property as well, allowing for subclasses of SafeDataReader in the future.

There's also a constructor that accepts the IDataReader object to be encapsulated as a parameter.

This means that ADO.NET code in a business object's DataPortal_Fetch() method might appear as follows:

```
Dim dr As New SafeDataReader(cm.ExecuteReader)
```

The ExecuteReader() method returns an object that implements IDataReader (such as SqlDataReader) that is used to initialize the SafeDataReader object. The rest of the code in DataPortal_Fetch() can use the SafeDataReader object just like a regular data reader object because it implements IDataReader. The benefit, though, is that the business object's data access code never has to worry about getting a null value from the database.

The implementation of IDataReader is a lengthy business—it contains a lot of methods—so I'm not going to go through all of it here. Instead I'll cover a few methods to illustrate how the overall class is implemented.

GetString

There are two overloads for each method that returns column data: one that takes an ordinal column position, and the other that takes the string name of the property. This second overload is a convenience, but makes the code in a business object much more readable. All the methods that return column data are "null protected" with code like this:

```
Public Function GetString(ByVal name As String) As String
  Dim index As Integer = Me.GetOrdinal(name)
  Return Me.GetString(index)
End Function

Public Overridable Function GetString(ByVal i As Integer) As String _
  Implements IDataReader.GetString

  If mDataReader.IsDBNull(i) Then
    Return ""
  Else
    Return mDataReader.GetString(i)
  End If
End Function
```

If the value in the database is null, the method returns some more palatable value—typically, whatever passes for "empty" for the specific data type. If the value isn't null, it simply returns the value from the underlying data reader object.

For String values, the empty value is String.Empty; for numeric types, it is 0; and for Boolean types, it is False. You can look at the full code for SafeDataReader to see all the translations.

Notice that the GetString() method that actually does the translation of values is marked as Overridable. This allows you to override the behavior of any of these methods by creating a subclass of SafeDataReader.

The GetOrdinal() method translates the column name into an ordinal (numeric) value, which can be used to actually retrieve the value from the underlying IDataReader object. GetOrdinal() looks like this:

```
Public Function GetOrdinal(ByVal name As String) As Integer _
  Implements System.Data.IDataReader.GetOrdinal

  Return mDataReader.GetOrdinal(name)
End Function
```

Every data type supported by IDataReader (and there are a lot of them) has a pair of methods that reads the data from the underlying IDataReader object, replacing null values with empty default values as appropriate.

GetDateTime and GetSmartDate

Most types have "empty" values that are obvious, but DateTime is problematic as it has no "empty" value:

```
Public Function GetDateTime(ByVal name As String) As Date
  Dim index As Integer = Me.GetOrdinal(name)
  Return Me.GetDateTime(index)
End Function

Public Overridable Function GetDateTime(ByVal i As Integer) As Date _
  Implements System.Data.IDataReader.GetDateTime
```

```
    If mDataReader.IsDBNull(i) Then
      Return Date.MinValue
    Else
      Return mDataReader.GetDateTime(i)
    End If
  End Function
```

The minimum date value is arbitrarily used as the "empty" value. This isn't perfect, but it does avoid returning a null value or throwing an exception. A better solution may be to use the SmartDate type instead of DateTime. To simplify retrieval of a date value from the database into a SmartDate, SafeDataReader implements two variations of a GetSmartDate() method:

```
  Public Function GetSmartDate(ByVal name As String) As SmartDate
    Dim index As Integer = Me.GetOrdinal(name)
    Return Me.GetSmartDate(index, True)
  End Function

  Public Overridable Function GetSmartDate(ByVal i As Integer) As SmartDate
    Return GetSmartDate(i, True)
  End Function

  Public Function GetSmartDate( _
    ByVal name As String, ByVal minIsEmpty As Boolean) As SmartDate

    Dim index As Integer = Me.GetOrdinal(name)
    Return Me.GetSmartDate(index, minIsEmpty)
  End Function

  Public Overridable Function GetSmartDate( _
    ByVal i As Integer, ByVal minIsEmpty As Boolean) As SmartDate

    If mDataReader.IsDBNull(i) Then
      Return New SmartDate(minIsEmpty)

    Else
      Return New SmartDate(mDataReader.GetDateTime(i), minIsEmpty)
    End If
  End Function
```

Data access code in a business object can choose either to accept the minimum date value as being equivalent to "empty," or to retrieve a SmartDate that understands the concept of an empty date:

```
  Dim myDate As SmartDate = dr.GetSmartDate(0)
```

or

```
  Dim myDate As SmartDate = dr.GetSmartDate(0, False)
```

GetBoolean

Likewise, there is no "empty" value for the Boolean type:

```
  Public Function GetBoolean(ByVal name As String) As Boolean
    Dim index As Integer = Me.GetOrdinal(name)
    Return Me.GetBoolean(index)
  End Function
```

```
Public Overridable Function GetBoolean(ByVal i As Integer) As Boolean _
  Implements System.Data.IDataReader.GetBoolean

  If mDataReader.IsDBNull(i) Then
    Return False
  Else
    Return mDataReader.GetBoolean(i)
  End If
End Function
```

The code arbitrarily returns a False value in this case.

Other Methods

The IDataReader interface also includes a number of methods that don't return column values, such as the Read() method:

```
Public Function Read() As Boolean Implements IDataReader.Read
  Return mDataReader.Read
End Function
```

In these cases, it simply delegates the method call down to the underlying data reader object for it to handle. Any return values are passed back to the calling code, so the fact that SafeDataReader is involved is entirely transparent.

The SafeDataReader class can be used to simplify data access code dramatically, any time an object is working with tables in which null values are allowed in columns where the application doesn't care about the difference between an empty and a null value. If your application *does* care about the use of null values, you can simply use the regular data reader objects instead.

DataMapper

Later in this chapter, you'll see the implementation of a CslaDataSource control that allows business developers to use Web Forms data binding with CSLA .NET–style business objects. When Web Forms data binding needs to insert or update data, it provides the data elements in the form of a dictionary object of name/value pairs. The name is the name of the property to be updated, and the value is the value to be placed into the property of the business object.

Copying the values isn't hard—the code looks something like this:

```
cust.FirstName = e.Values("FirstName").ToString
cust.LastName = e.Values("LastName").ToString
cust.City = e.Values("City").ToString
```

Unfortunately, this is tedious code to write and debug; and if your object has a lot of properties, this can add up to a lot of lines of code. An alternative is to use reflection to automate the process of copying the values.

■Tip If you feel that reflection is too slow for this purpose, you can continue to write all the mapping code by hand. Keep in mind, however, that data binding uses reflection extensively anyway, so this little bit of additional reflection is not likely to cause any serious performance issues.

A similar problem exists when building Web Services. Business objects should not be returned directly as a result of a web service, as that would break encapsulation. In such a case, your business object interface would become part of the web service interface, preventing you from ever adding or changing properties on the object without running the risk of breaking any clients of the web service.

Instead, data should be copied from the business object into a DTO, which is then returned to the web service client. Conversely, data from the client often comes into the web service in the form of a DTO. These DTOs are often created based on WSDL or an XSD defining the contract for the data being passed over the web service.

The end result is that the code in a web service has to map property values from business objects to and from DTOs. That code often looks like this:

```
cust.FirstName = dto.FirstName
cust.LastName = dto.LastName
cust.City = dto.City
```

Again, this isn't hard code to write, but it's tedious and could add up to many lines of code.

The DataMapper class uses reflection to help automate these data-mapping operations, from either a collection implementing IDictionary or an object with Public properties.

In both cases, it is possible or even likely that some properties can't be mapped. Business objects often have read-only properties, and obviously it isn't possible to set those values. Yet the IDictionary or DTO may have a value for that property. It is up to the business developer to deal on a case-by-case basis with properties that can't be automatically mapped.

The DataMapper class will accept a list of property names to be ignored. Properties matching those names simply won't be mapped during the process. Additionally, DataMapper will accept a Boolean flag that can be used to suppress exceptions during the mapping process. This can be used simply to ignore any failures.

Setting Values

The core of the DataMapper class is the SetValue() method. This method is ultimately responsible for putting a value into a specified property of a target object:

```
Private Sub SetValue( _
  ByVal target As Object, ByVal propertyName As String, _
  ByVal value As Object)

  Dim propertyInfo As PropertyInfo = _
    target.GetType.GetProperty(propertyName)
  Dim pType As Type = Utilities.GetPropertyType(propertyInfo.PropertyType)
  If value Is Nothing Then
    propertyInfo.SetValue(target, value, Nothing)

  Else
    If pType.Equals(value.GetType) Then
      ' types match, just copy value
      propertyInfo.SetValue(target, value, Nothing)

    Else
      ' types don't match, try to coerce types
      If pType.Equals(GetType(Guid)) Then
        propertyInfo.SetValue(target, New Guid(value.ToString), Nothing)

      Else
        propertyInfo.SetValue(target, _
          Convert.ChangeType(value, pType), Nothing)
      End If
    End If
  End If
End Sub
```

Reflection is used to retrieve a `PropertyInfo` object corresponding to the specified property on the target object. The specific type of the property's return value is retrieved using a `GetPropertyType()` helper method in the `Utilities` class. That helper method exists to deal with the possibility that the property could return a value of type `Nullable(Of T)`. If that happens, the real underlying data type (behind the `Nullable(Of T)` type) must be returned. Here's the `GetPropertyType()` method:

```
Public Function GetPropertyType(ByVal propertyType As Type) As Type

  Dim type As Type = propertyType
  If (type.IsGenericType AndAlso _
    (type.GetGenericTypeDefinition Is GetType(Nullable))) Then

    Return type.GetGenericArguments(0)
  End If

  Return type
End Function
```

If `Nullable(Of T)` isn't involved, then the original type passed as a parameter is simply returned. But if `Nullable(Of T)` *is* involved, then the first generic argument (the value of T) is returned instead:

```
  Return type.GetGenericArguments(0)
```

This ensures that the actual data type of the property is used rather than `Nullable(Of T)`.

Back in the `SetValue()` method, the `PropertyInfo` object has a `SetValue()` method that sets the value of the property, but it requires that the new value have the same data type as the property itself.

Given that the values from an `IDictionary` collection or a DTO may not exactly match the property types on a business object, `DataMapper.SetValue()` attempts to coerce the original type to the property type before setting the property on the target object.

To do this, it retrieves the type of the target property. If the new value is not `Nothing`, then the type of the new value is compared to the type of the property to see if they match:

```
If pType.Equals(value.GetType) Then
  ' types match, just copy value
  propertyInfo.SetValue(target, value, Nothing)
```

If they do match, then the property is set to the new value. If they don't match, then there's an attempt to coerce the new value to the same type as the property:

```
  ' types don't match, try to coerce types
  If pType.Equals(GetType(Guid)) Then
    propertyInfo.SetValue(target, New Guid(value.ToString), Nothing)

  Else
    propertyInfo.SetValue(target, _
      Convert.ChangeType(value, pType), Nothing)
  End If
```

For most common data types, the `Convert.ChangeType()` method will work fine. It handles string, date, and primitive data types in most cases. But `Guid` values won't convert using that technique (because `Guid` doesn't implement `IConvertible`), so they are handled as a special case, by using `ToString()` to get a string representation of the value, and using that to create a new instance of a `Guid` object.

If the coercion fails, `Convert.ChangeType()` will throw an exception. In such a case, the business developer will have to manually set that particular property; adding that property name to the list of properties ignored by `DataMapper`.

Mapping from IDictionary

A collection that implements IDictionary is effectively a name/value list. The DataMapper.Map()
method assumes that the names in the list correspond directly to the names of properties on the
business object to be loaded with data. It simply loops through all the keys in the dictionary,
attempting to set the value of each entry into the target object:

```
Public Sub Map( _
  ByVal source As System.Collections.IDictionary, _
  ByVal target As Object, _
  ByVal suppressExceptions As Boolean, _
  ByVal ParamArray ignoreList() As String)

  Dim ignore As New List(Of String)(ignoreList)
  For Each propertyName As String In source.Keys
    If Not ignore.Contains(propertyName) Then
      Try
        SetValue(target, propertyName, source.Item(propertyName))

      Catch ex As Exception
        If Not suppressExceptions Then
          Throw New ArgumentException( _
            String.Format("{0} ({1})", _
            My.Resources.PropertyCopyFailed, propertyName), ex)
        End If
      End Try
    End If
  Next
End Sub
```

While looping through the key values in the dictionary, the ignoreList is checked on each
entry. If the key from the dictionary is in the ignore list, then that value is ignored.

Otherwise, the SetValue() method is called to assign the new value to the specified property
of the target object.

If an exception occurs while a property is being set, it is caught. If suppressExceptions is True,
then the exception is ignored; otherwise it is wrapped in an ArgumentException. The reason for wrapping it in a new exception object is so the property name can be included in the message returned to
the calling code. That bit of information is invaluable when using the Map() method.

Mapping from an Object

Mapping from one object to another is done in a similar manner. The primary exception is that the
list of source property names doesn't come from the keys in a dictionary, but rather must be retrieved
from the source object.

Note The Map() method can be used to map to or from a business object.

The GetSourceProperties() method retrieves the list of properties from the source object:

```
Private Function GetSourceProperties( _
  ByVal sourceType As Type) As PropertyInfo()
```

```
    Dim result As New Generic.List(Of PropertyInfo)
    Dim props As PropertyDescriptorCollection = _
      TypeDescriptor.GetProperties(sourceType)
    For Each item As PropertyDescriptor In props
      If item.IsBrowsable Then
        result.Add(sourceType.GetProperty(item.Name))
      End If
    Next
    Return result.ToArray
  End Function
```

This method filters out methods that are marked as <Browsable(False)>. This is useful when the source object is a CSLA .NET–style business object, as the IsDirty, IsNew, and similar properties from BusinessBase are automatically filtered out. The result is that GetSourceProperties() returns a list of properties that are subject to data binding.

First, reflection is invoked by calling the GetProperties() method to retrieve a collection of PropertyDescriptor objects. These are similar to the more commonly used PropertyInfo objects, but they are designed to help support data binding. This means they include an IsBrowsable property that can be used to filter out those properties that aren't browsable.

A PropertyInfo object is added to the result list for all browsable properties, and then that result list is converted to an array and returned to the calling code.

The calling code is an overload of the Map() method that accepts two objects rather than an IDictionary and an object:

```
Public Sub Map( _
  ByVal source As Object, _
  ByVal target As Object, _
  ByVal suppressExceptions As Boolean, _
  ByVal ParamArray ignoreList() As String)

  Dim ignore As New List(Of String)(ignoreList)
  Dim sourceProperties As PropertyInfo() = _
    GetSourceProperties(source.GetType)
  For Each sourceProperty As PropertyInfo In sourceProperties
    Dim propertyName As String = sourceProperty.Name
    If Not ignore.Contains(propertyName) Then
      Try
        SetValue(target, propertyName, _
          sourceProperty.GetValue(source, Nothing))

      Catch ex As Exception
        If Not suppressExceptions Then
          Throw New ArgumentException( _
            String.Format("{0} ({1})", _
            My.Resources.PropertyCopyFailed, propertyName), ex)
        End If
      End Try
    End If
  Next
End Sub
```

The source object's properties are retrieved into an array of PropertyInfo objects:

```
Dim sourceProperties As PropertyInfo() = _
  GetSourceProperties(source.GetType)
```

Then the method loops through each element in that array, checking each one against the list of properties to be ignored. If the property isn't in the ignore list, the SetValue() method is called to set the property on the target object. The GetValue() method on the PropertyInfo object is used to retrieve the value from the source object:

```
SetValue(target, propertyName, _
    sourceProperty.GetValue(source, Nothing))
```

Exceptions are handled (or ignored) just like they are when copying from an IDictionary.

While the DataMapper functionality may not be useful in all cases, it is useful in *many* cases, and can dramatically reduce the amount of tedious data-copying code a business developer needs to write to use data binding in Web Forms or to implement Web Services.

Reporting

When discussing report generation and objects, it is important to divide the idea of report generation into two groups: small reports and large reports.

Some enterprise resource planning (ERP) and manufacturing resource planning (MRP) systems make exactly this distinction: small reports are often called *lists*, while large reports are called *reports*. Lists can be generated at any time and are displayed immediately on the client, while reports are typically generated in the background and are later displayed through a viewer or printed out.

Of course, the exact delineation between a "small" and a "large" report varies. Ultimately, small reports require small enough amounts of data that it's reasonable to transfer that data to the client immediately upon a user request. Large reports require too much data to transfer to the client immediately, or they take too long to generate to have the user's machine (or browser) tied up while waiting for it to complete.

The problem faced with reporting is twofold. First, pulling back large amounts of data from the server to the client just to generate a report is slow. In fact, it is a just a poor idea and should be avoided. Large reports should be generated using report engines that physically run on or near the database server to minimize the amount of data transferred across the network.

Second, for reports that require smaller data sets that *can* be efficiently returned to the client machine, few of the major report engine tools support data binding against custom objects. Reports generated with popular tools such as Crystal Reports or Active Reports can only be generated against ADO.NET objects such as the DataSet.

■**Tip** To be fair, these report engines also work in an "unbound" mode, in which you have the opportunity to supply the data to populate the report manually. This technique can certainly be used with business objects. You can write code to pull the data out of your objects and provide that data to the report engine as it generates the report. The trouble is that this is a lot of work, especially when compared to just binding the report to a DataSet.

Microsoft SQL Server 2005 Reporting Services and Developer Express Xtra Reports both support data binding against objects in a manner similar to Windows Forms. Ideally, in the future, more of the major report engine vendors will support data binding against objects just like Windows Forms and Web Forms do, but that's not the case today. At present, you can either generate the report from a DataSet or use the engines in unbound mode and provide the data manually.

To enable the use of major report-generation tools, the ObjectAdapter class implements a converter to load a DataSet with data from objects. It allows you to convert an object into a DataSet. You can then generate reports in standard report engines such as Crystal Reports or Active Reports by using that DataSet.

This approach is useful for lists, but not reports. By my definition, lists require relatively small amounts of data, so it's acceptable to transfer that data to a client and generate the report there. Reports, on the other hand, require processing large amounts of data, and the closer you can do this to the database, the better. In this case, directly using Crystal Enterprise or some other server-based reporting tool to generate the report physically close to or in the database is often the best solution.

ObjectAdapter

The Csla.Data.ObjectAdapter class is a utility that generates a DataSet (or more accurately, a DataTable in a DataSet) based on an object (or a collection of objects). This isn't terribly difficult, because reflection can be used to get a list of the properties or fields on the objects, and then loop through the objects' properties to populate the DataTable with their values.

ObjectAdapter is somewhat similar to a data adapter object such as OleDbDataAdapter, in that it implements a Fill() method that fills a DataSet with data from an object or a collection.

To implement a Fill() method that copies data from a source, such as a business object, into a DataSet, ObjectAdapter needs to support a certain amount of basic functionality. In ADO.NET, data is stored in a DataTable, and then that DataTable is held in a DataSet. This means that object data will be copied into a DataTable object.

To do this, ObjectAdapter needs to get a list of the properties exposed by the source object. That list will be used to define the list of columns to be created in the target DataTable object. Alternatively, it will also support the concept of a preexisting DataTable that already contains columns. In that case, ObjectAdapter will attempt to find properties in the source object that match the columns that already exist in the target DataTable object.

Also, rather obviously, the data values from the original data source must be retrieved. Reflection will be used to do this because it allows dynamic retrieval of the values.

Operational Scope

Figure 5-5 illustrates the possible data sources supported by the ObjectAdapter class.

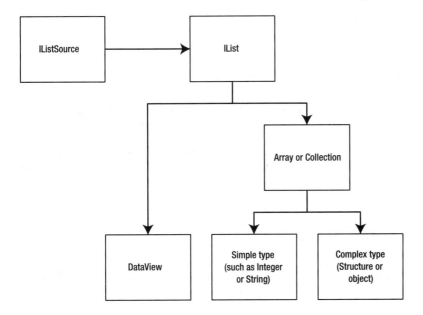

Figure 5-5. *Data sources supported by ObjectAdapter*

▉Tip The code could be simplified by only supporting binding to an object—but by supporting *any* valid data source (including ADO.NET objects, or arrays of simple values), it provides a more flexible solution.

Ultimately, a list of column, property, or field names will be retrieved from the data source, whether that be a DataView, an array or a collection, simple types (such as Integer or String), or complex types (such as a Structure or an object).

In the end, all data sources implement the IList interface that's defined in the .NET Framework. However, sometimes some digging is required to find that interface; or it must be added by creating a collection. Some data source objects, such as a DataSet, don't expose IList directly. Instead, they expose IListSource, which can be used to get an IList. In the case of simple types such as a string or a business object, an ArrayList is created and the item is placed inside it, thus providing an IList with which to work.

Fill Method

Like the OleDbDataAdapter, the ObjectAdapter implements a Fill() method (actually, several overloads of Fill() for easy use). In the end, though, they all route to a single Fill() method that fills a DataTable from data in a source object:

```
Public Sub Fill(ByVal dt As DataTable, ByVal source As Object)
    If source Is Nothing Then
        Throw New ArgumentException(My.Resources.NothingNotValid)
    End If

    Dim columns As List(Of String) = GetColumns(source)
    If columns.Count < 1 Then Exit Sub

    ' create columns if needed
    For Each column As String In columns
        If Not dt.Columns.Contains(column) Then
            dt.Columns.Add(column)
        End If
    Next

    ' get an IList and copy the data
    CopyData(dt, GetIList(source), columns)
End Sub
```

The first thing this method does is get a list of column names (typically, the public properties and fields) from the data source. It does this by calling a GetColumns() method (which will be covered later).

Next, the target DataTable is checked to ensure that it has a column corresponding to every column name retrieved from GetColumns(). If any columns are missing, they are added to the DataTable:

```
For Each column As String In columns
    If Not dt.Columns.Contains(column) Then
        dt.Columns.Add(column)
    End If
Next
```

This ensures that all properties or fields from the data source have a column in the DataTable so they can be copied. With that done, all that remains is to initiate the copy of data from the source object to the DataTable:

```
CopyData(dt, GetIList(source), columns)
```

Unfortunately, this is complicated slightly by the fact that the source object could be one of several object types. The GetIList() method sorts that out and ensures that it is an IList that is passed to the CopyData() method.

GetIList() looks like this:

```vb
Private Function GetIList(ByVal source As Object) As IList

  If TypeOf source Is IListSource Then
    Return CType(source, IListSource).GetList

  ElseIf TypeOf source Is IList Then
    Return CType(source, IList)

  Else
    ' they gave us a regular object - create a list
    Dim col As New ArrayList
    col.Add(source)
    Return CType(col, IList)
  End If
End Function
```

If the source object implements the IListSource interface, then its GetList() method is used to retrieve the underlying IList. This is typically the case with a DataTable, for instance.

If the source object directly implements IList, then it is simply cast and returned.

Otherwise, the source object is assumed to be a simple type (such as String), a Structure, or an object. In order to return an IList in this case, an ArrayList is created, the source object is added to the ArrayList, and it is returned as the result. Since ArrayList implements IList, the end result is that an IList is returned.

■**Note** This is the same technique used by the BindingSource object in Windows Forms data binding when a simple type or object is provided as a data source for data binding.

Getting the Column Names

The Fill() method calls a GetColumns() method to retrieve a list of the column names from the source object. If the source object is an ADO.NET DataView, it really will return a list of column names. But more commonly, the source object will be a business object, in which case the list of public properties and fields is returned.

GetColumns Method

The GetColumns() method determines the type of the source object and dispatches the work to type-specific helper methods:

```vb
Private Function GetColumns( _
  ByVal source As Object) As List(Of String)

  Dim result As List(Of String)
  ' first handle DataSet/DataTable
  Dim innerSource As Object
  Dim iListSource As IListSource = TryCast(source, IListSource)
  If iListSource IsNot Nothing Then
    innerSource = iListSource.GetList
```

```
      Else
        innerSource = source
      End If

      Dim dataView As DataView = TryCast(innerSource, DataView)
      If dataView IsNot Nothing Then
        result = ScanDataView(CType(innerSource, DataView))
      End If

      ' now handle lists/arrays/collections
      Dim iEnumerable As IEnumerable = _
        TryCast(innerSource, IEnumerable)
      If iEnumerable IsNot Nothing Then
        Dim childType As Type = _
          Utilities.GetChildItemType(innerSource.GetType)
        result = ScanObject(childType)

      Else
        ' they gave us a regular object
        result = ScanObject(innerSource.GetType)
      End If
      Return result
    End Function
```

As in `GetIList()`, if the source object implements `IListSource`, then its `GetList()` method is called to retrieve the underlying `IList` object.

ScanDataView Method

Next, that object is checked to see if it is a `DataView`. If so, a `ScanDataView()` method is called to pull the column names off the `DataView` object:

```
    Private Function ScanDataView(ByVal ds As DataView) As List(Of String)

      Dim result As New List(Of String)

      Dim field As Integer

      For field = 0 To ds.Table.Columns.Count - 1
        result.Add(ds.Table.Columns(field).ColumnName)
      Next
      Return result
    End Function
```

This is the simplest scenario, since the `DataView` object provides an easy interface to retrieve the list of columns.

GetChildItemType Method

If the source object isn't a `DataView`, but does directly implement the `IEnumerable` interface, then the type of the child object is retrieved using a helper method from the `Utilities` class, named `GetChildItemType()`:

```
      Dim iEnumerable As IEnumerable = _
        TryCast(innerSource, IEnumerable)
      If iEnumerable IsNot Nothing Then
        Dim childType As Type = _
          Utilities.GetChildItemType(innerSource.GetType)
        result = ScanObject(childType)
```

The `Utilities.GetChildItemType()` helper method checks to see if the type is an array. If so, it returns the array's element type—otherwise, it scans the properties of `listType` to find the default property (otherwise known as an indexer):

```
Public Function GetChildItemType(ByVal listType As Type) As Type
  Dim result As Type = Nothing
  If listType.IsArray Then
    result = listType.GetElementType()
  Else
    Dim indexer As DefaultMemberAttribute = _
      CType(Attribute.GetCustomAttribute(listType, _
      GetType(DefaultMemberAttribute)), DefaultMemberAttribute)
    If indexer IsNot Nothing Then
      For Each prop As PropertyInfo In listType.GetProperties( _
        BindingFlags.Public Or _
        BindingFlags.Instance Or _
        BindingFlags.FlattenHierarchy)
        If prop.Name = indexer.MemberName Then
          result = Utilities.GetPropertyType(prop.PropertyType)
        End If
      Next
    End If
  End If
  Return result
End Function
```

The default property can be identified because it will have the `<DefaultMember()>` attribute added by the compiler. If a default property is found, the type returned by that default property is returned as a result. If neither the array nor default property approaches work, then it isn't possible to determine the type of the child object, so `null` is returned.

ScanObject Method

Back in the `GetColumns()` method, a `ScanObject()` method is called, passing the type of the child object as a parameter. The `ScanObject()` uses reflection against that type. If you recall, the `GetColumns()` method itself might also call `ScanObject()` if it detects that the source object wasn't a collection but was a single, complex `Structure` or object:

```
' the source is a regular object
result = ScanObject(innerSource.GetType)
```

The `ScanObject()` method uses reflection much like you've seen in other methods within the framework. But in this case, it not only assembles a list of public properties, but also of public fields:

```
Private Function ScanObject(ByVal sourceType As Type) As List(Of String)
  Dim result As New List(Of String)

  ' retrieve a list of all public properties
  Dim props As PropertyInfo() = sourceType.GetProperties()
  If UBound(props) >= 0 Then
    For column As Integer = 0 To UBound(props)
      If props(column).CanRead Then
        result.Add(props(column).Name)
      End If
    Next
  End If
```

```
' retrieve a list of all public fields
Dim fields As FieldInfo() = sourceType.GetFields()
If UBound(fields) >= 0 Then
  For column As Integer = 0 To UBound(fields)
    result.Add(fields(column).Name)
  Next
End If

Return result
End Function
```

Given that this code is similar to other code you've seen earlier in the book, I won't go through it in detail. In the end, it returns a list of column names by finding the names of all public properties and fields.

Copying the Data

The last step in the Fill() method is to call a CopyData() method to copy the data from the source list to the DataTable. The list of column names from GetColumns() is also passed as a parameter, and that list is used to retrieve the data from each item in the source list.

```
Private Sub CopyData( _
  ByVal dt As DataTable, _
  ByVal ds As IList, ByVal columns As List(Of String))

  ' load the data into the DataTable
  dt.BeginLoadData()
  For index As Integer = 0 To ds.Count - 1
    Dim dr As DataRow = dt.NewRow
    For Each column As String In columns
      Try
        dr(column) = GetField(ds(index), column)

      Catch ex As Exception
        dr(column) = ex.Message
      End Try
    Next
    dt.Rows.Add(dr)
  Next
  dt.EndLoadData()
End Sub
```

Before doing any changes to the DataTable object, its BeginLoadData() method is called. This tells the DataTable that a batch of changes are about to happen, so it suppresses its normal event-handling process. This not only makes the changes more efficient to process, but avoids the possibility of the UI doing a refresh for every little change to the DataTable.

Then the method loops through all the items in the source list. For each item, a new DataRow object is created, the values are copied from the source object, and the DataRow is added to the DataTable. The GetField() method, which is key to this process, is discussed in the following section.

When all the data has been copied into the DataTable, its EndLoadData() method is called. This tells the object that the batch of changes is complete so it can resume its normal event, index, and constraint processing.

GetField Method

The workhorse of CopyData() is the GetField() method. This method retrieves the specified column property or field value from the source object. Given that the source object could be a simple or complex type, GetField() is relatively long:

```
Private Shared Function GetField( _
  ByVal obj As Object, ByVal fieldName As String) As String

  Dim result As String
  Dim dataRowView As DataRowView = TryCast(obj, DataRowView)
  If dataRowView IsNot Nothing Then
    ' this is a DataRowView from a DataView
    result = dataRowView.Item(fieldName).ToString

  ElseIf TypeOf obj Is ValueType AndAlso obj.GetType.IsPrimitive Then
    ' this is a primitive value type
    result = obj.ToString

  Else
    Dim tmp As String = TryCast(obj, String)
    If tmp IsNot Nothing Then
      ' this is a simple string
      result = obj.ToString

    Else
      ' this is an object or Structure
      Try
        Dim sourcetype As Type = obj.GetType

        ' see if the field is a property
        Dim prop As PropertyInfo = sourcetype.GetProperty(fieldName)

        If prop Is Nothing OrElse Not prop.CanRead Then
          ' no readable property of that name exists - check for a field
          Dim field As FieldInfo = sourcetype.GetField(fieldName)

          If field Is Nothing Then
            ' no field exists either, throw an exception
            Throw New System.Data.DataException( _
              My.Resources.NoSuchValueExistsException & " " & fieldName)

          Else
            ' got a field, return its value
            result = field.GetValue(obj).ToString
          End If

        Else
          ' found a property, return its value
          result = prop.GetValue(obj, Nothing).ToString
        End If
```

```
        Catch ex As Exception
          Throw New System.Data.DataException( _
            My.Resources.ErrorReadingValueException & " " & fieldName, ex)
        End Try
      End If
    End If
    Return result
  End Function
```

One of the supported data sources is an ADO.NET DataView. A DataView contains a list of DataRowView objects. Because of this, GetField() handles DataRowView objects as follows:

```
Dim dataRowView As DataRowView = TryCast(obj, DataRowView)
If dataRowView IsNot Nothing Then
  ' this is a DataRowView from a DataView
  result = dataRowView.Item(fieldName).ToString
```

The source list might also be an array of simple values such as Integer. In that case, a simple value is returned:

```
ElseIf TypeOf obj Is ValueType AndAlso obj.GetType.IsPrimitive Then
  ' this is a primitive value type
  result = obj.ToString
```

Similarly, the data source might be an array of String data, as shown here:

```
Dim tmp As String = TryCast(obj, String)
If tmp IsNot Nothing Then
  ' this is a simple string
  result = obj.ToString
```

If the data source was none of these, then it's a more complex type—a Structure or an object. In this case, there's more work to do, since reflection must be used to find the property or field and retrieve its value. The first thing to do is get a Type object in order to provide access to type information about the source object, as follows:

```
    ' this is an object or Structure
    Try
      Dim sourcetype As Type = obj.GetType
```

The code then checks to see if there's a Property with the name of the specified column, as shown here:

```
      ' see if the field is a property
      Dim prop As PropertyInfo = sourcetype.GetProperty(fieldName)
      If prop Is Nothing OrElse Not prop.CanRead Then
```

If there's no such property (or if the property isn't readable), then the assumption is that there's a matching field instead. However, if there *is* a readable property, its value is returned:

```
      Else
        ' found a property, return its value
        result = prop.GetValue(obj, Nothing).ToString
```

On the other hand, if no readable property is found, then a similar process is used to look for a field:

```
        ' no readable property of that name exists - check for a field
        Dim field As FieldInfo = sourcetype.GetField(fieldName)
        If field Is Nothing Then
```

If there's no field by this name, then an exception is thrown to indicate that the GetField() method was unsuccessful:

```
Throw New System.Data.DataException( _
    My.Resources.NoSuchValueExistsException & " " & fieldName)
```

However, if there is a matching field, then its value is returned, as follows:

```
' got a field, return its value
result = field.GetValue(obj).ToString
```

If any other exception occurs during the process, it is caught and included as an inner exception. The reason for doing this is so the exception message can include the field name that failed to make debugging easier:

```
Catch ex As Exception
  Throw New System.Data.DataException( _
    My.Resources.ErrorReadingValueException & " " & fieldName, ex)
End Try
```

The end result is that the GetField() method will return a property or field value from a row in a DataView, from an array of simple values, or from a Structure or an object.

At this point, the ObjectAdapter is complete. Client code can use the Fill() methods to copy data from virtually any object or collection of objects into a DataTable. Once the data is in a DataTable, commercial reporting engines such as Crystal Reports or Active Reports can be used to generate reports against the data.

Windows Data Binding

Much of the focus in Chapter 3 was on ensuring that business objects support Windows Forms data binding. That support from the objects is useful, but can be made even more useful by adding some functionality to each form. This can be done using a type of Windows Forms control called an *extender control*.

Extender controls are added to a form, and they in turn add properties and behaviors to other controls on the form, thus extending those other controls. A good example of this is the ErrorProvider control, which extends other controls by adding the ability to display an error icon with a tooltip describing the error.

ReadWriteAuthorization

Chapter 3 added authorization code to business objects, making them aware of whether each property can be read or changed. The CanReadProperty() and CanWriteProperty() methods were made Public so that code outside the object could easily determine whether the current user is allowed to get or set each property on the object. One primary user of this functionality is the UI, which can decide to alter its appearance to give users clues as to whether they are able to view or alter each piece of data.

While this could be done by hand for each control on every form, the ReadWriteAuthorization control helps automate the process of building a UI that enables or disables controls based on whether properties can be read or changed.

If a control is bound to a property, and the user does not have read access to that property due to authorization rules, the ReadWriteAuthorization control will disable that control. It also adds a handler for the control's Format event to intercept the value coming from the data source, substituting an empty value instead. The result is that data binding is prevented from displaying the data to the user.

Similarly, if the user doesn't have write access to a property, ReadWriteAuthorization will attempt to mark any controls bound to that property as being read-only (or failing that, disabled); ensuring that the user can't attempt to alter the property value.

Like all Windows Forms components, extender controls inherit from System.ComponentModel. Component. Additionally, to act as an extender control, the ReadWriteAuthorization control must implement the IExtenderProvider interface:

```
<DesignerCategory("")> _
<ProvideProperty("ApplyAuthorization", GetType(Control))> _
Public Class ReadWriteAuthorization
  Inherits System.ComponentModel.Component

  Implements IExtenderProvider

  Public Sub New(ByVal container As System.ComponentModel.IContainer)
    container.Add(Me)
  End Sub
```

The <ProvideProperty()> attribute is quite important. It specifies that ReadWriteAuthorization extends components of type Control by adding an ApplyAuthorization property to them. In other words, when a ReadWriteAuthorization control is on a form, all *other* controls on the form get a dynamically added ApplyAuthorization property. Figure 5-6 shows a text box control's Properties window with the dynamically added ApplyAuthorization property.

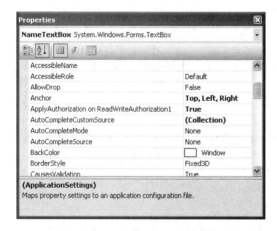

Figure 5-6. *ApplyAuthorization property added to textBox1*

The UI developer can set this property to True or False to indicate whether the ReadWriteAuthorization control should apply authorization rules to that particular control. You'll see how this works as the control is implemented.

The <DesignerCategory()> attribute is just used to help Visual Studio decide what kind of visual designer to use when editing the control. The value used here specifies that the default designer should be used.

The class also implements a constructor that accepts an IContainer parameter. This constructor is required for extender controls, and is called by Windows Forms when the control is instantiated. Notice that the control adds itself to the container as required by the Windows Forms infrastructure.

IExtenderProvider

The `IExtenderProvider` interface defines just one method: `CanExtend()`. This method is called by Windows Forms to ask the extender control whether it wishes to extend any given control. Windows Forms automatically calls `CanExtend()` for every control on the form:

```
Public Function CanExtend( _
  ByVal extendee As Object) As Boolean _
  Implements IExtenderProvider.CanExtend

  If IsPropertyImplemented(extendee, "ReadOnly") OrElse _
      IsPropertyImplemented(extendee, "Enabled") Then
    Return True

  Else
    Return False
  End If
End Function
```

The `ReadWriteAuthorization` control can extend any control that implements either a `ReadOnly` or an `Enabled` property. This covers most controls, making `ReadWriteAuthorization` broadly useful. If the potential target control implements either of these properties, a `True` result is returned to indicate that the control will be extended.

The `IsPropertyImplemented()` method is a helper that uses reflection to check for the existence of the specified properties on the target control:

```
Private Shared Function IsPropertyImplemented(ByVal obj As Object, _
  ByVal propertyName As String) As Boolean

  If obj.GetType.GetProperty(propertyName, _
    BindingFlags.FlattenHierarchy Or _
    BindingFlags.Instance Or _
    BindingFlags.Public) IsNot Nothing Then

    Return True

  Else
    Return False
  End If
End Function
```

ApplyAuthorization Property

The `<ProvideProperty()>` attribute on `ReadWriteAuthorization` specified that an `ApplyAuthorization` property would be dynamically added to all controls extended by `ReadWriteAuthorization`. Of course, the controls being extended really have no knowledge of this new property or what to do with it. All the behavior associated with the property is contained within the extender control itself.

The extender control manages the `ApplyAuthorization` property by implementing both `GetApplyAuthorization()` and `SetApplyAuthorization()` methods. These methods are called by Windows Forms to get and set the property value for each control that has been extended. The `Get` and `Set` are automatically prepended by Windows Forms to call these methods.

To manage a list of the controls that have been extended, a `Dictionary` object is used:

```
Private mSources As New Dictionary(Of Control, Boolean)

Public Function GetApplyAuthorization( _
  ByVal source As Control) As Boolean

  If mSources.ContainsKey(source) Then
    Return mSources.Item(source)

  Else
    Return False
  End If

End Function

Public Sub SetApplyAuthorization( _
  ByVal source As Control, ByVal value As Boolean)

  If mSources.ContainsKey(source) Then
    mSources.Item(source) = value
  Else
    mSources.Add(source, value)
  End If
End Sub
```

When Windows Forms indicates that the ApplyAuthorization property has been set for a particular extended control, the SetApplyAuthorization() method is called. This method records the value of the ApplyAuthorization property for that particular control, using the control itself as the key value within the Dictionary.

Conversely, when Windows Forms needs to know the property value of ApplyAuthorization for a particular control, it calls GetApplyAuthorization(). The value for that control is retrieved from the Dictionary object and returned. If the control can't be found in the Dictionary, then False is returned, since that control is obviously not being extended.

The end result here is that the ReadWriteAuthorization control maintains a list of all the controls it extends, along with their ApplyAuthorization property values. In short, it knows about all the controls it will affect, and whether it should be affecting them or not.

Applying Authorization Rules

At this point, the extender control's basic plumbing is complete. It gets to choose which controls to extend, and maintains a list of all the controls it does extend, along with the ApplyAuthorization property value for each of those controls.

When the UI developer wants to enforce authorization rules for the whole form, she can do so by triggering the ReadWriteAuthorization control. To allow this, the control implements a ResetControlAuthorization() method. This method is Public, so it can be called by code in the form itself. Typically, this method will be called immediately after a business object has been loaded and bound to the form, or immediately after the user has logged into or out of the application. It is also a good idea to call it after adding a new business object to the database, since some objects will change their authorization rules to be different for an old object than for a new object. You'll see how this works in Chapter 9 in the Windows Forms UI for the sample application.

The ResetControlAuthorization() method loops through all the items in the list of extended controls. This is the Dictionary object maintained by Get/SetApplyAuthorization, as discussed earlier. The ApplyAuthorization value for each control is checked, and if it is true, then authorization rules are applied to that control:

```
Public Sub ResetControlAuthorization()
  For Each item As KeyValuePair(Of Control, Boolean) In mSources
    If item.Value Then
      ' apply authorization rules
      ApplyAuthorizationRules(item.Key)
    End If
  Next
End Sub
```

To apply the authorization rules, the code loops through the target control's list of data bindings. Each `Binding` object represents a connection between a property on the control and a data source, so it is possible to get a reference to the data source through the `DataSource` property:

```
Private Sub ApplyAuthorizationRules(ByVal control As Control)
  For Each binding As Binding In control.DataBindings
    ' get the BindingSource if appropriate
    If TypeOf binding.DataSource Is BindingSource Then
      Dim bs As BindingSource = CType(binding.DataSource, BindingSource)
      ' get the BusinessObject if appropriate
      If TypeOf bs.DataSource Is Csla.Core.BusinessBase Then
        Dim ds As Csla.Core.BusinessBase = _
          CType(bs.DataSource, Csla.Core.BusinessBase)
        ' get the object property name
        Dim propertyName As String = _
          binding.BindingMemberInfo.BindingField

        ApplyReadRules(control, binding, propertyName, _
          ds.CanReadProperty(propertyName))
        ApplyWriteRules(control, binding, propertyName, _
          ds.CanWriteProperty(propertyName))

      ElseIf TypeOf bs.DataSource Is Csla.Core.IReadOnlyObject Then
        Dim ds As Csla.Core.IReadOnlyObject = _
          CType(bs.DataSource, Csla.Core.IReadOnlyObject)
        ' get the object property name
        Dim propertyName As String = _
          binding.BindingMemberInfo.BindingField

        ApplyReadRules(control, binding, propertyName, _
          ds.CanReadProperty(propertyName))
      End If
    End If
  Next
End Sub
```

If the data source is a subclass of `Csla.Core.BusinessBase`, then both the `ApplyReadRules()` and `ApplyWriteRules()` methods are called to change the target control's state based on whether the current user is authorized to read and write the property. If the data source implements `Csla.Core.IReadOnlyObject`, then only the `ApplyReadRules()` method is called, as it is assumed that all properties are read-only due to the nature of the object itself. It is also assumed that the UI developer is only using read-only controls for these read-only property values.

Notice that both `ApplyReadRules()` and `ApplyWriteRules()` accept the target control, the `Binding` object, the property name, and a Boolean indicating whether the user is authorized to perform the particular operation (read or write). This ensures that these methods have all the information they need to know how to alter the target control's appearance.

ApplyReadRules Method

Finally, we get to the heart of the matter: altering the target control. If the user is not allowed to read the property value, the target control must not display the value. To prevent display of the value, two things are done to the target control: it is disabled, and any values coming from the data source to the control are intercepted and replaced with an empty value.

Disabling the control is easily accomplished by setting its Enabled property to False. All controls have an Enabled property, so this is not an issue. Intercepting all values from the data source before they reach the control is more complex. Fortunately, data binding offers a solution through the Format event. All Binding objects have both Format and Parse events, which can be used to alter data as it moves from the data source to the control and then back to the data source.

The Format event is raised after the data value has been read from the data source, but *before* the value is provided to the control. The idea is that a UI developer can handle this event and use it to format the value for display. In this case, however, the value will simply be replaced with a default empty value instead, thus ensuring that the control never gets the real value that the user isn't authorized to see.

To handle the Format event, a method is required:

```vb
Private Sub ReturnEmpty( _
  ByVal sender As Object, ByVal e As ConvertEventArgs)
  e.Value = GetEmptyValue(e.DesiredType)
End Sub

Private Function GetEmptyValue(ByVal desiredType As Type) As Object
  Dim result As Object = Nothing
  If desiredType.IsValueType Then
    result = Activator.CreateInstance(desiredType)
  End If
  Return result
End Function
```

The ReturnEmpty() method handles the Format event. It then calls GetEmptyValue() to get an empty value appropriate for the data type of the value read from the data source. That empty value is returned through e.Value. The result is that data binding puts this empty value—rather than the original value from the data source—into the control.

Within the ApplyReadRules() method, if the user is not authorized to read the property, the control is disabled and the event handler is set up:

```vb
ctl.Enabled = False
AddHandler binding.Format, AddressOf ReturnEmpty

' clear the value displayed by the control
Dim propertyInfo As PropertyInfo = _
  ctl.GetType.GetProperty(binding.PropertyName, _
    BindingFlags.FlattenHierarchy Or _
    BindingFlags.Instance Or _
    BindingFlags.Public)
If propertyInfo IsNot Nothing Then
  propertyInfo.SetValue(ctl, _
    GetEmptyValue( _
      Utilities.GetPropertyType(propertyInfo.PropertyType)), _
      New Object() {})
End If
```

Of course, the control might have already contained a value, and if so, that value must be removed. To do this, the type of the property value is retrieved using reflection, and the

GetEmptyValue() method is called to get an appropriate empty value. This value is then placed into the control, overwriting any previous value the control may have had.

The reverse of the process occurs if the user *is* allowed to read the property. In that case, the control is enabled and the Format event handler is removed:

```
Dim couldRead As Boolean = ctl.Enabled
ctl.Enabled = True
RemoveHandler binding.Format, AddressOf ReturnEmpty
If Not couldRead Then binding.ReadValue()
```

Additionally, if the control was disabled before this code was run, it is assumed that the control doesn't contain a valid value. The ReadValue() method on the Binding object is called to force data binding to reload the control with the value from the data source.

ApplyWriteRules Method

The ApplyWriteRules() method is very similar to ApplyReadRules(), but takes a slightly different approach. In this case, users may be able to view the data, but they certainly can't be allowed to edit the data. If the control implements a ReadOnly property, then it can be set to False; otherwise, the control must be entirely disabled through the use its Enabled property.

As an optimization, if the control is a Label, the method immediately exits. Because Label controls are so common, and they are read-only by definition, it is worth this special check.

The preference is to use the control's ReadOnly property if it is implemented by the control. Reflection is used to get a PropertyInfo object corresponding to the control's ReadOnly property:

```
' enable/disable writing of the value
Dim propertyInfo As PropertyInfo = _
  ctl.GetType.GetProperty("ReadOnly", _
    BindingFlags.FlattenHierarchy Or _
    BindingFlags.Instance Or _
    BindingFlags.Public)
If propertyInfo IsNot Nothing Then
  Dim couldWrite As Boolean = _
    Not CBool(propertyInfo.GetValue(ctl, New Object() {}))
  propertyInfo.SetValue(ctl, Not canWrite, New Object() {})
  If Not couldWrite AndAlso canWrite Then binding.ReadValue()
```

If a ReadOnly property is found, then it is set to True or False depending on whether the user is allowed or denied write access to the business object property:

```
propertyInfo.SetValue(ctl, Not canWrite, New Object() {})
```

First, though, the value of the control's ReadOnly property is retrieved. If it is False, that means that the user was *already* able to edit the control—the user could write, so couldWrite is True. This is important, because if the user was *unable* to edit the control, and now *is* able to edit the control, data binding needs to be told to reload the data from the data source into the control:

```
If Not couldWrite AndAlso canWrite Then binding.ReadValue()
```

Otherwise, it is possible for the user to be placed into an empty control even though there really is a value in the business object's property.

If the control doesn't have a ReadOnly property, then the Enabled property is used as a fallback. The same procedure is used, just with the Enabled property instead:

```
Dim couldWrite As Boolean = ctl.Enabled
ctl.Enabled = canWrite
If Not couldWrite AndAlso canWrite Then binding.ReadValue()
```

The end result is that when the user is denied write access to a business object's property, controls bound to that property are either set to ReadOnly or are disabled. And if the user is denied read access to a business object's property, controls bound to that property are disabled and empty values are placed in the control, rather than any real values from the business object.

BindingSourceRefresh

The BindingSourceRefresh control is also an extender control, but its purpose is quite different from the ReadWriteAuthorization control. It turns out that there's a quirk (either a bug or an odd implementation choice) in the way Windows Forms data binding works. The BindingSourceRefresh control helps work around this quirk.

The quirk is that when data is changed in a business object, data binding doesn't always display the changes in the controls on the form. This occurs in the following sequence of events:

1. The user edits a value in a bound control.

2. Data binding puts the user's new value into the business object.

3. The business object alters the value in the property Set block.

4. The business object raises its PropertyChanged event.

You would expect that data binding would handle the PropertyChanged event, realize that the property's data has changed, and then update the control with the new value. And that does happen for all controls *except the current control*. In other words, the PropertyChanged event causes data binding to refresh all *other* controls on the form except the control that initiated the change in the first place.

Obviously, this can be problematic. Consider a TextBox control that is bound to a business object property that uses a SmartDate. Remember that SmartDate accepts the + character and replaces it with tomorrow's date. Due to this data binding quirk, when the user enters a + character, that value is put into the business object, which translates it to tomorrow's date—but that new value is not displayed to the user. The user continues to see the + character.

What's even more confusing for users is that if they edit a *different* control, then the previous control will be updated with tomorrow's date. Remember that data binding updates everything except the current control when it gets a PropertyChanged event.

This is the problem BindingSourceRefresh is intended to solve. It does so by interacting with the BindingSource control that manages the data binding for a given business object. While ReadWriteAuthorization extended controls like TextBox and Label, BindingSourceRefresh extends BindingSource controls.

The plumbing code in this control is virtually identical to ReadWriteAuthorization. It inherits from Component and implements IExtenderProvider:

```
<DesignerCategory("")> _
<ProvideProperty("ReadValuesOnChange", GetType(BindingSource))> _
Public Class BindingSourceRefresh
  Inherits System.ComponentModel.Component

  Implements IExtenderProvider
```

In this case, however, controls on the form gain a new ReadValuesOnChange property. The CanExtend() method returns True only for BindingSource controls:

```
Public Function CanExtend(ByVal extendee As Object) As Boolean _
  Implements IExtenderProvider.CanExtend

  If TypeOf extendee Is BindingSource Then
    Return True
```

```
    Else
      Return False
    End If
End Function
```

The control also implements GetReadValuesOnChange() and SetReadValuesOnChange() methods, using a private Dictionary to keep track of the property values for each extended control. This is the same concept as was used in ReadWriteAuthorization, with one twist. When SetReadValuesOnChange() is called, it not only stores the ReadValuesOnChange property value, but it immediately interacts with the control being extended:

```
Public Sub SetReadValuesOnChange( _
  ByVal source As BindingSource, ByVal value As Boolean)

  If mSources.ContainsKey(source) Then
    mSources.Item(source) = value
  Else
    mSources.Add(source, value)
  End If
  If value Then
    'hook
    AddHandler source.BindingComplete, AddressOf Source_BindingComplete
  Else
    'unhook
    RemoveHandler source.BindingComplete, AddressOf Source_BindingComplete
  End If
End Sub
```

What it is doing here is adding or removing an event handler for the BindingSource control's BindingComplete event. This event is raised by a BindingSource control after all controls have had their values updated through data binding.

Well, all controls except the current one, of course. The Source_BindingComplete() method takes the extra step of forcing the BindingSource control to refresh the value for the *current* binding as well:

```
Private Sub Source_BindingComplete( _
  ByVal sender As Object, ByVal e As BindingCompleteEventArgs)

  e.Binding.ReadValue()
End Sub
```

The BindingComplete event includes a BindingCompleteEventArgs parameter, and that parameter includes a reference to the currently active Binding object. It is this Binding object that *isn't* refreshed automatically when data binding gets a PropertyChanged event from the underlying data source. By calling its ReadValue() method, this code forces data binding to read the value from the data source and update the current control's display as well.

The BindingSourceRefresh control should be used to force data refreshes for all BindingSource controls bound to detail forms. It isn't necessary when only complex controls such as a GridView or ListBox are bound to the object. You'll see this control in action in Chapter 9.

Web Forms Data Binding

Web Forms data binding in ASP.NET 2.0 is bidirectional, meaning that data is copied from the data source into the web form's controls, and then from those controls back into the data source (either a preexisting instance, or a newly created instance) on a postback. This is powerful, as it simplifies both the display and update of data.

Unfortunately, the data source controls provided with ASP.NET are not designed to work with objects that contain business logic—meaning that they aren't useful when working with CSLA .NET business objects. To overcome this limitation, the `CslaDataSource` control is an ASP.NET data source control that is designed to work with objects containing business logic. This control allows the full use of Web Forms data binding with rich business objects.

Data source controls in ASP.NET have two major areas of functionality: runtime and design time. Runtime functionality is the actual data binding implementation—it copies data from the data source to the controls and back again. Design time functionality exists to support Visual Studio 2005, allowing developers to graphically create web pages using common controls like the `DataGridView` and `DetailsView` when they are bound to the data source control.

It turns out that implementing runtime functionality is relatively straightforward, but providing design time functionality is more complex. Table 5-6 lists the classes required to implement the `CslaDataSource` control's runtime and design time support.

Table 5-6. *Classes Required to Implement the CslaDataSource Control*

Class	Description
Csla.Web.CslaDataSource	The data source control itself; used directly by the UI developer
Csla.Web.CslaDataSourceView	Provides the actual implementation of data binding for `CslaDataSource`
Csla.Web.CslaDataSourceDesigner	The Visual Studio designer for `CslaDataSource`
Csla.Web.CslaDesignerDataSourceView	Provides schema information and sample data for the designer
Csla.Web.ObjectSchema	The schema object for a business object, responsible for returning an instance of `ObjectViewSchema`
Csla.Web.ObjectViewSchema	Provides actual information about a business object; specifically information about all the business object's bindable properties
Csla.Web.Design.ObjectFieldInfo	Maintains information about a specific field in the object schema

The detailed design issues around building an ASP.NET data source control are outside the scope of this book. Nonetheless, I'll walk quickly through the code in these classes to call out the highlights of the implementation.

First, though, it is helpful to understand the relationship between all these classes. Figure 5-7 shows how they are related.

The UI developer drags a `CslaDataSource` control onto a Web Form and interacts with it. While in Visual Studio, all that interaction is actually coordinated by `CslaDataSourceDesigner`, though in reality all the hard work is done by `CslaDesignerDataSourceView`.

When a control such as `GridView` is bound to the `CslaDataSource`, it requests schema information about the data source. This schema information is created and returned by the `ObjectSchema`, `ObjectViewSchema`, and `ObjectFieldInfo` objects.

Finally, at runtime, the web form interacts with `CslaDataSource` to perform the actual data binding. All the hard work is actually handled by `CslaDataSourceView`, an instance of which is managed by the `CslaDataSource` control.

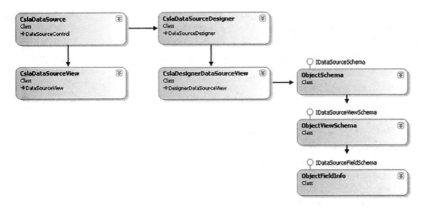

Figure 5-7. *Relationship between the classes in CslaDataSource*

CslaDataSource

The CslaDataSource class is the primary entry point at both design time and runtime. This is the object that a developer places on his web form when building a page. But really it is primarily a coordinator that connects all the pieces of the data source control together.

This starts with the declaration of the class itself, in which a <Designer()> attribute is used to connect CslaDataSource to CslaDataSourceDesigner within Visual Studio:

```
<Designer(GetType(Csla.Web.Design.CslaDataSourceDesigner))> _
<ToolboxData("<{0}:CslaDataSource runat=""server""></{0}:CslaDataSource>")> _
Public Class CslaDataSource
  Inherits DataSourceControl
```

Within the class itself, the code is largely concerned with providing the ASP.NET data binding infrastructure with a reference to the CslaDataSourceView object, and relaying events from the CslaDataSourceView back to the UI. Basically, CslaDataSource is merely a go-between at runtime, and a way of finding CslaDataSourceDesigner at design time.

The only bit of functionality that a UI developer will see is that CslaDataSource declares and raises four events. The UI developer must respond to these events to provide the interaction with the business object. Table 5-7 lists the events.

Table 5-7. *Events Raised by the CslaDataSource Control*

Event	Description
SelectObject	Requests that the UI provide a reference to the business object that is the data source
InsertObject	Requests that the UI insert a new business object based on the data from the form
UpdateObject	Requests that the UI update a business object with the data from the form, based on the key value provided
DeleteObject	Requests that the UI delete the business object based on the key value provided

These four events are directly analogous to the four method names required by the ASP.NET ObjectDataSource. Rather than using reflection to invoke a set of methods, I opted to raise events, as I feel that this is an easier programming model. With the ObjectDataSource, the UI developer must implement four methods (or defer to those in an ADO.NET TableAdapter); while with CslaDataSource, the developer simply handles these four events.

There is a custom EventArgs object for each of the events: SelectObjectArgs, InsertObjectArgs, UpdateObjectArgs, and DeleteObjectArgs, respectively. Each one provides properties that are used within the event handler.

Handling the Events in a Page

For instance, a SelectObject event handler may look like this:

```
Protected Sub CustomerDataSource_SelectObject( _
  ByVal sender As Object, ByVal e As Csla.Web.SelectObjectArgs) _
  Handles CustomerDataSource.SelectObject

  e.BusinessObject = Customer.NewCustomer()
End Sub
```

Notice that SelectObjectArgs defines a BusinessObject property, which must be set to the object that is to be used as a data source.

A typical UpdateObject event handler is a bit different:

```
Protected Sub CustomerDataSource_UpdateObject( _
  ByVal sender As Object, ByVal e As Csla.Web.UpdateObjectArgs) _
  Handles CustomerDataSource.UpdateObject

  Dim obj As Customer = Customer.GetCustomer(e.Keys("Id").ToString)
  Csla.Data.DataMapper.Map(e.Values, obj)
  obj.Save()
  e.RowsAffected = 1
End Sub
```

The e.Keys value is a name/value list of key values. The Id key value is used to load the customer object from the database, and then the DataMapper class is used to map the values from e.Values (another name/value list) to the properties of the object.

If you wanted to implement a type of field-level concurrency, the e.OldValues list contains the values from the data source when the form was loaded.

InsertObjectArgs exposes only e.Values, while DeleteObjectArgs exposes only e.Keys. The usage of both these events is comparable to UpdateObject:

```
Protected Sub CustomerDataSource_InsertObject( _
  ByVal sender As Object, ByVal e As Csla.Web.InsertObjectArgs) _
  Handles CustomerDataSource.InsertObject

  Dim obj As Customer = Customer.NewCustomer()
  Csla.Data.DataMapper.Map(e.Values, obj)
  obj.Save()
  e.RowsAffected = 1
End Sub

Protected Sub CustomerDataSource_DeleteObject( _
  ByVal sender As Object, ByVal e As Csla.Web.DeleteObjectArgs) _
  Handles CustomerDataSource.DeleteObject

  Customer.DeleteCustomer(e.Keys("Id").ToString)
  e.RowsAffected = 1
End Sub
```

All the custom `EventArgs` objects except `SelectObjectArgs` include a `RowsAffected` property that the event handler should set to indicate how many rows of data were affected by the operation.

In Chapter 10, you'll see complete examples of these event handlers, including exception handling and the use of `Session` to reduce the number of hits on the database.

Event Declaration

Each event is declared in `CslaDataSource`, along with a method to raise that event. For instance, here's the `SelectObject` event and related method:

```
Public Event SelectObject As EventHandler(Of SelectObjectArgs)

Friend Sub OnSelectObject(ByVal e As SelectObjectArgs)
  RaiseEvent SelectObject(Me, e)
End Sub
```

`EventHandler(Of T)` is a generic template in the .NET Framework that simplifies the declaration of event handler type events. Notice that the `OnSelectObject()` method is `Friend` in scope. It will only be called by `CslaDataSourceView`, and shouldn't be visible to UI or business developers.

CslaDataSourceView

The real work of data binding at runtime is handled by the `CslaDataSourceView`. ASP.NET gets a reference to this object through `CslaDataSource`, but it is this object that actually interacts with the data source. The object maintains a reference to the `CslaDataSource` control that created it, along with the assembly name and type name of the business object to which it is bound:

```
Public Class CslaDataSourceView
  Inherits DataSourceView

  Private mOwner As CslaDataSource
  Private mTypeName As String
  Private mTypeAssemblyName As String
```

The class inherits from `System.Web.UI.DataSourceView`, and so is required (at a minimum) to override the `ExecuteSelect()` method. It also overrides `ExecuteInsert()`, `ExecuteUpdate()`, and `ExecuteDelete()`.

ASP.NET calls these methods to trigger the appropriate operation at the appropriate time. For instance, when a control's data binding requires data, ASP.NET invokes the `ExecuteSelect()` method, and when data is to be inserted, it invokes the `ExecuteInsert()` method.

ExecuteInsert

`CslaDataSourceView` doesn't actually do much work. Rather, it calls methods on `CslaDataSource` to have it raise the four data access methods. The event handlers in the page then do the real work. For instance, here's the `ExecuteInsert()` method:

```
Protected Overrides Function ExecuteInsert( _
  ByVal values As System.Collections.IDictionary) As Integer

  ' tell the page to insert the object
  Dim args As New InsertObjectArgs(values)
  mOwner.OnInsertObject(args)
  Return args.RowsAffected
End Function
```

An instance of `InsertObjectArgs` is created and initialized with the `values` list. This is a list of name/value pairs for all the data elements from the web page (provided by ASP.NET), which presumably correspond to properties on the business object.

Then the `OnInsertObject()` method on `CslaDataSource` is called. That method simply raises the `InsertObject` method so the web form can handle the event to create a new business object and insert it into the database.

ExecuteSelect

The `ExecuteUpdate()` and `ExecuteDelete()` methods are quite similar, but `ExecuteSelect()` is a bit more complex:

```
Protected Overrides Function ExecuteSelect( _
  ByVal arguments As System.Web.UI.DataSourceSelectArguments) As _
  System.Collections.IEnumerable

  ' get the object from the page
  Dim args As New SelectObjectArgs
  mOwner.OnSelectObject(args)
  Dim obj As Object = args.BusinessObject

  Dim result As Object
  If arguments.RetrieveTotalRowCount Then
    If obj Is Nothing Then
      result = 0

    ElseIf TypeOf obj Is IList Then
      result = CType(obj, IList).Count

    ElseIf TypeOf obj Is IEnumerable Then
      Dim temp As IEnumerable = CType(obj, IEnumerable)
      Dim count As Integer = 0
      For Each item As Object In temp
        count += 1
      Next
      result = count

    Else
      result = 1
    End If

  Else
    result = obj
  End If

  ' if the result isn't IEnumerable then
  ' wrap it in a collection
  If Not TypeOf result Is IEnumerable Then
    Dim list As New ArrayList
    list.Add(result)
    result = list
  End If

  ' now return the object as a result
  Return CType(result, IEnumerable)
End Function
```

The first bit of complexity comes because ExecuteSelect() can be called either to retrieve a data source or to retrieve the number of rows in the data source. If it is asked to retrieve the row count, the method still must call OnSelectObject() on CslaDataSource so the UI event handler can return the business object:

```
' get the object from the page
Dim args As New SelectObjectArgs
mOwner.OnSelectObject(args)
Dim obj As Object = args.BusinessObject
```

These lines of code are run in every case. If the business object is to be retrieved, then it is returned as a result, but if the row count was requested, then the following code is used to get the number of items in the business object and return that number as a result, rather than the business object itself:

```
If arguments.RetrieveTotalRowCount Then
  If obj Is Nothing Then
    result = 0

  ElseIf TypeOf obj Is IList Then
    result = CType(obj, IList).Count

  ElseIf TypeOf obj Is IEnumerable Then
    Dim temp As IEnumerable = CType(obj, IEnumerable)
    Dim count As Integer = 0
    For Each item As Object In temp
      count += 1
    Next
    result = count

  Else
    result = 1
  End If
```

If the business object reference is Nothing, there are zero rows of data. If the object implements the IList interface, the count is simply retrieved from the object; while if it only implements IEnumerable, the code loops through all items in the list and counts them. Otherwise, the business object is not a collection at all, so obviously the result is 1.

Regardless of whether the method is returning the business object or the row count, Web Forms data binding requires that the data source be IEnumerable—the most basic interface for a collection or list in .NET. The challenge is that many business objects are simple objects, like Customer or Invoice; and of course, the row count is a simple int value. These values don't implement IEnumerable, and so can't be directly returned as a result.

The ExecuteSelect() method overcomes this issue by checking to see if the result to be returned implements IEnumerable; if not, it wraps the result in an ArrayList collection:

```
' if the result isn't IEnumerable then
' wrap it in a collection
If Not TypeOf result Is IEnumerable Then
  Dim list As New ArrayList
  list.Add(result)
  result = list
End If

' now return the object as a result
Return CType(result, IEnumerable)
```

In most cases, the end result is that the business object created by the UI event handler is returned as a result (possibly wrapped in an ArrayList object). In other cases, the row count is returned instead, as requested by ASP.NET.

The CslaDataSource and CslaDataSourceView classes are the only ones required to support run-time operations. But they don't provide designer support within Visual Studio, and that is an integral part of the web development experience. That's where the rest of the classes come into play.

CslaDataSourceDesigner

The CslaDataSourceDesigner class is the counterpart to CslaDataSource. Like CslaDataSource, CslaDataSourceDesigner is little more than a switchboard, routing calls to the CslaDesignerDataSourceView object where the real work occurs.

In its role as go-between, CslaDataSourceDesigner maintains references to the CslaDataSource control itself, and to the CslaDesignerDataSourceView object:

```
Public Class CslaDataSourceDesigner
  Inherits DataSourceDesigner

  Private mControl As CslaDataSource = Nothing
  Private mView As CslaDesignerDataSourceView = Nothing
```

CslaDataSourceDesigner is also responsible for telling the Web Forms page designer what capabilities are supported by the control. For instance, the CanRefreshSchema property is used by Visual Studio to determine whether the refresh schema option is available for the data source control, as in Figure 5-8. CslaDataSource does support this capability, so the property returns True:

```
Public Overrides ReadOnly Property CanRefreshSchema() As Boolean
  Get
    Return True
  End Get
End Property
```

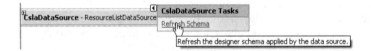

Figure 5-8. *Refresh schema link enabled for a CslaDataSource control*

As with CslaDataSource and CslaDataSourceView, however, the real work of providing design time support is handled by the view class: CslaDesignerDataSourceView.

CslaDesignerDataSourceView

The CslaDesignerDataSourceView object is really in control of what capabilities Visual Studio offers to the developer for a given data source. This object is responsible for providing the information listed in Table 5-8.

Table 5-8. *Information Provided by CslaDesignerDataSourceView*

Information	Description
Object schema	Schema information describing the properties of the data source (business object)
Sample data	Sample data for display in controls during design time; must match the object schema
Object capabilities	Flags indicating whether the data source supports various capabilities (such as insert, update, and delete)
Control capabilities	Flags indicating whether the control supports various capabilities (such as retrieving the row count)

Object Schema

The object schema information is created and returned through the ObjectSchema class, so CslaDesignerDataSourceView merely needs to delegate the work:

```
Public Overrides ReadOnly Property Schema() As IDataSourceViewSchema
  Get
    Return New ObjectSchema( _
      mOwner.DataSourceControl.TypeAssemblyName, _
      mOwner.DataSourceControl.TypeName).GetViews(0)
  End Get
End Property
```

I'll discuss ObjectSchema shortly. The schema information returned here is used by Visual Studio so that controls like DetailsView can be aware of the columns/properties provided by the data source, along with their data types and other information.

Sample Data

More interesting is the GetDesignTimeData() method, which returns sample data to populate controls like GridView at design time. This method is really the heart of CslaDesignerDataSourceView:

```
Public Overrides Function GetDesignTimeData( _
    ByVal minimumRows As Integer, _
    ByRef isSampleData As Boolean) As IEnumerable

  Dim schema As IDataSourceViewSchema = Me.Schema
  Dim result As New DataTable

  ' create the columns
  For Each item As IDataSourceFieldSchema In schema.GetFields
    result.Columns.Add(item.Name, item.DataType)
  Next

  ' create sample data
  For index As Integer = 1 To minimumRows
    Dim values(result.Columns.Count - 1) As Object
    Dim colIndex As Integer = 0
    For Each col As DataColumn In result.Columns
      If col.DataType.Equals(GetType(String)) Then
        values(colIndex) = "abc"
```

```
      ElseIf col.DataType.Equals(GetType(Date)) Then
        values(colIndex) = Today.ToShortDateString
      ElseIf col.DataType.Equals(GetType(Boolean)) Then
        values(colIndex) = False
      ElseIf col.DataType.IsPrimitive Then
        values(colIndex) = index
      ElseIf col.DataType.Equals(GetType(Guid)) Then
        values(colIndex) = Guid.Empty
      ElseIf col.DataType.IsValueType Then
        values(colIndex) = _
          Activator.CreateInstance(col.DataType)
      Else
        values(colIndex) = Nothing
      End If
      colIndex += 1
    Next
    result.LoadDataRow(values, LoadOption.OverwriteChanges)
  Next

  isSampleData = True
  Return CType(result.DefaultView, IEnumerable)
End Function
```

The data returned by this method must be in an `IEnumerable` list. The easiest way to create a set of tabular data is to use an ADO.NET `DataTable` object, so this method calls the `Schema` property to get an `ObjectViewSchema` object (which implements the `IDataSourceViewSchema` interface) representing the schema of the business object. That information is then used to construct a `DataTable` with columns matching the properties of the business object:

```
Dim schema As IDataSourceViewSchema = Me.Schema
Dim result As New DataTable

' create the columns
For Each item As IDataSourceFieldSchema In schema.GetFields
  result.Columns.Add(item.Name, item.DataType)
Next
```

The `minimumRows` parameter passed into the method indicates the number of rows of sample data that are to be created. With an empty `DataTable` created, the code simply loops to create the specified number of rows, inserting each one into the `DataTable`. Each common data type is provided with a default value that is displayed to the developer at design time. Then the `DefaultView` for the `DataTable` is returned as an `IEnumerable` value so that the data can be displayed.

Figure 5-9 shows an example of sample data displayed in a `DetailsView` control.

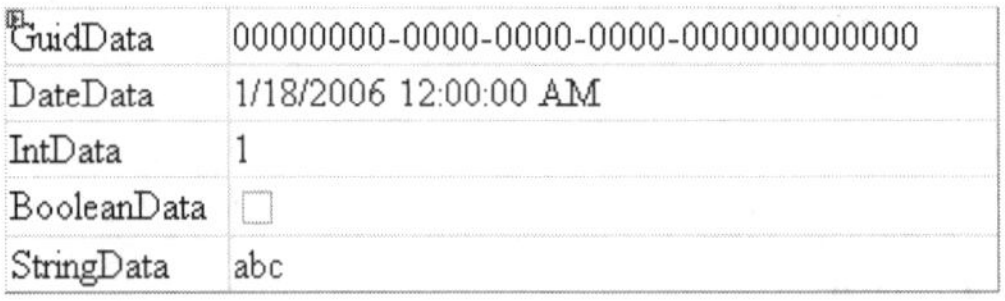

GuidData	00000000-0000-0000-0000-000000000000
DateData	1/18/2006 12:00:00 AM
IntData	1
BooleanData	☐
StringData	abc

Figure 5-9. *Sample data displayed in a DetailsView control*

Object Capabilities

Visual Studio needs to know the capabilities of the data source so that it can provide the UI developer with appropriate options at design time. Specifically, it relies on the following properties:

- CanDelete
- CanInsert
- CanUpdate

Figure 5-10 shows how these properties are used by Visual Studio to provide the set of options to the business developer.

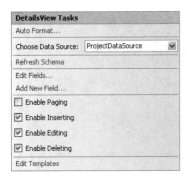

Figure 5-10. *Data source options presented to the developer by Visual Studio*

The options to enable inserting, editing (updating), and deleting are all driven by the properties discussed here. If CanInsert returns False, for instance, then the Enable Inserting option won't be visible to the business developer within Visual Studio.

Both BusinessBase and BusinessListBase are used to create editable objects, thus automatically supporting delete, insert, and update operations. Recall that in Chapter 3 both these classes implement the Csla.Core.IEditableObject interface, making it easy to determine if the business object class is one of these types. For instance, the CanUpdate property looks like this:

```
Public Overrides ReadOnly Property CanUpdate() As Boolean
  Get
    Dim objType As Type = CslaDataSource.GetType( _
      mOwner.DataSourceControl.TypeAssemblyName, _
      mOwner.DataSourceControl.TypeName)
    If GetType(Csla.Core.IUndoableObject).IsAssignableFrom(objType) Then
      Return True

    Else
      Return False
    End If
  End Get
End Property
```

The CanDelete and CanInsert properties are similar. The property calls a GetType() method on CslaDataSource to retrieve a Type object representing the type of the business object. Here's the code for that helper method in CslaDataSource:

```
Friend Overloads Shared Function [GetType]( _
  ByVal assemblyName As String, ByVal typeName As String) As Type

  If Len(assemblyName) > 0 Then
    Dim asm As Assembly = Assembly.Load(assemblyName)
    Return asm.GetType(typeName, True, True)

  Else
    Return Type.GetType(typeName, True, True)
  End If
End Function
```

This helper method accepts the assembly name and type name, and then uses reflection to load the assembly and get a Type object for the specified type.

This Type object is then used by the CanUpdate property to determine whether the business type implements Csla.Core.IEditableObject:

```
If GetType(Csla.Core.IUndoableObject).IsAssignableFrom(objType) Then
```

If so, the property returns True; otherwise it returns False—assuming that the business object is a read-only object.

Control Capabilities

The capabilities of the control itself must also be returned. These capabilities are reflected by the following properties:

- CanRetrieveTotalRowCount
- CanPage
- CanSort

Visual Studio uses these options in the same way it uses the object capabilities discussed earlier: to control the options available to the UI developer.

Earlier in the chapter, the ExecuteSelect() method in CslaDataSourceView included code to support retrieval of the row count, so CanRetrieveTotalRowCount will return True.

The other two methods will return False because CslaDataSource doesn't include code to manage paging or sorting of data.

This completes CslaDesignerDataSourceView, which is used by the Web Form designer in Visual Studio to provide the UI developer with a rich design time experience. Of course, the Schema property in this class relies entirely on the capabilities provided by the ObjectSchema class.

ObjectSchema

Following the theme set forth by CslaDataSource and CslaDataSourceDesigner, ObjectSchema is primarily a go-between or coordinator. It delegates all the real work to ObjectViewSchema.

When ObjectSchema is instantiated, it accepts the assembly and type names for the business class, and those are stored in instance fields:

```
Private mTypeAssemblyName As String = ""
Private mTypeName As String = ""

Public Sub New(ByVal assemblyName As String, ByVal typeName As String)
  mTypeAssemblyName = assemblyName
  mTypeName = typeName
End Sub
```

The GetViews() method then creates and returns an instance of ObjectViewSchema, which is also provided with the assembly and type name for the business object:

```
Public Function GetViews() As _
  System.Web.UI.Design.IDataSourceViewSchema() _
  Implements System.Web.UI.Design.IDataSourceSchema.GetViews

  Return New IDataSourceViewSchema() _
    {New ObjectViewSchema(mTypeAssemblyName, mTypeName)}
End Function
```

ObjectViewSchema is responsible for retrieving and returning the business object's schema information.

ObjectViewSchema

ObjectViewSchema implements the System.Web.UI.Design.IDataSourceViewSchema interface, making it responsible for retrieving and exposing the schema information about the data source (in this case, the business object). To that end, ObjectViewSchema maintains the assembly and type name for the business object:

```
Public Class ObjectViewSchema
  Implements IDataSourceViewSchema

  Private mTypeAssemblyName As String = ""
  Private mTypeName As String = ""
```

ASP.NET retrieves the schema information by calling the GetFields() method defined by the IDataSourceViewSchema interface. This method returns an array of objects that implement the IDataSourceFieldSchema interface from the System.Web.UI.Design namespace. The ObjectFieldInfo class discussed later implements this interface.

The GetFields() method is the only Public method in ObjectViewSchema:

```
Public Function GetFields() As _
  System.Web.UI.Design.IDataSourceFieldSchema() _
  Implements System.Web.UI.Design.IDataSourceViewSchema.GetFields

  Dim result As New Generic.List(Of ObjectFieldInfo)
  Dim t As Type = CslaDataSource.GetType(mTypeAssemblyName, mTypeName)
  If GetType(IEnumerable).IsAssignableFrom(t) Then
    ' this is a list so get the item type
    t = Utilities.GetChildItemType(t)
  End If
  Dim props As PropertyDescriptorCollection = _
    TypeDescriptor.GetProperties(t)
  For Each item As PropertyDescriptor In props
    If item.IsBrowsable Then
      result.Add(New ObjectFieldInfo(item))
    End If
  Next
  Return result.ToArray
End Function
```

This method gets a Type object representing the business object type by calling the CslaDataSource.GetType() helper method discussed earlier. It then checks to see if that type is a collection, and if so, it calls the GetChildItemType() helper method from the Utilities class to find the type of the child objects in that collection:

```
Dim t As Type = CslaDataSource.GetType(mTypeAssemblyName, mTypeName)
If GetType(IEnumerable).IsAssignableFrom(t) Then
  ' this is a list so get the item type
  t = Utilities.GetChildItemType(t)
End If
```

At this point, the method has a Type object corresponding to the type of business object (either the object itself, or the child objects in a collection). The method then gets a collection of PropertyDescriptor objects, each one representing a property of the business object:

```
Dim props As PropertyDescriptorCollection = _
  TypeDescriptor.GetProperties(t)
```

Each of the PropertyDescriptor methods is checked to see if the corresponding property is marked as <Browsable(False)>, in which case the IsBrowsable property will return False. Those properties are ignored. All other properties are used to create an instance of an ObjectFieldInfo object, which represents that property's schema information:

```
For Each item As PropertyDescriptor In props
  If item.IsBrowsable Then
    result.Add(New ObjectFieldInfo(item))
  End If
```

In the end, an array of these ObjectFieldInfo objects is returned as a result:

```
Return result.ToArray
```

Each element in this array contains schema information about a business object property that is available for data binding.

ObjectFieldInfo

The ObjectFieldInfo class maintains schema information about a single property on a business object. One of these objects is created for each bindable property on a business object, and is returned to ASP.NET through the GetFields() method of ObjectViewSchema.

The ObjectFieldInfo class implements the System.Web.UI.Design.IDataSourceFieldSchema interface as required by ASP.NET. This is a lengthy interface that defines a number of properties that provide information about the column/property. Many of these properties are designed specifically for columns from a DataTable, and have little meaning when applied to elements of a business object's interface, while others are valid in both cases.

The ObjectFieldInfo class maintains a set of instance fields to hold information about the business object property:

```
Public Class ObjectFieldInfo
  Implements System.Web.UI.Design.IDataSourceFieldSchema

  Private mField As PropertyDescriptor
  Private mPrimaryKey As Boolean
  Private mIsIdentity As Boolean
  Private mIsNullable As Boolean
  Private mLength As Integer

  Public Sub New(ByVal field As PropertyDescriptor)
    mField = field
    GetDataObjectAttribute()
  End Sub
```

Most of these values come from a <DataObjectField()> attribute that the business object developer can apply to properties of a business object.

DataObjectField Attribute

The `<DataObjectField()>` attribute comes from the `System.ComponentModel` namespace and can be used on a business object's property like this:

```
<DataObjectField(True, True, False)> _
Public ReadOnly Property Id() As Guid
  Get
    CanReadProperty(True)
    return mId
  End Get
End Property
```

In this example, the attribute specifies that the `Id` property is a primary key, represents the identity of the object, and is not nullable. Table 5-9 lists the possible parameters for the `<DataObjectField()>` attribute.

Table 5-9. *Parameters for the DataObjectField() Attribute*

Parameter	Description
primaryKey	Indicates whether the property acts as a primary key value for the object
isIdentity	Indicates whether the property uniquely identifies the object within a parent collection
isNullable	Indicates whether the property is nullable
length	Provides the maximum length of the property in bytes

The `GetDataObjectAttributes()` helper method retrieves this attribute from the business object's property and sets the corresponding instance fields:

```
Private Sub GetDataObjectAttribute()
  Dim attribute As DataObjectFieldAttribute = _
      CType(mField.Attributes.Item(GetType(DataObjectFieldAttribute)), _
      DataObjectFieldAttribute)
  If (Not attribute Is Nothing) Then
    With attribute
      mPrimaryKey = .PrimaryKey
      mIsIdentity = .IsIdentity
      mIsNullable = .IsNullable
      mLength = .Length
    End With
  End If
End Sub
```

Each of these values is exposed as a property through the `IDataSourceFieldSchema` interface. For instance, here's the `PrimaryKey` property:

```
Public ReadOnly Property PrimaryKey() As Boolean _
  Implements System.Web.UI.Design.IDataSourceFieldSchema.PrimaryKey
  Get
    Return mPrimaryKey
  End Get
End Property
```

Visual Studio can use these properties to assist the UI developer in building an appropriate interface for the business object's properties.

The Nullable property is a bit more complex, however, because it is sometimes possible to detect that a property is nullable even without the use of the <DataObjectField()> attribute. This is due to the nullable support built into .NET 2.0:

```
Public ReadOnly Property Nullable() As Boolean _
  Implements System.Web.UI.Design.IDataSourceFieldSchema.Nullable
  Get
    Dim t As Type = Me.mField.PropertyType
    If Not t.IsValueType OrElse mIsNullable Then
      Return True
    End If
    If t.IsGenericType Then
      Return (t.GetGenericTypeDefinition Is GetType(Nullable))
    End If
    Return False
  End Get
End Property
```

A property can be nullable if it is a reference type or if mIsNullable is True. It can also be nullable if the property is declared using the Nullable(Of T) generic type.

Other Property Information

The IDataSourceFieldSchema interface defines other properties as well. Some of these properties have little meaning for a business object. For instance, there's no way to determine meaningful values for Scale and Precision based on a business object's property, so these just return -1:

```
Public ReadOnly Property Scale() As Integer _
  Implements System.Web.UI.Design.IDataSourceFieldSchema.Scale
  Get
    Return -1
  End Get
End Property
```

Other properties can be determined based on information from the PropertyDescriptor object passed into the ObjectFieldInfo constructor. That PropertyDescriptor object provides information about the specific business object property. The property's name, for instance, can be directly retrieved:

```
Public ReadOnly Property Name() As String _
  Implements System.Web.UI.Design.IDataSourceFieldSchema.Name
  Get
    Return mField.Name
  End Get
End Property
```

Getting the Property's Data Type

The DataType property is a bit complex. It must deal with the possibility that the business object's property was declared with the Nullable(Of T) generic type. Fortunately, the Utilities. GetPropertyType() method discussed earlier in the chapter deals with that case, so it is called to ensure that the correct type is returned:

```
Public ReadOnly Property DataType() As System.Type _
  Implements System.Web.UI.Design.IDataSourceFieldSchema.DataType
  Get
    Return Utilities.GetPropertyType(mField.PropertyType)
  End Get
End Property
```

The `ObjectSchema`, `ObjectViewSchema`, and `ObjectFieldInfo` objects combine to provide ASP.NET with schema information about the business object when requested through the `CslaDesignerDataSourceView` object's `Schema` property.

Together with all the other classes related to `CslaDataSource`, the end result is a fully functional data source control that understands CSLA .NET–style business objects. UI developers can use this control to leverage the data binding support of ASP.NET Web Forms when working with rich business objects.

Conclusion

This chapter concludes creation of the CSLA .NET framework. Over the past three chapters, you have learned how to support a wide variety of functionality to support the development of business objects. This chapter combined a wide range of capabilities, including the following:

- Additional business base classes
- Custom authentication
- Collection sorting
- Date handling
- Common business rules
- Data access
- Reporting
- Windows data binding
- Web data binding

Combined with the support for editable and read-only business objects from Chapter 3, and the data access and mobile object support from Chapter 4, these capabilities make it relatively easy to build a powerful object-oriented business layer for an application.

The remainder of the book will focus on how to use this framework to create business objects, as well as a variety of UIs for those objects, including Windows Forms, Web Forms, and Web Services.

CHAPTER 6

■ ■ ■

Object-Oriented Application Design

Chapters 1 and 2 discussed the concepts behind distributed, object-oriented systems, and the .NET technologies that make them practical to implement with reasonable effort. Then, Chapters 3 through 5 covered the design and implementation of CSLA .NET, a framework upon which you can build distributed, object-oriented applications; thereby avoiding the complexities of the underlying technologies while creating each business class or user interface.

Chapter 7 will discuss the basic structure of business objects based on CSLA .NET. Chapter 8 will put that knowledge to use to implement a set of sample business objects for an application to track projects and resources assigned to projects. Chapter 9 will walk through the implementation of a Windows Forms UI, and in Chapter 10, a Web Forms UI will be implemented based on these objects. Chapter 11 will discuss the creation of a Web Services interface so the business objects can be used by other applications through the standard SOAP protocol.

This chapter will focus on the object-oriented application design process, using a sample scenario and application that will be implemented through the rest of the book. The design process in this chapter will result in a design for the business objects, and for an underlying database.

Obviously, the challenge faced in designing and building a sample application in a book like this is that the application must be small enough to fit into the space available, and yet be complex enough to illustrate the key features I want to cover. To start with, here's a list of the key features that I want to focus on:

- Creation of a business object

- Implementation of business validation rules

- Implementation of business authorization rules

- Transactional and nontransactional data access

- Parent-child relationships between objects

- Many-to-many relationships between objects

- Use of name/value lists

- Use of custom CSLA .NET authentication

In this chapter, I'll focus on the design of the application by using some example user scenarios, which are generally referred to as *use cases*. Based on those use cases, I'll develop a list of potential business objects and relationships. This information will be refined to develop a class design for the application. Based on the scenarios and object model, a relational database will be designed to store the data.

As I mentioned in Chapter 2, object-oriented design and relational design aren't the same process, and you'll see in this case how they result in two different models. To resolve these models, the business objects will include object-relational mapping (ORM) when they are implemented in

Chapter 8. This ORM code will reside in the `DataPortal_XYZ` methods of the business objects, and will translate the data between the relational and object-oriented models as each object is retrieved or updated.

Application Requirements

There are many ways to gather application requirements, but in general there are three main areas of focus from which you can choose:

- Data analysis and data flow
- UI design and storyboarding
- Business concept and process analysis

The oldest of the three is the idea that an application can be designed by understanding the data it requires, and how that data must flow through the system. While this approach can work, it isn't ideal when trying to work with object-oriented concepts, because it focuses less on business ideas and more on raw data. It's often a very good analysis approach when building applications that follow a data-centric architecture.

■**Note** The data-focused analysis approach often makes it hard to relate to users well. Very few users understand database diagrams and database concepts, so there's a constant struggle as the business language and concepts are translated into and out of relational, data-oriented language and concepts.

The idea of basing application analysis around the UI came into vogue in the early-to-mid 1990s with the rise of rapid application development (RAD) tools such as Visual Basic, PowerBuilder, and Delphi. It was subsequently picked up by the web development world, though in that environment, the term "storyboarding" was often used to describe the process. UI-focused analysis has the benefit of being very accessible to the end user—users find it very easy to relate to the UI and how it will flow.

The drawback to this approach is that there's a tendency for business validation and processing to end up being written directly into the UI. Not that this *always* happens, but it's a very real problem—primarily because UI-focused analysis frequently revolves around a UI prototype, which includes more and more business logic as the process progresses, until developers decide just to use the prototype as the base for the application, since so much work has already been done.

■**Tip** Obviously, people can resist this trend and make UI-focused design work, but it takes a great deal of discipline. The reality is that a lot of great applications end up crippled because this technique is used.

Another drawback to starting with the UI is that users often see the mocked-up UI in a demonstration and assume that the application is virtually complete. They don't realize that the bulk of the work comes from the business and data access logic that must still be created and tested *behind* the UI. The result is that developers are faced with tremendous and unrealistic time pressure to deliver on the application, since from the user's perspective, it's virtually complete already.

The third option is to focus on business concepts and process flow. This is the middle road in many ways, since it requires an understanding of how the users will interact with the system, the processes that the system must support, and (by extension) the data that must flow through the system to make it all happen. The benefit of this approach is that it's very business focused, allowing both the analyst and the end users to talk the language of business, thereby avoiding computer concepts and terminology. It also lends itself to the creation of object-oriented designs, because the entities and concepts developed during analysis typically turn into objects within the application.

The drawback to this approach is that it doesn't provide users with the look and feel of the UI, or the graphical reinforcement of how the system will actually work from their perspective. Nor does it produce a clear database design, thereby leaving the database analyst to do more work in order to design the database.

Personally, I use a blend of the business concept and UI approaches. I place the strongest emphasis on the business concept and process flow, while providing key portions of the UI via a prototype, so that the user can get the feel of the system. Since end users have such a hard time relating to database diagrams, I almost never use data-focused analysis techniques, instead leaving the database design process to flow from the other analysis techniques.

In this chapter, I'll make use of the business concept and process-flow techniques. It's difficult to storyboard the application at this stage, because we'll be developing both Windows Forms and Web Forms user interfaces, along with a web service application interface. The starting point, then, is to create a set of use case descriptions based on how the users (or other applications) will interact with the system.

Use Cases

Let's create a set of imaginary use cases for the project-tracking system. In a real application, these would be developed by interviewing key users and other interested parties. The use cases here are for illustration purposes.

■**Tip** This application is relatively simple. A real project-tracking system would undoubtedly be more complex, but it is necessary to have something small enough to implement within the context of this book. Remember that my focus is on illustrating how to use CSLA .NET to create business objects, child objects, and so forth.

Though not mentioned specifically in the following use cases, this system will be designed to accommodate large numbers of users. In Chapter 9, for instance, the Windows Forms UI will use the mobile object features of CSLA .NET to run the application in a physical n-tier deployment with an application server. This physical architecture will provide for optimum scalability. In Chapter 10, the Web Forms UI will make use of the CSLA .NET framework's ability to run the application's UI, business logic, and data access all on the web server. Again, this provides the highest-scaling and best-performing configuration, because you can easily add more web servers as needed to support more users.

Project Maintenance

Since this is a project-tracking system, there's no surprise that the application must work with projects. Here are some use cases describing the users' expectations.

Adding a Project

A project manager can add projects to the system. Project data must include key information, including the project's name, description, start date, and end date. A project can have a unique project number, but this isn't required, and the project manager shouldn't have to deal with it. The project's name is the field by which projects are identified by users, so every project must have a name.

The start and end dates are optional. Many projects are added to the system so that a list of them can be kept, even though they haven't started yet. Once a project has been started, it should have a start date, but no end date. When the project is complete, the project manager can enter an end date. These dates will be used to report on the average lengths of the projects, so obviously the end date can't be earlier than the start date.

Every project also has a list of the resources assigned to it (see the "Assigning a Resource" section later in this chapter).

Editing a Project

Project managers can edit any existing projects. The manager chooses from a list of projects, and can then edit that project. They need the ability to change the project's start and end dates, as well as its description. They also need to be able to change the resources assigned to the project (see the "Assigning a Resource" section later in this chapter).

Removing a Project

Project managers or administrators must be able to remove projects. There is no need to keep historical data about deleted projects, so such data should be completely removed from the system. The user should just choose from a list of projects, confirm his choice, and the project should be removed.

Resource Maintenance

At this point, the system not only tracks projects, but also tracks the resources assigned to each project. For the purposes of this simple example, the only project resources tracked are the people assigned to the projects. With further questioning of the users, a set of use cases revolving around the resources can be developed, without reference (yet) to the projects in which they may be involved.

Adding a Resource

We don't want to replicate the Human Resources (HR) database, but we can't make use of the HR database because the HR staff won't give us access. We just want to be able to keep track of the people we can assign to our projects. All we care about is the person's name and employee ID. Obviously, each person must have an employee ID and a valid name.

Resources can be added by project managers or supervisors. It would be really nice to be able to assign a person to a project at the same time as the person is being added to the application (see the "Assigning a Resource" section later in this chapter).

Editing a Resource

Sometimes, a name is entered incorrectly and needs to be fixed, so project managers and supervisors need to be able to change the name.

Removing a Resource

When an employee is let go or moves to another division, we want to be able to remove him from the system. Project managers, supervisors, and administrators should be able to do this. Once they're gone, we don't need any historical information, so they should be totally removed.

Assigning a Resource

As we were talking to the users to gather information about the previous use cases, the users walked through the requirements for assigning resources to projects. Since this process is common across several other processes, we can centralize it into a use case that's referenced from the others.

The project managers and supervisors need to be able to assign a resource to a project. When we do this, we need to indicate the role that the resource is playing in the project. We have a list of the roles, but we might need to change the list in the future. We also want to know when the resource was assigned to the project.

Sometimes, a resource will switch from one role to another, so we need to be able to change the role at any time. Equally, a resource can be assigned to several projects at one time. (We often have people working part-time on several projects at once.)

Lastly, we need to be able to remove an assignment. This happens when an employee is let go or moves to another division (see the "Removing a Resource" section earlier in this chapter); but we also often move people around from project to project. There's no need to keep track of who used to be on a project, because we only use this system for tracking current projects and the resources assigned to them right now.

Maintaining a List of Roles

Resources are assigned to projects to fill a specific role. The list of possible roles needs to be maintainable by end users: specifically administrators.

External Access

During conversations with users, we discovered that a number of them are highly technical, and are already skeptical of our ability to create all the UI options they desire. They indicated high interest in having programmatic access to the database, or to our business objects. In other words, we have some power users who are used to programming in Access and know a bit of VBA, and they want to write their own reports, and maybe their own data entry routines.

■Tip This same scenario would play out if there's a requirement to provide access to the application to business partners, customers, vendors, or any external application outside our immediate control.

Obviously, there are serious issues with giving other people access to the application's database—especially read-write access. Unless *all* the business logic is put into stored procedures, this sort of access can't be safely provided.

Likewise, there are issues with providing direct access to the business objects. This is safer in some ways, because the objects implement the business logic and validation; but it's problematic from a maintenance perspective. If other people are writing code to interact directly with the business objects, then the objects can't be changed without breaking their code. Since the other people are outside of our control, it means that the project tracker application can never change its object model.

Of course, this is totally unrealistic. It is a virtual guarantee that there will be future enhancements and requests for changes to the system, which will undoubtedly require changes to the business objects. Fortunately, Web Services offers a clean solution. If web services are treated just like any another interface (albeit a programmatic one) to the application, they can be used to easily provide access to the application without allowing external programs to directly interact with the application's database or business objects.

In Chapter 11, I'll revisit these ideas, showing how to implement a set of web services so that external applications can safely interact with the application in a loosely coupled manner.

Object Design

At this point, the key requirements for the application have been gathered from the use cases. Based on these use cases, it is possible to create an object-oriented design. There are a variety of techniques used in object-oriented design (you may have heard of CRC cards and decomposition, in addition to others), and in this chapter, I'll use ideas from both decomposition and CRC cards. A form of decomposition will be used to identify the "nouns" in the use cases, and then narrow down which of these are actual business objects. These objects will be described in terms of their class, responsibility, and collaborators (CRC).

Initial Design

The first step in the process, then, is to assemble a list of the nouns in the use case write-ups. By using a bit of judgment, you can eliminate a few nouns that are obviously not objects, but still end up with a good-sized list of potential business objects or entities, as shown in Table 6-1.

Table 6-1. *Potential Entities Discovered in the Initial Design*

Project manager	Project	Project number
Project name	Start date	End date
Administrator	List of projects	Employee
Resource	Employee name	Employee ID
Supervisor	List of assignments	Role
List of roles	Assignment	Date assigned
List of resources	List of assigned resources	

Using your understanding of the business domain (and probably through further discussion with business users and fellow designers), the options can be narrowed. Some of these aren't objects, but rather data elements or security roles. These include the following:

- Project manager
- Administrators
- Supervisor

■**Tip** I am assuming there's already an object to deal with a user's role. Such an object will be created by sub-classing the `Csla.Security.BusinessPrincipalBase` class later in the chapter. But these security roles should not be confused with the role a resource (person) plays on a project—they're two very different concepts.

Pulling out these nouns, along with those that are likely to be just data fields (such as project name and employee ID), you can come up with a smaller list of likely business objects, allowing you to start creating a basic class diagram or organizing the classes using CRC cards. Table 6-2 lists the high-level CRC data for each potential object.

Table 6-2. *Potential Objects and Their Associated Class Names*

Potential Class	Responsibility	Collaborators
Project	Adds and edits a valid project	ProjectResources
Resource	Adds and edits a valid resource	ResourceAssignments, Employee
Employee	Adds and edits a valid employee	None
ProjectList	Gets a read-only list of projects	Project
ResourceList	Gets a read-only list of resources	Resource
ProjectResources	Maintains a list of resources assigned to a project	Resource, RoleList
ResourceAssignments	Maintains a list of projects to which a resource is assigned	Project, RoleList
RoleList	Gets a read-only list of roles	Role
Role	Provides read-only role data	None
RoleEditList	Maintains a list of roles in the system	RoleEdit
RoleEdit	Adds and edits a valid role	None

One key aspect of CRC-based design is that an object's responsibility should be short and to the point. Long, complex responsibility descriptions are an indication that the object model is flawed, and that the complicated object should probably be represented by a set of simpler objects that collaborate to achieve the goal.

The diagram should also include relationships between the entities in the diagram. For the most part, these relationships can be inferred from the use case descriptions—for instance, we can infer that a "list of projects" will likely contain Project objects; and that a Project object will likely contain a "list of assigned resources," which in turn will likely contain Resource objects.

Note that I use the word *likely* here, rather than *will*. We're still very much in a fluid design stage here, so nothing is yet certain. We have a list of potential objects, and we're inferring a list of potential relationships.

Figure 6-1 is an illustration of how these objects relate to each other.

Looking at the CRC list and this diagram, there is some indication that there's more work to do. There are several issues that you should look for and address, including duplicate objects, trivial objects, objects that have overly complex relationships in the diagram, and places that can be optimized for performance.

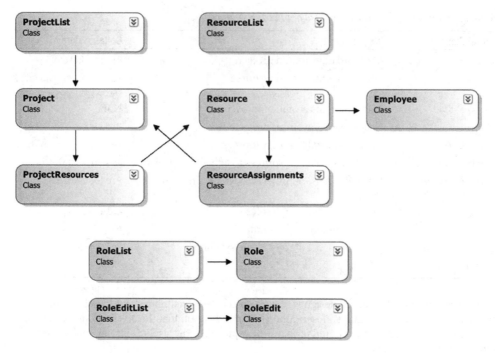

Figure 6-1. *Possible class diagram for the project tracker application*

Revising the Design

The following list indicates some of the things to address:

- Resource and Employee could be duplicates. It isn't clear that Resource adds anything to Employee, so the two can probably be merged into one class.

- Based on the use case description, we know that RoleList is a name/value list, which directly implies the Role is just a name/value placeholder. Given Csla.NameValueListBase, this can be simplified.

- The relationship between Project, ProjectResources, Resource, and ResourceAssignments is very complex. In fact, it forms a loop of references, which is always a danger sign.

- The RoleList object isn't used by any other objects in the model. Given that the use cases indicate that resources are assigned to projects based on a specific role, this is suspicious.

- The use cases for ProjectList and ResourceList indicate that they're primarily used for selection of objects, not for editing all the projects or resources in the system. Actually loading all the Project or Resource objects just so that the user can make a simple selection is expensive, performance-wise, so this design should be reviewed.

- It is clear that when the list of roles is edited, any RoleList objects need to know about the changes so that they can read the new data. This is not explicitly stated in a use case, but is an inferred requirement.

In the early stages of *any* object-design process, there will be duplicate objects, or potential objects that end up being mere data fields in other objects. Usually, a great deal of debate will ensue during the design phase as all the people involved in the design process thrash out which objects are real, which are duplicates, and which should be just data fields. This is healthy and important, though obviously some judgment must be exercised to avoid *analysis paralysis*, whereby the design stalls entirely due to the debate.

Let's discuss this in a bit more detail.

Duplicate Objects

First, you should identify duplicate objects that have basically the same data and relationships (like Resource and Employee). In this case, Employee can be eliminated in favor of Resource, since that's the term used most often in the use case descriptions (and thus, presumably, most used by the end users).

In most scenarios, the end users will have numerous terms for some of their concepts. It's your job, as part of the analysis process, to identify when multiple terms really refer to the same concepts (objects) and to clarify and abstract the appropriate meaning.

Trivial Objects

The Role object may not be required either. Fundamentally, a Role is just a string value, presumably with an associated key value. This is the specific scenario for which the NameValueListBase class in the CSLA .NET framework is designed. That base class makes it easy to implement name/value lists.

■Tip My characterization of the Role value is based on the use cases assembled earlier. If you intuitively feel that this is overly simplistic or unrealistic, then you should revisit the use cases and your users to make sure that you haven't missed something. For the purposes of this book, I'll assume that the use cases are accurate, and that the Role field really is a simple name/value pair.

Note that I'm not suggesting elimination of the RoleEdit class. While NameValueListBase can be used to create read-only name/value lists, RoleEdit and RoleEditList are used to *edit* the role data. They can't be automated away like a simple name/value pair.

Like the process of removing duplicates, the process of finding and removing trivial objects is as much an art as it is a science. It can be the cause of plenty of healthy debate!

Overly Complex Relationships

Although it's certainly true that large and complex applications often have complex relationships between classes and objects, those complex relationships should always be carefully reviewed.

As a general rule, if relationship lines are crossing each other or wrapping around each other in a diagram like Figure 6-1, you should review those relationships to see if they need to be so complex. Sometimes, it's just the way things have to be, but more often, this is a sign that the object model needs some work. Though relying on the aesthetics of a diagram may sound a bit odd, it is a good rule of thumb.

In this case, there's a pretty complex relationship between Project, ProjectResources, Resource, and ResourceAssignments. It is, in fact, a circular relationship, in which all these objects refer to the other objects in an endless chain. In a situation like this, you should always be looking for a way to simplify the relationships. What you'll often find is that the object model is missing a class: one that doesn't necessarily flow directly from the use cases, but is required to make the object model workable.

The specific problem caused by the circular relationship in Figure 6-1 becomes very apparent when an object is to be loaded from the database. At that time it will typically also load any child objects it contains. With an endless loop of relationships, that poses a rather obvious problem!

There must be some way to short-circuit the process, and the best way to do this is to introduce another object into the mix.

In the object model thus far, what's missing is a class that actually represents the assignment of a resource to a project. At this point, there's no object responsible for assigning a resource to a project, so there's an entire behavior from the use cases that's missing in the object model.

Additionally, there's data described in the use cases that isn't yet reflected in the object model, such as the role of a resource on a particular project, or the date that the resource was assigned to a project. These data fields can't be kept in the Project object, because a project will have many resources filling many different roles at different times. Similarly, they can't be kept in the Resource object, because a resource may be assigned to many projects at different times and in different roles.

Adding an Assignment Class

The need for another object—an Assignment object—is clear. This object's responsibility is to *assign a resource to a project*.

Figure 6-2 shows an updated diagram, including the changes thus far.

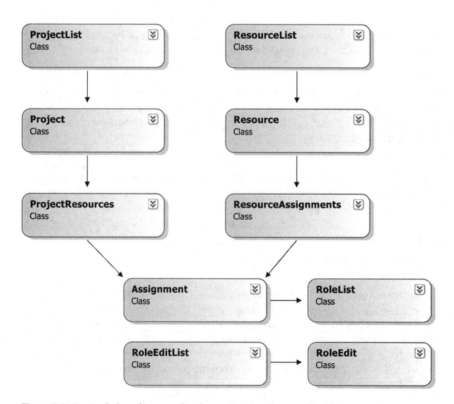

Figure 6-2. *Revised class diagram for the project tracker application*

However, we're still not done. The Assignment class itself just became overly complex, because it's used within two different contexts: from the list of resources assigned to a project, and from the list of projects to which a resource is assigned. This is typically problematic. Having a single object as a child of two different collections makes for very complicated implementation and testing, and should be avoided when possible.

Beyond that, think about its responsibility in the diagram in Figure 6-2. `Assignment` is now responsible for *assigning a resource to a project AND for associating a project with a resource.* When used from `ProjectResources`, it has the first responsibility, and when used from `ResourceAssignments`, it has the second responsibility. Sure, the responsibilities are similar, but they are different enough that it matters.

There's also an issue with data. A `Project` object uses the `ProjectResources` collection to get a list of resources assigned to the project. This implies that the `Assignment` object contains information about the resource assigned to the project.

Yet a `Resource` object uses the `ResourceAssignments` collection to get a list of projects to which the resource is assigned. This implies that the `Assignment` object contains information about the project to which the resource is assigned.

The fact that both behavioral and data conflicts exist means that the object model remains flawed.

There are two possible solutions. The list objects (`ProjectResources` and `ResourceAssignments`) could be combined into a single list of `Assignment` objects, or there could be two different objects representing assignments. To resolve this, we need to think about the different behaviors that are required when approaching the concept of assignments from `Project` and from `Resource`.

Assigning a Resource to a Project

Based on the use cases, resources can be assigned to projects. This implies that the user has identified the project and wishes to assign a resource to it. It also implies that a project has a collection of assigned resources: hence the `ProjectResources` collection in the object model.

But what behavior and information would a user expect from the items in the `ProjectResources` collection?

Certainly, one behavior is to return the list of resources assigned to the project. Another behavior is to allow a new resource to be assigned to the project, implying something like an `Assign()` method that accepts the `Id` property from a `Resource`.

It is also worth considering what information should be provided to the user. When viewing or editing a `Project`, the list of assigned resources should probably show something like this:

- Resource ID
- Resource name
- Date assigned to the project
- Role of the resource on the project

This means that `ProjectResources`, and the items returned by `ProjectResources`, might look something like Figure 6-3.

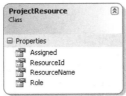

Figure 6-3. *The ProjectResources collection and the ProjectResource child object*

Though not visible in Figure 6-3, the `Assign()` method accepts a `resourceId` parameter to identify the resource being assigned to the project.

Given this analysis, let's consider the behaviors and information required to assign a project to a resource—basically the same process, but starting with a `Resource` instead of a `Project`.

Assigning a Project to a Resource

The use cases provide for the idea that a user could start by identifying a resource rather than a project. In this case, the user can still associate a project with the resource by selecting a project. This implies that the `Resource` object has a collection of projects to which the resource is assigned. The object model thus far represents this collection as `ResourceAssignments`.

Let's consider the behaviors and information for the `ResourceAssignments` collection and the items it would contain.

In this case, the user starts with a `Resource` and wishes to assign the resource to a project. So the `ResourceAssignments` object will have a couple behaviors: listing the projects to which the resource is assigned, and assigning the resource to a new project. This can probably be handled by an `AssignTo()` method that accepts the `Id` property of a `Project`.

The items in `ResourceAssignments` have the behavior of returning information about the project assigned to the resource. The information of value to a user is likely the following:

- Project ID
- Project name
- Date assigned to the project
- Role of the resource on the project

Figure 6-4 shows the potential `ResourceAssignments` object and what its items might look like.

Figure 6-4. *The ResourceAssignments collection and the ResourceAssignment child object*

The `AssignTo()` method accepts a `projectId` parameter to identify the project to which the resource should be assigned.

Can the Classes Be Merged?

It is important to notice that the objects described by Figure 6-3 and Figure 6-4 are *similar*, but they are not the same. Yet they do share at least some common information, if not behavior. Both child classes contain `Assigned` and `Role` properties, implying that there's commonality between them.

Such commonality is *not* justification for combining the two classes into one, because their behaviors are distinctly different. The items in `ProjectResources` have one responsibility: managing information about a resource assigned to a project. The items in `ResourceAssignments` have a different responsibility: managing information about a project to which a resource is assigned.

While this difference may seem subtle, it is a difference nonetheless. It is tempting to consider that the two classes could be merged into one, as shown in Figure 6-5.

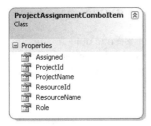

Figure 6-5. *Merged child items with assignment information*

Of course, ProjectName isn't valid if the user got to this object from a Project object, but it is valid if she got here through a Resource object. The same is true for several other properties.

Perhaps business logic could be added to properties to throw exceptions if they were called from an inappropriate context. But the obvious complexity of this sort of logic should give you pause. The problem is that one object is trying to handle more than one responsibility. Such a scenario means that the object model is flawed. Going down such a path will lead to complex, hard-to-maintain code.

Note Historically, this sort of complex code was referred to as spaghetti code. It turns out that with improper object design, it is *very* possible to end up with spaghetti code in business objects. The result is terrible, and is exactly what *good* object design is intended to prevent!

It should be quite clear at this point that merging the two collections or their child objects into a single set of objects isn't the right answer. They have different responsibilities, and so they should be separate objects.

But this leaves one glaring issue: what about the common properties and any common business logic they might require? How can two objects use the same data without causing duplication of business logic?

Dealing with Common Behaviors and Information

When designing relational databases, it is important to normalize the data. There are many aspects to normalization, but one of the most basic and critical is avoiding redundant data. A given data element should exist *exactly once* in the data model. And that's great for relational modeling.

Unfortunately, many people struggle with object design because they try to apply relational thinking to objects. But object design is *not the same* as relational design. Where the goal with relational design is to avoid duplication of data, the goal of object design is quite different.

There's no problem with a data field being used or exposed by different objects. I realize this may be hard to accept. We've all spent so many years being trained to think relationally that it's often very hard to break away and think in terms of objects. Yet creating a good object model *requires* changing this mode of thought.

Caution Object design isn't about normalizing data. It is about normalizing *behavior*.

The goal in object design is to ensure that a given *behavior* exists only once within the object model. Simple examples of behavior include the idea of a string being required, or one value being larger than another. More complex behaviors might be the calculation of a tax or discount amount.

Each behavior should exist only once in the object model, though it may be *used* from many different objects.

This is why collaboration is so critical to good object design. For example, one object—the DiscountCalculator—will implement the complex calculation for a discount. Many other objects may need to determine the discount, and so they collaborate with DiscountCalculator to find that value. In this manner, the behavior exists exactly once in the model.

Dealing with Common Information

So the real question isn't whether the Assigned and Role *properties* can be put into a common object—that's relational thinking. Instead, the question is whether those properties have common *behaviors* (business rules or logic) that can be put into a common object.

As it turns out, the Role property must be validated to ensure that any new value is a real role. Since the Role property can be set in both ProjectResource and ResourceAssignment, that behavior could be duplicated.

A better answer is to normalize that behavior, putting it into a central object. Let's call this new object Assignment, since it will be responsible for centralizing the code common to assignments of projects to resources, and resources to projects. Then both ProjectResource and ResourceAssignment can collaborate with Assignment to ensure that the Role property is validated.

This means that Assignment will contain the rule method that implements the role-validation behavior. In Chapter 3, the CSLA .NET framework defined the RuleHandler delegate to support exactly this type of scenario.

Given a ValidRole() rule method in Assignment, both ProjectResource and ResourceAssignment merely have to associate that rule method with their Role properties to share the common behavior. Figure 6-6 illustrates this relationship.

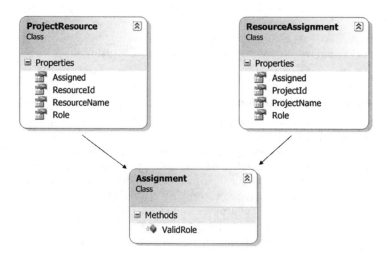

Figure 6-6. *ProjectResource and ResourceAssignment collaborating with Assignment*

The code to do exactly this is in Chapter 8.

Dealing with Common Behaviors

The responsibility of the Assignment object from Figure 6-6 is to manage the association between a project and resource.

This means that the `Assignment` object's behavior could include the idea of associating a project with a resource. This is a broader behavior than that provided by `ProjectResources`, which assigns a resource to a project; or by `ResourceAssignments`, which assigns a project to a resource. In fact, the behavior of `Assignment` is more general, and encompasses the needs of both other objects.

Of course, the real work of dealing with a resource assigned to a project, or a project associated with a resource, is handled by the `ProjectResource` and `ResourceAssignment` classes. The collection classes really just add and remove these child objects, leaving it to the child objects to handle the details.

The end result is that `ProjectResource`, to fulfill its behavior, can ask `Assignment` to do the actual work, as shown in Figure 6-7. The same is true of `ResourceAssignment`. The implication is that `Assignment` could have a method such as `AddAssignment()` that accepts a project's `Id` property and a resource's `Id` property, along with the role the resource will play on the project.

■**Tip** Object models should be simple and intuitive, even when underlying behaviors are complex. By centralizing common behaviors using objects internal to the business layer, a simpler and more tailored public interface can be exposed to the UI developer.

Similarly, `ProjectResource` and `ResourceAssignment` have behaviors that involve removing a resource from a project or removing a project from a resource. `Assignment`, then, will have a more general behavior to remove an association between a project and a resource.

Figure 6-7 shows the full extent of `Assignment`, including all the methods that implement behaviors common to both `ProjectResource` and `ResourceAssignment`.

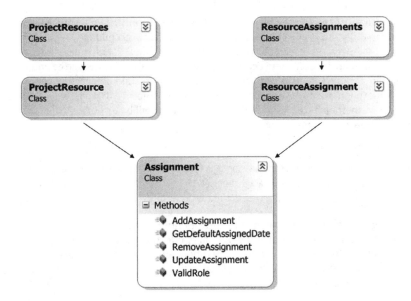

Figure 6-7. *Objects collaborating with Assignment*

At this point, all the common behaviors from `ProjectResource` and `ResourceAssignment` have been normalized into a single location in the object model.

Optimizing for Performance

Part of object design includes reviewing things to ensure that the model won't lead to poor performance. This isn't really a single step in the process, as much as something that should be done on a
continual basis during the whole process. However, once you think the object model is complete,
you should always pause to review it for performance issues.

One primary performance issue with many object models deals with the use of relational
thinking when designing the objects. Normalizing data within the object model is perhaps the
most common flaw causing performance issues. Due to the design of ProjectResource,
ResourceAssignment, and Assignment, the object model has already eliminated this issue by normalizing behavior instead of data. This helps avoid loading entire business objects just to display a
couple of common data elements.

There is, however, another performance issue in the model. The ProjectList and
ResourceList collection objects, as modeled, retrieve collections of Project and Resource business
objects so that some of their data can be displayed in a list. Based on the use cases, the user then
selects one of the objects and chooses to view, edit, or remove that object.

From a purely object-oriented perspective, it's attractive to think that you could just load a
collection of Project objects and allow the user to pick the one he wants to edit. However, this
could be very expensive, because it means loading all the data for *every* Project object, including
each project's list of assigned resources, and so forth. As the user adds, edits, and removes Project
objects, you would potentially have to maintain your collection in memory too.

Practical performance issues dictate that you're better off creating a read-only collection that
contains only the information needed to create the user interface. (This is one of the primary reasons why CSLA .NET includes the ReadOnlyListBase class, which makes it very easy to create such
objects.)

This stems from behavioral design. The responsibility of a Resource object is to add and edit
a valid resource. The responsibility of a ResourceList object is to get a read-only list of resources.
It is clear that these responsibilities are in conflict. To use a Resource object as a child of
ResourceList, it would need to be read-only—yet its whole purpose is to add and edit data!

Obviously ResourceList and ProjectList must contain child objects other than Resource and
Project. Instead, the ProjectList and ResourceList objects should contain child objects that contain only the data to be displayed, in read-only format. These new child objects will have
responsibilities appropriate to their purpose. ResourceInfo, for instance, will be responsible for
returning read-only information about a resource.

■**Tip** As discussed earlier, if there are common business rules or logic for properties exposed in such read-only
objects, the common behaviors should be normalized into another object.

Figure 6-8 shows the two collection objects with their corresponding read-only child objects.

The ProjectInfo object is responsible for providing read-only information about a project,
while the ResourceInfo object provides read-only information about a resource. By loading the
minimum amount of data required to meet these responsibilities, these objects provide a high-
performance solution and follow good behavioral object design.

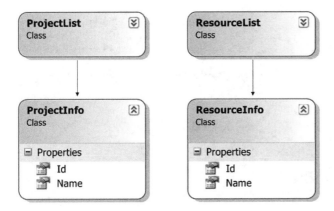

Figure 6-8. *The read-only collection objects, ProjectList and ResourceList*

Inter-Object Collaboration

The object model has a RoleList object, responsible for providing a read-only list of role data. It also has a Roles object, responsible for editing the list of roles in the application. While these two objects have very distinct responsibilities, they do have a point of interaction that should be addressed.

Though not required by any use case from a user, the RoleList object can, and probably should, be cached. The list of roles won't change terribly often, and yet the RoleList object will be used frequently to populate UI controls and to validate data from the user. There's no sense hitting the database every time to get the same data over and over.

You'll see how to easily implement the caching in Chapter 8, but first, there's a design issue to consider: what happens when the user edits the list of roles using the Roles object? In such a case, the RoleList object will be inaccurate.

■**Note** There's a related issue too, which is when *another user* edits the list of roles. That issue is harder to solve, and requires either periodic cache expiration or some mechanism by which the database can notify the client that the roles have changed. Solving this problem is outside the scope of this discussion, however.

It is relatively trivial to have the Roles object notify RoleList to tell it that the data has changed. In such a case, RoleList can simply invalidate its cache so the data is reloaded on the next request. Again, the implementation of this behavior is shown in Chapter 8.

From an object model perspective, however, this means that there is interaction between Roles and RoleList. From a CRC perspective, this means that Roles collaborates with RoleList to expire the cache when appropriate.

Reviewing the Design

The final step in the object design process is to compare the new class diagram with the original use case descriptions in order to ensure that everything described in each use case can be accomplished through the use of these objects. Doing so helps to ensure that the object model covers all the user requirements. The complete object model is shown in Figure 6-9, with the updated CRC information shown in Table 6-3.

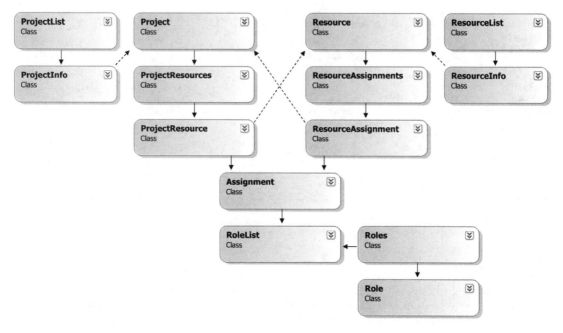

Figure 6-9. *Final project tracker object model*

The solid-lined arrows in Figure 6-9 indicate collaboration between objects, illustrating how many of them work together to provide the required functionality. The dashed lines show *navigation* between objects. For instance, if you have a ProjectInfo object, it is possible to navigate from there to a Project, typically by calling a GetProject() method.

While navigation between objects isn't strictly necessary, it is often of great benefit to UI developers. Consider that a UI developer will get access to a ProjectInfo object when the user selects a project from a control in the UI. In most cases, the next step is to load the associated Project so that the user can view or edit the data. Providing navigational support directly in the object model makes this trivial to implement within the UI.

Table 6-3. *Final List of Objects and Their Responsibilities*

Potential Class	Responsibility	Collaborators
Project	Adds and edits a valid project	ProjectResources, CommonRules
ProjectResources	Maintains a list of resources assigned to a project	ProjectResource
ProjectResource	Manages assignment of a resource to a project	Assignment, CommonRules, Resource
Resource	Adds and edits a valid resource	ResourceAssignments, CommonRules
ResourceAssignments	Maintains a list of projects to which a resource is assigned	ResourceAssignment
ResourceAssignment	Manages a project to which a resource is assigned	Assignment, CommonRules, Project
Assignment	Manages association of a project and a resource	RoleList

Potential Class	Responsibility	Collaborators
ProjectList	Gets a read-only list of projects	ProjectInfo
ProjectInfo	Provides read-only information for a project	Project
ResourceList	Gets a read-only list of resources	ResourceInfo
ResourceInfo	Provides read-only information for a resource	Resource
RoleList	Gets a read-only list of roles	None
Roles	Maintains a list of roles in the system	Role, RoleList
Role	Adds and edits a valid role	None

If you review the use cases, you should find that the objects can be used to accomplish all of the tasks and processes described in the following list:

- Users can get a list of projects.
- Users can add a project.
- Users can edit a project.
- Users can remove a project.
- Users can get a list of resources.
- Users can add a resource.
- Users can edit a resource.
- Users can remove a resource.
- Users can assign a resource to a project (and vice versa).
- When a resource is assigned to a project, users can specify the role that the resource will play on the project.

Custom Authentication

Though the objects required to service the business problem have been designed, there's one area left to address. For this application, I want to show how to use custom authentication. Perhaps this requirement became clear due to a user requirement to support users external to our organization; users that aren't in our corporate domain or Active Directory (AD).

The topic of authentication has been discussed several times in the book thus far, and you should remember that CSLA .NET supports Windows integrated (AD) authentication—in fact, that's the default. But it also supports custom authentication, allowing the business developer to create custom .NET principal and identity objects that authenticate the user using credentials stored in a database, LDAP server, or other location.

To this end, the object model will include two objects: PTPrincipal and PTIdentity. They are shown in Figure 6-10.

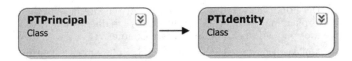

Figure 6-10. *Business objects subclassing BusinessListBase*

PTPrincipal is a .NET principal object, and acts as the primary entry point for custom authentication and role-based authorization. PTIdentity is a .NET identity object and is responsible for representing the user's identity.

At this point, the object model can be considered complete.

Using CSLA .NET

The class diagrams created so far have focused entirely on the business domain—which is a good thing. Ideally, you should always start by focusing on business issues, and deferring much of the technical design to a later stage in the process. Users typically don't understand (or care about) the technical issues behind the scenes, such as how you are going to implement the Cancel buttons, or how to retrieve data from the database.

Of course, the business developer cares about these issues—but these issues can be dealt with after the basic object modeling is complete, once you have a good understanding of the business issues and confidence that your model can meet the requirements laid out in the use cases.

At this point in the book, we also have the significant advantage of having designed and built a business framework. This means spending less time figuring out how to design or implement the features included in the framework. By relying on CSLA .NET, developers gain the benefits listed in Table 6-4.

Table 6-4. *Benefits Gained by Using CSLA .NET*

Feature	Description
Smart data	Business data is encapsulated in objects along with its associated business logic, so developers are never working with raw, unprotected data, and all business logic is centralized for easy maintenance.
Easy object creation	Developers use standard .NET object-oriented programming techniques to create business objects.
Flexible physical configuration	Data access runs locally or on an application server, without changing business code.
Object persistence	Clearly defined methods contain all data access code.
Optimized data access	Objects only persist themselves if their data has been changed. It's easy to select between various transaction technologies to balance between performance and features.
Optional n-level undo capabilities	Support for complex Windows Forms interfaces is easy, while also supporting high-performance web interfaces.
Business rule management	Reduces the code required to implement business rules.
Authorization rule management	Reduces the code required to implement per-property authorization.
Simple UI creation	With full support for both Windows Forms and Web Forms data binding, minimal code is required to create sophisticated user interfaces (see Chapters 9 and 10).
Web service support	Developers can readily create a web service interface for the application, so that other applications can directly tap into the application's functionality (see Chapter 11).
Custom authentication	Makes it easy to select between Windows integrated security and CSLA .NET custom security. It's also easy to customize CSLA .NET custom security to use preexisting security databases. In either case, standard .NET security objects are used, providing a standard way to access user security information.

To use CSLA .NET, developers merely need to determine which base classes to inherit from when creating each business class. For example, some business objects will be editable objects that can be loaded directly by the user. These need to inherit from BusinessBase, as shown in Figure 6-11.

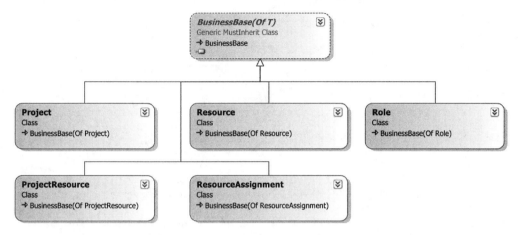

Figure 6-11. *Business objects subclassing BusinessBase*

By subclassing BusinessBase, all these objects gain the full set of business object capabilities implemented in Chapters 3 through 5.

The model also includes objects that are *collections* of business objects, and they should inherit from BusinessListBase, as shown in Figure 6-12.

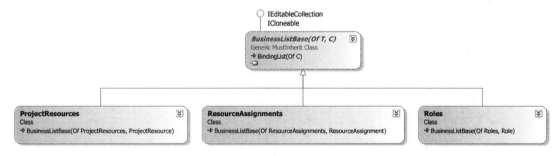

Figure 6-12. *Business objects subclassing BusinessListBase*

BusinessListBase supports the undo capabilities implemented for BusinessBase; the two base classes work hand in hand to provide this functionality.

As shown in Figure 6-13, the two objects that list read-only data for the user inherit from ReadOnlyListBase.

This base class provides the support objects need for retrieving data from the database *without* the overhead of supporting undo or business rule tracking. Those features aren't required for read-only objects.

The ProjectInfo and ResourceInfo classes don't inherit from any CSLA .NET base classes. As you'll see in Chapters 7 and 8, they must be marked with the <Serializable()> attribute, but they don't need to inherit from a special base class just to expose a set of read-only properties.

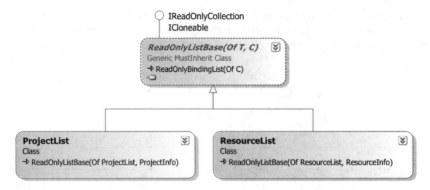

Figure 6-13. *Read-only list objects subclassing ReadOnlyListBase*

Next, there's the RoleList object, which is a read-only list of name/value data. Although this *could* be implemented using ReadOnlyListBase, Chapter 5 added a better alternative into the framework—the NameValueListBase class, as shown in Figure 6-14.

This base class is designed to make it as easy as possible to create read-only lists of text values, so it's ideal for building the RoleList class.

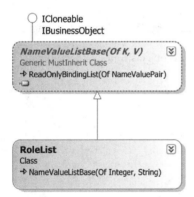

Figure 6-14. *RoleList subclassing NameValueListBase*

Finally, there are the two custom authentication objects: PTPrincipal and PTIdentity. Figure 6-15 shows these objects along with their CSLA .NET base classes.

PTPrincipal inherits from Csla.Security.BusinessPrincipalBase, ensuring that it implements the System.Security.Principal.IPrincipal interface, and also that it will work with the data portal, as implemented in Chapter 4. A required property from the IPrincipal interface is Identity, which provides a reference to a .NET identity object—in this case, PTIdentity.

The PTIdentity object inherits from ReadOnlyBase. It exposes only read-only data, and so this is a natural fit.

All of these classes will be implemented in Chapter 8. During that process, you'll see how to use the CSLA .NET framework to simplify the process of creating business objects.

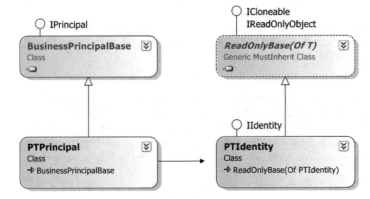

Figure 6-15. *Objects supporting custom authentication*

Database Design

It's a rare thing to be able to design a database specifically for an application. More often than not, the databases already exist, and developers must deal with their existing design. At best, you might be able to add some new tables or columns.

This is one reason why ORM is a key concept for object-oriented development. The object model designed earlier in the chapter matches the business requirements without giving any consideration to the database design. An important step in the development process is to create code that translates the data from the databases into the objects, and vice versa. That code will be included in Chapter 8 as the business objects are implemented.

In *this* chapter, let's create a database for use by the project-tracking application. One thing to note is that even though the database is created specifically for this application, the data model will not match the object model exactly. A good relational model and a good object model are almost never the same thing.

■**Tip** Speaking of good relational models, I strongly recommend that database design be done by a professional DBA, not by software developers. While many software developers are reasonably competent at database design, there are many optimizations and design choices that are better made by a DBA. The database design shown here is that of a software developer, and I'm sure a DBA would see numerous ways to improve or tweak the results to work better in a production setting.

To make development and testing relatively easy, this will be a SQL Server 2005 Express database. As you'll see in Chapter 8, you write the data access code for each object, so neither CSLA .NET nor your business objects are required to use SQL Server 2005 Express or any other specific database. You can use any data storage technology you choose behind your objects. In most cases, your applications will use production database servers such as SQL Server 2005 Enterprise Edition, Oracle, or DB2, rather than the more limited Express Edition used here.

The database will include tables, along with some stored procedures to enable database access from code. Additionally, there will be a second database to contain security information for use by the PTIdentity object.

■**Tip** If you're using a database other than SQL Server 2005 Express, you should translate the table creation and stored procedures to fit with your environment. You can find the database, table, and stored procedure scripts in the PTData project in the code download from www.apress.com.

While stored procedures may or may not offer any performance benefits, I believe they are a critical part of any business application. Stored procedures provide an abstract, logical interface to the database. They provide a level of indirection between the business objects and the underlying table structures, and thus they reduce coupling between the data management and business layers in your application. In short, stored procedures help make applications more maintainable over time.

That said, you'll notice that none of these stored procedures are complex, and every effort is made to keep business logic out of the database and in the business objects. Putting the business logic in both the objects and the database is just another way to duplicate business logic, which increases maintenance costs for the application as a whole.

Creating the Databases

The PTracker database will contain tables and stored procedures to persist the data for the business objects in the object model designed earlier in the chapter. This is a SQL Server 2005 Express database, and so you can think of it as being just another file in your project.

To create the database, open Visual Studio and create a new Class Library project named PTDB. I won't have you build this project at any point, so the project settings and Class1.vb file can be ignored. The purpose of this project is just so you can use Visual Studio to set up the database.

Choose Project ➤ Add New Item, and choose the SQL Database option. As shown in Figure 6-16, name the file and click Add.

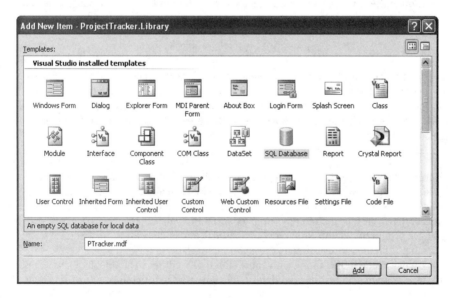

Figure 6-16. *Adding the PTracker database in Visual Studio*

Visual Studio will force you to walk through the process of creating a `DataSet` for the new database. You can walk through or cancel that wizard as you choose. It is not required for anything covered in this book.

Repeat the process to add a `Security.mdf` database as well. The end result is that you'll have two databases in the project—and more importantly, in the Server Explorer window, as shown in Figure 6-17.

Figure 6-17. *The PTracker and Security databases in Server Explorer*

Table creation can also be done within Server Explorer: just right-click the Tables node under the database, and choose New Table. This will bring up a table designer in VS .NET, with which you can define the columns for the new table.

Once the columns, keys, and indexes have been set up, save the changes by closing the designer or clicking the Save button in the toolbar. At this point, you'll be prompted to provide a name for the table, and it will be added to the database.

PTracker Database

Follow this process to add each of the following four tables to the database.

Roles

The `Roles` table will store the list of possible roles a resource can fill when assigned to a project—it simply contains an `Id` value and the name of the role. Figure 6-18 shows the VS .NET designer with these columns added, and the `Id` column configured as the primary key.

Column Name	Data Type	Allow Nulls
Id	int	☐
Name	varchar(50)	☐
LastChanged	timestamp	☐
		☐

Figure 6-18. *Design of the Roles table*

Notice that none of the columns allow `null` values. There's no business requirement to differentiate between an empty value and one that was never entered, so `null` values would make no sense.

The table also has a `LastChanged` column, which will be used to implement optimistic, first-write-wins concurrency in Chapter 8. It is of type `timestamp`, and so provides a unique, auto-incrementing value every time a row is inserted or updated. All the tables in the `PTracker` database will have this type of column.

Projects

The `Projects` table will contain the data for each project in the system. The columns for this table are shown in Figure 6-19.

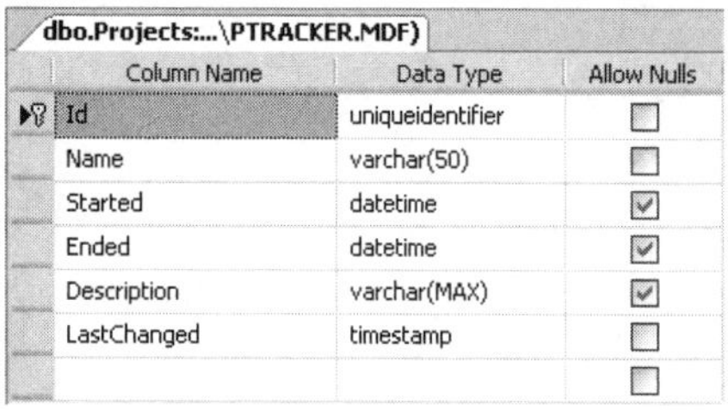

dbo.Projects:...\PTRACKER.MDF)		
Column Name	Data Type	Allow Nulls
Id	uniqueidentifier	☐
Name	varchar(50)	☐
Started	datetime	☑
Ended	datetime	☑
Description	varchar(MAX)	☑
LastChanged	timestamp	☐
		☐

Figure 6-19. *Design of the Projects table*

The `Id` column is set up as the primary key, and it's of type `uniqueidentifier`, which is a `Guid` type in .NET.

There are many ways to create primary key columns in tables, including using auto-incrementing numeric values or user-assigned values. However, the use of a `uniqueidentifier` is particularly powerful when working with object-oriented designs. Other techniques don't assign the identifier until the data is added to the database, or they allow the user to provide the value, which means that you can't tell if it collides with an existing key value until the data is added to the database. With a `uniqueidentifier`, however, the business developer can write code to assign the primary key value to an object as the object is created. There's no need to wait until the object is inserted into the database to get or confirm the value. If the value isn't assigned ahead of time, the database will supply the value.

Notice that the two `datetime` fields allow null values. The `null` value is used here to indicate an empty value for a date. The `Description` column is also allowed to be `null`. This isn't because of any business requirement, but rather because it is quite common for database columns to allow `null` values in cases in which they're meaningless. Chapter 8 will illustrate how to easily ignore any `null` values in this column.

The `Description` column is of type `varchar(MAX)`, so that it can hold a blob of text data. This field allows the user to enter a lengthy description of the project, if so desired.

Resources

The `Resources` table will hold the data for the various resources that can be assigned to a project. The columns for this table are shown in Figure 6-20.

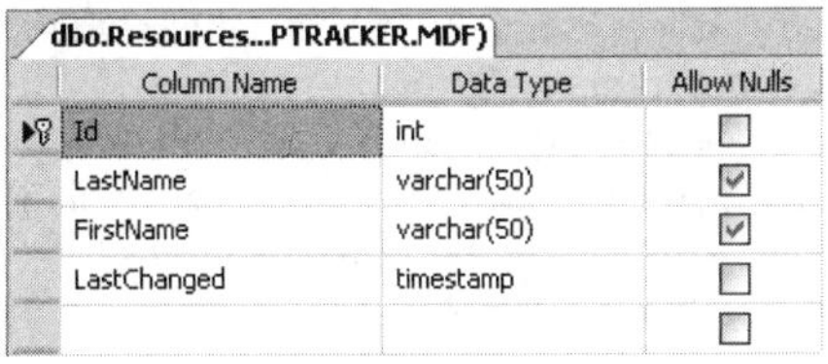

Figure 6-20. *Design for the Resources table*

Once again, the `Id` column is the primary key—it's an `int` that is configured as an identity column using the Column Properties window, as shown in Figure 6-21.

Figure 6-21. *Making the Id column an identity column*

This table has now been given an identity key; the code in Chapter 8 will demonstrate how to support this concept within your business objects.

As with the `Description` field in the `Projects` table, the `LastName` and `FirstName` columns allow `null` values even though they have no business meaning. Again, this is merely to illustrate how to build business objects to deal with real-world database designs and their intrinsic flaws.

Assignments

Finally, there's the `Assignments` table. A many-to-many relationship exists between projects and resources—a project can have a number of resources assigned to it, and a resource can be assigned to a number of projects.

The way you can represent this relationally is to create a *link table* that contains the primary keys of both tables. In this case, it will also include information about the relationship, including the date of the assignment and the role that the resource plays in the project, as shown in Figure 6-22.

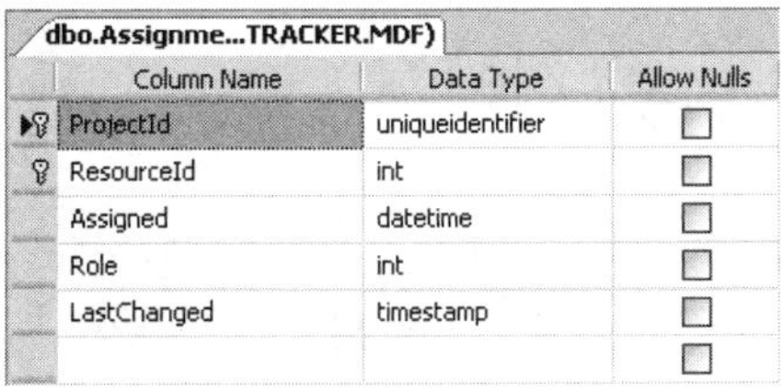

Figure 6-22. *Design for the Assignments table*

The first two columns here are the primary keys from the `Projects` and `Resources` tables; when combined, they make up the primary key in the link table. Though the `Assigned` column is of `datetime` type, `null` values are not allowed. This is because this value can't be empty—a valid date is always required. The `Role` column is also a foreign key, linking back to the `Roles` table. The data in this table will be used to populate the `ProjectResource` and `ResourceAssignment` objects discussed earlier in the chapter.

This really drives home the fact that a relational model isn't the same as an object-oriented model. The many-to-many relational design doesn't match up to the object model that represents much of the same data. The objects are designed around normalization of behavior, while the data model is designed around normalization of data.

Database Diagrams

Server explorer in Visual Studio supports the creation of database diagrams, which are stored in the database. These diagrams not only illustrate the relationships between tables, but also tell SQL Server how to enforce and work with those relationships.

Under the `PTracker.mdf` node in Server Explorer, there's a node for Database Diagrams. Right-click this entry and choose New Diagram. Visual Studio will prompt you for the tables to be included in the diagram. Highlight all of them, and click Add and Close.

The result is a designer window in which the tables are shown as a diagram. You can drag and drop columns from tables to other tables in order to indicate relationships. For example, drag and drop the `Id` field from `Projects` to the `ProjectID` field in the `Assignments` table. This will bring up a Tables and Columns dialog box, in which you can specify the nature of this relationship, as shown in Figure 6-23. Click OK to create the relationship.

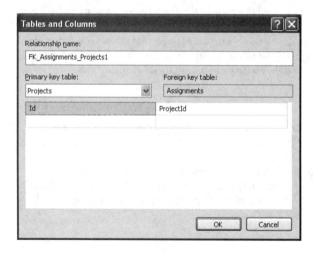

Figure 6-23. *Creating a relationship between Assignments and Projects*

Do the same to link the `Resources` table to `Assignments`. You can also link the `Roles` table's `Id` column to the `Role` column in `Assignments`, thereby allowing the database to ensure that only valid roles can be added to the table.

The resulting diagram should appear in a way that's similar to Figure 6-24.

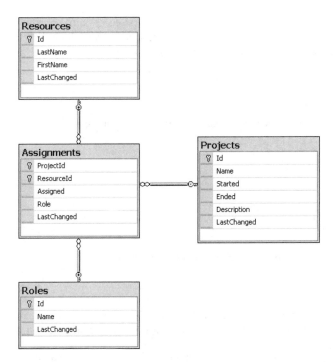

Figure 6-24. *Database diagram for the PTracker database*

Save the diagram to the database, naming it `PTrackerRelationships`. VS .NET will then ask whether to update the tables. Remember that these relationships are reflected as formal constraints within the database itself, so this diagram directly impacts the database design.

Stored Procedures

Whenever possible, database access should be performed through stored procedures. Stored procedures offer powerful security control over the database, and—perhaps most importantly—provide an abstraction layer between the physical structure of the database and the logical way in which it is used. The business objects created in Chapter 8 will make use of stored procedures for their database interaction.

You can use Server Explorer to add the stored procedures to the database by right-clicking the Stored Procedures node under the database, and choosing Add New Stored Procedure. This will bring up a designer window in which you can write the stored procedure code. When you close the designer, the stored procedure will be added to the database.

getProjects

The `getProjects` procedure will return the project data to populate the `ProjectList` object as follows:

```
CREATE PROCEDURE getProjects
AS
  SELECT    Id, Name
  FROM      Projects
  RETURN
```

It simply returns basic data about all of the projects in the system. The use cases didn't specify details about the order in which the projects should be listed in a project list, so I haven't included an ORDER BY clause here. Developers may have to do so during the testing process, as users typically add such requirements during that phase.

existsProject

The existsProject procedure is used to determine if a project's data is in the database:

```
CREATE PROCEDURE dbo.existsProject
  (
   @id uniqueidentifier
  )
AS
  SELECT COUNT(*)
  FROM Projects WHERE Id=@id
  RETURN
```

The procedure just returns the number of projects with a matching Id value.

getProject

The getProject procedure retrieves the information for a single project. This is a relatively complex proposition, since a Project object needs to retrieve not only the core project data, but also the list of resources assigned to the project.

This *could* be done by making two stored procedures and calling both of them to populate the business objects, but this can be reduced to a single database call by putting both SELECT statements in a single stored procedure. The stored procedure will then return two result sets, which can be read within the business object's code:

```
CREATE PROCEDURE getProject
  (
    @id uniqueidentifier
  )
AS
  SELECT Id,Name,Started,Ended,
    Description,LastChanged
  FROM Projects
  WHERE Id=@id

  SELECT ResourceId,LastName,
    FirstName,Assigned,Role,
    Assignments.LastChanged AS LastChanged
  FROM Resources,Assignments
  WHERE ProjectId=@id AND ResourceId=Id
  RETURN
```

Notice how the second SELECT statement merges data from both the Assignments table and the Resources table. Remember that the ProjectResource object will expose some resource data as read-only properties, so that data must be returned here.

To some degree, I'm putting ORM logic in the stored procedures by designing them to make it easy for the data access code in each business object to populate the objects. This isn't essential—you could write more complex code in the business objects—but it *is* a good idea, when you can do it.

> **■Tip** In many cases, applications must be built without the option of altering the structure of the database, or even its stored procedures. When that happens, all of the ORM logic must be written within the business objects. The end result is the same; it's merely a matter of where the ORM logic resides.

addProject

The addProject procedure is called to add a record to the Projects table, as follows:

```
CREATE PROCEDURE addProject
  (
    @id uniqueidentifier,
    @name varchar(50),
    @started datetime,
    @ended datetime,
    @description text,
    @description varchar(MAX),
    @newLastChanged timestamp output
  )
AS
  INSERT INTO Projects
  (Id,Name,Started,Ended,Description)
  VALUES
  (@id,@name,@started,@ended,@description)

  SELECT @newLastChanged = LastChanged
  FROM Projects WHERE Id=@id
  RETURN
```

Note that this only adds the record to the Projects table; a separate stored procedure adds records to the Assignments table.

This stored procedure not only includes an INSERT statement, but also a SELECT statement that loads an output parameter value. This is required to support concurrency. Recall that all the tables in the database include a timestamp column, which is automatically incremented each time a row is inserted or updated. As you'll see in Chapter 8, the business object must keep track of this value. Since the value changes any time the row changes, the value is returned as the result of any INSERT or UPDATE operation.

updateProject

Not only are records added to the Projects table, but the application must allow them to be changed. The updateProject procedure provides this capability, as shown here:

```
CREATE PROCEDURE updateProject
  (
    @id uniqueidentifier,
    @name varchar(50),
    @started datetime,
    @ended datetime,
    @description varchar(MAX),
    @lastChanged timestamp,
    @lastChanged timestamp,
    @newLastChanged timestamp output
  )
```

```
AS
  UPDATE Projects
  SET
    Name=@name,
    Started=@started,
    Ended=@ended,
    Description=@description
  WHERE Id=@id
    AND LastChanged=@lastChanged
  IF @@ROWCOUNT = 0
    RAISERROR('Row has been edited by another user', 16, 1)

  SELECT @newLastChanged = LastChanged
  FROM Projects WHERE Id=@id
  RETURN
```

Again, this procedure only updates the record in the Projects table; the related records in the Assignments table are updated separately.

Notice the @lastChanged parameter required by the procedure. This represents the last known timestamp value for the row. In Chapter 8, you'll see how this value is maintained by the business object.

When the object attempts to update the row, it provides the last known value for the LastChanged column. If that value hasn't changed in the database, then no other user has updated the row since the object read its data. But if the value *has* changed in the database, then some other user did change the data in the row since the object read the data. First-write-wins optimistic concurrency specifies that this second update can't be allowed, because it could overwrite changes made by that other user.

The UPDATE statement itself uses this parameter in the WHERE clause to ensure that the row is only updated if the value matches. The procedure then checks to see if the row was actually updated. If no rows were updated, it raises an error, which shows up as a database exception in the data access code of the business object.

On the other hand, if the update goes through and the row is changed, then a SELECT statement is executed to return the *new* value of the LastChanged column as an output parameter, so that the object can maintain the new value to allow possible future updates.

deleteProject

The deleteProject procedure deletes the appropriate record from the Projects table, and also removes any related records from the Assignments table. When creating the relationships between tables in the database diagram, the default is to *not* automatically cascade deletions to child tables:

```
CREATE PROCEDURE deleteProject
  (
    @id uniqueidentifier
  )
AS
  DELETE Assignments
  WHERE ProjectId=@id

  DELETE Projects
  WHERE Id=@id
  RETURN
```

If you set up your table relationships to cascade deletes automatically, then obviously the preceding stored procedure would only delete the data in the Projects table.

Though this procedure updates multiple tables, it does *not* include transactional code. Although you *could* manage the transaction at this level, you can gain flexibility by allowing the business object to manage the transaction.

Using the CSLA .NET framework, you have the option to run the data access code within a System.Transactions transactional context, to run it within an Enterprise Services distributed transaction, or to manually manage the transaction. When using either System.Transactions or Enterprise Services, transactional statements in the stored procedures will cause exceptions to occur. If you opt to handle the transactions manually, you can choose to put the transactional statements here in the stored procedure, or use an ADO.NET Transaction object within the business object's data access code.

addAssignment

When adding or editing a project or a resource, the user may also add or change the associated data in the Assignments table. The addAssignment procedure adds a new record as follows:

```
CREATE PROCEDURE addAssignment
  (
    @projectID uniqueidentifier,
    @resourceID varchar(10),
    @assigned datetime,
    @role int,
    @newLastChanged timestamp output
  )
AS
  INSERT INTO Assignments
  (ProjectId,ResourceId,Assigned,Role)
  VALUES
  (@projectId,@resourceId,@assigned,@role)

  SELECT @newLastChanged = LastChanged
  FROM Assignments
  WHERE ProjectId=@projectId AND ResourceId=@resourceId
  RETURN
```

This procedure may be called during the adding or editing of either a Project or a Resource object in the application.

Like addProject, this procedure ends with a SELECT statement that returns the new value of the LastChanged column for the row as an output parameter. This value must be maintained by the business object to allow for future updates of the row using the updateAssignment stored procedure.

updateAssignment

Likewise, there's a requirement to *update* records in the Assignments table:

```
CREATE PROCEDURE updateAssignment
  (
    @projectId uniqueidentifier,
    @resourceId int,
    @assigned datetime,
    @role int,
    @lastChanged timestamp,
    @newLastChanged timestamp output
  )
```

```
AS
  UPDATE Assignments
  SET
    Assigned=@assigned,
    Role=@role
  WHERE ProjectId=@projectId AND ResourceId=@resourceId
    AND LastChanged=@lastChanged
  IF @@ROWCOUNT = 0
    RAISERROR('Row has been edited by another user', 16, 1)

  SELECT @newLastChanged = LastChanged
  FROM Assignments
  WHERE ProjectId=@projectId AND ResourceId=@resourceId
  RETURN
```

As with addAssignment, this may be called when updating data from either a Project or a Resource object.

Notice the @lastChanged parameter. It is used in the same way the parameter was used in updateProject: to implement first-write-wins optimistic concurrency. If the UPDATE statement succeeds, the new value of the LastChanged column is returned as a result through an output parameter so that the business object can maintain the new value.

deleteAssignment

As part of the process of updating a project or resource, it is possible that a specific record will be deleted from the Assignments table. An assignment is a child entity beneath a project or resource; and a user can remove a resource from a project, or a project from a resource. In either case, that specific assignment record must be removed from the database:

```
CREATE PROCEDURE deleteAssignment
  (
    @projectId uniqueidentifier,
    @resourceId int
  )
AS
  DELETE Ass ignments
  WHERE ProjectId=@projectId AND ResourceId=@resourceId
  RETURN
```

This completes the operations that can be performed on the Assignments data. Notice that there's no getAssignments procedure. This is because assignments are always children of a project and a resource. The business objects never retrieve just a list of assignments, except as part of retrieving a project or resource. The getProject procedure, for instance, also retrieves a list of assignments associated with the project.

getResources

The ResourceList object needs to be able to retrieve a list of basic information about all the records in the Resources table, as follows:

```
CREATE PROCEDURE getResources
AS
  SELECT Id,LastName,FirstName
  FROM Resources
  RETURN
```

This information will be used to populate the read-only ResourceList business object.

existsResource

The `existsResource` procedure is used to determine if a resource's data is in the database:

```
CREATE PROCEDURE dbo.existsResource
  (
   @id int
  )
AS
  SELECT COUNT(*)
  FROM Resources WHERE Id=@id
  RETURN
```

Like `existsProject`, the procedure just returns the number of resource rows with a matching Id value.

getResource

The `Resource` object needs to be able to get detailed information about a specific record in the Resources table, along with its associated data from the `Assignments` table. This is very similar to the `getProject` procedure. Here, too, two result sets are returned from the stored procedure:

```
CREATE PROCEDURE getResource
  (
   @id int
  )
AS
  SELECT Id,LastName,FirstName,LastChanged
  FROM Resources
  WHERE Id=@id

  SELECT ProjectId,Name,Assigned,Role,
     Assignments.LastChanged AS LastChanged
  FROM Projects,Assignments
  WHERE ResourceId=@id AND ProjectId=Id
  RETURN
```

The second `SELECT` statement returns data not only from the `Assignments` table, but also from the `Projects` table. This data will be provided as read-only properties in the `ResourceAssignment` object. By combining the two `SELECT` statements into a single stored procedure, the `Resource` object can make a single database call to retrieve all the data it requires.

addResource

When a new `Resource` object is created and saved, its data needs to be inserted into the Resources table:

```
CREATE PROCEDURE addResource
  (
   @lastName varchar(50),
   @firstName varchar(50),
   @newId int output,
   @newLastChanged timestamp output
  )
```

```
AS
  INSERT INTO Resources
  (LastName,FirstName)
  VALUES
  (@lastName,@firstName)

  SELECT @newId = Id, @newLastChanged = LastChanged
  FROM Resources WHERE Id=SCOPE_IDENTITY()
  RETURN
```

Remember that the Id column in the Resources table is an identity column. This means its value is automatically assigned by the database when a new row is inserted. The built-in SCOPE_IDENTITY() function is used to retrieve the generated key value, and that value is returned in an output parameter, as a result of the stored procedure. In Chapter 8, you'll see how this value is retrieved by the Resource object so that the object becomes aware of the new value. Also, as in addProject, the new value for the LastChanged column is returned to the object.

The associated addAssignment procedure, which can be used to add related records to the Assignments table, was created earlier.

updateResource

Likewise, there's a need to update data in the Resources table, as shown here:

```
CREATE PROCEDURE updateResource
  (
    @id int,
    @lastName varchar(50),
    @firstName varchar(50),
    @lastChanged timestamp,
    @newLastChanged timestamp output
  )
AS
  UPDATE Resources
  SET
    LastName=@lastName,
    FirstName=@firstName
  WHERE Id=@id
    AND LastChanged=@lastChanged
  IF @@ROWCOUNT = 0
    RAISERROR('Row has been edited by another user', 16, 1)

  SELECT @newLastChanged = LastChanged
  FROM Resources WHERE Id=@id
  RETURN
```

This procedure will be called when an existing Resource object is edited and saved.

deleteResource

A Resource object can be removed from the system. This means removing not only the record from the Resources table, but also the associated records from the Assignments table, as shown here:

```
CREATE PROCEDURE deleteResource
  (
    @id int
  )
AS
  DELETE Assignments
  WHERE ResourceId=@id

  DELETE Resources
  WHERE Id=@id
  RETURN
```

This procedure works the same as deleteProject.

getRoles

The getRoles procedure will return the list of roles to populate the RoleList and Roles objects as follows:

```
CREATE PROCEDURE [dbo].[getRoles]
AS
  SELECT Id,Name,LastChanged
  FROM Roles
  RETURN
```

All the role data is returned as a result of this procedure. Though RoleList and Roles use the data differently, they both use the same set of values.

addRole

The addRole procedure adds a new entry to the Roles table:

```
CREATE PROCEDURE [dbo].[addRole]
  (
    @id int,
    @name varchar(50),
    @newLastChanged timestamp output
  )
AS
  INSERT INTO Roles
  (Id,Name)
  VALUES
  (@id,@name)

  SELECT @newLastChanged = LastChanged
  FROM Roles WHERE Id=@id
  RETURN
```

This stored procedure is called by the Role object when it needs to insert its data into the database. As with the other add procedures, this one returns the new value of the LastChanged column for use by the business object.

updateRole

The updateRole procedure updates an existing entry in the Roles table:

```
CREATE PROCEDURE [dbo].[updateRole]
  (
    @id int,
    @name varchar(50),
    @lastChanged timestamp,
    @newLastChanged timestamp output
  )
AS
  UPDATE Roles
  SET
    Name=@name
  WHERE Id=@id
    AND LastChanged=@lastChanged
  IF @@ROWCOUNT = 0
    RAISERROR('Row has been edited by another user', 16, 1)

  SELECT @newLastChanged = LastChanged
  FROM Roles WHERE Id=@id
  RETURN
```

This stored procedure is called by the Role object when it needs to update the data in the database.

deleteRole

The deleteRole procedure removes an entry from the Roles table:

```
CREATE PROCEDURE [dbo].[deleteRole]
  (
    @id int
  )
AS
  DELETE Roles
  WHERE Id=@id
  RETURN
```

This stored procedure is called by the Role object when it needs to remove a row of data from the database.

At this point, stored procedures exist to do every bit of data access. In Chapter 8, the business objects will implement data access code using ADO.NET that makes use of these stored procedures.

Security Database

With the PTracker database complete, let's wrap up the chapter by creating the tables and stored procedures for the Security database. This database will be used by the PTIdentity object to perform custom authentication of a user's credentials. Assuming the user is valid, the user's roles will be loaded into the business object so they can be used for authorization as the application is used.

The PTPrincipal and PTIdentity objects will be implemented in Chapter 8. In most cases, you'll be creating similar custom security objects—but designed to use your preexisting security database tables. The database created in this chapter and the objects created in Chapter 8 exist primarily to demonstrate the basic process required for creating your own objects.

Figure 6-25 shows the two tables in the database, along with their relationship.

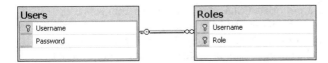

Figure 6-25. *Database diagram for the Security database*

In the Users table, Username and Password are both varchar(20) columns, as is the Role column in the Roles table. Only the Password column allows null values. All other values are required. Of course, a password should be required as well, but for this simple example, it is left as optional.

Finally, there's a Login stored procedure:

```
CREATE PROCEDURE Login
  (
    @user varchar(20),
    @pw varchar(20)
  )
AS
  SELECT Username
  FROM Users
  WHERE Username=@user AND Password=@pw;

  SELECT R.Role
  FROM Users AS U INNER JOIN Roles AS R ON
      R.UserName = U.UserName
  WHERE U.Username = @user and U.Password = @pw
  RETURN
```

This procedure is called by PTIdentity to authenticate the user and retrieve the user's list of roles. As you'll see in Chapter 8, PTIdentity determines whether the user's credentials are valid or not by finding out whether any data is returned from this stored procedure. If no data is returned, then the user's credentials are assumed to be invalid and the user is not authenticated.

On the other hand, if the stored procedure does return data, then PTIdentity stores that data, especially the list of roles to which the user belongs. This list of security roles (not to be confused with the project roles from the PTracker database) is then used for authorization throughout the application. The CanReadProperty() and CanWriteProperty() methods on each business object rely on this data.

Conclusion

This chapter has started the process of building a sample application that will make use of the CSLA .NET framework. It's a simple project-tracking application that maintains a list of projects and a list of resources, and allows the resources to be assigned to the projects.

The application's design used an object-oriented analysis technique that involved creating use cases that described the various ways in which the users need to interact with the system. Based on the use cases, and by using elements of CRC-style design, a list of potential business objects was created and refined.

That object list was then used to create a preliminary class diagram that showed the classes, their key data fields, and their relationships. Based on the diagram, our understanding of the business domain, and the use cases, we were able to refine the design to arrive at a final class diagram that describes the business classes that will comprise the application.

The next step was to determine the appropriate CSLA .NET base classes from which each business object should inherit. The editable business objects inherit from `BusinessBase`, and the collections of editable child objects inherit from `BusinessListBase`. The lists of read-only data inherit from `ReadOnlyListBase`, each of which contain simple child objects that don't inherit from a CSLA .NET base class at all. The list of simple name/value role data inherits from `NameValueListBase`.

Finally, a simple relational database was created to store the data for the application. In most applications, the database already exists, but in this case, we had the luxury of creating a database from scratch. Even so, it's interesting to note the differences between the object model and the relational model, thus highlighting the fact that a good object-oriented model and a good relational model are almost never the same.

Chapter 7 will discuss the basic structure of each type of business object directly supported by CSLA .NET. The chapter will also walk through a code template for each type. Then, Chapter 8 will implement the business objects designed in this chapter, and Chapter 9 will show how to build a Windows Forms UI based on those objects. In Chapter 10, a comparable Web Forms UI will be built, and Chapter 11 will walk through the construction of a Web Services interface that reuses the exact same objects. Finally, Chapter 12 will show how to host the server-side data portal components on various application server technologies.

■ ■ ■

CHAPTER 7

Using the CSLA .NET Base Classes

This chapter will discuss, in detail, how to implement business objects based on the CSLA .NET framework. To a large degree, this chapter will tie together everything in the book so far; it will illustrate how to write code to create business objects, and make the most of the thought, design, and coding that's been covered.

Chapter 8 will implement the objects for the sample application designed in Chapter 6. But before jumping headlong into implementing actual business objects, it is important to have a solid understanding of how to use each of the base classes provided by the framework implemented in Chapters 3 through 5.

This chapter will cover the life cycle of each type of business object in general terms. Then I'll get into code, creating a basic template showing the structure of each type of object:

- Editable root
- Editable child
- Editable, "switchable" (i.e., root or child) object
- Editable root collection
- Editable child collection
- Read-only object
- Read-only collection
- Command object
- Name/value list

Though the templates are not complete business object implementations, each one illustrates the basic structure you need to follow when creating that type of business object. You can use this information to create class templates or code snippets for use in Visual Studio to make your development experience more productive.

Business Object Life Cycle

Before getting into the code structure for the business objects, it's worth spending some time to understand the life cycle of those objects. By life cycle, I mean the sequence of methods and events that occur as the object is created and used. Although it isn't always possible to predict the business properties and methods that might exist on an object, there's a set of steps that occur during the lifetime of *every* business object.

Typically, an object is created by UI code, whether that's Windows Forms, Web Forms, or a web service. Sometimes, an object may be created by another object, which will happen when there's a *using* relationship between objects, for instance.

Object Creation

Whether editable or read-only, all root objects go through the same basic creation process. (Root objects are those that can be directly retrieved from the database, while child objects are retrieved within the context of a root object, though never directly.)

As I discussed in Chapter 4, it's up to the root object to invoke methods on its child objects and child collections so that they can load their own data from the database. Usually, the root object actually calls the database and gets all the data back, and then provides that data to the child objects and collections so that they can populate themselves. From a purely object-oriented perspective, it might be ideal to have each object encapsulate the logic to get its own data from the database, but in reality it's not practical to have each object independently contact the database to retrieve one row of data.

Root Object Creation

Root objects are created by calling a *factory method*, which is a method that's called in order to create an object. These will be Shared methods on the class. The Shared method will use the data portal to load the object with default values. The following steps outline the process of creating a new root object:

1. The factory method is called.

2. The factory method calls DataPortal.Create() to get the business object.

3. The data portal uses its channel adapter and message router functionality as described in Chapter 4; the result is that the data portal creates a new instance of the business object.

4. The business object can do basic initialization in the constructor.

5. The DataPortal_Create() method is called, and this is where the business object implements data access code to load its default values.

6. The business object is returned.

7. From the business object's perspective, two methods are called, as follows:

    • The default constructor

    • DataPortal_Create()

This is illustrated in Figure 7-1.

If the object *doesn't* need to retrieve default values from the database, the <RunLocal()> attribute can be used to short-circuit the data portal so the object initialization occurs locally.

To the UI code, of course, there's no difference—that code just calls the factory method and gets an object back:

```
Dim root As Root = Root.NewRoot()
```

From the business object's perspective, most of the work occurs in the DataPortal_Create() method, where the object's values are initialized.

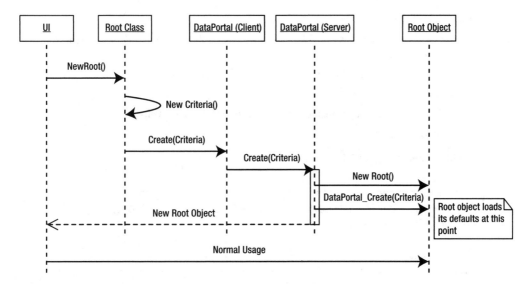

Figure 7-1. *Creating a root object*

Child Object Creation

Child objects are usually created when the UI code calls an Add() method on the collection object that contains the child object. Ideally, the child class and the collection class will be in the same assembly, so the Shared factory methods on a child object can be scoped as Friend, rather than Public. This way, the UI can't directly create the object, but the collection object *can* create the child when the UI calls the collection's Add() method.

The CSLA .NET framework doesn't actually dictate this approach. Rather, it's a design choice on my part because I feel that it makes the use of the business objects more intuitive from the UI developer's perspective. It's quite possible to allow the UI code to create child objects directly, by making the child factory methods Public; the collection's Add() method would then accept a pre-built child object as a parameter. I think that's less intuitive, but it's perfectly valid, and you can implement your objects that way if you choose.

■**Note** Child objects can optionally be created through data binding, in which case the addition is handled by overriding the AddNewCore() method in the collection class.

As with the root objects, you may or may not need to load default values from the database when creating a child object.

■**Tip** If you don't need to retrieve default values from the database, you could have the collection object create the child object directly, using the New keyword. For consistency, however, it's better to stick with the factory method approach so that all objects are created the same way.

The steps to create a child object that *doesn't* need to load itself with default values from the database are as follows:

1. The factory method (Friend scope) is called.

2. The factory method creates the object locally by using the New keyword and possibly passing parameter values.

3. The child object does any initialization in the constructor method.

4. The child object is returned.

5. From the child object's perspective, only one method is called, as follows:

   - Any constructor

This is illustrated in Figure 7-2.

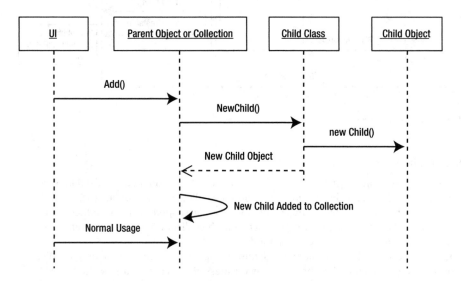

Figure 7-2. *Child object–creation process with no data access*

Once the child object has been created and added to the parent, the UI code can access the child via the parent's interface. Typically, the parent will provide a default property that allows the UI to access child objects directly.

Though the factory method is called by the parent object rather than the UI code, this is the same *process* that's used to create a root object. The same is true if the object needs to load itself with default values from the database.

1. The factory method (Friend scope) is called.

2. The factory method calls DataPortal.Create() to get the child business object.

3. The data portal uses its channel adapter and message router functionality as described in Chapter 4; the result is that the data portal creates a new instance of the business object.

4. The child object can do basic initialization in the constructor method.

5. The DataPortal_Create() method is called, and this is where the child object implements data access code to load its default values.

6. The child object is returned. Again, the factory method is called by the collection object rather than the UI, but the rest of the process is the same as with a root object.

7. From the child object's perspective, two methods are called, as follows:

- The default constructor
- `DataPortal_Create()`

This is illustrated in Figure 7-3.

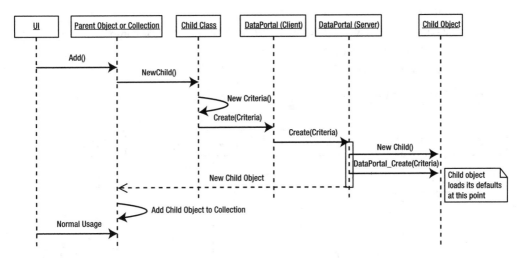

Figure 7-3. *Creating a child object using data access*

Note that in either of these cases, the UI code is the same: it calls the `Add()` method on the parent object, and then interacts with the parent's interface to get access to the newly added child object. The UI is entirely unaware of how the child object is created (and possibly loaded with default values).

Also note that the *parent* object is unaware of the details. All it does is call the factory method on the child class and receive a new child object in return. All the details about *how* the child object got loaded with default values are encapsulated within the child class.

Object Retrieval

Retrieving an existing object from the database is similar to the process of creating an object that requires default values from the database. Only a root object can be retrieved from the database directly by code in the user interface. Child objects are retrieved along with their parent root object, not independently.

Root Object Retrieval

To retrieve a root object, the UI code simply calls the `Shared` factory method on the class, providing the parameters that identify the object to be retrieved. The factory method calls `DataPortal.Fetch()`, which in turn creates the object and calls `DataPortal_Fetch()`, as follows:

1. The factory method is called.

2. The factory method calls `DataPortal.Fetch()` to get the business object.

3. The data portal uses its channel adapter and message router functionality as described in Chapter 4; the result is that the data portal creates a new instance of the business object.

4. The business object can do basic initialization in the constructor method.

5. The `DataPortal_Fetch()` method is called; this is where the business object implements data access code to retrieve the object's data from the database.

6. The business object is returned.

7. From the business object's perspective, two methods are called, as follows:

   - The default constructor
   - `DataPortal_Fetch()`

Figure 7-4 illustrates the process.

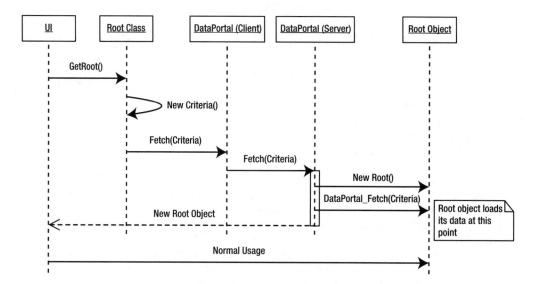

Figure 7-4. *Retrieving an existing root object*

It's important to note that the root object's `DataPortal_Fetch()` is responsible not only for loading the business object's data, but also for starting the process of loading the data for its child objects.

Chapter 6 implemented stored procedures to return the root object's data *and also all the child object data*—two result sets from a single stored procedure. This means that when the root object calls the stored procedure to retrieve its data, it will also get the data for its child objects, so it must cause those to be created as well.

The key thing to remember is that the data for the *entire* object, including its child objects, is retrieved when `DataPortal_Fetch()` is called. This avoids having to go back across the network to retrieve each child object's data individually. Though the root object gets the *data*, it's up to each child object to populate itself based on that data. Let's dive one level deeper and discuss how child objects load their data.

Child Object Retrieval

The retrieval of a child object is quite different from the retrieval of a root object, because the data portal isn't directly involved. Instead, as stated earlier, the root object's `DataPortal_Fetch()` method is responsible for loading not only the root object's data, but also the data for all child objects. It then calls methods on the child objects, passing the preloaded data as parameters so the child objects can load their fields with data. The sequence of events goes like this:

1. The root object's `DataPortal_Fetch()` creates the child *collection* using a `Shared` factory method on the collection class (scoped as `Friend`), and it passes a data reader object as a parameter.

2. The child collection implements a `Private` constructor to load its data. This method uses the data reader provided as a parameter.

3. The child collection's constructor loops through the records in the data reader, performing the following steps for each record:

   a. The child collection creates a child object by calling a factory method on the child class, passing the data reader as a parameter.

   b. The child object's factory method calls its own `Private` constructor, passing the data reader as a parameter, to load itself with data.

   c. The collection object adds the child object to its collection.

4. At the end of the data reader, the child collection and all child objects are fully populated.

Figure 7-5 is a sequence diagram that illustrates how this works. Note that this diagram occurs *during the process of loading the root object's data*. This means that this diagram is really an expansion of the previous sequence diagram for retrieving a root object!

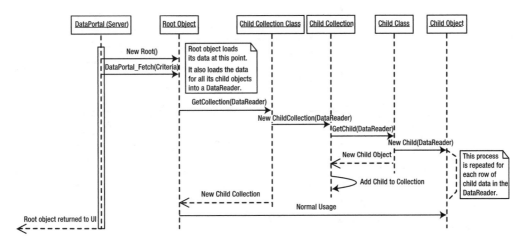

Figure 7-5. *Loading child objects with data*

Updating Editable Objects

For read-only objects, retrieval is the only data access concept required. Editable business objects and editable collections (those deriving from `BusinessBase` and `BusinessListBase`) support update, insert, and delete operations as well.

Adding and Editing Root Objects

After an object is created or retrieved, the user will work with the object, changing its values by interacting with the user interface. At some point, the user may click the OK or Save button, thereby triggering the process of updating the object into the database. The sequence of events at that point is as follows:

1. The UI calls the Save() method on the business object.

2. The Save() method calls DataPortal.Update().

3. DataPortal.Update() calls the DataPortal_Insert() or DataPortal_Update() method on the business object as appropriate; those methods contain the data access code needed to insert or update the data into the database.

4. During the insert or update process, the business object's data may change.

5. The updated business object is returned as a result of the Save() method.

6. From the business object's perspective, two methods are called:
    - Save()
    - Either DataPortal_Insert() or DataPortal_Update()

Figure 7-6 illustrates this process.

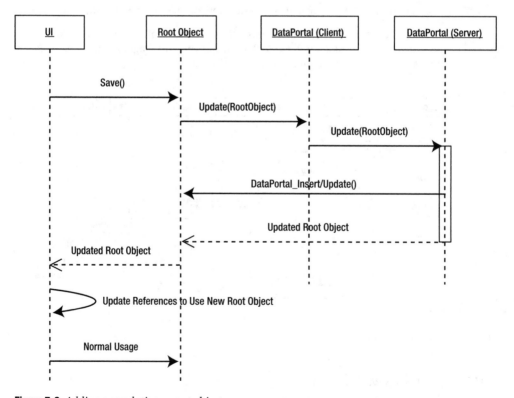

Figure 7-6. *Adding or updating a root object*

The Save() method is implemented in BusinessBase and BusinessListBase, and typically requires no change or customization. Remember that the framework's Save() method includes checks to ensure that objects can only be saved if IsValid and IsDirty are True. This helps to optimize data access by preventing the update of invalid or unchanged data.

■**Tip** If you don't like this behavior, your business class can override the framework's Save() method and replace that logic with other logic.

All the data access code that handles the saving of the object is located in DataPortal_Insert() or DataPortal_Update(). Recall that in Chapter 4 the data portal implementation included logic to check the object's IsNew and IsDeleted properties to properly route any update operation to the appropriate DataPortal_XYZ method. Deleting a root object will be discussed later.

■**Note** It's important to recall that when the server-side DataPortal is remote, the updated root object returned to the UI is a *new* object. The UI *must* update its references to use this new object in lieu of the original root object.

Note that the DataPortal_XYZ methods are responsible not only for saving the object's data, but also for starting the process of saving all the *child object* data. Calling the data portal does not save child objects; they are saved because their root parent object directly calls Friend-scoped Insert(), Update(), or DeleteSelf() methods on each child collection or object, thereby causing them to save their data.

Adding, Editing, and Deleting Child Objects

Child objects are inserted, updated, or deleted as part of the process of updating a root parent object. To support this concept, child collections implement a Friend method named Update(). Child objects within a collection implement Friend methods, named Insert(), Update(), and DeleteSelf(), that can be called by the collection during the update process. It is helpful for related root, child, and child collection classes to be placed in the same project (assembly) so that they can use Friend scope in this manner.

The sequence of events to add, edit, or delete a child object is as follows:

1. The root object's DataPortal_XYZ method calls the child collection's Update() method; the parent object is passed as a parameter so that child objects can use root object property values as needed (such as for foreign key values).

2. The child collection's Update() method loops through all the deleted child objects in the collection, calling each deleted object's DeleteSelf() method.

3. The child collection's Update() method loops through all its active child objects, calling each child object's Insert() or Update() method based on the child object's IsNew property value.

4. At this point, all the child object data has been inserted, updated, or deleted as required.

5. From the perspective of the child *collection* object, just one method is called, as follows:
   - Update()

6. From the perspective of each child object, one of three methods is called, as follows:
   - Insert()
   - Update()
   - DeleteSelf()

Figure 7-7 illustrates this process. Remember that this diagram is connected with the previous diagram showing the update of a root object. The events depicted in this diagram occur as a result of the root object's DataPortal_Insert() or DataPortal_Update() being called, as shown earlier in Figure 7-6.

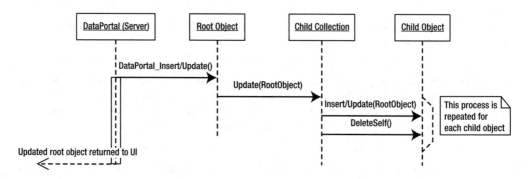

Figure 7-7. *Adding, updating, and deleting child objects in a collection*

The Insert() and Update() methods often accept parameters. Typically, the root object's primary key value is a required piece of data when saving a child object (since it would be a foreign key in the table), and so a reference to the root object is typically passed as a parameter to the collection's Update() method, and then to each child object's Insert() or Update() method.

Passing a reference to the root object is better than passing any specific property value, because it helps to decouple the root object from the child object. Using a reference means that the root object doesn't know or care what actual data is required by the child object during the update process—that information is encapsulated within the child class.

Also, when implementing transactions manually using ADO.NET, rather than System. Transactions or Enterprise Services, the ADO.NET transaction object will also need to be passed as a parameter so that each child object can update its data within the same transaction as the root object.

■**Tip** In most cases, the use of System.Transactions will provide the best trade-off between performance and simplicity of data access code.

Deleting Root Objects

While child objects are deleted within the context of the root object that's being updated, deletion of root objects is a bit different. Recall that the data portal was implemented to support both *immediate* and *deferred* deletion of a root object.

Immediate Deletion

Immediate deletion occurs when the UI code calls a Shared delete method on the business class, providing parameters that define the object to be deleted: typically, the same criteria that would be used to retrieve the object.

Most applications will use immediate deletion for root objects. The sequence of events flows like this:

1. The Shared delete method is called.

2. The Shared delete method calls DataPortal.Delete().

3. DataPortal.Delete() creates the business object using reflection.

4. DataPortal.Delete() calls the DataPortal_Delete() method on the business object, which contains the code needed to delete the object's data (and any related child data, and so on).

5. From the business object's perspective, two methods are called, as follows:

   • The default constructor

   • DataPortal_Delete()

Figure 7-8 illustrates the process of immediate deletion.

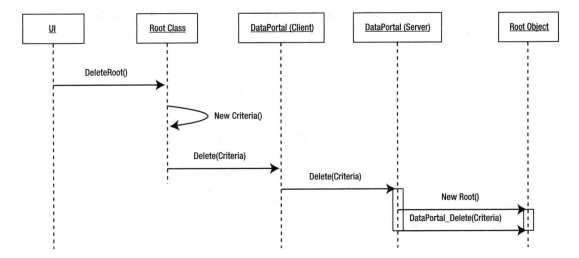

Figure 7-8. *Immediate deletion of a root object*

Since this causes the deletion of a root object, the delete process must also remove any data for child objects. This can be done through ADO.NET data access code, through a stored procedure, or by the database (if cascading deletes are set up on the relationships). In the example application, child data is deleted by the stored procedures created in Chapter 6.

Deferred Deletion

Deferred deletion occurs when the business object is loaded into memory and the UI calls a method on the object to mark it for deletion. Then when the Save() method is called, the object is deleted rather than being inserted or updated.

The sequence of events flows like this:

1. The object is loaded by the UI.

2. The UI calls a method to mark the object for deletion (that method must call MarkDeleted()).

3. The UI calls the object's Save() method.

4. The Save() method invokes the data portal just like it does to do an insert or update (as discussed earlier).

5. The data portal ultimately calls the object's DataPortal_DeleteSelf() method.

6. Typically, the DataPortal.DeleteSelf() method calls the object's DataPortal_Delete() method, which contains the code needed to delete the object's data (and any related child data, and so on).

7. From the business object's perspective, one method is called, as follows:

- DataPortal_DeleteSelf()

Figure 7-9 illustrates the process of deferred deletion. Note that this is a simplified diagram, since the complete process is analogous to adding or updating a root object as discussed earlier.

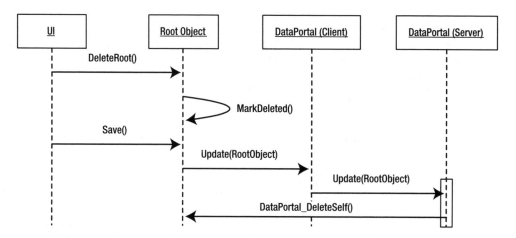

Figure 7-9. *Deferred deletion of a root object*

The CSLA .NET framework supports both deletion models to provide flexibility for the UI developer. It is up to the business object author to decide which model to support by implementing either a Shared or an instance delete method on the object.

Disposing and Finalizing Objects

Most business objects contain moderate amounts of data in their fields. For these, the default .NET default garbage collection behavior is fine. With that behavior, you don't know exactly when an object will be destroyed and its memory reclaimed. But that's almost always OK, because this is exactly what garbage collection is designed to do.

However, the default garbage collection behavior may be insufficient when objects hold onto "expensive" or unmanaged resources until they're destroyed. These resources include things like open database connections, open files on disk, synchronization objects, handles, and any other objects that already implement IDisposable. These are things that need to be released as soon as possible in order to prevent the application from wasting memory or blocking other users who might need to access a file or reuse a database connection. If business objects are written properly, most of these concerns should go away. Data access code should keep a database connection open for the shortest amount of time possible, and the same is true for any files the object might open on disk. However, there are cases in which business objects can legitimately contain an expensive resource—something like a multi-megabyte image in a field, perhaps.

Implementing IDisposable

In such cases, the business object should implement the IDisposable interface, which will allow the UI code to tell the business object to release its resources. This interface requires that the object implement a Dispose() method to actually release those resources:

```
<Serializable()> _
Public Class MyBusinessClass
  Inherits BusinessBase(Of MyBusinessClass)

  Implements IDisposable

  Private mDisposedValue As Boolean

  Protected Sub Dispose(ByVal disposing As Boolean)
    If Not mDisposedValue Then
      If disposing Then
        ' free unmanaged resources
      End If
    End If
    ' free shared unmanaged resources
    mDisposedValue = True
  End Sub

  Public Sub Dispose() Implements IDisposable.Dispose
    Dispose(True)
    GC.SuppressFinalize(Me)
  End Sub

  Protected Overrides Sub Finalize()
    Dispose(False)
  End Sub
End Class
```

The UI code can now call the object's Dispose() method (or employ a Using statement) when it has finished using the object, at which point the object will release its expensive resources.

Note, however, that if a business object is retrieved using a *remote* data portal configuration, the business object would be created and loaded on the server. It's then returned to the client as discussed in Chapter 4. The result, however, is that there's a copy left in memory on the server.

Because of this, there's no way to call the business object's Dispose() method on the server. To avoid this scenario, any time that the data portal may be configured to run outside of the client process, the business object designs *must* avoid any requirement for a Dispose() method. Happily, this is almost never an issue with a properly designed business object, since all database connections or open files should be closed in the same method from which they were opened.

■**Note** If you're calling a remote data portal, you must avoid object designs that require IDisposable. Alternatively, you can modify the SimpleDataPortal class to explicitly call Dispose() on your business objects on the server.

Business Class Structure

As you've seen, business objects follow the same sequence of events for creation, retrieval, and updates. Because of this, there's a structure and a set of features that are common to all of them. Although the structure and features are common, however, the actual code will vary for each business object. Due to the consistency in structure, however, there's great value in providing some foundations that make it easier for the business developer to know what needs to be done.

Also, there are differences between editable and read-only objects, and between root and child objects. After discussing the features common to all business objects, I'll create "templates" to illustrate the structure of each type of business object that you can create based on CSLA .NET.

Common Features

There are some common features or conventions that should be followed when coding any business classes that will inherit from the CSLA .NET base classes. These are as follows:

- `<Serializable()>` attribute
- Common regions
- `Private` default constructor
- `Criteria` class

Let's briefly discuss each of these requirements.

The Serializable Attribute

All business objects must be unanchored so that they can move across the network as needed. This means that they must be marked as serializable by using the `<Serializable()>` attribute, as shown here:

```
<Serializable()> _
Public Class MyBusinessClass

End Class
```

This is required for all business classes that inherit from any of the CSLA .NET base classes. It's also required for any objects that are referenced by business objects. If a business object references an object that isn't serializable, then you must be sure to mark its field with the `<NonSerialized()>` attribute to prevent the serialization process from attempting to serialize that object. If you don't do this, the result will be a runtime exception from the .NET Framework.

Common Regions

When writing code in VS .NET, the `#Region` directive can be used to place code into collapsible regions. This helps organize the code, and allows you to look only at the code pertaining to a specific type of functionality.

All business collection classes will have a common set of regions, as follows:

- *Factory Methods*
- *Data Access*

and so classes derived from `BusinessListBase` and `ReadOnlyListBase` will follow this basic structure:

```
<Serializable()> _
Public Class MyCollectionClass
  Inherits Csla.baseclass(Of MyCollectionClass, MyChildType)

  #Region " Factory Methods "

  #End Region

  #Region " Data Access "

  #End Region
End Class
```

All non-collection (editable and read-only) classes will have the following set of regions:

- *Business Methods*
- *Validation Rules*
- *Authorization Rules*
- *Factory Methods*
- *Data Access*

This means that the skeletal structure of a business object, with these regions, is as follows:

```
<Serializable()> _
Public Class MyBusinessClass
  Inherits Csla.baseclass(Of MyBusinessClass)

  #Region " Business Methods "

  #End Region

  #Region " Validation Rules "

  #End Region

  #Region " Authorization Rules "

  #End Region

  #Region " Factory Methods "

  #End Region

  #Region " Data Access "

  #End Region
End Class
```

Command objects that inherit from CommandBase will have the following regions:

- *Authorization Rules*
- *Client-side Code*
- *Factory Methods*
- *Server-side Code*

```
<Serializable()> _
Public Class MyCommandClass
  Inherits Csla.CommandBase

  #Region " Authorization Rules "

  #End Region

  #Region " Client-side Code "

  #End Region

  #Region " Factory Methods "

  #End Region

  #Region " Server-side Code "

  #End Region
End Class
```

And name/value list objects that inherit from NameValueListBase will typically have the following regions:

- *Factory Methods*
- *Data Access*

```
<Serializable()> _
Public Class MyListClass
  Inherits Csla.NameValueListBase(Of KeyType, ValueType)

  #Region " Factory Methods "

  #End Region

  #Region " Data Access "

  #End Region
End Class
```

The *Business Methods* region will contain the methods that are used by UI code (or other client code) to interact with the business object. This includes any properties that allow retrieval or changing of values in the object, as well as methods that operate on the object's data to perform business processing.

The *Validation Rules* region will contain the AddBusinessRules() method, and any custom rule methods required by the object.

The *Authorization Rules* region will contain the AddAuthorizationRules() method. It will also contain a standard set of Shared methods indicating whether the current user is authorized to get, add, save, or delete this type of business object.

The *Factory Methods* region will contain the Shared factory methods to create or retrieve the object, along with the Shared delete method (if the object is an editable root object). It will also contain the default constructor for the class, which must be scoped as non-Public (i.e., Private or Protected) to force the use of the factory methods when creating the business object.

The *Data Access* region will contain the DataPortal_XYZ methods. It will also contain the Criteria class used to create, retrieve, or delete the object.

Your business objects may require other code that doesn't fit neatly into these regions, and you should feel free to add extra regions if needed. But these regions cover the vast majority of code required by typical business objects, and in most cases they're all you'll need.

Private Default Constructor

All business objects will be implemented to make use of the class-in-charge scheme discussed in Chapter 1. Factory methods are used in lieu of the New keyword, which means that it's best to prevent the use of New, thereby forcing the UI developer to use the factory methods instead.

The data portal mechanism, as implemented in Chapter 4, requires business classes to include a default constructor. As I reviewed the create, fetch, update, and delete processes for each type of object earlier in this chapter, each sequence diagram showed how the server-side data portal created an instance of the business object. This is done using a technique that requires a default constructor.

By making the default constructor Private or Protected (and by not creating other Public constructors), you ensure that UI code must use the factory methods to get an instance of any object:

```
' ...
#Region " Factory Methods "

Private Sub New()
  ' require use of factory methods
End Sub

#End Region
' ...
```

This constructor both prevents the New keyword from being called by code outside this class and provides the data portal with the ability to create the object via reflection. Your classes might also include other constructors, but this one is required for all objects.

Criteria Class

Root objects must have a Criteria class. Also, any child object that loads its own default values from the database can have an optional Criteria class if needed.

Criteria classes can be nested classes within the business class or they can inherit from Csla. CriteriaBase. In most cases, it is simplest to nest the Criteria class within the business class. The Csla.CriteriaBase approach is intended primarily for use with code-generation tools.

The Criteria class simply contains the data that's required to identify the specific object to be retrieved or the default data to be loaded. Since it's passed by value to the data portal, this class must be marked as <Serializable()>.

Tip Technically, the Criteria class can have *any* name, as long as it's <Serializable()>, and is either nested in the business class or inherits from CriteriaBase. Some objects may have more than one criteria class, each one defining a different set of criteria that can be used to retrieve the object.

Since this class is no more than a way to ferry data to the data portal, it doesn't need to be fancy. Typically, it's implemented with a constructor to make it easier to create and populate the object all at once. For example, here's a Criteria class that includes an EmployeeID field:

```
' ...
#Region " Data Access "

<Serializable()> _
Private Class Criteria
  Private mEmployeeId As String
  Public ReadOnly Property EmployeeId() As String
    Get
      Return mEmployeeId
    End Get
  End Property

  Public Sub New(ByVal employeeId As String)
    mEmployeeId = employeeId
  End Sub
End Class
' ...
```

An equivalent criteria class can be created by subclassing CriteriaBase (only the changed lines are in bold):

```
<Serializable()> _
Public Class MyBusinessClass
  Inherits Csla.baseclass(Of MyBusinessClass)

  ' ...
  #Region " Data Access "

  <Serializable()> _
  Protected Class Criteria
    Inherits Csla.CriteriaBase
    Private mEmployeeId As String
    Public ReadOnly Property EmployeeId() As String
      Get
        Return mEmployeeId
      End Get
    End Class

    Public Sub New(ByVal employeeId As String)
      MyBase.New(GetType(MyBusinessClass))
      mEmployeeId = employeeId
    End Sub
  End Class
  ' ...
```

All Criteria classes are constructed using one of these two schemes. Nested criteria classes are scoped as Private because they are only needed within the context of the business class. The CriteriaBase class is typically used by code-generation tools, in which case the class is typically Protected in scope so that it is available to subclasses as well.

Note Code generation is outside the scope of this book. For good information on code generation, including the rationale behind CriteriaBase, please refer to Kathleen Dollard's book, *Code Generation in Microsoft .NET* (Apress, 2004).

Even though the Criteria object is passed through the data portal, it's passed as a type Object, so the DataPortal code doesn't need access to the object's code. This is ideal, because it means that UI developers, or other business object developers, won't see the Criteria class, thus improving the business object's overall encapsulation.

The Criteria classes shown thus far include a constructor that accepts the criteria data value. This is done to simplify the code that will go into the Shared factory methods. Rather than forcing the business developer to create a Criteria object and then load its values, this constructor allows the Criteria object to be created and initialized in a single statement. In many cases, this means that a Shared factory method will contain just one line of code! For instance:

```
Public Shared Function GetProject(ByVal id As Guid) As Project
  Return DataPortal.Fetch(Of Project)(New Criteria(id))
End Sub
```

Many Criteria classes will contain a single value (as in the examples here), but they can be more complex, providing for more control over the selection of the object to be retrieved. If you have a root collection in which you're directly retrieving a collection of child objects, the Criteria class may not define a single object, but rather act as a search filter that returns the collection populated with all matching child objects.

In other cases, an object may have no criteria data at all. In that case, a Criteria class is still required, but it would be empty:

```
<Serializable()> _
Private Class Criteria

End Class
```

The factory methods can still create an instance of this Criteria class and pass it to the data portal. In this case, the Criteria object doesn't provide any criteria data beyond the type of the business object to be retrieved. This is typically used when retrieving a root collection object for which you want all the child objects in the database returned at all times. I'll use this technique to create the ProjectList and ResourceList collection classes in Chapter 8.

Class Structures

At this point in the chapter, I've walked through the life cycle of typical business objects, so you know the sequence of events that will occur as they are created, retrieved, updated, and deleted. I've also discussed the code concepts and structures that are common to all business classes. Now let's dive in and look at the specific coding structure for each type of business class that you can create based on the CSLA .NET framework. These include the following:

- Editable root
- Editable child
- Editable, "switchable" (i.e., root or child) object
- Editable root collection
- Editable child collection
- Read-only object
- Read-only collection
- Command object
- Name/value list

For each of these object types, I'll create the basic starting code that belongs in the class. In a sense, these are the templates from which business classes can be built.

■**Tip** You can use this code to create either snippets or class templates for use in Visual Studio. The `Csla\` `Snippets` subdirectory in the code download (available from www.apress.com) contains a set of sample snippets you may find valuable.

Editable Root Business Objects

The most common type of object will be the editable root business object, since any object-oriented system based on CSLA .NET will typically have at least one root business object or root collection. (Examples of this type of object include the `Project` and `Resource` objects discussed in Chapter 8.) These objects often contain collections of child objects, as well as their own object-specific data.

As well as being common, an editable object that's also a root object is the most complex object type, so its code template covers all the possible code regions. The basic structure for an editable root object, with example or template code in each region, is as follows:

```vb
<Serializable()> _
Public Class EditableRoot
  Inherits BusinessBase(Of EditableRoot)

#Region " Business Methods "

  ' TODO: add your own fields, properties and methods
  Private mId As Integer

  Public Property Id() As Integer
    Get
      CanReadProperty(True)
      Return mId
    End Get
    Set(ByVal value As Integer)
      CanWriteProperty(True)
      If mId <> value Then
        mId = value
        PropertyHasChanged()
      End If
    End Set
  End Property

  Protected Overrides Function GetIdValue() As Object
    Return mId
  End Function

#End Region

#Region " Validation Rules "

  Protected Overrides Sub AddBusinessRules()

    ' TODO: add validation rules
    'ValidationRules.AddRule(Nothing, "")

  End Sub
```

```vb
#End Region

#Region " Authorization Rules "

  Protected Overrides Sub AddAuthorizationRules()

    ' TODO: add authorization rules
    'AuthorizationRules.AllowWrite("", "")

  End Sub

  Public Shared Function CanAddObject() As Boolean
    Return ApplicationContext.User.IsInRole("")
  End Function

  Public Shared Function CanGetObject() As Boolean
    Return ApplicationContext.User.IsInRole("")
  End Function

  Public Shared Function CanEditObject() As Boolean
    Return ApplicationContext.User.IsInRole("")
  End Function

  Public Shared Function CanDeleteObject() As Boolean
    Return ApplicationContext.User.IsInRole("")
  End Function

#End Region

#Region " Factory Methods "

  Public Shared Function NewEditableRoot() As EditableRoot
    Return DataPortal.Create(Of EditableRoot)()
  End Function

  Public Shared Function GetEditableRoot(ByVal id As Integer) As EditableRoot
    Return DataPortal.Create(Of EditableRoot)(New Criteria(id))
  End Function

  Public Shared Sub DeleteEditableRoot(ByVal id As Integer)
    DataPortal.Delete(New Criteria(id))
  End Sub

  Private Sub New()
    ' require use of factory methods
  End Sub

#End Region

#Region " Data Access "

  <Serializable()> _
  Private Class Criteria
    Private mId As Integer
    Public ReadOnly Property Id() As Integer
      Get
        Return mId
```

```vb
      End Get
    End Property
    Public Sub New(ByVal id As Integer)
      mId = id
    End Sub
  End Class

  Private Overloads Sub DataPortal_Create(ByVal criteria As Criteria)
    ' load default values
  End Sub

  Private Overloads Sub DataPortal_Fetch(ByVal criteria As Criteria)
    ' load values
  End Sub

  Protected Overrides Sub DataPortal_Insert()
    ' insert values
  End Sub

  Protected Overrides Sub DataPortal_Update()
    ' update values
  End Sub

  Protected Overrides Sub DataPortal_DeleteSelf()
    DataPortal_Delete(New Criteria(mId))
  End Sub

  Private Overloads Sub DataPortal_Delete(ByVal criteria As Criteria)
    ' delete values
  End Sub

#End Region

End Class
```

You must define the class, including making it serializable, giving it a name, and having it inherit from BusinessBase.

The *Business Methods* region includes all member or instance field declarations, along with any business-specific properties and methods. These properties and methods typically interact with the instance fields, performing calculations and other manipulation of the data based on the business logic.

Notice the GetIdValue() method, which is required when inheriting from BusinessBase. This method should return a unique identifying value for the object. The value is directly returned by the default ToString() method in BusinessBase, and is used in the implementation of the Equals() and GetHashCode() methods as well. For details, refer to Chapter 3.

The *Validation Rules* region, at a minimum, overrides the AddBusinessRules() method. In this method, you call ValidationRules.AddRule() to associate rule methods with properties. This region may also include custom rule methods for rules that aren't already available in Csla.Validation.CommonRules or in your own library of rule methods.

The *Authorization Rules* region overrides the AddAuthorizationRules() method and implements a set of Shared authorization methods.

The AddAuthorizationRules() method should include calls to methods on the AuthorizationRules object: AllowRead(), AllowWrite(), DenyRead(), and DenyWrite(). Each one associates a property with a list of roles that are to be allowed read and write access to that property.

The Shared authorization methods are CanGetObject(), CanAddObject(), CanEditObject(), and CanDeleteObject(). These methods should check the current user's roles to determine whether the user is in a role that allows or denies the particular operation. The purpose of these methods is so the UI developer can easily determine whether the current user can get, add, update, or delete this type of object. That way, the UI can enable, disable, or hide controls to provide appropriate visual cues to the end user.

Since these are Shared methods, there's no way to make them part of the BusinessBase class, and they must be directly declared and implemented in each business class.

In the *Factory Methods* region, there are Shared factory methods to create, retrieve, and delete the object. Of course, these are just examples that must be changed as appropriate. The parameters accepted and Criteria object used must be tailored to match the identifying criteria for your particular business object.

Finally, the *Data Access* region includes the Criteria class and the DataPortal_XYZ methods. These methods must include the code to load defaults, retrieve object data, update object data, and delete object data, as appropriate. In most cases, this will be done through ADO.NET, but this code could just as easily be implemented to read or write to an XML file, call a web service, or use any other data store you can imagine.

The <RunLocal()> attribute is for objects that *do not* load default values from the database when they are created. The use of the <RunLocal()> attribute on DataPortal_Create() is optional, and is used to force the data portal to always run the method locally. When this attribute is used, the DataPortal_Create() method should *not* access the database, because it may not be running in a physical location where the database is available.

The <Transactional()> attributes on the methods that insert, update, or delete data specify that those methods should run within a System.Transactions transactional context. You may opt instead to use the TransactionTypes.EnterpriseServices setting to run within a COM+ distributed transaction, or TransactionTypes.Manual to handle your own transactions using ADO.NET.

■**Tip** Many organizations use an abstract, metadata-driven data access layer. In environments like this, the business objects don't use ADO.NET directly. This works fine with CSLA .NET, since the data access code in the DataPortal_XYZ methods can interact with an abstract data access layer just as easily as it can interact with ADO.NET directly.

The key thing to note about this code template is that there's very little code in the class that's not related to the business requirements. Most of the code implements business properties, validation, and authorization rules or data access. The bulk of the nonbusiness code (code not specific to your business problem) is already implemented in the CSLA .NET framework.

Immediate or Deferred Deletion

As implemented in the template, the UI developer can delete the object by calling the Shared delete method and providing the criteria to identify the object to be deleted. Another option is to implement *deferred* deletion, whereby the object must be retrieved, marked as deleted, and then updated in order for it to be deleted. The object's data is then deleted as part of the update process.

To support deferred deletion, simply remove the Shared delete method:

```
'Public Shared Sub DeleteEditableRoot(ByVal id As Integer)
'   DataPortal.Delete(New Criteria(id))
'End Sub
```

Then, the only way to delete the object is by calling the Delete() method on an instance of the object and updating that object to the database by calling Save().

Editable Child Business Objects

Most applications will have some editable child objects, or even grandchild objects. Examples of these include the ProjectResource and ResourceAssignment objects. In many cases, the child objects are contained within a child collection object, which I'll discuss later. In other cases, the child object might be referenced directly by the parent object. Either way, the basic structure of a child object is the same; in some ways, this template is very similar to the editable root:

```vb
<Serializable()> _
Public Class EditableChild
  Inherits BusinessBase(Of EditableChild)

#Region " Business Methods "

  ' TODO: add your own fields, properties and methods
  Private mId As Integer

  Public Property Id() As Integer
    Get
      CanReadProperty(True)
      Return mId
    End Get
    Set(ByVal value As Integer)
      CanWriteProperty(True)
      If mId <> value Then
        mId = value
        PropertyHasChanged()
      End If
    End Set
  End Property

  Protected Overrides Function GetIdValue() As Object
    Return mId
  End Function

#End Region

#Region " Validation Rules "

  Protected Overrides Sub AddBusinessRules()
    ' TODO: add validation rules
    'ValidationRules.AddRule(Nothing, "")
  End Sub

#End Region

#Region " Authorization Rules "

  Protected Overrides Sub AddAuthorizationRules()
    ' TODO: add authorization rules
    'AuthorizationRules.AllowWrite("", "")
  End Sub

#End Region

#Region " Factory Methods "
```

```vbnet
  Friend Shared Function NewEditableChild() As EditableChild
    ' TODO: change to use New keyword if not loading defaults
    'Return New EditableChild
    Return DataPortal.Create(Of EditableChild)()
  End Function

  Friend Shared Function GetEditableChild( _
    ByVal dr As SqlDataReader) As EditableChild
    Return New EditableChild(dr)
  End Function

  Private Sub New()
    MarkAsChild()
  End Sub

  Private Sub New(ByVal dr As SqlDataReader)
    MarkAsChild()
    Fetch(dr)
  End Sub

#End Region

#Region " Data Access "

  Protected Overrides Sub DataPortal_Create(ByVal criteria As Object)
    ' TODO: load default values, or remove method
  End Sub

  Private Sub Fetch(ByVal dr As SqlDataReader)
    ' TODO: load values
    MarkOld()
  End Sub

  Friend Sub Insert(ByVal parent as Object)
    ' TODO: insert values
    MarkOld()
  End Sub

  Friend Sub Update(ByVal parent as Object)
    ' TODO: update values
    MarkOld()
  End Sub

  Friend Sub DeleteSelf()
    ' TODO: delete values
    MarkNew()
  End Sub

#End Region

End Class
```

As with all business classes, this one is serializable and inherits from a CSLA .NET base class. The fact that it is a child object is specified by the MarkAsChild() method calls in each constructor within the object.

The *Business Methods* region is the same as with a root object: it simply implements the properties and methods required by the business rules. Similarly, the *Validation Rules* region is the same as with a root object.

The *Authorization Rules* region is simpler, as it only implements the AddAuthorizationRules() method. Control over retrieving, adding, updating, and deleting child objects is controlled by the parent object or collection, so no Shared methods are needed here for that purpose.

The *Factory Methods* region is a bit different. The factory methods are Friend rather than Public, as they should only be called by the parent object, not by the UI code. Also, there's no need for a Shared delete method because BusinessBase implements a DeleteChild() method that is automatically called by BusinessListBase when the child is removed from a collection.

Notice that the NewEditableChild() method invokes the data portal to create the child object. This allows the child object to load itself with default values from the database when it is created. I'll discuss an alternative approach that avoids using the database shortly.

The GetEditableChild() method uses the New keyword to create an instance of the child object. See how it accepts a data reader as a parameter and passes it to the constructor. The idea is that the parent object will have already retrieved the necessary data from the database, and is providing it to the child object through this parameter. That parameterized constructor then calls a Fetch() method in the *Data Access* region where the object loads its data.

If you are using a data store other than a relational database, the data reader parameter would be replaced by some other type of object. For instance, if the object's data is being loaded from an XML document, the parameter would likely be an XmlNode that contains the child object's data.

The biggest difference from a root object comes in the *Data Access* region. The DataPortal_Create() method is implemented to support the loading of default values from the database on the creation of a new child object, but no other DataPortal_XYZ methods are implemented.

Instead, there's a Private Fetch() method to load the object with data, and Friend methods named Insert(), Update(), and DeleteSelf() to handle insert, update, and delete operations. These mirror the functionality of the DataPortal_XYZ methods, but they are called by the parent object rather than by the data portal.

Notice that Insert() and Update() both accept a reference to the parent object as a parameter. The assumption is that any child object will need data from the parent while being inserted or updated into the database. Most often, the parent contains a foreign key value required by the child object during data access.

Note Typically, the parent parameter will be strongly typed, based on the class of the parent object itself.

As an example, the ProjectResource child object will need the Id property from its parent Project object so that it can store it as a foreign key in the database. By getting a reference to its parent Project object, the ProjectResource gains access to that value as needed.

The Fetch(), Insert(), and Update() methods all call MarkOld() when they are done, because the object's data in memory matches that in the database at those points, so the object is neither new nor dirty. The DeleteSelf() method calls MarkNew() as it completes, because the object's primary key value is *not* in the database at that point, so the object qualifies as a new object.

Object Creation Without Defaults

As implemented, the template uses DataPortal.Create() to load the child object with default values from the database. As discussed earlier, if the object doesn't need to load default values from the database, the code can be implemented more efficiently by changing the Shared factory method to create the child object directly:

```
Friend Shared Function NewEditableChild() As EditableChild
  Return New EditableChild
End Function
```

Then the DataPortal_Create() method can be removed, since it won't be used. The default constructor is then used to set any default values that are hard-coded into the class.

Switchable Objects

It's possible that some classes must be instantiated as root objects on some occasions and as child objects on others. This can be handled by conditionally calling MarkAsChild(), based on how the object is being created.

■**Note** In most cases, the need for a switchable object indicates a flawed object model. While there are exceptions for which this makes sense, you should carefully examine your object model to see if there's a simpler solution before implementing a switchable object.

Conditionally calling MarkAsChild() typically *can't* be done in the default constructor, because there's no way to determine whether the object is being created as a root or a child object at that point. Instead, you need to go back to your object's life cycle to see where you *can* make this decision. In fact, since the default is for an object to be a root object, all you need to do is determine the paths by which a *child* object can be created, and make sure to call MarkAsChild() only in those cases.

The template for creating a "switchable" object is the same as the editable root template, with the following exceptions:

- Dual criteria objects
- Dual create and fetch factory methods
- Dual create and fetch data access methods

Let's discuss each change in turn.

Dual Criteria Classes

The object's criteria must now include a flag to indicate whether the object is being created as a root or a child object (this is in addition to any object-specific criteria fields in this class). This can be done either by adding an actual flag field to the Criteria class or by creating a second criteria class. I prefer the second approach as it makes the code simpler overall.

Remember that for a child object, the criteria class is only used for the create operation, and so it typically doesn't need any actual criteria data. The result is that there are two criteria classes; for example:

```
<Serializable()> _
Private Class RootCriteria
  Private mId As Integer
  Public ReadOnly Property Id() As Integer
    Get
      Return mId
    End Get
  End Property
```

```
    Public Sub New(ByVal id As Integer)
      mId = id
    End Sub

    Public Sub New()

    End Sub
  End Class

  <Serializable()> _
  Private Class ChildCriteria

  End Class
```

These two classes will be used to differentiate the way the object should be created.

Dual Factory Methods

Instead of single factory methods to create and retrieve the object, there will be two methods for each operation: one Public, the other Friend.

```
    Public Shared Function NewSwitchable() As SwitchableObject
      Return DataPortal.Create(Of SwitchableObject)(New RootCriteria())
    End Function

    Friend Shared Function NewSwitchableChild() As SwitchableObject
      Return DataPortal.Create(Of SwitchableObject)(New ChildCriteria())
    End Function

    Public Shared Function GetSwitchableRoot( _
      ByVal id As Integer) As SwitchableObject

      Return DataPortal.Create(Of SwitchableObject)(New RootCriteria(id))
    End Function

    Friend Shared Function GetSwitchableChild( _
      ByVal dr As SqlDataReader) As SwitchableObject

      Return New SwitchableObject(dr)
    End Function
```

Notice how the NewSwitchable() methods are each designed. The Public version (used to create a root object) uses the RootCriteria object, while the Friend version (called by a parent object to create a child object) uses ChildCriteria. The DataPortal_Create() methods, which follow, are called based on the type of the criteria object.

The two GetSwitchable() methods are even more different. The Public one is called by UI code to retrieve a root object. In this case, the data portal is called to retrieve the object based on the supplied criteria. The Friend one follows the pattern for child objects, accepting a data reader from the parent object and passing it along to a Private constructor, which in turn calls a Private Fetch() method.

Dual Data Access Methods

The data access methods that handle create and fetch operations are different for a root and child object. Because of this, these methods are duplicated in a switchable object. In most cases, they can delegate to a shared implementation that is private to the class. For instance:

```
Private Overloads Sub DataPortal_Create(ByVal criteria As RootCriteria)
  DoCreate()
End Sub

Private Overloads Sub DataPortal_Create(ByVal criteria As ChildCriteria)
  MarkAsChild()
  DoCreate()
End Sub

Private Sub DoCreate()
  ' load default values from database here
End Sub
```

Notice how the overload of `DataPortal_Create()` that accepts a `ChildCriteria` object calls `MarkAsChild()`, while the other does not. This ensures that the object is marked as a child object when appropriate.

Similarly, the data-retrieval operations are duplicated:

```
Private Overloads Sub DataPortal_Fetch(ByVal criteria As RootCriteria)
  ' TODO: create data reader to load values
  Using dr As SqlDataReader = Nothing
    DoFetch(dr)
  End Using
End Sub

Private Sub Fetch(ByVal dr As SqlDataReader)
  MarkAsChild()
  DoFetch(dr)
End Sub

Private Sub DoFetch(ByVal dr As SqlDataReader)
  ' TODO: load values
End Sub
```

If the object is being loaded from the UI, then it is treated as a root object and `DataPortal_Fetch()` is called, passing in appropriate criteria. This method opens the database, and sets up and executes a database command object to get back a data reader. That data reader is then passed to a central `DoFetch()` helper method to copy the data from the data reader into the object's fields.

On the other hand, if the object is being loaded from a parent object as a child, then its parameterized constructor is called, which in turn calls the `Fetch()` method. This method calls `MarkAsChild()` to mark the object as a child, and then the `DoFetch()` helper is called to copy the data from the data reader into the object's fields.

Object Creation Without Defaults

When creating the object using the `New` keyword instead of calling `DataPortal.Create()`, the `Friend` factory method can directly call `MarkAsChild()`, as shown here:

```
Friend Shared Function NewSwitchableChild() As SwitchableObject
  Dim obj As New SwitchableObject
  obj.MarkAsChild()
  Return obj
End Function
```

From the parent object's perspective, there's no difference—it just calls the factory method; but this approach is faster because it doesn't load default values from the database.

Editable Root Collection

At times, applications need to retrieve a collection of child objects directly. To do this, you need to create a root collection object. For instance, the application may have a Windows Forms UI consisting of a DataGridView control that displays a collection of Contact objects. If the root object is a collection of child Contact objects, the UI developer can simply bind the collection to the DataGridView, and the user can do in-place editing of the objects within the grid.

This approach means that all the child objects are handled as a single unit in terms of data access. They are loaded into the collection to start with, so the user can interact with all of them, and then save them all at once when all edits are complete. This is only subtly different from having a regular root object that has a collection of child objects. Figure 7-10 shows the regular root object approach on the left and the collection root object approach on the right.

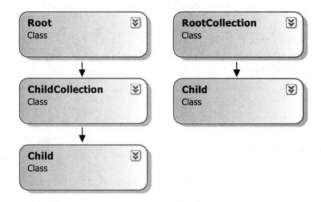

Figure 7-10. *Comparing simple root objects (left) and collection root objects (right)*

This approach isn't recommended when there are large numbers of potential child objects, because the retrieval process can become too slow, but it can be very useful in cases where you can specify criteria to limit the number of objects returned. To create an editable root collection object, use a template like this:

```
<Serializable()> _
Public Class EditableRootList
  Inherits BusinessListBase(Of EditableRootList, EditableChild)

#Region " Authorization Rules "

  Public Shared Function CanAddObject() As Boolean
    ' TODO: customize to check user role
    Return ApplicationContext.User.IsInRole("")
  End Function

  Public Shared Function CanGetObject() As Boolean
    ' TODO: customize to check user role
    Return ApplicationContext.User.IsInRole("")
  End Function

  Public Shared Function CanEditObject() As Boolean
    ' TODO: customize to check user role
    Return ApplicationContext.User.IsInRole("")
  End Function
```

```vb
  Public Shared Function CanDeleteObject() As Boolean
    ' TODO: customize to check user role
    Return ApplicationContext.User.IsInRole("")
  End Function

#End Region

#Region " Factory Methods "

  Public Shared Function NewEditableRootList() As EditableRootList
    Return New EditableRootList()
  End Function

  Public Shared Function GetEditableRootList(ByVal id As Integer) As EditableRootList
    Return DataPortal.Fetch(Of EditableRootList)(New Criteria(id))
  End Function

  Private Sub New()
    ' require use of factory methods
  End Sub

#End Region

#Region " Data Access "

  <Serializable()> _
  Private Class Criteria
    Private mId As Integer
    Public ReadOnly Property Id() As Integer
      Get
        Return mId
      End Get
    End Property
    Public Sub New(ByVal id As Integer)
      mId = id
    End Sub
  End Class

  Private Overloads Sub DataPortal_Fetch(ByVal criteria As Criteria)

    ' TODO: load values
    RaiseListChangedEvents = False
    Using dr As SqlDataReader = Nothing
      While dr.Read
        Add(EditableChild.GetEditableChild(dr))
      End While
    End Using
    RaiseListChangedEvents = True

  End Sub

  Protected Overrides Sub DataPortal_Update()

    RaiseListChangedEvents = False
    For Each item As EditableChild In DeletedList
      item.DeleteSelf()
    Next
    DeletedList.Clear()
```

```
    For Each item As EditableChild In Me
      If item.IsNew Then
        item.Insert(Me)

      Else
        item.Update(Me)
      End If
    Next
    RaiseListChangedEvents = True

  End Sub

#End Region

End Class
```

The *Authorization Rules* region contains the standard `Shared` methods discussed earlier for editable root objects. Since collection objects don't have detailed properties, there's no need or support for the `AddAuthorizationRules()` method.

The *Factory Methods* region implements factory methods to create, retrieve, and (optionally) delete the collection. The create method simply uses the `New` keyword to create an instance of the collection. There's no need to load default values for the collection itself. The retrieve and delete methods rely on the data portal to do much of the work, ultimately delegating the call to the appropriate `DataPortal_XYZ` method.

In the *Data Access* region, the `DataPortal_Fetch()` method is responsible for getting the data from the database, typically via a data reader. It then calls the `Shared` factory method of the child class for each row in the data reader, thereby allowing each child object to load its data. The `Shared` factory method in the child class calls its own `Private` constructor to actually load the data from the data reader.

The `DataPortal_Update()` method must loop through all the child objects contained in the deleted object collection, calling each object's `DeleteSelf()` method in turn. An alternative is to have the collection object dynamically generate a SQL statement to delete all the items in the `DeleteList` with a single call. The specific implementation is up to the business developer and may vary depending on the database design.

Once the child objects have been deleted from the database, that list is cleared. Then the active child objects are either inserted or updated based on their `IsNew` property value.

■Note It's critical that the *deleted* child objects be processed first.

It's quite possible for the user to delete a child object from the collection, and then add a new child object *with the same primary key value*. This means that the collection will have the original child object marked as deleted in the list of deleted child objects, and the new child object in the list of active objects. This new object will have its `IsNew` property set to `True` because it's a new object. If the original child object isn't deleted first, the insertion of the new child object will fail.

Thus, the code first processes the list of deleted child objects, and then moves on to process the list of active child objects.

Both the `DataPortal_Fetch()` and `DataPortal_Update()` methods set the `RaiseListChangedEvents` property to `False` before changing the collection, and then restore it to `True` once the operation is complete. Setting this property to `False` tells the base `BindingList(Of T)` class to stop raising the `ListChanged` event. When doing batches of updates or changes to a collection, this can increase performance.

Editable Child Collection

The most common type of collection is one that is contained within a parent object to manage a collection of child objects for that parent; like ProjectResources and ResourceAssignments in the sample application.

■Tip Note that the parent object here might be a root object, or it might be a child itself—child objects can be nested, if that's what the business object model requires. In other words, this concept supports not only root-child, but also child-grandchild and grandchild-to-great-grandchild relationships.

A child collection class inherits from BusinessListBase and calls MarkAsChild() during its creation process to indicate that it's operating in child mode. This also means that it won't be directly retrieved or updated by the DataPortal, but instead will be retrieved or updated by its parent object:

```
<Serializable()> _
Public Class EditableChildList
  Inherits BusinessListBase(Of EditableChildList, EditableChild)

#Region " Factory Methods "

  Friend Shared Function NewEditableChildList() As EditableChildList
    Return New EditableChildList
  End Function

  Friend Shared Function GetEditableChildList( _
    ByVal dr As SqlDataReader) As EditableChildList

    Return New EditableChildList(dr)
  End Function

  Private Sub New()
    MarkAsChild()
  End Sub

  Private Sub New(ByVal dr As SqlDataReader)
    MarkAsChild()
    Fetch(dr)
  End Sub

#End Region

#Region " Data Access "

  Private Sub Fetch(ByVal dr As SqlDataReader)

    RaiseListChangedEvents = False
    While dr.Read
      Add(EditableChild.GetEditableChild(dr))
    End While
    RaiseListChangedEvents = True

  End Sub

  Friend Sub Update(ByVal parent As Object)
```

```
RaiseListChangedEvents = False
For Each item As EditableChild In DeletedList
  item.DeleteSelf()
Next
DeletedList.Clear()

For Each item As EditableChild In Me
  If item.IsNew Then
    item.Insert(parent)

  Else
    item.Update(parent)
  End If
Next
RaiseListChangedEvents = True

End Sub

#End Region

End Class
```

As you can see, this code is very similar to a root collection in structure. The differences start with the factory methods. Since only a parent object can create or fetch an instance of this class, the Shared factory methods are scoped as Friend. The Shared method to create an object simply returns a new collection object. As with the EditableChild template, the constructor calls MarkAsChild() to indicate that this is a child object.

Likewise, the Shared method to load the child collection with data creates a new collection object and then calls a parameterized constructor just like in the EditableChild template. That constructor calls a Fetch() method to load the data.

The Update() method is identical to the DataPortal_Update() method in the EditableRootList. It loops through the list of deleted child objects, calling their DeleteSelf() methods, and then loops through the active child objects, calling Insert() or Update() as appropriate.

Notice, however, that the Update() method accepts a reference to the parent object as a parameter, and this value is provided to the child objects' Insert() and Update() methods. As discussed earlier, this allows the child objects to use data from the parent object as needed for things like foreign key values and so forth.

Read-Only Business Objects

Sometimes, an application may need an object that provides data in a read-only fashion. For a read-only list of data, there's ReadOnlyListBase; but if the requirement is for a single object containing read-only data, it should inherit from ReadOnlyBase. This is one of the simplest types of object to create, since it does nothing more than retrieve and return data, as shown here:

```
<Serializable()> _
Public Class ReadOnlyRoot
  Inherits ReadOnlyBase(Of ReadOnlyRoot)

#Region " Business Methods "

  Private mId As Integer
```

```vb
  Public ReadOnly Property Id() As Integer
    Get
      CanReadProperty(True)
      Return mId
    End Get
  End Property

  Protected Overrides Function GetIdValue() As Object

    Return mId

  End Function

#End Region

#Region " Authorization Rules "

  Protected Overrides Sub AddAuthorizationRules()

    ' TODO: add authorization rules
    'AuthorizationRules.AllowRead("", "")

  End Sub

  Public Shared Function CanGetObject() As Boolean
    ' TODO: customize to check user role
    'Return ApplicationContext.User.IsInRole("")
    Return True
  End Function

#End Region

#Region " Factory Methods "

  Public Shared Function GetReadOnlyRoot(ByVal id As Integer) As ReadOnlyRoot
    Return DataPortal.Create(Of ReadOnlyRoot)(New Criteria(id))
  End Function

  Private Sub New()
    ' require use of factory methods
  End Sub

#End Region

#Region " Data Access "

  <Serializable()> _
  Private Class Criteria
    Private mId As Integer
    Public ReadOnly Property Id() As Integer
      Get
        Return mId
      End Get
    End Property
    Public Sub New(ByVal id As Integer)
      mId = id
    End Sub
  End Class
```

```
Private Overloads Sub DataPortal_Fetch(ByVal criteria As Criteria)
  ' load values
End Sub
```

```
#End Region
```

```
End Class
```

Like other business objects, a read-only object will have instance fields that contain its data. It will typically also have read-only properties or methods that allow client code to retrieve values. As long as they don't change the state of the object, these may even be calculated values.

Like editable objects, read-only objects must override the GetIdValue() method and provide a unique identifying value for the object. This value is used by the Equals(), GetHashCode(), and ToString() implementations in the ReadOnlyBase class. If those implementations are inadequate for your needs, you can override them and provide your own implementations.

The AddAuthorizationRules() method only needs to add roles for read access, since no properties should be implemented to allow altering of data. It also includes a CanGetObject() method so that the UI can enable or disable options based on that result.

In the *Factory Methods* region, there's just one factory method that retrieves the object by calling DataPortal.Fetch(). This means there's also a Criteria class, which should be modified to contain the criteria data needed to select the correct object for retrieval.

The *Data Access* region just contains DataPortal_Fetch(). Of course, there's no need to support updating or deleting of a read-only object.

Read-Only Collections of Objects

Applications commonly retrieve read-only collections of objects. The CSLA .NET framework includes the ReadOnlyListBase class to help create read-only collections. It throws an exception any time there's an attempt to change which items are in the collection by adding or removing objects.

■**Note** The template shown here is for the most common scenario: a read-only root collection. You can adapt this to provide a read-only child collection if desired.

However, there's no way for the collection object to stop client code from interacting with the child objects themselves. Typically, the items in the collection will expose only read-only properties and methods. If read-write objects are put into the collection, client code will be able to alter their data. A read-only collection only guarantees that objects can't be added or removed from the collection.

The child objects may be derived from ReadOnlyBase, but more often they will be simple objects that don't inherit from any CSLA .NET base class. The only requirements for these child objects is that they are implemented with read-only properties and that they are marked as <Serializable()>.

The code for a typical read-only collection object looks like this:

```
<Serializable()> _
Public Class ReadOnlyList
    Inherits ReadOnlyListBase(Of ReadOnlyList, ReadOnlyChild)
```

```
#Region " Authorization Rules "
```

```vb
  Public Shared Function CanGetObject() As Boolean
    ' TODO: customize to check user role
    'Return ApplicationContext.User.IsInRole("")
    Return True
  End Function

#End Region

#Region " Factory Methods "

  Public Shared Function GetList(ByVal filter As String) As ReadOnlyList
    Return DataPortal.Fetch(Of ReadOnlyList)(New Criteria(filter))
  End Function

  Private Sub New()
    ' require use of factory methods
  End Sub

#End Region

#Region " Data Access "

  <Serializable()> _
  Private Class Criteria

    Private mFilter As String
    Public ReadOnly Property Filter() As String
      Get
        Return mFilter
      End Get
    End Property

    Public Sub New(ByVal filter As String)
      mFilter = filter
    End Sub
  End Class

  Protected Overrides Sub DataPortal_Fetch(ByVal criteria As Object)

    RaiseListChangedEvents = False
    IsReadOnly = False
    ' load values
    Using dr As SqlDataReader = Nothing
      While dr.Read
        Add(ReadOnlyChild.GetReadOnlyChild(dr))
      End While
    End Using
    IsReadOnly = True
    RaiseListChangedEvents = True

  End Sub

#End Region

End Class
```

In the *Authorization Rules* region, there's just the CanGetObject() method for use by UI code.

In the *Factory Methods* region, there's a factory method to return a collection loaded with data. It calls DataPortal.Fetch(), and so there's a Criteria class as well as a Private constructor. This is no different from the classes you've looked at already.

Finally, the DataPortal_Fetch() method loads the object with data from the database. To do this, the IsReadOnly flag is set to False, the data is loaded from the database, and then IsReadOnly is set to True. When IsReadOnly is set to True, any attempt to add or remove items from the collection will result in an exception being thrown. Temporarily setting it to False allows the code to insert all the appropriate child objects into the collection.

Also note that RaiseListChangedEvents is set to False and then True in a similar manner. To improve performance, this suppresses the raising of ListChanged events while the data is being loaded.

Command Objects

Command objects can be used in many ways. They may be called directly by UI code to execute arbitrary code on the application server, but even more often they are used *within* other business objects to execute code on the application server. A primary example is when a normal editable business object wants to implement an Exists() command. You'll see an example of this concept in the Project and Resource objects in Chapter 8.

If the UI is to directly use the object, the class will be Public, while if it is to be used within the context of another business object, it will be a Private nested class within that business object. Either way, the structure of a command object is the same, as shown here:

```
<Serializable()> _
Public Class CommandObject
  Inherits CommandBase

#Region " Authorization Rules "

  Public Shared Function CanExecuteCommand() As Boolean

    ' to see if user is authorized
    'Return Csla.ApplicationContext.User.IsInRole("")
    Return True

  End Function

#End Region

#Region " Client-side Code "

  Private mResult As Boolean

  Public ReadOnly Property Result() As Boolean
    Get
      Return mResult
    End Get
  End Property

  Private Sub BeforeServer()
    ' implement code to run on client
    ' before server is called
  End Sub
```

```vb
    Private Sub AfterServer()
      ' implement code to run on client
      ' after server is called
    End Sub

#End Region

#Region " Factory Methods "

  Public Shared Function TheCommand() As Boolean

    Dim cmd As New CommandObject
    cmd.BeforeServer()
    cmd = DataPortal.Execute(Of CommandObject)(cmd)
    cmd.AfterServer()
    Return cmd.Result

  End Function

  Private Sub New()
    ' require use of factory methods
  End Sub

#End Region

#Region " Server-side Code "

  Protected Overrides Sub DataPortal_Execute()

    ' implement code to run on server
    ' here - and set result value(s)
    mResult = True

  End Sub

#End Region

End Class
```

This class structure is quite a bit different from anything you've seen so far.

The *Authorization Rules* region isn't bad—it just implements a CanExecuteCommand() method so that the UI can easily determine whether the current user is authorized to execute the command.

The *Factory Methods* region is similar in structure to many of the other templates shown thus far, but its implementation is different. Rather than passing a Criteria object to the server, the Execute() method creates and initializes an instance of the command object itself. That instance is then sent to the server through the data portal, which invokes the DataPortal_Execute() method on the server.

The Execute() method also calls the BeforeServer() and AfterServer() methods, which are found in the *Client-side Code* region.

The idea behind this is that the command object can be initialized on the client with any data required to perform the server-side processing. In fact, the object could do some processing or data gathering on the client before or after it is transferred to the server through the data portal. The client-side code may be as complex as needed to prepare to run the server-side code.

Then the data portal moves the object to the application server and calls the DataPortal_ Execute() method in the *Server-side Code* region. The code in this method runs on the server and can do any server-side work. This might be something as simple as doing a quick database lookup, or it might be a complex server-side workflow. The code in this method can create and interact with other business objects (all on the server of course). It can interact directly with the database, or any other server-side resources, such as the server's file system or third-party software installed on the server.

Command objects are powerful because they provide high levels of flexibility for running both client and server code in a coordinated manner.

Name/Value List Objects

Perhaps the simplest business object to create is a name/value list that inherits from the NameValueListBase class in the CSLA .NET framework. The base class provides almost all the functionality needed, except the actual data access and factory method.

Because name/value list data is often very static, changing rarely, it is often desirable to cache the data. This can be done in the factory method, as shown in the template:

```
<Serializable()> _
Public Class NameValueList
  Inherits NameValueListBase(Of Integer, String)

#Region " Factory Methods "

  Private Shared mList As NameValueList

  Public Shared Function GetList() As NameValueList
    If mList Is Nothing Then
      mList = DataPortal.Fetch(Of NameValueList) _
        (New Criteria(GetType(NameValueList)))
    End If
    Return mList
  End Function

  Public Shared Sub InvalidateCache()
    mList = Nothing
  End Sub

  Private Sub New()
    ' require use of factory methods
  End Sub

#End Region

#Region " Data Access "

  Protected Overrides Sub DataPortal_Fetch(ByVal criteria As Object)

    RaiseListChangedEvents = False
    IsReadOnly = False
    ' TODO: load values
    Using dr As SqlDataReader = Nothing
      While dr.Read
        Add(New NameValueListBase(Of Integer, String). _
          NameValuePair(dr.GetInt32(0), dr.GetString(1)))
      End While
    End Using
    IsReadOnly = True
    RaiseListChangedEvents = True
```

```
  End Sub

#End Region

End Class
```

The *Factory Methods* region declares a `Shared` field to hold the list once it is retrieved. Notice how the factory method returns the cached list if it is present; only calling the data portal to retrieve the data if the list is `Nothing`. There's also an `InvalidateCache()` method that can be called to force a reload of the data if needed.

This caching behavior is optional—if it doesn't fit your need, then use a factory method like this:

```
Public Shared Function GetNameValueList() As NameValueList
  Return DataPortal.Fetch(Of NameValueList) _
    (New Criteria(GetType(NameValueList)))
End Function
```

The *Data Access* region contains only a `DataPortal_Fetch()` method, which connects to the database and retrieves the name/value data. The `NameValueListBase` class defines a strongly typed `NameValuePair` class, which is used to store each element of data. For each row of data from the database, a `NameValuePair` object is created and added to the collection.

Notice the use of the `IsReadOnly` property to temporarily unlock the collection and then relock it so it becomes read-only once the data has been loaded. The `RoleList` class in the sample application in Chapter 8 illustrates a complete implementation of a name/value list.

Conclusion

This chapter has discussed the basic concepts and requirements for all business classes based on CSLA .NET. I discussed the life cycle of business objects, and walked through the creation, retrieval, update, and delete processes.

The basic structure of each type of business class was covered. There are common requirements, including making all the classes serializable, implementing a common set of code regions for clarity of code, including a `Private` constructor, and having a nested `Criteria` class. There are also specific structures or templates for each type of business object, including the following:

- Editable root
- Editable child
- Switchable object
- Editable root collection
- Editable child collection
- Read-only object
- Read-only collection
- Command object
- Name/value list

Chapter 8 will implement the sample project tracker application classes based on these concepts and templates.

Business Object Implementation

This chapter will implement the business objects designed in Chapter 6 by following the business object coding structures from Chapter 7. This chapter will illustrate how to write code to create business objects that enjoy all the features and capabilities built into the CSLA .NET framework. The great thing is that almost all the code in the business objects will be business focused. Each business class will largely consist of three areas:

- UI-focused business properties and methods
- Shared factory methods to support the class-in-charge model (as discussed in Chapter 1)
- Data access methods (DataPortal_XYZ, as discussed in Chapter 4)

The object model created in Chapter 6 includes editable objects and collections, parent-child collection relationships, read-only lists, a name/value list, and command objects. It also makes use of custom authentication, requiring the creation of custom principal and identity objects. The custom identity object will be a read-only object.

In the end, the sample application makes use of every CSLA .NET base class available.

In this chapter, I won't walk through all the code in the ProjectTracker business object library. Instead, I'll focus on providing examples of how to implement common types of business objects and how to establish various object relationships. For the complete code, please refer to the code download for this book, available at www.apress.com.

ProjectTracker Objects

Chapter 6 covered the creation of an object model for the sample project-tracking application. This object model, shown in Figure 8-1, includes some editable root business objects (Project and Resource), some editable child objects (ProjectResource and ResourceAssignment), some collections of child objects (ProjectResources and ResourceAssignments), and a name/value list (RoleList). It also includes two read-only collections (ProjectList and ResourceList) and an editable root collection (Roles).

The solid arrows indicate using relationships, where one object uses another for some purpose—either as a parent-child relationship or for collaboration. The dashed lines indicate navigation, where a method exists so that the UI developer can easily get a reference to the target object. Of course, Chapter 6 has complete details on the object model.

By implementing these objects, you should get a good feel for the practical process of taking the class templates from Chapter 7 and applying them to the creation of real business classes.

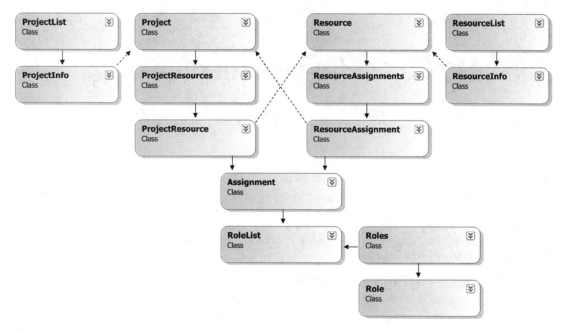

Figure 8-1. *ProjectTracker application classes*

Setting Up the Project

Technically, business classes can be placed in a Class Library, Windows Application, or website-type project in Visual Studio. But to get the full advantages of mobile objects and the CSLA .NET framework, they really must be placed in a Class Library project.

By putting the business classes in a DLL, it becomes possible for the business objects to be used by various different "front ends." This is important, because Chapters 9 through 11 will use exactly the same business DLL to create Windows Forms, Web Forms, and Web Services interfaces. It's equally important in "real-world" applications, since they too often have multiple interfaces. Even if an application starts with a single interface, the odds are good that at some time in the future, it will need a new one.

I prefer to collect all my projects under a single Visual Studio solution, including the business library, the Windows and Web UI projects, and the Web Service project. To this end, you'll find all the code in a ProjectTracker20vb solution in the code download, with each project and website contained inside.

The ProjectTracker.Library Class Library project is a library of business classes based on the design from Chapter 6. This library contains all the business logic for the ProjectTracker application.

The code in ProjectTracker.Library uses the CSLA .NET framework, and so the project references Csla.dll. This is a file reference that is set up through the Add Reference dialog box, as shown in Figure 8-2.

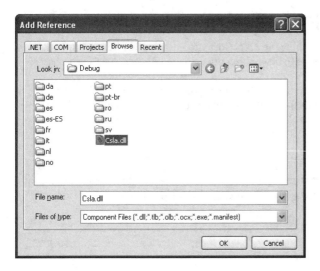

Figure 8-2. *Referencing the Csla.dll assembly*

This makes the CSLA .NET framework available for use within the project, and is typically all that is required.

However, remember that Csla.dll includes code that might run in Enterprise Services (COM+). In particular, this includes both the ServicedDataPortal and EnterpriseServicesPortal components of the data portal, as discussed in Chapter 4. If you choose to use the Enterprise Services features, then you may need to reference System.EnterpriseServices.dll as well.

The specific case in which this is required is if you configure the data portal to run locally in the client process *and* you mark your DataPortal_XYZ methods with <Transactional (TransactionTypes.EnterpriseServices)>. This combination causes the direct use of a ServicedComponent within the client process, and so requires a reference to System. EnterpriseServices.dll. It also has the side effect of requiring that Csla.dll be registered with COM+, which is handled automatically if the user is an administrator on the client workstation, but otherwise must be done manually by an administrator using the regsvcs.exe command line utility (or as part of a standard msi setup process).

■**Note** Enterprise Services (COM+) isn't supported on Windows 98 or Windows ME. If you plan to configure the data portal to run locally in the client process on older client workstations, you must not use the <Transactional (TransactionTypes.EnterpriseServices)> attribute on your data access methods.

If you don't use the <Transactional(TransactionTypes.EnterpriseServices)> attribute on your DataPortal_XYZ methods, no code will use Enterprise Services in the client process, and so you don't have to worry about these details.

I'll discuss the use of the EnterpriseServicesPortal through the data portal in Chapter 12, as it has its own unique set of requirements.

Business Class Implementation

The business classes implemented here follow the object-oriented design created in Chapter 6. That chapter identified not only the classes to be created, but also which CSLA .NET base classes each one will subclass.

I'll walk through the first few classes in detail. The other classes will be very similar, so for those, I'll discuss only the key features. Of course, the complete code for all classes is available in the code download for the book.

Project

The Project class is an editable root class that represents a single project in the application. It will follow the EditableRoot template, as discussed in Chapter 7. This means that it inherits from BusinessBase, as shown in Figure 8-3.

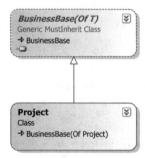

Figure 8-3. *The Project class subclasses BusinessBase*

Since this is the first business class to be created, I'll walk through the code in complete detail. You can assume that subsequent classes follow a similar structure overall.

The Project class will use a number of .NET and CSLA .NET features. To make this easier, a number of namespaces are imported at the project level (through the References tab in the My Project designer). These include:

- System.Data
- System.Data.SqlClient
- Csla
- Csla.Data

These references are used to simplify the code in the class. For instance, the data access code will interact with SQL Server, so the project needs to import the System.Data.SqlClient namespace. And of course, CSLA .NET features are used, so namespaces are brought in for that as well.

The class itself is contained within the default ProjectTracker.Library namespace and is declared as follows:

```
<Serializable()> _
Public Class Project
  Inherits BusinessBase(Of Project)
```

The `BusinessBase` class requires one generic type parameter. This is the type of the business object itself, and is used to provide strongly typed `Save()` and `Clone()` methods for the object as discussed in Chapter 3.

The class will contain the standard code regions discussed in Chapter 7:

- *Business Methods*
- *Validation Rules*
- *Authorization Rules*
- *Factory Methods*
- *Data Access*

The class also has a region named *Exists*. This region implements an `Exists()` method that can be used to determine if a specific project's data exists in the database. I'll discuss the code in the *Exists* region at the end of the chapter.

Let's walk through each region in turn.

Business Methods

The *Business Methods* region includes the declaration of all instance fields, along with the properties and methods that implement business logic around those fields. Since `Project` is a parent class, it will also include some special code designed to work well with its child objects.

Instance Field Declarations

The field declarations are as follows:

```
Private mId As Guid = Guid.NewGuid
Private mName As String = ""
Private mStarted As New SmartDate
Private mEnded As New SmartDate(False)
Private mDescription As String = ""
Private mTimestamp(7) As Byte

Private mResources As ProjectResources = _
  ProjectResources.NewProjectResources()
```

The `String` fields are all initialized to `""`. By default, the value would be `Nothing`, but that causes problems with data binding, especially in Windows Forms. It is very important that `String` type instance fields be initialized to some non-`Nothing` value.

Note All `String` instance fields should be initialized with a default value when they're declared. This is because Windows Forms data binding throws a runtime exception when attempting to data bind against string properties that return `Nothing`.

Also notice that the date values are of type `SmartDate`, rather than just `DateTime`. The object is taking advantage of the `Csla.SmartDate` class that understands empty dates. The code specifies that `mStarted` should treat an empty date as the minimum possible date value, while `mEnded` will treat it as the maximum value.

Each `Project` object contains a collection of `ProjectResource` child objects. When a `Project` object is created, an empty child collection is also created by calling the appropriate factory method on the collection. The NewProjectResources() method creates an empty collection, ensuring that child objects can be added as required.

The result is that the instance fields are declared and initialized so the object is immediately useful for things like data binding, setting property values, or adding child objects.

Read-Only Properties

The bulk of the code in the *Business Methods* region for most objects will be the properties. Some objects may include complex methods implementing business logic, but virtually all objects include properties to allow the UI to view or update the object's values.

The Id property of the Project is read-only. It also represents the object's unique primary key value in the database:

```
<System.ComponentModel.DataObjectField(True, True)> _
Public ReadOnly Property Id() As Guid
  Get
    CanReadProperty(True)
    Return mId
  End Get
End Property
```

Since this is the primary key for the data in the database, the value can also be considered to be a unique identifier for the object itself. The DataObjectField attribute is used to specify that the property is both a primary key and an identity value. This attribute is used by data binding, and in particular by the CslaDataSource ASP.NET control created in Chapter 5. The attribute is optional, but is useful for helping to identify the nature of primary key properties.

Notice the use of the CanReadProperty() method in the get block. This code uses the overload created in Chapter 3, telling the method to throw a System.Security.SecurityException if the current user is not authorized to read the property. This is the simplest way to use the authorization functionality built into CSLA .NET. You could also opt to manually check the result with code like this:

```
If CanReadProperty() Then
  Return mId
Else
  ' take appropriate action
End If
```

This approach allows you to do something other than throw the default exception. You would write your code in the Else clause to cover the case in which the user isn't authorized to read the property. A third approach, which avoids the use of System.Diagnostics to determine the name of the property, is as follows:

```
If CanReadProperty("Id") Then
  Return mId
Else
  ' take appropriate action
End If
```

Notice that in this case, the name of the property is specified as literal text. This reduces the maintainability of the code, but has a marginal performance benefit by avoiding the System.Diagnostics call used by the previous overloads. You can determine whether the performance gain is worth the maintainability loss for your particular application.

Tip If you are using code generation or code snippets to create your business classes, there's no real cost to using a literal value here. Since the code generator creates the code automatically, the likelihood of bugs due to typos is very small, and you may opt to use the literal in order to gain optimal performance.

The Id property illustrates several things: a read-only property, a primary identity key value, and the use of the CanReadProperty() calling options.

Read-Write Properties

Now let's try something a bit more interesting by creating a read-write property, Name:

```
Public Property Name() As String
  Get
    CanReadProperty(True)
    Return mName
  End Get
  Set(ByVal Value As String)
    CanWriteProperty(True)
    If mName <> Value Then
      mName = Value
      PropertyHasChanged()
    End If
  End Set
End Property
```

Since this is neither a primary key nor an identity value, there's no immediate need to use the DataObjectField attribute. You may still opt to use this attribute on your properties to provide this extra information for other purposes, such as automated unit testing.

The Get block is virtually identical to that in the Id property. In fact, the Get block for properties will always be the same—the only difference being the name of the instance field that's returned.

The Set block deserves some discussion, however. First, notice the CanWriteProperty() method call. The options for calling CanWriteProperty() are the same as for CanReadProperty(), so you can take more control or use a literal name for the property if you so desire. Regardless, the idea is that the object's property value is only changed if the user is authorized to write to this property.

Assuming the user is authorized to change the property value, the code checks to see if the provided value is actually new. If it's the same as the value already in the object, then there's no sense in any work being done.

So, if the user is authorized to change the value, and the value is different from what is already in the object, then the new value is stored in the object. It is important to realize that this occurs *before* any validation code runs. This means that the object could end up storing *invalid values*. That's OK, though, because the object has an IsValid property that can be used to determine whether any validation rules are currently being violated by values in the object.

The PropertyHasChanged() method is where the validation rules are actually invoked. This method performs a sequence of steps:

1. It checks the validation rules for the property.

2. It sets the object's IsDirty flag to True.

3. It raises a PropertyChanged event for data binding.

Like `CanReadProperty()`, the `PropertyHasChanged()` method uses `System.Diagnostics` to determine the name of the current property, which incurs a marginal performance hit. If this is a problem for you, the code can be changed to provide the literal name of the property:

```
PropertyHasChanged("Name")
```

Again, this is a trade-off between performance and maintainability; you'll have to determine which is most important for your application.

The validation rules to be checked are associated with the property in the `AddBusinessRules()` method, which is implemented later in the chapter. Most rule methods assume that the value to be validated is already in the object's property, which is why it is important that the instance field be set to the new value before the validation rules are invoked.

The `IsDirty` property indicates whether the object's data has been changed. Since a new value has been put into the object, this property must now return `True`.

Finally, since the object's data has changed, any UI bound to the object through data binding must update its display. This is done by raising a `PropertyChanged` event, as discussed in Chapter 3. The `PropertyHasChanged()` method takes care of this automatically.

■**Note** Whenever the value of an instance field changes, you need to call `PropertyHasChanged()` for any properties that have changed values. This ensures that the object's state and the state of any data-bound UI components are changed or updated as appropriate.

You can also have other objects handle the `PropertyChanged` event if they need to respond to a change in a business object's state. For instance, this technique can be used to automatically have a parent object recalculate values when its child objects are changed.

Most read-write properties look just like the preceding `Name` property. For instance, here's the `Description` property:

```
Public Property Description() As String
  Get
    CanReadProperty(True)
    Return mDescription
  End Get
  Set(ByVal Value As String)
    CanWriteProperty(True)
    If mDescription <> Value Then
      mDescription = Value
      PropertyHasChanged()
    End If
  End Set
End Property
```

Notice that it is identical to the `Name` property, other than working with a different instance field. The vast majority of property methods will look exactly like this. In fact, you can find a code snippet for both read-only and read-write properties in the `Snippets` subdirectory in the CSLA .NET code download.

■**Tip** You can manually install the snippet files for use in Visual Studio 2005. By default, you should copy them to the `Visual Basic\My Code Snippets` directory under `My Documents\Visual Studio 2005\ Code Snippets`. I typically put them in a `Csla` directory beneath `My Code Snippets`.

SmartDate Properties

So far, you've seen how to implement properties for type Guid and String. Most types follow this same approach, with obvious small variation for formatting of values and so forth. But dates are a tougher issue.

One way to deal with dates is to expose them as DateTime values directly. This works well for date values that are required, for which an empty date isn't an option. And of course, it only works well if you are binding the property to a date-aware control. Unfortunately, most of the date-aware controls don't allow the user to just type a free-form date value, and so they aren't really very good for any sort of heads-down data entry scenarios.

The SmartDate class from Chapter 5 is intended to help solve this dilemma by making it easy for a business class to expose a date value as a String, yet also be able to treat it like a date. Additionally, SmartDate allows for empty date values—it gives you the option of treating an empty date as the smallest or largest possible date for the purposes of comparison.

The Started and Ended properties utilize the SmartDate data type. Here's the Started property:

```
Public Property Started() As String
  Get
    CanReadProperty(True)
    Return mStarted.Text
  End Get
  Set(ByVal Value As String)
    CanWriteProperty(True)
    If mStarted <> Value Then
      mStarted.Text = Value
      ValidationRules.CheckRules("Ended")
      PropertyHasChanged()
    End If
  End Set
End Property
```

I'll discuss the CheckRules() method call shortly. First, let's focus on how the property is constructed. Notice that it is a String property, so it can be data bound to any text input control. This means the user can enter the date value in any format that can be parsed, including the shortcuts added to SmartDate in Chapter 5 (such as + for tomorrow).

The Get block returns the Text property of the mStarted field, thus returning the date value as a string, formatted based on the format string set in mStarted (by default it is d, the short date format).

The Set block sets the Text property, automatically triggering the parsing algorithm built into SmartDate. That way, the value is stored as a date internal to SmartDate itself. This is important because it allows SmartDate values to be compared to each other, as well as to DateTime values. This comparison capability will be used later when the validation rules are implemented in Project.

The end result is that the UI sees a String property, but all the features and functionality of a date type are available inside the business class.

The Ended property is declared the same way, but works with the mEnded field instead.

Interdependent Properties

Sometimes an object will have properties that are interdependent, or at least have interdependent validation logic. The Started and Ended properties are good examples of this case. Later on, you'll see how to implement a business validation rule saying that the value of Ended must not be earlier than the value of Started—a project can't end before it begins.

This complicates matters slightly, because a change to either property can affect the validity of the other value. Suppose that Started and Ended begin with valid dates, but then Ended is changed to a date earlier than Started. At that point, the Ended property is invalid; but so is the Started property. Because the properties are interdependent, *both* should become invalid when the interdependent rule is violated. Similarly, if the interdependent rule later becomes unbroken, both properties should become valid.

This is the purpose behind the CheckRules() method call in the Started property's Set block:

```
Set(ByVal Value As String)
  CanWriteProperty(True)
  If mStarted <> Value Then
    mStarted.Text = Value
    ValidationRules.CheckRules("Ended")
    PropertyHasChanged()
  End If
End Set
```

Remember that this code is in the Started property, and the call to CheckRules() is specifically forcing the validation rules for the Ended property to be executed. The Set block in the Ended property is a mirror image:

```
Set(ByVal Value As String)
  CanWriteProperty(True)
  If mEnded <> Value Then
    mEnded.Text = Value
    ValidationRules.CheckRules("Started")
    PropertyHasChanged()
  End If
End Set
```

In each case, the property value is updated based on the new input, and then the validation rules for the other interdependent property are checked. Then PropertyHasChanged() runs, which checks the validation rules for *this* property. This code simply ensures that, in addition to the current property, the interdependent property's rules are checked as well.

The result is that any interdependent business rules are run on both properties, so both properties will become invalid or valid as appropriate.

Child Collection Properties

The final business property in this region provides client code with access to the collection of child objects:

```
Public ReadOnly Property Resources() As ProjectResources
  Get
    Return mResources
  End Get
End Property
```

The collection itself is exposed as a read-only property, but since it is an editable collection derived from BusinessListBase, the UI code will be able to add and remove child items as needed.

Overriding GetIdValue

The BusinessBase class defines a MustOverride GetIdValue() method. This means that the method must be implemented by any subclass, such as Project. The purpose behind the GetIdValue() method is to allow BusinessBase to implement the standard System.Object overrides: Equals(), GetHashCode(), and ToString().

To do this, some unique identifier for the object is required, and so this is the value that is returned from GetIdValue():

```
Protected Overrides Function GetIdValue() As Object
    Return mId
End Function
```

Remember from Chapter 3 that this value must not return Nothing, or else an exception will be thrown by the BusinessBase class. The value you return from this method is used to determine if this object is equal to another object of the same type (i.e., is this Project object equal to another Project object?). It is also returned as the result of ToString(), so anyone calling ToString() on a Project will get that object's mId value as a result (in string form of course).

While you *must* override GetIdValue() because it is MustOverride, overriding ToString(), Equals(), and GetHashCode() is entirely optional. Default overrides for these methods already exist in BusinessBase. If your object has different requirements for any of these three methods, it can directly override *those* methods and provide its own implementation.

Overriding IsValid and IsDirty

Before we move on, there's one last bit of work that this region must include. Project is a parent object that has a collection of child objects, and so the default behavior for IsValid and IsDirty from BusinessBase won't work.

■Note The default IsValid and IsDirty properties must be enhanced for all objects that subclass BusinessBase and contain child objects.

A parent object is valid only if it is in a valid state *and* if all of its child objects are in a valid state. Likewise, a parent object is dirty if its own data has been changed *or* if any of its child objects or collections have been changed. To handle this properly, the IsValid and IsDirty methods must be overridden to provide a slightly more sophisticated implementation of each:

```
Public Overrides ReadOnly Property IsValid() As Boolean
    Get
        Return MyBase.IsValid AndAlso mResources.IsValid
    End Get
End Property

Public Overrides ReadOnly Property IsDirty() As Boolean
    Get
        Return MyBase.IsDirty OrElse mResources.IsDirty
    End Get
End Property
```

In the case of IsValid, the Project object is checked to see if it is invalid. If it is, then the result is False and there's no need to check the child collection. Otherwise, the child collection's IsValid property is checked, which triggers a check of all the child objects it contains. If any child object is invalid, then the result is False.

IsDirty is similar. In this case, the Project object is checked, and if it has been changed, then the result is True. But if the Project itself hasn't been changed, then the child collection object's IsDirty property is checked, triggering a check of all child objects it contains. If any child object has been changed, then the result is True.

Validation Rules

The *Validation Rules* region implements the AddBusinessRules() method to associate validation rules to properties of the business object. As discussed in Chapter 3, validation rules are implemented as rule methods that conform to the Csla.Validation.RuleHandler delegate.

This region also implements any custom rule methods for the object. The rule methods provided in Csla.Validation.CommonRules are designed to handle most common validation requirements, but some objects have rules that aren't implemented in the CommonRules class.

AddBusinessRules

Let's look first at the AddBusinessRules() implementation:

```
Protected Overrides Sub AddBusinessRules()
  ValidationRules.AddRule( _
    AddressOf Validation.CommonRules.StringRequired, "Name")
  ValidationRules.AddRule( _
    AddressOf Validation.CommonRules.StringMaxLength, _
    New Validation.CommonRules.MaxLengthRuleArgs("Name", 50))

  ValidationRules.AddRule(AddressOf StartDateGTEndDate, "Started")
  ValidationRules.AddRule(AddressOf StartDateGTEndDate, "Ended")
End Sub
```

This method is automatically invoked by the CSLA .NET framework any time validation rules need to be associated with the object's properties. The method should only contain a series of ValidationRules.AddRule() method calls as shown here.

Each call to AddRule() associates a validation rule with a property. In the simple case, this means associating a rule method like StringRequired to a property like Name:

```
ValidationRules.AddRule( _
  AddressOf Validation.CommonRules.StringRequired, "Name")
```

With this done, any time PropertyHasChanged() is called by the Name property, or ValidationRules.CheckRules() is called anywhere in the object, the rule will be applied to the Name property by executing the StringRequired method. The implementation for this method was covered in Chapter 5.

■**Note**   The rule will also be applied if ValidationRules.CheckRules() is called with no parameters, as that causes the validation rules for *all* properties to be checked.

Other rules are a bit more complex, requiring extra parameter values to operate. This is the case with the StringMaxLength rule, for instance:

```
ValidationRules.AddRule( _
  AddressOf Validation.CommonRules.StringMaxLength, _
  New Validation.CommonRules.MaxLengthRuleArgs("Name", 50))
```

Notice that in this case, a MaxLengthRuleArgs object is created, supplying both the name of the property against which the rule is to be run and the maximum length for a valid String.

Both of the rules so far have been in the CommonRules class. But Project has a custom rule method as well: StartDateGTEndDate. This rule is associated with both the Started and Ended properties:

```
ValidationRules.AddRule(AddressOf StartDateGTEndDate, "Started")
ValidationRules.AddRule(AddressOf StartDateGTEndDate, "Ended")
```

As you'll see, this custom rule compares the two date values to ensure that the project doesn't end before it begins.

Custom Rule Methods

Chapter 5 discussed the `CommonRules` class and the rule methods it contains. The basic concepts behind implementing a rule method were discussed at that time. The core requirement for all rule methods is that they conform to the `Csla.Validation.RuleHandler` delegate signature. They also must return `True` if the rule is unbroken and `False` if it is broken. Additionally, if the rule is broken, `e.Description` should be set to provide a human-readable description of the problem.

None of the rules in `CommonRules` are designed to ensure that one `SmartDate` value is greater than another, and so `Project` implements this as a custom rule:

```
Private Function StartDateGTEndDate( _
  ByVal target As Object, ByVal e As Validation.RuleArgs) As Boolean

  If mStarted > mEnded Then
    e.Description = "Start date can't be after end date"
    Return False

  Else
    Return True
  End If
End Function
```

This rule method is comparable to those in the `CommonRules` class, but it doesn't use reflection to do its work. It doesn't need to because it is *inside* the `Project` class and thus has direct access to all the fields in the object. The code can directly access the `mStarted` and `mEnded` instance fields to do the comparison.

If the project start date is greater than the project end date, then the rule is broken and the method returns `False`; otherwise it returns `True`.

This method is invoked by the `PropertyHasChanged()` and `CheckRules()` calls in the `Set` blocks of the `Started` and `Ended` properties.

It is important to notice that this rule method uses two different property values in the object, thus creating an interdependent relationship between those properties. The property implementations discussed earlier included extra code to deal with this interdependency, and that type of code is required any time you implement a single rule method that deals with multiple property values.

Authorization Rules

The *Authorization Rules* region implements the `AddAuthorizationRules()` method, along with a standard set of `Shared` methods for use by the UI.

AddAuthorizationRules

Like `AddBusinessRules()`, the `AddAuthorizationRules()` method is called automatically by the CSLA .NET framework any time the authorization rules for the object need to be configured. This method contains only a series of calls to `AuthorizationRules`, specifying which security roles are allowed or denied read and write access to each property:

```
Protected Overrides Sub AddAuthorizationRules()
  AuthorizationRules.AllowWrite("Name", "ProjectManager")
  AuthorizationRules.AllowWrite("Started", "ProjectManager")
  AuthorizationRules.AllowWrite("Ended", "ProjectManager")
  AuthorizationRules.AllowWrite("Description", "ProjectManager")
End Sub
```

In this example, there are no restrictions on who can read properties, so there are no calls to AllowRead() or DenyRead(). Recall from Chapter 3 that if no roles are specified for allow or deny, then *all* users are allowed access.

■**Tip** If the default implementation for authorization as implemented in Chapter 3 doesn't meet your needs, the business object can override the CanReadProperty() and CanWriteProperty() methods from BusinessBase, and you can implement your own algorithm.

But there are restrictions on who can change property values. In particular, only users in the ProjectManager role are allowed to change any properties on the object, so each property is associated with this role. For instance:

```
AuthorizationRules.AllowWrite("Name", "ProjectManager")
```

Remember, the ProjectManager role is a security role, and so it is either a Windows domain or Active Directory group, or a custom security role loaded when the user is authenticated. This sample application uses custom authentication, so the user's roles come from a SQL Server database.

The AllowWrite() method, like all the methods on AuthorizationRules, accepts the property name, followed by a comma-separated list of the roles allowed to alter this property. The list of roles is a ParamArray parameter, making it easy to specify several roles on one line.

Authorization Methods

The CanReadProperty() and CanWriteProperty() methods make it easy to implement authorization on a per-property basis, both within the object's property code and from the UI (remember that these two methods are Public in scope). While this is important, it isn't enough.

A typical UI will have menus or links that allow the user to view, add, edit, and remove data in various ways. If the user isn't authorized to do those things, then the menus or links should be hidden or disabled in the UI, providing the user with clear visual cues that they aren't allowed to perform the action.

The implication is that the UI needs some way to know ahead of time whether a user will be allowed to view, add, edit, or delete a given type of data; or in this case, object. It makes no sense to force the UI to create an *instance* of the object to find out what the user is authorized to do; instead, Shared methods are implemented so that the UI can effectively ask the business *class*. This is the purpose behind the following methods:

- CanGetObject()
- CanAddObject()
- CanEditObject()
- CanDeleteObject()

While it would be nice if these methods were part of a standard interface, it isn't possible to define Shared methods through an interface, so that's not an option. Nor is it possible to define Shared methods in a base class like BusinessBase and then override them in a subclass. Instead, it is necessary to manually implement them in every business class.

■**Note** Of course, you can change the names of these methods to suit your own needs. The only thing to keep in mind is that they should be named the same on every one of your business objects to simplify the creation and maintenance of your UI code.

Each of the methods simply checks the user's roles to determine if the user is in a role authorized to perform the operation. For instance, here's the CanAddObject() method:

```
Public Shared Function CanAddObject() As Boolean
  Return Csla.ApplicationContext.User.IsInRole("ProjectManager")
End Function
```

Only users in the ProjectManager role are allowed to add Project objects to the application. The CanDeleteObject() method is a bit more complex:

```
Public Shared Function CanDeleteObject() As Boolean
  Dim result As Boolean
  If Csla.ApplicationContext.User.IsInRole("ProjectManager") Then
    result = True
  End If
  If Csla.ApplicationContext.User.IsInRole("Administrator") Then
    result = True
  End If
  Return result
End Function
```

Based on the use cases from Chapter 6, users in either the ProjectManager or Administrator roles are allowed to delete Project objects.

These methods will be used in Chapters 9 and 10 to enable and disable various menu options and links to provide the user with visual cues as to what options are available based on their role. The methods will also be used later in this chapter so that the Project object's methods prevent unauthorized users from retrieving, updating, or deleting the object.

Factory Methods

The next step in creating the object is to write the code that will allow the UI to create, retrieve, and delete a Project object. As discussed in Chapter 1, factory methods are used to provide these capabilities.

Additionally, the default constructor is declared with non-Public scope (either Private or Protected) to force the use of the factory methods for creating or retrieving the object. While this is not strictly necessary, it is a good thing to do. Without making the constructor Private, it is far too easy for a UI developer to forget to use the factory method and to instead use the New keyword to create the object—leading to bugs in the UI code.

Finally, though it isn't technically a *factory* method, the Save() method from BusinessBase is overridden to add authorization checking.

Factory Methods

Let's start by looking at the factory methods themselves:

```
Public Shared Function NewProject() As Project
  If Not CanAddObject() Then
    Throw New System.Security.SecurityException( _
      "User not authorized to add a project")
  End If
  Return DataPortal.Create(Of Project)()
End Function

Public Shared Function GetProject(ByVal id As Guid) As Project
  If Not CanGetObject() Then
    Throw New System.Security.SecurityException( _
      "User not authorized to view a project")
  End If
  Return DataPortal.Fetch(Of Project)(New Criteria(id))
End Function

Public Shared Sub DeleteProject(ByVal id As Guid)
  If Not CanDeleteObject() Then
    Throw New System.Security.SecurityException( _
      "User not authorized to remove a project")
  End If
  DataPortal.Delete(New Criteria(id))
End Sub
```

The NewProject() method creates a new instance of Project, which loads default values from the database if required. To do this, it simply calls DataPortal.Create() to trigger the data portal process, as discussed in Chapter 7 and implemented in Chapter 4. First though, the CanAddObject() method is called to determine whether the user is authorized to add a new Project to the system. If the user isn't authorized, there's no sense even creating a new instance of the object.

■**Tip** Ideally, this authorization exception would never be thrown. Good UI design dictates that the UI should hide or disable the options that would allow a user to add a new object if they aren't authorized to do so. If that is done properly, the user should never be able to even attempt to create a new object if they aren't authorized. This call to CanAddObject() is defensive, and exists just in case a bug creeps into the UI.

The GetProject() factory method retrieves an existing Project object, which is populated with data from the database. This method accepts the primary key value for the data as a parameter and passes it to DataPortal.Fetch() through a new Criteria object. The Criteria object will be discussed later.

The data portal ultimately creates a new Project object and calls its DataPortal_Fetch() method to do the actual data access. The Criteria object is passed through this process, so the DataPortal_Fetch() method will have access to the Guid key value.

Of course, the CanGetObject() method is called first to ensure that the user is authorized to view the data.

There's also a Shared method to allow immediate deletion of a Project. The CanDeleteObject() method is called first to ensure that the user is authorized to delete the data. DeleteProject() accepts the primary key value for the data and uses it to create a Criteria object. It then calls DataPortal.Delete() to trigger the deletion process, ultimately resulting in the object's DataPortal_Delete() method being invoked to do the actual deletion of the data.

Non-Public Constructor

As noted earlier, all business objects must include a default constructor, as shown here:

```
Private Sub New()
  ' require use of factory methods
End Sub
```

This is straight out of the template from Chapter 7. It ensures that client code must use the factory methods to create or retrieve a `Project` object, and it provides the data portal with a constructor that it can call via reflection.

Overriding Save

The default implementation for `Save()` is good—it checks to ensure that the object is valid and dirty before saving. But it isn't sufficient in all cases, especially when there's authorization logic to be applied. Checking authorization on the client is ideal because it means that no attempt to save the object occurs if the user isn't authorized.

Keep in mind, however, that `Save()` is called for adding, updating, *and* deleting the object. The authorization checks must take that into account:

```
Public Overrides Function Save() As Project
  If IsDeleted AndAlso Not CanDeleteObject() Then
    Throw New System.Security.SecurityException( _
      "User not authorized to remove a project")

  ElseIf IsNew AndAlso Not CanAddObject() Then
    Throw New System.Security.SecurityException( _
      "User not authorized to add a project")

  ElseIf Not CanEditObject() Then
    Throw New System.Security.SecurityException( _
      "User not authorized to update a project")
  End If
  Return MyBase.Save
End Function
```

There are three different security checks here based on the state of the object. If the object is marked for deletion, `CanDeleteObject()` is checked. If the object is new, then `CanAddObject()` is checked, and otherwise, `CanEditObject()` is checked.

As with the checks in the factory methods, this authorization code *shouldn't* ever throw an exception, because the UI should have prevented the user from getting this far. But bugs occur, so these checks are very important. And in Chapter 11, you'll see how these checks are directly leveraged when implementing a web service interface.

In the end, if the user is allowed to do the delete, add, or update operation, then `MyBase.Save()` is called to do the actual work.

Data Access

The *Data Access* region defines the `Criteria` object used by the factory methods, and implements the `DataPortal_XYZ` methods that support the creation, retrieval, addition, updating, and deletion of a `Project` object's data. Because this is an editable object, it will implement all the possible methods:

- `DataPortal_Create()`
- `DataPortal_Fetch()`

- DataPortal_Insert()
- DataPortal_Update()
- DataPortal_DeleteSelf()
- DataPortal_Delete()

First though, let's look at the Criteria class.

Criteria

The factory methods discussed earlier create instances of a Criteria object. Factory methods use a Criteria object to pass the criteria required to load the object through the data portal to the corresponding DataPortal_XYZ method. The criteria data for a Project is a Guid value: its primary key in the database.

The criteria data for a simple object is often a single value—though your database may use multipart keys, in which case it would include multiple values. Criteria data for collection objects is often more complex, since it typically provides a filter rather than a specific key value.

The Criteria class itself is Private, since it is only used within Project. Also, it is a *nested* class, which allows the data portal to determine that this is criteria for a Project object. An alternative would be to have it inherit from Csla.CriteriaBase, in which case the business object type would be specified in the constructor. However, the CriteriaBase option is designed primarily for use by code generation tools, and so the nested class approach is used here:

```
<Serializable()> _
Private Class Criteria

    Private mId As Guid
    Public ReadOnly Property Id() As Guid
      Get
        Return mId
      End Get
    End Property

    Public Sub New(ByVal id As Guid)
      mId = id
    End Sub
End Class
```

Notice that the class is marked with the <Serializable()> attribute, so the data portal can transfer the object from the client to the server as needed.

To make the factory methods easier to implement, this class includes a constructor that accepts the criterion as a parameter. That value is stored within the object and is exposed as a read-only property. The DataPortal_XYZ methods will make use of this property value to interact with the appropriate data in the database.

With the Criteria class defined, let's move on to discuss the DataPortal_XYZ methods themselves.

In this sample application, the data access code is relatively straightforward. Keep in mind, however, that these routines could be much more complex, interacting with multiple databases, merging data from various sources, and doing whatever is required to retrieve and update data in your business environment.

Handling Transactions

As discussed in Chapters 2 and 4, the data portal supports three transactional models: manual, Enterprise Services, and System.Transactions. The preferred model for performance and simplicity is System.Transactions, and so that is the model used in the sample application.

This means that each method that updates data will be decorated with the <Transactional (TransactionTypes.TransactionScope)> attribute. Since this tells the data portal to wrap the code in a TransactionScope object, there's no need to write any ADO.NET or stored procedure transactional code. All the transaction details are handled by the TransactionScope object from System. Transactions.

As you look at the data access code, notice that it never actually *catches* any exceptions. The code leverages Using blocks to ensure that database connection, command, and data reader objects are disposed properly, but no exceptions are caught. The reasons for this are twofold:

- First, the code uses the <Transactional()> attribute, which causes it to run within a System. Transactions transactional context. An exception automatically causes the transaction to be rolled back, which is exactly the desired result. If the exceptions were caught, then the transaction wouldn't be rolled back, and the application would misbehave.

- Second, if an exception occurs, normal processing shouldn't continue. Instead, the client code needs to be notified that the operation failed, and why. Returning the exception to the client code allows the client code to know that there was a problem during data access. The client code can then choose how to handle the fact that the object couldn't be created, retrieved, updated, or deleted. Remember that the original exception is wrapped in a DataPortalException, which includes extra information that can be used by the client when handling the exception.

DataPortal_Create

The DataPortal_Create() method is called by the data portal when it is asked to create a new Project object. In some cases, this method will load the new object with default values from the database, and in simpler cases, it may load hard-coded defaults or set no defaults at all.

The Project object has no need for loading default values, so the DataPortal_Create() method simply loads some default, hard-coded values rather than talking to the database:

```
<RunLocal()> _
Private Overloads Sub DataPortal_Create(ByVal criteria As Criteria)
  mId = Guid.NewGuid
  Started = CStr(Today)
  ValidationRules.CheckRules()
End Sub
```

The method is decorated with the <RunLocal()> attribute because it doesn't do any data access, but rather sets hard-coded or calculated default values. If the method *did* load default values from the database, then the <RunLocal()> attribute would not be applied, causing the data portal to run the code on the application server. With the <RunLocal()> attribute on the method, the data portal short-circuits its processing and runs this method locally.

■Tip In a more complex object, in which default values come from the database, this method would contain ADO.NET code that retrieves those values and uses them to initialize the object's fields. In that case, the <RunLocal()> attribute would *not* be used.

Notice how the code directly alters the instance fields of the object. For instance, the mId field is set to a new Guid value. Since the Id property is read-only, this is the only way to load the Id property with a new value. While the Started property is read-write and could be set through the property, it is more efficient and consistent to directly set the mStarted field.

Since not all properties can be set, it is best to be consistent and always set fields directly. Additionally, the ValidationRules.CheckRules() call will apply all the validation rules in the entire object. Setting a property causes the validation rules for that property to be checked, so setting property values would cause validation rules to be run twice, which is wasteful. Setting the fields and then calling CheckRules() means validation rules are run only once.

Of course, the default values set in a new object might not conform to the object's validation rules. In fact, the Name property starts out as an empty String value, which means it is invalid, since that is a required property. Remember that this was specified in the AddBusinessRules() method by associating this property with the StringRequired rule method.

To ensure that all validation rules are run against the newly created object's data, ValidationRules.CheckRules() is called. Calling this method with no parameters causes it to run all the validation rules associated with all properties of the object, as defined in the object's AddBusinessRules() method.

The end result is that the new object has been loaded with default values, and those values have been validated. The new object is then returned by the data portal to the factory method (NewProject() in this case), which typically returns it to the UI code.

DataPortal_Fetch

More interesting and complex is the DataPortal_Fetch() method, which is called by the data portal to tell the object that it should load its data from the database (or other data source). The method accepts a Criteria object as a parameter, which contains the criteria data needed to identify the data to load:

```
Private Overloads Sub DataPortal_Fetch(ByVal criteria As Criteria)
  Using cn As New SqlConnection(Database.PTrackerConnection)
    cn.Open()
    Using cm As SqlCommand = cn.CreateCommand
      cm.CommandType = CommandType.StoredProcedure
      cm.CommandText = "getProject"
      cm.Parameters.AddWithValue("@id", criteria.Id)

      Using dr As New SafeDataReader(cm.ExecuteReader)
        dr.Read()
        With dr
          mId = .GetGuid("Id")
          mName = .GetString("Name")
          mStarted = .GetSmartDate("Started", mStarted.EmptyIsMin)
          mEnded = .GetSmartDate("Ended", mEnded.EmptyIsMin)
          mDescription = .GetString("Description")
          .GetBytes("LastChanged", 0, mTimestamp, 0, 8)

          ' load child objects
          .NextResult()
          mResources = ProjectResources.GetProjectResources(dr)
        End With
      End Using
    End Using
  End Using
End Sub
```

This method is not marked with either the `<RunLocal()>` or `<Transactional()>` attributes. Since it does interact with the database, `<RunLocal()>` is inappropriate. That attribute could prevent the data portal from running this code on the application server, causing runtime errors when the database is inaccessible. Also, since this method doesn't update any data, it doesn't need transactional protection, and so there's no need for the `<Transactional()>` attribute.

You should also notice that no exceptions are caught by this code. If the requested Id value doesn't exist in the database, the result will be a SQL exception, which will automatically flow back through the data portal to the UI code, contained within a `DataPortalException`. This is intentional, as it allows the UI to have full access to the exception's details so that the UI can decide how to notify the user that the data doesn't exist in the database.

The first thing the method does is open a connection to the database:

```
Using cn As New SqlConnection(Database.PTrackerConnection)
  cn.Open()
```

`Database.PTrackerConnection` is a call to a helper class in `ProjectTracker.Library`. This helper simply abstracts the process of retrieving the database connection string. It uses `System.Configuration` to get the data, and looks like this:

```
Public ReadOnly Property PTrackerConnection() As String
  Get
    Return ConnectionStrings("PTracker").ConnectionString
  End Get
End Property
```

Because the `ConfigurationManager` is used in this code, a reference to `System.Configuration.dll` is required by `ProjectTracker.Library`. This `PTrackerConnection` property is merely a convenience to simplify the code in business objects. You may use a similar concept in your code if you choose.

Then, within a `Using` block, a `SqlCommand` object is initialized to call the `getProject` stored procedure:

```
Using cm As SqlCommand = cn.CreateCommand
  cm.CommandType = CommandType.StoredProcedure
  cm.CommandText = "getProject"
  cm.Parameters.AddWithValue("@id", criteria.Id)
```

Note the use of the `criteria` parameter. This is the `Criteria` object that was created in the `GetProject()` factory method, and so it provides access to the criteria data supplied to the factory method by the UI. The `SqlCommand` object is then executed to return a data reader:

```
Using dr As New SafeDataReader(cm.ExecuteReader)
```

Rather than using a `SqlDataReader`, this code creates an instance of the `Csla.Data.SafeDataReader` class. This provides automatic protection from errant `null` values in the data, and also enables support for the `SmartDate` data type.

The data reader is then used to populate the object's fields like this:

```
With dr
  mId = .GetGuid("Id")
  mName = .GetString("Name")
  mStarted = .GetSmartDate("Started", mStarted.EmptyIsMin)
  mEnded = .GetSmartDate("Ended", mEnded.EmptyIsMin)
  mDescription = .GetString("Description")
  .GetBytes("LastChanged", 0, mTimestamp, 0, 8)
```

The `SmartDate` values are retrieved using the `SafeDataReader` object's `GetSmartDate()` method, which automatically handles the translation of `null` values into appropriate empty date values.

Also notice that the LastChanged column is retrieved and placed into the mTimestamp Byte array. This value is never exposed outside the object, but is maintained for later use if the object is updated. Recall from Chapter 6 that LastChanged is a timestamp value in the database table, and is used by the updateProject stored procedure to implement first-write-wins optimistic concurrency. The object must be able to provide updateProject with the original timestamp value that was in the table when the data was first loaded.

At this point, the Project object's fields have been loaded. But Project contains a collection of child objects, and they need to be loaded as well. Remember that the getProject stored procedure returns *two* result sets: the first with the project's data; the second with the data for the child objects. The NextResult() method of the data reader moves to the second result set so that the child collection object can simply loop through all the rows, creating a child object for each:

```
.NextResult()
mResources = ProjectResources.GetProjectResources(dr)
End With
```

Now that the object contains data loaded directly from the database, it is an "old" object. The definition of an old object is that the primary key value in the object matches a primary key value in the database. In Chapter 4, the data portal was implemented to automatically call the object's MarkOld() method after DataPortal_Fetch() is complete. That ensures that the object's IsNew and IsDirty properties will return False.

DataPortal_Insert

The DataPortal_Insert() method handles the case in which a new object needs to insert its data into the database. It is invoked by the data portal as a result of the UI calling the object's Save() method when the object's IsNew property is True.

As with all the methods that change the database, this one is marked with the <Transactional()> attribute to ensure that the code is transactionally protected:

```
<Transactional(TransactionalTypes.TransactionScope)> _
Protected Overrides Sub DataPortal_Insert()
  Using cn As New SqlConnection(Database.PTrackerConnection)
    cn.Open()
    Using cm As SqlCommand = cn.CreateCommand
      cm.CommandText = "addProject"
      DoInsertUpdate(cm)
    End Using
  End Using
  ' update child objects
  mResources.Update(Me)
End Sub
```

As with DataPortal_Fetch(), this method opens a connection to the database and creates a SqlCommand object. However, it turns out that both the addProject and updateProject stored procedures take almost the same set of parameters. To consolidate code, a DoInsertUpdate() helper method is called to load the common parameters and to execute the SqlCommand object. That method looks like this:

```
Private Sub DoInsertUpdate(ByVal cm As SqlCommand)
  With cm
    .CommandType = CommandType.StoredProcedure
    .Parameters.AddWithValue("@id", mId)
    .Parameters.AddWithValue("@name", mName)
    .Parameters.AddWithValue("@started", mStarted.DBValue)
    .Parameters.AddWithValue("@ended", mEnded.DBValue)
```

```
      .Parameters.AddWithValue("@description", mDescription)
      Dim param As New SqlParameter("@newLastChanged", SqlDbType.Timestamp)
      param.Direction = ParameterDirection.Output
      .Parameters.Add(param)

      .ExecuteNonQuery()

      mTimestamp = CType(.Parameters("@newLastChanged").Value, Byte())
    End With
  End Sub
```

The DataPortal_Insert() method already set the stored procedure name on the SqlCommand object, so this helper method only needs to add parameters to the object, loading it with the object's data. It then executes the stored procedure.

Recall from Chapter 6 that both the addProject and updateProject stored procedures perform a SELECT statement to return the updated LastChanged column value. This value is read as a result of the stored procedure call so that the object can update the mTimestamp field with the new value from the database. As with DataPortal_Fetch(), the object needs to have the current value of the timestamp for any future updates to the database.

Back in DataPortal_Insert(), once the insert operation is complete, the Project object's data is in the database. However, a Project contains child objects, and their data must be added to the database as well. This is handled by calling an Update() method on the child collection object:

```
mResources.Update(Me)
```

This method is scoped as Friend and is intended for use only by the Project object. It loops through all the child objects in the collection, inserting each one into the database. You'll see the code for this Update() method later in the chapter.

Once DataPortal_Insert() is complete, the data portal automatically invokes the MarkOld() method on the object, ensuring that the IsNew and IsDirty properties are both False. Since the object's primary key value in memory now matches a primary key value in the database, it is not new; and since the rest of the object's data values match those in the database, it is not dirty.

DataPortal_Update

The DataPortal_Update() method is very similar to DataPortal_Insert(), but it is called by the data portal in the case that IsNew is False. It too opens a database connection and creates a SqlCommand object, and then calls DoInsertUpdate() to execute the updateProject stored procedure:

```
<Transactional(TransactionalTypes.TransactionScope)> _
Protected Overrides Sub DataPortal_Update()
  If MyBase.IsDirty Then
    Using cn As New SqlConnection(Database.PTrackerConnection)
      cn.Open()
      Using cm As SqlCommand = cn.CreateCommand
        cm.CommandText = "updateProject"
        cm.Parameters.AddWithValue("@lastChanged", mTimestamp)
        DoInsertUpdate(cm)
      End Using
    End Using
  End If
  ' update child objects
  mResources.Update(Me)
End Sub
```

However, the updateProject stored procedure requires one extra parameter not required by addProject: the timestamp value for the LastChanged column:

```
cm.Parameters.AddWithValue("@lastChanged", mTimestamp)
```

This is required for the first-write-wins optimistic concurrency implemented by the stored procedure. The goal is to ensure that multiple users can't overwrite each other's changes to the data. Other than adding this one extra parameter to the SqlCommand object, the DataPortal_Update() method is very similar to DataPortal_Insert().

DataPortal_DeleteSelf

The final method that the data portal may invoke when the UI calls the object's Save() method is DataPortal_DeleteSelf(). This method is invoked if the object's IsDeleted property is True and its IsNew property is False. In this case, the object needs to delete itself from the database.

Remember that there are two ways objects can be deleted: through immediate or deferred deletion. Deferred deletion is when the object is loaded into memory, its IsDeleted property is set to True, and Save() is called. Immediate deletion is when a factory method is called and passes criteria identifying the object to the DataPortal.Delete() method.

In the case of immediate deletion, the data portal ultimately calls DataPortal_Delete(), passing the Criteria object to that method so it knows which data to delete. Deferred deletion calls DataPortal_DeleteSelf(), passing no Criteria object because the object is fully populated with data already.

■**Note** Implementing the DataPortal_DeleteSelf() method is only required if your object supports deferred deletion. In the Project object, deferred deletion is *not* supported, but I am implementing the method anyway to illustrate how it is done.

The simplest way to implement DataPortal_DeleteSelf() is to create a Criteria object and delegate the call to DataPortal_Delete():

```
<Transactional(TransactionalTypes.TransactionScope)> _
Protected Overrides Sub DataPortal_DeleteSelf()
  DataPortal_Delete(New Criteria(mId))
End Sub
```

You might wonder why the data portal couldn't do this for you automatically. But remember that the data portal has no idea what values are required to identify your business object's data. Even if you assume that GetIdValue() returns the complete primary key value for the object, there's no automatic way by which the data portal can create and properly initialize the specific Criteria object for every business object you might create. Thus, you must create the Criteria object and pass it to DataPortal_Delete().

DataPortal_Delete

The final data portal method is DataPortal_Delete(). This method is called from two possible sources—if immediate deletion is used, the UI will call the Shared deletion method, which will call DataPortal_Delete(); and if deferred deletion is used, then DataPortal_Delete() is called by DataPortal_DeleteSelf(). A Criteria object is passed as a parameter, identifying the data to be deleted. Then it's just a matter of calling the deleteProject stored procedure as follows:

```
<Transactional(TransactionalTypes.TransactionScope)> _
Private Overloads Sub DataPortal_Delete(ByVal criteria As Criteria)
  Using cn As New SqlConnection(Database.PTrackerConnection)
    cn.Open()
    Using cm As SqlCommand = cn.CreateCommand
      With cm
        .Connection = cn
        .CommandType = CommandType.StoredProcedure
        .CommandText = "deleteProject"
        .Parameters.AddWithValue("@id", criteria.Id)
        .ExecuteNonQuery()
      End With
    End Using
  End Using
End Sub
```

The method just opens a database connection, configures a SqlCommand object to call the deleteProject stored procedure, and executes the command.

In the download code, you'll also see a code region for an Exists command, which I'll discuss later in the chapter.

ProjectResources

A Project object contains a collection of child objects, each one representing a resource assigned to the project. The collection is maintained by a ProjectResources collection object, which is created by inheriting from Csla.BusinessListBase. The ProjectResources class has three regions:

- *Business Methods*
- *Factory Methods*
- *Data Access*

The *Business Methods* region contains the Assign() method that assigns a resource to the project. It also contains some helpful overloads of common methods, such as a Contains() method that accepts the Id value of a Resource. This is useful because the Contains() method provided by BusinessListBase() only accepts a ProjectResource object; but as you'll see in Chapters 9 and 10, the UI code needs to see if the collection contains a ResourceInfo object based on its Id value.

The *Factory Methods* region contains a set of Friend-scoped factory methods for use by the Project object in creating and loading the collection with data. Finally, the *Data Access* region implements code to load the collection with data, and to save the child objects in the collection into the database.

Before getting into the regions, let's take a look at the class declaration:

```
<Serializable()> _
Public Class ProjectResources
  Inherits BusinessListBase(Of ProjectResources, ProjectResource)
```

Like all business classes, this one is serializable. It also inherits from a CSLA .NET base class—in this case, BusinessListBase. The BusinessListBase class requires two generic type parameters.

The first one is the type of the collection itself. That value is used to provide strongly typed methods such as Clone() and Save().

The second one is the type of the child objects contained within the collection. That value is used to make the collection itself strongly typed and affects many methods on the collection, including the Item property, Remove(), Contains(), and others.

Business Methods

The *Business Methods* region contains a set of methods that provide business functionality for use by UI code. In many cases, these methods are overloads of methods common to all collections, but they accept parameters that provide much simpler use for the UI developer. The methods are listed in Table 8-1.

Table 8-1. *Business Methods in ProjectResources*

Method	Description
Assign	Assigns a resource to the project
GetItem	Returns a child object based on a resource Id value
Remove	Removes a child object based on a resource Id value
Contains	Searches for a child object based on a resource Id value
ContainsDeleted	Searches for a deleted child object based on a resource Id value

Of all these methods, only Assign() is truly required. All the other methods merely provide simpler access to the collection's functionality. Still, that simpler access translates into much less code in the UI, so it is well worth implementing in the object.

Assign

The Assign() method assigns a resource to the project. It accepts a resource Id value as a parameter, and adds a new ProjectResource object to the collection representing the assignment of the resource:

```
Public Sub Assign(ByVal resourceId As Integer)
  If Not Contains(resourceId) Then
    Dim resource As ProjectResource = _
      ProjectResource.NewProjectResource(resourceId)
    Me.Add(resource)

  Else
    Throw _
      New InvalidOperationException("Resource already assigned to project")
  End If
End Sub
```

A resource can only be assigned to a project one time, so the collection is first checked to see if it contains an entry with that same resource Id value. Notice that the simpler Contains() overload is useful—I'll get to its implementation shortly.

Assuming the resource isn't already assigned, a new ProjectResource child object is created and initialized by calling the NewProjectResource() factory method. Notice that the resource Id value is passed to the new child object, establishing the proper connection between the project and resource. The child object is then added to the collection, completing the process.

This means the UI code to add a resource to a project looks like this:

```
project.Resources.Assign(resourceId)
```

where resourceId is the primary key of the Resource to be assigned.

GetItem

Collections have an Item property that provides access to individual items in the collection based on a numeric index value. It is often also useful to be able to get at a specific child object based on other data in the child objects themselves. In this case, it will be necessary to retrieve a child item based on the Id property of the resource that was assigned to the project, and this requires a method that accepts the Id property and returns the corresponding child object:

```
Public Function GetItem(ByVal resourceId As Integer) As ProjectResource
  For Each res As ProjectResource In Me
    If res.ResourceId = resourceId Then
      Return res
    End If
  Next
  Return Nothing
End Function
```

In principle, this method operates much like a default Item property—but the Item property's parameter is a positional index, while the GetItem() method's parameter indicates the Id value of the resource. Simply overloading the Item property would be a cleaner solution, but this isn't possible because the Item property accepts an Integer, and so does this new "overload." The result would be a duplicate method signature, and so this must be a method rather than an overload of the Item property.

Remove, Contains, and ContainsDeleted

Collections that inherit from BusinessListBase automatically have Remove(), Contains(), and ContainsDeleted() methods. Each of these accepts a reference to a child object as a parameter, and often that is sufficient.

For this collection, however, it turns out that the UI code in Chapters 9 and 10 is much simpler if it is possible to remove or check for a child object based on a resource Id property value rather than a child object reference. To provide this capability, each of these three methods is overloaded with a different implementation. For instance, here's the Remove() method:

```
Public Overloads Sub Remove(ByVal resourceId As Integer)
  For Each res As ProjectResource In Me
    If res.ResourceId = resourceId Then
      Remove(res)
      Exit For
    End If
  Next
End Sub
```

This method accepts the resourceId value as a parameter, and that value is used to locate the child object (if any) in the collection. The Contains() and ContainsDeleted() overloads follow the same basic approach.

Not all collections will need overloads of this type, but such overloads are often useful to simplify the use of the collection and reduce code in the UI.

Factory Methods

The *Factory Methods* region contains two factory methods and a Private constructor, much like the Project class.

Factory Methods

The two factory methods are declared as `Friend` scope since they are not for use by the UI code. Rather, they are intended for use by the `Project` object that contains the collection:

```
Friend Shared Function NewProjectResources() As ProjectResources
  Return New ProjectResources
End Function

Friend Shared Function GetProjectResources( _
  ByVal dr As SafeDataReader) As ProjectResources

  Return New ProjectResources(dr)
End Function
```

In both cases, the factory methods simply use the `New` keyword to create and return a new instance of the collection object.

The `NewProjectResources()` method returns an empty, new collection. This method is called by `Project` when a new `Project` object is created.

`GetProjectResources()` is used to load the collection with child objects based on data from the database. It is called from `DataPortal_Fetch()` in the `Project` class when a `Project` object is in the process of being loaded from the database. This method accepts a data reader as a parameter, and that data reader is provided to the constructor, which is responsible for loading the collection with data. That parameterized constructor is found in the *Data Access* region.

Constructor

The default constructor, called from `NewProjectResources()`, is located in the *Factory Methods* region, just like it is in the template from Chapter 7:

```
Private Sub New()
  MarkAsChild()
End Sub
```

The fact that `MarkAsChild()` is called here is very important. Remember that the `ProjectResources` collection is contained within a `Project` object and is a child of that `Project`. Due to this, the collection object must be marked as a child object as it is created. The `BusinessListBase` code relies on this information to make sure that the object behaves properly as a child of another object.

The `GetProjectResources()` factory method also calls a constructor, passing it a data reader object:

```
Private Sub New(ByVal dr As SafeDataReader)
  MarkAsChild()
  Fetch(dr)
End Sub
```

This method also calls `MarkAsChild()`, and then calls a `Fetch()` method, which will actually load the object's data from the data reader.

Data Access

The *Data Access* region in a child collection object is quite different from that of any root object like `Project`. Remember that the data portal never directly interacts with child objects, leaving it instead to the root object to initiate all data access in its children. In this case, that means that the

`Project` object is responsible for initiating all data access activity in its child `ProjectResources` collection.

Recall that in the `DataPortal_XYZ` methods of `Project`, calls were made to the `GetProjectResources()` factory method and to an `Update()` method on the collection.

Loading Data

In the `DataPortal_Fetch()` method of `Project`, a call is made to the `GetProjectResources()` factory method in `ProjectResources`. That factory method calls a parameterized constructor, passing a data reader that contains the collection of data for the child objects to be loaded into the collection. That constructor then calls the following `Fetch()` method to load the object with data:

```
Private Sub Fetch(ByVal dr As SafeDataReader)
  Me.RaiseListChangedEvents = False
  While dr.Read()
    Me.Add(ProjectResource.GetResource(dr))
  End While
  Me.RaiseListChangedEvents = True
End Sub
```

This method loops through all the items in the data reader, using each row of data to create a new `ProjectResource` child object. I'll discuss the `GetResource()` factory method later in the chapter, but you can see that it accepts the data reader object as a parameter so the new child object can populate itself with data from the current row.

As discussed in Chapter 7, the `RaiseListChangedEvents` property is set to `False` and then `True` to suppress the `ListChanged` events that would otherwise be raised as each item is added.

Updating Data

The `DataPortal_Insert()` and `DataPortal_Update()` methods of `Project` call the collection's `Update()` method. This method is `Friend` in scope, as it is intended only for use by the parent `Project` object. The `Update()` method is responsible for deleting, inserting, and updating all the child objects in the collection into the database. More precisely, it is responsible for asking each *child* object to do the appropriate operation.

This means looping through both the list of child objects marked for deletion and the list of active objects that may require insert or update operations:

```
Friend Sub Update(ByVal project As Project)
  Me.RaiseListChangedEvents = False
  ' update (thus deleting) any deleted child objects
  For Each obj As ProjectResource In DeletedList
    obj.DeleteSelf(project)
  Next
  ' now that they are deleted, remove them from memory too
  DeletedList.Clear()

  ' add/update any current child objects
  For Each obj As ProjectResource In Me
    If obj.IsNew Then
      obj.Insert(project)

    Else
      obj.Update(project)
    End If
  Next
  Me.RaiseListChangedEvents = True
End Sub
```

First, the code loops through the list of deleted child objects, telling each one to remove its data from the database:

```
For Each obj As ProjectResource In DeletedList
  obj.DeleteSelf(project)
Next
```

Once that's done, the DeletedList is cleared:

```
DeletedList.Clear()
```

This is done because the items have actually been deleted from the database, and so they are no longer needed in memory either. This step keeps the objects in memory in sync with the data in the database.

Then the code loops through all the child objects in the active list. These objects are obviously not marked for deletion (or they would have been in DeletedList), so they are either inserted or updated based on their individual IsNew property values:

```
For Each obj As ProjectResource In Me
  If obj.IsNew Then
    obj.Insert(project)

  Else
    obj.Update(project)
  End If
Next
```

In many ways, this approach mirrors the behavior of the data portal as implemented in Chapter 4. The state of the child object is used to determine which specific data access method to call.

This completes the ProjectResources collection code.

ProjectResource

A Project contains a child collection: ProjectResources. The ProjectResources collection contains ProjectResource objects. As designed in Chapter 6, each ProjectResource object represents a resource that has been assigned to the project.

Also remember from Chapter 6 that ProjectResource shares some behaviors with ResourceAssignment, and those common behaviors were factored out into an Assignment object. As you look through the code in ProjectResource, you'll see calls to the behaviors in Assignment, as ProjectResource collaborates with that other object to implement its own behaviors. I'll discuss the Assignment class after ProjectResource.

ProjectResource is an editable child object, and so that is the template (from Chapter 7) that I'll follow here. Editable child objects have the following code regions:

- *Business Methods*
- *Validation Rules*
- *Authorization Rules*
- *Factory Methods*
- *Data Access*

The class is declared as follows:

```
<Serializable()> _
Public Class ProjectResource
  Inherits BusinessBase(Of ProjectResource)

  Implements IHoldRoles
```

As with Project, the class inherits from BusinessBase, providing the type of the business object itself as the type parameter.

The class also implements an interface: IHoldRoles. This interface will be defined in the Assignments class later in the chapter, and it defines a Role property. This interface will be used by code that validates the Role property value.

Business Methods

The *Business Methods* region is constructed in the same manner as Project. It contains instance field declarations and any properties or methods that interact with those fields.

The instance fields used in this object are as follows:

```
Private mResourceId As Integer
Private mFirstName As String = ""
Private mLastName As String = ""
Private mAssigned As New SmartDate(Today)
Private mRole As Integer
Private mTimestamp(7) As Byte
```

As with Project, notice that string fields are initialized to an empty value.

The properties declared in this class are identical in structure to those in the Project class, so I won't list their code here. They call the CanReadProperty() method in the Get blocks and the CanWriteProperty() method in the Set blocks. Also in the Set blocks, once the value has been updated, the PropertyHasChanged() method is called to trigger validation rules, set the object's IsDirty property to True, and raise the PropertyChanged event for data binding.

This object includes one property that's unique: FullName. This property is a combination of the FirstName and LastName properties, and provides an easy way to get at a preformatted combination of the two:

```
Public ReadOnly Property FullName() As String
  Get
    If CanReadProperty("FirstName") AndAlso CanReadProperty("LastName") Then
      Return LastName & ", " & FirstName
    Else
      Throw _
        New System.Security.SecurityException("Property read not allowed")
    End If
  End Get
End Property
```

Because this property returns values from two other properties, the CanReadProperty() method is explicitly called for those two properties. This helps simplify the authorization rules for the object as a whole, and prevents a user from accidentally seeing a value they aren't authorized to view.

Validation Rules

The *Validation Rules* region is much like that in Project, in that it implements the AddBusinessRules() method and could include custom rule methods. In this case, however, the one custom rule required by ProjectResource is also required by ResourceAssignment. Since the rule is a form of common behavior, its implementation is located in the Assignment class. So the only code here is AddBusinessRules():

```
Protected Overrides Sub AddBusinessRules()
  ValidationRules.AddRule(AddressOf Assignment.ValidRole, "Role")
End Sub
```

The ValidRole rule from the Assignment class is associated with the Role property. That rule is designed to ensure that the Role property is set to a value corresponding to a role in the RoleList collection (which will be discussed later in the chapter). The IHoldRoles interface will be used to allow the ValidRule method to access the Role property.

Authorization Rules

The *Authorization Rules* region implements the AddAuthorizationRules() method, establishing the roles authorized to read and write each property. For this object, the only restriction is that the Role property can only be changed by a ProjectManager:

```
Protected Overrides Sub AddAuthorizationRules()
  AuthorizationRules.AllowWrite("Role", "ProjectManager")
End Sub
```

The CanReadProperty() and CanWriteProperty() method calls in all the properties automatically check any authorization settings established here.

Factory Methods

Like ProjectResources, this object has two factory methods scoped as Friend. These methods are intended for use only by the parent object: ProjectResources.

The NewProjectResource() factory method accepts a resourceId value as a parameter. That value is used to retrieve the corresponding Resource object from the database:

```
Friend Shared Function NewProjectResource( _
  ByVal resourceId As Integer) As ProjectResource

  Return New ProjectResource( _
    Resource.GetResource(resourceId), RoleList.DefaultRole)
End Function
```

The Resource object is needed to initialize the new ProjectResource object with all its data, including the resource's first and last name.

Also notice how the default role is retrieved from the RoleList class by calling a DefaultRole() method. It is the responsibility of the RoleList object to deal with the details around roles, including what role is the default for a newly assigned resource.

The constructor method called here initializes the new object based on the information provided.

The GetResource() factory method is called by ProjectResources as it is being loaded with data from the database. Recall that ProjectResources gets a data reader and loops through all the rows in that data reader, creating a new ProjectResource for each row. To do this, it calls the GetResource() factory method:

```
Friend Shared Function GetResource( _
  ByVal dr As SafeDataReader) As ProjectResource

  Return New ProjectResource(dr)
End Function
```

Again, the data reader is passed through to a constructor, which loads the object's fields with data from the current row in the data reader.

Constructor

All business objects must have a non-`Public` default constructor. Since `ProjectResource` is a child of `ProjectResources`, the constructor must call `MarkAsChild()`:

```
Private Sub New()
  MarkAsChild()
End Sub
```

As with `ProjectResources`, this ensures that the object behaves properly as a child of another object.

When a resource is newly assigned to a project, the `NewProjectResource()` factory method is called. It, in turn, calls a constructor to initialize the new object:

```
Private Sub New(ByVal resource As Resource, ByVal role As Integer)
  MarkAsChild()
  With resource
    mResourceId = .Id
    mLastName = .LastName
    mFirstName = .FirstName
    mAssigned.Date = Assignment.GetDefaultAssignedDate
    mRole = role
  End With
End Sub
```

As with all constructors in a child object, `MarkAsChild()` is called to mark this as a child object. Then the object's fields are set to appropriate values based on the `Resource` object and default role value passed in as parameters.

Finally, the `GetProjectResource()` factory method calls a constructor to create the object, passing a data reader object as a parameter:

```
Private Sub New(ByVal dr As SafeDataReader)
  MarkAsChild()
  Fetch(dr)
End Sub
```

This method calls `MarkAsChild()` to mark the object as a child object, and then calls a `Fetch()` method to do the actual data loading.

Data Access

The *Data Access* region contains the code to initialize a new instance of the class when created as a new object or loaded from the database. It also contains methods to insert, update, and delete the object's data in the database.

Loading an Existing Object

When a `Project` is being loaded from the database, it calls `ProjectResources` to load all the child objects. `ProjectResources` loops through all the rows in the data reader supplied by `Project`, creating a `ProjectResource` child object for each row. That data reader is ultimately passed into the `Fetch()` method where the object's fields are set:

```
Private Sub Fetch(ByVal dr As SafeDataReader)
  With dr
    mResourceId = .GetInt32("ResourceId")
    mLastName = .GetString("LastName")
    mFirstName = .GetString("FirstName")
    mAssigned = .GetSmartDate("Assigned")
```

```
        mRole = .GetInt32("Role")
        .GetBytes("LastChanged", 0, mTimestamp, 0, 8)
    End With
    MarkOld()
End Sub
```

This code is very similar to the code in Project to load the object's fields from the data reader. Each field is loaded, including the timestamp value for this row in the database; thus enabling implementation of first-write-wins optimistic concurrency for the child objects, as well as the Project object itself.

Notice the call to MarkOld() at the end of the method. Since the object is now populated with data directly from the database, it is not new or dirty. The MarkOld() method sets the IsNew and IsDirty property values to False. In root objects, this is handled by the data portal; but in child objects, you need to manually call the method.

Inserting Data

When ProjectResources is asked to update its data into the database, it loops through all the child objects. Any child objects with IsDeleted set to False and IsNew set to True have their Insert() method called. The child object is responsible for inserting its own data into the database:

```
Friend Sub Insert(ByVal project As Project)
    ' if we're not dirty then don't update the database
    If Not Me.IsDirty Then Exit Sub

    Using cn As New SqlConnection(Database.PTrackerConnection)
        cn.Open()
        mTimestamp = Assignment.AddAssignment( _
            cn, project.Id, mResourceId, mAssigned, mRole)
        MarkOld()
    End Using
End Sub
```

If the object's data hasn't been changed, then the database isn't altered. There's no sense updating the database with the same values it already contains.

In Chapter 6, the object design process revealed that ProjectResource and ResourceAssignment both create a relationship between a project and a resource using the same data in the same way. Due to this, the Insert() method delegates most of its work to an AddAssignment() method in the Assignment class.

You may be wondering why this method opens a connection to the database. Didn't Project open a connection already? If you look back at the Project class, you'll see that its code closes the connection before updating any child objects. I'm relying on the database connection pooling available in .NET to make this code perform well.

Later in the chapter, I'll show how the Resource object and its ResourceAssignment child objects are implemented to share a common database connection. That complicates the code a bit, but may offer some minor performance gains. By looking at both approaches, you can choose which one suits your needs the best.

Updating Data

The Update() method is very similar to Insert(). It too opens a database connection and then delegates the call to a method in the Assignment class: UpdateAssignment(). This is because the data updated by ProjectResource is the same as ResourceAssignment, so the common behavior is factored out into the Assignment class.

Deleting Data

Finally, there's the `DeleteSelf()` method. Like `Update()` and `Insert()`, it too opens a database connection and delegates the work to the `Assignment` class. There is one important difference in this method, however, in that it not only skips out if `IsDirty` is `False`, but also if `IsNew` is `True`:

```
If Me.IsNew Then Exit Sub
```

The reason for checking `IsNew` is to prevent the code from trying to delete data in the database that the object knows isn't there. Remember that the definition of a "new" object is one in which the object's primary key value in memory doesn't exist in the database. If it isn't in the database, then there's no sense trying to delete it.

This completes the `ProjectResource` class, and really the whole `Project` object family. Of course, you don't quite have the whole picture yet, because `ProjectResource` collaborates with both `Assignment` and `RoleList` to do its work. I'll discuss those classes next.

Assignment

The `Assignment` class contains the behaviors common to both `ProjectResource` and `ResourceAssignment`, as designed in Chapter 6. Figure 8-4 shows the collaboration relationship between these objects.

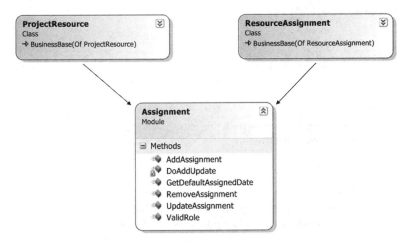

Figure 8-4. *Objects collaborating with Assignment*

Since `Assignment` only implements behaviors and contains no data, it is declared as a `Module`:

Friend Module Assignment

Notice that it doesn't inherit from any CSLA .NET base classes. It has no need, since it is merely a collection of common behaviors. Specifically, it contains a business method, a custom validation rule, and a set of data access methods.

Business Methods

When a resource is associated with a project, the date of that association is recorded. Though it may seem somewhat trivial, the code to determine that date value is a common behavior between ProjectResource and ResourceAssignment, so it is implemented in the Assignment class:

```
Public Function GetDefaultAssignedDate() As Date
  Return Today
End Function
```

This is an example of the concept of normalization of behavior I discussed in Chapter 6.

Validation Rules

Similarly, both ProjectResource and ResourceAssignment have a Role property, allowing the role of the resource on the project to be changed. When that value is changed, it must be validated. Of course, this is handled by implementing a rule method conforming to the RuleHandler delegate defined by CSLA .NET. This is common behavior, so it is implemented in Assignment:

```
Public Function ValidRole( _
  ByVal target As Object, ByVal e As RuleArgs) As Boolean

  Dim role As Integer = CType(target, IHoldRoles).Role

  If RoleList.GetList.ContainsKey(role) Then
    Return True

  Else
    e.Description = "Role must be in RoleList"
    Return False
  End If
End Function
```

This method uses the IHoldRoles interface to retrieve the value of the Role property from the specified target object. This interface is defined like this:

```
Friend Interface IHoldRoles
  Property Role() As Integer
End Interface
```

Notice that the interface is Friend in scope. It is only used within this assembly by the ValidRole() method, so there's no need to expose it as a public interface. Since both ProjectResource and ResourceAssignment implement this interface, the ValidRole() method has strongly typed access to the Role property on both objects.

Using the retrieved role value, the RoleList collection is asked whether it contains an entry with that value as a key. If it does, then the role is valid; otherwise, it is not valid, so e.Description is set to indicate the nature of the problem and False is returned as a result.

The RoleList object automatically caches the list of roles, so only the first call to GetList() by the application goes to the database, and subsequent calls are handled from the in-memory cache.

Data Access

The Assignment class also implements the data access behaviors common between both ProjectResource and ResourceAssignment. The AddAssignment() and UpdateAssignment() methods are very similar, in that they both create a SqlCommand object and then call a DoAddUpdate() helper method. Here's the UpdateAssignment() method:

```
Public Function UpdateAssignment(ByVal cn As SqlConnection, _
  ByVal projectId As Guid, ByVal resourceId As Integer, _
  ByVal assigned As SmartDate, ByVal newRole As Integer, _
  ByVal timestamp() As Byte) As Byte()

  Using cm As SqlCommand = cn.CreateCommand()
    cm.CommandText = "updateAssignment"
    cm.Parameters.AddWithValue("@lastChanged", timestamp)
    Return DoAddUpdate( _
      cm, projectId, resourceId, assigned, newRole)
  End Using
End Function
```

The only differences between UpdateAssignment() and AddAssignment() are the name of the
stored procedure to be called and the fact that AddAssignment() doesn't add a timestamp parameter
to the SqlCommand object. The timestamp value is only needed for updates to deal with optimistic
concurrency.

All the real work occurs in DoAddUpdate():

```
Private Function DoAddUpdate(ByVal cm As SqlCommand, _
  ByVal projectId As Guid, ByVal resourceId As Integer, _
  ByVal assigned As SmartDate, _
  ByVal newRole As Integer) As Byte()

  cm.CommandType = CommandType.StoredProcedure
  cm.Parameters.AddWithValue("@projectId", projectId)
  cm.Parameters.AddWithValue("@resourceId", resourceId)
  cm.Parameters.AddWithValue("@assigned", assigned.DBValue)
  cm.Parameters.AddWithValue("@role", newRole)
  Dim param As New SqlParameter("@newLastChanged", SqlDbType.Timestamp)
  param.Direction = ParameterDirection.Output
  cm.Parameters.Add(param)

  cm.ExecuteNonQuery()

  Return CType(cm.Parameters("@newLastChanged").Value, Byte())
End Function
```

This method loads the parameters into the SqlCommand object and then executes it to call the
proper stored procedure. Both the addAssignment and updateAssignment stored procedures were
implemented in Chapter 6 to return the updated timestamp value for the row. That value is returned
as an output parameter so the business object can store the new value.

The Assignment class illustrates how to normalize behavior through collaboration, helping to
ensure that a given behavior is only implemented once within the business layer.

RoleList

The final object used by Project, ProjectResources, ProjectResource, and Assignment is the
RoleList collection. This is a name/value list based on the Roles table from Chapter 6. The name
(key) values are of type Integer, while the values are the String names of each role.

The CSLA .NET framework includes the NameValueListBase class to help simplify the creation
of name/value list objects. Such objects are so common in business applications that it is worth
having a base class to support this one specialized scenario.

Chapter 7 includes a template for name/value list classes, and RoleList will follow that template. It includes the *Business Methods*, *Factory Methods*, and *Data Access* regions. The class is
declared like this:

```
<Serializable()> _
Public Class RoleList
  Inherits NameValueListBase(Of Integer, String)
```

Notice the generic type parameters. The first specifies the data type of the name or key, while the second specifies the data type of the value. These data types are used to define the name and value types of the NameValuePair child objects contained in the collection.

Business Methods

The only business method in this class is DefaultRole(), which returns the default role for a resource newly assigned to a project. Not all name/value collections will provide a method to specify the default role, but it is often helpful. Recall that this method is used by ProjectResource as a new ProjectResource object is created. Here's the method:

```
Public Shared Function DefaultRole() As Integer
  Dim list As RoleList = GetList()
  If list.Count > 0 Then
    Return list.Items(0).Key

  Else
    Throw New NullReferenceException( _
      "No roles available; default role can not be returned")
  End If
End Function
```

The implementation in this application is very simplistic, as it just returns the first item in the collection. In a more complex application, the default value might be specified in the database.

Factory Methods

As in the template from Chapter 7, RoleList implements a form of caching to minimize load on the database. The GetList() factory method stores the collection in a Shared field and returns it if the object has already been loaded. It only goes to the database if the cache field is Nothing:

```
Private Shared mList As RoleList

Public Shared Function GetList() As RoleList
  If mList Is Nothing Then
    mList = DataPortal.Fetch(Of RoleList) _
      (New Criteria(GetType(RoleList)))
  End If
  Return mList
End Function
```

Remember that NameValueListBase defines a Criteria class, so one doesn't need to be declared in every business class. As long as no filtering is required, that basic Criteria class can be used; and it meets the needs of RoleList just fine.

■**Note** If you do need to filter the name/value list results, you'll need to declare your own criteria class in the *Data Access* region just like you would with any other root object.

In case the cache needs to be flushed at some point, there's also an `InvalidateCache()` method:

```
Public Shared Sub InvalidateCache()
  mList = Nothing
End Sub
```

By setting the `Shared` cache value to `Nothing`, the cache is reset. The next time any code calls the `GetList()` method, the collection will be reloaded from the database. This `InvalidateCache()` method will be called by the `Roles` collection later in the chapter.

Of course, there's also a non-`Public` constructor in the class to enforce the use of the factory method to retrieve the object.

Data Access

Finally, there's the `DataPortal_Fetch()` method that loads the data from the database into the collection:

```
Private Overloads Sub DataPortal_Fetch(ByVal criteria As Criteria)
  Me.RaiseListChangedEvents = False
  Using cn As New SqlConnection(Database.PTrackerConnection)
    cn.Open()
    Using cm As SqlCommand = cn.CreateCommand
      cm.CommandType = CommandType.StoredProcedure
      cm.CommandText = "getRoles"

      Using dr As New SafeDataReader(cm.ExecuteReader)
        IsReadOnly = False
        With dr
          While .Read()
            Me.Add(New NameValuePair( _
              .GetInt32("id"), .GetString("name")))
          End While
        End With
        IsReadOnly = True
      End Using
    End Using
  End Using
  Me.RaiseListChangedEvents = True
End Sub
```

As with the `DataPortal_Fetch()` method in `Project`, the code here opens a connection to the database, sets up a `SqlCommand` object, and executes it to get a `SafeDataReader` object. The code then loops through that data reader and creates a new `NameValuePair` object for each row.

Since the collection is normally read-only, the `IsReadOnly` property is set to `False` before loading the data and then restored to `True` once the data has been loaded.

The result is a fully populated name/value list containing the data from the `Roles` table in the database.

This completes the `Project` object family, including all collaboration objects. Next, I'll walk briefly through the `Resource` object family.

Resource and Related Objects

The other primary root object in the object model is `Resource`. Like `Project`, a `Resource` object can be directly created, retrieved, or updated. It also contains a list of child objects.

Since I've already walked through the creation of an editable root business object in detail, there's no need to do the same for the Resource class. However, there are two primary areas of difference that should be discussed.

Where the Projects table uses a uniqueidentifier as a primary key, the Resources table uses an int identity column. This means that the database is responsible for assigning the primary key value for any new Resource objects.

Additionally, just to show how it is done, I have implemented the Resource, ResourceAssignments, and ResourceAssignment objects to share a common database connection. Where every object in the Project family opens and closes its own database connection, the objects in the Resource family pass a common SqlConnection object between them when doing data access. While this complicates the code somewhat, it may offer some minor performance gains. You can choose the approach that best fits your needs.

Using an Identity Column

Many databases are designed to use identity columns, where the database is responsible for assigning primary key values to rows of data as they are inserted. While the Guid approach used in Project is somewhat simpler to implement, Resource illustrates how to work with identity columns.

The changes are limited to the *Data Access* region of the code, and in particular the DataPortal_Insert() method. Where the updateResource stored procedure simply returns the updated timestamp for the row, addResource also returns the newly created identity value:

```
SELECT Id, LastChanged FROM Resources WHERE Id=SCOPEmIdENTITY()
```

This means DataPortal_Insert() needs to retrieve that value and update the object's mId field:

```
<Transactional(TransactionalTypes.TransactionScope)> _
Protected Overrides Sub DataPortal_Insert()
  Using cn As New SqlConnection(Database.PTrackerConnection)
    cn.Open()
    Using cm As SqlCommand = cn.CreateCommand
      With cm
        .CommandType = CommandType.StoredProcedure
        .CommandText = "addResource"
      With cm
        .Parameters.AddWithValue("@lastName", mLastName)
        .Parameters.AddWithValue("@firstName", mFirstName)
        Dim param As New SqlParameter("@newId", SqlDbType.Int)
        param.Direction = ParameterDirection.Output
        .Parameters.Add(param)
        param = New SqlParameter("@newLastChanged", SqlDbType.Timestamp)
        param.Direction = ParameterDirection.Output
        .Parameters.Add(param)

        .ExecuteNonQuery()

        mId = CInt(.Parameters("@newId").Value)
        mTimestamp = CType(.Parameters("@newLastChanged").Value, Byte())
      End With

      ' update child objects
      mAssignments.Update(cn, Me)
    End With
  End Using
  End Using
End Sub
```

The method opens the database connection and sets up the `SqlCommand` object. When the command is executed, it returns both the `@newId` and `@newLastChanged` column values, which are used to set the `mId` and `mTimestamp` fields in the object. The result is that the `Resource` object's `Id` property reflects the value assigned by the database as soon as the data is added to the database.

Notice that the child objects are updated *after* this value has been retrieved, which means that all the child `ResourceAssignment` objects will have access to their parent object's `Id` value. This is important since they use this value as a foreign key.

Sharing a Database Connection

If you look at the preceding `DataPortal_Insert()` method, you'll notice that the child object collection's `Update()` method is called *before* the database connection is closed. In fact, the `SqlConnection` object is passed as a parameter to the `Update()` method along with a reference to the `Resource` object itself:

```
mAssignments.Update(cn, Me)
```

The idea behind this is to make the connection available to the child objects so a connection doesn't have to be opened and closed for each object.

The .NET Framework provides database connection pooling, so talking about "opening and closing" database connections isn't really meaningful. Just because your code "closes" or "disposes" a `SqlConnection` object doesn't mean the connection is actually closed; in fact, it usually isn't closed, but rather is simply returned to the connection pool for later reuse.

What this means is that it typically isn't worth worrying about the frequency of opening and closing the database connection, since your code is really just reusing an already open connection anyway.

But if you want to eke out that tiny extra bit of performance, you may want to share the connection. Also, if you are implementing manual ADO.NET transactions, you'll want to follow the flow of code I'm showing here; though you would pass the `SqlTransaction` object as a parameter rather than the `SqlConnection` object. `SqlTransaction` objects contain a reference to the underlying `SqlConnection`, so passing a `SqlTransaction` provides all the information needed to initialize `SqlCommand` objects to use the same connection and transaction.

The principle remains consistent, however. The `Update()` method in `ResourceAssignments` accepts the open `SqlConnection` object and passes it to each `ResourceAssignment` child object's data access method:

```
Friend Sub Update(ByVal cn As SqlConnection, ByVal resource As Resource)
  Me.RaiseListChangedEvents = False
  ' update (thus deleting) any deleted child objects
  For Each item As ResourceAssignment In DeletedList
    item.DeleteSelf(cn, resource)
  Next
  ' now that they are deleted, remove them from memory too
  DeletedList.Clear()

  ' add/update any current child objects
  For Each item As ResourceAssignment In Me
    If item.IsNew Then
      item.Insert(cn, resource)

    Else
      item.Update(cn, resource)
    End If
  Next
  Me.RaiseListChangedEvents = True
End Sub
```

Finally, in the Insert(), Update(), and DeleteSelf() methods of ResourceAssignment, this open connection is used. For instance, here's the Insert() method:

```
Friend Sub Insert(ByVal cn As SqlConnection, ByVal resource As Resource)
  ' if we're not dirty then don't update the database
  If Not Me.IsDirty Then Exit Sub

  mTimestamp = Assignment.AddAssignment( _
    cn, mProjectId, resource.Id, mAssigned, mRole)
  MarkOld()
End Sub
```

As with ProjectResource, the real work is delegated to the Assignment class. But notice that no database connection is opened in this Insert() method because an open connection was passed in as a parameter.

The ResourceAssignments and ResourceAssignment objects are otherwise totally comparable to ProjectResources and ProjectResource, so I won't cover their code in detail here. You can look at the code for these classes by downloading the code for the book.

ProjectList and ResourceList

The ProjectList and ResourceList classes are both read-only collections of read-only data. They exist to provide the UI with an efficient way to get a list of projects and resources for display to the user.

On the surface, it might seem that you could simply retrieve a collection of Project or Resource objects and display their data. But that would mean retrieving a lot of data that the user may never use. Instead, it's more efficient to retrieve a small set of read-only objects for display purposes, and then retrieve an actual Project or Resource object once the user has chosen which one to use.

The CSLA .NET framework includes the ReadOnlyListBase class, which is designed specifically to support this type of read-only list. Such a collection typically contains objects that inherit from ReadOnlyBase.

Because these two read-only collections are so similar in implementation, I'm only going to walk through the ResourceList class in this chapter. You can look at the code for ProjectList in the code download.

The ResourceList class inherits from Csla.ReadOnlyListBase:

```
<Serializable()> _
Public Class ResourceList
  Inherits ReadOnlyListBase(Of ResourceList, ResourceInfo)
```

ReadOnlyListBase requires two generic type parameters. The first is the type of the collection object itself and is used to create the strongly typed Clone() method.

The second is the type of the child objects contained in the collection: ResourceInfo. This is a separate class that implements simple read-only properties to expose the resource data. Let's quickly look at that class before continuing with the implementation of ResourceList itself.

ResourceInfo Class

The ResourceList class is a collection of ResourceInfo objects. Each ResourceInfo object provides read-only access to a subset of data from the Resources table. The class is defined like this:

```
<Serializable()> _
Public Class ResourceInfo
  Inherits ReadOnlyBase(Of ResourceInfo)
```

It inherits from ReadOnlyBase, which requires one generic type parameter: the type of the business object. This type parameter is used to implement the strongly typed Clone() method. By inheriting from ReadOnlyBase, the class automatically gains implementations of the standard System.Object overrides: Equals(), GetHashCode(), and ToString().

The class implements a *Business Methods* region and a *Constructors* region. There's no need for *Data Access*, because the data will be loaded by the ResourceList parent collection.

Business Methods

The ResourceInfo object exposes two properties: Id and Name:

```
Private mId As Integer
Private mName As String

Public Property Id() As Integer
  Get
    Return mId
  End Get
  Friend Set(ByVal Value As Integer)
    mId = Value
  End Set
End Property

Public Property Name() As String
  Get
    Return mName
  End Get
  Friend Set(ByVal Value As String)
    mName = Value
  End Set
End Property

Protected Overrides Function GetIdValue() As Object
  Return mId
End Function
```

Notice that the properties are read-only, so the values can't be changed by UI code. The implementation of GetIdValue() is required by ReadOnlyBase, and it should return a unique value for the child object within the collection. This value is used to implement the standard System.Object overrides.

In this particular case, the default implementation of ToString() isn't sufficient. While the unique identifier for this object comes from mId, the ToString() method should return the value from mName. To resolve this, the ToString() method is overridden:

```
Public Overrides Function ToString() As String
  Return mName
End Function
```

This is important, because when the collection is data bound to a list control like a ListBox, it is the ToString() value that will be displayed to the user.

Constructors

The class has two constructors: the default constructor to prevent direct creation of the object, and a parameterized constructor used by ResourceList to load the object with data:

```
Private Sub New()
  ' require use of factory methods
End Sub

Friend Sub New(ByVal dr As SafeDataReader)
  mId = dr.GetInt32("Id")
  mName = String.Format("{0}, {1}", _
    dr.GetString("LastName"), dr.GetString("FirstName"))
End Sub
```

The first constructor exists merely to prevent the UI developer from accidentally using the New keyword to create an instance of this class. The result is that the UI developer is prevented from directly creating an instance of the object.

The second constructor is called by DataPortal_Fetch() in ResourceList to initialize the new child object with data for display.

This completes the ResourceInfo object. It is a very small, simple object designed to efficiently expose read-only data to the UI for display. Now let's return to the implementation of the ResourceList class, which contains a collection of these ResourceInfo objects.

Factory Methods

The ResourceList collection exposes one factory method: GetResourceList(). This factory method simply uses the data portal to retrieve the list of data. For this example, no criteria is used, so the entire list is retrieved:

```
Public Shared Function GetResourceList() As ResourceList
  Return DataPortal.Fetch(Of ResourceList)(New Criteria)
End Function
```

Of course, there's also a non-Public constructor to require the use of the factory method.

Data Access

The GetResourceList() factory method calls the data portal, which in turn ultimately calls the ResourceList object's DataPortal_Fetch() method to load the collection with data. The Criteria object passed from the factory to DataPortal_Fetch() is the simplest implementation possible:

```
<Serializable()> _
Private Class Criteria
  ' no criteria - we retrieve all resources
End Class
```

Since no criteria values are required, the class is just an empty implementation. The class itself is still required, because the data portal uses it to determine what type of object is to be retrieved when DataPortal.Fetch() is called.

The DataPortal_Fetch() method itself is like the others you've seen in the chapter:

```
Private Overloads Sub DataPortal_Fetch(ByVal criteria As Criteria)
  RaiseListChangedEvents = False
  Using cn As New SqlConnection(Database.PTrackerConnection)
    cn.Open()
    Using cm As SqlCommand = cn.CreateCommand
      With cm
        .CommandType = CommandType.StoredProcedure
        .CommandText = "getResources"
```

```
      Using dr As New SafeDataReader(.ExecuteReader)
        IsReadOnly = False
        While dr.Read()
          Dim info As New ResourceInfo(dr)
          Me.Add(info)
        End While

        IsReadOnly = True
      End Using
    End With
  End Using
End Using
RaiseListChangedEvents = True
End Sub
```

It opens a connection to the database, sets up a SqlCommand, and executes that command to get back a SafeDataReader object. The code then loops through the data reader, creating an instance of ResourceInfo for each row of data:

```
      Dim info As New ResourceInfo(dr)
      Me.Add(info)
```

The data reader object is passed to each new object's constructor so it can initialize itself with data as appropriate. Once each child object has been created and initialized, it is added to the collection.

Since ResourceList is a read-only collection, the IsReadOnly property is set to False before loading the data and True once the loading is complete.

The end result is a fully populated list of the resources in the database that can be displayed to the user by the UI.

Roles

The RoleList object provides a read-only, cached list of roles that a resource can hold when assigned to a project. But that list of roles needs to be maintained, and that is the purpose behind the Roles collection. This is an editable root collection that contains a list of editable child Role objects.

The Roles class illustrates how to create an editable root collection based on the template code from Chapter 7. The class inherits from BusinessListBase:

```
<Serializable()> _
Public Class Roles
  Inherits BusinessListBase(Of Roles, Role)
```

The first generic type parameter specifies the type of the collection itself, while the second provides the type of the child objects contained in the collection.

An editable root collection has *Business Methods*, *Authorization Rules*, *Factory Methods*, and *Data Access* regions. By this point, you've seen good examples of each region, so I'll just focus on the parts that are unique for a root collection. For instance, the *Authorization Rules* region includes only the Shared authorization rules discussed earlier in the chapter, so I'll bypass talking about that code here.

Business Methods

The Roles class implements an overloaded Remove() method that accepts a role's Id value rather than a Role object. This simplifies removal of child objects, especially in the Web Forms UI that will be created in Chapter 10.

```
Public Overloads Sub Remove(ByVal id As Integer)
  For Each item As Role In Me
    If item.Id = id Then
      Remove(item)
      Exit For
    End If
  Next
End Sub
```

It also implements a GetRoleById() method to retrieve a child Role object based on the role Id value:

```
Public Function GetRoleById(ByVal id As Integer) As Role
  For Each item As Role In Me
    If item.Id = id Then
      Return item
    End If
  Next
  Return Nothing
End Function
```

Again, this exists to simplify the creation of the Web Forms UI.

Finally, and probably of most interest, is the AddNewCore() override:

```
Protected Overrides Function AddNewCore() As Object
  Dim item As Role = Role.NewRole
  Add(item)
  Return item
End Function
```

When using Windows Forms data binding, it is possible to allow grid controls to automatically add new items to a collection when the user moves to the last row of the grid. The collection object itself controls whether this option is available, and the Roles collection supports the concept. Turning the option on is done in the collection's constructor, but if the option is turned on, then the object *must* override AddNewCore(), as shown here.

■**Note** This option is not enabled for ProjectResources or ResourceAssignments because it isn't possible to add a new ProjectResource or ResourceAssignment child object to those collections without first gathering extra information from the user (specifically the resource or project to be assigned). You can only allow a grid control to add new child objects if you can implement AddNewCore() to create a new child object with no user interaction.

The AddNewCore() method is called by data binding when a new item needs to be added to the collection. The method is responsible for creating a new child object, adding it to the collection, and returning it as a result.

It is important to realize that this puts a serious constraint on the child objects, since it must be possible to create them without user input. In other words, it must be possible to create a child object based purely on default values provided by your code or from the database. If your child object has a parameterless factory method (like the NewRole() method in the preceding AddNewCore() method) for creating a new object, then you are ready to go.

Factory Methods

The *Factory Methods* region implements a GetRoles() factory method, which just calls the data portal like the other factory methods you've seen. It also implements a non-Public constructor to require use of the factory method. But the constructor contains an extra line of code that is quite important:

```
Private Sub New()
  Me.AllowNew = True
End Sub
```

AllowNew is a Protected property defined by BindingList; the base class of BusinessListBase. Setting this to True allows Windows Forms data binding to automatically add new child objects to the collection. Typically, this happens when the collection is bound to an editable grid control in the UI. Table 8-2 lists the properties you can use to control the behavior of an editable collection.

Table 8-2. *Properties Used to Control an Editable Collection*

Property	Description
AllowNew	If True, Windows Forms data binding can automatically add new child objects to the collection. It requires that you override the AddNewCore() method, and defaults to False.
AllowEdit	If True, Windows Forms data binding will allow in-place editing of child objects in a grid control. It defaults to True.

Though a collection can opt to implement a Shared delete method to delete all the items in the database, that isn't a requirement for Roles, so it doesn't have such a method.

Data Access

The *Data Access* region has some unique code. The reason for this is not that the collection is an editable root, but rather that the Roles collection needs to invalidate the cache of any RoleList object when the list of roles is changed. In other words, when Save() is called on a Roles collection, any cached RoleList object must be reloaded from the database to get the new values.

Other than this requirement, the data access code is quite straightforward, so let's focus on the cache invalidation code.

Invalidating the Client-Side Cache

First, the Save() method itself is overridden. This is partially because it implements authorization code just like you saw in the Project class. But it also adds code to invalidate the RoleList cache:

```
Public Overrides Function Save() As Roles
  ' see if save is allowed
  If Not CanEditObject() Then
    Throw New System.Security.SecurityException( _
      "User not authorized to save roles")
  End If

  ' do the save
  Dim result As Roles
  result = MyBase.Save()
  ' this runs on the client and invalidates
  ' the RoleList cache
  RoleList.InvalidateCache()
  Return result
End Function
```

The bold lines show where the cache is invalidated. Notice that it happens *after* the call to MyBase.Save(), because that is the point at which you know that the database has been updated.

But there's a subtler detail to putting the code at this location. Remember that MyBase.Save() invokes the data portal, which potentially transfers the object to an application server to save its data. By the time the MyBase.Save() method returns, the updated object has been returned to the client.

In other words, putting the code in this particular location ensures that it is the client-side cache that is invalidated by calling RoleList.InvalidatedCache().

Invalidating the Server-Side Cache

Perhaps even subtler is the fact that there could be a cached RoleList collection on *both the client and server*. Keep in mind that CSLA .NET enables mobile objects, and that means that business object code can run on the client and on the server. If a business object has server-side code that uses a RoleList, that will cause a RoleList object to be created and cached *on the server*.

If you look back at the ValidRole() rule method in Assignment, you'll see that it calls the GetList() factory on RoleList, loading a list of roles. If any business rule validation occurs for either a ProjectResource or ResourceAssignment object on the server, that would cause the list to be loaded and cached on the server. Though that doesn't occur in ProjectTracker, it is a very common scenario in many applications.

The great thing about the way the mobile objects works is that caching the RoleList on client and server is automatic. You'll note that there's no special code to make that happen. But it does mean a bit of extra work in the Roles collection to ensure that any server-side cache is also flushed.

Recall from Chapter 4 that the data portal will optionally invoke the DataPortal_OnDataPortalInvoke() and DataPortal_OnDataPortalInvokeComplete() methods if your business object implements them. The former is invoked before any DataPortal_XYZ method is called, and the latter is invoked afterward. You can use this method to run code on the server after the DataPortal_Update() method is complete:

```
Protected Overrides Sub DataPortal_OnDataPortalInvokeComplete( _
  ByVal e As Csla.DataPortalEventArgs)

  If ApplicationContext.ExecutionLocation = _
    ApplicationContext.ExecutionLocations.Server Then
    ' this runs on the server and invalidates
    ' the RoleList cache
    RoleList.InvalidateCache()
  End If
End Sub
```

Of course, the data portal could be configured to run the "server-side" code locally in the client process, in which case there's no point invalidating the cache here, since the Save() method will take care of it. That's why the code checks the ExecutionLocation to see if it's actually running on an application server. If so, it calls RoleList.InvalidateCache() to invalidate any server-side cache of role data.

Role

The Roles object is an editable root collection that contains a list of editable child Role objects. Each Role object is an editable child, and so it is very similar in structure to ProjectResource and ResourceAssignment.

The design decision that makes this object unique and interesting is that its key value, Id, is a user-entered value. Unlike Project (in which the value is automatically generated by the object) or Resource (in which the value is generated by the database), this object's key value must be directly entered by the user.

From a data access perspective, this isn't overly complex. The Roles table views the Id column as a primary key, so it already ensures that duplicate values aren't allowed in the database. Of course, sending the object all the way to the database to find out about a validation rule being violated is wasteful. It is far better to detect the condition as soon as a duplicate key value is entered.

Additionally, the user shouldn't have to guess to find an appropriate value when adding a new role to the application. When a new Role object is created, it can set its Id property to an appropriate default value.

Setting a Default Value

The Id property contains code to find a default value if the Id property has never been set to a value:

```
Public Property Id() As Integer
  Get
    CanReadProperty(True)
    If Not mIdSet Then
      ' generate a default id value
      mIdSet = True
      Dim parent As Roles = CType(Me.Parent, Roles)
      Dim max As Integer = 0
      For Each item As Role In parent
        If item.Id > max Then
          max = item.Id
        End If
      Next
      mId = max + 1
    End If
    Return mId
  End Get
  Set(ByVal value As Integer)
    CanWriteProperty(True)
    If Not mId.Equals(value) Then
      mIdSet = True
      mId = value
      PropertyHasChanged()
    End If
  End Set
End Property
```

If the Id property is read, and it hasn't been set prior to this point, then the code loops through the objects in the parent Roles collection to find the maximum value for any existing Id property, and then it sets mId to that value plus one:

```
Dim parent As Roles = CType(Me.Parent, Roles)
Dim max As Integer = 0
For Each item As Role In parent
  If item.Id > max Then
    max = item.Id
  End If
Next
mId = max + 1
```

Your first thought might be that this should be done in the object's constructor. The problem with that is that the Parent property in the base class isn't set to a valid value when the constructor runs.

■**Note** Both the data portal and .NET serialization create the object using constructors that can't provide parameters such as the parent object reference. This is why, as discussed in Chapter 3, `BusinessListBase` includes code to call a `SetParent()` method on its child objects at key points in the object's life cycle.

Since the default value can't be set in the constructor, it is set in the `Id` property on the first request for the value—unless the value has been set previously, either through the property `Set` block or when the data was loaded from the database.

Preventing Duplicate Values

The requirement to have no duplicate `Id` property values is simply a validation rule and so it is implemented as a rule method in the `Role` object's *Validation Rules* region:

```
Private Function NoDuplicates(ByVal target As Object, _
  ByVal e As Csla.Validation.RuleArgs) As Boolean

  Dim parent As Roles = CType(Me.Parent, Roles)
  For Each item As Role In parent
    If item.Id = mId AndAlso Not ReferenceEquals(item, Me) Then
      e.Description = "Role Id must be unique"
      Return False
    End If
  Next
  Return True
End Function
```

When this rule is run, it loops through the list of `Role` objects in the parent `Roles` collection to see if any other child object has the same `Id` value. If there's a match, the method returns `False`; otherwise it returns `True`.

The rule method is associated with the `Id` property in the `AddBusinessRules()` method:

```
Protected Overrides Sub AddBusinessRules()
  ValidationRules.AddRule( _
    AddressOf Csla.Validation.CommonRules.StringRequired, "Name")
  ValidationRules.AddRule(AddressOf NoDuplicates, "Id")
End Sub
```

This custom rule ensures that duplicate `Id` values are caught as they are entered, so that the data doesn't have to be sent to the database to find out about the problem. As you'll see in Chapter 9, this is particularly nice in a Windows Forms UI, since the user gets instant and automatic feedback about what is wrong.

Implementing Exists Methods

The first object discussed in the chapter was `Project`, and I covered all the code in that class except for the `Exists()` command implementation. Many objects can benefit from implementation of an `Exists()` command, as it allows the UI to quickly and easily determine if a given object's data is in the database without having to fully instantiate the object itself. Ideally, a UI developer could write conditional code like this:

```
If Project.Exists(productId) Then
```

Implementing an `Exists()` command also provides an opportunity to make use of `Csla.CommandBase` to create a command object. This makes sense, since all an `Exists()` command needs to do is run a stored procedure in the database and report on the result.

Exists Method

The Project class itself has a Shared method called Exists(), which is Public, so it can be called from UI code:

```
Public Shared Function Exists(ByVal id As Guid) As Boolean
  Dim result As ExistsCommand
  result = DataPortal.Execute(Of ExistsCommand)(New ExistsCommand(id))
  Return result.Exists
End Function
```

While this code is somewhat like other factory methods, it is different in one key way. It creates an instance of an ExistsCommand object, and has the data portal execute the object on the application server:

```
result = DataPortal.Execute(Of ExistsCommand)(New ExistsCommand(id))
```

Notice how the id parameter value is used to initialize the ExistsCommand object as it is created. The important thing to understand is that the ExistsCommand object is created and initialized on the client, and then the data portal transfers the object to the server where the object's DataPortal_ Execute() method is run.

This means that a command object can do work on the client, then do work on the server, and then do more work on the client. In this particular case, it is initialized on the client, executes a stored procedure on the server, and then exposes the result as a property back on the client.

That result value is returned as the result of the Exists() method.

ExistsCommand Class

The real work occurs in the command object itself: ExistsCommand. The ExistsCommand class inherits from Csla.CommandBase and is declared as a Private nested class within Project:

```
<Serializable()> _
Private Class ExistsCommand
  Inherits CommandBase
```

Not all command objects are nested within other business classes, but in this case, it makes sense. There's no need for the UI developer to be aware of the ExistsCommand class or its implementation details; they only need to know about the Project.Exists() method.

In other cases, you may have Public command objects that are directly used by the UI. A good example would be a ShipOrder object that is responsible for shipping a sales order. It is quite realistic to expect that the UI would want to directly ship a sales order, and so there's value in being able to call a ShipOrder.Ship(orderId) method.

Command objects, whether Public or Private, tend to be very simplistic in terms of their structure. ExistsCommand declares some instance fields, one property, and a constructor:

```
Private mId As Guid
Private mExists As Boolean

Public ReadOnly Property Exists() As Boolean
  Get
    Return mExists
  End Get
End Property

Public Sub New(ByVal id As Guid)
  mId = id
End Sub
```

The constructor initializes the `mId` field, so that value is available when the command is executed on the server. The `mExists` field is set as a result of the command running on the server and is exposed through the `Exists` property.

The code that runs on the server is entirely contained within the `DataPortal_Execute()` method:

```
Protected Overrides Sub DataPortal_Execute()
  Using cn As New SqlConnection(Database.PTrackerConnection)
    cn.Open()
    Using cm As SqlCommand = cn.CreateCommand
      cm.CommandType = CommandType.Text
      cm.CommandText = "SELECT Id FROM Projects WHERE Id=@id"
      cm.Parameters.AddWithValue("@id", mId)

      Dim count As Integer = CInt(cm.ExecuteScalar)
      mExists = (count > 0)
    End Using
  End Using
End Sub
```

Of course, the code in `DataPortal_Execute()` could be as complex as you require. It might create and interact with business objects on the server; or it might use server-side resources such as the file system, a high-powered CPU or specialized third-party hardware, or software installed on the server. In this case, the code works directly against the database to execute the `existsProject` stored procedure to determine if the data exists in the database:

```
Dim count As Integer = CInt(cm.ExecuteScalar)
mExists = (count > 0)
```

Really, the data portal does most of the hard work with command objects. When `DataPortal.Execute()` is called on the client, the command object is copied to the server and its `DataPortal_Execute()` method is invoked. Once that method completes, the data portal copies the object back to the client, thus allowing the client to get any information out of the command object.

The `Exists()` command in the `Resource` class is implemented in the same manner.

At this point, you should understand how all the business objects in `ProjectTracker.Library` are implemented. The only classes yet to be discussed are the ones supporting custom authentication.

Custom Authentication

Applications may use either Windows integrated (AD) or custom authentication.

Using Windows integrated security requires no extra coding in the business layer, and the only code required in the UI is to tell .NET to use Windows authentication, by calling `AppDomain.CurrentDomain.SetPrincipalPolicy()` in Windows Forms, or in the `web.config` file for Web Forms or Web Services.

Custom authentication requires some extra code in the business layer, however, because custom principal and identity classes must be created. The details of the design were discussed in Chapter 6, so I'll focus on the implementation here.

PTPrincipal

`PTPrincipal` is a custom principal object that can be assigned as the current principal on the `Thread` object and in the `HttpContext`. Chapters 9 and 10 will demonstrate how to configure the `Thread` and `HttpContext` to use this object in the UI, but first you should understand how the `PTPrincipal` class is created.

Within .NET, the principal object is the centerpiece for authorization. The object must implement System.Security.Principal.IPrincipal, which defines an Identity property and an IsInRole() method. Default implementations are implemented in Csla.Security. BusinessPrincipalBase, and so PTPrincipal inherits from that class:

```
<Serializable()> _
Public Class PTPrincipal
  Inherits Csla.Security.BusinessPrincipalBase
```

Principal objects typically have a constructor that accepts the identity object that represents the user's identity, and PTPrincipal is no exception:

```
Private Sub New(ByVal identity As IIdentity)
  MyBase.New(identity)
End Sub
```

The BusinessPrincipalBase class also has a constructor that requires an identity object. This object is used to implement the Identity property in that base class, so it doesn't need to be implemented in PTPrincipal.

The IsInRole() method is a bit more complex, however. To implement this method, the principal object must have the list of roles to which the user belongs. Of course, the identity object actually represents the user's identity and profile, and so it most likely contains the list of roles for the user as well. Certainly, that is how I choose to implement my custom objects, and so PTIdentity maintains the user's roles. This means that PTPrincipal can simply delegate the call to its identity object:

```
Public Overrides Function IsInRole(ByVal role As String) As Boolean
  Dim identity As PTIdentity = DirectCast(Me.Identity, PTIdentity)
  Return identity.IsInRole(role)
End Function
```

The result indicates whether the user is in the specified role or not.

Login and Logout

The UI will need to collect the user's credentials and initiate any login or logout process. However, the actual login and logout process can be encapsulated within PTPrincipal to help simplify the code in the UI. To do this, Shared methods named Login() and Logout() are implemented in the class. This allows the UI to write code like this:

```
If PTPrincipal.Login(username, password) Then

End If
```

and this:

```
PTPrincipal.Logout
```

Login

The Login() method is the more complex of the two. It creates an instance of PTIdentity and uses that identity object to create a new PTPrincipal object:

```
Public Shared Function Login( _
  ByVal username As String, ByVal password As String) As Boolean

  Dim identity As PTIdentity = PTIdentity.GetIdentity(username, password)
  If identity.IsAuthenticated Then
```

```
      Dim principal As New PTPrincipal(identity)
      Csla.ApplicationContext.User = principal
   End If
   Return identity.IsAuthenticated
End Function
```

Notice that `PTIdentity` has a factory method; in fact, it is derived from `Csla.ReadOnlyBase` and so is a full-fledged business object. The `username` and `password` parameters are passed to the `PTIdentity` object's factory method. Of course, the factory method calls the data portal, which ultimately invokes the `DataPortal_Fetch()` method in `PTIdentity`. As you'll see, that method validates the credentials against the database.

With a `PTIdentity` object created, its `IsAuthenticated` property can be checked to see if the user's credentials were valid. If they were valid, the identity object is used to create a new `PTPrincipal` object, and that object is set to be the current principal by using the `ApplicationContext` object's `User` property, as discussed in Chapter 4:

```
      Dim principal As New PTPrincipal(identity)
      Csla.ApplicationContext.User = principal
```

If the credentials weren't valid, then the current principal value is left unchanged.

In any case, the `IsAuthenticated` value is returned as a result so that the UI code can take appropriate steps based on whether the user was successfully logged in or not.

Logout

The `Logout()` method is much simpler. All it needs to do is ensure that the current principal value is set to an unauthenticated principal object—that means a principal object whose identity object has an `IsAuthenticated` property which returns `False`:

```
Public Shared Sub Logout()
  Dim identity As PTIdentity = PTIdentity.UnauthenticatedIdentity
  Dim principal As New PTPrincipal(identity)
  Csla.ApplicationContext.User = principal
End Sub
```

To achieve this result, an unauthenticated `PTIdentity` object is created by calling a special factory method for that purpose. That identity object is then used to create a new `PTPrincipal` object, and it is set as the current principal by setting `ApplicationContext.User`.

The reason for creating an unauthenticated `PTPrincipal` rather than an unauthenticated `GenericPrincipal` (a built-in .NET type) is to support anonymous or guest users. Recall from Chapter 4 that the data portal will only accept principal objects that subclass `BusinessPrincipalBase` when custom authentication is used. This means the data portal will throw an exception if a `GenericPrincipal` is passed to the application server. So if the application is to support anonymous (i.e., unauthenticated) users, then the principal must be an unauthenticated `PTPrincipal`, as shown here.

PTIdentity

As you've seen, `PTPrincipal` isn't overly complex. It leaves most of the work to `PTIdentity`, including implementing the `IsInRole()` functionality and verification of the user's credentials.

`PTIdentity` is a read-only object, and so it inherits from `Csla.ReadOnlyBase`. It is also a .NET identity object, so it must implement `System.Security.Principal.IIdentity`:

```
<Serializable()> _
Public Class PTIdentity
  Inherits ReadOnlyBase(Of PTIdentity)

  Implements IIdentity
```

Being a read-only root object, PTIdentity follows the appropriate template from Chapter 7, including *Business Methods*, *Factory Methods*, and *Data Access* regions. It doesn't implement an *Authorization Rules* region because it has no authorization rules.

Business Methods

Because PTIdentity implements the IIdentity interface, it is required to implement the AuthenticationType, IsAuthenticated, and Name properties:

```
Private mIsAuthenticated As Boolean
Private mName As String = ""

Public ReadOnly Property AuthenticationType() As String _
  Implements System.Security.Principal.IIdentity.AuthenticationType
  Get
    Return "Csla"
  End Get
End Property

Public ReadOnly Property IsAuthenticated() As Boolean _
  Implements System.Security.Principal.IIdentity.IsAuthenticated
  Get
    Return mIsAuthenticated
  End Get
End Property

Public ReadOnly Property Name() As String _
  Implements System.Security.Principal.IIdentity.Name
  Get
    Return mName
  End Get
End Property
```

These are all read-only properties and are quite straightforward. Also, because it is a subclass of ReadOnlyBase, the class must implement the GetIdValue() method:

```
Protected Overrides Function GetIdValue() As Object
  Return mName
End Function
```

Finally, the code in PTPrincipal requires that PTIdentity implement an IsInRole() method to determine whether the user is in a specified role:

```
Private mRoles As New List(Of String)

Friend Function IsInRole(ByVal role As String) As Boolean
  Return mRoles.Contains(role)
End Function
```

This method is Friend in scope because it is only intended for use by PTPrincipal. All it does is determine whether the specified rule exists in the list of roles for the user. That list is populated in DataPortal_Fetch(), assuming the user's credentials are valid.

Factory Methods

Like all read-only root objects, PTIdentity implements a factory method so it can be created. In fact, it implements two factory methods: one to verify a set of credentials, and one to return an unauthenticated identity object to support the concept of anonymous users.

The UnauthenticatedIdentity() factory method is simple:

```
Friend Shared Function UnauthenticatedIdentity() As PTIdentity
  Return New PTIdentity
End Function
```

Because mIsAuthenticated defaults to False, mName defaults to an empty value, and mRoles defaults to being an empty list, simply creating an instance of the object is enough to provide an unauthenticated identity object with no username and no roles.

The GetIdentity() factory, on the other hand, creates a Criteria object and calls the data portal so that the DataPortal_Fetch() method can verify the supplied username and password parameter values:

```
Friend Shared Function GetIdentity( _
  ByVal username As String, ByVal password As String) As PTIdentity

  Return DataPortal.Fetch(Of PTIdentity)(New Criteria(username, password))
End Function
```

This is a standard factory method to retrieve an object populated from the database.

Data Access

The DataPortal_Fetch() method actually performs the authentication: verifying the user's credentials against the values in the database. In a real application, you should store passwords as hashed or encrypted values; but for a sample application, it is simpler to store them as clear text.

The Criteria object passed from the GetIdentity() factory method to DataPortal_Fetch() is the most complex in the application:

```
<Serializable()> _
Private Class Criteria
  Private mUsername As String
  Private mPassword As String

  Public ReadOnly Property Username() As String
    Get
      Return mUsername
    End Get
  End Property

  Public ReadOnly Property Password() As String
    Get
      Return mPassword
    End Get
  End Property

  Public Sub New(ByVal username As String, ByVal password As String)
    mUsername = username
    mPassword = password
  End Sub
End Class
```

Of course, "complex" is a relative term. Obviously, there's nothing overly complex about a class that exposes two read-only properties. But this illustrates how the Criteria object concept can be used to pass complex criteria to the DataPortal_XYZ methods as needed.

The DataPortal_Fetch() method itself accepts this Criteria object and calls the Login stored procedure created in Chapter 6:

```
Private Overloads Sub DataPortal_Fetch(ByVal criteria As Criteria)
  Using cn As New SqlConnection(Database.SecurityConnection)
    cn.Open()
    Using cm As SqlCommand = cn.CreateCommand
      cm.CommandText = "Login"
      cm.CommandType = CommandType.StoredProcedure
      cm.Parameters.AddWithValue("@user", criteria.Username)
      cm.Parameters.AddWithValue("@pw", criteria.Password)
      Using dr As SqlDataReader = cm.ExecuteReader()
        If dr.Read() Then
          mName = criteria.Username
          mIsAuthenticated = True
          If dr.NextResult Then
            While dr.Read
              mRoles.Add(dr.GetString(0))
            End While
          End If

        Else
          mName = ""
          mIsAuthenticated = False
        End If
      End Using
    End Using
  End Using
End Sub
```

The method uses standard ADO.NET data access code. It opens a connection to the database (calling a Database.SecurityConnection helper to get the connection string for the security database). Then it sets up a SqlCommand object, loading it with the Username and Password properties from the Criteria object.

When the command is executed, the resulting data reader object will either contain data or it won't—if it contains data, then the user's credentials were valid, otherwise they were invalid. Given valid credentials, the object's fields are loaded with data from the database, and the list of roles are loaded into the mRoles collection:

```
        mName = criteria.Username
        mIsAuthenticated = True
        If dr.NextResult Then
          While dr.Read
            mRoles.Add(dr.GetString(0))
          End While
        End If
```

On the other hand, if the credentials were not valid, the object's fields are set to appropriate values for an unauthenticated identity:

```
        mName = ""
        mIsAuthenticated = False
        mRoles.Clear()
```

The end result is a populated PTIdentity object: either authenticated or unauthenticated. Either way, the object is returned to the client where it can be used to create a PTPrincipal object to support authorization activities within the business objects and the UI.

Conclusion

This chapter implemented the business objects designed in Chapter 6, using the templates and concepts discussed in Chapter 7. The result is ProjectTracker.Library, the business layer for the sample ProjectTracker application, including the following:

- Project
- ProjectResources
- ProjectResource
- Resource
- ResourceAssignments
- ResourceAssignment
- Assignment
- RoleList
- Roles
- Role

The library also includes classes to support custom authentication:

- PTPrincipal
- PTIdentity

This business library will be used to create Windows Forms, Web Forms, and Web Services interfaces in the next three chapters.

CHAPTER 9

Windows Forms UI

Up to this point, the focus has been on the business layer of the application. Chapters 6 through 8 walked through the design and creation of business objects and logic. Now let's shift gears and look at how a user interface can be created based on those business objects. This chapter will describe a Windows Forms interface.

Windows Forms is a flexible technology that can be used to create a great many types of user interfaces, as evidenced by the fact that there are entire books on Windows Forms UI development. I won't rehash that sort of material in this book; what I want to focus on here is how to make effective use of business objects and collections to create Windows Forms displays and entry forms.

When creating the CSLA .NET framework, quite a bit of effort was spent to allow business objects to support Windows Forms development. The business objects themselves are focused on modeling the business behaviors described in the use cases from Chapter 6. At the same time, the fact that they inherit from CSLA .NET base classes means they possess quite a few important features that are very useful for creating a Windows Forms UI. Most important is the support for Windows Forms data binding. Although you could certainly write your own code to move the data between properties of business objects and the controls on a form, it's far easier to use data binding whenever possible.

The user interface is centered around user controls. Each form will be created as a user control, rather than a `Form` object. That way, each form can be dynamically loaded into many styles of interface, including the multiple document interface (MDI), multipane user interfaces such as Microsoft Outlook, the single document interface (SDI), and other styles. The style in this chapter uses a single `Form` object that hosts the controls, showing just one at a time. This provides the user with a simple, easily understandable interface.

The important thing is that the chapter will illustrate the use of user controls, and how to dynamically host them. You can easily adapt this code to implement a wide variety of different UI styles.

But above all, my focus in this chapter is to show how easy it is to create an interface, given that the business objects already implement all the business logic, including validation, manipulation, authorization, and data access. The result is that there's only minimal code in the UI, and that code is focused only on user interaction.

The chapter starts by laying out the basic design of the interface, and then walks through the common behaviors of the menu, status display, and authentication. Once that's done, I'll discuss the creation of forms to view and edit data using the `DataGridView` and detail controls. I'll also show how to create and use dialog forms.

Interface Design

The UI application can be found within the `ProjectTracker` solution. The project is named `PTWin`. The design of the `PTWin` interface is that of a single main form with a menu and status bar. This main form dynamically loads user controls and displays them to the user. Figure 9-1 shows what the main form looks like.

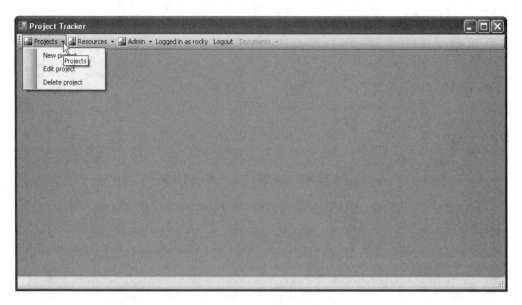

Figure 9-1. *Appearance of the main form*

Notice that the menu bar includes menus that deal with projects, resources, roles, and authentication. When the user chooses a menu option, a user control is dynamically loaded into the main area of the form. Figure 9-2 shows the application while the user is editing a project.

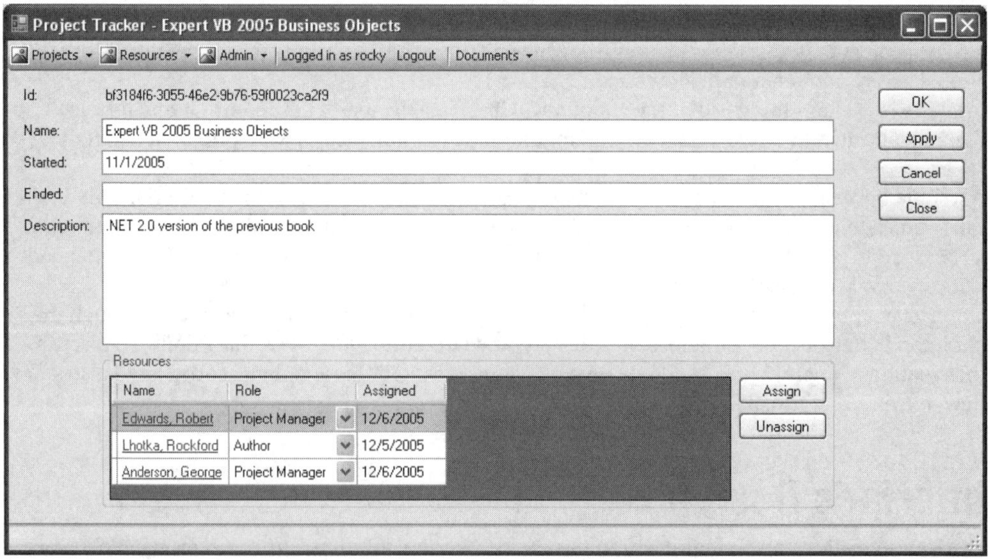

Figure 9-2. *Editing a project*

Of course, there are some dialog windows used to collect input from the user as well, but the bulk of the application's functionality centers around the use of user controls hosted by the main form.

Table 9-1 lists the forms and controls that make up the interface.

Table 9-1. *Forms and User Controls in PTWin*

Form/Control	Type	Description
MainForm	Form	The main form for the application
LoginForm	Form	A login dialog to collect user credentials
RolesEdit	Control	Allows the user to edit the list of roles
ProjectSelect	Form	A dialog prompting the user to select from a list of projects
ProjectEdit	Control	Allows the user to view, add, or edit a project
ResourceSelect	Form	A dialog prompting the user to select from a list of resources
ResourceEdit	Control	Allows the user to view, add, or edit a resource

It is very important that you understand that all the data binding and business functionality covered in this chapter works *exactly the same* with regular forms as it does with user controls. I am using user controls in this chapter because I think it is a best practice for Windows Forms UI design, but this has *no impact* on the way data binding is used to create the UI against the business objects created in Chapter 8.

The user control approach taken in this chapter gives you a great deal of flexibility. You can host the user controls, as shown in this chapter, you can host them in child forms in an MDI interface, or you can host them in panes in a multipane interface. In short, by creating your "forms" as user controls, you gain the flexibility to use them in many different types of UI design.

User Control Framework

Dynamically loading a user control isn't difficult. The code needs to follow this basic process:

1. Create the control.

2. Add the control to the form's Controls collection.

3. Set the control's properties for size/position.

4. Make the control visible (Visible = True).

5. Set the control's z-order (BringToFront()).

This is simple enough—however, integrating the user controls into the main form display nicely requires some extra work. In particular, the UI in this chapter supports the following:

- A Documents menu

- Notification when the user logs in or out

- Bringing an existing control forward when appropriate

- Centralized status text and cursor handling

Let's quickly discuss what I mean by each of these bullet points. If you look at Figure 9-1, you'll notice that there's a Documents item on the menu bar, but it's disabled. In Figure 9-2, it's enabled. This is because there's now a document (user control) loaded in the application. In fact, multiple documents can be loaded at the same time, and this Documents menu allows the user to switch between them.

■**Note** This application uses a Documents menu rather than a Windows menu because the menu allows the user to switch between various documents, not between windows. If you were creating a user interface in which the user chooses to display or arrange different windows, you would name the menu "Windows."

Both figures also show that the user is logged in with the name rocky, and that there's a Logout button available on the menu bar. Look back at Figure 9-2 and notice how the user is allowed to edit the fields in the form. Now look at Figure 9-3, in which the user is *not* allowed to edit any of the fields.

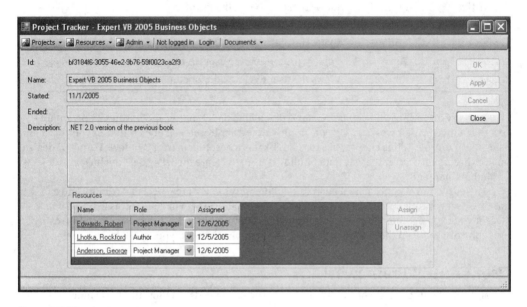

Figure 9-3. *Viewing a project*

The reason for this is that the user isn't logged in. This is clearly shown in the menu bar, which now has a Login button instead of a Logout button.

To make this authorization behavior work, the main form must be able to notify all the loaded user controls when the current user logs in or out. That way, each user control can enable and disable its controls based on the authorization properties of the business object being edited by the form. The hard work is actually handled by the ReadWriteAuthorization control created in Chapter 5. Still, each user control must be notified about the fact that the user logged in or out so that the authorization code can be triggered.

If the user has a number of documents open in the application, he can only see the one in front—the active document. He could easily try to open the same document a second time, and this should result in the already open document being brought to the front to be the new active document.

For instance, suppose the user opens project A. Then he opens some other projects and resources, so project A is no longer active. Then suppose the user again tries to open project A. In that case, the application won't open a *new* document—rather, it will find the already open document for project A and will make it the active document.

Finally, as the user interacts with a document, many things may happen, some of which can take a while. The user may load or save data, start a complex computing task, or any number of things that may take some time. When this happens, the main form's status bar should show text telling the user what is going on, and the mouse cursor should change to indicate that the application is busy.

It is not good to write code in every user control to handle the details of the Documents menu. This code must detect login/logout activity, avoid duplicate documents, and display status to the user. That is all plumbing code that should be written once and reused by user controls.

Although my intent with this chapter isn't to create a full-blown Windows Forms UI framework, these issues must be addressed for a basically decent user experience.

User Control Design

The user will primarily interact with user controls hosted within the main form. In Visual Studio, each user control is really just like a regular form. Visual Studio even provides a user control designer surface, which you can use to create the user control just like you would normally create a form.

In order to support the features discussed in the previous section, each user control needs some common functionality. To provide this functionality with the minimum amount of manual coding, the PTWin project includes a WinPart control. Each user control inherits from WinPart, rather than directly from UserControl.

The WinPart base control implements behaviors common to all user controls that are to be hosted in the main form, including the following:

- Overrides for common System.Object methods
- Event notification for the process of closing
- Event notification when the current user's principal object is changed

By inheriting from WinPart, a user control can often include no extra code beyond a simple GetIdValue() method, which must be implemented to return a unique identifier for the instance of the user control. In most cases, this method simply returns the business object being edited by the form.

All other code in a typical user control centers around user interaction—dealing with button clicks, text changes, and so forth.

Application Configuration

The application needs to provide some basic configuration information through the application's configuration file.

In the client application configuration file, you can either provide connection strings so that the application can interact with the database directly, or you can configure the data portal to communicate with a remote application server. The basic concept here was discussed in Chapter 4 when the channel adapter implementation was covered. Recall that the data portal supports three possible channels: remoting, Enterprise Services, and Web Services. You can create your own channels as well if none of these meet your needs.

In Chapter 1, I discussed the trade-offs between performance, scalability, fault tolerance, and security that come with various physical n-tier configurations. The most scalable solution for an intelligent client UI is to use an application server to host the data access layer, while the most *performant* solution is to run the data portal locally in the client process. In this chapter, I'll show first how to run the data portal locally, and then remotely using each available channel. Chapter 12 will demonstrate how to create the three types of remote data portal hosts for use by the PTWin application.

The configuration is controlled by the application's configuration file. In the Visual Studio project, this is named App.config.

■**Note** Naming the file App.config is important. VS .NET will automatically copy the file into the appropriate Bin directory, changing the name to match that of the program. In this case, it will change the name to PTWin. exe.config as it copies it into the Bin directories. This occurs each time the project is built in Visual Studio.

The App.config file is an XML file that contains settings to configure the application. You use different XML depending on how you want the application configured.

Authentication

The way authentication is handled by CSLA .NET is controlled through the configuration file:

```
<?xml version="1.0" encoding="utf-8" ?>
<configuration>
  <appSettings>
    <add key="CslaAuthentication" value="Csla" />
  </appSettings>
</configuration>
```

The CslaAuthentication key shown here specifies the use of custom authentication. Chapter 8 implemented the PTPrincipal and PTIdentity classes specifically to support custom authentication, and the UI code in this chapter will use custom authentication as well.

If you want to use Windows authentication, change the configuration to the following:

```
<add key="CslaAuthentication" value="Windows" />
```

Of course, that change would require coding changes. To start, the PTPrincipal and PTIdentity classes should be removed from ProjectTracker.Library, as they would no longer be needed. Also, the login/logout functionality implemented in this chapter would become unnecessary. Specifically, the Login form and the code to display that form would be removed from the UI project.

Local Data Portal

The configuration file also controls how the application uses the data portal. To make the client application interact directly with the database, use the following (with your connection string changed to the connection string for your database):

```
<?xml version="1.0" encoding="utf-8" ?>
<configuration>
  <appSettings>
    <add key="CslaAuthentication" value="Csla" />
  </appSettings>
  <connectionStrings>
    <add name="PTracker" connectionString="your connection string"
      providerName="System.Data.SqlClient" />
    <add name="Security" connectionString="your connection string"
      providerName="System.Data.SqlClient" />
  </connectionStrings>
</configuration>
```

Because LocalProxy is the default for the data portal, no actual data portal configuration is required, so the only settings in the configuration file are to control authentication and to provide the database connection strings.

Remote Data Portal (with Remoting)

To make the data portal use an application server and communicate using the remoting channel, use the following configuration:

```xml
<?xml version="1.0" encoding="utf-8" ?>
<configuration>
  <appSettings>
    <add key="CslaAuthentication" value="Csla" />
    <add key="CslaDataPortalProxy"
      value="Csla.DataPortalClient.RemotingProxy, Csla"/>
    <add key="CslaDataPortalUrl"
      value="http://localhost/RemotingHost/RemotingPortal.rem"/>
  </appSettings>
  <connectionStrings>
  </connectionStrings>
</configuration>
```

The key lines for remoting configuration are in bold. Of course, you need to change localhost to the name of the application server on which the data portal host is installed. Also, the RemotingHost text needs to be replaced with the name of your virtual root on that server.

Before using this configuration, the remoting host virtual root must be created and configured. I'll show how this is done in Chapter 12.

Remote Data Portal (with Enterprise Services)

Similarly, to use the Enterprise Services channel, the configuration would look like this:

```xml
<?xml version="1.0" encoding="utf-8" ?>
<configuration>
  <appSettings>
    <add key="CslaAuthentication" value="Csla" />
    <add key="CslaDataPortalProxy"
      value="EnterpriseServicesHost.EnterpriseServicesProxy,
                EnterpriseServicesHostvb"/>
  </appSettings>
  <connectionStrings>
  </connectionStrings>
</configuration>
```

Before using this configuration, an Enterprise Services host must be created and registered with COM+. The resulting COM+ application must be registered with COM on each client workstation. The basic steps were discussed in Chapter 4, and I'll show how this is done in Chapter 12.

Remote Data Portal (with Web Services)

Finally, to use Web Services, the configuration would look like this:

```xml
<?xml version="1.0" encoding="utf-8" ?>
<configuration>
  <appSettings>
    <add key="CslaAuthentication" value="Csla" />
    <add key="CslaDataPortalProxy"
      value="Csla.DataPortalClient.WebServicesProxy, Csla"/>
```

```
    <add key="CslaDataPortalUrl"
      value="http://localhost/WebServicesHost/WebServicePortal.asmx"/>
  </appSettings>
  <connectionStrings>
  </connectionStrings>
</configuration>
```

As with remoting, you need to change `localhost` and `WebServicesHost` to the actual server name and virtual root name used by your application. Also, the virtual root and Web Service `asmx` file must be created and configured. I'll show how this is done in Chapter 12.

The most important thing to realize about the application configuration is that the data portal can be changed from local to remote (using any of the network channels) with no need to change any UI or business object code.

PTWin Project Setup

The UI application can be found within the `ProjectTracker` solution. The project is named `PTWin`.

The project references the `ProjectTracker.Library` project, along with `Csla.dll`.

`ProjectTracker.Library` is a project reference, while `Csla.dll` is a file reference. When building applications using the CSLA .NET framework, it is best to establish a file reference to the framework assembly, but use project references between the UI and any business assemblies. This makes debugging easier overall, because it helps prevent accidental changes to the CSLA .NET framework project while enabling fluid changes to both the business objects and UI code.

Let's go through the creation of the Windows Forms UI. First, I'll discuss the code in the main form and the `WinPart` base control. Then I'll cover the process of logging a user in and out.

With the common code out of the way, I'll discuss the process of maintaining the roles and project data in detail. At that point, you should have a good understanding of how to create lookup dialogs, and both grid-based and detail forms.

User Control Framework

The main edit forms in the application are user controls that inherit from the `WinPart` base control. This base control provides functionality that is used by the main form when it needs to interact with the user controls it contains. The end result is that the main form can implement the Documents menu, notify user controls when the user logs in or out, and handle other basic interactions the user would expect.

WinPart

All user controls that are to be displayed on `MainForm` must inherit from the `WinPart` base control. This control adds common behaviors used by the code in `MainForm` to manage the display. It inherits from `UserControl`:

```
Public Class WinPart
  Inherits System.Windows.Forms.UserControl
```

GetIdValue

Somewhat like the `BusinessBase` class in CSLA .NET, `WinPart` implements a `GetIdValue()` method that should be overridden by all user controls. The value returned in this method is used as a unique identifier for the control, and is used to implement the standard `System.Object` overrides of `Equals()`, `GetHashCode()`, and `ToString()`. The `GetIdValue()` method is declared like this:

```
Protected Overridable Function GetIdValue() As Object
  Return Nothing
End Function
```

The Equals() method is a bit odd, as it has to act differently at design time than at runtime:

```
Public Overrides Function Equals(ByVal obj As Object) As Boolean
  If Me.DesignMode Then
    Return MyBase.Equals(obj)
  Else
    Dim id As Object = GetIdValue()
    If Me.GetType.Equals(obj.GetType) AndAlso id IsNot Nothing Then
      Return CType(obj, WinPart).GetIdValue.Equals(id)

    Else
      Return False
    End If
  End If
End Function
```

When controls are loaded into Visual Studio at design time, they don't run in the same environment as when they're loaded into the running application. Sometimes this can cause odd errors in your code at design time, and this is one such case. It seems that Visual Studio calls the Equals() method at design time in such a way that the new implementation of the method throws an exception. Checking the DesignMode property allows the code to see if the control is being used in Visual Studio, so it can just use the default behavior from the base class.

Closing the Control

When a user control is closed, it needs to notify MainForm so that the control can be gracefully removed from the list of active user controls. To do this, WinPart declares an event and implements a Close() method:

```
Public Event CloseWinPart As EventHandler

Protected Sub Close()
  RaiseEvent CloseWinPart(Me, EventArgs.Empty)
End Sub
```

This way, the UI code in the user control can call the Close() method to close the user control. Raising the CloseWinPart event tells MainForm to remove the control from the active list and dispose the user control.

Login/Logout Notification

Finally, when the user logs into or out of the application, MainForm needs to notify all active user controls of that change. This is required so that the UI code in each user control can perform any authorization activities based on the new user identity.

As you'll see shortly, MainForm loops through all active user controls when the user logs in or out, calling an OnCurrentPrincipalChanged() method on each user control. This method is implemented in WinPart:

```
Protected Friend Overridable Sub OnCurrentPrincipalChanged( _
  ByVal sender As Object, ByVal e As EventArgs)

  RaiseEvent CurrentPrincipalChanged(sender, e)
End Sub
```

It is both `Overridable` and raises a `CurrentPrincipalChanged` event, declared as follows:

```
Protected Event CurrentPrincipalChanged As EventHandler
```

If the developer of a user control needs to respond to a login/logout event, they can either override `OnCurrentPrincipalChanged()` or handle the `CurrentPrincipalChanged` event. Either way, they'll be notified that the `CurrentPrincipal` property of the `Thread` object has changed.

MainForm

The `MainForm` form is the core of the application in that it provides the menu and status bar, and hosts the user controls for display to the user. It coordinates the flow of the entire application. Figure 9-4 shows the layout of `MainForm`.

Figure 9-4. *MainForm layout*

The Resources menu has three items comparable to those in the Projects menu, while the Admin menu has a single item: Edit Roles. The code behind each of these menu items will be discussed later in the chapter as the business functionality is implemented. For now, I want to focus on hosting the user controls, the Documents menu, the status bar, and the Login button.

Hosting the User Controls

What isn't immediately obvious from Figure 9-4 is that the main region of the form contains a `Panel` control. All the user controls are actually contained within this `Panel` control rather within than `MainForm` itself. This is done so that resizing events can be handled more easily, and the overall hosting process can be simplified.

The `Panel` control's `Dock` property is set to `Fill`, so it automatically fills the available space in the form, even if the form is resized.

Loading/Adding User Controls

When a new user control is dynamically loaded (because the user chooses to view/edit a project, resource, or role), it needs to be created, added to the host's Controls collection, positioned, and sized to fit the client area of MainForm. The same thing happens when MainForm is resized, since all the user controls it contains need to be resized accordingly.

This process is split into two parts: adding a user control and showing a user control. The reason for the split is that when a new user control is added, it must be displayed. But already-loaded user controls also must be displayed through the Documents menu.

The AddWinPart() method adds a user control to the Panel control:

```
Private Sub AddWinPart(ByVal part As WinPart)
  AddHandler part.CloseWinPart, AddressOf CloseWinPart
  part.BackColor = ToolStrip1.BackColor
  Panel1.Controls.Add(part)
  Me.DocumentsToolStripDropDownButton.Enabled = True
  ShowWinPart(part)
End Sub
```

Remember that all user controls will inherit from the WinPart base control—hence the naming of the AddWinPart() method and the type of the parameter.

The CloseWinPart() method is hooked to handle the user control's CloseWinPart event. I'll discuss this method shortly—but for now, you should know that its purpose is to properly remove the user control from MainForm.

The user control's BackColor property is set to match the color scheme of MainForm. Then, the user control is added to the Controls collection of the panel. This effectively adds the user control to the form. Then ShowWinPart() is called to display the user control.

Finally, the Documents menu option is enabled. At this point, it's known that there's at least one user control hosted by MainForm, so the Documents menu should be available to the user.

The ShowWinPart() method makes sure that the user control is properly positioned and sized; then it makes it visible:

```
Private Sub ShowWinPart(ByVal part As WinPart)
  part.Dock = DockStyle.Fill
  part.Visible = True
  part.BringToFront()
  Me.Text = "Project Tracker - " & part.ToString
End Sub
```

Remember that the Panel control's Dock property is set to Fill, so the Panel control automatically fills the available space—even when MainForm is resized. The user control is contained within the Panel control and its Dock property is also set to Fill. This means that the user control is automatically resized along with the Panel control, so it always fills the client area of MainForm.

Next, the user control is made visible and is brought to the front: its z-order is set so that the user control is on top of all other controls in the Panel control. These two steps ensure that the user control is visible and active.

Finally, the caption text of MainForm itself is changed to reflect the ToString() value of the newly active user control. If you look back at Figures 9-2 and 9-3, you'll notice that MainForm displays the name of the Project object being edited. You'll see how this flows from the ToString() value of the user control later in the chapter.

Removing User Controls

Recall how the AddWinPart() method sets up the CloseWinPart() method to handle the user control's CloseWinPart event. That event is raised by the user control when it is closed, and MainForm uses the event to properly remove the user control from the Panel control's Controls collection:

```
Private Sub CloseWinPart(ByVal sender As Object, ByVal e As EventArgs)
  Dim part As WinPart = CType(sender, WinPart)
  RemoveHandler part.CloseWinPart, AddressOf CloseWinPart
  part.Visible = False
  Panel1.Controls.Remove(part)
  part.Dispose()
  If DocumentCount = 0 Then
    Me.DocumentsToolStripDropDownButton.Enabled = False
    Me.Text = "Project Tracker"

  Else
    ' Find the first WinPart control and set
    ' the main form's Text property accordingly.
    ' This works because the first WinPart
    ' is the active one.
    For Each ctl As Control In Panel1.Controls
      If TypeOf ctl Is WinPart Then
        Me.Text = "Project Tracker - " + CType(ctl, WinPart).ToString
        Exit For
      End If
    Next
  End If
End Sub
```

When a user control is removed, other work is required as well. The user control's `Dispose()` method is called, and the caption text on `MainForm` is reset (because there's almost certainly a new active user control now). If there's no longer an active user control, then the caption text is set accordingly.

Also notice that the `CloseWinPart` event is unhooked. This is an important step, because handling an event sets up an object reference behind the scenes, and failing to unhook events can cause memory leaks (by keeping objects in memory when they are no longer needed).

Resizing User Controls

When `MainForm` is resized, the `Panel` control's `Resize` event is automatically raised. The following code handles that event to resize all the hosted user controls:

```
Private Sub Panel1_Resize( _
  ByVal sender As Object, ByVal e As System.EventArgs) Handles Panel1.Resize

  For Each ctl As Control In Panel1.Controls
    If TypeOf ctl Is WinPart Then
      ctl.Size = Panel1.ClientSize
    End If
  Next
End Sub
```

With the ability to add, remove, and resize user controls, the code in `MainForm` covers most of the capabilities required. Of course, there's the implementation of the Documents menu itself to consider.

Documents Menu

The Documents menu is a drop-down menu listing all the active documents (user controls) currently hosted by the main form. If there are no active user controls, then the menu is disabled. When the user selects an item from the list, that particular user control becomes the active user control.

The DropDownOpening event is raised when the user clicks the Documents menu option to open the list. Handling this event allows the code to populate the list *before* it is displayed to the user:

```
Private Sub DocumentsToolStripDropDownButton_DropDownOpening( _
  ByVal sender As Object, ByVal e As System.EventArgs) _
  Handles DocumentsToolStripDropDownButton.DropDownOpening

  Dim items As ToolStripItemCollection = _
    DocumentsToolStripDropDownButton.DropDownItems
  For Each item As ToolStripItem In items
    RemoveHandler item.Click, AddressOf DocumentClick
  Next
  items.Clear()
  For Each ctl As Control In Panel1.Controls
    If TypeOf ctl Is WinPart Then
      Dim item As New ToolStripMenuItem()
      item.Text = CType(ctl, WinPart).ToString
      item.Tag = ctl
      AddHandler item.Click, AddressOf DocumentClick
      items.Add(item)
    End If
  Next
End Sub
```

Remember that the menu item is only enabled if there are one or more items in the Controls collection of the Panel control. Notice that a reference to each user control is put into the Tag property of the corresponding ToolStripMenuItem object.

If the user clicks an item in the list, a Click event is raised and handled to make the selected user control the active control:

```
Private Sub DocumentClick(ByVal sender As Object, ByVal e As EventArgs)
  Dim ctl As WinPart = CType(CType(sender, ToolStripItem).Tag, WinPart)
  ShowWinPart(ctl)
End Sub
```

The Tag property of the menu item references the user control associated with that item, so this code needs only to cast the Tag value and make the control visible by calling the ShowWinPart() method discussed earlier.

This wraps up the code in MainForm that deals with the user controls and the Documents menu. Now let's see how the status bar display and mouse cursor changes are handled.

Status Bar

MainForm has a StatusStrip control at the bottom, so the user can be informed about any long-running activity that is occurring. Also, when a long-running activity is going on, the mouse cursor should be changed to indicate that the application is busy.

An easy way to handle this is to create an object that implements IDisposable. This object would update both the status display and mouse cursor, and then reset them when it is disposed. The result is that anywhere in the UI, code can be written like this:

```
Using busy As New StatusBusy("Working…")
  ' do long-running task here
End Using
```

When the object is created, it sets the status display on MainForm, and it resets the text when it is disposed. Similarly, when the object is created, it sets the mouse cursor to a busy cursor, and resets it when disposed.

To do this, it needs to be able to access the MainForm object. Fortunately VB 2005 supports default instances for forms. If your application has exactly one instance of a specific form, such as MainForm, then you can just refer to it by name anywhere in the project. Using this feature, the MainForm object can be used by any code in the UI, including the StatusBusy class:

```
Public Class StatusBusy

  Implements IDisposable

  Private mOldStatus As String
  Private mOldCursor As Cursor

  Public Sub New(ByVal statusText As String)

    mOldStatus = MainForm.StatusLabel.Text
    MainForm.StatusLabel.Text = statusText
    mOldCursor = MainForm.Cursor
    MainForm.Cursor = Cursors.WaitCursor

  End Sub

  ' IDisposable
  Private disposedValue As Boolean = False ' To detect redundant calls

  Protected Overridable Sub Dispose(ByVal disposing As Boolean)
    If Not Me.disposedValue Then
      If disposing Then
        MainForm.StatusLabel.Text = mOldStatus
        MainForm.Cursor = mOldCursor
      End If
    End If
    Me.disposedValue = True
  End Sub

  Public Sub Dispose() Implements IDisposable.Dispose
    ' Do not change this code.
    ' Put cleanup code in Dispose(ByVal disposing As Boolean) above.
    Dispose(True)
    GC.SuppressFinalize(Me)
  End Sub
End Class
```

When a StatusBusy object is created, it sets the status text and mouse cursor, storing the old values for later use:

```
mOldStatus = MainForm.StatusLabel.Text
MainForm.StatusLabel.Text = statusText
mOldCursor = MainForm.Cursor
MainForm.Cursor = Cursors.WaitCursor
```

Then, when the object is disposed, the status text and cursor are reset to their previous values:

```
MainForm.StatusLabel.Text = mOldStatus
MainForm.Cursor = mOldCursor
```

This is one of the simplest ways to implement powerful status notification and cursor handling for the user in a Windows Forms UI.

Login Button

The final bit of common functionality implemented in MainForm allows the user to log into or out of the application. It is important to realize that the ProjectTracker application allows unauthorized or guest users to view certain data, and so the user can interact with the application even if they haven't logged in.

The login process is triggered when the application first loads, and when the user clicks the Login button on the menu. In both cases, a DoLogin() method is called to handle the actual login/logout behavior:

```
Private Sub DoLogin()
  ProjectTracker.Library.Security.PTPrincipal.Logout()

  If Me.LoginToolStripButton.Text = "Login" Then
    LoginForm.ShowDialog(Me)
  End If

  Dim user As System.Security.Principal.IPrincipal = _
    Csla.ApplicationContext.User

  If user.Identity.IsAuthenticated Then
    Me.LoginToolStripLabel.Text = "Logged in as " & user.Identity.Name
    Me.LoginToolStripButton.Text = "Logout"

  Else
    Me.LoginToolStripLabel.Text = "Not logged in"
    Me.LoginToolStripButton.Text = "Login"
  End If

  ' reset menus, etc.
  ApplyAuthorizationRules()

  ' notify all documents
  For Each ctl As Control In Panel1.Controls
    If TypeOf ctl Is WinPart Then
      CType(ctl, WinPart).OnCurrentPrincipalChanged(Me, EventArgs.Empty)
    End If
  Next
End Sub
```

Before doing anything else, this method ensures that the CurrentPrincipal property of the Thread is set to an unauthenticated PTPrincipal object:

```
ProjectTracker.Library.Security.PTPrincipal.Logout()
```

This way, if the user's credentials are invalid, she can at least use the application as an unauthenticated user. Recall that the data portal requires that the principal object inherit from Csla.Security.BusinessPrincipalBase. PTPrincipal meets this requirement, and so the current principal is set to an unauthenticated PTPrincipal object by calling the Logout() method.

Next, the text of the button on the menu is checked. If the text is Login, then a login process is initiated. The login process is actually handled by a Login dialog form, which is shown to the user as a modal dialog. That dialog prompts the user for her credentials and calls PTPrincipal.Login() (as implemented in Chapter 8) to validate them.

The result is that the CurrentPrincipal property on the Thread object will either be an authenticated PTPrincipal or an unauthenticated PTPrincipal. The status of the principal object is used to determine whether the user is logged in or not:

```
If user.Identity.IsAuthenticated Then
  Me.LoginToolStripLabel.Text = "Logged in as " & user.Identity.Name
  Me.LoginToolStripButton.Text = "Logout"

Else
  Me.LoginToolStripLabel.Text = "Not logged in"
  Me.LoginToolStripButton.Text = "Login"
End If
```

If the user was authenticated, then the button text is changed to Logout and the user's name is displayed in the menu. Otherwise, the button text is changed to Login, and text indicating that the user isn't logged in is displayed.

In any case, an ApplyAuthorizationRules() method is called so that MainForm can update its display based on the user's identity (or lack thereof). Then all the active user controls are notified that the principal has changed:

```
' reset menus, etc.
ApplyAuthorizationRules()

' notify all documents
For Each ctl As Control In Panel1.Controls
  If TypeOf ctl Is WinPart Then
    CType(ctl, WinPart).OnCurrentPrincipalChanged(Me, EventArgs.Empty)
  End If
Next
```

Each user control is responsible for handling this event and responding appropriately. Recall that the WinPart base control implements the OnCurrentPrincipalChanged() method and subsequently raises a Protected event to the code in the user control.

The ApplyAuthorizationRules() method in MainForm is responsible for enabling and disabling menu items. This method is somewhat long and repetitive, so I won't show the whole thing, but here's the code to enable/disable one menu item:

```
Me.NewProjectToolStripMenuItem.Enabled = _
  Project.CanAddObject
```

Notice how the actual authorization check is delegated to the Shared method of the Project business class. These methods were discussed in Chapter 8, and were implemented specifically to enable scenarios like this. The idea is that MainForm has no idea whether particular users or roles are authorized to add Project objects. Instead, the Project class itself has that knowledge, and MainForm simply asks Project whether the current user is authorized.

The end result is good separation of concerns: Project is concerned with whether users can and can't add objects, while MainForm is concerned with the UI details of enabling and disabling controls.

Login Form

The DoLogin() method in MainForm calls a Login dialog form to collect and authenticate the user's credentials. After gathering credentials from the user, this dialog form will call PTPrincipal.Login() to do the authentication itself.

Figure 9-5 shows the Login form layout.

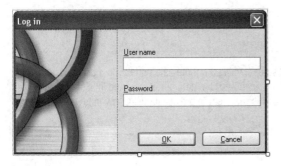

Figure 9-5. *Layout of the Login form*

All the work occurs when OK is clicked. At that point, the credentials entered by the user are verified:

```
Private Sub OK_Click( _
  ByVal sender As System.Object, ByVal e As System.EventArgs) _
  Handles OK.Click

  Using busy As New StatusBusy("Verifying credentials...")
    ProjectTracker.Library.Security.PTPrincipal.Login( _
      Me.UsernameTextBox.Text, Me.PasswordTextBox.Text)
  End Using
  Me.Close()
End Sub
```

Notice the use of the StatusBusy object to update the status text and mouse cursor. Also notice the simplicity of this code. Since PTPrincipal.Login() does all the work of authenticating the user, there's just not much work to do in the UI. This is a theme you'll see throughout the rest of the chapter.

Using Windows Integrated Security

If you wanted to use Windows integrated security, you wouldn't need a login form because the client workstation already knows the user's identity. Instead, you would need to add a bit of code to MainForm so that as it loads, the CurrentPrincipal is configured with a WindowsPrincipal object.

The following code shows how to detect the authentication mode and adapt to use either Windows or custom authentication appropriately:

```
Private Sub MainForm_Load( _
  ByVal sender As System.Object, ByVal e As System.EventArgs) _
  Handles MyBase.Load

  If Csla.ApplicationContext.AuthenticationType = "Windows" Then
    AppDomain.CurrentDomain.SetPrincipalPolicy( _
      System.Security.Principal.PrincipalPolicy.WindowsPrincipal)

  Else
    DoLogin()
  End If
  If DocumentCount = 0 Then
    Me.DocumentsToolStripDropDownButton.Enabled = False
  End If
  ApplyAuthorizationRules()
End Sub
```

Calling `SetPrincipalPolicy()` to set the `WindowsPrincipal` option tells the .NET runtime to return the current `WindowsPrincipal` object for the `CurrentPrincipal` property of the `Thread`.

■Note If you use Windows integrated security, and you are using a remote data portal, you *must* make sure to change the server configuration file to also use Windows security. If the data portal is hosted in IIS, the virtual root must be set to disallow anonymous access, thereby forcing the client to provide IIS with the Windows identity from the client workstation via integrated security.

Business Functionality

With the common functionality in `MainForm`, `WinPart`, `StatusBusy` and `Login` covered, we can move on to the business functionality itself. As I mentioned earlier, I'll walk through the `RolesEdit` user control, the `ProjectSelect` dialog, and the `ProjectEdit` user control in some detail. `ResourceSelect` and `ResourceEdit` are available in the download and follow the same implementation approach.

All of these forms and user controls will be created using the new data binding capabilities built into Visual Studio 2005. These capabilities allow the UI developer to literally drag-and-drop business classes or properties onto the form to create the controls and set up data binding. The developer productivity gained through this approach is simply amazing.

The detail edit forms (`ProjectEdit` and `ResourceEdit`) will also make use of the `ReadWriteAuthorization` and `BindingSourceRefresh` controls created in Chapter 5, as well as the standard Windows Forms `ErrorProvider` control. All three controls are *extender controls*, adding important extra capabilities to the other controls on each form or user control.

Let's start by looking at the business code in `MainForm` that displays the other forms and user controls.

MainForm

You've already seen the code in `MainForm` that exists to provide common functionality around the user controls, authentication, and authorization. But the form also implements the menu options to add, edit, and delete project and resource data, and to edit the list of roles.

Displaying User Controls

Thanks to the common code discussed earlier, none of these menu options are difficult to implement. For instance, when the user chooses the menu option to edit the list of roles, the code simply checks to see if the `RolesEdit` user control is already loaded. If it is, the existing user control is made active; otherwise, a new one is created and displayed:

```vb
Private Sub EditRolesToolStripMenuItem_Click( _
  ByVal sender As System.Object, ByVal e As System.EventArgs) _
  Handles EditRolesToolStripMenuItem.Click

  ' see if this form is already loaded
  For Each ctl As Control In Panel1.Controls
    If TypeOf ctl Is RolesEdit Then
      ShowWinPart(CType(ctl, WinPart))
      Exit Sub
    End If
  Next
```

```
' it wasn't already loaded, so show it
AddWinPart(New RolesEdit)
End Sub
```

A slightly more complex variation occurs when the user clicks the menu to add a project or resource. In both cases, a new instance of the appropriate business object is created and is passed to a new instance of the appropriate user control. For example, when the user opts to add a new project, this code is run:

```
Private Sub NewProjectToolStripMenuItem_Click( _
  ByVal sender As System.Object, ByVal e As System.EventArgs) _
  Handles NewProjectToolStripMenuItem.Click

  Using busy As New StatusBusy("Creating project...")
    AddWinPart(New ProjectEdit(Project.NewProject))
  End Using
End Sub
```

`Project.NewProject()` is called to create the new `Project` object, and it is then passed to the constructor of a `ProjectEdit` user control. That user control, now populated with data from the `Project` object, is then added to the list of active user controls and displayed.

Editing an Existing Object

Even more complex is the process of editing an existing project or resource. This is because in both cases, the user must be prompted to select the specific item to edit. The `ProjectSelect` and `ResourceSelect` dialog forms are used to prompt the user for the particular object he wishes to edit. Here's the code behind the menu option to edit a resource:

```
Private Sub EditResourceToolStripMenuItem_Click( _
  ByVal sender As System.Object, ByVal e As System.EventArgs) _
  Handles EditResourceToolStripMenuItem.Click

  Dim dlg As New ResourceSelect
  dlg.Text = "Edit Resource"
  If dlg.ShowDialog = Windows.Forms.DialogResult.OK Then
    ' get the project id
    ShowEditResource(dlg.ResourceId)
  End If
End Sub
```

The code for editing a project is virtually identical, but obviously uses `ProjectSelect` instead.

This code displays the dialog using the `ShowDialog()` method and checks its result value. If the user clicks the OK button in the dialog, then the selected `ResourceId` value is retrieved from the dialog form and is passed to a `ShowEditResource()` method.

`ShowEditResource()` checks to see if this resource is already visible in a user control, and if so, it makes that the active user control. Otherwise, the method takes care of retrieving the business object from the database and adding a new `ResourceEdit` user control to `MainForm`:

```
Public Sub ShowEditResource(ByVal resourceId As Integer)
  ' see if this project is already loaded
  For Each ctl As Control In Panel1.Controls
    If TypeOf ctl Is ResourceEdit Then
      Dim part As ResourceEdit = CType(ctl, ResourceEdit)
      If part.Resource.Id.Equals(resourceId) Then
        ' project already loaded so just
        ' display the existing winpart
```

```
          ShowWinPart(part)
          Exit Sub
        End If
      End If
    Next

    ' the resource wasn't already loaded
    ' so load it and display the new winpart
    Using busy As New StatusBusy("Loading resource...")
      Try
        AddWinPart(New ResourceEdit(Resource.GetResource(resourceId)))

      Catch ex As Csla.DataPortalException
        MessageBox.Show(ex.BusinessException.ToString, _
          "Error loading", MessageBoxButtons.OK, _
          MessageBoxIcon.Exclamation)

      Catch ex As Exception
        MessageBox.Show(ex.ToString, _
          "Error loading", MessageBoxButtons.OK, _
          MessageBoxIcon.Exclamation)
      End Try
    End Using
  End Sub
```

The code to find an existing `ResourceEdit` user control for this resource loops through all the controls hosted in the `Panel` control. Those items that are of type `ResourceEdit` are checked to see if the `Resource` object they are editing has the same `Id` value as the one just selected by the user.

Assuming no matching `ResourceEdit` user control is found, the requested `Resource` object is loaded from the database. This object is passed to a new `ResourceEdit` user control, which is displayed in `MainForm`:

```
AddWinPart(New ResourceEdit(Resource.GetResource(resourceId)))
```

Any exceptions are handled so that the user is notified about the problem; otherwise, the user is free to move ahead and view or edit the `Resource` object's data.

Deleting an Object

Deleting a project or resource is a similar process. The user is prompted to select the item to delete. Then he is asked if he is sure he wants to delete the item, and finally the item is deleted. The code to delete projects and resources is quite comparable; here's the code to delete a `Resource` object:

```
Private Sub DeleteResourceToolStripMenuItem_Click( _
  ByVal sender As System.Object, ByVal e As System.EventArgs) _
  Handles DeleteResourceToolStripMenuItem.Click

  Dim dlg As New ResourceSelect
  dlg.Text = "Delete Resource"
  If dlg.ShowDialog = Windows.Forms.DialogResult.OK Then
    ' get the resource id
    Dim resourceId As Integer = dlg.ResourceId

    If MessageBox.Show("Are you sure?", "Delete resource", _
      MessageBoxButtons.YesNo, MessageBoxIcon.Question, _
      MessageBoxDefaultButton.Button2) = _
      Windows.Forms.DialogResult.Yes Then
```

```
        Using busy As New StatusBusy("Deleting resource...")
          Try
            Resource.DeleteResource(resourceId)

          Catch ex As Csla.DataPortalException
            MessageBox.Show(ex.BusinessException.ToString, _
              "Error deleting", MessageBoxButtons.OK, _
              MessageBoxIcon.Exclamation)

          Catch ex As Exception
            MessageBox.Show(ex.ToString, _
              "Error deleting", MessageBoxButtons.OK, _
              MessageBoxIcon.Exclamation)
          End Try
        End Using
      End If
    End If
  End Sub
```

Though this looks like a lot of code, there are really only a couple lines of importance—the rest provide the user with feedback during the process or implement exception handling. To start with, the user is prompted for the Resource to delete:

```
Dim dlg As New ResourceSelect
dlg.Text = "Delete Resource"
If dlg.ShowDialog = Windows.Forms.DialogResult.OK Then
```

If the user clicks the OK button, the ResourceId value is retrieved from the ResourceSelect dialog form, and the user is asked if he is sure he wants to delete the object. Assuming he confirms the deletion, the Resource class is used to delete the object:

```
            Resource.DeleteResource(resourceId)
```

Because the business classes implement all the data access, the code in the UI is entirely focused on the user experience—not on adding, retrieving, or deleting data.

RolesEdit

The RolesEdit user control allows an authorized user to edit the roles a resource can hold when assigned to a project. The simplest way to create such data maintenance forms is with the DataGridView control, because it can be directly bound to an editable root collection object such as ProjectTracker.Library.Roles.

Using a Business Class As a Data Source

To bind controls to an object, choose the Data ➤ Add New Data Source menu option in Visual Studio to bring up the Data Source Configuration Wizard. Choose the Object option in the first step, as shown in Figure 9-6.

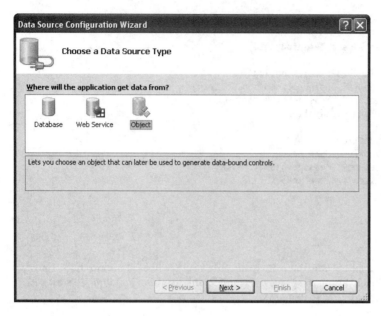

Figure 9-6. *Choosing an object data source*

The next step in the wizard is to select the business class that will be the data source. All types in the current project and any referenced projects are listed. As shown in Figure 9-7, they are grouped by namespace.

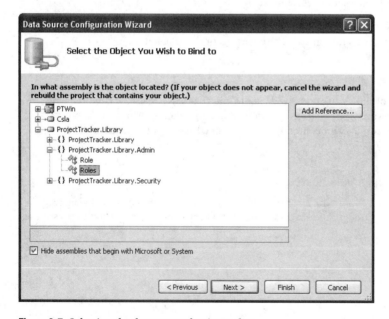

Figure 9-7. *Selecting the data source business class*

■**Tip** This wizard uses reflection to get this list, so the assemblies must be compiled before the classes will show up in this list. Make sure to build your solution *before* running the Data Source Configuration Wizard.

At this point, you can finish the wizard to add the class as a data source. The data sources appear in the Data Sources window. If this window isn't available, you can open it by using the Data ➤ Show Data Sources menu item in Visual Studio. Figure 9-8 shows the Data Sources window after all the root classes from Chapter 8 have been added as data sources.

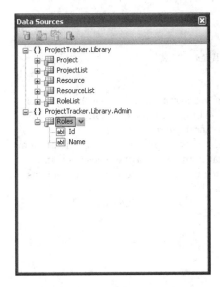

Figure 9-8. *ProjectTracker.Library classes in the Data Sources window*

Notice how the classes are grouped by namespace to help you find them more easily. The illustration in Figure 9-8 shows the Roles class expanded to show its properties. When doing drag-and-drop data binding, you can drag entire classes or individual properties onto the form.

In the case of the RolesEdit user control, the entire class was dragged onto the form, causing Visual Studio to create a DataGridView control. This control is bound to a rolesBindingSource object, which was also automatically added by Visual Studio. The resulting display is shown in Figure 9-9.

■**Tip** The BindingSource controls appear in the component tray at the bottom of the designer in Visual Studio.

The new data binding in Windows Forms uses BindingSource controls. These controls sit between all the data-bound controls in the UI and the actual data source object—in this case, Roles.

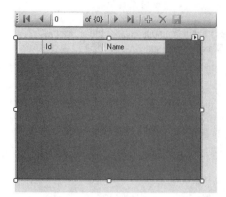

Figure 9-9. *RolesEdit user control with data-bound DataGridView*

The first thing you might notice about Figure 9-9 is the ToolStrip control across the top. This BindingNavigator control is added by Visual Studio when you drag your first data source onto the form, and it provides VCR-like behaviors for the associated BindingSource control.

I don't use any BindingNavigator controls in the ProjectTracker application. To get rid of them, you can select them in the designer or in the component tray at the bottom of the designer, and press the Delete key. Of course, there's still the need for Save and Cancel buttons, so I add them as normal Button controls. Figure 9-10 shows the resulting form layout.

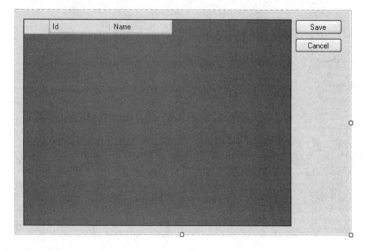

Figure 9-10. *Final layout of the RolesEdit user control*

Looking at Figure 9-10, you'll see that data binding automatically picked up the properties from the child object, Role, contained within the Roles collection. Thanks to the <Browsable(False)> attributes applied to the CSLA .NET base class properties in Chapter 3, they are automatically ignored by data binding, so only the actual business properties appear.

WinPart Code

One drawback to using a custom base control rather than UserControl is that Visual Studio has no direct support for adding subclasses of a custom control. So what you need to do to add a WinPart-derived user control is choose the Project ➤ Add User Control menu option to add a standard user control to the project. Then change the control to inherit from WinPart instead of UserControl. This means the declaration of RolesEdit looks like this:

```
Public Class RolesEdit
  Inherits WinPart
```

The one bit of code that every subclass of WinPart needs to implement is the GetIdValue() method. Since there can really only be one instance of EditRoles, it simply returns human-readable text for display in the Documents menu:

```
Protected Overrides Function GetIdValue() As Object
  Return "Edit Roles"
End Function
```

This allows the WinPart base control to automatically handle the System.Object overrides for the user control. For instance, this text is returned through the user control's ToString() method, which is used by MainForm to populate the display of the Documents menu.

Authorization

The RolesEdit authorization code is perhaps the simplest in the application. This user control doesn't support a read-only mode, so if the user isn't authorized to edit the list of roles, then the form can't be available.

MainForm already disables the menu to prevent the user from getting to the user control if she isn't authorized, but there's still the possibility that the user could log out while the user control is loaded. In that case, the user control needs to close itself to prevent the now unauthorized user from editing the roles. To implement this, the CurrentPrincipalChanged event is handled:

```
Private Sub RolesEdit_CurrentPrincipalChanged( _
  ByVal sender As Object, ByVal e As System.EventArgs) _
  Handles Me.CurrentPrincipalChanged

  If Not Roles.CanEditObject Then
    Me.Close()
  End If
End Sub
```

The Roles class is asked whether the current user is authorized to edit the object, and if the user isn't authorized, then the user control is immediately closed.

Loading the Form

When the RolesEdit user control is loaded, it retrieves a new Roles object and makes it the current data source for the rolesBindingSource object; which in turn means it becomes the current data source for the DataGridView control:

```
Private mRoles As Admin.Roles

Private Sub RolesEdit_Load( _
  ByVal sender As System.Object, ByVal e As System.EventArgs) _
  Handles MyBase.Load
```

```
    Try
      mRoles = Admin.Roles.GetRoles

    Catch ex As Csla.DataPortalException
      MessageBox.Show(ex.BusinessException.ToString, _
        "Error loading", MessageBoxButtons.OK, _
        MessageBoxIcon.Exclamation)

    Catch ex As Exception
      MessageBox.Show(ex.ToString, _
        "Error loading", MessageBoxButtons.OK, _
        MessageBoxIcon.Exclamation)
    End Try

    If mRoles IsNot Nothing Then
      Me.RolesBindingSource.DataSource = mRoles
    End If
  End Sub
```

Most of this code exists to gracefully handle exceptions. Only two lines really matter:

```
    mRoles = Admin.Roles.GetRoles
```

and

```
    Me.RolesBindingSource.DataSource = mRoles
```

The first retrieves the Roles object, and the second sets the data source using that object. Setting the DataSource property of the BindingSource control automatically connects all the data-bound controls on the form to the underlying data source object. The result is that data in the object is displayed in the controls and is available for editing by the user.

Of course, the exception-handling code is important too. If an exception occurs during the normal data portal processing, including within the DataPortal_Fetch() method of the Roles object, a Csla.DataPortalException will be thrown. To get at the original exception thrown by the business code, use the BusinessException property. Remember that you can also use the BusinessObject property to get a reference to the business object as it was when the exception was thrown—a fact that can be very useful for debugging.

It is far less likely that any other exception will be thrown, but I've included code showing how to catch those exceptions as well. If you look at the client-side DataPortal code from Chapter 4, you'll see that very little code executes that can throw exceptions other than a DataPortalException, so other types of exceptions typically only occur during development and debugging.

Saving the Data

When the user clicks the Save button, the data needs to be saved. This is the most complex bit of processing the UI developer should have to write. The complexity comes because the object may be updated during the update process, and it is possible for the update process to fail part of the way through—possibly leaving the object in an invalid or indeterminate state.

For instance, suppose Jeff edits a number of roles in the Roles object. And suppose Marie has edited the *last* role in the list and saved her change. When Jeff saves his changes, all the data will be saved (updating the timestamp values in each Role object) until the update process hits that last role. At that point, a concurrency issue is detected and an exception is thrown. The database transaction handles rolling back the *database* to a valid state, but all those Role objects now have invalid timestamp values in memory. Somehow the Roles object needs to be reset to the state it was in before Save() was called.

Another issue occurs if the data portal is configured to run locally in the client process. In that case, the object is *not* serialized to a server, but is rather updated in place on the client. It is possible that the business object could raise PropertyChanged or ListChanged events while it is being updated, causing the UI to refresh during the data update process. Not only does that incur performance costs, but sometimes code in the UI might respond to those events in ways that cause bugs.

To avoid these issues, the following process is followed:

1. Turn off events from the BindingSource controls.

2. Clone the business object.

3. Save the *clone* of the business object.

4. Rebind the BindingSource controls to the *new* object returned from Save(), if necessary.

5. Turn on events from the BindingSource controls.

Turning off and on the events from the BindingSource controls ensures that any events from the data source won't be cascaded up to the UI during the update process. This is important, because otherwise an exception will occur when rebinding the BindingSource controls to the new object returned from Save(). As you'll see, this rebinding requires that the DataSource property first be set to Nothing, which of course isn't a valid data source for the UI.

The reason for cloning the business object is so *an exact copy* of the object can be saved to the database. It is this exact copy of the object that has its fields changed during the update process. If the update fails, then the *original* object remains intact and unchanged, but if the update succeeds, then the Save() method returns the successfully updated version of the object, including any new field values.

Here's the code for the Save button on the RolesEdit user control:

```
Private Sub SaveButton_Click( _
  ByVal sender As System.Object, ByVal e As System.EventArgs) _
  Handles SaveButton.Click

  Me.RolesBindingSource.RaiseListChangedEvents = False
  Dim temp As Admin.Roles = mRoles.Clone
  Try
    mRoles = temp.Save
    Me.Close()

  Catch ex As Csla.DataPortalException
    MessageBox.Show(ex.BusinessException.ToString, _
      "Error saving", MessageBoxButtons.OK, _
      MessageBoxIcon.Exclamation)

  Catch ex As Exception
    MessageBox.Show(ex.ToString, _
      "Error saving", MessageBoxButtons.OK, _
      MessageBoxIcon.Exclamation)

  Finally
    Me.RolesBindingSource.RaiseListChangedEvents = True
  End Try
End Sub
```

The first line of code turns off event processing for the BindingSource control:

```
Me.RolesBindingSource.RaiseListChangedEvents = False
```

You would do this for every `BindingSource` control on the form if there were more than one. In `ProjectEdit`, for instance, there are two such controls bound to editable data.

The next line of code creates a clone of the business object:

```
Dim temp As Admin.Roles = mRoles.Clone
```

This is easily done, since all CSLA .NET business objects automatically support the `Clone()` method. Remember that this method copies the object and all child objects it contains. In this case, it copies the `Roles` object and all the `Role` objects in the collection.

Then the *copy* of the object is saved:

```
mRoles = temp.Save
```

Notice that the result of the `Save()` method is stored in the original `mRoles` field, which overwrites the original value. If no exception occurs during the `Save()` call, the original object is replaced by the resulting updated object. Remember that most insert and update operations do change the object's data, at least updating the `timestamp` values for concurrency.

If the user control was not immediately closed, you would rebind the `BindingSource` object to the new business object returned from the `Save()` method by adding these lines of code immediately after the `Save()` method call:

```
Me.RolesBindingSource.DataSource = Nothing
Me.RolesBindingSource.DataSource = mRoles
```

You can't simply set the `DataSource` property to a new object. You must first set the property to `Nothing`, and then to the new object. If you don't do this, the `BindingSource` will not bind to the new object and will silently remain bound to the old object, resulting in hard-to-debug problems in your application.

In this case, the form is closed immediately upon successfully saving the data, so the UI is not re-bound. Instead, the user control's `Close()` method is called:

```
Me.Close()
```

The `Save()` call and closing of the user control (or rebinding of the `BindingSource` control) occurs in a `Try` block. If an exception occurs during the `Save()` call, the `mRoles` field will *not* be set to a new value, meaning it will retain the original value it had to start with.

Additionally, in the case of an exception, the user control isn't closed (or if the UI is being re-bound, that rebinding won't occur). This means that the `BindingSource` control will still be bound to the original, unchanged, object. This is exactly the desired behavior, since it means that the UI controls are still bound to an object in a valid state (even though it apparently can't be saved for some reason). The `Catch` blocks contain code to display the exception details to the user as discussed earlier.

Finally, whether an exception occurs or not, event handling is reenabled for the `BindingSource` control:

```
Me.RolesBindingSource.RaiseListChangedEvents = True
```

This must occur for data binding to behave properly, either against the newly updated object, or in the case of an exception, the original object.

Simplified Saving with a Remote Data Portal

If you *know* that you'll be using a remote data portal rather than running the data portal locally in the client process, you can avoid some of the work I just discussed. This is because when you use a remote data portal, the object is automatically copied from the client to the application server, effectively doing the cloning for you.

In that case, the Save button code would look like this:

```
Private Sub SaveButton_Click( _
  ByVal sender As System.Object, ByVal e As System.EventArgs) _
  Handles SaveButton.Click

  Me.RolesBindingSource.RaiseListChangedEvents = False
  Try
    mRoles = mRoles.Save
    Me.Close()

  Catch ex As Csla.DataPortalException
    MessageBox.Show(ex.BusinessException.ToString, _
      "Error saving", MessageBoxButtons.OK, _
      MessageBoxIcon.Exclamation)

  Catch ex As Exception
    MessageBox.Show(ex.ToString, _
      "Error saving", MessageBoxButtons.OK, _
      MessageBoxIcon.Exclamation)

  Finally
    Me.RolesBindingSource.RaiseListChangedEvents = True
  End Try
End Sub
```

Notice that the Clone() method call is gone, and the original object in mRoles is saved directly. If this succeeds without an exception, a newly updated copy of the object is returned from Save(), and the BindingSource controls are re-bound to that new object.

But if an exception *does* occur, then no new object is returned and the mRoles field will continue to point to the original object, as it was before Save() was called! Similarly, an exception will prevent the rebinding of the BindingSource controls, so they continue to point to the original object as well.

Again, this alternate approach is valid if you *only* use a remote data portal configuration. But in that case, it is a good change to make since it avoids making an extra clone of the object before calling Save(), and so is better for performance.

If you are (or might be) using a local data portal configuration, you should manually clone the object to ensure that the UI ends up bound to a valid object in the case of an exception during data processing.

Closing the Form

Since the mRoles field is local to the RolesEdit user control, closing the user control is as simple as calling the Protected Close() method:

```
Private Sub CancelButton_Click( _
  ByVal sender As System.Object, ByVal e As System.EventArgs) _
  Handles CancelButton.Click

  Me.Close()
End Sub
```

As you'll see, more complex user controls like ProjectEdit require a bit more work before closing.

This completes the code in RolesEdit. The important thing to note about this form is the comparative simplicity of the code. It implements GetIdValue(), loads the business object and makes it a data source, and implements code to save the object. All the authorization, validation, and other business logic is entirely in the business object, leaving the code in the UI to focus purely on user interaction.

Project List

When the user wants to edit or remove a project from the system, she'll need to be presented with a list of projects. The ProjectList business object was created for this purpose, so the infrastructure already exists to retrieve the project data. All the UI needs to do is provide a dialog box to display the information.

The user may be prompted to select a project from the list in various places in the application, so the dialog form will be very focused: it will simply display the list of projects and allow the user to select one. This way, the form can be reused anywhere the user must choose a project. Figure 9-11 shows the layout of the ProjectSelect form.

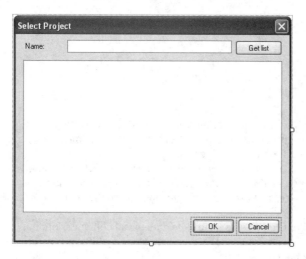

Figure 9-11. *Layout of the ProjectSelect form*

Displaying the Data

When the form is loaded, it populates its display with a list of projects:

```vb
Private Sub ProjectSelect_Load( _
  ByVal sender As System.Object, ByVal e As System.EventArgs) _
  Handles MyBase.Load

  DisplayList(ProjectList.GetProjectList)

End Sub

Private Sub DisplayList(ByVal list As ProjectList)

  Dim sortedList As New Csla.SortedBindingList(Of ProjectInfo)(list)
  sortedList.ApplySort("Name", ListSortDirection.Ascending)
  Me.ProjectListBindingSource.DataSource = sortedList
End Sub
```

Notice how the `DisplayList()` helper method uses `SortedBindingList` to sort the results before they are displayed:

```
Dim sortedList As New Csla.SortedBindingList(Of ProjectInfo)(list)
sortedList.ApplySort("Name", ListSortDirection.Ascending)
```

The user can also get a filtered list of projects. The `NameTextBox` control allows for optional filtering of the displayed list. This value will be provided to the `GetProjectList()` factory method of `ProjectList` when the associated button is clicked:

```
Private Sub GetListButton_Click( _
  ByVal sender As System.Object, ByVal e As System.EventArgs) _
  Handles GetListButton.Click

  DisplayList(ProjectList.GetProjectList(NameTextBox.Text))
End Sub
```

In this case, `DisplayList()` is passed a *filtered* `ProjectList` object, and its data is sorted and displayed to the user.

Data Binding the ListBox

The primary control on the form is a simple `ListBox` that is data bound to the `ProjectList` object. This binding was set up using drag-and-drop binding from the Data Sources window.

Recall that dragging the `Roles` collection onto the designer resulted in a `DataGridView` control. That is the default control, but you can change that in the Data Sources window before dragging the data source onto the designer. Doing that requires customizing the list of controls available from the Data Sources window. Figure 9-12 shows the Customize menu option you would use.

Figure 9-12. *Customization option in the Data Sources window*

This option brings up a dialog in which you can specify which controls should be available in the menu for your data source. You would then select that option from the list and drag the object onto the form.

But I think it is easier to use connect-the-dots data binding instead. To do this, just drag a `ListBox` control from the normal toolbox onto the designer. Size and position it as you desire, then drag the `ProjectList` object from the Data Sources window onto the *already existing* `ListBox` control.

Visual Studio adds a `ProjectListBindingSource` control to the designer, and the data binding properties of the `ListBox` control are automatically linked to that `BindingSource` control.

Either approach is fine, and the end result is the same: your form has a `ListBox` control that is data bound to the `ProjectList` business object. Figure 9-13 shows the Data properties for the `ListBox` control.

Figure 9-13. *Data properties for the ListBox control*

The DataSource property points to the ProjectListBindingSource control. Again, this follows the new data binding approach, with which UI controls are bound to BindingSource controls, which in turn are bound to the underlying data source itself.

Also notice the DisplayMember and ValueMember properties. DisplayMember indicates the property value from the data source that will be displayed to the user. ValueMember indicates the property from the data source that will be invisibly maintained for each item in the ListBox control.

The ListBox control has a SelectedValue property that you can use to get the ValueMember value for the currently selected item in the ListBox. This makes it very easy to retrieve the Id value for the project that the user selected from the list.

Selecting a Project

When ProjectSelect is displayed, it presents the user with a list of projects. At this point, the user can either select one and click OK, or click Cancel. Either way, the DialogResult property is set and the form is closed. For instance, here's the code for the Cancel button:

```
Private Sub Cancel_Button_Click( _
  ByVal sender As System.Object, ByVal e As System.EventArgs) _
  Handles Cancel_Button.Click

  Me.Close()
End Sub
```

The DialogResult property is set to Cancel (because the DialogResult property of the Cancel button is set to Cancel) and the form is closed. The code that displayed this dialog in the first place can retrieve the DialogResult value like this:

```
If dlg.ShowDialog = DialogResult.OK Then
```

The `DialogResult` value from the dialog form's code flows through as the result of the `ShowDialog()` method call in this calling code.

If the user clicks the OK button, things are a bit more interesting. The code behind the OK button stores the `SelectedValue` property from the `ListBox` control, sets the `DialogResult` value, and closes the form:

```
Private mProjectId As Guid

Private Sub OK_Button_Click( _
  ByVal sender As System.Object, ByVal e As System.EventArgs) _
  Handles OK_Button.Click

  mProjectId = CType(Me.ProjectListListBox.SelectedValue, Guid)
  Me.Close()
End Sub
```

The value of `SelectedValue` needs to be stored so that it can be retrieved by the calling code. After all, the reason this `ProjectSelect` dialog was called in the first place was to allow the user to select that value! The OK button's `DialogResult` property is set to `OK`, indicating that the user clicked the OK button, and then the form is closed to return control to the code that called the dialog.

The final bit of code is a read-only `ProjectId` property:

```
Public ReadOnly Property ProjectId() As Guid
  Get
    Return mProjectId
  End Get
End Property
```

It is important to realize that closing a form doesn't destroy the object; it merely causes the form to no longer be displayed. This means that the code that created and displayed the `ProjectSelect` dialog still has a valid reference to the `ProjectSelect` dialog object, even after it has been closed. The calling code can then retrieve the selected `ProjectId` value, somewhat like this:

```
Dim projectId As Guid
Using dlg As New ProjectSelect
  If dlg.ShowDialog = DialogResult.OK Then
    projectId = dlg.ProjectId
  End If
End Using
```

With this small bit of effort, the `ProjectSelect` dialog is complete and can be used any time the user needs to select a project. The form is highly reusable, because `ProjectSelect` doesn't care what's done with the selected value; it simply allows the user to select a project.

ProjectEdit

The final item I'll cover in detail is the `ProjectEdit` user control. In some ways, this is like `RolesEdit`, because it inherits from `WinPart` and is hosted in `MainForm`. But the goal here is to show how a detail form can be created, along with using a `DataGridView` for editing child objects.

Figure 9-14 shows the layout of the `ProjectEdit` user control.

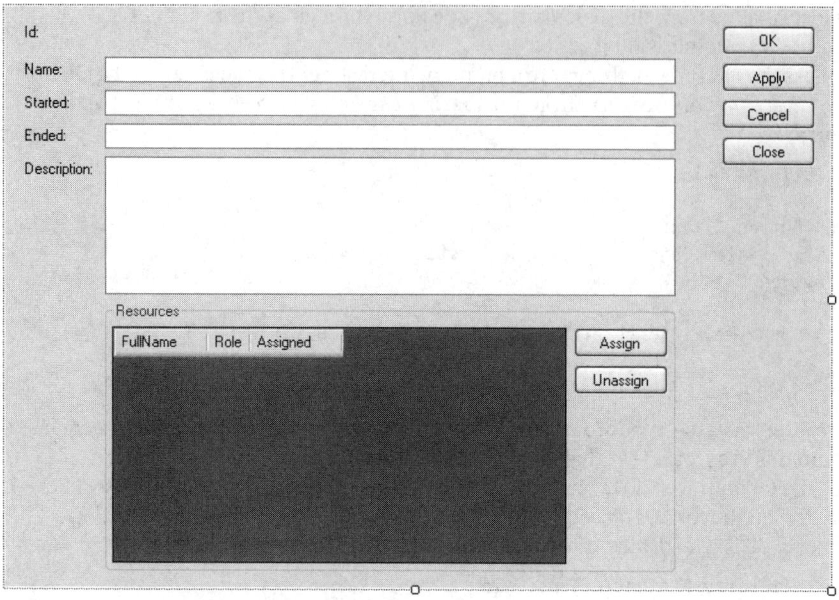

Figure 9-14. *Layout of the ProjectEdit user control*

As you can see, this form has a set of Label and TextBox controls so the user can view and edit information in the Project object itself. It also uses a DataGridView control to display the ProjectResource objects. That DataGridView will also allow the user to change the role a resource plays on a project. Additionally, the values in the FullName column will be displayed as hyperlinks to make it easy for the user to bring up the associated ResourceEdit user control for that resource.

Implementing the functionality behind this form is more complex than RolesEdit or ResourceSelect. But still, the focus is entirely on user interaction and the flow of the UI, not on authorization, validation, or other business behaviors already implemented in the business objects.

Creating the Controls

The controls shown in Figure 9-14 were all added using drag-and-drop data binding. The Label and TextBox controls were added by dragging the Project object from the Data Sources window onto the designer, after setting some options in the Data Sources window.

Binding to the Project Class

Figure 9-15 shows the Data Sources window with the Projects node expanded and being changed to create a details form.

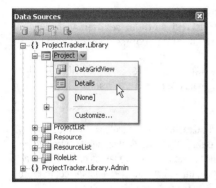

Figure 9-15. *Project node ready to create a details form*

Notice the icon next to the Project node: it represents a details form rather than the default grid display icon you see next to ProjectList, Resource, and the other object nodes. This change occurred because I chose the Details option from the menu for the Project node.

When an object is set to use details mode, the individual control types of the properties for that object come into play. When the object is dragged onto the designer, controls for each property will be created. In fact, a pair of controls is created: a Label displaying the property name and another control to display the property value itself. This second control is indicated by the icons you see next to each property node in the Data Sources window.

The Id property on a Project object is read-only, and so it should be displayed in a Label rather than an editable control. Figure 9-16 shows how the Id property's control is changed from TextBox to Label.

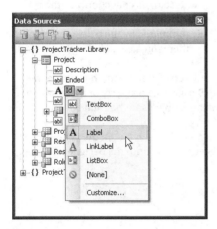

Figure 9-16. *Changing the Id property to display in a Label*

Once the object node is set to details mode and all its properties are set to use the correct control types, the object is simply dragged onto the designer. Visual Studio creates a ProjectBindingSource, all the controls for the properties, and of course the BindingNavigator control.

You can then resize and reposition the controls to get the display you require. The layout in Figure 9-14 shows the result after I've repositioned the controls, resized them, set their Anchor properties, and changed their tab order to match the new layout. And of course, I've removed the BindingNavigator control.

But at no point did I need to worry about setting up the data binding for any controls; Visual Studio handled that automatically. My only concern is the appearance of the UI itself.

■**Note** If you prefer, you could put the controls on the form manually, directly from the toolbox. Then you could use connect-the-dots binding to drag each object property from the Data Sources window onto the controls to set up the data binding. Or if you really like manual work, you could manually set the data properties on each control through the Properties window. Regardless of which approach you take, the results are the same: the controls are data bound to the ProjectBindingSource control, which in turn will be bound to a Project object.

You may be wondering why the Started and Ended properties are bound to TextBox controls rather than a specialized date-entry control. As discussed in Chapter 5, it is often preferable to allow the user to enter dates as he or she chooses—especially for heads-down data entry. Given the extra parsing capabilities of SmartDate, this makes even more sense, since the user can simply press -, ., or + to get yesterday, today, or tomorrow's date.

■**Tip** If you prefer to use a specialized date-entry control, you are best off avoiding the use of SmartDate, and instead exposing the business object properties using the DateTime data type directly.

Adding a RoleListBindingSource Control

Before configuring the DataGridView control that is bound to the Resources collection, another BindingSource control is required. The Roles column in the grid is a combo box column, listing the available roles a resource can play on a project. This list is easily populated by the RoleList object created in Chapter 8—but for it to be available for data binding, there must be a BindingSource control in the component tray.

You can drag a BindingSource control onto the designer directly from the toolbox (it's in the Data group of the toolbox). Figure 9-17 shows how to set the DataSource property of the new control to the RoleList object (assuming you've added your business objects to the Data Sources window as discussed earlier in this chapter).

I've also changed the name of the control to RoleListBindingSource to match the default naming convention used by Visual Studio when an object is dragged directly onto the designer.

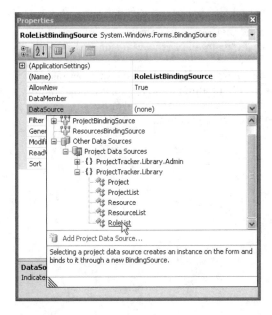

Figure 9-17. *Setting the DataSource property on a BindingSource control*

Binding to the Resources Collection

You've already seen how to create a `DataGridView` in the `RolesEdit` form. The only difference in `ProjectEdit` is that the Resources node *within* the Project node represents the child objects. It is that node that you drag onto the designer to create the `DataGridView` control and set up the data binding.

Notice that a `ResourcesBindingSource` control is automatically added in the component tray, and the `DataGridView` control is bound to that new `BindingSource` control. Each business object must have its own `BindingSource` control because each `BindingSource` control is responsible for managing the information in a single object or collection.

Some design work is required to get the `DataGridView` control to appear as desired. By default, it shows all the properties of the `ProjectResource` objects, as shown in Figure 9-18.

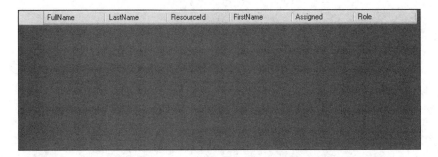

Figure 9-18. *Default display of the DataGridView for the Resources collection*

This doesn't match the appearance of the control shown in Figure 9-14. Given the `FullName` property, there's no need to also display `FirstName` and `LastName`. Additionally, the end user shouldn't have to see the `ResourceId` property, since it is really an internal value for use by the application itself.

On top of those simple formatting changes, the FullName column should be a hyperlink column so that the user can click on a name to open an editor for that resource. And the Role column needs to be a combo box so that the user can select the role from a list of valid options.

To make these changes, edit the columns in the control by choosing the Edit Columns option, as shown in Figure 9-19.

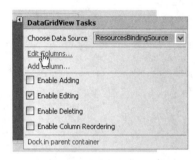

Figure 9-19. *Choosing the Edit Columns option for a DataGridView control*

Using the Edit Columns dialog, you can remove and rearrange columns to get the desired appearance. You can also change the column properties and types for specific columns. For instance, the ResourceId column has its `Visible` property set to `False`, and the FullName column has its column type changed to `DataGridViewLinkColumn`.

The most interesting change is to the Role column, which is changed to a `DataGridViewComboBoxColumn`. Making this change means that the data source used to populate the list of items must be specified. Figure 9-20 shows the data properties for this column.

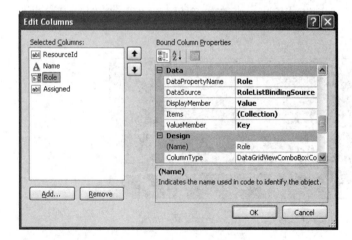

Figure 9-20. *Data properties for the Role column*

The DataSource property is set to the RoleListBindingSource control discussed earlier. You can also just set up the data binding entirely from within the Edit Columns dialog, in which case RoleListBindingSource would be added by Visual Studio at this point, instead of manually like I demonstrated earlier.

Also notice that the DisplayMember and ValueMember properties are set to appropriate values. DisplayMember indicates which property of the data source will be displayed to the user, while ValueMember indicates the property of the data source that will be associated with the Role property of the ProjectResource object in the grid's row.

In other words, each row of the DataGridView represents a single ProjectResource object, which has a Role property of type int. That property is bound to the Role column in the grid, and is linked to the ValueMember property of the RoleList object. The end result is that the DisplayMember value corresponding to the ValueMember from the Role property is shown to the user. And if the user selects a different item, that item's ValueMember is used to set the Role property of the ProjectResource object.

ErrorProvider Control

The ProjectEdit user control includes an ErrorProvider control in the component tray. This extender control is bound to the same data source as the detail controls on the form, and it automatically displays information about any validation errors in the business object. Figure 9-21 shows the case in which a project's Ended property has been set to an earlier date than the Started property.

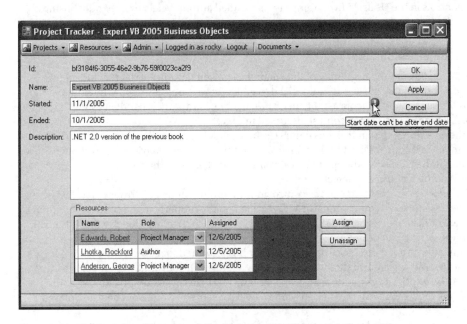

Figure 9-21. *The ErrorProvider control displaying validation error information*

The error icons next to the two date fields, along with the tooltip text, come from the ErrorProvider control. Of course, it gets its information from the Project object itself—through the IDataErrorInfo interface implemented by BusinessBase in Chapter 3.

The ErrorProvider control was simply dragged from the toolbox onto the designer, and its DataSource property set to the ProjectBindingSource control, as shown in Figure 9-22.

Figure 9-22. *Properties for the ErrorProvider control*

The important property here is DataSource, which is set to the same BindingSource control as the detail controls in the UI itself. Everything else is handled automatically by either the business object or the ErrorProvider control itself.

ReadWriteAuthorization Control

In Figures 9-2 and 9-3, at the beginning of the chapter, I showed how the ProjectEdit display changes based on whether the user is authorized to edit a Project object or not. While some manual coding is required to achieve that effect, much of the hard work is handled by the Csla. Windows.ReadWriteAuthorization control discussed in Chapter 5.

Like the ErrorProvider control, this control is an extender control, meaning that it adds extra behaviors to normal controls like Label and TextBox. In this case, the behaviors are to change those controls so that they disallow editing or even viewing of data based on the authorization rules specified in the underlying business object.

You'll find a ReadWriteAuthorization control in the component tray of ProjectEdit. Just by being on the designer, this control adds an ApplyAuthorization property to the controls for editing project data. For instance, Figure 9-23 shows the new ApplyAuthorization property that has been added to the NameTextBox control.

By setting this property to True, the UI developer has indicated that the ReadWriteAuthorization control should automatically set this control's ReadOnly property to True if the user isn't authorized to edit the Name property. If the user isn't even authorized to *read* the property value, the ReadWriteAuthorization control will prevent the value from being displayed at all.

I'll discuss the code used to trigger the authorization behaviors later, but as you'll see, the ReadWriteAuthorization control radically simplifies the process of creating the UI.

Figure 9-23. *ApplyAuthorization property on the NameTextBox control*

BindingSourceRefresh Control

The final control I want to discuss is the `Csla.Windows.BindingSourceRefresh` control. This control was discussed in Chapter 5, and it exists to work around an unfortunate behavior in Windows Forms data binding.

The issue occurs when the user edits a value in a control, such as a `TextBox`, and tabs off that control. The data in the control is put into the business object's property through data binding. But if the object then *changes* the value, that change is not shown in the UI. This is particularly problematic with the `SmartDate` properties on the `Project` object, since the user could enter +, expecting to see tomorrow's date. But due to this issue, the user would continue to see the + character even though the business object *does have* the right date value internally!

The `BindingSourceRefresh` control is designed to eliminate this issue. You'll find this control in the component tray of the designer. Unlike `ErrorProvider` and `ReadWriteAuthorization`, which add behaviors to controls like `Label` or `TextBox`, this control adds behaviors to the `BindingSource` controls on the form.

For instance, Figure 9-24 shows the `ProjectBindingSource` control with the new `ReadValuesOnChange` property. This property should be set to `True` for any `BindingSource` controls used by detail controls like `TextBox`. It can be set to `False` for `BindingSource` controls that only provide data to a list or grid control like `DataGridView`, because those controls don't have the same quirky behavior.

At this point, you should understand how all the detail and grid controls were added to `ProjectEdit`. You should also understand how the `RoleListBindingSource` is used to populate the combo box display in the `DataGridView`, and how the three extender controls are used to easily implement advanced features. Now let's discuss the code behind the form.

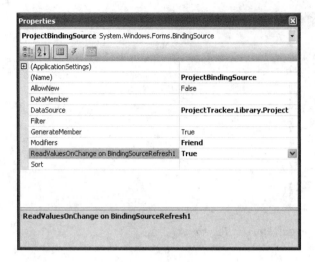

Figure 9-24. *The ReadValuesOnChange property on the ProjectBindingSource control*

WinPart Code

Because `ProjectEdit` inherits from `WinPart`, it must override the `GetIdValue()` method:

```
Protected Overrides Function GetIdValue() As Object
    Return mProject
End Function
```

Remember that this method is supposed to return a unique identifying value for the user control; and the best thing to use is the business object being edited. By using the business object itself as the unique identifier, the code in `MainForm` can ensure that any attempt by the user to open a second user control to edit the same `Project` object will simply result in the original user control being brought to the forefront.

There's one more thing to do, though. Recall that `MainForm` calls `ToString()` on the identifier value to populate the display in the Documents menu. Yet calling `ToString()` on a `Project` object will return the object's `Id` value: a `Guid`. This is obviously not desirable, since it would be preferable to show the object's `Name` property value. To solve this, the `ToString()` method is overridden to return that value:

```
Public Overrides Function ToString() As String
    Return mProject.Name
End Function
```

This way, the Documents menu will show the project's `Name` rather than its `Id`.

Loading the User Control

A parameterized constructor is used to create the form, allowing the calling code to pass in a reference to the `Project` object that is to be viewed or edited. This constructor sets the `DataSource` properties of the `BindingSource` controls to initiate data binding:

```
Private WithEvents mProject As Project

Public Sub New(ByVal project As Project)

  InitializeComponent()

  mProject = project
  mProject.BeginEdit()

  Me.RoleListBindingSource.DataSource = RoleList.GetList
  Me.ProjectBindingSource.DataSource = mProject

  ApplyAuthorizationRules()
End Sub
```

First though, it stores the object reference in an instance field for later use. It also calls the business object's BeginEdit() method, thus invoking the n-level undo capability discussed in Chapter 3. This method call tells the object to take a snapshot of its current state, so the object can be restored to this exact state later if the user clicks the Cancel or Close button without saving the data first.

With that done, data binding is initialized:

```
Me.RoleListBindingSource.DataSource = RoleList.GetList
Me.ProjectBindingSource.DataSource = mProject
```

The DataSource property of RoleListBindingSource is set to a RoleList object. If this is the first time GetList() has been called, this will incur a call to the database; otherwise, the collection is returned from the cache implemented in Chapter 8.

The DataSource property of projectBindingList is set to the Project object passed into the constructor as a parameter. By accepting this object as a parameter, ProjectEdit can be used to add new objects, or edit or view existing objects. It isn't concerned with where the object came from, just that it is a Project object that is to be displayed or edited. This technique increases the reusability of the ProjectEdit user control.

Notice that the DataSource of ResourcesBindingSource is not explicitly set. This is because the Windows Forms designer understands the relationship between the Project object and its Resources property, and sets up the binding automatically.

The last line of code in the constructor calls ApplyAuthorizationRules(), which is responsible for applying all authorization rules to the controls on the form.

Authorization Rules

Authorization rules are applied in two cases: as the form loads, and any time the user logs into or out of the application. This second scenario causes a CurrentPrincipalChanged event to be raised, and that event is handled in the code:

```
Private Sub ProjectEdit_CurrentPrincipalChanged( _
  ByVal sender As Object, ByVal e As System.EventArgs) _
  Handles Me.CurrentPrincipalChanged

  ApplyAuthorizationRules()
End Sub
```

Like in the constructor, the ApplyAuthorizationRules() method is called to actually apply the rules and update the display. Of course, not much code is required in ApplyAuthorizationRules() because the ReadWriteAuthorization control will do most of the hard work. The only real code in the method exists to deal with the various buttons on the form (which aren't data bound) and the DataGridView control:

```
Private Sub ApplyAuthorizationRules()
  ' have the controls enable/disable/etc
  Me.ReadWriteAuthorization1.ResetControlAuthorization()

  Dim canEdit As Boolean = _
    ProjectTracker.Library.Project.CanEditObject

  ' enable/disable appropriate buttons
  Me.OKButton.Enabled = canEdit
  Me.ApplyButton.Enabled = canEdit
  Me.Cancel_Button.Enabled = canEdit
  Me.AssignButton.Enabled = canEdit
  Me.UnassignButton.Enabled = canEdit

  ' enable/disable role column in grid
  Me.ResourcesDataGridView.Columns(2).ReadOnly = Not canEdit
End Sub
```

The call to ResetControlAuthorization() tells the ReadWriteAuthorization control to loop through all the detail controls and apply authorization rules to any that have their ApplyAuthorization property set to True. Recall from Chapter 5 that ReadWriteAuthorization relies entirely on the CanReadProperty() and CanWriteProperty() methods of the business object to determine whether the current user is authorized to read or write each property. Thus, this one line of code is able to completely enable or disable all the detail controls on the whole form.

The code then enables or disables the buttons that would allow the user to save the object. The Shared method CanEditObject() is called to ask the Project class itself whether the current user can edit project data, so the UI really has no idea about the authorization rules themselves; its only concern is to properly update the display to give the user appropriate visual cues.

Finally, if the user isn't authorized to edit project data, the Roles column in the DataGridView is set to be read-only. Not that the user could save any changes they might make, but there's no sense letting the user think they can change values when they can't actually save them.

Saving the Data

Notice that ProjectEdit has four buttons: Save, Apply, Cancel, and Close. Normally, an application wouldn't have all these buttons, but I want to illustrate how each one is implemented so you understand the options available to you when implementing detail forms. The goal is to highlight some of the capabilities of the n-level undo functionality discussed in Chapter 3.

The actual save process is the same for a Project object as it was for the Roles object earlier in the chapter:

1. Turn off events from the BindingSource controls.

2. Clone the business object.

3. Save the *clone* of the business object.

4. Rebind the BindingSource controls to the *new* object returned from Save().

5. Turn on events from the BindingSource controls.

The SaveProject() method implements this process. Because this form supports both the Save and Apply buttons, the rebinding of the UI controls is optional. Rebinding the UI is controlled by a rebind parameter passed to the method:

```vb
Private Sub SaveProject(ByVal rebind As Boolean)
  Using busy As New StatusBusy("Saving...")
    ' stop the flow of events
    Me.ProjectBindingSource.RaiseListChangedEvents = False
    Me.ResourcesBindingSource.RaiseListChangedEvents = False

    ' do the save
    Dim temp As Project = mProject.Clone
    temp.ApplyEdit()
    Try
      mProject = temp.Save
      mProject.BeginEdit()
      If rebind Then
        ' rebind the UI
        Me.ProjectBindingSource.DataSource = Nothing
        Me.ResourcesBindingSource.DataSource = Me.ProjectBindingSource
        Me.ProjectBindingSource.DataSource = mProject
        ApplyAuthorizationRules()
      End If

    Catch ex As Csla.DataPortalException
      MessageBox.Show(ex.BusinessException.ToString, _
        "Error saving", MessageBoxButtons.OK, _
        MessageBoxIcon.Exclamation)

    Catch ex As Exception
      MessageBox.Show(ex.ToString, _
        "Error saving", MessageBoxButtons.OK, _
        MessageBoxIcon.Exclamation)

    Finally
      Me.ProjectBindingSource.RaiseListChangedEvents = True
      Me.ResourcesBindingSource.RaiseListChangedEvents = True
    End Try
  End Using
End Sub
```

The BindingSource controls that are bound to the business objects about to be updated have their events turned off:

```vb
Me.ProjectBindingSource.RaiseListChangedEvents = False
Me.ResourcesBindingSource.RaiseListChangedEvents = False
```

Then the Project object is cloned and ApplyEdit() is called on the clone. Remember that BeginEdit() was called in the constructor, causing the business object to take a snapshot of its data. At this point, the user has obviously decided that he like the changes he has made, so the snapshot is no longer required. Calling ApplyEdit() commits the changes to the object *in memory*, in preparation for saving those changes to the database.

As with the Roles object, it is the clone that is saved, so if any exception occurs during the Save() call, the original object remains intact and valid. On the other hand, if no exception occurs during the Save() call, the mProject field is updated with a reference to a Project object that contains the updated data.

The BeginEdit() method is called on this new Project object, telling the object that it is about to be edited so that it can take a snapshot of its values. This is the same as in the constructor, and is the key to making n-level undo function properly. Having the object take a snapshot of its data before it is edited allows the Cancel button to be implemented properly (as discussed later).

The BindingSource controls are then re-bound to this new object:

```
Me.ProjectBindingSource.DataSource = Nothing
Me.ResourcesBindingSource.DataSource = Me.ProjectBindingSource
Me.ProjectBindingSource.DataSource = mProject
```

Again, binding to the Resources property is handled automatically, though you do need to explicitly *unbind* ResourcesBindingSource by setting its DataSource property to Me.ProjectBindingSource.

With that done, the ApplyAuthorizationRules() method is called. The reason for this is that authorization rules for a new object could be different from an old object; and now that the object has been saved to the database, its status could have changed. Remember that the authorization rules are *inside the object*, not in the UI. The UI code should call ApplyAuthorization() rules any time an object might be expected to change its authorization rules.

Before exiting the SaveProject() method, whether an exception occurred or not, the BindingSource controls have their event handling turned back on:

```
Me.ProjectBindingSource.RaiseListChangedEvents = True
Me.ResourcesBindingSource.RaiseListChangedEvents = True
```

All business objects should be saved following this same basic flow. Also remember the discussion from the Roles object regarding how you can avoid calling Clone() if you know that the data portal will *always* be configured to use an application server.

▌Note The process is a bit different for Web Forms and Web Services interfaces.

With the SaveProject() method, the code behind the buttons now becomes quite straightforward. The only difference between the Save and Apply buttons is whether the user control is closed after the data is saved:

```
Private Sub OKButton_Click(ByVal sender As System.Object, _
  ByVal e As System.EventArgs) Handles OKButton.Click

  SaveProject(False)
  Me.Close()
End Sub

Private Sub ApplyButton_Click(ByVal sender As System.Object, _
  ByVal e As System.EventArgs) Handles ApplyButton.Click

  SaveProject(True)
End Sub
```

Recall that the SaveProject() method calls ApplyEdit() on the object before saving it to the database, which applies any changes made by the user. It also calls BeginEdit() before rebinding the object to the UI, so n-level undo is always available. Finally, the object is only re-bound to the UI if the rebind parameter is True, so the rebinding is only done when the Apply button is clicked.

The Close and Cancel buttons are also quite similar:

```
Private Sub Cancel_Button_Click(ByVal sender As System.Object, _
  ByVal e As System.EventArgs) Handles Cancel_Button.Click

  mProject.CancelEdit()
End Sub
```

```
Private Sub CloseButton_Click(ByVal sender As System.Object, _
  ByVal e As System.EventArgs) Handles CloseButton.Click

  mProject.CancelEdit()
  Me.Close()
End Sub
```

Both call the CancelEdit() method on the Project object, telling the object to restore its state to the point when BeginEdit() was last called. The only difference is that the Close button causes the user control to be closed, while the Cancel button leaves it open.

The call to CancelEdit() in the Close button is important. At first glance, it might seem unnecessary, but remember that in some types of UI, *other forms* could be displaying this same object at the same time. Calling CancelEdit() here ensures that the displays in those other forms are updated to reflect the reversal of any edits done to the object's state.

You can play with the Apply and Cancel buttons to experiment with n-level undo. Run the application and edit a project. Then make some changes to various data, possibly even adding or removing ProjectResource child objects in the DataGridView. Then click the Cancel button to see all your changes go away as the object restores its state to the last BeginEdit() call.

Or make some changes, click Apply, and then make some more changes. Then click Cancel to see the object reset itself to the point at which Apply was clicked (because that caused BeginEdit() to be called).

Most UI styles don't require the full capabilities of n-level undo, but almost all Windows Forms UI designs need at least single-level undo. The n-level undo capabilities provided by CSLA .NET enable both simple and advanced UI scenarios with a common code base.

Editing a Resource

The DataGridView has a FullName column, which is set to be a hyperlink. When the user clicks on an item in this column, the application should open a ResourceEdit user control so the user can view or edit the data for that resource.

▪**Note** I won't discuss ResourceEdit in detail, but you can look at the code in the download. It is fundamentally equivalent to ProjectEdit in its construction.

Getting the correct Resource object is easy, because the ProjectResource object implements a GetResource() method. When the user clicks the hyperlink, the code gets the selected ResourceId value from the DataGridView control and passes that value to the ShowEditResource() method on MainForm:

```
Private Sub ResourcesDataGridView_CellContentClick( _
  ByVal sender As System.Object, _
  ByVal e As System.Windows.Forms.DataGridViewCellEventArgs) _
  Handles ResourcesDataGridView.CellContentClick

  If e.ColumnIndex = 1 And e.RowIndex > -1 Then
    Dim resourceId As Integer = _
      CInt(Me.ResourcesDataGridView.Rows(e.RowIndex).Cells(0).Value)
    MainForm.ShowEditResource(resourceId)
  End If
End Sub
```

Calling `ShowEditResource()` is important, because if this `Resource` object is already being edited in a `ResourceEdit` user control, then that user control will be made active. Otherwise, the `Resource` object will be loaded from the database and displayed in a new `ResourceEdit` user control.

The end result is that the user can easily navigate to any of the resources assigned to the project. Comparable functionality exists in the `ResourceEdit` user control, which allows the user to easily navigate to any project to which the resource is assigned.

Assigning and Unassigning Resources

The last bit of functionality in the application is the ability to add and remove child `ProjectResource` objects from the `Resources` collection. Editing of the child objects is handled automatically by data binding, but there are buttons on the user control to allow the user to assign and unassign resources on the project.

The user is prompted to select the resource to assign to the project by using the `ResourceSelect` dialog form:

```
Private Sub AssignButton_Click(ByVal sender As System.Object, _
  ByVal e As System.EventArgs) Handles AssignButton.Click

  Dim dlg As New ResourceSelect
  If dlg.ShowDialog = DialogResult.OK Then
    Try
      mProject.Resources.Assign(dlg.ResourceId)

    Catch ex As InvalidOperationException
      MessageBox.Show(ex.ToString, _
        "Error assigning", MessageBoxButtons.OK, _
        MessageBoxIcon.Information)

    Catch ex As Exception
      MessageBox.Show(ex.ToString, _
        "Error assigning", MessageBoxButtons.OK, _
        MessageBoxIcon.Exclamation)
    End Try
  End If
End Sub
```

If the user clicks the OK button in the dialog, the `ResourceId` value is retrieved from the dialog and passed to the `Assign()` method of the `Resources` collection. Remember from Chapter 8 that this `Assign()` method takes care of all the details of assigning a resource to a project.

When the new item is added to the `Resources` collection, the data binding support built into the `Csla.BusinessListBase` class automatically notifies the UI that the collection has changed, so the `DataGridView` immediately displays the new row of data.

The Unassign button finds the `DataGridView` row currently selected and retrieves the `ResourceId` value from that row. The `Remove()` method on the `Resources` collection is then called to remove that item from the collection:

```
Private Sub UnassignButton_Click(ByVal sender As System.Object, _
  ByVal e As System.EventArgs) Handles UnassignButton.Click

  If Me.ResourcesDataGridView.SelectedRows.Count > 0 Then
    Dim resourceId As Integer = _
      CInt(Me.ResourcesDataGridView.SelectedRows(0).Cells(0).Value)
    mProject.Resources.Remove(resourceId)
  End If
End Sub
```

Remember that n-level undo is active, so the item is not *really* deleted, but rather is moved to the DeletedList within the collection. If the user later clicks the Cancel or Close buttons, the item will be restored to the collection. Similarly, any newly added items will be automatically removed from the collection when those buttons are clicked.

Conclusion

This chapter has walked through the process of creating a basic Windows Forms UI using the business objects from Chapter 8. Obviously, there are many ways to create a UI using Windows Forms, so the goal of this chapter was to highlight how you can use data binding to easily create grid-based and detail forms to view and edit object data.

The ProjectEdit user control also illustrates how to leverage the n-level undo support built into CSLA .NET business objects. This capability is also used by the DataGridView control to provide in-place editing of data.

The key point to take from this chapter is that when you create your business layer using business objects, the UI developer doesn't need to worry about validation or authorization rules, data access, or most other complex issues. The UI developer can focus on user interaction, the look and feel of the application, and so forth. The result is a high degree of separation between the UI layer and the business layer.

At the same time, because the objects use the data portal mechanism to retrieve and update data, the application is able to exploit the capabilities of mobile objects: running business logic on both the client workstation and an application server as appropriate. Better still, you can simply change the application configuration file to switch between various physical n-tier configurations to meet different performance, scalability, reliability, and security requirements. Chapter 12 will show how to implement the various application server hosts for each network channel.

First though, Chapter 10 will cover the implementation of a Web Forms UI based on the same set of business objects. Although there are obvious differences between the Windows Forms and Web Forms environments, total reuse of the business logic and data access code is achieved in the move from one UI type to the next.

Web Forms UI

Chapter 9 covered the creation of a Windows Forms UI based on the `ProjectTracker` business objects. But .NET also supports web development through ASP.NET and the Web Forms technology. In this chapter, the same business objects are used to create a Web Forms interface with functionality comparable to the Windows Forms interface.

While Web Forms can be used to create many different user interfaces, this chapter isn't intended to act as a tutorial on web development in ASP.NET. Instead, I'll focus on how business objects are used within a web application, including state management and data binding.

Tip ASP.NET is the .NET web server component that hosts web forms, web services, and other server-side handlers in Internet Information Services (IIS). ASP.NET is a very broad and flexible technology. Web forms are hosted within ASP.NET and provide "normal" web development capabilities.

As with the Windows Forms interface in Chapter 9, I won't walk through the details of every web form in the application. Instead, I'll walk through a representative sample to illustrate key concepts.

In particular, I'll discuss the following:

- Basic site design
- The use of forms-based authentication
- Adding and editing roles
- Adding and editing project data

However, before getting into the design and development of the Web Forms UI itself, I need to discuss some of the basic concepts around the use of business objects in web development.

Web Development and Objects

Historically, the world of web development has been strongly resistant to the use of "stateful" objects behind web pages, and not without reason. In particular, using such objects without careful forethought can be very bad for website performance. Sometimes, however, it's suggested that instead of a stateful object, you should use a `DataSet`—which is itself a very large, stateful object! Most people don't think twice about using one of those for web development.

Clearly then, stateful objects aren't inherently bad—it's how they're designed and used that matters. Business objects can be very useful in web development, but it is necessary to look carefully at how such objects are conceived and employed.

■Note Objects *can* work very well in web development, if they're designed and used properly.

In general terms, web applications can choose from three basic data access models, as shown in Figure 10-1.

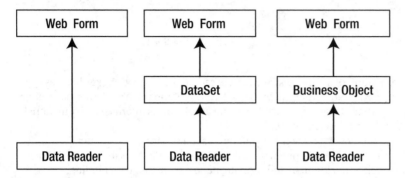

Figure 10-1. *The three basic data access models*

Using the data reader directly can be very beneficial if the data set is relatively small and the page processing is fast, because the data is taken directly from the database and put it into the page. There's no need to copy the data into an in-memory container (such as a DataSet or business object) before putting it into the page output. This is illustrated in Figure 10-2.

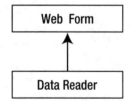

Figure 10-2. *Data flowing directly from a data reader into a web form*

However, if the data set is large or the page processing is slow, using a data reader becomes a less attractive option. Using one requires the database connection to remain open longer, causing an increase in the number of database connections required on the server overall, and thereby decreasing scalability.

Direct use of a data reader also typically leads to code that's harder to maintain. A data reader doesn't offer the ease of use of the DataSet or a business object. Nor does it provide any business logic or protection for the data, leaving it up to the UI code to provide all validation and other business processing.

■Note In most cases, use of the DataSet or a business object will offer better scalability when compared to direct use of a data reader, and will result in code that's easier to maintain.

Having discounted the use of a data reader in all but a few situations, the question becomes whether to use the DataSet or a business object as a stateful, in-memory data container. These options are similar in that the data is loaded from a data reader into the stateful object, and from there into the page, as illustrated in Figure 10-3.

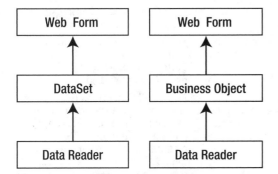

Figure 10-3. *Data loaded into an intermediate object, followed by the web form*

This means that, in general, you can expect similar performance characteristics from the DataSet and business objects. However, business objects are often actually more *lightweight* than the ADO.NET DataSet object. This is because business objects are specific to the data they contain, and don't need to retain all the metadata required by the DataSet object.

Better yet, business objects provide access not only to the application's data, but also to its *business logic*. As discussed in Chapter 1, business objects can be thought of as *smart data*. They encapsulate the business logic and the data so that the UI doesn't need to worry about potential data misuse.

Overall, business objects provide the high-scalability characteristics of the DataSet, without the overhead. They offer a better use of database connections than the data reader, though at the cost of some performance in certain situations. When compared to both other technologies, business objects enable a much higher level of reuse and easier long-term maintenance, making them the best choice overall.

State Management

The Achilles' heel of web development is state management. The original design of web technology was merely for document viewing, not the myriad purposes for which it's used today. Because of this, the issue of state management was never thought through in a methodical way. Instead, state management techniques have evolved over time in a relatively ad hoc manner.

Through this haphazard process, some workable solutions have evolved, though each requires trade-offs in terms of performance, scalability, and fault tolerance. The primary options at your disposal are as follows:

- State is maintained on the web server.
- State is transferred from server to client to server on each page request.
- State is stored in temporary files or database tables.

Whether you use a DataSet, a data reader, or business objects to retrieve and update data is immaterial here—ultimately, you're left to choose one of these three state management strategies. Table 10-1 summarizes the strengths and weaknesses of each.

Table 10-1. *State Management Strategies*

Approach	Strengths	Weaknesses
State stored on web server	Easy to code and use. Works well with business objects.	Use of global fields/data is poor programming practice. Scalability and fault tolerance via a web farm requires increased complexity of infrastructure.
State transferred to/from client	Scalability and fault tolerance are easily achieved by implementing a web farm.	Hard to code, requires a lot of manual coding to implement. Performance can be a problem over slow network links.
State stored in file/database	Scalability and fault tolerance are easily achieved by implementing a web farm. A lot of state data or very complex data can be easily stored.	Increased load on database server since state is retrieved/stored on each page hit. Requires manual coding to implement. Data cleanup must be implemented to deal with abandoned state data.

As you can see, all of these solutions have more drawbacks than benefits. Unfortunately, in the more than ten years that the Web has been a mainstream technology, no vendor or standards body has been able to provide a comprehensive solution to the issue of dealing with state data. All you can do is choose the solution that has the lowest negative impact on your particular application.

Let's go into some more detail on each of these techniques, in the context of using business objects behind web pages.

State on the Web Server

First, you can choose to keep state on the web server. This is easily accomplished through the use of the ASP.NET Session object, which is a name/value collection of arbitrary data or objects. ASP.NET manages the Session object, ensuring that each user has a unique Session, and that the Session object is available to all Web Forms code on any page request.

This is by far the easiest way to program web applications. The Session object acts as a global repository for almost any data that you need to keep from page to page. By storing state data on the web server, you enable the type of host-based computing that has been done on mainframes and minicomputers for decades.

As I've already expressed, however, there are drawbacks. Session is a *global* repository for each user, but as any experienced programmer knows, the use of global fields is very dangerous and can rapidly lead to code that's hard to maintain. If you choose to use Session to store state, you must be disciplined in its use to avoid these problems.

The use of Session also has scalability and fault tolerance ramifications.

Using a Web Farm in ASP.NET

Achieving scalability and fault tolerance typically requires implementation of a web farm: two or more web servers that are running exactly the same application. It doesn't matter which server handles each user page request, because all the servers run the same code. This effectively spreads the processing load across multiple machines, thus increasing scalability. You also gain fault tolerance, since if one machine goes down, the remaining server(s) will simply take over the handling of user requests.

What I just described is a fully load-balanced web farm. However, because state data is often maintained directly on each web server, the preceding scenario isn't possible. Instead, web farms are often configured using "sticky sessions." Once a user starts using a specific server, the user remains on that server because that's where their data is located. This provides *some* scalability, because the processing load is still spread across multiple servers, but it provides very limited fault tolerance. If a server goes down, all the users attached to that server also go down.

To enable a fully load-balanced web farm, *no* state can be maintained on *any* web server. As soon as user state is stored on a web server, users become attached to that server to the extent that only that server can handle their web requests. By default, the ASP.NET Session object runs on the web server in the ASP.NET process. This provides optimal performance because the state data is stored in process with the application's code, but this approach doesn't allow implementation of a fully load-balanced web farm.

Instead, the Session object can be run in a separate process on the same web server. This can help improve fault tolerance, since the ASP.NET process can restart, and users won't lose their state data. However, this still doesn't result in a fully load-balanced web farm, so it doesn't help with scalability. Also, there's a performance cost because the state data must be serialized and transferred from the state management process to the ASP.NET process (and back again) on every page request.

As a third option, ASP.NET allows the Session object to be maintained on a dedicated, separate server, rather than on any specific web server. This *state server* can maintain the state data for all users, making it equally accessible to all web servers in a web farm. This *does* mean that you can implement a fully load-balanced web farm, in which each user request is routed to the least-loaded web server. As shown in Figure 10-4, no user is ever "stuck" on a specific web server.

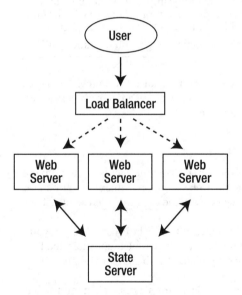

Figure 10-4. *Load-balanced web server farm with centralized state server*

With this arrangement, you can lose a web server with minimal impact. Obviously, users in the middle of having a page processed on that particular server will be affected, but all other users should be redirected to the remaining live servers transparently. All the users' Session data will remain available.

As with the out-of-process option discussed previously, the Session object is serialized so that it can be transferred to the state server machine efficiently. This means that all objects referenced by Session are also serialized—which isn't a problem for CSLA .NET–style business objects, since they're marked as <Serializable()>.

> ■**Note** When using this approach, all state *must* be maintained in `<Serializable()>` objects.

In this arrangement, fault tolerance is significantly improved, but if the state server goes down, then all user state is lost. To help address this, you can put the `Session` objects into a SQL Server database (rather than just into memory on the state server), and then use clustering to make the SQL Server fault tolerant as well.

Obviously, these solutions are becoming increasingly complex and costly, and they also worsen performance. By putting the state on a separate state server, the application now incurs network overhead on each page request, since the user's `Session` object must be retrieved from the state server by the web server so that the Web Forms code can use the `Session` data. Once each page is complete, the `Session` object is transferred back across the network to the state server for storage.

Table 10-2 summarizes these options.

Table 10-2. *Session Object Storage Locations*

Location of State Data	Performance, Scalability, and Fault Tolerance
`Session` in process	High performance; low scalability; low fault tolerance; web farms must use sticky sessions; fully load-balanced web farms not supported
`Session` out of process	Decreased performance; low scalability; improved fault tolerance (ASP.NET process can reset without losing state data); web farms must use sticky sessions; fully load-balanced web farms not supported
`Session` on state server	Decreased performance; high scalability; high fault tolerance

In conclusion, while storing state data on the web server (or in a state server) provides the simplest programming model, you must make some obvious sacrifices with regard to complexity and performance in order to achieve scalability and fault tolerance.

Transferring State to or from the Client

The second option to consider is transferring all state from the server to the client, and back to the server again, on each page request. The idea here is that the web server never maintains any state data—it gets all state data along with the page request, works with the data, and then sends it back to the client as part of the resulting page.

This approach provides high scalability and fault tolerance with very little complexity in your infrastructure: since the web servers never maintain state data, you can implement a fully load-balanced web farm without worrying about server-side state issues. On the other hand, there are some drawbacks.

First of all, all the state data is transferred over what is typically the slowest link in the system: the connection between the user's browser and the web server. Moreover, that state is transferred *twice* for each page: from the server to the browser, and then from the browser back to the server. Obviously, this can have serious performance implications over a slow network link (like a modem), and can even affect an organization's overall network performance due to the volume of data being transferred on each page request.

The other major drawback is the complexity of the application's *code*. There's no automatic mechanism that puts all state data into each page; you must do that by hand. Often this means creating hidden fields on each page in which you can store state data that's required, but that the user shouldn't see. The pages can quickly become very complex as you add these extra fields.

This can also be a security problem. When state data is sent to the client, that data becomes potentially available to the end user. In many cases, an application's state data will include internal information that's not intended for direct consumption by the user. Sometimes, this information may be sensitive, so sending it to the client could create a security loophole in the system. Although you could encrypt this data, that would incur extra processing overhead and could increase the size of the data sent to/from the client, so performance would be decreased.

To avoid such difficulties, applications often minimize the amount of data stored in the page by re-retrieving it from the original database on each page request. All you need to keep in the page, then, is the key information to retrieve the data and any data values that have changed. Any other data values can always be reloaded from the database. This solution can dramatically increase the load on your database server, but continues to avoid keeping any state on the web server.

In conclusion, while this solution offers good scalability and fault tolerance, it can be quite complex to program, and can often result in a lot of extra code to write and maintain. Additionally, it can have a negative performance impact, especially if your users connect over low-speed lines.

State in a File or Database

The final solution to consider is the use of temporary files (or database tables of temporary data) in which you can store state data. Such a solution opens the door to other alternatives, including the creation of data schemas that can store state data so that it can be retrieved in parts, reported against, and so forth. Typically, these activities aren't important for state data, but they *can* be important if you want to keep the state data for a long period of time.

Most state data just exists between page calls, or at most, for the period of time during which the user is actively interacting with the site. Some applications, however, keep state data for longer periods of time, thereby allowing the user's "session" to last for days, weeks, or months. Persistent shopping carts and wish lists are examples of long-term state data that's typically stored in a meaningful format in a database.

Whether you store state as a single BLOB of data or in a schema, storing it in a file or a database provides good scalability and fault tolerance. It can also provide better performance than sending the state to and from the client workstation, since communicating with a database is typically faster than communicating with the client. In situations like these, the state data isn't kept on the client or the web server, so you can create fully load-balanced web farms, as shown in Figure 10-5.

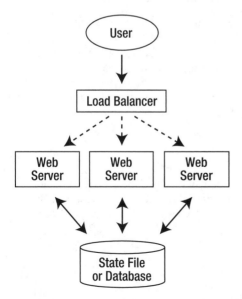

Figure 10-5. *Load-balanced web farm with centralized state database*

■Tip As I mentioned earlier, one way to implement a centralized state database is to use the ASP.NET `Session` object and configure it so that the data is stored in a SQL Server database. If you just want to store arbitrary state data as a single chunk of data in the database, then this is probably the best solution.

The first thing you'll notice is that this diagram is virtually identical to the state server diagram discussed earlier, and it turns out that the basic model and benefits are indeed consistent with that approach. The application gains scalability and fault tolerance because you can implement a web farm, whereby the web server that's handling each page request retrieves state from the central database. Once the page request is complete, the data is stored in the central state database. Using clustering technology, you can make the database server itself fault tolerant, thereby minimizing it as a single point of failure.

In conclusion, though this approach offers a high degree of scalability and fault tolerance, if you implement the retrieval and storage of the state data by hand, it increases the complexity of your code. There are also performance implications, since all state data is transferred across a network and back for each page request—and then there's the cost of storing and retrieving the data in the database itself.

In the final analysis, determining which of the three solutions to use depends on the specific requirements of your application and environment. For most applications, using the ASP.NET `Session` object to maintain state data will offer the easiest programming model and the most flexibility. You can achieve optimal performance by running it in process with your pages, or achieve optimal scalability and fault tolerance by having the `Session` object stored in a SQL Server database on a clustered database server. There are shades of compromise in between.

■Note ASP.NET allows you to switch between three different state-handling models by simply changing the website's `web.config` file (assuming you already have a SQL Server database server available in your environment). For an excellent overview of this feature, see "Understanding session state modes + FAQ" in Microsoft's ASP.NET forums (`http://forums.asp.net/7504/ShowPost.aspx`).

The key is that CSLA .NET–style business objects are serializable, so the `Session` object can serialize them as needed. Even if you choose to implement your own BLOB-based file or data-storage approach, the fact that the objects are serializable means that the business objects can be easily converted to a byte stream that can be stored as a BLOB. If the objects were not serializable, the options would be severely limited.

For the sample application, I'll use the `Session` object to help manage state data; but I'll use it sparingly, because overuse of global fields is a cardinal sin!

Interface Design

The UI application can be found within the `ProjectTracker` solution. The project is named `PTWeb`. The `PTWeb` interface uses a master page to provide consistency across all the pages in the site. The `Default.aspx` page provides a basic entry point to the website. Figure 10-6 shows what the page layout looks like.

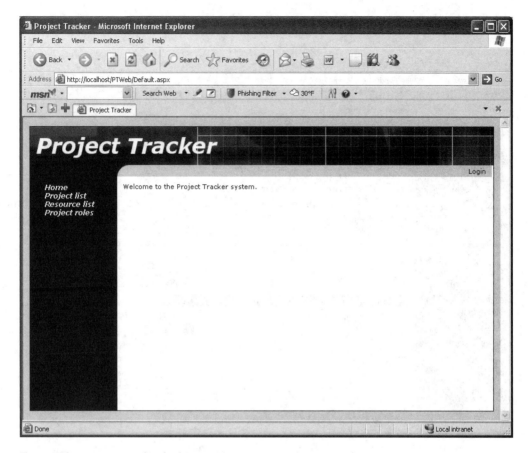

Figure 10-6. *Appearance of Default.aspx*

Notice that the navigation area on the left provides links dealing with projects, resources, and roles. An authentication link is provided near the top-right of the page. When the user clicks a link, the user is directed to an appropriate content page. Figure 10-7 shows the user editing a project.

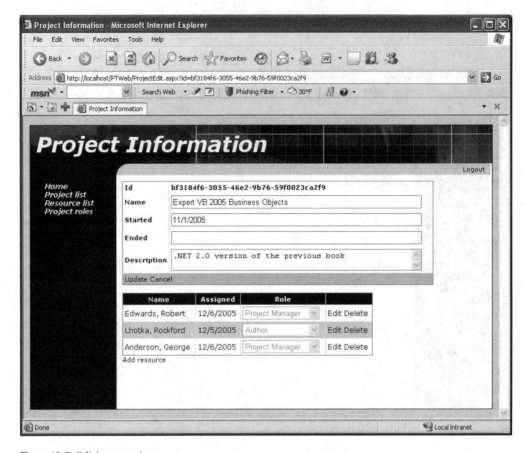

Figure 10-7. *Editing a project*

Table 10-3 lists the forms and controls that make up the interface.

Table 10-3. *Web Forms in PTWeb*

Form/Control	Description
Default	The main page for the application
Login	A login page to collect user credentials
RolesEdit	Allows the user to edit the list of roles
ProjectList	Allows the user to select and delete projects
ProjectEdit	Allows the user to view, add, or edit a project
ResourceList	Allows the user to select and delete resources
ResourceEdit	Allows the user to view, add, or edit a resource

All of the pages dealing with business data use the *exact same* objects as the Windows Forms UI in Chapter 9. The same ProjectTracker.Library assembly created in Chapter 8 is used for the Windows, web, and Web Services interfaces in this book. The web forms using those objects are built using data binding, relying on the CslaDataSource control discussed in Chapter 5.

Application Configuration

The site needs to provide some basic configuration information through the web.config file. This includes configuring the data portal or database connection strings. It also includes configuring the CslaDataSource control.

In the web.config file, you can either provide connection strings so that the site can interact with the database directly, or you can configure the data portal to communicate with a remote application server. The basic concept here was discussed in Chapter 4 when the channel adapter implementation was covered. Recall that the data portal supports three possible channels: remoting, Enterprise Services, and Web Services. You can create your own channels as well if none of these meet your needs.

In Chapter 1, I discussed the trade-offs between performance, scalability, fault tolerance, and security that come with various physical n-tier configurations. In most cases, the optimal solution for a web UI is to run the data portal locally in the client process. However, for security reasons, it may be desirable to run the data portal remotely on an application server. Chapter 12 will demonstrate how to create the three types of remote data portal hosts for use by the PTWeb application.

The web.config file is an XML file that contains settings to configure the website. You use different XML depending on how you want the site configured.

CslaDataSource Control

The data binding in this chapter will rely on the CslaDataSource control discussed in Chapter 5. In order to use this control in Web Forms, the site needs to define a control prefix for any controls in Csla.dll. I'll use the prefix csla.

This prefix is defined either in each web form, or in web.config. Since most pages will use the control, it is best to define the prefix in web.config so that it's available site-wide. You'll find this element within the <pages> element:

```
<controls>
  <add tagPrefix="csla" namespace="Csla.Web" assembly="Csla"/>
</controls>
```

This globally defines the csla prefix to refer to the Csla.Web namespace from Csla.dll. With this done, all pages in the website can use the prefix like this:

```
<csla:CslaDataSource id="MyDataSource" runat="server"/>
```

Authentication

The way authentication is handled by CSLA .NET is controlled through web.config:

```
<?xml version="1.0" encoding="utf-8" ?>
<configuration>
  <appSettings>
    <add key="CslaAuthentication" value="Csla" />
  </appSettings>
</configuration>
```

The CslaAuthentication key shown here specifies the use of custom authentication. Chapter 8 implemented the PTPrincipal and PTIdentity classes specifically to support custom authentication, and the UI code in this chapter will use custom authentication as well.

If you want to use Windows authentication, change the configuration to this:

```
<add key="CslaAuthentication" value="Windows" />
```

Of course, that change would require coding changes. To start, the `PTPrincipal` and `PTIdentity` classes should be removed from `ProjectTracker.Library`, as they would no longer be needed. Also, the login/logout functionality implemented in this chapter would become unnecessary. Specifically, the `Login` form and the code to display that form would be removed from the UI project.

Local Data Portal

The `web.config` file also controls how the application uses the data portal. To have the website interact directly with the database, use the following (with your `connection string` changed to the connection string for your database):

```
<?xml version="1.0" encoding="utf-8" ?>
<configuration>
  <appSettings>
    <add key="CslaAuthentication" value="Csla" />
  </appSettings>
  <connectionStrings>
    <add name="PTracker" connectionString="your connection string"
      providerName="System.Data.SqlClient" />
    <add name="Security" connectionString="your connection string"
      providerName="System.Data.SqlClient" />
  </connectionStrings>
```

Because `LocalProxy` is the default for the data portal, no actual data portal configuration is required, so the only settings in the configuration file are to control authentication and to provide the database connection strings.

■**Tip** In the code download for this book, the `PTracker` and `Security` database files are in the solution directory, not in the website's `App_Data` directory. This means that you can't use a local data portal from the website without first copying the database files into the `App_Data` directory and changing the connection strings accordingly.

Remote Data Portal (with Remoting)

To have the data portal use an application server and communicate using the remoting channel, the configuration would look like this:

```
<?xml version="1.0" encoding="utf-8" ?>
<configuration>
  <appSettings>
    <add key="CslaAuthentication" value="Csla" />
    <add key="CslaDataPortalProxy"
      value="Csla.DataPortalClient.RemotingProxy, Csla"/>
    <add key="CslaDataPortalUrl"
      value="http://localhost/RemotingHost/RemotingPortal.rem"/>
  </appSettings>
  <connectionStrings>
  </connectionStrings>
```

The key lines for remoting configuration are in bold. Of course, you need to change `localhost` to the name of the application server on which the data portal host is installed, and the `RemotingHost` text needs to be replaced with the name of your virtual root on that server.

Before using this configuration, the remoting host virtual root must be created and configured. I'll show how this is done in Chapter 12.

Remote Data Portal (with Enterprise Services)

Similarly, to use the Enterprise Services channel, the configuration would look like this:

```
<?xml version="1.0" encoding="utf-8" ?>
<configuration>
  <appSettings>
    <add key="CslaAuthentication" value="Csla" />
    <add key="CslaDataPortalProxy"
      value="EnterpriseServicesHost.EnterpriseServicesProxy,
                  EnterpriseServicesHostvb"/>
  </appSettings>
  <connectionStrings>
  </connectionStrings>
```

Before using this configuration, an Enterprise Services host must be created and registered with COM+. The resulting COM+ application must be registered with COM on each client workstation. The basic steps were discussed in Chapter 4, and I'll show how this is done in Chapter 12.

Remote Data Portal (with Web Services)

Finally, to use Web Services, the configuration would look like this:

```
<?xml version="1.0" encoding="utf-8" ?>
<configuration>
  <appSettings>
    <add key="CslaAuthentication" value="Csla" />
    <add key="CslaDataPortalProxy"
      value="Csla.DataPortalClient.WebServicesProxy, Csla"/>
    <add key="CslaDataPortalUrl"
      value="http://localhost/WebServicesHost/WebServicePortal.asmx"/>
  </appSettings>
  <connectionStrings>
  </connectionStrings>
```

As with remoting, you need to change localhost and WebServicesHost to the actual server name and virtual root name used by your application. Also, the virtual root and web service asmx file must be created and configured. I'll show how this is done in Chapter 12.

The most important thing to realize about the site configuration is that the data portal can be changed from local to remote (using any of the network channels) with no need to change any UI or business object code.

PTWeb Site Setup

The UI application can be found within the ProjectTracker solution. The project is named PTWeb.

The site references the ProjectTracker.Library project, as shown in Figure 10-8. This causes Visual Studio to automatically put the associated Csla.dll files into the Bin directory as well, because Csla.dll is referenced by ProjectTracker.Library.

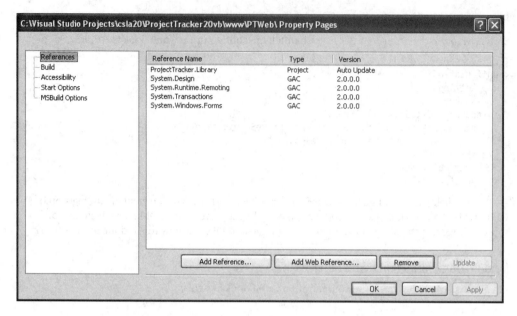

Figure 10-8. *Referencing ProjectTracker.Library*

Hosting in IIS

The PTWeb website will only run within IIS, not within the ASP.NET Development Server (commonly known as Cassini or VS Host). The reason for this is explained later in the chapter, in the "Forms-Based Authentication" section.

To host a website in IIS during development, you need to take the following steps:

1. Set up a virtual root in IIS that points to the directory containing the PTWeb project files.

2. Set the virtual root to use ASP .NET 2.0, using the ASP.NET tab of the virtual root properties dialog in the IIS management console.

3. Set the website's start options using the project properties dialog in Visual Studio 2005. Change the setting to use a custom server so it starts up using IIS with a URL such as http://localhost/PTWeb.

With the basic website setup complete, let's go through the creation of the Web Forms UI. First, I'll discuss the use of a master page, and then I'll cover the process of logging a user in and out using forms-based authentication.

With the common code out of the way, I'll discuss the process of maintaining the roles and project data in detail. At that point, you should have a good understanding of how to create both grid-based and detail pages.

Master Page

To ensure that all pages in the site have the same basic layout, navigation, and authentication options, a *master page* is used. The master page provides these consistent elements, and all the rest of the pages in the site are *content pages*. This means they fit within the context of the master page itself, adding content where appropriate.

Look back at Figures 10-6 and 10-7 to see the visual appearance of the pages. Both `Default.aspx` and `ProjectEdit.aspx` are content pages, adding their content to that already provided by `MasterPage.master`:

```
<%@ Master Language="VB" CodeFile="MasterPage.master.vb"
  Inherits="MasterPage" %>
<!DOCTYPE html PUBLIC "-//W3C//DTD XHTML 1.1//EN"
  "http://www.w3.org/TR/xhtml11/DTD/xhtml11.dtd">
<html xmlns="http://www.w3.org/1999/xhtml" xml:lang="en">
<head runat="server">
  <title>Untitled Page</title>
  <meta http-equiv="Content-Type" content="text/html;
    charset=iso-8859-1" />
</head>
<body>
  <form id="form1" runat="server">
  <div id="mainTable">
    <div id="header">
      <asp:Label ID="PageTitle" runat="server">
      </asp:Label>
    </div>
    <div id="navigation">
      <div id="navigationContent">
        <asp:TreeView ID="TreeView1" runat="server"
          DataSourceID="SiteMapDataSource1"
          ShowExpandCollapse="False" SkipLinkText="" >
          <NodeStyle CssClass="nav" />
        </asp:TreeView>
      </div>
    </div>
    <div id="subnavigation">
      <div id="logout">
        <asp:LoginStatus ID="LoginStatus1"
          runat="server"/>
      </div>
    </div>
    <div id="content">
      <asp:ContentPlaceHolder id="ContentPlaceHolder1"
        runat="server">
      </asp:ContentPlaceHolder>
    </div>
  </div>
  <asp:SiteMapDataSource ID="SiteMapDataSource1" runat="server"
    ShowStartingNode="False" />
  </form></body>
</html>
```

`MasterPage.master` defines the header/title bar at the top of the page. The area immediately beneath the header/title bar contains the `Login` button, and there is a navigation area down the left. Perhaps most importantly, it also defines a content area containing a `ContentPlaceHolder` control:

```
<asp:ContentPlaceHolder id="ContentPlaceHolder1"
    runat="server">
</asp:ContentPlaceHolder>
```

This is the area where content pages provide their content, and it is the main body of the page. You'll see how each content page provides content for this area later in the chapter.

Theme Support

ASP.NET 2.0 supports the concept of themes for a website, where the visual appearance of the site is defined by a *theme*: a group of files in a theme-specific subdirectory beneath the App_Themes directory in the virtual root. A theme is a group of style sheets, graphics, and control skins that describe the appearance of a site. A given site can have many themes, and you can even allow the user to choose between them if you so desire.

Notice how all of the regions in the master page are set up using div tags. No appearance characteristics are specified in the page itself. Instead, the actual appearance is defined by a CSS style sheet contained within the current theme for the site. The PTWeb site includes and uses a Basic theme. The use of the Basic theme is set up in web.config:

```
<pages theme="Basic" styleSheetTheme="Basic">
```

The theme property sets the default runtime theme, while styleSheetTheme sets the theme for use at design time in Visual Studio. The styleSheetTheme property should be removed when the website is deployed to a production server.

The files defining this theme are in the App_Themes/Basic folder beneath the virtual root. You should notice that the names of the css and skin files match the name of the theme folder itself. Having the names match allows ASP.NET to automatically realize that it needs to use these files when the theme is selected for the website. The files in this theme are listed in Table 10-4.

Table 10-4. *Files in the Basic Theme*

File	Description
Basic.css	The style sheet for the site
Basic.skin	The skins for GridView, DetailsView, and Login controls
Images\background.jpg	The background graphic for the header region
Images\corner.png	The graphic for the rounded corner in the upper-left

Combined, these files define the look and feel of the site. This includes defining the appearance of the regions in MasterPage.master. For instance, the header region is defined in the css file like this:

```
#header
{
  background-image: url('images/background.jpg');
  background-repeat: no-repeat;
  height: 64px;
  line-height: 60px;
  text-align: left;
  color: #FFFFFF;
  font-family:
  Verdana, Arial, Helvetica, sans-serif;
  font-size: 36px;
  font-weight: bold;
  font-style: italic;
  padding-left: 10px
}
```

A control skin defines the appearance of specific controls in the website, such as GridView, TextBox, and so forth. For instance, the appearance of the Login control is defined in the skin file like this:

```
<asp:Login runat="server" BackColor="#DEDEDE" BorderColor="Black"
    BorderStyle="Solid" BorderWidth="1px" Font-Names="Verdana"
    Font-Size="10pt">
    <TitleTextStyle BackColor="Black" Font-Bold="True"
        Font-Names="Verdana" Font-Size="10pt"
        ForeColor="White" />
</asp:Login>
```

Each type of control in Web Forms has different options you can set in a skin file, allowing you to set the appearance of each control in many ways.

By making the site theme-enabled, you can easily change the appearance of the site later by creating a new theme directory and similar theme files, and setting the theme property in web.config to use the new theme.

Header Region

The header region of the page is the title area across the top. It contains a single Label control named PageTitle. This control displays the title of the current content page, based on the Title property set for that page. The following code is included in MasterPage.master to load this value:

```
Protected Sub Page_Load( _
    ByVal sender As Object, ByVal e As System.EventArgs) Handles Me.Load

    PageTitle.Text = Page.Title
End Sub
```

As each content page loads, not only does the Load event for the content page run, but so does the Load event for the master page. This means that code can be placed in the master page to run when *any* content page is loaded—in this case, to set the title at the top of the page.

Navigation Region

The navigation region displays the navigation links down the left side of each page. To do this, a web.sitemap file and associated SiteMapDataSource control are used to load the overall structure of the site into memory. This data is then data bound to a TreeView control for display to the user.

The web.sitemap file is an XML file that contains a node for each page to be displayed in the navigation region:

```
<?xml version="1.0" encoding="utf-8" ?>
<siteMap
    xmlns="http://schemas.microsoft.com/AspNet/SiteMap-File-1.0" >
    <siteMapNode url="" title=""  description="">
        <siteMapNode url="~/Default.aspx" title="Home"
                    description="Main page" />
        <siteMapNode url="~/ProjectList.aspx" title="Project list"
                    description="Project list" />
        <siteMapNode url="~/ResourceList.aspx" title="Resource list"
                    description="Resource list" />
        <siteMapNode url="~/RolesEdit.aspx" title="Project roles"
                    description="Project roles" />
    </siteMapNode>
</siteMap>
```

The site map concept can be used to define hierarchical website structures, but in this case, I'm using it to define a flat structure. Notice how each <siteMapNode> element defines a page—except the first one. That root node is required in the file, but since I'm defining a flat structure, it really doesn't represent a page and is just a placeholder. If you were to define a hierarchical page structure, that node would typically point to Default.aspx.

Notice that MasterPage.master includes a SiteMapDataSource control:

```
<asp:SiteMapDataSource ID="SiteMapDataSource1" runat="server"
ShowStartingNode="False" />
```

This special data control automatically reads the data from the web.sitemap file and makes it available to controls on the page. The ShowStartingNode property is set to False, indicating that the root node in web.sitemap is to be ignored. That's perfect, because that node is empty and shouldn't be displayed.

In this case, a TreeView control in the navigation region is bound to the SiteMapDataSource, so it displays the items listed in web.sitemap to the user.

LoginStatus Control

In the subnavigation region of MasterPage.master, you'll see a LoginStatus control:

```
<asp:LoginStatus ID="LoginStatus1"
    runat="server"/>
```

This is one of the login controls provided with ASP.NET 2.0, and its purpose is to allow the user to log into and out of the site. The control automatically displays the word Login if the user is logged out, and Logout if the user is logged in. When clicked, it also automatically redirects the user to a login web page defined in web.config. I'll cover the web.config options later.

Because the control automatically directs the user to the appropriate login page to be logged in, no code is required for that process. However, code is required to handle the case in which the user clicks the control to be logged out. This code goes in the master page:

```
Protected Sub LoginStatus1_LoggingOut( _
  ByVal sender As Object, _
  ByVal e As System.Web.UI.WebControls.LoginCancelEventArgs) _
  Handles LoginStatus1.LoggingOut

  ProjectTracker.Library.Security.PTPrincipal.Logout()
  Session("CslaPrincipal") = Csla.ApplicationContext.User
  System.Web.Security.FormsAuthentication.SignOut()
End Sub
```

This code covers a lot of ground. First, the Logout() method of PTPrincipal is called, which sets the current principal on the current Thread object to an unauthenticated PTPrincipal object. This was discussed in Chapter 8 and used in PTWin in Chapter 9.

However, when the user is logged in, their principal object is stored in a Session field so it can be easily reloaded on every page request. The details on how this works are discussed later in the chapter. When the user logs out, that Session field is updated to reference the new principal object.

■**Note** If you want to avoid Session, you can choose to reload the user's identity and roles from the security database on every page request. While that avoids the use of Session, it can put a substantial workload on your security database server. In PTWeb, I have opted to use Session to minimize the load on the database.

The final step is to tell ASP.NET itself that the user is no longer authenticated. This is done by calling FormsAuthentication.SignOut(). This method invalidates the security cookie used by ASP.NET to indicate that the user has been authenticated. The result is that ASP.NET sees the user as unauthenticated on all subsequent page requests.

This covers the logout process, but the login process requires some more work. While the LoginStatus control handles the details of directing the user to a login page, that page must be created.

Login Page

Like the PTWin smart client, the PTWeb site is designed to use custom authentication, so I can illustrate the custom authentication support provided by CSLA .NET. I'll also briefly discuss the use of Windows integrated security and the ASP.NET membership service.

In Web Forms, when using custom authentication, you need to configure the site appropriately using web.config, and implement a login web page to collect and validate the user's credentials. That's the purpose behind Login.aspx.

Forms-Based Authentication

When using forms-based authentication, users are often automatically redirected to a login form before being allowed to access any other pages. Alternatively, anonymous users can be allowed to use the site, and they can choose to log into the site to gain access to extra features or functionality. The specific behaviors are defined by web.config.

Before moving on, remember that the following implementation only works within IIS. The ASP.NET Development Server provided with Visual Studio has various limitations; among them is the inability to load custom security objects from assemblies in the Bin directory. This means you can't use the ASP.NET Development Server to test or debug custom principal objects, custom membership providers, or other custom security objects if they're in an assembly referenced from the project.

Though this is an unfortunate limitation, it can be argued that the ASP.NET Development Server is not intended for anything beyond hobbyist or casual usage, and that IIS should be used for any serious business development.

Note An alternative solution is to install the assembly containing your custom principal and identity classes into the .NET Global Assembly Cache (GAC). For PTWeb, this would mean giving ProjectTracker.Library a strong name and using the gacutil.exe command line utility to install the assembly into the GAC. ProjectTracker. Library would need to be updated in the GAC after each time you build the assembly. I find that using IIS is a far simpler solution than using the GAC.

Configuring the Site

Using forms-based security in ASP.NET means that web.config includes elements like this:

```
<authentication mode="Forms">
  <forms loginUrl="Login.aspx" name="ptracker"/>
</authentication>
<authorization>
  <allow users="*"/>
</authorization>
```

This tells ASP.NET to use forms-based authentication (mode="Forms"), yet to allow unauthenticated users (<allow users="*"/>).

> **Note** To require users to log in before seeing *any* pages, replace `<allow users="*"/>` with `<deny users="?"/>`.

It is important that you also ensure that the security on the virtual root itself (within IIS) is configured to allow anonymous users. If IIS blocks anonymous users, then it doesn't really matter what kind of security you use within ASP.NET.

> **Note** Remember that IIS security runs *first*, and then any ASP.NET security is applied.

With the `web.config` options shown previously, users can use the site without logging in, but the concept of logging in is supported. The goal is the same as with `PTWin` in Chapter 9: allow all users to perform certain actions, and allow authenticated users to perform other actions based on their roles.

When a user chooses to log in, the `<forms>` tag specifies that he will be directed to `Login.aspx`, which will collect and validate their credentials. Figure 10-9 shows the appearance of `Login.aspx`.

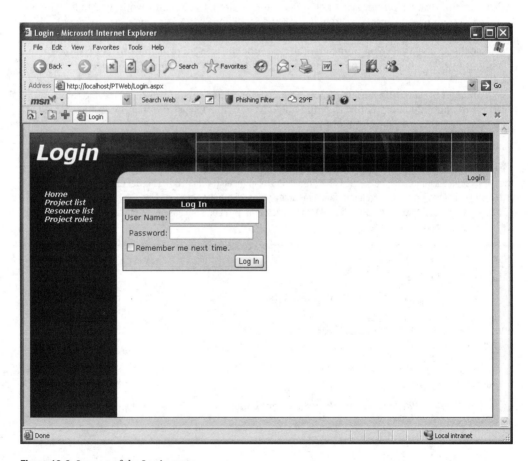

Figure 10-9. *Layout of the Login page*

Now this is where things get kind of cool. There is *no code* behind `Login.aspx`. This page uses the ASP.NET `Login` control:

```
<asp:Login ID="Login1" runat="server">
</asp:Login>
```

This control is designed to automatically use the default ASP.NET membership provider for the site.

■**Caution** The user's credentials flow from the browser to the web server in clear text—they are not automatically encrypted. Due to this, it is recommended that `Login.aspx` be accessed over an SSL (Secure Sockets Layer) connection so that data traveling to and from the browser is encrypted during the login process.

You *can* write code to handle the events of the `Login` control if you desire, but a membership provider offers a cleaner solution overall. Of course, the membership provider that comes with ASP.NET doesn't understand `PTPrincipal` and `PTIdentity` objects, so `PTWeb` includes its own custom membership provider.

Custom Membership Provider

A membership provider is an object that inherits from `System.Web.Security.MembershipProvider` to handle all aspects of membership. These aspects include:

- Validating user credentials
- Adding a new user
- Deleting a user
- Changing a user's password
- And more . . .

Of course, `PTPrincipal` doesn't understand all these things, and `ProjectTracker.Library` doesn't implement a full set of membership objects either. If you want to support all these capabilities, you should create your own security library with appropriate objects.

But `PTPrincipal` *does* understand how to validate a user's credentials. Fortunately, it is possible to implement a subset of the complete membership provider functionality, and that's what I do in `PTWeb`.

The `PTMembershipProvider` class is in the `App_Code` directory, so ASP.NET automatically compiles it and makes it available to the website. This class inherits from `MembershipProvider` and overrides the `ValidateUser()` method:

```
Public Class PTMembershipProvider
  Inherits MembershipProvider

  Public Overrides Function ValidateUser( _
    ByVal username As String, ByVal password As String) As Boolean

    If PTPrincipal.Login(username, password) Then
      System.Web.HttpContext.Current.Session("CslaPrincipal") = _
        Csla.ApplicationContext.User
      Return True
```

```
      Else
        Return False
      End If
    End Function

    ' other methods …
  End Class
```

All other methods are overridden to throw an exception indicating that they aren't implemented by this provider.

Notice how the ValidateUser() method already accepts username and password parameters. This is convenient because the Login() method of PTPrincipal accepts those parameters as well. The code simply calls the Login() method and records the result; True if the user was logged in, False otherwise.

Remember from Chapter 8 that the Login() method sets the User property of Csla. ApplicationContext, thus automatically setting either the Thread object's CurrentPrincipal property or the HttpContext.Current.User property to an authenticated PTPrincipal if the user's credentials were valid; otherwise, it is set to an unauthenticated PTPrincipal. Since this code will be running within ASP.NET, it is the HttpContext value that is set to the user's principal.

The code then sets a Session field, CslaPrincipal, to contain this principal value so that it will be available to subsequent pages.

Then the result value is returned. The ASP.NET membership infrastructure relies on this return value to know whether the user's credentials were valid or not.

Before this custom membership provider can be used, it must be defined in web.config as follows:

```
<membership defaultProvider="PTMembershipProvider">
  <providers>
    <add name="PTMembershipProvider"
      type="PTMembershipProvider"
      enablePasswordRetrieval="false"
      enablePasswordReset="false"
      requiresQuestionAndAnswer="false"
      applicationName="/"
      requiresUniqueEmail="false"
      passwordFormat="Clear"
      description="Stores and retrieves membership
        data using CSLA .NET business objects."
    />
  </providers>
</membership>
```

By making PTMembershipProvider the default provider, this definition tells ASP.NET to automatically use it for any membership activities, including validating a user's credentials.

Reloading the Principal

At this point, you've seen how the user can log in or out using the LoginStatus control on the master page. And you've seen how Login.aspx and the custom membership provider are used to gather and validate the user's credentials.

But how does the principal object carry forward from page to page? Remember that the web technologies are stateless by default, and it is up to the web developer to manually implement state management as she chooses. Unfortunately, this extends to the user's identity as well.

The forms-based security infrastructure provided by ASP.NET writes an encrypted cookie to the user's browser. That cookie contains a security ticket with a unique identifier for the user, the user's name, and an expiration time. This cookie flows from the browser to the web server on each page request, so that basic information is available.

Notice, however, that the cookie doesn't include the principal and identity objects. That is because those objects could be quite large, and in some cases, might not even be serializable. Though PTPrincipal and PTIdentity are serializable, they could still be large enough to pose a problem if you tried to write them to the cookie. Cookies have a size limit, and remember that PTIdentity contains an array with all the role names for the user. Given a large number of roles or lengthy role names, this could easily add up to a lot of bytes of data.

Note It is possible to serialize the principal and identity objects into the cookie (if the objects are serializable). Doing so isn't recommended, however, due to the size limitations on cookies.

It is quite possible to reload PTPrincipal and PTIdentity from the security database on every page request. Remember that the ASP.NET security cookie contains the username value, and you already know that the user was authenticated. All you would need is another stored procedure in the database that returns the user information based on username alone; no password would be provided or checked. Similarly, another Shared method like Login() would be implemented in PTPrincipal to load the objects based only on the username value.

There are two drawbacks to this. First, reloading this data from the security database on every page request could cause a serious performance issue. The security database could get overloaded with all the requests. Second, there's an obvious security risk in implementing methods that allow loading user identities without having to supply the password. While that functionality wouldn't be exposed to the end user, it makes it easier for accidental bugs or malicious back-door code to creep into your website.

This is why I use Session to store the principal object in PTWeb. The user's credentials are validated, and the resulting principal object is placed in a Session field named CslaPrincipal. On all subsequent page requests, this value is retrieved from Session and is used to set both the current Thread and HttpContext object's principals.

The work occurs in Global.asax, as this file contains the event handlers for all events leading up to a page being processed. In this case, it is the AcquireRequestState event that is used:

```
Protected Sub Application_AcquireRequestState( _
    ByVal sender As Object, ByVal e As System.EventArgs)

  Dim principal As System.Security.Principal.IPrincipal
  Try
    principal = _
      CType(Session("CslaPrincipal"), System.Security.Principal.IPrincipal)

  Catch
    principal = Nothing
  End Try

  If principal Is Nothing Then
    ' didn't get a principal from Session, so
    ' set it to an unauthenticted PTPrincipal
    ProjectTracker.Library.Security.PTPrincipal.Logout()

  Else
    ' use the principal from Session
    Csla.ApplicationContext.User = principal
  End If
End Sub
```

The reason for using the `AcquireRequestState` event, rather than the more obvious `AuthenticateRequest` event, is that `Session` isn't initialized when `AuthenticateRequest` is raised, but it usually is initialized when `AcquireRequestState` is raised.

The code first attempts to retrieve the principal object from `Session`. This can result in an exception if `Session` doesn't exist, and so the value would end up being `Nothing`. Also, if this is the first page request by the user, the `Session` field will return `Nothing`. So the outcome is either a valid `PTPrincipal` object or `Nothing`.

If the resulting `principal` value is `Nothing`, `PTPrincipal.Logout()` is called to set the current principal as an unauthenticated `PTPrincipal`, and the `HttpContext` is set to use that same principal object. This supports the idea of an unauthenticated anonymous guest user. Both the web and business library code have access to valid, if unauthenticated, principal objects, and can apply authorization code as needed. Additionally, by having the current principal be a valid `PTPrincipal` object, a remote data portal can be invoked and the application server will impersonate the unauthenticated user identity so *that* code can apply authorization rules as well.

On the other hand, if a principal object is retrieved from `Session`, then that value is set as the current principal.

Using Windows Integrated Security

If you wanted to use Windows integrated security, you wouldn't need `Login.aspx`, the custom membership provider, or the code in `Global.asax`, because the user's identity is already known. The user provided his Windows credentials to the browser, which in turn provided them to the web server.

This means that the virtual root in IIS must be configured to disallow anonymous users, thus forcing the user to provide credentials to access the site. It is IIS that authenticates the user and allows authenticated users into the site.

To have ASP.NET use the Windows identity from IIS, `web.config` must be configured correctly:

```
<authentication mode="Windows"/>
<identity impersonate="true"/>
```

The authentication mode is set to `Windows`, indicating that ASP.NET should defer all authentication to the IIS host. Setting the `impersonate` property to `true` tells ASP.NET to impersonate the user authenticated by IIS.

■**Note** If you use Windows integrated security, and you are using a remote data portal, you *must* make sure to change the application server configuration file to also use Windows security. If the data portal is hosted in IIS, the virtual root must be set to disallow anonymous access, thereby forcing the client to provide IIS with the Windows identity from the web server via integrated security.

Using the ASP.NET Membership Service

ASP.NET 2.0 not only supports the broad concept of membership as used previously, but it provides a complete membership service, including all the code to make it work.

The membership service is most often used with the SQL membership provider that comes with ASP.NET. This provider requires that you use a predefined database schema, along with the membership objects provided by Microsoft to manage and interact with the database. By default, ASP.NET will use a Microsoft SQL Server 2005 Express database in the virtual root's `App_Data` directory, but you can override that behavior to have it use another Microsoft SQL Server database if needed.

The other membership provider shipped with ASP.NET is a connector to Active Directory (AD). It does the same thing, but stores the user information in AD instead of a SQL database.

Using the Membership Service with a Local Data Portal

If you are running the data portal in the client process, you can use the SQL membership provider without any special effort. In that case, the web server will interact directly with the database.

Of course, you don't need PTPrincipal or PTIdentity, because ASP.NET provides its own principal and identity types. Similarly, you don't need to manually handle the logout event of the LoginStatus control or put any code in Global.asax.

In short, it just works. All the authorization code in CSLA .NET will use the ASP.NET principal object to call IsInRole(), so all the prebuilt authorization functionality just works.

Using the Membership Service with a Remote Data Portal

Things are a bit more complex if you are using a remote data portal on an application server. There are two things to consider here. First, the SQL membership provider talks directly to the security database, knowing nothing about application servers. If you want to use the application server, the approach taken in PTWeb is better. Second, the data portal will only accept principal objects that inherit from Csla.Security.BusinessPrincipalBase, and of course the ASP.NET membership principal types don't do that.

The first problem is one of application architecture, and you need to decide if it makes sense for you to have the security mechanism talk directly to a database while your business code uses an application server to talk to the business database.

The second problem can be overcome with just a bit of code. You need to wrap the ASP.NET membership principal in a CSLA .NET–style principal. There are two parts to this. First, you need a custom principal class; second, you need to add some code to Global.asax.

A custom principal class to wrap the ASP.NET principal object would look like this:

```
<Serializable()> _
Public Class MembershipPrincipal
  Inherits Csla.Security.BusinessPrincipalBase

  Private mPrincipal As System.Security.Principal.IPrincipal

  Public Sub New(ByVal principal As System.Security.Principal.IPrincipal)
    MyBase.New(principal.Identity)
    mPrincipal = principal
  End Sub

  Public Overrides Function IsInRole(ByVal role As String) As Boolean
    Return mPrincipal.IsInRole(role)
  End Function
End Class
```

The code in Global.asax takes the ASP.NET principal and wraps it in a MembershipPrincipal:

```
Protected Sub Application_AcquireRequestState( _
  ByVal sender As Object, ByVal e As System.EventArgs)

  Csla.ApplicationContext.User =
    New MembershipPrincipal(HttpContext.Current.User)
End Sub
```

This code sets the ApplicationContext object's User property to use the new MembershipPrincipal. This way, the original user information and list of roles are preserved, but the actual principal object used by the application inherits from BusinessPrincipalBase. The result is that the data portal can impersonate the web user on the application server.

At this point, you should have an understanding of how the website is organized. It references `ProjectTracker.Library` and uses a master page and theme to provide a consistent, manageable appearance for the site. It also uses a mix of ASP.NET login controls and the prebuilt `ProjectTracker` security objects to implement custom authentication.

Now let's move on and discuss the pages that provide actual business behaviors.

Business Functionality

With the common functionality in the master page, `Login.aspx`, and `Global.asax` covered, it is possible to move on to the business functionality itself. As I mentioned earlier, I'll walk through the `RolesEdit`, `ProjectList`, and `ProjectEdit` web forms in some detail. `ResourceList` and `ResourceEdit` are available in the download and follow the same implementation approach.

All of these web forms will be created using the new data binding capabilities built into ASP.NET 2.0 and the `CslaDataSource` control discussed in Chapter 5. These capabilities allow the web developer to easily link controls on the form to business objects and their properties. The developer productivity gained through this approach is simply amazing.

Other key technologies I'll be using are the `MultiView` control and the associated `View` control. These controls make it easy for a single page to present multiple views to the user, and are often very valuable when building pages for editing data.

Finally, remember that all these pages are content pages. This means that they fit within the context of a master page—in this case, `MasterPage.master`. As you'll see, the tags in a content page are a bit different from those in a simple web form.

RolesEdit Form

The `RolesEdit.aspx` page is a content page, so its `Page` directive looks like this:

```
<%@ Page Language="VB" MasterPageFile="~/MasterPage.master"
  AutoEventWireup="false" CodeFile="RolesEdit.aspx.vb"
  Inherits="RolesEdit" title="Project Roles" %>
```

Notice the `MasterPageFile` property, which points to `MasterPage.master`. Also notice the `Title` property, which sets the page's title. It is this value that is used in the master page's `Load` event handler to set the title text in the `header` region of the page.

Figure 10-10 shows what the page looks like in Visual Studio.

The grey Content title bar across the top of the main page body won't be visible at runtime. It is visible at design time to remind you that you are editing a content area in the page. If you look at the page's source, you'll see that all the page content is contained within a `Content` control:

```
<asp:Content ID="Content1"
  ContentPlaceHolderID="ContentPlaceHolder1" Runat="Server">
  <%-- page content goes here --%>
</asp:Content>
```

The `ContentPlaceHolderID` property links this content to the `ContentPlaceHolder1` control in the master page. This scheme means that a master page can define multiple content placeholders, and a content page can have multiple `Content` controls—one for each placeholder.

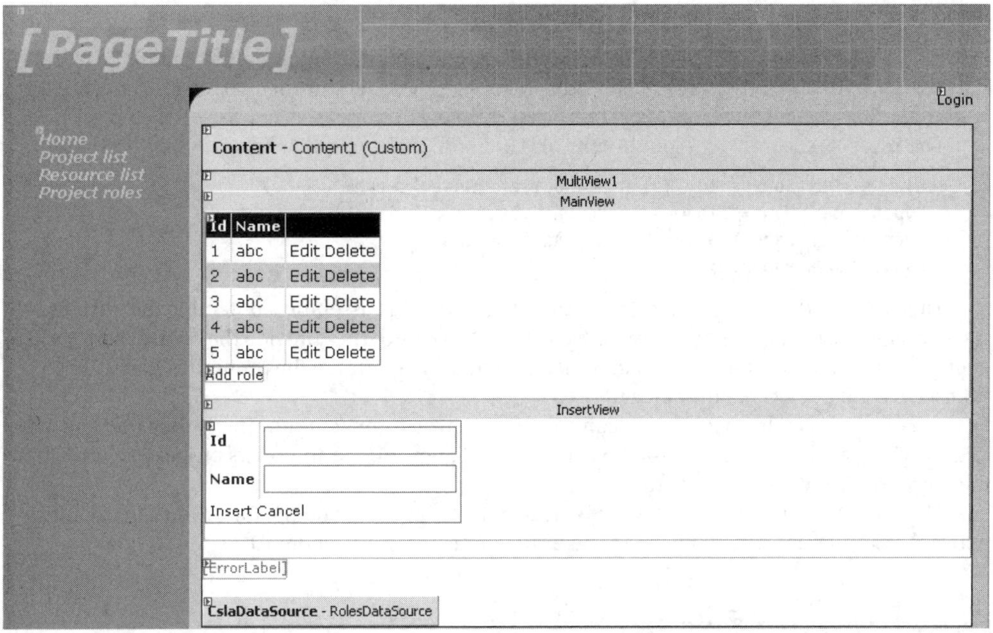

Figure 10-10. *Layout of the RolesEdit page*

MultiView Control

The MultiView control contains two View controls, named MainView and InsertView. Only one of these views will be active (visible) at any time, so this form really defines two different views for the user.

Within your code, you select the view by setting the ActiveViewIndex property of the MultiView control to the numeric index of the appropriate View control. Of course, using a numeric value like this doesn't lead to maintainable code, so within the page, I define an enumerated type with text values corresponding to each View control:

```
Private Enum Views
  MainView = 0
  InsertView = 1
End Enum
```

The Views type will be used to change the page view as needed.

Error Label

Beneath the MultiView control in Figure 10-10 is a Label control with its ForeColor set to Red. The purpose behind this control is to allow the page to display error text to the user in the case of an exception.

As you'll see, the data access code uses Try...Catch blocks to catch exceptions that occur during any data updates (insert, update, or delete). The text of the exception is displayed in ErrorLabel so it is visible to the user.

Using a Business Object As a Data Source

In Chapter 5, I discussed the CslaDataSource control, and how it overcomes the limitations of the standard ObjectDataSource control. The RolesEdit page uses this control, making it relatively easy to bind the Roles collection from ProjectTracker.Library to a GridView control on the page.

The RolesDataSource data source control is defined on the page like this:

```
<csla:CslaDataSource ID="RolesDataSource" runat="server"
  TypeAssemblyName="ProjectTracker.Library"
  TypeName="ProjectTracker.Library.Admin.Roles">
</csla:CslaDataSource>
```

The TypeAssemblyName and TypeName properties define the assembly containing the business class and the business class type, respectively. These two properties provide the control with enough information so that it can load the Roles type and determine the properties that will be exposed by child objects in the collection.

Of course, to get this data source control onto the web form, you can simply drag the CslaDataSource control from the toolbox onto the designer surface and set its properties through the Properties window in Visual Studio.

Then, when the GridView and DetailsView controls are placed on the form, you can use their pop-up Tasks menu to select the data source control, as shown in Figure 10-11.

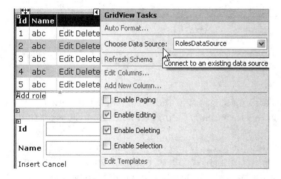

Figure 10-11. *Choosing a data source for a GridView or DetailsView*

You can either write the tags yourself or use the designer support built into Visual Studio.

Caching the Object in Session

To optimize the performance of the website, business objects are stored in Session. While they could be retrieved directly from the database when needed, storing them in Session reduces the load on the database server.

To minimize the number of objects maintained in Session, all pages use the same Session field to store their business objects: currentObject. This way, only one business object is stored in Session at any time, and that is the object being actively used by the current page.

Of course, browsers have a Back button, which means that the user could navigate back to some previous page that expects to be using a different type of object than the current page. For instance, the user could be editing a Project object, and then start editing a Resource object. Session would have originally contained the Project, but then would contain the Resource.

If the user then used the Back button to return to the ProjectEdit page, Session could still have the Resource object in the currentObject field. This possibility is very real, and must be dealt with by checking the type of the object retrieved from Session to see if it is the type the page actually needs. If not, then the correct object must be retrieved from the database.

In RolesEdit, the GetRoles() method performs this task:

```
Private Function GetRoles() As ProjectTracker.Library.Admin.Roles
  Dim businessObject As Object = Session("currentObject")
  If businessObject Is Nothing OrElse _
    Not TypeOf businessObject Is ProjectTracker.Library.Admin.Roles Then
    businessObject = _
      ProjectTracker.Library.Admin.Roles.GetRoles
    Session("currentObject") = businessObject
  End If
  Return CType(businessObject, ProjectTracker.Library.Admin.Roles)
End Function
```

The code retrieves the currentObject item from Session. If the result is Nothing, or if the resulting object isn't a Roles object, then a new Roles object is retrieved by calling the Roles.GetRoles() factory method. That newly retrieved object is placed in Session, making it the current object.

In any case, a valid Roles object is returned as a result.

Selecting an Object

The SelectObject event is raised when the web page needs data from the data source—the Roles object, in this case. The page must handle the event and return the requested data object:

```
Protected Sub RolesDataSource_SelectObject( _
  ByVal sender As Object, ByVal e As Csla.Web.SelectObjectArgs) _
  Handles RolesDataSource.SelectObject

  Dim obj As ProjectTracker.Library.Admin.Roles = GetRoles()
  e.BusinessObject = obj
End Sub
```

The GetRoles() helper method is called to retrieve the Roles collection object. Then the Roles object is returned to the RolesDataSource control by setting the e.BusinessObject property. The data source control then provides this object to the ASP.NET data binding infrastructure so it can be used to populate any UI controls bound to the data control. In this case, that's the GridView control in MainView. That control is declared like this:

```
<asp:GridView ID="GridView1" runat="server"
  AutoGenerateColumns="False"
  DataSourceID="RolesDataSource"
  DataKeyNames="Id">
  <Columns>
    <asp:BoundField DataField="Id" HeaderText="Id"
      ReadOnly="True" SortExpression="Id" />
    <asp:BoundField DataField="Name" HeaderText="Name"
      SortExpression="Name" />
    <asp:CommandField ShowDeleteButton="True"
      ShowEditButton="True" />
  </Columns>
</asp:GridView>
```

The DataSourceID property establishes data binding to the RolesDataSource control.

The DataKeyNames property specifies the name of the property on the business object that acts as a primary key for the object. For a Role object, this is Id. Remember the use of the DataObjectField attribute on the Id property in Chapter 8, which provides a hint to Visual Studio that this property is the object's unique key value.

The first two columns in the GridView control are bound to properties from the data source: Id and Name, respectively. The third column is a CommandField, which automatically adds Delete and Edit links next to each element in the list. The Delete link automatically triggers DeleteObject to delete the specified object. The Edit link puts the row into in-place edit mode, allowing the user to edit the data in the selected row. If the user accepts his updates, the UpdateObject event is automatically raised. No code beyond that handling those events is required to support either of these links.

Of course, you don't have to deal with all these tags if you don't want to. Most of the code in the CslaDataSource control exists to support the graphical designer support in Visual Studio. Look back at Figure 10-10 and notice how the GridView control displays the Id, Name, and command columns. I configured the control entirely using the Visual Studio designer and setting properties on the controls.

Figure 10-12 shows the Fields dialog for the GridView control.

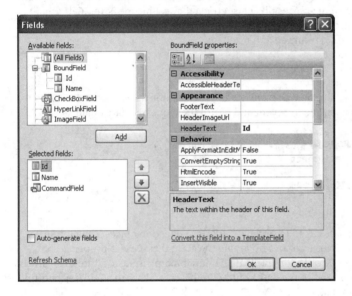

Figure 10-12. *Fields dialog for a GridView control*

Notice that the Available fields box contains a list of the potentially bound fields from the data source: Id and Name. The CslaDataSource control's designer support returns this list by using reflection against the data source object as discussed in Chapter 5. You can use this dialog to choose which columns are displayed, to control the way they are displayed, to rearrange their order, and more.

Inserting an Object

The MainView contains not only a GridView control, but also a LinkButton control named AddRoleButton. This button allows the user to add a new Role object to the Roles collection. To do this, the current View is changed to InsertView:

```
Protected Sub AddRoleButton_Click( _
  ByVal sender As Object, ByVal e As System.EventArgs) _
  Handles AddRoleButton.Click
```

```
  Me.DetailsView1.DefaultMode = DetailsViewMode.Insert
  MultiView1.ActiveViewIndex = Views.InsertView
End Sub
```

This changes the page to appear as shown in Figure 10-13.

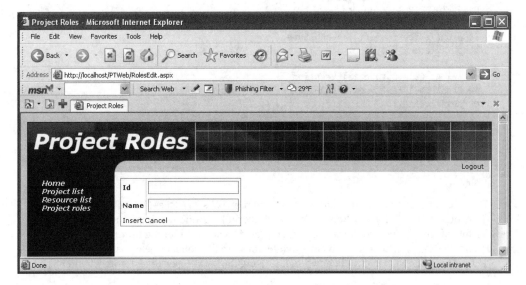

Figure 10-13. *The RolesEdit.aspx page when a new role is being added*

Look at the address bar in the browser; see how it is still RolesEdit.aspx even though the display is entirely different from Figure 10-10. This illustrates the power of the MultiView control, which allows a user to remain on a single page to view, edit, and insert data.

The control shown here is a DetailsView control, which is data bound to the same RolesDataSource control as the GridView earlier. This control is declared in a manner very similar to the GridView:

```
<asp:DetailsView ID="DetailsView1" runat="server"
  AutoGenerateRows="False" DataSourceID="RolesDataSource"
  DefaultMode="Insert" Height="50px" Width="125px"
  DataKeyNames="Id">
  <Fields>
    <asp:BoundField DataField="Id" HeaderText="Id"
      SortExpression="Id" />
    <asp:BoundField DataField="Name" HeaderText="Name"
      SortExpression="Name" />
    <asp:CommandField ShowInsertButton="True" />
  </Fields>
</asp:DetailsView>
```

It is bound to RolesDataSource, and its DataKeyNames property specifies that the Id property is the unique identifier for the object. The <Fields> elements define the rows in the control much as columns are defined in a GridView.

If the user enters values for a new role and clicks the Insert link in the DetailsView control, the InsertObject event is raised by RolesDataSource. This event is handled in the page to add the new role to the Roles collection:

```
Protected Sub RolesDataSource_InsertObject( _
  ByVal sender As Object, ByVal e As Csla.Web.InsertObjectArgs) _
  Handles RolesDataSource.InsertObject

  Try
    Dim obj As Roles = GetRoles()
    Dim role As Role = obj.AddNew
    Csla.Data.DataMapper.Map(e.Values, role)
    Session("currentObject") = obj.Save
    e.RowsAffected = 1

  Catch ex As Csla.DataPortalException
    Me.ErrorLabel.Text = ex.BusinessException.Message
    e.RowsAffected = 0

  Catch ex As Exception
    Me.ErrorLabel.Text = ex.Message
    e.RowsAffected = 0
  End Try
End Sub
```

This code retrieves the current `Roles` object and then calls its `AddNew()` method to add a new child `Role` object. Recall that in Chapter 8 the `AddNewCore()` method was implemented to enable easy adding of child objects to the collection. The `Public AddNew()` method ultimately results in a call to `AddNewCore()`, which adds an empty child object to the collection.

This new child object is populated with data using the `DataMapper` object from Chapter 5:

```
Csla.Data.DataMapper.Map(e.Values, role)
```

All new values entered by the user are provided to the event handler through `e.Values`. The `Map()` method uses reflection to copy those values to the corresponding properties on the object. If you want to avoid this use of reflection, you can replace this line with code like this:

```
role.Id = CInt(e.Values("Id"))
role.Name = CStr(e.Values("Name"))
```

For this simple object, this code isn't too onerous, but for larger objects you could end up writing a lot of code to copy each value into the object's properties.

Either way, once the data from `e.Values` has been put into the object's properties, the object's `Save()` method is called to update the database.

Note This follows the typical web model of updating the database any time the user performs any action, and results in a lot more database access than the equivalent Windows Forms implementation from Chapter 9. You could defer the call to `Save()` by putting a Save button on the form and having the user click that button to commit all changes.

Once the `Save()` method is complete, the resulting (updated) `Roles` object is put into `Session`. This is very important because the result of `Save()` is a *new* `Roles` object, and that new object must be used in place of the previous one on subsequent pages. For instance, the newly added role data generated a new `timestamp` value in the database, which can only be found in this new `Roles` object.

This completes the insert operation, but the `MultiView` control is still set to display the `InsertView`. It needs to be reset to display `MainView`. That is done by handling the `ItemInserted` event from the `DetailsView` control:

```
Protected Sub DetailsView1_ItemInserted( _
  ByVal sender As Object, _
  ByVal e As System.Web.UI.WebControls.DetailsViewInsertedEventArgs) _
  Handles DetailsView1.ItemInserted

  MultiView1.ActiveViewIndex = Views.MainView
  Me.GridView1.DataBind()
End Sub
```

The `ActiveViewIndex` is changed so that the `MainView` is displayed when the page refreshes. Also, the `GridView` control in `MainView` is told to refresh its data by calling its `DataBind()` method.

Calling `DataBind()` causes the `GridView` to refresh its display so that it shows the newly added `Role` object. Behind the scenes, this triggers a call to `RolesDataSource`, causing it to raise its `SelectObject` event.

Figure 10-13 also shows a Cancel link. If the user clicks that link, she likewise needs to be returned to `MainView`. When the user clicks Cancel, it triggers a `ModeChanged` event on the `DetailsView` control:

```
Protected Sub DetailsView1_ModeChanged( _
  ByVal sender As Object, ByVal e As System.EventArgs) _
  Handles DetailsView1.ModeChanged

  MultiView1.ActiveViewIndex = Views.MainView
End Sub
```

So, whether the user clicks Insert or Cancel, she ends up back at the main display of the list of roles.

Updating an Object

As shown in Figure 10-10, the `CommandField` column in the `GridView` control includes both Delete and Edit links for each row. I'll get to the Delete link shortly, but for now let's focus on the Edit link. When the user clicks the Edit link on a row, the `GridView` allows the user to edit that row's data, as shown in Figure 10-14.

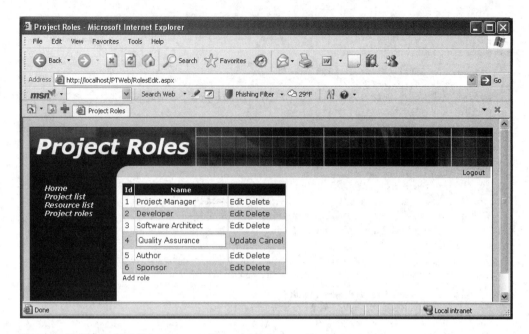

Figure 10-14. *The RolesEdit.aspx page when a role is being edited*

The user can edit the Name column only. The Id column is set to read-only:

```
<asp:BoundField DataField="Id" HeaderText="Id"
    ReadOnly="True" SortExpression="Id" />
```

When done, the user can click either the Update or Cancel links on the row. If the user clicks Update, then the UpdateObject event is raised by RolesDataSource to trigger the data update. This event is handled in the page:

```
Protected Sub RolesDataSource_UpdateObject( _
  ByVal sender As Object, ByVal e As Csla.Web.UpdateObjectArgs) _
  Handles RolesDataSource.UpdateObject

  Try
    Dim obj As Roles = GetRoles()
    Dim role As Role = obj.GetRoleById(CInt(e.Keys.Item("Id")))
    role.Name = e.Values.Item("Name").ToString
    Session("currentObject") = obj.Save
    e.RowsAffected = 1

  Catch ex As Csla.DataPortalException
    Me.ErrorLabel.Text = ex.BusinessException.Message
    e.RowsAffected = 0

  Catch ex As Exception
    Me.ErrorLabel.Text = ex.Message
    e.RowsAffected = 0
  End Try
End Sub
```

This code is quite similar to that for the insert operation discussed earlier, though in this case, the specific Role object that was edited is retrieved from the collection:

```
Dim role As Role = obj.GetRoleById(CInt(e.Keys.Item("Id")))
```

e.Keys contains all the values from the page that correspond to the properties defined in the GridView control's DataKeyNames property. Recall that the only property set in DataKeyNames was Id, so that's the only value provided through e.Keys. This value is passed to the GetRoleById() method to retrieve the correct Role object.

■**Note** Update and delete operations *require* that appropriate business object property names be specified in the GridView or DetailsView control's DataKeyNames property.

Since only one property can be edited, I opted not to use DataMapper and to set the property value manually. However, in a more complex edit scenario in which many properties are edited, you may choose to use DataMapper to simplify the code.

Finally, the Roles object's Save() method is called to commit the user's changes to the database. As with the insert process, the new Roles object returned from Save() is put into Session for use on all subsequent page requests.

Deleting an Object

Having seen how the update process works, you can probably guess how the delete process works. The user can click the Delete link next to a row in the GridView control. When they do so, RolesDataSource raises the DeleteObject event, which is handled in the page:

```
Protected Sub RolesDataSource_DeleteObject( _
  ByVal sender As Object, ByVal e As Csla.Web.DeleteObjectArgs) _
  Handles RolesDataSource.DeleteObject

  Try
    Dim obj As Roles = GetRoles()
    Dim id As Integer = CInt(e.Keys.Item("Id"))
    obj.Remove(id)
    Session("currentObject") = obj.Save
    e.RowsAffected = 1

  Catch ex As Csla.DataPortalException
    Me.ErrorLabel.Text = ex.BusinessException.Message
    e.RowsAffected = 0

  Catch ex As Exception
    Me.ErrorLabel.Text = ex.Message
    e.RowsAffected = 0
  End Try
End Sub
```

The Id value for the Role object to delete is retrieved from e.Keys and used to call the Remove() method on the Roles collection. Recall from Chapter 8 that this overload of Remove() accepts the Id value of the Role object.

Of course, the child object is merely marked for deletion, and isn't removed until the Save() method is called on the Roles object itself. Again, the resulting Roles object returned from Save() is put into Session for use on subsequent page requests.

At this point, you should understand the basic process for creating a grid-based data form that supports viewing, inserting, editing and deleting data. The only thing left to do in RolesEdit is to add support for authorization.

Authorization

The RolesEdit authorization code is perhaps the simplest in the application. If the user isn't authorized to edit the Roles object, then the CommandField column in the GridView control shouldn't be shown; and if the user can't add a new role, then the LinkButton for adding a new object shouldn't be shown.

When the page is loaded, an ApplyAuthorizationRules() method is called:

```
Protected Sub Page_Load( _
  ByVal sender As Object, ByVal e As System.EventArgs) Handles Me.Load

  If Not IsPostBack Then
    ApplyAuthorizationRules()

  Else
    Me.ErrorLabel.Text = ""
  End If
End Sub

Private Sub ApplyAuthorizationRules()
  Me.GridView1.Columns( _
    Me.GridView1.Columns.Count - 1).Visible = Roles.CanEditObject
  Me.AddRoleButton.Visible = Roles.CanAddObject
End Sub
```

The ApplyAuthorizationRules() method asks the Roles class whether the current user is authorized to edit the object or add new roles. If the user isn't authorized, then the appropriate controls' Visible properties are set to False, and the controls are thereby hidden.

Since the user is then unable to put the GridView control into edit mode or ask it to delete an item, the display effectively becomes read-only. Similarly, without the LinkButton for adding a new item, the user can't switch the MultiView to InsertView; so again the page becomes a simple read-only page.

As you can see, creating a simple grid-based edit page requires relatively little work. You add a data control, bind the GridView and possibly a DetailsView control to the data, and write a bit of code. Most of the code in this page exists to react to user actions as they indicate that data is to be inserted, edited, or deleted.

ProjectList Form

The ProjectList web form is responsible for displaying the list of projects to the user and allowing the user to choose a specific project to view or edit. From this page, the user can also delete a project and choose to add a new project. Figure 10-15 shows the layout of ProjectList.

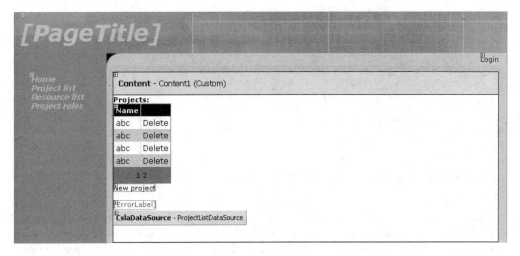

Figure 10-15. *Layout of ProjectList*

It is important to realize that the `GridView` control actually has *three* columns: Id, Name, and the `CommandField` column with the Delete links:

```
<Columns>
  <asp:BoundField DataField="Id" HeaderText="Id"
    SortExpression="Id" Visible="False" />
  <asp:HyperLinkField DataNavigateUrlFields="Id"
    DataNavigateUrlFormatString="ProjectEdit.aspx?id={0}"
    DataTextField="Name" HeaderText="Name" />
  <asp:CommandField ShowDeleteButton="True"
    SelectText="Edit" />
</Columns>
```

The Id column has its `Visible` property set to `False`, so it is there, but invisible. Also notice that the Name column is a `HyperLinkField`, not a simple `BoundField`. This makes each project name appear to the user as a hyperlink, though in reality it is more like a `LinkButton`—when the user clicks a project name, a `SelectedIndexChanged` event is raised from the `GridView` control.

Also of importance is the fact that the `GridView` control's `DataKeyNames` property is set to Id, so the Id property is specified as the unique identifier for each row of data. Without setting this property, the Delete link can't work.

The view, edit, and add operations are all handled by `ProjectEdit`, so `ProjectList` is really just responsible for redirecting the user to that other page as appropriate. The delete operation is handled directly from `ProjectList` through a `CommandField` column in the `GridView` control.

Notice that the `GridView` control displays paging links near the bottom. This is because paging is enabled for the control, as shown in Figure 10-16.

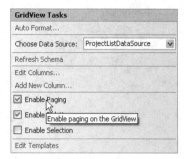

Figure 10-16. *Enabling paging for the GridView control*

You can also set the GridView control's PageSize property to control how many items are shown on each page. All the paging work is done by the GridView control itself, which is fine because the ProjectList business object will be maintained in Session, so the user can move from page to page without hitting the database each time.

Figure 10-17 shows the properties of the CslaDataSource control used on the page.

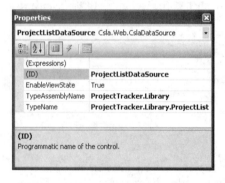

Figure 10-17. *Properties for the ProjectListDataSource control*

Like the RolesDataSource control in RolesEdit, the TypeAssemblyName and TypeName properties are set to point to the appropriate class within ProjectTracker.Library. This data source control will be used to retrieve the list of projects and to delete a project if the user clicks a Delete link.

Loading the Data

When the GridView control needs data, it asks ProjectListDataSource for the data. The data source control in turn raises its SelectObject event, which is handled in the page:

```
Protected Sub ProjectListDataSource_SelectObject( _
  ByVal sender As Object, ByVal e As Csla.Web.SelectObjectArgs) _
  Handles ProjectListDataSource.SelectObject

  e.BusinessObject = GetProjectList()
End Sub
```

As in `RolesEdit`, this page caches the business object in `Session`. The details of that process are handled by `GetProjectList()`:

```
Private Function GetProjectList() As ProjectTracker.Library.ProjectList
  Dim businessObject As Object = Session("currentObject")
  If businessObject Is Nothing OrElse _
      Not TypeOf businessObject Is ProjectList Then
    businessObject = ProjectTracker.Library.ProjectList.GetProjectList
    Session("currentObject") = businessObject
  End If
  Return CType(businessObject, ProjectTracker.Library.ProjectList)
End Function
```

This method is the same as the `GetRoles()` method discussed earlier, except that it ensures that a valid `ProjectList` object is returned instead of a `Roles` object.

This code allows the `GridView` control to populate itself with pages of data for display as needed.

Viewing or Editing a Project

The `Name` column in the `GridView` control was set up as a `HyperLinkField`, meaning that the user sees the values as a set of hyperlinks. If the user clicks on one of the project names, the browser directly navigates to the `ProjectEdit.aspx` page, passing the selected `Id` value as a parameter on the URL.

Adding a Project

The `ProjectList` page contains a `LinkButton` to allow the user to add a new project. If the user clicks this button, a `Click` event is raised:

```
Protected Sub NewProjectButton_Click( _
  ByVal sender As Object, ByVal e As System.EventArgs) _
  Handles NewProjectButton.Click

  'allow user to add a new project
  Response.Redirect("ProjectEdit.aspx")
End Sub
```

The `ProjectEdit` page takes care of viewing, editing, and adding `Project` objects, so all this code does is redirect the user to `ProjectEdit`. Notice that no parameter is provided to the page on the URL, and this is what tells `ProjectEdit` to create a new `Project` rather than to view or edit an existing one.

Deleting a Project

The `GridView` control has a `CommandField` column, which automatically creates a Delete link for each row of data. If the user clicks a Delete link, the `GridView` deletes that row of data by calling its data source control, `ProjectListDataSource`. The result is a `DeleteObject` event handled in the page:

```
Protected Sub ProjectListDataSource_DeleteObject( _
  ByVal sender As Object, ByVal e As Csla.Web.DeleteObjectArgs) _
  Handles ProjectListDataSource.DeleteObject

  Try
    ProjectTracker.Library.Project.DeleteProject( _
      New Guid(e.Keys("Id").ToString))
    e.RowsAffected = 1
```

```
    Catch ex As Csla.DataPortalException
      Me.ErrorLabel.Text = ex.BusinessException.Message
      e.RowsAffected = 0

    Catch ex As Exception
      Me.ErrorLabel.Text = ex.Message
      e.RowsAffected = 0
    End Try
  End Sub
```

Again, the `DataKeyNames` property being set in the `GridView` means that the `Id` column value from the row automatically flows into this event handler through `e.Keys`. That value is converted to a `Guid` object so that the `Shared DeleteProject()` method on the `Project` class can be called. The result is immediate deletion of the related project data.

Authorization

Having discussed all the core business functionality of the page, let's look at the authorization code. Like in `RolesEdit`, the authorization rules themselves are in the business class, and the UI code simply uses that information to enable and disable various UI controls as the page loads:

```
  Protected Sub Page_Load( _
    ByVal sender As Object, ByVal e As System.EventArgs) Handles Me.Load

    If Not IsPostBack Then
      ApplyAuthorizationRules()

    Else
      Me.ErrorLabel.Text = ""
    End If
  End Sub

  Private Sub ApplyAuthorizationRules()
    Me.GridView1.Columns( _
      Me.GridView1.Columns.Count - 1).Visible = _
      Project.CanDeleteObject
    NewProjectButton.Visible = _
      ProjectTracker.Library.Project.CanAddObject
  End Sub
```

When the page is loaded, the `ApplyAuthorizationRules()` method makes sure that the `CommandField` column in the `GridView` is only visible if the user is authorized to delete `Project` objects. It also hides the `NewProjectButton` control if the user isn't allowed to add `Project` objects.

The end result is that a user who can't delete or add data is still allowed to view the list of projects, and they can even click on a project's name to get more details in the `ProjectEdit` page.

ProjectEdit Form

At this point, you've seen how to create two different types of grid-based web forms. The pages so far have illustrated in-place editing, adding of new items, and displaying a list of items for selection or deletion. The final web form I'll discuss in this chapter is `ProjectEdit`, which is a detail form that allows the user to view and edit details about a specific object.

Like `RolesEdit`, this form uses a `MultiView` control. Figure 10-18 shows the `MainView` layout, and Figure 10-19 shows the `AssignView` layout. There's also a `Label` control and some `CslaDataSource` controls on the page itself, below the `MultiView`. These are shown in Figure 10-20.

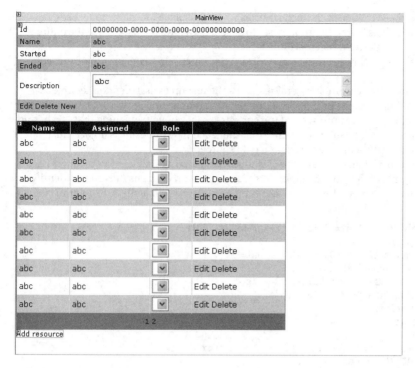

Figure 10-18. *Layout of MainView in ProjectEdit*

MainView includes a DetailsView control to allow display and editing of the Project object's properties. This control is data bound to the ProjectDataSource control shown in Figure 10-20, and so it is effectively data bound to the current Project object.

The Id row is set to read-only, since the Project object's Id property is a read-only property. The Description row is a TemplateField, which allows the use of a TextBox control with its TextMode property set to MultiLine:

```
<asp:TemplateField HeaderText="Description"
  SortExpression="Description">
  <EditItemTemplate>
    <asp:TextBox ID="TextBox1" TextMode="MultiLine"
      Width="100%" runat="server"
      Text='<%# Bind("Description") %>'></asp:TextBox>
  </EditItemTemplate>
  <InsertItemTemplate>
    <asp:TextBox ID="TextBox1" TextMode="MultiLine"
      Width="100%" runat="server"
      Text='<%# Bind("Description") %>'></asp:TextBox>
  </InsertItemTemplate>
  <ItemTemplate>
    <asp:TextBox ID="TextBox1" TextMode="MultiLine"
      ReadOnly="true" Width="100%" runat="server"
      Text='<%# Bind("Description") %>'></asp:TextBox>
  </ItemTemplate>
</asp:TemplateField>
```

Notice that even the ItemTemplate, which controls what is displayed in view mode, uses a TextBox control—but with its ReadOnly property set to true. This allows the user to see the entire text of the Description property, even if it is quite long.

Finally, the DetailsView control has a CommandField row, which allows the user to delete, edit, and add a Project.

Beneath the DetailsView control is a GridView to list the resources assigned to the project. This control is data bound to the ResourcesDataSource control shown in Figure 10-20. It is effectively data bound to the Resources property of the current Project object; meaning that it is bound to a collection of ProjectResource objects. Remember that each type of business object must have its own CslaDataSource control in order to act as a data source.

The GridView control also has an ResourceId column, which is not visible. Its DataKeyNames property is set to ResourceId, specifying that the ResourceId column contains the unique identifying value for each row. The Name and Assigned columns are read-only, while the Role column is a TemplateField:

```
<asp:TemplateField HeaderText="Role" SortExpression="Role">
  <EditItemTemplate>
    <asp:DropDownList ID="DropDownList1" runat="server"
      DataSourceID="RoleListDataSource"
      DataTextField="Value" DataValueField="Key"
      SelectedValue='<%# Bind("Role") %>'>
    </asp:DropDownList>
  </EditItemTemplate>
  <ItemTemplate>
    <asp:DropDownList ID="DropDownList2" runat="server"
      DataSourceID="RoleListDataSource"
      DataTextField="Value" DataValueField="Key"
      Enabled="False" SelectedValue='<%# Bind("Role") %>'>
    </asp:DropDownList>
  </ItemTemplate>
</asp:TemplateField>
```

Notice how the DropDownList controls are data bound to the RoleListDataSource control shown in Figure 10-20. This data source control provides access to a RoleList business object, so the DropDownList controls are populated with the list of roles a resource can play on a project. This way, ASP.NET does all the hard work of mapping the Key values for each role to the corresponding human-readable text value. The numeric Key values are stored in the business objects, while the text values are displayed on the page.

The GridView control also has a CommandField column so that the user can edit or remove assignments. Of course, "remove" in this case really means unassign, but those details are handled by the business object, not the UI.

Finally, there's a LinkButton to allow the user to assign a new resource to the project. When the user clicks that button, the view is switched so that the user see AssignView, where he or she can select the resource to assign. The layout of that view is shown in Figure 10-19.

AssignView is comparatively straightforward. It contains a GridView control that is data bound to the ResourceListDataSource control. Effectively, this means the GridView is bound to a ResourceList business object, so it displays the list of resources to the user. The CommandField column in the GridView provides a Select link, so the user can select the resource to be assigned.

There's also a LinkButton at the bottom to allow the user to cancel the operation and return to MainView without assigning a resource at all.

Finally, Figure 10-20 shows the bottom of the page, beneath the MultiView control.

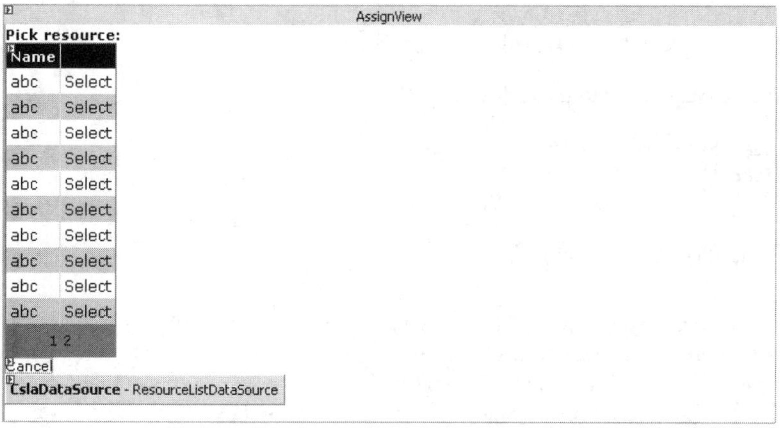

Figure 10-19. *Layout of AssignView in ProjectEdit*

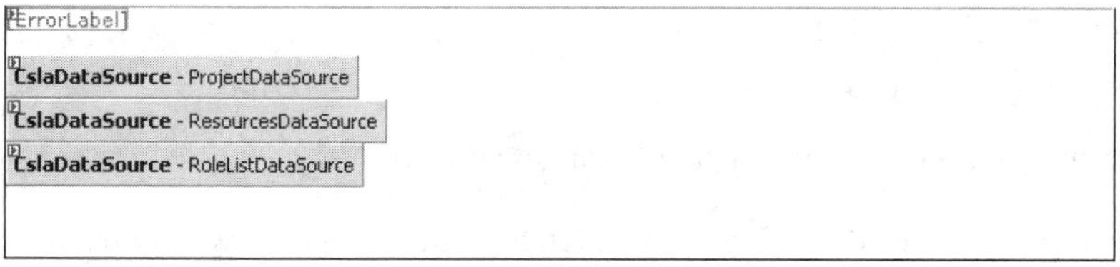

Figure 10-20. *Other controls in ProjectEdit*

The `CslaDataSource` controls are used by the various `DetailsView` and `GridView` controls discussed previously. And of course, the `ErrorLabel` control is a simple `Label` control that has its `ForeColor` property set to `Red`. The exception-handling code in the form uses this control to display details about any exceptions to the user.

Now let's go through the implementation of the page. I'll do this a bit differently than with the previous pages, because by now you should understand how the pieces fit together using data binding.

Caching the Project Object in Session

The `RolesEdit` and `ProjectList` forms implement methods to retrieve the central business object from `Session`, or to retrieve it from the database as necessary. This not only implements a type of cache to reduce load on the database, but it provides support for the browser's Back button as well. The same thing is done in `ProjectEdit`:

```
Private Function GetProject() As Project
  Dim businessObject As Object = Session("currentObject")
  If businessObject Is Nothing OrElse _
      Not TypeOf businessObject Is Project Then
    Try
      Dim idString As String = Request.QueryString("id")
      If Not String.IsNullOrEmpty(idString) Then
        Dim id As New Guid(idString)
        businessObject = Project.GetProject(id)
```

```
      Else
        businessObject = Project.NewProject
      End If
      Session("currentObject") = businessObject

    Catch ex As System.Security.SecurityException
      Response.Redirect("ProjectList.aspx")
    End Try
  End If
  Return CType(businessObject, Project)
End Function
```

As before, if there's no object in Session, or if the object isn't a Project, then a Project is retrieved from the database. But the code here is a bit more complex than in the other forms.

Notice that the Request.QueryString property is used to get the id value (if any) passed in on the page's URL. If an id value is passed into the page, then that value is used to retrieve an existing Project:

```
      Dim id As New Guid(idString)
      businessObject = Project.GetProject(id)
```

Otherwise, a new Project is created for the page:

```
      businessObject = Project.NewProject
```

Either way, the resulting object is placed into Session and is also returned as a result from the method.

It is possible for a user to navigate directly to ProjectEdit.aspx, providing no id value on the URL. In such a case, the user might not be authorized to add a Project, and so a SecurityException would result. In that case, the user is simply redirected to the ProjectList page, where he can safely view the list of projects.

Saving a Project

In this form, the Project object is saved in many scenarios, including:

- Inserting the project

- Editing the project

- Assigning a resource

- Unassigning a resource

- Deleting the project

To simplify the code overall, the SaveProject() method handles the common behaviors in all those cases:

```
  Private Function SaveProject(ByVal project As Project) As Integer
    Dim rowsAffected As Integer
    Try
      Session("currentObject") = project.Save()
      rowsAffected = 1

    Catch ex As Csla.Validation.ValidationException
      Dim message As New System.Text.StringBuilder
      message.AppendFormat("{0}<br/>", ex.Message)
```

```
    If project.BrokenRulesCollection.Count = 1 Then
      message.AppendFormat("* {0}: {1}", _
        project.BrokenRulesCollection(0).Property, _
        project.BrokenRulesCollection(0).Description)

    Else
      For Each rule As Csla.Validation.BrokenRule In _
          project.BrokenRulesCollection
        message.AppendFormat( _
          "* {0}: {1}<br/>", rule.Property, rule.Description)
      Next
    End If
    Me.ErrorLabel.Text = message.ToString
    rowsAffected = 0

  Catch ex As Csla.DataPortalException
    Me.ErrorLabel.Text = ex.BusinessException.Message
    rowsAffected = 0

  Catch ex As Exception
    Me.ErrorLabel.Text = ex.Message
    rowsAffected = 0
  End Try
  Return rowsAffected
End Function
```

This method accepts the Project as a parameter and calls its Save() method. As always, the resulting object is placed in Session to replace the old version of the object. In case of an exception, the ErrorLabel text is updated.

The code here is the same as in the other pages, but it is worth consolidating in this page (and in ResourceEdit) because of the many places the Project object is saved.

ProjectDataSource

The ProjectDataSource control takes care of data binding that deals with the Project object itself. The page handles its DeleteObject, InsertObject, SelectObject, and UpdateObject events. For instance, the SelectObject handler looks like this:

```
Protected Sub ProjectDataSource_SelectObject( _
  ByVal sender As Object, ByVal e As Csla.Web.SelectObjectArgs) _
  Handles ProjectDataSource.SelectObject

  e.BusinessObject = GetProject()
End Sub
```

Thanks to the GetProject() method discussed earlier, this method is very simple to implement. The delete, insert, and update events are also comparatively simple due to the SaveProject() method. For instance, here's the InsertObject event handler:

```
Protected Sub ProjectDataSource_InsertObject( _
  ByVal sender As Object, ByVal e As Csla.Web.InsertObjectArgs) _
  Handles ProjectDataSource.InsertObject

  Dim obj As Project = GetProject()
  Csla.Data.DataMapper.Map(e.Values, obj, "Id")
  e.RowsAffected = SaveProject(obj)
End Sub
```

The current Project object is retrieved from Session (or pulled from the database), and the new values entered by the user are mapped into the object's properties using the DataMapper from Chapter 5. Then SaveProject() is called to save the project and update Session with the newly updated data.

The update operation works in a similar manner, so I won't detail it here.

Deleting the Project

DeleteObject is a bit different:

```
Protected Sub ProjectDataSource_DeleteObject( _
  ByVal sender As Object, ByVal e As Csla.Web.DeleteObjectArgs) _
  Handles ProjectDataSource.DeleteObject

  Try
    Project.DeleteProject(New Guid(e.Keys("Id").ToString))
    Session("currentObject") = Nothing
    e.RowsAffected = 1

  Catch ex As Csla.DataPortalException
    Me.ErrorLabel.Text = ex.BusinessException.Message
    e.RowsAffected = 0

  Catch ex As Exception
    Me.ErrorLabel.Text = ex.Message
    e.RowsAffected = 0
  End Try
End Sub
```

If the user clicks the link in the DetailsView control to delete the project, the DeleteObject event is raised. e.Keys contains the Id row value from the DetailsView, because the DataKeyNames property on the control is set to Id. This value is used to create a Guid, which is then passed to the Shared DeleteProject() method to delete the project. Of course, this immediately deletes the Project using the data portal, and so proper exception handling is implemented to display any exception messages in ErrorLabel.

Once the Project has been deleted, it makes no sense to leave the user on ProjectEdit. If the delete operation is successful, the DetailsView control raises an ItemDeleted event:

```
Protected Sub DetailsView1_ItemDeleted( _
  ByVal sender As Object, _
  ByVal e As System.Web.UI.WebControls.DetailsViewDeletedEventArgs) _
  Handles DetailsView1.ItemDeleted

  Response.Redirect("ProjectList.aspx")
End Sub
```

The user is simply redirected to ProjectList, where she should no longer see the deleted project in the list.

ResourcesDataSource

The ResourcesDataSource control takes care of data binding dealing with the Resources collection from the Project object. The GridView control in MainView is bound to this control, and the page handles its DeleteObject, SelectObject, and UpdateObject events.

There's no need to handle the InsertObject event, because the GridView isn't used to dynamically add ProjectResource objects to the collection. I'll discuss adding a new child object shortly.

The SelectObject event handler returns the collection of ProjectResource objects for the Project:

```
Protected Sub ResourcesDataSource_SelectObject( _
  ByVal sender As Object, ByVal e As Csla.Web.SelectObjectArgs) _
  Handles ResourcesDataSource.SelectObject

  Dim obj As Project = GetProject()
  e.BusinessObject = obj.Resources
End Sub
```

It first gets the current Project object by calling GetProject(). Then it simply provides the Resources collection to the data source control, which in turn provides it to any UI controls requiring the data.

The DeleteObject and UpdateObject event handlers are worth exploring a bit. The DeleteObject handler gets the ResourceId value from the GridView control through e.Keys and uses that value to remove the ProjectResource object from the collection:

```
Protected Sub ResourcesDataSource_DeleteObject( _
  ByVal sender As Object, ByVal e As Csla.Web.DeleteObjectArgs) _
  Handles ResourcesDataSource.DeleteObject

  Dim obj As Project = GetProject()
  Dim rid As Integer = CInt(e.Keys("ResourceId"))
  obj.Resources.Remove(rid)
  e.RowsAffected = SaveProject(obj)
End Sub
```

The current Project object is retrieved, and then the Remove() method is called on the Resources collection to remove the specified child object. SaveProject() is then called to commit the change.

UpdateObject is a bit more complex:

```
Protected Sub ResourcesDataSource_UpdateObject( _
  ByVal sender As Object, ByVal e As Csla.Web.UpdateObjectArgs) _
  Handles ResourcesDataSource.UpdateObject

  Dim obj As Project = GetProject()
  Dim rid As Integer = CInt(e.Keys("ResourceId"))
  Dim res As ProjectResource = obj.Resources.GetItem(rid)
  Csla.Data.DataMapper.Map(e.Values, res)
  e.RowsAffected = SaveProject(obj)
End Sub
```

In this case, the actual child object is retrieved from the Resources collection. Then the values entered into the GridView by the user are pulled from e.Values and are mapped into the child object using DataMapper. And finally, SaveProject() is called to commit the changes.

Assigning a Resource to the Project

The GridView isn't used to insert new ProjectResource child objects, so ResourcesDataSource will never raise its InsertObject method. Users are allowed to assign a new user to the project by clicking a LinkButton control. In that case, the MultiView is changed to display AssignView so that the user can select the resource to be assigned:

```
Protected Sub AddResourceButton_Click( _
  ByVal sender As Object, ByVal e As System.EventArgs) _
  Handles AddResourceButton.Click

  Me.MultiView1.ActiveViewIndex = Views.AssignView
End Sub
```

Once AssignView is displayed, the user can either select a resource or click the Cancel button. If the user selects a resource, the resource is assigned to the project:

```
Protected Sub GridView2_SelectedIndexChanged( _
  ByVal sender As Object, ByVal e As System.EventArgs) _
  Handles GridView2.SelectedIndexChanged

  Dim obj As Project = GetProject()
  Try
    obj.Resources.Assign(CInt(Me.GridView2.SelectedDataKey.Value))
    If SaveProject(obj) > 0 Then
      Me.GridView1.DataBind()
      Me.MultiView1.ActiveViewIndex = Views.MainView
    End If

  Catch ex As InvalidOperationException
    ErrorLabel.Text = ex.Message
  End Try
End Sub
```

To make the assignment, the current Project object is retrieved. Then the Resources collection's Assign() method is called, passing the SelectedDataKey value from the GridView control as a parameter. This GridView control, which displays the list of resources, has its DataKeyNames property set to Id, so SelectedDataKey returns the Id value of the selected resource.

Once the assignment is made, SaveProject() is called to commit the change. If SaveProject() succeeds, it will return a value greater than 0. And in that case, the GridView control in MainView, which displays the list of assigned resources, is told to refresh its data by calling DataBind(). Remember that ASP.NET tries to optimize data access, and so GridView and DetailsView controls don't refresh their data from the data source on every postback. You need to explicitly call DataBind() to force this refresh to occur.

Several things could go wrong during this whole process. The resource might already be assigned, or the SaveProject() method could fail due to some data error. Of course, SaveProject() already does its own exception handling and displays any exception messages to the user through the ErrorLabel control.

But if the user attempts to assign a duplicate resource to the project, the Assign() method will raise an InvalidOperationException. This is caught and the message text is displayed to the user. Notice that in that case, the user is *not* sent back to MainView, but remains on AssignView so that the user can choose a different resource to assign if desired.

The simplest course of action occurs if the user clicks the Cancel LinkButton control:

```
Protected Sub CancelAssignButton_Click( _
  ByVal sender As Object, ByVal e As System.EventArgs) _
  Handles CancelAssignButton.Click

  Me.MultiView1.ActiveViewIndex = Views.MainView
End Sub
```

In that case, the user is simply directed back to the MainView display.

RoleListDataSource

RoleListDataSource is used by the GridView control in MainView. It provides access to the list of roles a resource can play on a project. This data isn't cached in the UI because the RoleList object handles caching automatically (see Chapter 8 for details). Also, because RoleList is read-only, the only event that needs to be handled is SelectObject:

```
Protected Sub RoleListDataSource_SelectObject( _
  ByVal sender As Object, ByVal e As Csla.Web.SelectObjectArgs) _
  Handles RoleListDataSource.SelectObject

  e.BusinessObject = RoleList.GetList
End Sub
```

The GetList() method returns the list of roles, either from the cache or the database. The beauty of this approach is that the UI code doesn't know or care whether the database was used to get the data; it just uses the result.

■**Note** Because the RoleList object is cached in a Shared field, the cached object is shared by *all users* of the website. A Shared field is global to the AppDomain, and so is effectively global to the entire website. In this case, that's a good thing, because it means the RoleList object is retrieved once for all users—but this is a detail you should keep in mind when working with data that should be per-user instead of shared.

ResourceListDataSource

The ResourceListDataSource is used by the GridView control in AssignView to display a list of resources in the database. It is bound to the ResourceList business object, which is read-only—meaning that only the SelectObject event needs to be handled:

```
Protected Sub ResourceListDataSource_SelectObject( _
  ByVal sender As Object, ByVal e As Csla.Web.SelectObjectArgs) _
  Handles ResourceListDataSource.SelectObject

  e.BusinessObject = ProjectTracker.Library.ResourceList.GetResourceList
End Sub
```

I'm making no special effort to cache the results of GetResourceList(), nor does that method do caching on its own. This is intentional.

Users will most likely come to ProjectEdit to view a project's details. Rarely will they opt to assign a new resource to a project—so I made a conscious decision here to keep my code simple and just get the list each time it is needed.

If it turns out later that users are assigning far more resources than anticipated, and that retrieving ResourceList is a performance bottleneck, then the implementation can be changed to do some caching—in the UI, or in ResourceList itself.

Either way, I tend to default to implementing simpler code, and only make it more complex when application usage patterns prove that some other solution is required.

Authorization

At this point, you've seen almost all the code in ProjectEdit. The rest of the code primarily deals with authorization, though there's a bit of UI magic as well.

When the page loads, an `ApplyAuthorizationRules()` method is called:

```
Protected Sub Page_Load( _
  ByVal sender As Object, ByVal e As System.EventArgs) Handles Me.Load

  If Not IsPostBack Then
    ApplyAuthorizationRules()

  Else
    Me.ErrorLabel.Text = ""
  End If
End Sub


Private Sub ApplyAuthorizationRules()

  ' project display
  If Project.CanEditObject Then
    Dim obj As Project = GetProject()
    If obj.IsNew Then
      Me.DetailsView1.DefaultMode = DetailsViewMode.Insert

    Else
      Me.DetailsView1.DefaultMode = DetailsViewMode.Edit
    End If
    Me.AddResourceButton.Visible = Not obj.IsNew

  Else
    Me.DetailsView1.DefaultMode = DetailsViewMode.ReadOnly
    Me.AddResourceButton.Visible = False
  End If
  Me.DetailsView1.Rows(Me.DetailsView1.Rows.Count - 1).Visible = _
    Project.CanEditObject

  ' resources display
  Me.GridView1.Columns(Me.GridView1.Columns.Count - 1).Visible = _
    Project.CanEditObject
End Sub
```

As with the previous forms, various controls, `GridView` columns, and `DetailsView` rows are made visible or invisible depending on the authorization values returned from the business objects.

Additionally, the mode of the `DetailsView` control is set based on the business object's `IsNew` property:

```
If obj.IsNew Then
  Me.DetailsView1.DefaultMode = DetailsViewMode.Insert

Else
  Me.DetailsView1.DefaultMode = DetailsViewMode.Edit
End If
```

This ensures that the user gets the right set of options in the `CommandField` row of the `DetailsView` control based on whether they are adding or editing the object.

Finally, it is possible for the object's authorization rules to change depending on whether it is new or old. Though not strictly an authorization rule, setting the `DetailsView` control's `DetailsViewMode` property, as shown previously, is an example. This means that when the object changes from new to old, then authorization rules should be rechecked.

The DetailsView control automatically raises an event when this happens. To be complete, the page actually handles both the ItemInserted and ItemUpdated events from the DetailsView control:

```
Protected Sub DetailsView1_ItemInserted( _
  ByVal sender As Object, _
  ByVal e As System.Web.UI.WebControls.DetailsViewInsertedEventArgs) _
  Handles DetailsView1.ItemInserted

  Dim project As Project = GetProject()
  Response.Redirect("ProjectEdit.aspx?id=" & project.Id.ToString)
End Sub

Protected Sub DetailsView1_ItemUpdated( _
  ByVal sender As Object, _
  ByVal e As System.Web.UI.WebControls.DetailsViewUpdatedEventArgs) _
  Handles DetailsView1.ItemUpdated

  ApplyAuthorizationRules()
End Sub
```

When an item is updated, the authorization rules are rechecked, ensuring that the display is appropriate for a new or an old object. The insert operation is a bit more complex, however, because the URL query string used to reach the page doesn't include the Project object's Id property value. By forcing the browser to redirect to the page with the Id value, the GetProject() method will work properly to retrieve the now-existing object from the database if needed.

As noted earlier, the ResourceEdit and ResourceList forms are very comparable to ProjectEdit and ProjectList, so I won't cover them in this chapter. You can look at their code in the download for the book. This completes the PTWeb UI, so you should now have a good understanding of how to create both Windows Forms and Web Forms interfaces based on business objects.

Conclusion

This chapter has discussed the creation of a basic Web Forms UI based on the business objects from Chapter 8. As with the Windows Forms technology in Chapter 9, there are many ways to create a Web Forms interface, and the one I've created here is just one option among many.

The key is that the business objects automatically enforce all business rules and provide business processing so that the UI doesn't need to include any of that code. As you can see, it is very possible to create two very different user interfaces based on exactly the same set of business objects, data access code, and database design.

As shown here, the website is configured for optimal performance, running the Session and the data portal in the same process as the web forms. You could increase scalability and fault tolerance by moving Session into its own process, or onto a state server. You could potentially increase security by running the data portal server components on a separate application server. In either case, all you need to do is change some settings in Web.config; the UI code and business objects will work in all these scenarios.

In Chapter 11, I'll show how you can create another type of interface to the business objects by using Web Services. Then Chapter 12 will show how to create remote data portal hosts for remoting, Enterprise Services, and Web Services.

CHAPTER 11

■■■

Web Services Interface

One of the most hyped technologies to be linked with .NET is Web Services. Over the past few years, this has evolved into the widely discussed concept of service-oriented architecture (SOA). All the hype and confusion around SOA has in turn given way to service orientation (SO), putting the concept more on a par with object orientation.

Regardless of your choice of terminology or views on SOA, there's no doubt that when web services are used appropriately, they are very useful. It's important to realize, however, that web services are fundamentally just a text format for data interchange—they're not designed to simplify the process of creating object-oriented systems.

In my view, web services are just another type of interface to applications. I've already discussed Windows Forms and Web Forms interfaces, which allow a user to access an application as shown in Figure 11-1.

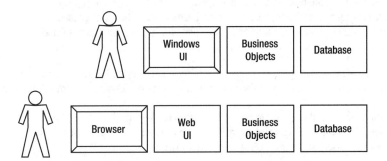

Figure 11-1. *Using Windows Forms and Web Forms interfaces*

Web services are another type of interface that the application can make available. The primary difference is that a web service interface is designed for use by other *applications*, not by users directly. Another application can use web services to get or update data in your application. This other application that's consuming your data may or may not have users of its own. This concept is illustrated in Figure 11-2.

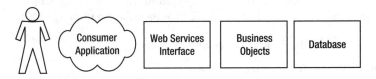

Figure 11-2. *Using a web service interface*

■**Note** I fully realize that Web Services is being sold as offering much more than just another type of interface to your application. As such, I'll discuss my rationale some more before implementing the web services in this chapter.

In this chapter, I'll provide a short overview of Web Services as a technology. Then I'll quickly review Web Services and SOA to lay out the two primary ways people approach the design of web services: service-oriented and component-based. Then I'll discuss the creation of a Web Services interface for the ProjectTracker business objects in order to illustrate how business objects can support the creation of web services. That implementation will illustrate how to create both service-oriented and component-based web services.

Overview of Web Services

At an abstract level, web services enable one application to call procedures or methods in another application. On the face of it, this is similar to the aims of Remote Procedure Call (RPC), DCOM, Remote Method Invocation (RMI), Internet Inter-ORB Protocol (IIOP), and .NET Remoting—all of these technologies enable one application to invoke procedures in another application.

■**Note** It's also possible to view these technologies as a way for two components in the same application to interact with each other. While this is definitely a common use for the other technologies I mention, it isn't the intended use of web services. Web services are designed for cross-application communication, not cross-component communication. This is because the focus of web services is interoperability. Due to this focus, web services don't offer the same performance or features as the other more platform-specific technologies listed.

Additionally, ASP.NET Web Services uses the Hypertext Transfer Protocol (HTTP) for communication between one application and another, and the SOAP standard for packaging the data transferred over HTTP.

The following discussion is intended to provide some high-level background information on Web Services. As you'll see, a typical .NET developer rarely needs to worry directly about these details, because the .NET Framework and Visual Studio take care of them.

The SOAP Standard

The SOAP standard defines the format and structure of the data packets (messages) that are sent back and forth between the applications involved. There are two primary types of message:

- A procedure call
- The results of a procedure call

When an application wants to call a procedure or a method in another application, it constructs a SOAP message that describes the method to be called and provides any parameter data. Any results from the procedure are likewise packed up into a SOAP message that's returned to the original application.

SOAP defines a couple of important things that must go into a message:

- The format of the data that's being transferred
- An envelope of metadata around the data that's being transferred

The SOAP data format is designed to be supported by virtually any platform. It defines a rich set of data types, including numbers, strings, arrays, and so forth. Data of these types can be encoded into a standard XML format that can be understood by any platform that supports SOAP. The format is designed for interoperability, which means that most platforms will have more complex data types or structures that can't be readily encoded into SOAP XML.

The SOAP envelope contains metadata describing the nature and purpose of the message. You can think of the envelope as being like a "header" for the actual data; it's a little like an HTTP header. The envelope, which is extensible, can be quite complex. This means that you can add arbitrary additional data into the envelope—a feature I'll use later in the chapter to pass security credentials along with each method call.

Message-Based Communication

A key point to remember is that SOAP only defines the XML that makes up the message; it doesn't describe how that message should be delivered from one application to another. It's up to some other mechanism to deliver a SOAP-formatted request message from one application (the consumer) to the other (the service). The service application then runs the requested procedure. Any results from that procedure are packaged into another SOAP-formatted message, which is returned to the consumer (as shown in Figure 11-3).

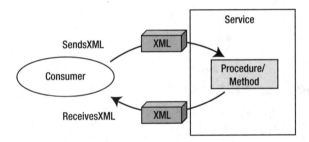

Figure 11-3. *XML messages are passed to and from the service.*

The most common approach today is for the applications to communicate via HTTP, but the SOAP data format can be transferred via email, MSMQ, raw sockets, text files, instant-messaging technology, or any other way that you can think of to get the data from one application to the other.

SOAP and Web Services

This, then, is where web services come into play. Web services allow consumers to connect to them using HTTP. Each procedure call is an isolated event in which the consumer connects to the service, makes the call, and gets back the result.

However, using web services over HTTP is about more than just passing SOAP XML messages back and forth. While that's at the core of the process, there are a number of supporting features that are very important, including the following:

- Describing the nature of a web service
- Generating consumer-side proxies for a web service
- Discovering the web services on a machine
- Managing directories of web services

Describing a web service means generating a list of all the procedures (often called *web methods*) that are available to consumers, along with the data types of the parameters those procedures require, and the data types of any return values. There's a standard for describing this information: Web Services Description Language (WSDL). WSDL is an XML dialect that *describes* a web service. When you (or Visual Studio on your behalf) need information about a web service, the first step is to retrieve a WSDL document.

The primary reason for retrieving a WSDL document is to create a consumer-side proxy for the web service: an object on the consumer machine that *looks like* the web service. Any method calls made on this proxy are automatically packaged into SOAP XML and sent to the service application, as shown in Figure 11-4. This is really no different from how you use client-side proxy objects in remoting, DCOM, or any other similar technology.

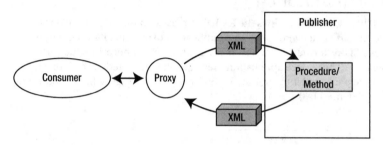

Figure 11-4. *Web service interaction is abstracted behind a proxy object.*

SOAP, Web Services, and the .NET Framework

Most .NET developers don't think about the creation of SOAP messages and envelopes. Nor do they really think about the details of delivering a SOAP message via HTTP. All this is handled by the .NET Framework and its support for web services.

To create a service (an application that exposes web services), you simply create a Web Services project in Visual Studio and write some code. Alternatively, you can just add a web service to an existing ASP.NET web application. In either case, apart from adding a couple of special attributes to the code, you don't usually have to do any difficult work.

For instance, you might write the following code in a web service within an ASP.NET application:

```
<System.Web.Services.WebService( _
  Namespace:="http://ws.lhotka.net/PTService/ProjectTracker")> _
Public Class ProjectTracker
  Inherits System.Web.Services.WebService

  <WebMethod(Description="Get Resource Name")> _
  Public Function GetResourceName(ByVal id As String) As String
    Return Resource.GetResource(id).Name
  End Function
End Class
```

Visual Studio automatically generates all the extra files needed to provide access to this method via Web Services. This includes the ability to generate WSDL descriptions for the web service dynamically.

Equally, a typical .NET developer doesn't need to worry about creating consumer-side proxy objects. When using Visual Studio, simply add a web reference to the web service. Visual Studio then automatically retrieves the WSDL describing the web service and generates the proxy. If you are not using Visual Studio, the .NET Framework offers the `soapsuds.exe` command line utility, which can also create the proxy.

Because of the tight integration of Web Services into the .NET Framework and Visual Studio, developers can avoid dealing with the details of publishing and consuming web services. This means that you can focus on how to use them in your business applications, rather than worrying about how to make them.

Now that you have a basic understanding of the technologies behind Web Services, let's discuss the two architectural worldviews most commonly used when discussing Web Services.

Web Services and SOA

No chapter on Web Services can avoid discussing the relationship (or lack thereof) between Web Services and SOA or SO.

SOA and SO purists argue up and down that service orientation and Web Services are separate, but somewhat related, things—that the concepts should be thought of more like salt and sugar. Both are useful on their own, and in some cases, they may be combined successfully.

Certainly, it is true that SOA is independent from Web Services. SOA is really independent from technology or any implementation-specific concepts. It describes a set of high-level architectural concepts and perhaps some best practices. You can use the ideas of SOA in business process engineering as easily as in software engineering. My point is that SOA is not a technology-related concept and *really* isn't connected with Web Services.

Service orientation, on the other hand, is an attempt to map some of those SOA concepts into technology—along the lines of mapping object orientation to technology. Ideally, service orientation encompasses analysis, architecture, design, and programming aspects of software.

Still, even service orientation isn't tied to Web Services, because a *service* can be implemented using a wide variety of technologies, including the following:

- Queuing software (such as MSMQ or MQSeries)
- Email (SMTP and POP)
- TCP sockets
- Instant messenger (IM) protocols such as Jabber
- Microsoft Enterprise Services
- .NET Remoting
- Web Services

I specifically put Web Services last to emphasize that it is but one option among many. Of course, the reality is that *most people* directly link Web Services to SOA or any other discussion of service orientation. If you bring up service orientation in a conversation, almost everyone will just *assume* you are talking only about Web Services.

This broadly accepted misunderstanding is unfortunate, and threatens to undermine the long-term benefits of service orientation.

Services vs. Components

A more productive way to frame the discussion is to look at the two competing ways to design a web service:

- As a component
- As a service

Though the difference between these two worldviews may seem subtle on the surface, they are very much in conflict. You will be best served if you choose one of the two worldviews and consistently use it in your web service design within a given application.

■**Note**   The example web services implemented later in this chapter are a mix of both approaches. They are not intended to convince you to mix the worldviews, but rather they are intended to show you how to implement either approach.

Keep in mind that my intent with this discussion is not to paint one worldview as being inherently superior to the other. Both are valid in different scenarios, though I must say that my personal bias does lean toward taking a service-oriented approach.

Web Services as Components

You can view a web service as a *component*, along the same lines that you would think of a component in MTS or COM+. This is totally logical, and is probably the most common way people look at web services.

A well-designed component is a collection of classes, each of which exposes a set of atomic, stateless methods. Typically, all the methods in a class are related to each other in some logical manner, though nothing really enforces that except good design practices. Table 11-1 defines the terms *atomic* and *stateless*.

Table 11-1. *Definition of Atomic and Stateless*

Term	Definition
Atomic	A method that has no dependencies on methods called prior to or subsequent to its being called
Stateless	A method that maintains no state, and so behaves consistently when called repeatedly with the same or different parameters

Having components implement atomic, stateless methods is a best practice that evolved as the industry used MTS and COM+ over the past decade. While those technologies support other models, it has become an accepted best practice to implement methods in this manner.

The classes and methods of a component define that component's *interface*. An interface is a strong contract that the component makes with all callers. That interface contract can't be changed without all calling code being changed as well.

You can think of a web service in exactly the same way. A web service contains one or more classes. Each class contains one or more methods. These methods should be designed to be atomic and stateless. This one-to-one match between the design view of a component and a web service is why most people design their web services just like they have designed MTS/COM+ components for the past many years.

In a service-oriented worldview, a web service has classes that expose methods. These methods, taken together, form an API (application program interface). The idea is that the web service is an application, and these methods describe how another application can interact.

However, the legacy of MTS/COM+ continues. Those technologies were widely used for client/server implementations, and the components they hosted were most commonly viewed as *part of* the application, not as a *separate* application.

Today, most people design their web services as part of a bigger application, not as a separate application. In other words, web services are most commonly used to implement a client/server model, rather than a service-oriented model.

These methods typically have a strongly typed, parameter-based signature. Each method can really be thought of as a procedure that is invoked by the client of the web service. For instance:

```
Public AddCustomer(ByVal id As Integer, ByVal firstName As String, _
  ByVal lastName As String, ByVal add1 As String, ByVal addr2 As String, _
  ByVal city As String, ByVal zipCode As String) As Boolean
```

This is natural when defining a strongly typed API for components, especially if those components are designed to be used in a client/server or an n-tier environment. The result is that web services become a way of remotely calling procedures. In very loose terms, they can be thought of as an RPC technology.

Thinking of web services as a way of implementing a strongly typed, contractual interface that is designed around an n-tier or a client/server model is exactly what I mean when I refer to component-based web service design.

Web Services As Services

You can also view a web service as a *service*. The fact that the word "service" is in the name of the technology might lead you to believe that they are *all* services, but that's not really true.

A service is an autonomous entity that performs some processing operation. You communicate with a service by sending and receiving *messages*. In today's world, those messages are almost always XML documents or fragments, though nothing in SOA mandates the use of XML.

Of course, web services *do* mandate the use of XML, so when implementing service-oriented web services, the messages are always XML. That said, .NET supports web services in such a way that you'll often interact with a strongly typed proxy object, rather than ever seeing the XML yourself.

Note I argue that this is a good thing. XML was never intended for human consumption, and a good programming toolset should always provide higher-level abstractions so programmers don't have to deal with XML directly.

Autonomy

The first big thing to realize is that services are *autonomous*. Technically, this means self-governing, but in the case of a service, it means totally independent. It means that the service is a thing unto itself and is *not* part of some other application. It is not a tier in an n-tier model.

This is entirely unlike the typical view of MTS/COM+ components, which are almost always viewed as being a tier in an n-tier or a client/server application.

Instead, a service is *an application*. Other applications (including other services) may interact with it, but the service stands alone.

The primary outcome of this view is that a service never trusts the data provided by any caller. I don't mean *trust* in just a security sense, but also in a semantic sense. Even data coming from an authenticated and authorized caller could be incorrect; either accidentally or maliciously. A service *always* validates and recalculates data from external sources. Services are paranoid.

Basing your services on business objects like those in this book works out well in this model, because all your business logic is in those objects. If the service merely provides an interface to the objects, then all the validation, calculation, and even authorization is automatically handled by the objects themselves.

Message-Based Communication

The other primary element of service orientation is that services communicate through *messages*. In short, this typically means that the method signature of a service-oriented web service looks like this:

```
Public Function AddCustomer(ByVal request As RequestMsg) As ResponseMsg
```

ResponseMsg and RequestMsg are formally defined message data types that represent XML messages sent between the caller and the service. In many cases, the messages are defined by an XSD schema.

Within a .NET application, however, the messages are almost always exposed as strongly typed proxy classes. So ResponseMsg might be defined like this:

```
Public Class ResponseMsg

  Private mResult As Boolean
  Public Property Result() As Boolean
    Get
      Return mResult
    End Get
    Set(ByVal value As Boolean)
      mResult = value
    End Set
  End Property
End Class
```

Notice that this is just a really fancy or complex way of returning the same Boolean value that was returned in the component-based AddCustomer() web method. The benefit here is that the return type starts out as a complex, formally defined type. It is comparatively easy to add more return information to ResponseMsg than it would be to return more information from the previous AddCustomer() implementation.

Similarly, RequestMsg would look something like this:

```
Public Class RequestMsg

  Private mId As Integer
  Public Property Id() As Integer
    Get
      Return mId
    End Get
    Set(ByVal value As Integer)
      mId = value
    End Set
  End Property
  ' other fields/properties go here…
End Class
```

Again, this is just another way of packaging all the parameters from the earlier AddCustomer() web method. And the benefit is the same; it is easier to add new elements to RequestMsg than to add them to the component-based model.

Perhaps more importantly is the benefit to versioning. The component-based approach suffers from the same limitation as COM did, in that you can't change the API. If your parameters are all exposed individually, the odds of having to change the API to add or change elements over time is quite high. To do this, you'll almost certainly end up creating AddCustomer2() and AddCustomerEx() methods—that sort of thing.

With a service-oriented message-based model, you can just add extra optional elements to `RequestMsg` and `ResponseMsg`. The API never changes, because the `AddCustomer()` method always accepts a single parameter and returns a single result.

Again, both the component-based and service-oriented worldviews are valid and useful in different scenarios. My goal here isn't to provide comprehensive coverage of SOA, SO, or even Web Services, as there are entire books on each of these topics. Rather, my goal is to provide you with some very basic background on the concepts before walking through the implementation of the web services to expose the `ProjectTracker` sample business objects.

Designing a Web Services Interface

In many ways, a Web Services interface is easier to construct than a Windows Forms or Web Forms interface because there's no need to worry about any issues of display or user interaction. Those are the responsibility of the calling application. All the web service needs to worry about is providing an interface that allows the developer of a consumer application to access the information and functionality provided by *this* application's business logic and data.

In designing a web service, the following four primary issues must be addressed:

- Whether to use a component-based or service-oriented design
- How to organize the web methods into classes
- What data to expose and accept
- How to handle authentication

Component-Based vs. Service-Oriented Design

I've already provided a high-level overview of these two models, and as I stated earlier in the chapter, I'll demonstrate both. In your applications, I recommend that you choose one model or the other and use it consistently, as that will provide a Web Services interface that is much easier to understand and consume.

It's possible to subdivide the `ProjectTracker` application's functionality in many different ways. For example, you could be very specific and provide a set of discrete services, such as those listed in Table 11-2.

Table 11-2. *Possible Web Methods*

Add project	Get project	Remove project	Change project name
Change project start date	Change project end date	Add resource	Get resource
Remove resource	Change resource first name	Change resource last name	Get list of projects
Get list of resources	Change project description	Add resource to project	Remove resource from project
Add project to resource	Remove project from resource	Change role of resource on project	and so on . . .

Following this approach, you could end up writing a rather large number of web methods! Although it's perfectly possible to do that, you might instead consider consolidating some of these operations into web methods with broader functionality, as follows:

- Get a list of projects
- Get details for a project
- Add or update a project
- Delete a project
- Get a list of resources
- Get details for a resource
- Add or update a resource
- Delete a resource

This is a smaller list of discrete operations, and by having fewer operations, there's less code to maintain. Moreover, this approach provides a higher level of abstraction—a consumer has no idea what happens when it requests details for a project, and over time you may change how that process works without having any impact on the consumers. Perhaps most importantly, having a small number of operations tends to improve performance, since a client application needs to make fewer cross-network method calls to get its work done.

The web methods implemented in this chapter fall into two categories. Those designed with a component-based approach are as follows:

- AddProject()
- EditProject()
- ChangeResource()
- AssignResource()

Those designed with a service-oriented, message-based approach are as follows:

- GetProjectList()
- GetProject()
- GetResourceList()
- GetResource()

This should give you an idea how both are handled.

Grouping Web Methods into Web Services

Under the .NET Framework, web methods are grouped together within a URL such as http://server/root/projecttracker.asmx, where projecttracker.asmx is the page or file that contains a class in the web service. Within a given virtual root on a given web server, there can be any number of such web service classes, each with its own set of web methods.

This, then, is a decision point in the design: should you put all the web methods into a single web service class, or put each web method in its own web service class, or something in between? Unfortunately, there's no hard-and-fast rule to guide the decision.

In this context, one way to view a web service is as a component that happens to be accessed via Internet technologies. A component is a container for similar groupings of functionality (COM or .NET components typically contain a group of related classes), so likewise a web service "component" should contain a group of related web methods. Of course, all the functionality in an application is related in some way; the question is whether it should be broken into multiple web services—perhaps one for project-related tasks and one for resource-related tasks.

However, there's another angle to this question that you need to consider before making a decision, and that's the consumer. Consumers don't reference an entire virtual root; they reference a specific web service (asmx file). The more granular you make the web service classes, the more different references the developer of the consumer will need to make in order to use the web methods.

Because of this, I prefer to group related web methods into web service classes based on the likely usage pattern of consumer developers. Since the web methods will all be related within the context of the ProjectTracker application, I'm following basic component design concepts; and since the web services are an interface to the application, I'm also taking into account the needs of the end user (the consumer application developer).

For the ProjectTracker sample application, this means putting all the web methods into a single web service class. They are all related to each other, so they naturally fit into a component. More importantly, it's likely that any consumer will be dealing with both projects and resources, and there's no sense in forcing the consumer developer to establish two separate references just to use all the web methods.

Returning and Accepting Data

The next issue is how to return complex business data. The data exists in the ProjectTracker. Library business objects, but it needs to be returned to the consumer via SOAP-formatted XML.

In many sample web services, the web methods return simple data types such as Integer or String, but that doesn't match the needs of most applications. In the ProjectTracker example, complex data must be returned, such as an array or a collection of project data. And the project data itself isn't a simple data type—it consists of multiple data fields.

There are a couple of approaches to consider, as follows:

- Returning the business objects directly, tying the data format directly to the object interface

- Using a formal facade to separate the data format from the business object interface

As you'll see, the more formal approach is superior, but to be thorough, let's discuss the first option, too.

Returning Business Objects Directly

It may seem tempting to return a business object (or an array of business objects) as a result of a web method. Why go through the work of copying the data from the business object into some formal data structure just so that data structure can be converted into XML to be returned to the consumer? After all, the .NET Web Services infrastructure can automatically examine a business class and convert all the Public read-write properties and Public fields of the object to XML, as shown in Figure 11-5.

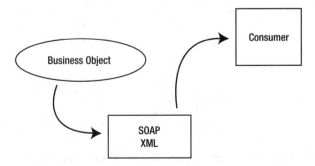

Figure 11-5. *Directly returning a business object's data to the consumer*

Unfortunately, there are two flaws with this approach that make it untenable. First and most important is the fact that doing this directly ties the business object's interface to the web service interface. This restricts the ability to change, enhance, and maintain business objects over time. If the business object is directly exposed, then the object's interface becomes part of the web service interface. This means that the object's interface is part of the contract established by publishing the web service. This is almost never acceptable, as it breaks any concept of encapsulation and separation of interface from implementation.

Second, make careful note of the fact that only the public, read-write properties, and public fields are exposed. Non-public properties aren't exposed. Read-only properties (such as Id on the Project and Resource objects) aren't exposed. This is because the Web Services implementation in ASP.NET relies on the XmlSerializer object to convert objects into and out of XML, and the XmlSerializer has limitations on what it will and won't serialize. Unless you're willing to compromise your object model's design specifically to accommodate the requirements of web service design, you won't be able to expose the data you choose via Web Services.

Beyond this, Web Services requires that objects to be converted to and from XML expose a public default constructor. If the class doesn't provide a public default constructor, you'll get a runtime exception when attempting to access the web service. The design of CSLA .NET business objects specifically precludes the use of public default constructors, as they always use Shared factory methods to create instances of the business objects.

Due to these drawbacks, directly exposing the business objects isn't a good practice. The answer instead is to create a facade around the business objects that can separate the public interface of the web service from the interface of the business objects. This facade can be constructed so that its properties and fields are always available for serialization into XML.

Returning Formal Data Structures

You can easily create a formal data structure to define the external interface of a web service by using a class. The data structure of the class will define the public interface of the web service, meaning that the web service interface is separate from the business object interface. The web service and this formal definition form a facade so that consumers of the web service don't know or care about the specific interface of the business object.

For instance, you can define a class that describes the data for a project like this:

```
Public Class ProjectData

  Private mId As Guid
  Private mName As String
  Private mStarted As String
  Private mEnded As String
  Private mDescription As String

  Public Property Id() As Guid
    Get
      Return mId
    End Get
    Set(ByVal value As Guid)
      mId = value
    End Set
  End Property
  ' remaining properties...
End Class
```

Then you can have the project-related web methods return a result of this type—or even an array of results of this type. When this is returned as a result from a web method, its data will be converted into SOAP-formatted XML that's returned to the consumer. Figure 11-6 illustrates what I'm talking about doing here.

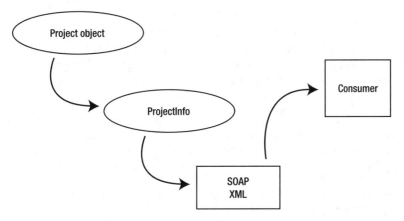

Figure 11-6. *Using a facade to define the data returned to the consumer*

When consumers reference the web service, they will gain access to the definition of this type via the WSDL data that's associated with the service. This means that the consumer will have information about the data being returned in a very clear and concise format.

■**Tip** When creating a consumer for the web service, Visual Studio uses this information to create a proxy class that mirrors the data structure. This gives consumer developers the benefits of IntelliSense, so that they can easily understand what data is required or returned from the web methods.

Authentication

The final consideration is authentication and security. Of course, there are many types and layers of security, but what I'm focusing on here is how to use either CSLA .NET or Windows integrated security to identify the users and their roles.

Even though the "user" in this case is a remote application, that application must still identify itself so that the business objects can apply their authorization rules. In short, a valid principal and identity object must be established to identify the calling application in some way.

The remote consumer may use a hard-coded username and password, or prompt its actual user for credentials. What that application does is entirely its business, and really has nothing to do with the web service. All the web service can do is ensure that the consumer provides valid credentials so a principal and identity can be created. The business objects contain the authentication rules to do the rest.

If you opt to use Windows integrated security, you'll need to configure IIS to disallow anonymous access to the virtual root containing the web service. You'll also add an <identity impersonate="true" /> element into the <system.web> section of the site's web.config file so that ASP.NET knows to impersonate the user account of the calling application. This will force the consumer to provide valid Windows credentials in order to interact with the web service.

No extra work is required in the web service or business object code, other than ensuring that the web.config file in the web service virtual root has the <appSettings> entry to configure CSLA .NET to use Windows security.

■**Tip** Windows integrated security is probably *not* a viable option in most cases. It's relatively unlikely that unknown clients on unknown platforms will be authenticated within your Windows domain. While the CSLA .NET architecture does support this option, using it would mean that consumers must start out with valid Windows domain accounts with which they can authenticate to your web server.

CSLA .NET security requires a bit more work, but avoids any necessity for the remote consumer (or its users) to have Windows domain user accounts in your environment. To implement CSLA .NET security, IIS should be left with the default configuration that allows anonymous users to access the virtual root. You must then include code in the web service to ensure that the calling code provides a username and password, which can be validated using the PTPrincipal class in the ProjectTracker.Library—just like in the Windows Forms and Web Forms interfaces.

The harder question is how to get the username and password from the consumer, and there are two basic approaches to an answer. The first of these is to have each web method include username and password parameters. Each time the consumer calls a web method, it would need to provide values for these two parameters (along with any other parameters the method requires). Within the web method, those two parameters could be passed to PTPrincipal.Login() to see if the credentials are valid.

Although this can work, it pollutes the parameter lists of all the web methods. Each method ends up with these two extra parameters that really have nothing to do with the method itself. This is far from ideal.

The other approach is to use the SOAP header to pass the information from consumer to server *outside* the context of the method, but as part of the same exchange of data. In other words, the username and password information will piggyback on the method call, but won't be part of the method call.

■**Tip** Web Services Extensions (WSE) offers a more advanced implementation of this concept. WSE includes the ability to encrypt the credentials over the network. In the future, Windows Communication Foundation (WCF or Indigo) will provide a similar advanced implementation. If you are going to pass credentials to web services, it is best to use one of these technologies that already provide the implementation.

This is a standard technique for passing extra information along with method calls. It's supported by the SOAP standard, and therefore by all SOAP-compliant client-development tools. What this means is that it's a perfectly acceptable approach—in fact, it's the preferred approach. I'll use it in the sample interface in this chapter.

One thing you need to keep in mind with this implementation is that the user's credentials are authenticated on every web service call. This could cause substantial load on your security database. Technologies such as WSE and WCF offer more advanced authentication options that may be more appropriate in many cases.

Web Service Implementation

The web service implementation can be found in the ProjectTracker solution. It is named PTWebService. As with the Windows Forms and Web Forms interfaces, I won't go through every method in detail. Instead I'll pick out some representative methods that highlight the concepts and you can examine the rest at your leisure.

Application Configuration

The website hosting the web service needs to provide some basic configuration information through the web.config file. In the web.config file, you can either provide connection strings so that the site can interact with the database directly, or you can configure the data portal to communicate with a remote application server.

The basic concept here was discussed in Chapter 4 when the channel adapter implementation was covered. Recall that the data portal supports four possible channels: local, remoting, Enterprise Services, and Web Services. You can create your own channels as well if none of these meet your needs.

In Chapter 1, I discussed the trade-offs between performance, scalability, fault tolerance, and security that come with various physical n-tier configurations. In most cases, the optimal solution for a web UI is to run the data portal locally in the client process. However, for security reasons, it may be desirable to run the data portal remotely on an application server. Chapter 12 will demonstrate how to create the three types of remote data portal hosts for use by the PTWeb application.

The web.config file is an XML file that contains settings to configure the website. You use different XML depending on how you want the site configured.

Authentication

The way authentication is handled by CSLA .NET is controlled through web.config:

```
<?xml version="1.0" encoding="utf-8" ?>
<configuration>
  <appSettings>
    <add key="CslaAuthentication" value="Csla" />
  </appSettings>
</configuration>
```

The CslaAuthentication key shown here specifies the use of custom authentication. Chapter 8 implemented the PTPrincipal and PTIdentity classes specifically to support custom authentication, and the UI code in this chapter will use custom authentication as well.

If you want to use Windows authentication, change the configuration to this:

```
<add key="CslaAuthentication" value="Windows" />
```

Of course, that change would require coding changes. To start, the PTPrincipal and PTIdentity classes should be removed from ProjectTracker.Library, as they would no longer be needed. Also, the virtual root would need to disallow anonymous users, and ASP.NET would need to be configured to impersonate the caller. Beyond that, the CslaCredentials custom SOAP header and related code discussed in this chapter would not be used.

Local Data Portal

To have the web service interact directly with the database, use the following (with your connection string changed to the connection string for your database):

```
<?xml version="1.0" encoding="utf-8" ?>
<configuration>
  <appSettings>
    <add key="CslaAuthentication" value="Csla" />
  </appSettings>
  <connectionStrings>
    <add name="PTracker" connectionString="your connection string"
      providerName="System.Data.SqlClient" />
    <add name="Security" connectionString="your connection string"
      providerName="System.Data.SqlClient" />
  </connectionStrings>
```

Because LocalProxy is the default for the data portal, no actual data portal configuration is required, so the only settings in the configuration file are to control authentication and to provide the database connection strings.

■**Tip** In the code download for this book (available at www.apress.com), the PTracker and Security database files are in the solution directory, not in the website's App_Data directory. This means that you can't use a local data portal from the website without first copying the database files into the App_Data directory and changing the connection strings accordingly.

Remote Data Portal (with Remoting)

To have the data portal use an application server and communicate using the remoting channel, the configuration would look like this:

```
<?xml version="1.0" encoding="utf-8" ?>
<configuration>
  <appSettings>
    <add key="CslaAuthentication" value="Csla" />
    <add key="CslaDataPortalProxy"
      value="Csla.DataPortalClient.RemotingProxy, Csla"/>
    <add key="CslaDataPortalUrl"
      value="http://localhost/RemotingHost/RemotingPortal.rem"/>
  </appSettings>
  <connectionStrings>
  </connectionStrings>
```

The key lines for remoting configuration are in bold. Of course, you need to change localhost to the name of your application server on which the data portal host is installed, and the RemotingHost text needs to be replaced with the name of your virtual root on that server.

Before using this configuration, the remoting host virtual root must be created and configured. I'll show how this is done in Chapter 12.

Remote Data Portal (with Enterprise Services)

Similarly, the configuration for using the Enterprise Services channel would look like this:

```
<?xml version="1.0" encoding="utf-8" ?>
<configuration>
  <appSettings>
    <add key="CslaAuthentication" value="Csla" />
    <add key="CslaDataPortalProxy"
      value="EnterpriseServicesHost.EnterpriseServicesProxy,
                  EnterpriseServicesHostvb"/>
  </appSettings>
  <connectionStrings>
  </connectionStrings>
```

Before using this configuration, an Enterprise Services host must be created and registered with COM+. The resulting COM+ application must be registered with COM on each client workstation. The basic steps were discussed in Chapter 4, and I'll show how this is done in Chapter 12.

Remote Data Portal (with Web Services)

Finally, the configuration for using Web Services would look like this:

```
<?xml version="1.0" encoding="utf-8" ?>
<configuration>
  <appSettings>
    <add key="CslaAuthentication" value="Csla" />
    <add key="CslaDataPortalProxy"
      value="Csla.DataPortalClient.WebServicesProxy, Csla"/>
    <add key="CslaDataPortalUrl"
      value="http://localhost/WebServicesHost/WebServicePortal.asmx"/>
  </appSettings>
  <connectionStrings>
  </connectionStrings>
```

As with remoting, you need to change localhost and WebServicesHost to the actual server name and virtual root name used by your application. Also, the virtual root and web service asmx file must be created and configured. I'll show how this is done in Chapter 12.

The most important thing to realize about the site configuration is that the data portal can be changed from local to remote (using any of the network channels) with no need to change any UI or business object code.

PTWebService Site Setup

The website references the ProjectTracker.Library project as shown in Figure 11-7. This causes Visual Studio to automatically put the associated Csla.dll files into the Bin directory as well, because Csla.dll is referenced by ProjectTracker.Library.

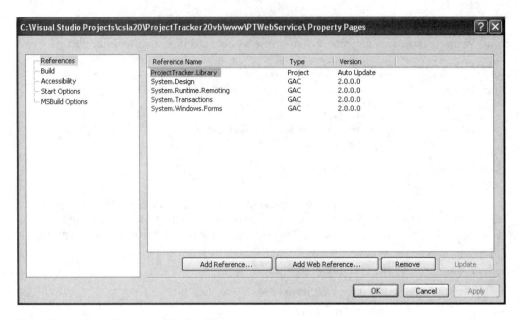

Figure 11-7. *Referencing ProjectTracker.Library*

Hosting in IIS

The PTWebService website will only run within IIS, not within ASP.NET Development Server (commonly known as Cassini or VS Host).

ASP.NET Development Server (provided with Visual Studio) has various limitations—among them is the inability to load custom security objects from assemblies in the Bin directory. This means you can't use ASP.NET Development Server to test or debug custom principal objects, custom membership providers, or other custom security objects if they are in an assembly referenced from the project.

Though this is an unfortunate limitation, it can be argued that ASP.NET Development Server is not intended for anything beyond hobbyist or casual usage, and that IIS should be used for any serious business development.

■**Note** An alternative solution is to install the assembly containing your custom principal and identity classes into the .NET Global Assembly Cache (GAC). For PTWebService, this would mean giving ProjectTracker. Library a strong name and using the gacutil.exe command line utility to install the assembly into the GAC. ProjectTracker.Library would need to be updated in the GAC after each time you build the assembly. I find that using IIS is a far simpler solution than using the GAC.

To host a website in IIS during development, you need to take the following steps:

1. Set up a virtual root in IIS, pointing to the directory containing the PTWebService project files.

2. Set the virtual root to use ASP .NET 2.0 using the ASP.NET tab of the Virtual Root Properties dialog in the IIS management console.

3. Set the website's start options using the Project Properties dialog in Visual Studio 2005. Change the setting to use a custom server so that it starts up using IIS with a URL such as http://localhost/PTWebService.

Now let's go through the creation of the web service interface. I'll start by discussing the authentication scheme, then move on to component-based web methods and wrap up by discussing service-oriented, message-based web methods. Once the web service has been covered, I'll briefly discuss the client application that calls the web service.

PTService

In .NET, a web service typically comes in two parts: the asmx file and an associated code file. The PTService.asmx file is really just a pointer to the code file:

```
<%@ WebService Language="VB"
  CodeBehind="~/App_Code/PTService.vb" Class="PTService" %>
```

All the interesting work happens in the code file, PTService.vb. This file can be found in the App_Code folder beneath the virtual root, and it contains the web service class, within which are all the web methods a consumer will use. I'll cover many of those web methods later, but here I want to show the declaration of the class itself:

```
<WebService(Namespace:="http://ws.lhotka.net/")> _
<WebServiceBinding(ConformsTo:=WsiProfiles.BasicProfile1_1)> _
<Global.Microsoft.VisualBasic.CompilerServices.DesignerGenerated()> _
Public Class PTService
  Inherits System.Web.Services.WebService
```

The class inherits from the WebService base class, and thus is a web service class. The <WebService()> attribute specifies the logical namespace for the web service. The domain name of the namespace is a meaningful value that corresponds to a specific organization. (You should use your organization's domain here instead of ws.lhotka.net.) This URI location doesn't need to exist, it just needs to be unique to your organization. Each web service needs a unique XML namespace to identify it so that client applications can distinguish it from other services on the Web.

The <WebServiceBinding()> attribute is placed here by Visual Studio when the web service is added to the application. It can be used to provide advanced control over the public interface exposed by the web service, and isn't directly relevant to this chapter.

Authentication

Earlier in the chapter, I discussed the authorization options available. While in a production application, you should probably use WSE or WCF, I'll show you how to pass credentials in the SOAP header using the web service support built into Visual Studio 2005.

To use custom authentication, include the following line in the <appSettings> element:

```
<add key="CslaAuthentication" value="Csla"/>
```

Tip You could also use the Windows integrated security model, as described earlier. However, if you decide to go down that route, you *must not* implement the security code shown here.

When using custom authentication, the Login() method of PTPrincipal will be called to validate the username and password values provided by the consumer that's calling the web service.

As discussed earlier, this could be done by putting username and password parameters on every web method, but that would pollute the parameter lists of the methods. Instead, a SOAP header can be used to transfer the values. This is a standard SOAP concept, and it's easily implemented in .NET code (on both the server and consumer).

■**Tip** Note that the username and password will be passed in clear text in the SOAP envelope. To encrypt this data for additional security, you may want to use the .NET Framework's cryptography support, expose the web service over SSL, or use WSE.

The following three steps are required in order to set up and use the SOAP header for security credentials:

1. Implement a SoapHeader class that defines the data required from the consumer.

2. Apply a <SoapHeader()> attribute to all web methods that require authentication, indicating that the web method requires the custom SOAP header.

3. Implement a method that takes the username and password values and uses them to authenticate the user, and set up the principal object on the current Thread.

Let's walk through the implementation of these steps.

CslaCredentials Class

SoapHeader is just a class that defines some fields of data that are to be included in the XML header data of a SOAP message. In this case, two values are needed: username and password. These values are passed in the SOAP header along with any method call requiring authentication. The SoapHeader class clearly defines this requirement:

```
Public Class CslaCredentials
  Inherits SoapHeader

  Public Username As String
  Public Password As String
End Class
```

The class itself is very simple—it just defines the two required data fields, as shown here:

```
Public Username As String
Public Password As String
```

More important is the fact that it inherits from System.Web.Services.Protocols.SoapHeader. This means that the CslaCredentials object's values will be automatically populated by the .NET runtime, based on the data in the SOAP header that's provided as part of the method call. To make this happen, a <SoapHeader()> attribute will be applied to each web method in the web service to indicate that the SOAP header data should be loaded into a CslaCredentials object.

Credentials Field

Within the PTService class, the code declares a CslaCredentials field, as follows:

```
Public Credentials As New CslaCredentials
```

This step is required because the actual data values will be placed into this object. There's no magic here—each web method that needs access to the user's credentials will have a <SoapHeader()> attribute that tells ASP.NET to load the SOAP header data into this specific object.

The use of this field, combined with the fact that the CslaCredentials class is Public in scope, means that the CslaCredentials type is included as part of the web service's WSDL definition.

The result is that any consumers referencing the web service will have full access to the type information, so they will clearly see the required username and password values.

> **Tip** When creating the consumer with Visual Studio, the consumer-side proxy class is created automatically for CslaCredentials, thus dramatically simplifying the process of providing the data. You'll see an example of this later in the chapter.

SoapHeader Attribute

With the SoapHeader class and corresponding field defined, any consumer that references the web service will have a clearly defined structure into which the username and password values can be placed. By default, web methods don't require SOAP headers. The <SoapHeader()> attribute is applied to a web method to indicate that it does require a specific SOAP header.

This attribute accepts a parameter that links the SOAP header to a specific SoapHeader field declared in the web service class—in this case, to the Credentials field of type CslaCredentials.

This means that any web methods requiring authentication will be declared like this:

```
<WebMethod(Description="A sample method")> _
<SoapHeader("Credentials")> _
Public Sub SampleMethod()
  ' Web method implementation code goes here
End Sub
```

When this method is invoked by a consumer, the .NET runtime uses reflection to find a field called Credentials. It then uses reflection against that Credentials field to discover its type. Based on that type information, it looks at the SOAP header data to find the SOAP header that matches that type, and takes the appropriate data out of the SOAP header and uses it to populate the field.

This SOAP XML might look something like this (the CslaCredentials header is displayed in bold):

```
POST /PTservice/projecttracker.asmx HTTP/1.1
Host: localhost
Content-Type: text/xml; charset=utf-8
Content-Length: 574
SOAPAction: "http://ws.lhotka.net/PTWebService/ProjectTracker/GetResourceList"

<?xml version="1.0" encoding="utf-8"?>
<soap:Envelope xmlns:xsi=http://www.w3.org/2001/XMLSchema-instance
    xmlns:xsd="http://www.w3.org/2001/XMLSchema"
    xmlns:soap="http://schemas.xmlsoap.org/soap/envelope/">
  <soap:Header>
    <CslaCredentials xmlns="http://ws.lhotka.net/PTWebService/ProjectTracker">
      <Username>string</Username>
      <Password>string</Password>
    </CslaCredentials>
  </soap:Header>
  <soap:Body>
    <GetResourceList xmlns="http://ws.lhotka.net/PTWebService/ProjectTracker" />
  </soap:Body>
</soap:Envelope>
```

That data is used to create a CslaCredentials object, which is provided to PTService through the Credentials field. Then the web method itself is called.

■**Note** Notice that the <SoapHeader()> attribute indicates a *required* SOAP header, so the web method can *only* be called by a consumer that provides this information.

This means that by the time the web method code is running, the Credentials field will be loaded with the username and password values provided by the consumer via the SOAP header.

Validating the Credentials

At this point, you should understand how to require a consumer to provide a username and a password, and how to make those values available to your web service code through a field declared in the web service class.

Given this information, it is now possible to use the username and password values to authenticate the caller by using PTPrincipal.Login(). This method was discussed in Chapter 8. It validates the caller's credentials and sets the current principal object to the resulting PTPrincipal. Since this code is running inside ASP.NET, Csla.ApplicationContext sets the HttpContext.Current.User property with this value.

As with the PTWeb interface in Chapter 10, it is also important to set the User property from the current HttpContext. Though the business objects and most of the .NET Framework rely on the Thread object to get the current principal, most web-related code relies on HttpContext.Current. User instead. Setting both values ensures that all code will use the same principal object.

The Security class in the App_Code directory contains a Login() helper method to take care of the details:

```
Public Sub Login(ByVal credentials As CslaCredentials)
  If Len(credentials.Username) = 0 Then
    Throw New System.Security.SecurityException( _
      "Valid credentials not provided")
  End If

  ' set to unauthenticated principal
  PTPrincipal.Logout()

  With credentials
    PTPrincipal.Login(.Username, .Password)
  End With

  If Not Csla.ApplicationContext.User.Identity.IsAuthenticated Then
    ' the user is not valid, raise an error
    Throw New System.Security.SecurityException("Invalid user or password")
  End If
End Sub
```

This method accepts the CslaCredentials object created by .NET and uses its values to call PTPrincipal.Login(). If the credentials are valid, then the current principal is set to use the new principal object. Otherwise, an exception is thrown to notify the caller that their credentials were invalid.

All of this work ensures that only valid, authenticated users gain access to the web methods, provided that those methods have the following structure:

```
<WebMethod(Description="A sample method")> _
<SoapHeader("Credentials")> _
Public Sub SampleMethod()
  ' user credentials required.
  Security.Login(Credentials)

  ' Web method implementation code goes here
End Sub
```

Web methods that don't require authentication simply don't use the `<SoapHeader()>` attribute or call `Security.Login()`. Instead they call a different method, `Security.UseAnonymous()`:

```
Public Sub UseAnonymous()
  ProjectTracker.Library.Security.PTPrincipal.Logout()
End Sub
```

Remember from Chapter 8 that `PTPrincipal.Logout()` sets the current principal value to an unauthenticated `PTPrincipal`. A remote data portal will only accept a principal object that inherits from `Csla.Security.BusinessPrincipalBase`, and so this code ensures that the current principal is such a principal object.

With the authentication scheme covered, let's move on to discuss the implementation of actual web methods.

Component-Based Web Methods

First, let's look at how you can construct component-based or API-style web methods. These are methods designed in much the same way you might have designed methods for MTS or COM+ components over the past decade or so. Each method accepts a set of strongly typed parameters and returns a strongly typed result.

In the `PTWebService` project, you'll find several methods of this type, including the following:

- `AddProject()`
- `EditProject()`
- `ChangeResourceName()`
- `AssignResource()`

All of these web methods follow the same basic structure, so I'll just walk through one of them: `AddProject()`.

AddProject

The `AddProject()` web method allows a caller to add a new project to the system. To avoid breaking encapsulation, the actual `Project` class is never exposed to the consumer of the web service. Instead, a set of detailed parameters are exposed, making it clear to the consumer what data is required when adding a project:

```
<WebMethod(Description:="Add a project")> _
<SoapHeader("Credentials")> _
Public Function AddProject( _
  ByVal name As String, ByVal started As String, ByVal ended As String, _
  ByVal description As String) As ProjectData
```

```
    ' user credentials required
    Security.Login(Credentials)

    Try
      Dim proj As Project = Project.NewProject
      With proj
        .Name = name
        .Started = started
        .Ended = ended
        .Description = description
      End With
      proj = proj.Save

      Dim result As New ProjectData
      Csla.Data.DataMapper.Map(proj, result, "Resources")
      Return result

    Catch ex As Csla.DataPortalException
      Throw ex.BusinessException

    Catch ex As Exception
      Throw New Exception(ex.Message)
    End Try
  End Function
```

Since this method alters data, it requires that the caller provide credentials for authentication:

```
<SoapHeader("Credentials")> _
```

The first thing the code does is validate these credentials:

```
Security.Login(Credentials)
```

If the credentials aren't valid, the Login() method throws an exception, so any code subsequent to this point can be assured that the credentials were valid.

However, it is important to realize that the Project object will still apply its normal *authorization* rules based on these credentials. In other words, the web method code is *not* responsible for preventing an unauthorized user from adding a new project, because the Project object itself takes care of those details.

Thanks to the fact that all validation and authorization is in the Project object, the web method code is very straightforward. It creates a new Project, loads the parameter values from the caller into the object's properties, and then calls the Save() method to commit the change:

```
    Dim proj As Project = Project.NewProject
    With proj
      .Name = name
      .Started = started
      .Ended = ended
      .Description = description
    End With
    proj = proj.Save
```

This is all within a Try...Catch block. Notice that the Catch blocks simply rethrow the exceptions. You could add logging code here if desired, but you should remember to rethrow the exception as well. When exceptions are thrown from within the web service class itself, the message text from the exception is automatically returned to the consumer so that it gets some information about what went wrong.

If no exception occurs and the Save() call succeeds, then the updated project data is returned to the caller. To do this, a ProjectData object is created, loaded with the data from the Project object, and returned as a result:

```
Dim result As New ProjectData
Csla.Data.DataMapper.Map(proj, result, "Resources")
Return result
```

The DataMapper functionality discussed in Chapter 5 is used to copy the values from Project into ProjectData. If you want to avoid that use of reflection, you can write code to manually copy each property value.

The first question you might ask is why this code doesn't simply return the Project object itself. But remember that this is problematic for three reasons. First, Project has at least one read-only property (Id), and that value wouldn't be returned, thanks to the way Web Services serializes objects into XML. Second, that would break encapsulation by directly tying the internal implementation of the web service to its external interface. Finally, the Project class doesn't have a default constructor, which means the XmlSerializer can't serialize the object.

ProjectData Class

The ProjectData class offers a clear, abstract, and formal interface to the caller that is *separate* from the interface of Project itself. The ProjectData class is a *data transfer object* (DTO). This means that it is composed purely of Public read-write properties, with no internal code. In other words, this class should exactly match the code created by Visual Studio when it creates a proxy class for a web service.

In fact, if you are using XSD schemas to define the XML transferred to and from the caller, you can generate this class using the xsd.exe command line utility. In PTWebService, I wrote the class by hand, and it looks like this:

```
Public Class ProjectData

  Private mId As Guid
  Private mName As String
  Private mStarted As String
  Private mEnded As String
  Private mDescription As String
  Private mResources As New Generic.List(Of ProjectResourceData)

  Public Property Id() As Guid
    Get
      Return mId
    End Get
    Set(ByVal value As Guid)
      mId = value
    End Set
  End Property
  ' other properties go here
End Class
```

You can get the complete code from the download for this book.

Not only does this class include properties corresponding to those of Project, but it also includes a List(Of ProjectResourceData) field. I'll discuss this later, as this class will also be used by GetProjectList() and GetProject().

As you can see, component-based methods like AddProject() are relatively easy to implement. They simply accept a set of strongly typed parameters, potentially call Security.Login(), and then let the business objects do all the hard work. The code in AddProject() relies on the fact that the Project object will throw exceptions for any authorization violations, and that its Save() method will throw an exception if the object's validation rules are violated by the data provided from the consumer.

Now let's move on to look at service-oriented, message-based web method implementations.

Service-Oriented Web Methods

As discussed earlier, the primary definition of a service-oriented web method is that it accepts and returns messages. These messages are typically XML structures, but within .NET they are represented as strongly typed classes. You can create these classes by hand, or generate them from an XSD schema by using the xsd.exe command line utility.

The service-oriented web methods in PTWebService include the following:

- GetProjectList()
- GetProject()
- GetResourceList()
- GetResource()

They all work essentially the same way, and so I'll only walk through two of them in this chapter: GetProjectList() and GetProject().

It is important to realize that even though my examples in this chapter focus on retrieving data, you can use service-oriented techniques to implement methods like AddProject() (described earlier). AddProject() could just as easily have accepted a single message, rather than a long list of parameters, as it does in this chapter. Similarly, the GetProject() implementation shown following could accept strongly typed parameters rather than a request message.

My point is that you can switch between models, and the code in this chapter is primarily intended to show you how to implement each approach so that you can choose which is appropriate for your application.

GetProjectList

The GetProjectList() web method is intended to return a list of the projects in the ProjectTracker application. A consumer application can use this data however it wishes, and this method will allow anonymous access with no authentication. Recall that the ProjectList business object applies no authorization rules, and both the PTWin and PTWeb interfaces allow anonymous users access to the list of projects (and the list of resources through ResourceList).

This method provides an opportunity to see the simplest message-based implementation, and also demonstrates how to create a web method that doesn't use the custom authentication mechanism implemented earlier:

```
<WebMethod(Description:="Get a list of projects")> _
Public Function GetProjectList() As ProjectData()
  ' anonymous access allowed
  Security.UseAnonymous()

  Try
    Dim list As ProjectList = ProjectList.GetProjectList
    Dim result As New List(Of ProjectData)
    For Each item As ProjectInfo In list
      Dim info As New ProjectData
      Csla.Data.DataMapper.Map(item, info)
      result.Add(info)
```

```
      Next
      Return result.ToArray

    Catch ex As Csla.DataPortalException
      Throw ex.BusinessException

    Catch ex As Exception
      Throw New Exception(ex.Message)
    End Try
  End Function
```

Notice that there's no <SoapHeader()> attribute and no call to Security.Login(). Instead there's a call to Security.UseAnonymous():

```
Security.UseAnonymous()
```

Thus, any consumer can call this web method and get back data.

■**Tip** If you are using Windows integrated security, then security is applied at the virtual root level by IIS and always applies to all web services within that virtual root. In that case, you do not have the flexibility to allow anonymous users for some methods and not for others.

The method accepts no parameters, because it always returns all the projects in the database. The result is returned as an array of ProjectData objects. The ProjectData class was discussed earlier, during the implementation of AddProject().

This array is populated by looping through all the items in a ProjectList object and using DataMapper to copy the properties from each ProjectTracker.Library.ProjectInfo child object in the collection to a List(Of ProjectData) object. That list is then converted to an array, which is returned as a result:

```
      Dim list As ProjectList = ProjectList.GetProjectList
      Dim result As New List(Of ProjectData)
      For Each item As ProjectInfo In list
        Dim info As New ProjectData
        Csla.Data.DataMapper.Map(item, info)
        result.Add(info)
      Next
      Return result.ToArray
```

Web Services can't serialize complex collection types into XML, but it can serialize arrays without a problem. That is the reason for converting the List(Of ProjectData) into an array before returning it as a result.

GetProject

The GetProject() web method is a bit more interesting, because it returns the list of resources assigned to the project along with the rest of the project's information. Again, viewing project data isn't a restricted behavior, so no authentication is required, and Security.UseAnonymous() is called:

```
<WebMethod(Description:="Get a project")> _
Public Function GetProject(ByVal request As ProjectRequest) As ProjectData
  ' anonymous access allowed
  Security.UseAnonymous()
```

```
    Try
      Dim proj As Project = Project.GetProject(request.Id)
      Dim result As New ProjectData
      Csla.Data.DataMapper.Map(proj, result, "Resources")
      For Each resource As ProjectResource In proj.Resources
        Dim info As New ProjectResourceData
        Csla.Data.DataMapper.Map(resource, info, "FullName")
        result.AddResource(info)
      Next
      Return result

    Catch ex As Csla.DataPortalException
      Throw ex.BusinessException

    Catch ex As Exception
      Throw New Exception(ex.Message)
    End Try
  End Function
```

The body of this method retrieves the `Project` object based on the information provided through the `request` parameter:

```
    Dim proj As Project = Project.GetProject(request.Id)
```

ProjectRequest Class

The parameter is of type `ProjectRequest`:

```
Public Class ProjectRequest

  Private mId As Guid

  Public Property Id() As Guid
    Get
      Return mId
    End Get
    Set(ByVal value As Guid)
      mId = value
    End Set
  End Property
End Class
```

You can think of this object in much the same way as you would a criteria object for the data portal. By using a complex type for a parameter rather than a simpler type like `Integer` or `Guid`, the `GetProject()` method is easier to extend or change over time. Due to the way Web Services serializes objects into and out of XML, you can add extra properties to `ProjectRequest` over time *without breaking existing consumers*. This type of flexibility is powerful, as it means the `GetProject()` method can evolve over time with less impact on consumers as compared to an API-style approach based on individual strongly typed parameters.

Unfortunately, you can't remove properties, rename them, or change their data types over time without forcing changes in the code that consumes your web service. The rules for changing Web Services interfaces are basically the same as the rules were for COM interfaces in Visual Basic 6; you can add to an interface, but any change or removal of *existing* interface elements will force consumers of your web service to update their software to compensate.

Copying the Properties

Once the Project object is available, DataMapper is used to copy the properties from Project into a ProjectData object:

```
Csla.Data.DataMapper.Map(proj, result, "Resources")
```

The ProjectData class was discussed earlier when creating the AddProject() web method.

Once the Project object's data has been copied, the code loops through all the ProjectResource objects in the Project object's Resources collection. Each of these objects has its property values mapped to a ProjectResourceData object, which is added to the ProjectData object:

```
For Each resource As ProjectResource In proj.Resources
  Dim info As New ProjectResourceData
  Csla.Data.DataMapper.Map(resource, info, "FullName")
  result.AddResource(info)
Next
```

You've seen the ProjectData class and how it contains a List(Of ProjectResourceData) field. The AddResource() method simply adds the item to this field:

```
Public Sub AddResource(ByVal resource As ProjectResourceData)
  mResources.Add(resource)
End Sub
```

Let's look at the ProjectResourceData class and how it is used in ProjectData. This will make it clear why the AddResource() method is implemented as shown here.

ProjectResourceData Class

ProjectResourceData is also a simple DTO:

```
Public Class ProjectResourceData

  Private mResourceId As Integer
  Private mFirstName As String
  Private mLastName As String
  Private mAssigned As String
  Private mRole As Integer

  Public Property ResourceId() As Integer
    Get
      Return mResourceId
    End Get
    Set(ByVal value As Integer)
      mResourceId = value
    End Set
  End Property
  ' other properties declared here
End Class
```

You can see the complete code in the download for this book. Each ProjectResourceData object contains the data to be returned to the consumer for each ProjectResource business object.

ProjectResources Property

The really interesting challenge, however, is that Web Services can't serialize a List(Of T) into XML; so back in ProjectData, the List(Of ProjectResourceData) field is exposed as a property using the following code:

```
Public Property ProjectResources() As ProjectResourceData()
  Get
    If mResources.Count > 0 Then
      Return mResources.ToArray

    Else
      Return Nothing
    End If
  End Get
  Set(ByVal value As ProjectResourceData())
    mResources = New Generic.List(Of ProjectResourceData)(value)
  End Set
End Property
```

Notice how this property exposes an array of type ProjectResourceData externally, but maintains a List(Of ProjectResourceData) internally. It is easier to deal with a List(Of T) than an array, which is why the internal representation is a List(Of T).

This is also why the AddResource() method is used to add elements to the List(Of ProjectResourceData) field. Since that field is never exposed publicly as a List(Of T), there's no way for the GetProject() method to directly add items to the list.

Back in GetProject(), the resulting ProjectData, along with its list of ProjectResourceData objects, is returned to the consumer as a result:

```
    Return result
```

As with all the other web methods, this one implements exception handling to rethrow any exceptions so that the exception message text is provided to the consumer for its use.

At this point, you should understand how to create component-based or API-style web methods. And you should understand how to create service-oriented, message-based web methods. You can look at the rest of the code in the code download for this book.

The result is that you now have a web service interface to some of the ProjectTracker functionality. Consumers can now call these web methods to interact with the application's business logic and data. These consumers may be running on any hardware platform or OS, and may be written in virtually any programming language. Those details don't matter in any meaningful way.

The important thing is that any consumers will interact with the ProjectTracker data *through* the business logic in the business objects, including validation, authentication, and authorization— thereby making it difficult for a consumer to misuse the data or functionality.

Web Service Consumer Implementation

The thing about creating web services is that it's not a very satisfying experience. There's nothing to see—no visual reinforcement that you've accomplished anything.

While ASP.NET includes functionality to generate a test page for web services automatically, that isn't of much use with PTWebService. The test page created by ASP.NET is only useful for testing web services that accept simple data types as parameters, and it doesn't have any provision for handling custom SOAP headers. This means the test page can only be used to call the GetProjectList(), GetResourceList(), and GetRoles() web methods.

■**Note** Remember that PTWebService uses custom authentication, and so you must host the website in IIS, not in ASP.NET Development Server. To do this, set up a virtual root in IIS pointing to the PTWebService directory in order to run the web service code.

Still, there is value in that, since you can use this capability to quickly determine whether your web service works at all. Simply use the browser to navigate to the web service asmx file. Enter http://localhost/PTWebService/PTService.asmx, for example, into the address box, and you'll get an informational display about the web service and its capabilities, similar to what's shown in Figure 11-8.

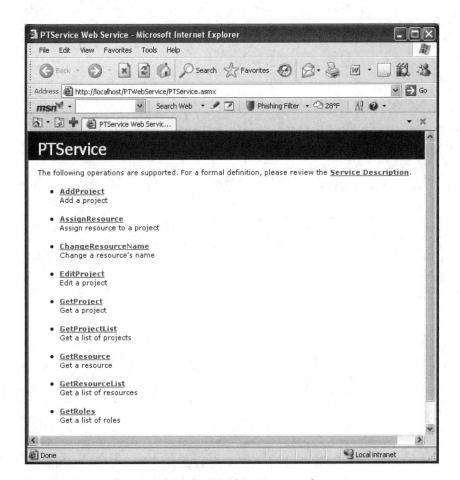

Figure 11-8. *Example output from the PTWebService test web page*

If you then click one of the links for a web method, you'll get details about that method. For instance, clicking the GetResourceList() method brings up a display similar to the one in Figure 11-9.

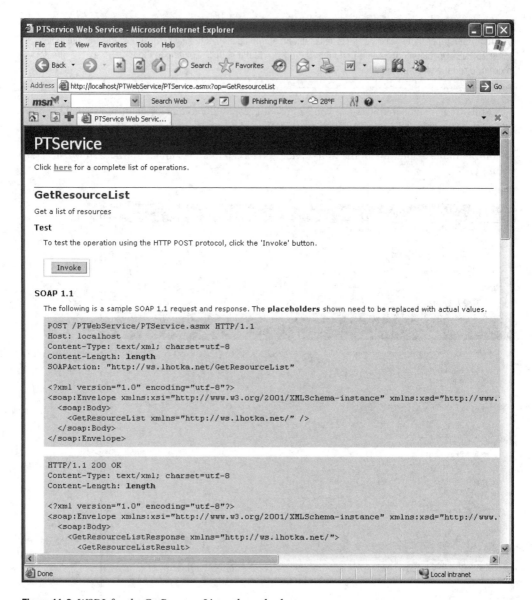

Figure 11-9. *WSDL for the GetResourceList web method*

With simple web methods, this display includes the ability to invoke the method from within the browser. For example, Figure 11-10 shows the result of clicking the Invoke button to execute the GetResourceList() web method.

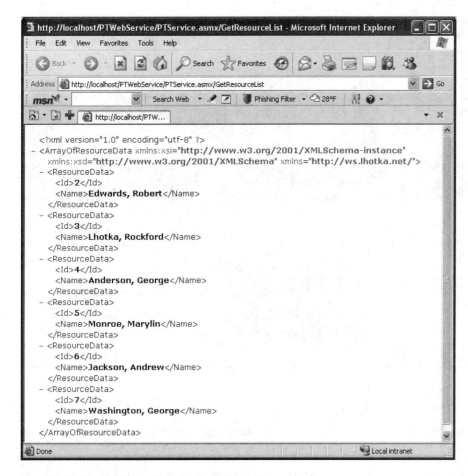

Figure 11-10. *Results of invoking the GetResourceList method*

Your results may vary, of course, depending on the data in your database.

A Simple Smart Client

To further illustrate how to call PTWebService, and in particular to show how to deal with the custom SOAP header for authentication, the ProjectTracker solution contains a PTServiceClient project. This is a bare-bones smart client application that acts as a consumer for PTWebService. Figure 11-11 shows what the application looks like when running.

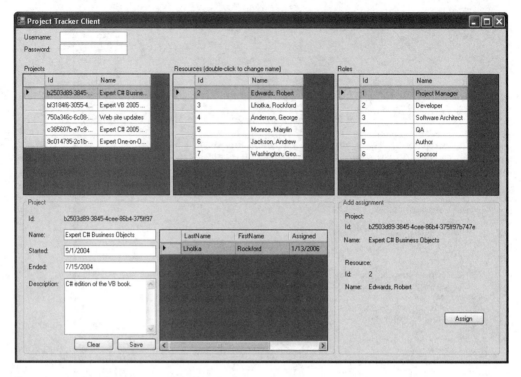

Figure 11-11. *The PTWebService client application*

My goal with this application isn't to create a complete consumer. I want to use this application to show how to consume a basic web service, and how to set up and pass credentials through the custom SOAP header.

As shown in Figure 11-12, `PTServiceClient` has a web reference to `PTService`.

Figure 11-12. *Web reference to PTService*

The URL behavior for this reference is set to Dynamic in the Properties window. This means that the URL for the web service is maintained in the app.config file:

```
<applicationSettings>
  <PTServiceClient.My.MySettings>
    <setting name="PTServiceClient_PTService_PTService"
             serializeAs="String">
      <value>http://localhost/PTWebService/PTService.asmx</value>
    </setting>
  </PTServiceClient.My.MySettings>
</applicationSettings>
```

The <applicationSettings> element is part of the configuration functionality provided by System.Configuration in .NET 2.0, and it is automatically used by Visual Studio when you set the URL behavior property to Dynamic for a web reference.

When you add a web reference to your project, Visual Studio uses the WSDL description for the web service to determine all the types it exposes, including CslaCredentials, ProjectData, and the other types accepted as parameters or returned as results from the web methods. Visual Studio uses this information to create proxy classes for all these types, so they can be used in the consumer code as though they were local classes.

Calling a Web Method

The data binding support in Windows Forms works against the proxy classes generated for a web service. This means you can add a type like ProjectData to the Data Sources window much like Project was added in Chapter 9. Figure 11-13 shows the Data Source Configuration Wizard listing all the types from the PTService web reference.

When you go to add a data source to the Data Sources window, the first step in the wizard includes the option to add a web service as a data source, as shown in Figure 11-14.

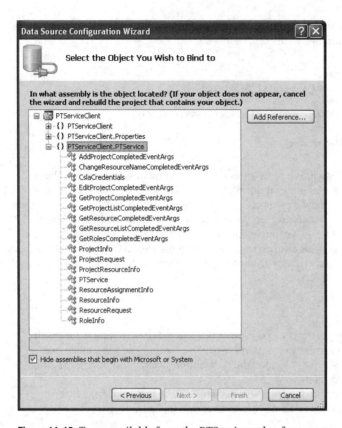

Figure 11-13. *Types available from the PTService web reference*

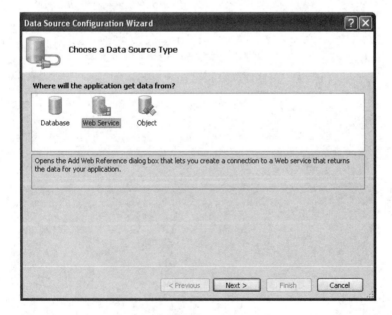

Figure 11-14. *Adding a web service as a data source*

While you can use this option, it gets you exactly the same result as if you manually add the web reference and then add the proxy objects as object data sources. In other words, web service proxy objects are always object data sources, regardless of whether you add them using the web service or object options in the Data Source Configuration Wizard.

Once the proxy types are in the Data Sources window, you can drag and drop them onto a form just like you would with any business object. This is how the `PTServiceClient` UI was built.

For each type you drag onto the form, Visual Studio creates a corresponding `BindingSource` object in the form's component tray. The UI controls are bound to the `BindingSource` control, and that `BindingSource` control is bound to your data.

Just like in Chapter 9, you need to write a bit of code to set the `DataSource` property of each `BindingSource` object. For instance, when the client's form loads, the following code is run:

```
Private Sub MainForm_Load( _
  ByVal sender As System.Object, ByVal e As System.EventArgs) _
  Handles MyBase.Load

  Using svc As New PTService.PTService
    Me.ProjectInfoBindingSource.DataSource = svc.GetProjectList
    Me.ResourceInfoBindingSource.DataSource = svc.GetResourceList
    Me.RoleInfoBindingSource.DataSource = svc.GetRoles
  End Using
End Sub
```

First, an instance of `PTService` is created:

```
Using svc As New PTService.PTService
```

Notice that it is within a `Using` block, so the object is properly disposed when the code is through with it. Then the project, resource, and role data is retrieved from the web service. Each resulting object is used to set a `DataSource` property, ultimately populating the three `DataGridView` controls across the top of the form shown in Figure 11-11.

Of course, this is the simple case, since these three web methods don't require authentication. Let's look at the case in which a method *does* require authentication using the custom SOAP header.

Providing Credentials for Authentication

To supply a SOAP header, the consumer needs to create an instance of the `SoapHeader` class; in this case, that means `CslaCredentials`. This object has its properties loaded with appropriate username and password values, and it is then attached to the consumer-side proxy for the web service.

To streamline this process throughout the client application, the code is centralized in a `SetCredentials()` helper method:

```
Private Sub SetCredentials(ByVal svc As PTService.PTService)
  Dim credentials As New PTService.CslaCredentials
  credentials.Username = UsernameTextBox.Text
  credentials.Password = PasswordTextBox.Text
  svc.CslaCredentialsValue = credentials
End Sub
```

First, a `CslaCredentials` object is created and loaded with values:

```
Dim credentials As New PTService.CslaCredentials
credentials.Username = UsernameTextBox.Text
credentials.Password = PasswordTextBox.Text
```

Because the `CslaCredentials` class was exposed by the web service, Visual Studio automatically created a consumer-side proxy class for it, used here.

The WSDL definition for the web service also indicated that there are web methods that require this as a SOAP header, so Visual Studio automatically added a CslaCredentialsValue property to the consumer-side proxy. To pass a CslaCredentials object to the server as a SOAP header, all you need to do is set this CslaCredentialsValue property!

```
svc.CslaCredentialsValue = credentials
```

With that done, it becomes relatively easy to call a web method that requires authentication. For instance, the following code is called to assign a resource to a project:

```
Using svc As New PTService.PTService
  SetCredentials(svc)
  Try
    ' do the assignment
    svc.AssignResource( _
      CInt(Me.ResourceIdLabel.Text), New Guid(Me.ProjectIdLabel.Text))
    ' refresh the detail view
    Dim request As New PTService.ProjectRequest
    request.Id = New Guid(Me.ProjectIdLabel.Text)
    Me.ProjectDetailBindingSource.DataSource = svc.GetProject(request)

  Catch ex As Exception
    MessageBox.Show(ex.Message, "Assign resource", _
      MessageBoxButtons.OK, MessageBoxIcon.Exclamation)
  End Try
End Using
```

As before, an instance of the web service proxy is created:

```
Using svc As New PTService.PTService
```

Before doing anything else, however, the credentials are attached to this object:

```
SetCredentials(svc)
```

Now all web method calls within this Using block will automatically have the custom SOAP header with the credentials passed to the server. So when AssignResource() is called, it can authenticate the credentials, and the business objects can authorize the action based on the roles for the supplied username:

```
svc.AssignResource( _
  CInt(Me.ResourceIdLabel.Text), New Guid(Me.ProjectIdLabel.Text))
```

Interestingly, the custom SOAP header is also passed to the subsequent GetProject() call:

```
Me.ProjectDetailBindingSource.DataSource = svc.GetProject(request)
```

This doesn't cause any problem. The GetProject() web method doesn't have a <SoapHeader()> attribute, so the custom SOAP header is simply ignored by the server-side code.

You can look through the rest of the client code in the code download for the book. At this point, however, you should understand how to set up web service proxy objects as data sources for Windows Forms, how to call simple web methods, and how to call web methods that require a custom SOAP header.

Conclusion

Web services enable the creation of another type of interface to business objects. Rather than exposing an interface directly to users, as with Windows forms or web forms, web services expose an interface for use by other, external applications. Those applications can call your web methods to leverage the business functionality and data provided by your application and its business objects.

You can design your web services along the lines of MTS or COM+ components, effectively creating a public API for your application. In such a case, most people tend to think of the web service as implementing a tier in an n-tier or a client/server model.

In many cases, it is better to follow service-oriented thinking, which specifies that a service (web service or otherwise) is an autonomous entity—an independent application, *not* a tier within a larger application. Service orientation also specifies that your web methods should communicate using a message-based approach, for which a web method accepts a complex type as a message, and returns a complex type as a resulting message.

In this chapter, I demonstrated how to create web methods using both approaches, so you can decide which works best in your application.

The example web service and client illustrate how you can expose all the functionality of your business objects without duplicating business logic in the web service interface itself. The validation, authentication, and other business logic is all encapsulated entirely in the business objects.

Chapter 12 will close the book by showing how to create remote data portal hosts for remoting, Web Services, and Enterprise Services. These remote hosts can be used by the Windows Forms, Web Forms, and Web Services interfaces you've seen in the last three chapters.

CHAPTER 12

■■■

Implementing Remote Data Portal Hosts

In Chapters 9 through 11, you saw how to implement Windows Forms, Web Forms, and Web Services interfaces to a common set of business objects. In each chapter, I briefly discussed the configuration options available in terms of running the server-side data portal components on the client or on an application server.

What I haven't discussed yet in detail is how to set up application servers to host the server-side data portal components and your business objects. As discussed in Chapter 4, the data portal implements a channel adapter pattern, allowing you to communicate from the client to the application server using .NET Remoting, Web Services, or Enterprise Services. It is also possible for you to create your own custom channel proxy and host if these standard technologies aren't sufficient for your needs.

It is my intent to provide a WCF (Windows Communication Foundation, or Indigo) channel proxy and host when that technology becomes available. You'll be able to find further information at www.lhotka.net/cslanet.

I want to be very clear, however, that I believe you should only use a remote data portal to achieve scalability, security, or fault tolerance objectives. As I discussed in Chapter 1, adding physical tiers to an application is a double-edged sword. You lose performance and increase complexity by adding tiers, so you should have a strong reason for doing so.

In this chapter, I will walk through the process of setting up and using three data portal application server hosts:

- .NET Remoting
- Web Services
- Enterprise Services

Though no code changes are required in your UI or business objects, each application server will require a slightly different set of steps to work.

In general terms, though, the process for each is similar:

1. Set up the host on the server.

2. Make your business object assembly available to that host.

3. Configure the client to use the new host.

To a large degree, the implementation of the data portal in Chapter 4 already took care of the hard parts, so these steps are relatively straightforward in each case.

Before creating each host, I want to spend a short time discussing why you might choose each of the channel technologies.

Data Portal Channel Comparison

Thanks to the way the data portal channel adapter functionality was implemented in Chapter 4, there is no functional difference between using .NET Remoting, Web Services, or Enterprise Services as used by your UI or business objects. In other words, you can switch between any of these channels and your application will continue to function in exactly the same manner.

So how do you decide which to use?

Factors for Comparison

As it turns out, there are some differences in performance and other behaviors, which you can use to decide between the channels. Table 12-1 lists the key differences.

Table 12-1. *Functional Comparison of Channel Technologies (1 = worst, 4 = best)*

Factor	Remoting	Web Services	Enterprise Services
Performance	3	2	4
Security	2	2	4
Host technology	IIS or custom	IIS	COM+
Firewall-friendliness	2	2	1
Ease of deployment	2	2	1
Ease of implementation	2	2	1

Notice that neither open standards nor interop are listed here. This is because the data portal is serializing *your business objects* across the network, so the only way that the data on the other end of the wire can be understood is if the data is deserialized back into *your business classes*. The data portal is an n-tier client/server concept, and neither interop nor XML standards on the network matter within this context.

■Tip If interop and readable XML are requirements for your application, you should use the concepts discussed in Chapter 11 to create a web service interface on top of your business objects.

However, for n-tier client/server applications, the factors listed in Table 12-1 are typically very important. Let's discuss each factor in turn.

Performance

When it comes to performance, you can find a wealth of opinions and a number of conflicting studies on the Web telling you what's faster and slower.

In general terms, though, you'll find that both remoting and Web Services are of relatively comparable performance. This makes sense because they are both web-based technologies and share a lot of common underpinnings within .NET. The reason I give remoting slightly higher marks than Web Services is because remoting transfers the serialized object data in a binary format that is substantially smaller than the Base64 encoded format used by Web Services.

■Tip You may be able to employ compression technologies when using Web Services to get similar or even smaller chunks of data on the network. Of course, that would mean an increase in CPU use on both client and server, so you need to test to see if this makes sense for you.

Perhaps more importantly, you'll find that Enterprise Services is *substantially* faster than either remoting or Web Services.

Of course, when it comes to performance, environmental factors make a big difference. What is your network topology? Your network load? Your server load? Due to these variables, you should do your own testing to determine which channel technology provides you with the best performance overall.

Security

The term "security" spans a wide area. In this case, I am talking about security in terms of knowing that the data came from the client, and whether the data is encrypted as it moves across the network between the client and server.

Both remoting and Web Services can use SSL (Secure Sockets Layer) communication over HTTP, which is typically the easiest and best way to provide a secure communication channel for these technologies.

If you are using the TCP channel and implement a custom host application, remoting also offers the ability to do its own encryption. This option is not available with the HTTP channel, so in that case you should use SSL.

Enterprise Services offers various levels of data encryption on the wire, and so has the most flexibility and capabilities in this area. Additionally, enabling secure communication using Enterprise Services is often easier than configuring SSL on a web server. If you are running in a Windows domain, just set your COM+ application properties as shown in Figure 12-1.

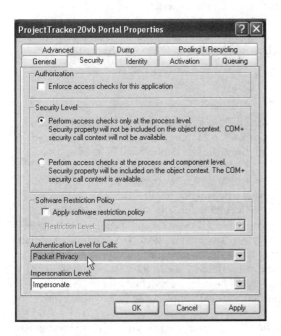

Figure 12-1. *Using packet privacy in Enterprise Services*

This is often far easier than the process required to enable SSL on a web server.

Host Technology

The host technology used by an application server can weigh heavily in some server environments. Some organizations disallow the use of IIS on certain types of servers.

Both remoting and Web Services can be hosted in IIS; technically within ASP.NET on IIS. This is an ideal configuration for remoting, since it gains all the benefits of running within IIS and ASP.NET. And it is the only real option for Web Services.

Remoting can also be hosted in a custom application of your design. Typically this would be a Windows service. I don't recommend this course of action, because you would need to duplicate a large percentage of IIS to achieve comparable levels of manageability, security, runtime monitoring, and so forth. In most cases, it is far preferable to use remoting within the context of IIS and ASP.NET.

Enterprise Services can only be hosted in COM+, because Enterprise Services is really just a wrapper around the existing COM+ services. This means that your server does *not* need IIS to host the data portal in Enterprise Services.

Firewall-Friendliness

Some organizations use internal firewall technology that makes the use of DCOM, and thus the Enterprise Services channel, problematic. The Enterprise Services channel uses DCOM as its network transport—and while it is technically possible to make DCOM work through a firewall, most organizations opt for a more firewall-friendly technology.

Both remoting and Web Services can use HTTP over port 80, and thus they are firewall-friendly by default. Even when using SSL, most firewalls allow that traffic as well.

When hosted in a custom host like a Windows Service, remoting can be configured to use raw TCP sockets over arbitrary ports. In that case, remoting would require extra firewall configuration to allow that traffic to flow. Again, I recommend hosting remoting in IIS, in which case this is not an issue.

Ease of Deployment

There are two aspects to deployment: client and server. Simple client deployment typically means that there is no need to register components, thus providing support for XCOPY deployment and ClickOnce. Server deployment is never "simple," but the goal is for deployment to be as easy and straightforward as possible.

When it comes to client deployment, both remoting and Web Services are trivial. Neither require special components or registration of any sort. They merely require that the client's configuration specify the data portal channel to be used, including the URL of the application server.

Enterprise Services is a bit more complex because the COM+ server application must be registered on the client. While this merely means running an extra `msi` installer on the client workstation or client web server, this extra step definitely complicates deployment of client applications.

On the server, all three technologies are relatively comparable. In the case of remoting (hosted in IIS) and Web Services, you need to set up and configure a virtual root in IIS. With Enterprise Services, you need to set up and configure a COM+ application using the server's Component Services tool.

Of course, if you choose to implement a custom host for remoting, it is up to you to ensure that server deployment and management is straightforward.

Ease of Implementation

Finally, there's the ease of implementation. As I mentioned earlier, neither your UI nor business object code varies depending on the data portal channel, so what I'm talking about here is the ease with which you implement the data portal host to run on the application server.

Remoting and Web Services have the edge here, because virtually all their implementation was done in Chapter 4. With remoting, all you need to do is add some lines to web.config on the server; while with Web Services, you need to create a one-line asmx file. Either approach is trivial.

Enterprise Services requires more work because COM+ has no concept of virtual roots. If you want to set up a COM+ application on the server with a unique name, you need a specific Enterprise Services component to put into that COM+ application. In other words, you can't put Csla.dll into COM+ multiple times and be able to configure each instance separately—something that you *can* do with virtual roots in IIS.

Due to this, you'll need to do some simple coding to create a unique Enterprise Services assembly for your particular application. Again, most of the work was done in Chapter 4, but this is an extra bit of work you need to do once for each business application you create (if you want to create an Enterprise Services data portal host).

In the final analysis, it is up to you which data portal channel technology to choose. The important thing to remember is that you can switch from one to the other without breaking your UI or business object code. This means you can try one channel and switch to another later if you determine it would better fit your needs. This flexibility will become particularly important once Microsoft releases WCF, since it should provide you with a largely transparent migration path to that technology.

.NET Remoting

The .NET Remoting technology provides good performance with easy deployment and configuration. This is typically my first choice when implementing a remote data portal. The easiest and best way to set up an application server to host your business objects through remoting is to use IIS and ASP.NET.

■Note As I mentioned earlier, I recommend hosting .NET Remoting within IIS and ASP.NET. While you can create your own custom remoting host, I won't discuss that option here.

To set up an application server for your application, follow these steps:

1. Create an empty web project in Visual Studio.

2. Add a reference to your business assembly or assemblies.

3. Ensure Csla.dll is in the Bin directory.

4. Add a web.config file.

5. Add a <system.runtime.remoting> element to expose the data portal.

6. Configure the client.

Let's walk through each step to set up a remoting host for the ProjectTracker sample application.

Implementation

The `ProjectTracker` solution in the code download for this book (available at www.apress.com) includes the virtual root and `web.config` file discussed in the following sections.

Creating the Virtual Root

The `RemotingHost` project in the `ProjectTracker` solution started out as an empty web project, created as shown in Figure 12-2.

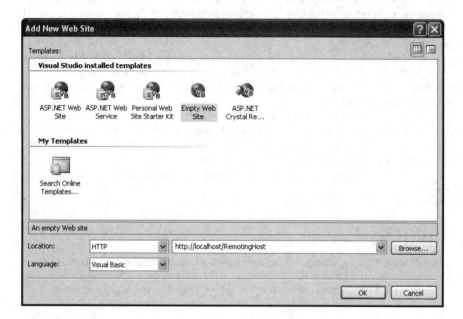

Figure 12-2. *Creating an empty website*

This allows Visual Studio to properly set up the directory as needed for ASP.NET.

Note You can use the ASP.NET Development Server during development if you choose. While hosting Web Forms and Web Services interfaces is problematic due to assembly load issues, I typically do my development for remoting using this host rather than IIS.

To this empty website I added the appropriate references, and a `web.config` file to configure remoting to expose the `Csla.Server.Hosts.RemotingProxy` class.

Referencing Assemblies

When running, the remoting host needs access to your business classes from your business assembly or assemblies. What this means in practice is that your business assemblies must be in the `Bin` subdirectory of the virtual root.

You can copy them there manually, but an easy way to get them into the `Bin` directory is to have the project reference them in Visual Studio. This way, any time you change your business objects and rebuild the solution, the updated assemblies are automatically copied into the Bin directory by Visual Studio.

The Csla.dll assembly must also be in the Bin directory. Since ProjectTracker.Library references Csla.dll, Visual Studio automatically copies it into the Bin directory because ProjectTracker. Library is referenced. If you opt to copy your business assemblies manually into the Bin directory, you'll need to either explicitly reference Csla.dll or manually copy it into the Bin directory as well.

Configuring web.config

With the virtual root set up and the required assemblies in the Bin directory, all that remains is to configure ASP.NET to use remoting. This is done by adding a <system.runtime.remoting> element to web.config. Of course, when starting with an empty website, you need to add a web.config file first.

The required <system.runtime.remoting> section looks like this:

```
<system.runtime.remoting>
  <application>
    <service>
      <wellknown mode="SingleCall" objectUri="RemotingPortal.rem"
            type="Csla.Server.Hosts.RemotingPortal, Csla"/>
    </service>
    <channels>
      <channel ref="http">
        <serverProviders>
          <provider ref="wsdl"/>
          <formatter ref="soap" typeFilterLevel="Full"/>
          <formatter ref="binary" typeFilterLevel="Full"/>
        </serverProviders>
      </channel>
    </channels>
  </application>
</system.runtime.remoting>
```

This configures ASP.NET to expose the Csla.Server.Hosts.RemotingPortal class such that clients can create instances of the class through remoting over HTTP.

Note There are many different options for configuring remoting. I won't cover them all here, but instead I'll focus only on those used in the previous configuration code. For more information on remoting, I recommend you look at Ingo Rammer's book, *Advanced .NET Remoting in VB .NET* (Apress, 2002).

When configuring remoting, the <wellknown> element identifies a server-side (anchored) class that can be used by clients. When using this element, you must decide between the two different operation modes:

- If the mode attribute is set to SingleCall, each method call from any client will cause the server to create a new object that will handle just that one method call. The object isn't reused in any way after that, and is destroyed automatically via the .NET garbage-collection mechanism.

- If the mode attribute is set to Singleton, all method calls from all clients will be handled by a single object running on the server. Many method calls may be handled on different threads at the same time, meaning that the application's code would have to be entirely safe for multithreading.

Implementing an object for the Singleton mode can be very complex, because you have to deal with multithreading issues. Typically, this means using thread-synchronization objects, which will almost always reduce performance and increase complexity.

For most server-side behavior, SingleCall is ideal because each method call is handled by a newly created object that has its own thread. You don't need to worry about threading issues, or about one client interfering with another in some way.

Having selected a mode, you need to define the URI that will be used to access the server-side object. This URI is combined with the server name and virtual root to construct a URL that clients can use to call the server. The URL is in the form http://yourserver/yourvroot/testserver.rem, where yourserver is the name of your server and yourvroot is the name of your virtual root.

■**Note** The .rem extension is important. When ASP.NET is installed on a server, it configures IIS to route .rem and .soap extensions to the remoting subsystem. Either extension will work, as they're both configured to do the same thing.

Finally, you need to tell the remoting subsystem which specific class and DLL this URL refers to. The type attribute is somewhat cryptic because it accepts a string that contains the full name (including namespaces) of the class, a comma, and then the name of the assembly (DLL) that contains the class. Note that the assembly name doesn't include the .dll extension.

With the well-known endpoint defined, clients can call the server. However, to allow for full serialization of complex object graphs, remoting must be told to allow any type to be serialized. This is the purpose behind the XML in the <channels> element. This XML sets the typeFilterLevel attribute to Full for both the SoapFormatter and BinaryFormatter in the .NET Framework. As these are the two formatters supported by remoting, this ensures that all serializable objects can flow through to the data portal.

Configuring the Client

At this point, the application server is configured and is ready for use by clients. The same application server can be used by Windows Forms, Web Forms, and Web Services clients—even all at once, if you choose. The only requirement is that both the application server and clients have the same version of your business assemblies installed.

To configure a Windows Forms client, you need to edit the app.config file. To configure either a Web Forms or Web Service client, you need to edit the web.config file.

In either case, the configuration file should contain the following bold lines:

```
<?xml version="1.0" encoding="utf-8" ?>
<configuration>
  <appSettings>
    <add key="CslaAuthentication" value="Csla" />
    <add key="CslaDataPortalProxy"
      value="Csla.DataPortalClient.RemotingProxy, Csla"/>
    <add key="CslaDataPortalUrl"
      value="http://localhost/RemotingHost/RemotingPortal.rem"/>
  </appSettings>
  <connectionStrings>
  </connectionStrings>
</configuration>
```

The CslaDataPortalProxy element specifies that the data portal should use the remoting channel, and the CslaDataPortalUrl element specifies the URL of the server. You'll need to replace localhost with the name (and possibly the TCP port) of your server, and RemotingHost with the name of your virtual root. Also remember that XML is case sensitive, so double-check to make sure you enter the text *exactly* as shown here.

Of course, web.config should also include the connection strings for the database in the <connectionStrings> element. You can see an example in the code download for the book.

Encrypting Data on a TCP Channel

If you do implement a custom remoting host and opt to use the TCP channel rather than the HTTP channel, you can optionally also include the following element within the <appSettings> block:

```
<add key="CslaEncryptRemoting"
     value="true"/>
```

Adding this element tells the RemotingProxy class to automatically encrypt data sent across the network. This option is not available when using the HTTP channel, so in that case, you should use SSL to secure the channel.

At this point, you should understand how to set up an application server to use remoting, and how to configure a client to use that server.

Web Services

Web Services is often preferred over remoting because it provides interoperability with external systems. That use of Web Services was discussed in Chapter 11, and really has no bearing on the data portal.

The data portal is designed to be an n-tier client/server technology that allows you to add a physical tier so your logical business layer can run on both the client and application server as needed. Because of this, the data portal isn't designed with interop in mind, but rather with high-level functionality to clone object graphs across the network. Thus, at first glance, the data portal and Web Services appear to be entirely incompatible.

Yet I am frequently asked to provide Web Services support for the data portal, primarily by architects and developers forced to use Web Services by management that doesn't understand its intended purpose. In other words, Web Services is sometimes mandated as a network transport even when the technology really make no sense. That is the primary reason CSLA .NET provides data portal support for Web Services.

As discussed in Chapter 4, the WebServicesProxy directly uses the BinaryFormatter to serialize the object graph for transmission. Although it does use Web Services to transport the data, the data itself is a byte array created and consumed by the BinaryFormatter on either end of the connection. By using this technique, the WebServicesProxy is able to provide all the high-level functionality of remoting or Enterprise Services while still technically using the Web Services network transport.

To set up an application server for your application, follow these steps:

1. Create a Web Services project in Visual Studio.

2. Add a reference to your business assembly or assemblies.

3. Ensure Csla.dll is in the Bin directory.

4. Edit the asmx file to refer to WebServicesProxy.

5. Configure the client.

Of course, web.config will also include the connection strings for the database in the <connectionStrings> element. You can see an example in the code download for the book.

■Note You can put the asmx file discussed here into almost any ASP.NET website. There's nothing special about web service projects or sites, so it is technically possible to even host the data portal web service through a website like PTWeb from Chapter 10 if you wanted. However, most people prefer to keep the data portal physically separate from their UI code.

Let's walk through each step to set up a Web Services host for the ProjectTracker sample application.

Implementation

The ProjectTracker solution in the code download for this book includes the Web Services project discussed here.

Creating the Web Service Project

The WebServicesHost project in the ProjectTracker solution was created as a web service project, as shown in Figure 12-3.

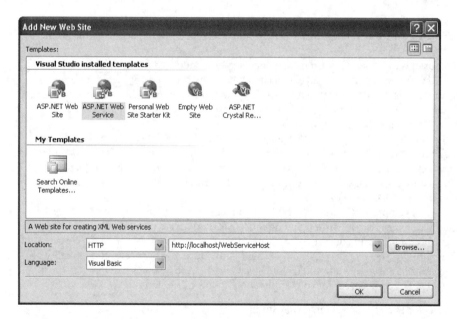

Figure 12-3. *Creating a web service project*

This allows Visual Studio to properly set up the directory as needed for ASP.NET.

■Note You can use ASP.NET Development Server during development if you choose. While hosting Web Forms and Web Services *interfaces* is problematic due to assembly load issues, it is not a problem when hosting the data portal. I typically do my development using this host rather than IIS.

I altered this basic web service website by adding the appropriate references and changing the asmx file to expose the `Csla.Server.Hosts.WebServicesProxy` class.

Referencing Assemblies

As when using remoting, the web service host needs access to your business classes from your business assembly or assemblies. What this means in practice is that your business assemblies must be in the `Bin` subdirectory of the virtual root.

Again, you can copy them manually, but an easy way to get them into the `Bin` directory is to have the project reference them in Visual Studio. That way, any time you change your business objects and rebuild the solution, the updated assemblies are automatically copied into the `Bin` directory by Visual Studio.

The `Csla.dll` assembly must also be in the `Bin` directory. Since `ProjectTracker.Library` references `Csla.dll`, Visual Studio automatically copies it into the `Bin` directory because `ProjectTracker.Library` is referenced. If you opt to copy your business assemblies manually into the `Bin` directory, you'll need to either explicitly reference `Csla.dll` or manually copy it into the `Bin` directory as well.

The asmx File

By default, a new web service project has a `Service1.asmx` file, and an associated `Service1.vb` file in the `App_Code` directory.

CSLA .NET already includes the `WebServicesProxy` class discussed in Chapter 4. It provides the full web service functionality required by the data portal, so all the website really needs is an asmx file referring to that code. To get such a file, you can either edit `Service1.asmx` or add a new asmx file to the project. In any case, the code-behind file (`Service1.vb`) can be deleted, as it won't be used.

In the `WebServicesHost` project, you'll find a `WebServicePortal.asmx` file with the following code:

```
<%@ WebService Language="VB" Class="Csla.Server.Hosts.WebServicePortal" %>
```

This points the `WebServicePortal` web service to use the code from Chapter 4, thus providing access to the data portal functionality.

Configuring the Client

At this point, the application server is configured and is ready for use by clients. The same application server can be used by Windows Forms, Web Forms, and Web Services clients—even all at once if you choose. The only requirement is that both the application server and clients have the same version of your business assemblies installed.

As with the previous options, to configure a Windows Forms client, you need to edit the `app.config` file. To configure either a Web Forms or Web Services client, you need to edit the `web.config` file.

In either case, the configuration file should contain the following bold lines:

```
<?xml version="1.0" encoding="utf-8" ?>
<configuration>
  <appSettings>
    <add key="CslaAuthentication" value="Csla" />
    <add key="CslaDataPortalProxy"
      value="Csla.DataPortalClient.WebServicesProxy, Csla"/>
    <add key="CslaDataPortalUrl"
      value="http://localhost/WebServicesHost/WebServicePortal.asmx"/>
  </appSettings>
```

```
<connectionStrings>
</connectionStrings>
</configuration>
```

The `CslaDataPortalProxy` element specifies that the data portal should use the Web Services channel, and the `CslaDataPortalUrl` element specifies the URL of the server. You'll need to replace `localhost` with the name of your server, and `WebServicesHost` with the name of your virtual root. Also remember that XML is case sensitive, so double-check to make sure you enter the text *exactly* as shown here.

At this point, you should understand how to set up an application server to use Web Services, and how to configure a client to use that server.

Enterprise Services

The Enterprise Services channel uses DCOM as its network transport. The primary advantage of DCOM is that it offers superior performance over Web Services and remoting. It is sometimes also easier to encrypt data on the wire using Enterprise Services than it is to set up SSL on web servers, which is how you would encrypt the data for remoting (using the IIS host) or Web Services.

Of the three technologies supported by CSLA .NET, Enterprise Services is the most complex to use, since it requires that you create a custom assembly for your application, and that you install that assembly into COM+ on the server. You must also register that COM+ application on each client before it can be used.

To set up an application server for your application, follow these steps:

1. Create an Enterprise Services proxy/host assembly for your application.

2. Reference `Csla.dll` and your business assemblies.

3. Install your proxy/host assembly into COM+ on the server.

4. Create a configuration directory for the code on the server.

5. Configure the COM+ application on the server.

6. Export the COM+ application to create and install `msi`.

7. Configure the client.

Let's walk through each step to set up an Enterprise Services host for the `ProjectTracker` sample application.

Creating the Proxy/Host Assembly

The `ProjectTracker` solution in the code download for this book includes the Enterprise Services proxy/host assembly and its related files as discussed here. Once I've walked through the steps to create the proxy/host assembly, I'll show how to install it in COM+ and how to export a client setup `msi` from COM+.

The proxy/host assembly is used by the client to call the server, so it contains a proxy object. The client calls that proxy object, which in turn calls the host object on the server. The assembly also contains the host object, which is actually installed in COM+ on the application server. This is illustrated in Figure 12-4.

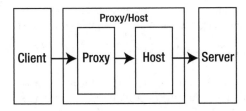

Figure 12-4. *Client calling the server through a proxy and host*

There are a number of steps to create the proxy/host assembly. Let's walk through each step.

Configuring the Class Library Project

The `EnterpriseServicesHostvb` project in the `ProjectTracker` solution is a normal Class Library project. It is designed so that it can be hosted in Enterprise Services, which means following these steps after creating a Class Library:

1. Reference `System.EnterpriseServices.dll`.

2. Sign the assembly.

3. Add an `EnterpriseServicesSettings.vb` file with special attributes.

In order to use the features of Enterprise Services, your assembly must reference `System.EnterpriseServices.dll`. Additionally, to be installed in COM+, the assembly must have a strong name, which really means that it must be signed with a key file by setting the project's properties as shown in Figure 12-5.

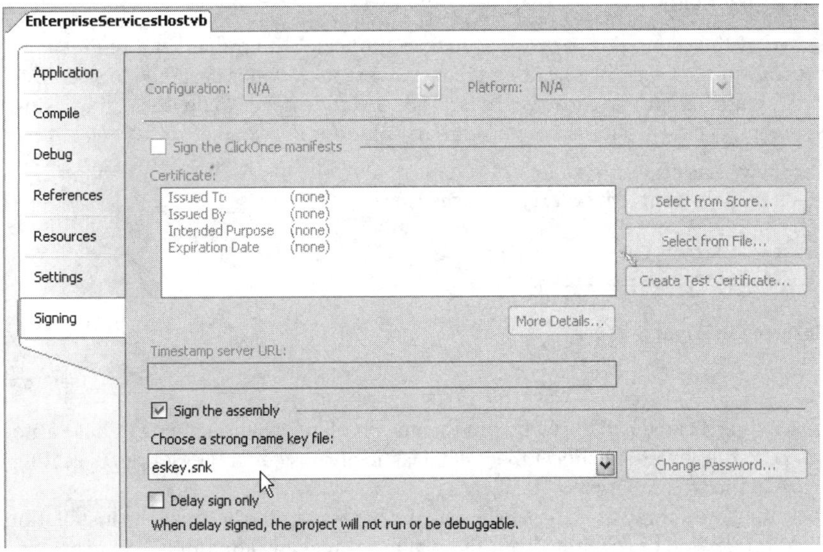

Figure 12-5. *Signing the assembly*

You can either create a key file directly within the project properties window or use a preexisting key file. Typically, an organization will have a common key file that is used to sign all assemblies created by that organization.

This allows the assembly to be installed in COM+ so that it is available through Enterprise Services.

The project also includes an `EnterpriseServicesSettings.vb` file. I added this file to the project as a class and simply replaced the class code with the special attributes required by Enterprise Services to define how the assembly should be treated by COM+. Here are the settings in that file:

```
<Assembly: ApplicationActivation(ActivationOption.Server)>
<Assembly: ApplicationName("ProjectTracker20vb Portal")>
<Assembly: Description("Project Tracker DataPortal host")>
<Assembly: ApplicationAccessControl(False)>
```

The `ApplicationActivation()` setting indicates that the assembly should run in a server process, not within the process that called the assembly. This is important, since the proxy/host assembly is to be hosted by COM+ on the server.

The `ApplicationName()` and `Description()` settings are optional, but are used to describe the COM+ component. Finally, the `ApplicationAccessControl()` setting indicates that COM+ shouldn't apply its own method-level security when clients try to call the data portal.

Referencing Assemblies

When running, the Enterprise Services data portal host needs access to your business classes from your business assembly or assemblies. To make them available, the proxy/host assembly references `ProjectTracker.Library`.

It also references `Csla.dll` so that the CSLA .NET framework is available both to the proxy/host code and for the business code in `ProjectTracker.Library`.

EnterpriseServicesProxy Class

The proxy class is used by the client-side `DataPortal` to communicate with the server. Chapter 4 covered the implementation of a base class, `EnterpriseServicesProxy`, that is designed to simplify the creation of a proxy class for your application. In fact, all *your* code needs to do is override a single method. Here's the proxy class from the `ProjectTracker` solution:

```
Public Class EnterpriseServicesProxy
  Inherits Csla.DataPortalClient.EnterpriseServicesProxy

  Protected Overrides Function GetServerObject() As _
    Csla.Server.Hosts.EnterpriseServicesPortal

    Return New EnterpriseServicesPortal
  End Function
End Class
```

The code from Chapter 4 can do all the work, but the one bit of information it doesn't have automatically is a reference to the server-side host object. That is the purpose of the `GetServerObject()` method: to return a reference to the server-side object.

Notice that the code here simply uses the `New` keyword. That is possible because the installation of the COM+ application's `msi` on the client will automatically redirect any attempt to create an `EnterpriseServicesPortal` object to the application server. This leverages the same location transparency capability provided by DCOM for the past decade or more.

As you'll see shortly, the client application's configuration file will reference this EnterpriseServicesProxy type, telling the data portal to use this custom class as a proxy for communication with the server. First, though, let's finish creating the proxy/host assembly itself.

EnterpriseServicesPortal Class

The host class runs within COM+ on the application server. Again, Chapter 4 discussed a base class, EnterpriseServicesPortal, that is designed to do all the actual work. That base class makes creation of a server-side host trivial, since all you need to do is create an empty class that inherits from the base:

```
<EventTrackingEnabled(True)> _
<ComVisible(True)> _
Public Class EnterpriseServicesPortal
  Inherits Csla.Server.Hosts.EnterpriseServicesPortal

  ' no code needed - implementation is in the base class
End Class
```

It may seem odd to create an empty class like this, but it is the class *name* and its containing assembly that are really important. Remember that COM+ has no concept of a virtual root, so there's no way to directly host Csla.dll multiple times in COM+. The EnterpriseServicesHostvb assembly and this EnterpriseServicesPortal class exist specifically to act as wrappers around Csla.dll to provide a unique name for COM+.

All the *functionality* is already written in CSLA .NET as discussed in Chapter 4.

Notice that this class is decorated with a couple of attributes. The <EventTrackingEnabled()> attribute tells COM+ to monitor the object and display tracking information in the component services console. In short, this attribute turns on the "spinning balls" in COM+. The <ComVisible()> attribute is required for making the class available to COM+. Remember that at its core, COM+ is still a COM-based technology.

That's all you need to do with this class. The fact that the assembly is signed, combined with the settings in the EnterpriseServicesSettings.vb file, means that the assembly can be built and installed into COM+. First, though, let's discuss how to configure the assembly—providing database connection strings, for instance.

COM+ Configuration Files

COM+ 1.5 and higher allows you to provide separate configuration files (essentially like app.config or web.config) for each COM+ application. This is an important feature available on Windows XP and Windows Server 2003 (and higher), because without it you could only provide one configuration file for *all* COM+-hosted .NET code.

To use this feature, you need to create two files for your Enterprise Services assembly:

- application.config
- application.manifest

The application.config file is actually named "application.config." It is a standard .NET config file that contains the normal .NET configuration that you would put into any app.config file, including the CSLA .NET configuration settings. For instance, it might look like this:

```
<?xml version="1.0" encoding="utf-8" ?>
<configuration>
  <appSettings>
    <add key="CslaAuthentication" value="Csla"/>
  </appSettings>
</configuration>
```

Most likely, you'll need to add a `<connectionStrings>` element with the connection strings for your database. You can see an example in the code download for this book.

The `application.manifest` file is required by Enterprise Services and looks like this:

```
<?xml version="1.0" encoding="UTF-8" standalone="yes"?>
<assembly xmlns="urn:schemas-microsoft-com:asm.v1" manifestVersion="1.0">
</assembly>
```

These two files are part of the `EnterpriseServicesHostvb` project in the `ProjectTracker` solution. However, when you deploy the assembly to the application server, these files need to go in a directory so that they can be referenced from COM+.

Installing the Proxy/Host into COM+

At this point, you've seen how to create the proxy/host assembly, including all the references and extra steps required to make it work with COM+. The final step is to register the assembly with COM+ on your application server, and then to configure the COM+ application.

Registering a .NET assembly into COM+ is done using the `regsvcs.exe` command line utility. In a Visual Studio 2005 command prompt window, navigate to the directory containing `EnterpriseServicesHostvb.dll` and type the following command:

```
> regsvcs EnterpriseServicesHostvb.dll
```

This will install the assembly into COM+. It will put the assembly into a COM+ application with the name based on the `ApplicationName` attribute in `EnterpriseServicesSettings.vb`: `ProjectTracker20vb Portal`. Figure 12-6 shows the result in the Component Services management console.

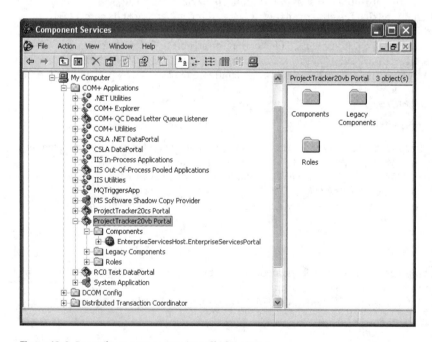

Figure 12-6. *Proxy/host component installed in COM+*

There are two key bits of configuration you should do before using the component. First, you should set the COM+ application to run under a user account appropriate for your environment. This is done in the properties window for the application, as shown in Figure 12-7.

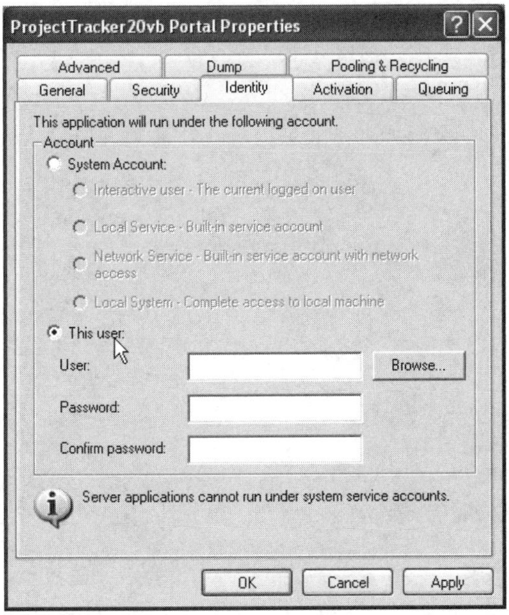

Figure 12-7. *Setting the identity account for the service*

As shown in Figure 12-7, you should change the identity for the application to a specific user account. That user account should have appropriate access to the database or other data sources (such as XML files) on your application server.

Second, you need to configure the application root directory property on the Activation tab in the Properties window, as shown in Figure 12-8.

The application root directory must point to the location on the server where you put the `application.config` and `application.manifest` files discussed earlier. Obviously, the user account you set up on the Identity tab must have access to this directory.

At this point, your application server is ready for use. The assembly is registered with COM+, and the COM+ application is set up appropriately for your environment. The next task is to make an `msi` install program that can be run on each client so they have access to the server component.

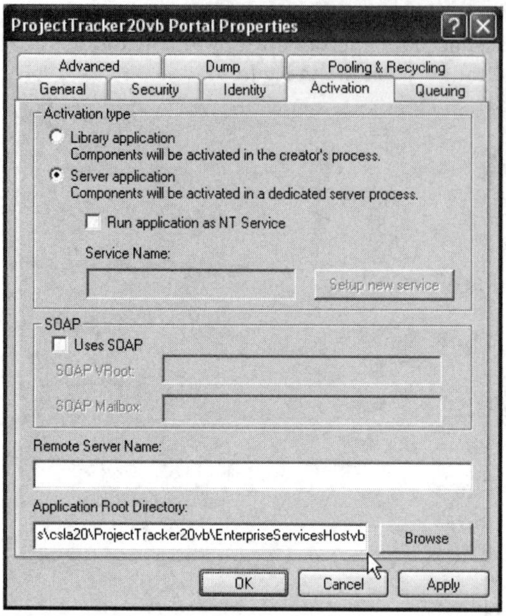

Figure 12-8. *Setting the application root directory for the component*

Creating the Setup Program

To create a setup program (msi) for your proxy/host assembly, you need to right-click the COM+ application node in the component services console; in this case, the ProjectTracker20vb Portal node. Choose Export from the pop-up menu. This brings up the Application Export Wizard. The important step in the wizard is shown in Figure 12-9.

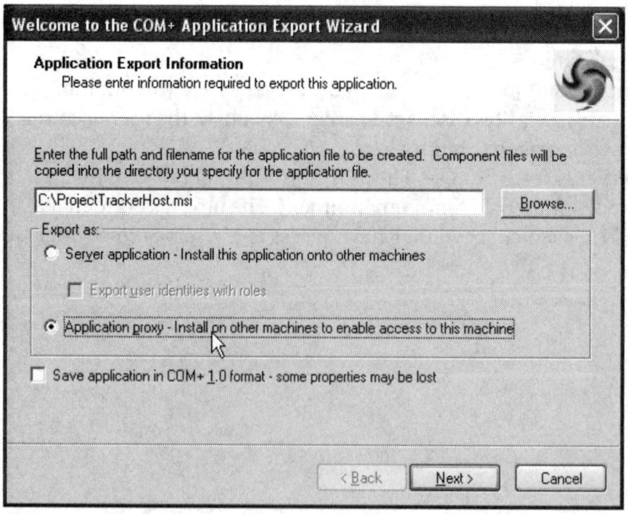

Figure 12-9. *Exploring the COM+ application to create a client install*

Make sure to choose the application proxy option, as shown in Figure 12-9, and provide a path and name for the `msi` file to be created. The result will be both `msi` and `cab` files that you can use to set up clients to use the server.

Client Setup

There are two steps to configure a client to use the Enterprise Services application server host, both of which are quite straightforward:

1. Run the COM+ application `msi`.
2. Configure the client application to use the host.

Installing the COM+ Application

To configure the client to use the COM+ application created earlier, simply run the `msi` file created through the Component Services Application Export Wizard. This registers the COM+ application on the client, including setting up the Windows registry entries necessary for the client to find the correct application server on the network.

Configuring the Client

The only remaining step is to configure the client application itself. The clients could be Windows Forms, Web Forms, and Web Services clients—even all at once if you choose. The only requirement is that both the application server and clients have the same version of your business assemblies installed.

To configure a Windows Forms client, you need to edit the `app.config` file. To configure either a Web Forms or Web Services client, you need to edit the `web.config` file.

In either case, the configuration file should contain the following highlighted lines:

```
<?xml version="1.0" encoding="utf-8" ?>
<configuration>
  <appSettings>
    <add key="CslaAuthentication" value="Csla" />
    <add key="CslaDataPortalProxy"
      value="EnterpriseServicesHost.EnterpriseServicesProxy,
                EnterpriseServicesHostvb"/>
  </appSettings>
  <connectionStrings>
  </connectionStrings>
</configuration>
```

The `CslaDataPortalProxy` element specifies that the data portal should use the proxy class created earlier: `EnterpriseServicesProxy`. Remember, this is not the CSLA .NET base class, but your custom class in your application's specific proxy/host assembly. Notice that the assembly name is `EnterpriseServicesHostvb` in the preceding example.

That's all there is to it. You don't need to specify the server name or any other details, because the Windows registry already contains that information based on the `msi` run in the previous step.

At this point, you should understand how to set up an application server to use Enterprise Services, and how to install the associated COM+ application on each client so that each client can use the server.

Conclusion

As discussed in Chapter 4, the data portal implements a channel adapter pattern, allowing you to select between four technologies for communicating with the server-side data portal components:

- Local
- Remoting
- Web Services
- Enterprise Services

It is also possible to create your own custom network channel by implementing `DataPortalClient.IDataPortalProxy` on the client, and `Server.IDataPortalServer` on the server, just as was done in Chapter 4 to create the four proxy/host combinations listed previously.

In this chapter, you've seen how to configure an application server to host each of the three remote channels: remoting, Web Services, and Enterprise Services. And you've seen how to configure client applications to use those hosts.

Whether you use a remote data portal or not, the framework and concepts discussed in this book should enable you to create applications using object-oriented design concepts while leveraging the power of .NET. Your objects will support data binding in Windows Forms and Web Forms, along with support for encapsulation of validation and authorization logic, in a clear and concise manner.

I've thoroughly enjoyed exploring these concepts with you, and wish you the best as you develop your software.

Code well, have fun!

Index

Find it faster at http://superindex.apress.com/